PSYCHOLOGY APPLIED TO WORK

An Introduction to Industrial and Organizational Psychology

PSYCHOLOGY APPLIED TO WORK

An Introduction to Industrial and Organizational Psychology

Paul M. Muchinsky

Iowa State University

Brooks/Cole Publishing Company
Pacific Grove, California

Brooks/Cole Publishing Company
A Division of Wadsworth, Inc.

© 1990 by Wadsworth, Inc., Belmont, California 94002. © 1987, 1983 by The Dorsey Press. All rights reserved. No part of this book may be reproduced, stored in a retrieval system, or transcribed, in any form or by any means—electronic, mechanical, photocopying, recording, or otherwise—without the prior written permission of the publisher, Brooks/ Cole Publishing Company, Pacific Grove, California 93950, a division of Wadsworth, Inc.

Printed in the United States of America

10 9 8 7 6 5 4 3

Library of Congress Cataloging in Publication Data

Muchinsky, Paul M.
  Psychology applied to work: an introduction to industrial and organizational psychology / Paul M. Muchinsky.
—3rd ed.
    p.   cm.
  Includes bibliographical references and index.
  ISBN 0-534-13032-1
  1. Psychology, Industrial.   2. Organizational behavior.
I. Title.
HF5548.8.M756   1990
158.7—dc20   89-22343
                                                                                                    CIP

Sponsoring Editor: *Philip L. Curson*
Editorial Assistant: *Heather L. Riedl*
Production Editor: *Timothy A. Phillips*
Manuscript Editor: *Betty G. Seaver*
Permissions Editor: *Carline Haga*
Interior and Cover Design: *Michael Rogondino*
Design Coordinator: *Vernon T. Boes*
Cover Photo: *Dawson Jones*
Art Coordinator: *Lisa Torri*
Interior Illustration: *Pat Rogondino*
Photo Researcher: *Doris F. Hill*
Typesetting: *Interactive Composition Corporation*
Cover Printing: *The Lehigh Press*
Printing and Binding: *Arcata Graphics/Fairfield*

To Carly
Thank you

Preface

There is an old saying, "If something is not broken, don't fix it." I recently heard an updated version of the saying: "If something is not broken, improve it." This third edition of my book represents an attempt to improve upon something that has been favorably received within the field of industrial/organizational psychology.

I strove to maintain three major aspects of the book that have contributed to its popularity. First, I like to write in an engaging, personal style. I feel it serves to bring the reader closer to material that can sometimes appear to be rather cold and sterile. One of the highest compliments I get from people is to be told my writing makes the material "interesting and enjoyable." I trust you will find this edition to be written in the same readable style as its predecessors.

Second, by its very nature industrial/organizational psychology is concerned with the generation of knowledge, as well as its application to solve real-world problems. That is, the field is directed toward both science and practice. When writing a book, one can easily stray too far in one direction or the other. I have tried to strike a balance between the two. I would be performing a disservice to the scientific aspect of our profession if I exclusively wrote a lengthy series of applications without explaining their conceptual bases. Likewise, it is difficult to imagine how abstract theories can ever be applied in practice if there is no attempt to provide illustration of their use. On many occasions I've had incredulous students ask me if "all this stuff can really be used in everyday life?" My answer is a resounding "Yes!" I have tried to capture both the science and practice of industrial/organizational psychology in writing this book.

Third, I have retained and further developed a number of instructional devices that I feel enhance the value of the book: case studies, field notes, photographs, cartoons, and summary tables. I believe they all serve to embellish the text material by increasing the avenues of learning.

Finally, I have added some new material—organizational theory, alcoholism and drug abuse in the workplace, genetic screening, computer-adaptive testing, organizational culture, emerging views of leadership, ergonomics, and much more—and deleted some dated material from the earlier edition. I hope you will find the material to be current and comprehensive. All in all, I believe this edition is a worthy successor to its predecessors.

I would like to thank a number of colleagues who served as reviewers for this edition. They were Janet Barnes-Farrell, University of Connecticut; John Binning,

Illinois State University at Normal; Douglas Cellar, DePaul University, Chicago, Illinois; Dean Frost, Portland State University; Larry Gregory, New Mexico State University; Shepard Insel, San Francisco State University; Karl Kuhnert, University of Georgia; Lynn Offerman, George Washington University, Washington, D.C.; David Weckler, San Jose State University; Ladd Wheeler, University of Rochester; and a special thanks to K.H.E. Kroemer, Virginia Polytechnic Institute. Their comments and suggestions were most gratefully received. I would also like to thank two of my graduate students, Laura Reichel and Judy Collins, for their invaluable assistance. My loyal secretary, Martha Behrens, once again typed the book in its entirety. Marty, the book, and I are all aging gracefully, but she more than I. Finally, to my children, Andrea and Brian, who represent two of the really good things in life, you kept asking me when I'd be done with the book. Well, here it is.

Paul M. Muchinsky

Contents

SECTION FOUR The Work Environment

List of Figures

List of Tables

PSYCHOLOGY APPLIED TO WORK

An Introduction to Industrial and Organizational Psychology

1
Introduction

1

Introduction

Psychology

Psychology is defined as the scientific study of behavior. It is a complex discipline involving the study of behavior of both animals and humans. It is a science because psychologists use the same rigorous methods of research found in other areas of scientific investigation. Some of their research is more biological in nature (as the effects of brain lesions on a rat's food consumption). Other research is more social in nature (as identifying the factors that lead to bystander apathy). Because psychology covers such a broad spectrum of content areas, it is difficult to have a clear and accurate image of what a psychologist does. Many people think that every psychologist "is a shrink," "has a black couch," "likes to discover what makes people tick," and so on. In fact, these statements usually refer to the specialty of clinical psychology—the diagnosis and treatment of mental illness or abnormal behavior. Most psychologists do not treat mental disorders, nor do they practice psychotherapy. In reality, psychologists are a very diversified lot with many specialized interests.

Many psychologists are united professionally through membership in the American Psychological Association (APA), a national organization. As of 1988, there were over 55,000 members, 67% men and 33% women. The diversification of interest among psychologists is reflected by the fact that there are 45 divisions of APA representing special-interest subgroups. Matarazzo (1987) notes there are not really 45 different specialty areas of psychology, just many fields in which the same basic psychological principles are applied. Though some members have no divisional affiliation, others belong to more than one. The APA publishes several journals, vehicles through which psychologists can communicate their research findings to other scholars. The APA also holds regional and national conventions, sets standards for graduate training in certain areas of psychology (that is, clinical, counseling, and school), develops and enforces a code of professional ethics, and helps psychologists find employment.

The APA has three classes of membership. An associate has a minimum of either two years of graduate work in psychology or a master's degree in psychology. A member has a Ph.D. degree based in part on a psychological dissertation. A fellow

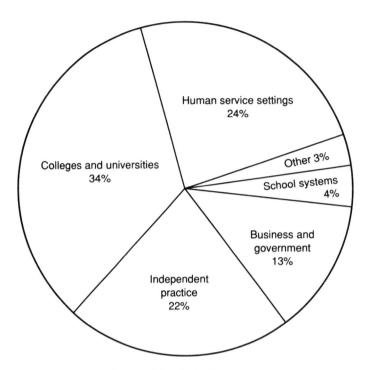

Figure 1–1   Employers of Psychologists

SOURCE: A. Howard et al., "The Changing Face of American Psychology: A Report from the Committee on Employment and Human Resources," *American Psychologist 41* (1986), pp. 1311–1327.

has a Ph.D. degree and a minimum of five years of subsequent professional experience, and is judged to have made exceptional scientific contributions in his or her area of expertise.

Figure 1–1 shows areas where psychologists are employed. Colleges and universities employ the greatest number, followed by human service settings. Most psychologists who specialize in basic areas (for example, experimental, social, developmental) are employed in colleges or universities. Many applied psychologists (those with training in clinical, counseling, industrial/organizational, school) work in nonacademic settings. In summary, psychology is a complex and varied profession whose members work in a wide variety of jobs.

Industrial/Organizational Psychology

One of the specialty areas of psychology is industrial/organizational (I/O) psychology (represented by Division 14 of APA, The Society for Industrial-Organizational Psychology). In 1988, there were about 2,500 members of Division 14, 85% male and 15% female. However, between 1975 and 1984 there has been an 18% increase in the

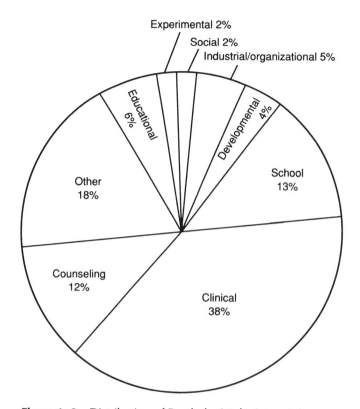

Experimental 2%
Social 2%
Industrial/organizational 5%
Educational 6%
Developmental 4%
School 13%
Other 18%
Counseling 12%
Clinical 38%

Figure 1–2 Distribution of Psychologists by Interest Area

SOURCE: J. Stapp, A. M. Tucker, & G. R. VandenBos, "Census of Psychological Personnel: 1983," *American Psychologist 40* (1985), pp. 1317–1351.

number of females entering the field of I/O psychology, the greatest increase in female representation across all areas of psychology (Howard et al., 1986).

I wish I could say that becoming an I/O psychologist was my childhood ambition, but such was not the case. I originally wanted to be a chemist, but in college it soon became apparent that I lacked the skills and talents needed for that discipline. By accident I took an introductory psychology course taught by an I/O psychologist. I was so impressed by his teaching that I wanted to emulate him and was soon embarked on a new career. My happenstance entry into the field of I/O psychology places me in some distinguished company. Stagner (1981) reported that industrial psychology was the second career choice of many past presidents of Division 14 of APA. Like me, they gave circumstance or luck as the reason for "finding" I/O psychology. Perhaps this book will serve as a catalyst for some students to select a career in I/O psychology rationally rather than depending on fate.

A master's degree is necessary to qualify as an I/O psychologist (and for membership in Division 14 of APA). However, many obtain a Ph.D. degree, and this gives them more expertise and professional mobility. Unlike some areas of psychology, job opportunities are extremely good for I/O psychologists.

The distribution of psychologists in the major subfields is shown in Figure 1–2.

According to the survey on which this figure is based, 5% of all psychologists are in the I/O area. Our relatively small representation in the total population of psychologists probably contributes to why some people are unaware of the I/O area. As can also be seen, half of all psychologists work in the specialty areas of clinical and counseling, which probably contributes to the stereotype of psychologists in general.

As a specialty area, I/O psychology has a more restricted definition than psychology as a whole. Guion (1965) defines industrial/organizational psychology as "the scientific study of the relationship between man and the world at work: the study of the adjustment people make to the places they go, the people they meet, and the things they do in the process of making a living" (p. 817). Blum and Naylor (1968) define it as "simply the application or extension of psychological facts and principles to the problems concerning human beings operating within the context of business and industry" (p. 4). Broadly speaking, the I/O psychologist is concerned with behavior in work situations.

There are two sides of I/O psychology: science and practice. I/O psychology is a legitimate field of scientific inquiry, concerned with advancing knowledge about people at work. As in any area of science, questions are posed by I/O psychologists to guide their investigation and they use scientific methods to obtain answers. They try to form the results of studies into meaningful patterns that will be useful in explaining behavior and to replicate findings to make generalizations about behavior. In this respect, I/O psychology is an academic discipline.

There is another side of I/O psychology, though—the professional side, which is concerned with the application of knowledge to solve real problems in the world of work. I/O psychological research findings can be used to hire better employees, reduce absenteeism, improve communication, increase job satisfaction, and solve countless other problems. Most I/O psychologists feel a sense of kinship with both sides: science and practice.

As an I/O psychologist, I am pleased that the results of my research can be put to some practical use. But by the same token, I am more than a technician—someone who goes through the motions of solving problems without knowing why they "work" and what their consequences will be. I/O psychology is more than just a tool for business leaders to use to make their companies more efficient. So the I/O psychologist has a dual existence. The well-trained I/O psychologist realizes that good application of knowledge can come only from *sound* knowledge and can therefore both contribute to knowledge and apply it.

Figure 1–3 shows the main work settings of I/O psychologists. They are represented across five areas, with business, academia, and consulting firms being the primary employers. But across these five areas, I/O psychologists are unevenly split as to their scientist/practitioner orientation. Universities employ more scientists; consulting firms employ more practitioners; business and government have a good mix of both.

This orientation difference has caused many problems in deciding the best way to train I/O psychologists. Should graduate programs train students as scientists or practitioners? This is important because practitioners need certain skills to be suc-

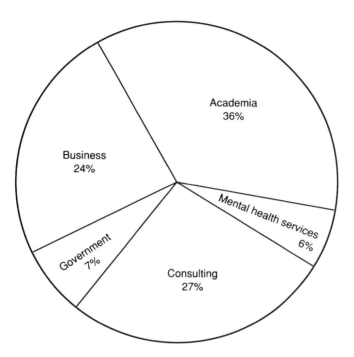

Figure 1–3 Principal Work Settings of I/O Psychologists

SOURCE: A. Howard, "Characteristics of Society Members," *The Industrial-Organizational Psychologist 23* (3), (1986), pp. 41–47.

cessful that the scientists do not, and vice versa (Mayfield, 1975). Such I/O psychologists as Meyer (1972), Naylor (1970), and Muchinsky (1973) have discussed the consequences of poorly trained students, the product of unintelligent handling of this dualism issue. While many "solutions" to the problem have been proposed (Task Force on the Practice of Psychology in Industry, 1971), no final blueprint has yet been devised. Some psychologists (Naylor, 1971) proposed adopting a strict "scientist" model of graduate training for all students. Others have proposed the separation of academic and professional training (Rodgers, 1964). I prefer the scientist end of the continuum for graduate training, but students who wish to become practitioners should have a chance to serve as interns in business or industry during this period (Muchinsky, 1976). Although training to become an I/O psychologist is an arduous process, the rewards in terms of challenging work, intellectual stimulation, and feelings of accomplishment are great.

Fields of I/O Psychology

Like psychology in general, I/O psychology is a diversified science containing several subspecialties (see Figure 1–4).

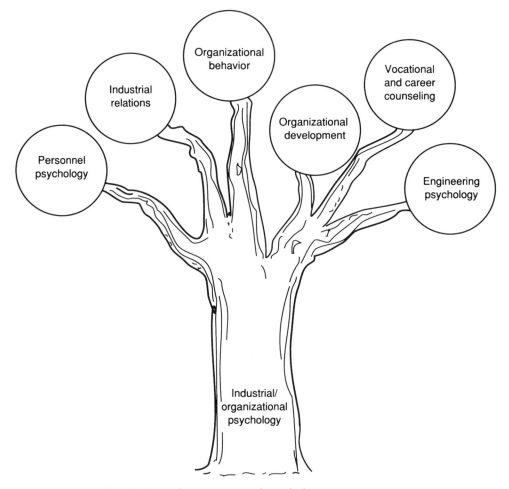

Figure 1–4   Fields of Industrial/Organizational Psychology

Personnel Psychology.   The word *personnel* means *people*. So personnel psychology is concerned with all aspects of applied individual differences. Among other things, personnel psychologists determine what human skills and talents are needed for certain jobs, how to assess potential employees, how to grade employee job perform-ance, and how to train workers to improve job performance. Personnel psychology is one of the oldest and most traditional activities of I/O psychologists. In fact, for many years personnel psychology and I/O psychology were synonymous. It was only after other topics caught the interest of I/O psychologists that personnel psy-chology became just a subspecialty of the total profession.

Organizational Behavior.   Almost all employees work within some organizational context. We know that organizations can influence the attitudes and behaviors of people associated with them. Work in this area concerns such factors as role-related behavior, pressures that groups can impose on individuals, personal feelings of commitment to an organization, and patterns of communication within an organization. There is a strong social influence in organizational behavior research because organizations are social collectivities. At the risk of overgeneralizing, personnel psychology is more concerned with individual-level issues (for example, who gets hired and who doesn't); organizational behavior is more concerned with social and group influences.

Engineering Psychology. Engineering psychology concerns the understanding of human performance in person-machine systems, including the design of equipment and machinery to enhance worker productivity and safety. Most tools, equipment, and machines are designed for a human to operate. However, humans have limitations in terms of strength, reaction time, coordination, sensory acuity, and so on. No one benefits if a machine's demands exceed the limits of human capabilities. Engineering psychology tries to modify the work environment to be compatible with human skills and talents. *Human factors psychology* and *ergonomics* are also names for this specialized field.

Vocational and Career Counseling. This subspecialty is a cross between counseling and I/O psychology; the counseling applies to people's problems at work. Industrial-oriented counselors help employees choose a rewarding and satisfying career path, resolve conflicts between work and nonwork interests, adjust to changing career interests, and prepare for retirement. I/O psychologists in this area may research these issues, or they may work for large organizations as in-house staff counselors.

Organization Development. I/O psychologists in this area are concerned with improving or changing (that is, "developing") organizations to make them more efficient. The I/O psychologist must be able to diagnose an organization's problems, recommend or enact changes, and then assess the effectiveness of the changes. Organization development involves the planned, deliberate change of an organization to resolve a particular problem; the change may involve people, work procedures, or technology. Organization development is the newest and least-structured subspecialty of I/O psychology. Organization development provides an exciting opportunity for some I/O psychologists to help organizations resolve or adapt to their problems.

Industrial Relations. The final specialty area of I/O psychology is industrial relations. Industrial relations deals with problems between employers and employees and usually involves a labor union. I/O psychologists interested in industrial relations address such issues as cooperation and conflict between work parties, resolving disputes in the work force, and bargaining or negotiating agreements between various segments of the work force. I/O psychologists in this area have close contact with specialists in labor relations; that is, people with knowledge of federal and state laws on employee rights, collective bargaining, and dispute settlement. Unlike some other areas of I/O psychology, industrial relations is heavily legislated, and a person who works in this area must have knowledge of these laws.

In summary, psychology as a discipline is composed of many specialty areas, one of which is I/O psychology. And I/O psychology consists of several subspecialities. While some of these subspecialties overlap, many are quite distinct from each other. Thus, I/O psychology is not really a single discipline. It is a mix of subspecialties bonded together by a concern for people at work. Each of the subspecialties of I/O psychology will be explored to various degrees in this book.

Licensing and Certification of Psychologists

What makes a psychologist a psychologist? What prevents people with no psychological training from passing themselves off as psychologists? One way professions offer high-quality service to the public is by regulating their own membership. Selective admission into the profession helps protect the public against quacks and charlatans who risk great damage not only to their clients but also to the profession they allegedly represent.

The practice of professional psychology is regulated by law in every state. When both the title and practice of psychology are regulated, the law is called a *licensing law*. When only the title of psychologist is regulated, the law is called a *certification law* (Hess, 1977). Laws limit licensure to those qualified to practice psychology as defined by state law. Each state has its own standards for licensure, and these are governed by regulatory boards. The major functions of any professional board are to determine the standards for admission into the profession and to conduct disciplinary actions involving violations of professional standards.

Typically, licensure involves educational, experience, examination, and administrative requirements. A doctoral degree in psychology from an approved program is usually required, as well as one or two years of supervised experience. Applicants must also pass an objective, written examination covering all areas of psychology. Specialty examinations (for example, in I/O psychology) usually are not given. Currently, psychologists must pass a uniform national examination to obtain a license (Hoffman, 1980). Finally, the applicant must meet citizenship and residency requirements and be of good moral character.

Psychologists disagree about how successful licensing laws have been in protecting the public. Some authors (Hess, 1977) are quite positive on the effects of licensing, some are pessimistic (Gross, 1978). Others have called for a greater separation between those involved in graduate education and those who serve on regulatory licensing boards (Matarazzo, 1977).

Licensing and certification are intended to ensure that clients receive services from qualified people (Fretz & Mills, 1980). However, scrupulous I/O psychologists can never guarantee results, and they should never try. Companies have been duped by consulting firms and individuals into believing a wide range of claims that simply cannot be substantiated. The problems that the I/O psychologist faces are too complex for guarantees. Reasonable expectations on the part of both the I/O psychologists and the company are the best way to avoid such difficulties.

There is currently a controversy regarding the licensure of I/O psychologists. The original purpose of licensure was to protect the public in the health care areas of psychology, such as clinical and counseling. Because I/O psychologists are not health care providers, there is not as pressing a need for licensure to protect the public (Howard & Lowman, 1985). Most states regard I/O psychologists as they do other types of applied psychologists who offer services to the public and thus require them to be licensed. However, some states regard I/O psychologists as having a sufficiently different mandate to prohibit them from obtaining licensure.

The History of I/O Psychology

It is always difficult to write *the* history of anything—there are different perspectives with different emphases. It is also a challenge to divide the historical evolution of a discipline into units of time. In some cases, time itself is a convenient watershed (decades or centuries); in others, major events serve as landmarks. In the case of I/O psychology, the two world wars were major catalysts for changing the discipline. This historical overview will show how the field of I/O psychology came to be what it is and how some key individuals and events helped shape it.[1]

The Early Years (1900–1916)

In its beginnings, what we know today as I/O psychology didn't even have a name—it was a merging of two forces that gathered momentum before 1900. One force was the pragmatic nature of some basic psychological research. Most psychologists at this time were strictly scientific and deliberately avoided studying problems that strayed outside the boundaries of pure research. However, a psychologist named W. L. Bryan published a paper (Bryan & Harter, 1897) about how professional telegraphers develop skill in sending and receiving Morse code. A few years later (1903) Bryan's presidential address to the American Psychological Association (Bryan, 1904) touched on having psychologists study "concrete activities and functions as they appear in everyday life" (p. 80). Bryan did not advocate studying problems found in industry per se but, rather, examining real skills as a base on which to develop scientific psychology. Bryan is not considered the father of I/O psychology but rather a precursor.[2]

---

[1] I am indebted to David C. Edwards and Kimberley Abbey, whose research provided much of the material for this section. A more detailed treatment of the history of I/O psychology can be found in the excellent books by Ferguson (1962) and Napoli (1981).

[2] The term *industrial psychology* was apparently used for the first time in Bryan's 1904 article. Ironically, it appeared in print only as a typographical error. Bryan was quoting a sentence he had written five years earlier (Bryan & Harter, 1899) in which he spoke of the need for more research in *individual* psychology. Instead, Bryan wrote industrial psychology and did not catch his mistake.

Walter Dill Scott. *Archives of the History of American Psychology*

The second major force in the evolution of the discipline came from the desire of industrial engineers to improve efficiency. They were concerned mainly with the economics of manufacturing and thus the productivity of industrial employees. Two industrial engineers, Frederick Taylor and Frank Gilbreth, redesigned jobs, developed training programs, and used selection methods to increase employee efficiency. Thus, the merging of psychology with applied interests and concern for increasing industrial efficiency was the ingredient for the emergence of I/O psychology. By 1910, "industrial psychology" (the "organizational" appendage did not become official until 1970) was a legitimate specialty area of psychology.

Three individuals stand out as the founding fathers of I/O psychology. They worked independently, and in fact their work barely overlapped. The major contributions of these individuals deserve a brief review.

Walter Dill Scott.   Scott, a psychologist, was persuaded to give a talk to some Chicago business leaders on the need for applying psychology to advertising. His talk was well received and led to the publication of two books, *The Theory of Advertising* (1903) and *The Psychology of Advertising* (1908). The first book dealt with suggestion and argument as means of influencing people. The second book was aimed at improving human efficiency with such tactics as imitation, competition, loyalty, and concentration. By 1911, he had increased his areas of interest and published two more books, *Influencing Men in Business* and *Increasing Human Efficiency in Business*. During World War I, Scott was instrumental in the application of personnel procedures within the Army.

Frederick W. Taylor. Stevens Institute of Technology

Frederick W. Taylor. Taylor was an engineer by profession. His formal schooling was limited, but through experience and self-training in engineering he went on to obtain many patents. As he worked himself up through one company as a worker, supervisor, and finally plant manager, Taylor realized the value of redesigning the work situation to achieve both higher output for the company and a higher wage for the worker. His best-known work is his book *Principles of Scientific Management* (1911). These principles of scientific management were (1) scientifically designing work methods for efficiency; (2) selecting the best workers and training them in new methods; (3) developing a cooperative spirit between managers and workers; and (4) sharing the responsibility of the design and conduct of work between management and worker. In perhaps the most famous example of his methods, Taylor showed that workers who handled heavy iron ingots (pig iron) could be more productive through the use of work rests. Training employees when to work and when to rest increased average worker productivity from 12.5 to 47 tons moved per day (with less reported fatigue), and this resulted in increased wages for them. The company also drastically increased efficiency by reducing costs from 9.2 cents per ton to 3.9 cents per ton.

As a consequence of this method, it was charged that Taylor inhumanely exploited workers for a higher wage and that great numbers of workers would be unemployed because fewer were needed. Because there was rampant unemployment at this time, the attacks on Taylor were virulent. Taylor's methods were eventually investigated by the Interstate Commerce Commission (ICC) and the U.S. House of Representatives. Taylor replied that increased efficiency led to greater, not lesser, prosperity, and that workers not hired for one job would be placed in another that

Hugo Münsterberg. Archives of the History of American Psychology

would better use their potential. The arguments were never really resolved—World War I broke out, and the controversy faded.

Hugo Münsterberg. Münsterberg was a German psychologist with traditional academic training. He was invited to Harvard University by the noted American psychologist William James. Münsterberg applied his experimental methods to a variety of problems, including perception and attention. He was a popular figure in American education, a gifted public speaker, and a personal friend of President Theodore Roosevelt. Münsterberg was interested in applying traditional psychological methods to practical problems of industry. His book *Psychology and Industrial Efficiency* (1913) was divided into three parts: selecting workers, designing work situations, and using psychology in sales. One of Münsterberg's most renowned studies involved determining what makes a safe trolley car operator. He systematically studied all aspects of the job, developed an ingenious laboratory simulation of a trolley car, and concluded that a good operator could comprehend simultaneously all of the influences that bear on the progress of the car. Some writers consider Münsterberg *the* father of industrial psychology.

When World War I broke out in Europe, Münsterberg supported the German cause. He was ostracized for his allegiance, and the emotional strain probably contributed to his death in 1916. Münsterberg's sudden departure from the field of industrial psychology created a scientific vacuum since he left no colleagues behind to continue in his work. Only the U.S. involvement in World War I gave some unity to the profession. The primary emphasis of the early work in I/O psychology was the economic gains that could be accrued by applying the ideas and methods of psychology to problems in business and industry. Business leaders began to employ psychologists, and some psychologists entered applied research. However, World War I caused a shift in the direction of industrial psychological research.

World War I (1917–1918)

World War I was a potent influence behind psychology's rise to respectability. Psychologists believed they could provide a valuable service to the nation, and some saw the war as a means of accelerating the profession's progress.

Robert Yerkes was the psychologist most instrumental in getting psychology into the war. As president of APA, he maneuvered the profession into assignments in the war effort. The APA suggested many proposals, including ways of screening recruits for mental deficiency and of assigning them to jobs within the army. Committees of psychologists investigated soldier motivation, morale, psychological problems of physical incapacity, and discipline. Yerkes continued to press his point that psychology could be of great help to our nation in time of war.

The army, in turn, was somewhat skeptical of the psychologists' claims. It eventually approved only a modest number of proposals mostly involving the assessment of recruits. Yerkes and other psychologists reviewed a series of general intelligence tests and eventually developed one that they called the Army Alpha. When they discovered that 30% of the recruits were illiterate, they developed the Army Beta, a special test for those who couldn't read English. Meanwhile, Walter Scott was doing research on the best placement of soldiers in the army. Some of his work involved classifying and placing enlisted soldiers, performance ratings of officers, and developing and preparing job duties and qualifications for over 500 jobs.

Plans for testing recruits proceeded at a slow pace. The army instructed its camps to build special testing sites and ordered all existing officers, officer candidates, and newly drafted recruits to be tested. Both the Army Alpha and Beta group intelligence tests were used, as were a few individual tests. The final order authorizing the testing program came from the adjutant general's office in August 1918. However, the Armistice was signed only three months later, and World War I was over. Testing was terminated just as it was finally organized and authorized. Because of this, the intelligence testing program didn't contribute as much to the war as Yerkes would have liked. Even though 1,726,000 individuals were ultimately tested in the program, actual use of the results was minimal.

While psychology's impact on the war effort was not substantial, the very process of giving psychologists so much recognition and authority was a great impetus to the profession. Psychologists were regarded as people who could make valuable contributions to society, and who could add to a company's (and in war, a nation's) prosperity.

Also in 1917, the oldest and most representative journal in the field of I/O psychology, the *Journal of Applied Psychology*, began publication. Some of the articles in the first volume included "Practical Relations between Psychology and the

War" by Hall, "Mentality Testing of College Students" by Bingham, and "The Moron as a War Problem" by Mateer. The first article published in the *Journal of Applied Psychology* not only summarized the prevailing state of industrial psychology at the time but also addressed the science-versus-practice issue that still faces I/O psychologists today.

> The past few years have witnessed an unprecedented interest in the extension of the application of psychology to various fields of human activity. . . . But perhaps the most strikingly original endeavor to utilize the methods and the results of psychological investigation has been in the realm of business. This movement began with the psychology of advertising. . . . Thence the attention of the applied psychologist turned to the more comprehensive and fundamental problem of vocational selection,—the question, namely, of making a detailed inventory of the equipment of mental qualities possessed by a given individual, of discovering what qualities are essential to successful achievement in a given vocation, and thus of directing the individual to the vocational niche which he is best fitted to fill. . . . Every psychologist who besides being a "pure scientist" also cherishes the hope that in addition to throwing light upon the problems of his science, his findings may also contribute their quota to the sum-total of human happiness; and it must appeal to every human being who is interested in increasing human efficiency and human happiness by the more direct method of decreasing the number of cases where a square peg is condemned to a life of fruitless endeavor to fit itself comfortably into a round hole [Hall, Baird, & Geissler, 1917, pp. 5–6].

After the war, there was a boom in the number of psychological consulting firms and research bureaus. The birth of these agencies ushered in the next era in I/O psychology.

Between the Wars (1919–1940)

Applied psychology emerged from the war as a recognized discipline. Society was beginning to realize that industrial psychology could solve practical problems. Following the war, several psychological research bureaus came into full bloom.

The Bureau of Salesmanship Research was developed by Walter Bingham at the Carnegie Institute of Technology. There was little precedent for this kind of cooperation between college and industry. The bureau intended to solve problems with psychological research techniques, problems that had never been examined scientifically. Twenty-seven companies cooperated with Bingham, each contributing $500 annually to finance applied psychological research. One of the early products of the bureau was a book, *Aids in Selecting Salesmen*. For several years, the bureau concentrated on selection, classification, and development of clerical and executive personnel as well as salesmen. When the Carnegie Institute stopped offering graduate work in psychology, the bureau was disbanded.

Another influential company during the period was the Psychological Corporation, founded by James Cattell in 1921. Cattell formed it as a business corporation and asked psychologists to buy stock in it. Its purpose was to advance psychology and promote its usefulness to industry. The corporation also served as a clearinghouse for information. As protection against quacks and charlatans, who were becoming increasingly prevalent, it provided companies with reference checks on any prospective psychologists. Unlike many agencies at the time, the Psychological Corporation remained in business. Over the years it changed its early mission, and today it is one of the country's largest publishers of psychological tests.

During the 1920s, the emphasis of industrial psychology was on testing, but the focus switched from mental testing of people in a laboratory setting to employment testing of industrial workers in field settings. The *Journal of Personnel Research* (later renamed *Personnel Journal*) began in this era, and has remained useful, especially for practitioners. Also the term *industrial psychology* achieved its own identity, as evidenced by the book by Viteles (1932).

In 1924 a series of experiments began at the Hawthorne Works of the Western Electric Company. Although they initially seemed of only minor scientific significance, they became classics in industrial psychology. In the opinion of many writers, the Hawthorne studies "represent the most significant research program undertaken to show the enormous complexity of the problem of production in relation to efficiency" (Blum & Naylor, 1968, p. 306).

The Hawthorne studies were a joint venture between Western Electric and several researchers from Harvard University (none of whom were industrial psychologists by training). The original study attempted to find the relationship between lighting and efficiency. The researchers installed various sets of lights in workrooms where electrical equipment was being produced. In some cases, the light was intense, in other cases, it was reduced to the equivalent of moonlight. Much to the researchers' surprise, productivity seemed to have no relationship to the level of illumination. The workers' productivity increased or remained at a satisfactory level whether the illumination was decreased, increased, or held constant. The results of the study were so bizarre that the researchers hypothesized some other factors as being responsible for productivity.

The results of the first study initiated four other major studies that occurred over a 12-year period: (1) relay assembly test room; (2) mass interviewing program; (3) bank wiring observation room; and (4) personnel counseling. (For more information on these studies, see the original text by Roethlisberger and Dickson [1943]). In essence, the Hawthorne studies revealed many previously unrecognized aspects about human behavior in a workplace. Researchers hypothesized that the results of the study were caused by the employees' desire to please them. Flattered at having distinguished investigators from Harvard University take the time to study them, the workers went out of their way to do what they thought would impress them—namely, to be highly productive. They therefore had produced a lot whether the room was too light or too dark. The researchers learned that factors other than purely technical ones (for example, illumination) influence productivity.

One of the major findings from the Hawthorne studies was a phenomenon

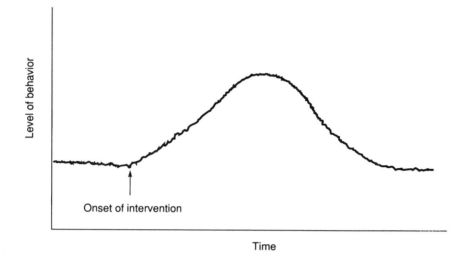

Figure 1–5 Graphic Portrayal of a Hawthorne Effect

labeled the *Hawthorne effect*. The workers' job performance began to improve following the start of the researchers' intervention and continued to do so because of the novelty of the situation; that is, the employees responded positively to the novel treatment they were getting from the researchers. Eventually, however, the novelty began to wear off, and productivity levels returned to their earlier level. This phenomenon of a change in behavior following the onset of novel treatment, and culminating in a gradual return to the previous level of behavior as the effect of novelty dissipates is an example of Hawthorne effect. However, as Adair (1984) has observed, the precise reason for the change in behavior (for example, the novelty of the situation, special attention, prestige from being selected for study) is not always clear.

A Hawthorne effect is represented graphically in Figure 1–5. Its significance is that sometimes behavior change is due just to a change in the environment (for example, the presence of the researchers) and not to the effect of some experimentally manipulated variable (for example, the amount of illumination). The psychological literature indicates that Hawthorne effects may last anywhere from a few days to two years, depending upon the situation. Throughout this book, research findings that appear attributable to Hawthorne effects will be cited.

The Hawthorne studies also revealed the existence of informal employee work groups and their controls on production, as well as the importance of employee attitudes, the value of having a sympathetic and understanding supervisor, and the need to treat workers as people instead of merely human capital. Their revelation of the complexity of human behavior opened up new vistas for industrial psychology, which for nearly 40 years had been dominated by the desire to improve company efficiency. Today the Hawthorne studies, while not considered "perfect" examples of field research, are regarded as the greatest single episode in the formation of industrial psychology. They also showed that researchers sometimes obtain totally unexpected results. Because the investigators were not tied to any one explanation, their studies took them into areas never before studied by industrial psychology and raised questions that otherwise might never have been asked. Industrial psychology was never the same again.

This era in industrial psychology ended with the coincidental conclusion of the Hawthorne studies and the outbreak of World War II. Industrial psychologists were now faced with an immense task: helping to mobilize a nation for a two-continent war.

World War II (1941–1945)

When the United States entered World War II, industrial psychologists were more prepared for their role in the war effort than they had been in 1917. By this time psychologists had studied the problems of employee selection and placement and had refined their techniques considerably.

Walter Bingham chaired the advisory committee on classification of military personnel that had been formed in response to the army's need for classification and training. Unlike World War I, this time the army approached the psychologists first. One of the committee's first assignments was to develop a test that could sift new recruits into a few broad categories based on their ability to learn the duties and responsibilities of a soldier. The test that was finally developed was the Army General Classification Test (AGCT), a benchmark in the history of group testing. The committee also worked on other projects, such as methods of selecting people for officer training, trade proficiency tests, and supplemental aptitude tests.

Psychologists also worked on the development and use of situational stress tests, a project undertaken by the United States Office of Strategic Services (OSS) (Murray & MacKinnon, 1946). The purpose of this testing program was to assess candidates for assignment to military intelligence units. During a three-day session of extremely intensive testing and observation, the candidates lived together in small groups under almost continual observation by members of the assessment staff. Specially constructed situational tests, many modeled after techniques developed in the German and British armies, were used to assess candidates in nontraditional ways. One test, for example, involved constructing a 5-foot cube from a collection of wooden poles, pegs, and blocks. It was impossible for one person to assemble the cube in the allotted time, so two "helpers" were provided. These were actually psychologists who played prearranged roles. One helper acted very passive and contributed little; the other obstructed work by making impractical suggestions and ridiculing and criticizing the candidate. Of course, no candidate could complete the project with this kind of "help." The real purpose of the test was not to see if the candidates could construct the cube but to assess their emotional and interpersonal reactions to stress and frustration. In general, the OSS assessment program was judged to be quite successful. Another area of work was in the selection and training of pilots to fly warplanes. The committee formed for this purpose consisted of psychologists, military personnel, and civilian pilots. The committee's policy was to move the traditional experimental test setting from the laboratory to the cockpit. Airplanes were outfitted with recording and monitoring devices to assess the problems and reactions of student pilots. The product of this research was twofold. Good candidates were selected and trained as pilots (the traditional domain of personnel psychology). Second, equipment was designed to make the pilots' job easier and safer (a contribution of the new field of engineering psychology).

Throughout the war, industrial psychology was also being used in civilian life. There was great increase in the use of employment tests in industry. Because the nation needed a productive work force, psychologists were also called on to help reduce employee absenteeism (Pickard, 1945). Industry discovered that it could use many of the techniques of industrial psychologists, especially in the areas of selection, training, and machine design, and it was particularly interested in the applications of social psychology. New methods of measuring soldier attitude and morale also could be applied to industry. In short, the techniques developed during the war could be applied to business and industry in peacetime. World War II was a springboard for refining industrial psychological techniques and honing the skills of applied psychology.

Each of the two world wars had a major effect on industrial psychology but in a somewhat different way. World War I helped form the profession and give it social acceptance. World War II helped develop and refine it. The next era in the history of I/O psychology saw the discipline evolve into subspecialties and attained higher levels of academic and scientific rigor.

Toward Specialization (1946–1963)

In this era, industrial psychology evolved into a legitimate field of scientific inquiry, having already established itself as an acceptable professional practice. More colleges and universities began to offer courses in "industrial psychology," and graduate degrees (both M.S. and Ph.D.) were soon given.

As with any evolving discipline, subspecialties of interest began to crystallize, and industrial psychology experienced a splintering effect. New journals emerged along with new professional associations. Engineering psychology, born during World War II, was recognized as a separate area, in part due to such seminal books as *Applied Experimental Psychology* (Chapanis, Garner, & Morgan, 1949) and the *Handbook of Human Engineering Data* (1949). Engineering psychology entered an explosive period of growth from 1950 to 1960. This was due mainly to research done in affiliation with the defense industries (Grether, 1968). Engineering psychology's heritage was a mixture of both experimental and industrial psychology, as seen in its early label, "applied experimental psychology." That part of industrial psychology specializing in personnel selection, classification, and training also got its own identity: "personnel psychology."

Sometime in the 1950s, interest grew in the study of organizations. Long the province of sociologists, this area caught the interest of psychologists. In the 1960s there was a stronger organizational flavor to industrial psychology research. Investigators gave more attention to social influences that impinge on behavior in organizations. Terms such as *organizational change* and *organization development* appeared in the literature regularly. Industrial psychology addressed a broader range of topics. Classic textbooks of the 1950s such as *Personnel and Industrial Psychology* by Ghiselli and Brown (1955) gave way in title (as well as substance) to books with more of an organizational thrust. Traditional academic boundaries between disciplines began to blur in this postwar period. Engineering psychology was a fusion of experimental and industrial psychology; organizational behavior a mix of industrial psychology, social psychology, and sociology. This melding of disciplines was healthy because it decreased the probability of narrow, parochial attempts to address complex areas of research.

Governmental Intervention (1964–Present)

In the late 1950s and early 1960s the nation was swept up in what became known as the "civil rights movement." As a nation we became more sensitized to the plight of minorities who had systematically been denied equal opportunities to various sectors of life, including housing, education, and employment. In 1964 Congress passed the Civil Rights Act, a far-reaching piece of legislation designed to reduce unfair discrimination against minorities. One component of the Civil Rights Act, Title VII, addressed the issue of discrimination in employment. The significance of the law to I/O psychologists was basically as follows. For years I/O psychologists were given a relatively free rein to use a wide variety of psychological assessment devices (that is, tests, interviews, and so on) to make employment decisions. The product of these employment decisions was the disproportionately small representation of minorities (most notably blacks and women) in the workplace, particularly above lower-level jobs. Therefore, since I/O psychologists contributed to making employment decisions, and since (historically) these decisions seemingly resulted in discrimination against minorities, the government would now enter the picture to monitor (and if necessary, remedy) the personnel practices of employers.

In essence, the profession of I/O psychology was placed "on trial" to demonstrate the appropriateness of its personnel selection methods. By 1978 the government had drafted a uniform set of employment guidelines to which employers were bound. Companies became legally mandated to demonstrate that their employment tests did not uniformly discriminate against any minority group. In addition, the new governmental standards were not limited to just paper-and-pencil tests or the personnel function of selection—they addressed *all* devices (interviews, tests, application blanks) used to make all types of personnel decisions (selection, placement, promotion, discharge, and so on).

The discipline of I/O psychology now had to direct itself to serving two ultimate authorities. The first authority is what all disciplines must serve—namely, that of performing high-quality work, be it in the area of scientific research or providing services to clients. However, the second authority was governmental scrutiny and evaluation. We now had to accept the consequences of being legally accountable for our actions. As a profession we would continue to evaluate ourselves, but governmental policies and agencies would also be utilized to judge our actions.

Much has been discussed about the overall effect of governmental intervention in the profession of I/O psychology. Some people believe it has been an impetus to our profession, compelling us to address issues and develop solutions that we might otherwise have ignored. Others believe that our profession has been compromised by the intrusion of political and legal influences that serve to deflect our activities into areas beyond our traditional domain. While I do not believe there is a simple answer to this complex question, for the most part I believe the impact of governmental scrutiny has been positive. Some of the greatest advances in our profession have been made in the past 10 to 15 years, and I attribute these advances, in part, to our being accountable to forces beyond our own profession. Legal oversight has, in my opinion, prompted I/O psychologists to broaden their horizons in terms of the problems they address and the solutions they propose. While I do believe that external pressures can have an inhibiting effect on some avenues of scientific research, for the most part I believe as a profession we are stronger and better as a result of the governmental intervention. In any case, the reality of being an I/O psychologist in the 1990s involves attentiveness to legal standards, parameters that our professional predecessors never had to deal with.

In retrospect, the history of I/O psychology is rich and diverse. We were born at the confluence of several forces, developed and grew through global conflict, and were woven into the societal fabric of which we are a part. Our history is relatively brief and our members are not great in number, but I believe I/O psychologists have contributed strongly to both the domains of economic and personal welfare. Today, I/O psychology is multidisciplinary with regard to both its content and methods of inquiry. Upon reflection, it was the same at the turn of the century—a confluence of interest in advertising research, industrial efficiency, and mental testing. In a sense, the evolution of I/O psychology is the chronicle of mushrooming interests along certain common dimensions as molded by a few seismic events.

Scope of the Book

This book explains the field of I/O psychology. While it does discuss some technical areas, it does not presume the student has an extensive background in psychology, applied measurement, or statistics.

There are four major sections to help the student identify homogeneous units of material. The first section gives the student some exposure to and appreciation of how scientists address research questions.

The second section involves personnel psychology. Chapter 3 addresses a crucial topic: evaluative standards, or what I/O psychologists call "criteria." Criterion development is one of the oldest and most intriguing areas of research in I/O psychology. Chapter 4 discusses psychological tests and other measures used to predict how well people will perform in some aspect of their work. Chapter 5 shows how psycholo-

MISS PEACH

gists make decisions about hiring employees and classifying them in certain jobs, and describes which factors influence their decisions. Chapter 6 concerns personnel training: how psychologists decide who needs training, on what aspects of their job they need it, types of training techniques, and whether or not training works. Chapter 7 discusses why a person's performance is evaluated, how it is done, and what problems arise in appraising different types of employees.

The third section of the book reflects the organizational influence in I/O psychology. Chapter 8 reviews the nature of organizations, how organizations are different from one another, and the effect they have on human behavior. Chapter 9 concerns employee attitudes and feelings of satisfaction at work. Chapter 10 explores the approaches investigators have used to understand what motivates behavior in the workplace. Chapter 11 is concerned with the process of leadership and the factors associated with its recognition. Chapter 12 addresses organizational communication and how it affects the way people behave at work.

The final section discusses the work environment. Chapter 13 is on work design and organization development. It shows how jobs can be designed (or redesigned) to make them more rewarding for both the company and the employee. Chapter 14 examines union/management relations: the employer/employee relationship, collective bargaining and the resolution of industrial disputes, and recent behavioral research on unions. Finally, Chapter 15 (working conditions) explores the areas of environmental stress, work design, and research on work schedules.

I can think of few other fields of work that are as critical to human welfare as I/O psychology. We spend more of our lifetimes engaged in working than any other activity. Thus, I/O psychology is devoted to understanding our major mission in life. As our nation faces increasing problems of economic productivity, the field of I/O psychology continues to contribute to making our world a better place in which to live. Indeed, Katzell and Guzzo (1983) reported that 87% of the psychological approaches to improving employee productivity have been successful. Additionally, the scientific contributions that I/O psychologists have made are regarded as sufficiently noteworthy to occasion revision of federal laws governing fair employment practices (Norton & Gustafson, 1982).

In general, we as professionals are striving to gain a complete understanding of the problems and issues associated with the world of work, embracing both quantitative and humanistic dimensions (Stagner, 1982). When students have finished reading this book, they should have a much better understanding of human behavior in the workplace. Perhaps some people will be stimulated enough to continue work in I/O psychology. It is a most challenging, rewarding, and useful profession.

MAJOR CHAPTER OBJECTIVES IN REVIEW

After having read this chapter, you should know:

1. How I/O psychology relates to the profession of psychology as a whole.

2. The major fields of I/O psychology.

3. Licensing and certification of psychologists.

4. The history of I/O psychology including major people, events, and eras.

2

Research Methods in I/O Psychology

We all have hunches or beliefs about the nature of human behavior. Some of us believe that red-haired people are temperamental, dynamic leaders are big and tall, blue-collar workers prefer beer to wine, the only reason people work is to make money, and the like. The list is endless. Which of these beliefs are true? The only way to find out is to conduct research, the systematic study of phenomena according to scientific principles. Much of this chapter is devoted to research methods used in I/O psychology. Understanding the research process helps people solve practical problems, apply the results of studies reported by others, and assess the accuracy of claims made about new practices, equipment, and so on (Stone, 1986).

I/O psychologists are continually faced with a host of practical problems. Knowledge of research methods gives us a better opportunity to find useful solutions to problems rather than merely stumbling across them by chance. An understanding of research methods will also help us apply the results of studies reported by others. Some factors promote the generalizability of research findings; others retard it. Finally, people often assert the superiority of some new technique or method; a knowledge of research methods will help determine which are only cheap gimmicks.

Kaplan (1964) suggests that there are three goals of science: description, explanation, and prediction. The descriptive function of science is like a photograph—a picture of a state of events. Researchers may make descriptions of levels of productivity, number of employees who quit during the year, average level of job satisfaction, and so on. The explanatory function of science is perhaps the most difficult to unravel; it is a statement of why events occur as they do. It tries to find causes: why production is at a certain level, why employees quit, why they are dissatisfied, and so forth. The last function of science is prediction. Researchers try to predict which employees will be productive, who are likely to quit, and who will be dissatisfied. This information is then used to select applicants who would be better employees.

This chapter will give the reader some insight into the research process in I/O psychology. The process begins with a statement of the problem and ends with the

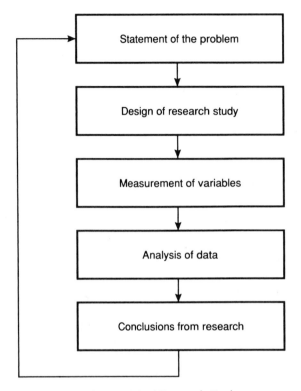

Figure 2–1   The Empirical Research Cycle

conclusions drawn from the research. This chapter should help you become a knowledgeable consumer of I/O psychological research.

The Empirical Research Process

Figure 2–1 shows the steps that are followed in conducting empirical research. The research process is basically a five-step procedure with an important feedback factor—that is, the results of the fifth step influence the first step in future research studies. The research process begins with a statement of the problem: What question or problem needs to be answered? Second, how do you design a study to answer the question? Third, how do you measure the variables and collect the necessary data? Fourth, how do you apply statistical procedures to analyze the data? (In other words, how do you make some sense out of all the information collected?) Finally, how do you draw conclusions from analyzing the data. Let's look at each of these steps in more detail.

Statement of the Problem

Questions that initiate research don't arise out of thin air. They are based on existing knowledge—your own and others' experiences with the problem, personal intuition or insight, or some formal theory. Most research begins with personal insight or intuition. As they conduct their studies, researchers become more familiar with the problem and may expand the scope of their questions. One person's research may stimulate similar research by someone else; thus, researchers often benefit from their colleagues' studies. After conducting much research on a topic, researchers may propose a theory about why the behavior occurs. The sequence that starts with data and culminates in theory is the *inductive* method of science. The opposite sequence is the *deductive* method. In the deductive method, a researcher first forms a theory (perhaps by intuition or by studying previous research) and then tests the theory by collecting data. If the theory is accurate, the data will support it; if inaccurate, they will not.

The value of theory in science is that it integrates and summarizes large amounts of information and provides a framework for the research. Despite the merits of theory, not all researchers agree on its value. The following quotes illustrate three different yet valid views:

1. "There is nothing quite so practical as a good theory."—*Kurt Lewin, noted social psychologist.*

2. "Research designed with respect to theory is likely to be wasteful."—*B. F. Skinner, noted experimental psychologist.*

3. "Theory, like mist on eyeglasses, obscures facts."—*Charlie Chan, noted fictional detective.*

Lewin's statement is often cited in psychology. Its essence is that a theory is useful for conducting research. A theory synthesizes information, organizes it into logical components, and directs the researcher's efforts in future studies. But Skinner believes that too much effort is spent on "proving" theories; that is, the theory is master of the research. Skinner feels that most theories eventually fall out of favor and that productive research does not require a theory. His position is an extreme case of empiricism. Charlie Chan thinks that researchers become too committed to proving their theories and become blinded to information that doesn't conform to what they want to believe. A good researcher doesn't let the theory obscure the facts. Rather than thinking of theories as "right" or "wrong," try to think of them in terms of their usefulness. A useful theory helps give meaning to the problem. It helps the subject matter make more sense.

The role of theory in I/O psychological research is quite mixed and depends on the subspecialty involved. Personnel psychology has been called "a lot of data but little theory"; organizational psychology has been called "a lot of theory but little data." Engineering psychology is almost completely devoid of theory, while organization development draws heavily on theories of social influence and change.

As an entire discipline, I/O psychology is not as dominated by theories as are other areas of psychology. In fact, I/O psychology has sometimes been referred to as the bastion of "dustbowl empiricism" by more theory-oriented psychologists. Such a statement is obviously a value judgment made by people who believe that theory is the best source for problem identification. Also, Miner (1984) believes that most I/O psychological theories have only modest value when judged by the standards of importance, empirical support, and usefulness. Theory is only one way to formulate a research problem: but other methods can also result in high-quality research. This is especially true in a pragmatic area like I/O psychology where some research problems come from everyday experiences in industry. If 50% of a company's work force quit every year, you don't need a theory to realize that this is a serious problem. Developing a carefully thought out research problem is far more important than which source (experience, theory, intuition) it came from.

Design of the Research Study

A research design is a plan for conducting a study. There are a number of strategies a researcher can use; the choice of method depends on the nature of the problem being studied. The strategies can be compared along several dimensions, but the two most important dimensions are (1) the naturalness of the research setting and (2) the investigator's degree of control over the study. No one strategy is the best under all conditions; there are always trade-offs.

1. *Naturalness of the Research Setting.* In some research strategies, the problem can be studied in the environment in which it naturally occurs. This is desirable because we don't want the research strategy being used to destroy or distort the phenomenon under study. Some research strategies appear phony because the problem is studied in unnatural ways. For example, the Hawthorne studies were conducted right in the plant with actual employees performing their normal jobs. However, there are studies that need not be conducted in a natural environment because the behavior under investigation is assumed to be independent of the setting. For example, an engineering psychology study testing whether people react faster to red or green lights could be conducted as appropriately in a laboratory as in a natural field setting.

2. *Degree of Control.* In some research strategies, the researcher has a high degree of control over the conduct of the study. In others, very little control is possible. In the Hawthorne studies the researchers could control the exact amount of lighting in the work area by installing (or removing) lights, though it turned out factors other than lighting affected the workers' performance. But suppose you want to study the relationship between people's ages and their attitude toward I/O psychology. You are particularly interested in comparing the attitudes of people over 40 with those under 40. You develop a questionnaire that asks their opinions about I/O psychology (is it interesting, difficult to understand, and so on), and you distribute the survey to your classmates. But it turns out that every person in the class is under 40. You have no information on the over-40 group, so you can't answer your research question. This

is an example of a low degree of control (you cannot control the age of the people in the study). Low control is particularly endemic to the survey questionnaire research strategy.

The following sections discuss the major research methods used in I/O psychology. Note that no one method is perfect—that is, none offers a high degree of both naturalism and control. The selection of a method is a function of the nature of the research problem being studied. Each method will be described, evaluated, and illustrated with an example.

Laboratory Experiment

Laboratory experiments are conducted in contrived settings as opposed to naturally occurring organizational settings. In a laboratory, the researcher has a high degree of control over the conduct of the study, especially those conditions associated with the observations of behavior. The experimenter designs the study to test how certain aspects of an actual working environment affect behavior. The laboratory setting must mirror certain dimensions of the natural environment where the behavior normally occurs. A well-designed laboratory experiment will have some of the conditions found in the natural environment but omit those that would never be present (Fromkin & Streufert, 1976).

A laboratory experiment has several *advantages*:

1. It is the best method for inferring causality; that is, the experimenter can eliminate or control for other explanations for the observed behavior. The experimenter can determine which variables influence other variables.

2. The measurement of behavior is usually very precise because it is observed under tightly controlled conditions.

3. Laboratory experiments can easily be replicated by other researchers because all the experimental conditions are measured and recorded.

But there are *disadvantages*:

1. Laboratory experiments may lack realism (that is, a high degree of similarity between the experimental conditions and the natural environment).

2. Some phenomena cannot be analyzed in a laboratory (for example, how riots affect individual behavior and attitudes).

3. Some variables may have a weaker impact in a laboratory than they do in a natural environment.

Example of the Method. Hegarty and Sims (1978) reported an example of a laboratory experiment in I/O psychology. In this study researchers wanted to know what factors cause people to behave unethically in business decisions. Specifically, they wanted to examine under what conditions would people agree to make kickbacks—that is, illegal payments of money in return for favorable treatment. The subjects in the study were 120 graduate students enrolled in a business college. They were told to pretend that they were sales managers for a large wholesaling company. Each subject had to decide how many salespeople to hire in his or her company because that factor would directly affect the company's profits. If too few were hired, the company would not be able to sell enough to be profitable. If too many were hired, the company would pay out more in salary than each salesperson would return in profit. But, if a salesperson paid a kickback to a purchasing agent, that salesperson's sales would increase and so would the company's profit.

Hegarty and Sims tested the effects of two factors on the practice of making kickbacks. One factor was the degree to which kickbacks would increase the company's profits. Some subjects were told that they could stop their salespeople from making kickbacks purely on moral grounds and that kickbacks had no effect on profit. Others were told that they could stop kickbacks, but it would probably decrease the company's profits. The second factor was a sense of competitiveness instilled in the subjects. Some subjects were not told how well other people were doing in the experiment (that is, how much profit the other subjects were making). Other subjects were told that if their profit performance was among the best of all subjects, they would each be paid an extra cash incentive.

The results of the study showed that if unethical behavior (i.e., making kickbacks) is rewarded, it is more likely to occur. It appears that subjects can "learn" to be unethical if such behavior enhances their position. Unethical behavior also increased when competitiveness was intensified. Subjects who were offered money for performing better approved kickbacks more readily than did others.

In evaluating this study, you can see both the advantages and disadvantages of a laboratory experiment. First, the researchers showed that two factors (the degree of reward and interpersonal competitiveness) directly caused people to behave in unethical ways. By controlling the only two variables in the experiment, they showed that increasing the reward for illegal behavior resulted in more illegal behavior—a big step toward explaining why it occurs. The researchers also based their results on objective empirical evidence, not speculation or guesswork.

However, the subjects were not really sales managers; they were students *pretending* to be sales managers. Would real sales managers act the same way? We do not know. Second, if this problem occurred in the real world, would the results have been the same? Would even more people approve of kickbacks if they had been threatened with being fired for failing to reach a certain profit level? We can only speculate about this because the study was not done in an actual company with real sales managers.

Field Experiment

A field experiment is a research strategy in which the manipulation of independent variables occurs in a natural setting (that is, the people in the study do not perceive the setting as having been created to conduct the research). As in a laboratory experiment, the researcher tests the effects of a few variables on the subjects' behavior. But there is also less control. In a laboratory experiment, all the variables are manipulated at the researcher's discretion and can be included or excluded according to the design of the study. However, in a field experiment, variables that occur in the natural setting are also part of the experiment. Though they add to the richness and realism of the field experiment, they also lessen the researcher's control.

The *advantages* of field experiments include the following:

1. Because field experiments are conducted in natural settings, they are very realistic, and the results are highly generalizable.

2. If the proper experimental design is used, the researcher may be able to *suggest* some causal inferences about the observed behavior.

3. Unlike laboratory experiments, field experiments can address broader research questions dealing with complex behavior in real-life contexts.

The *disadvantages* of field experiments include the following:

1. Because there is less control in field experiments, it is difficult to measure variables precisely.

2. Sometimes the individuals or groups of people may refuse to participate in the study.

3. Researchers often can't gain access to a business or industrial setting—the "natural environment" for a field experiment.

Example of the Method. Latham and Kinne (1974) reported a study that used the field experiment as a research method. It examined how a one-day training program on goal setting affected the job performance of pulpwood workers. The subjects in the study were 20 pulpwood logging crews. Their behavior was observed as they performed their normal job duties harvesting lumber in a forest. The experimenters split the subjects into two groups of 10 crews each. They matched the two groups on a number of factors so that they would be equal in terms of ability and experience. One group was given a one-day course in how to set production goals—that is, how many cords of wood to harvest per hour. The other group was not given any special instructions, and worked in the usual way. The experimenters then monitored the job performance of the wood crews over the next three months. Results showed that the crews who were trained to set production goals for themselves harvested significantly more wood than the other crews. The study supported the use of goal setting in an industrial context.

The major strength of this study in terms of demonstrating the field experiment method was that the context was very real. Actual workers were used in the context of their everyday jobs. The setting was a forest, not a laboratory where the subjects would have been pretending to be there. While the study's design was not complex enough to rule out competing explanations for the observed behavior, it did allow the researchers to conclude that the goal-setting technique probably caused the increase in job performance.

This study also illustrates some of the weaknesses of the field experiment method. Some workers who were supposed to participate in the goal-setting group decided not to. This forced the researchers to redesign part of the study. Also, few I/O psychologists would be able to influence a company to change its work operations for research purposes. (In fact, one of the authors of this study was employed by the lumber company, so this undoubtedly had some effect on the company's willingness to participate.)

Field Study

Like field experiments, field studies involve the study of people in intact, naturally occurring environments as opposed to those specifically created for research purposes (for example, laboratory experiments). Unlike the field experiment, the field study gives the researcher very little control over the study. The researcher cannot select certain variables to manipulate (like the effect of goal setting in the Latham and Kinne field experiment) because variables are not manipulated at all; rather, the researcher relies on self-reports of subjects or some other nonmanipulative measure. In some cases, research based upon field studies is exploratory in nature. Ideas that have been generated as a result may be translated into hypotheses, which in turn are tested formally in a field or laboratory experiment.

Because field studies occur in natural environments, they are high in realism. The researcher's presence may distort the nature of the variables being studied, so he or she must remain as *unobtrusive* as possible. In most cases, field study data are obtained through questionnaires or interviews. But while the researcher's presence can be minimized, it can never be totally eliminated.

The *advantages* of the field study are:

1. Field studies are very realistic because they are conducted in naturally occurring environments.

2. Data on a large number of variables can be collected at the same time.

3. The researcher's impact in the study is not nearly as great as in other research strategies.

The *disadvantages* of the field study include:

1. Variables cannot be manipulated by the researcher and their effects systematically studied, so the method does not permit causality to be assessed.

2. Companies may not give permission to conduct a field study.

3. The measurement of the variables is not as precise as in laboratory experiments.

Example of the Method.   Muldrow and Bayton (1979) conducted a study to investigate the accuracy of decision making in male and female executives. One hundred male managers and one hundred female managers working in federal agencies in Washington, D.C., completed a questionnaire assessing how people decide to hire a new person in an organization. The subjects were given descriptions of three hypothetical job applicants. Their task was to review the information on each applicant and then pick one of the three to hire. The questionnaire asked the subjects to describe what information about the applicants led them to make the decisions they did and how they felt about their choices.

After this, each subject completed additional questionnaires that assessed personality, willingness to take risks, and strength of sex-role perceptions (that is, questions about what is "typical" male and female behavior). Their responses were analyzed to see if there was any relationship between the response to the decision-making problem and the other variables (personality of the subject, inclination for risk taking, and the like). The findings showed that the most accurate decision makers were those who were confident about their decision and had taken more time to reach it. They also showed that the male and female executives were equal in terms of their decision-making ability. But there were differences between males and females in how they went about making decisions. The female executives were less willing to take risks, and they held stronger sex-role perceptions. The researchers concluded that certain variables are consistently associated with making correct managerial decisions, and that males and females are equally competent in making decisions.

The task used in this study was "natural" for the subjects. The subjects answered the questionnaires in their own offices. And the decision-making task (hiring a new person) was something they performed as a normal part of their jobs. While the subjects in this study probably do not routinely complete questionnaires about their personalities, they undoubtedly did a large amount of report writing, questionnaire taking, and general paperwork. Thus, the researchers were not asking the subjects to engage in behavior they typically would not use on the job. Also, the study allowed the researchers to examine many variables at once—decision-making ability, personality, risk-taking propensity, and sex-role perceptions—rather than confining them to only one or two.

This example also brings out the weaknesses of the field study. The researchers could not prove that abundant confidence in one's decisions *causes* good decisions. Nor could they say that more accurate decisions are reached after lengthy contemplation. Perhaps factors other than those examined in this study caused the results. The researchers say only that certain variables were associated with making accurate decisions. A second major drawback of the field study method pertains to the difficulty of obtaining permission to conduct the research. In this study, one of the authors worked for the federal government, which is probably why the government permitted it. An I/O psychologist does not *have* to be employed by a company to get permission for a field study, but having some "contacts" in a company greatly helps.

Sample Survey

A researcher using the sample survey research strategy collects information directly from subjects in a standardized manner. The survey is conducted in a natural rather than a contrived setting. The data are usually collected by a questionnaire, interview,

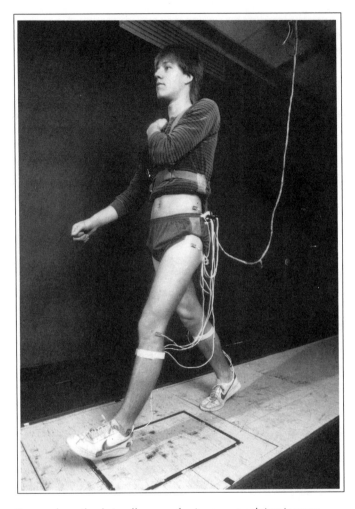

Research methods in all areas of science are relying increasingly on computers. Pictured is a man wired with infra-red sensors for computer analysis of his walk.

Cameramann International

or observation. Whatever technique is used, the researcher must be sure that it is used systematically (that is, that each person in the study answers the same set of questions). Variables are simply measured (not manipulated) by the researcher. This method is a good way to generate ideas that may later be tested more formally in a field or laboratory experiment.

The *advantages* of the sample survey method include:

1. The method is high in realism since data are collected in a naturally occurring environment.

2. The results of sample surveys often yield new hypotheses that might be tested by another method.

3. A number of sample survey techniques (for example, questionnaires, interviews, and observation) may be used alone or in combination.

    Some of the *disadvantages* of the method are that:

1. The researcher has little control over the variables in the study. Because no variables are manipulated experimentally, the method does not permit any inferences about causality.

2. People are becoming less willing to respond to surveys. If a questionnaire is used, only a low proportion is usually returned. A typical questionnaire (with no follow-up reminder to the respondents) has a return rate of less than 50%.

3. Because some people do not respond to surveys, the responses of those people who do may be biased or unrepresentative of the group as a whole.

Example of the Method. Two Canadian researchers (Goodale & Aagaard, 1975) conducted a survey to assess workers' reactions to switching from a five-day workweek to a four-day workweek with longer hours per day. The researchers sent a questionnaire to several hundred employees of a large company that had recently switched to the four-day workweek. Each employee was asked to rate several aspects of his or her job with the four-day work schedule compared to the former five-day one. Questions involved absenteeism, psychological reactions to the longer workday, work performance, attitudes toward work, changes in leisure life, and feelings of overall satisfaction.

The results showed that most employees were enthusiastic and positive about the four-day workweek. Younger workers were more positive than older ones. Managers and supervisors were quite negative, both in their own attitudes and in how they perceived their employees' performance. The researchers concluded that the four-day workweek would be successful *except* where (1) employees must meet and work in groups, (2) customer service was provided five days per week, (3) supervisors felt the need to be available during all working hours, and (4) a majority of employees were relatively old.

One of the strengths of this study was that the data were collected in a very real

THE WIZARD OF ID   by Brant parker and Johnny hart

TABLE 2–1 *Comparison of Empirical Research Strategies*

	Laboratory Experiment	Field Experiment	Field Study	Sample Survey
Control (potential for testing causal relationships)	High	Moderate	Low	Low
Realism (naturalness of setting)	Low	High	High	High

environment. Employees were asked to evaluate a work schedule that affected their lives every day. Also, the data provided many ideas that might be pursued in future studies. For example, what changes could be made so that supervisors would like the four-day workweek? Are the positive reactions likely to continue, or were they the results of a Hawthorne effect?

The disadvantages of the method in this case were that the researchers could not experimentally manipulate any factors. They could not have half the employees work the four-day schedule and the other half five days and then compare the two sets of responses. They could not test what caused the older workers to dislike the four-day workweek—were they more inflexible than younger workers, or are they just more used to working five days? What is not apparent from this study is the problem of the return rate and potentially biased results. Goodale and Aagaard had little trouble getting responses back. Other researchers are not always so lucky. The results of some well-planned and well-intentioned sample surveys have to be discarded because the return rate is too small to be meaningfully interpreted.

Table 2–1 compares the four research methods on two major dimensions: researcher control and realism. No method is high on both factors. There is always a trade-off; a researcher may sacrifice realism for control or vice versa, depending upon the study's objectives. Choice of strategy should be guided by the purpose of the research and the resources available. A well-trained I/O psychologist is versed in all four of these research methods and knows the advantages and disadvantages of each.

Measurement of Variables

After developing a study design, the researcher must next enact it and measure the variables of interest. A *variable* is a symbol that can assume a range of numerical values. *Quantitative* variables (age, time, and so on) are those inherently numerical (21 years or 16 minutes). *Qualitative* variables (sex, race, and the like) are not inherently numerical, but they can be "coded" to give them numerical meaning: female=0, male=1, or white=0, black=1, Hispanic=2, Oriental=3; and so forth. For research purposes, it doesn't matter what numerical values are given to the qualitative variables, because they merely identify these variables for measurement purposes.

The term *variable* is often used in conjunction with other terms in I/O psychological research. Four such terms that will be used throughout this book are *independent, dependent, predictor,* and *criterion* variables.

Independent and *dependent* variables are associated in particular with experi-

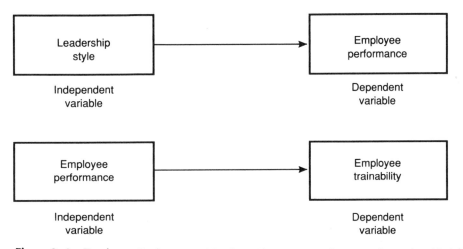

Figure 2–2 Employee Performance Used as Either a Dependent or Independent Variable .

mental (laboratory or field) research strategies. Independent variables are those that are manipulated or controlled by the researcher. They are chosen by the experimenter, set or manipulated to occur at a certain level, and then examined to assess their effect on some other variable. In the laboratory experiment by Hegarty and Sims (1978), two independent variables were used: (1) the degree to which kickbacks increased company profits, and (2) the degree of competition among the subjects. In the field experiment by Latham and Kinne (1974) one independent variable was used: the effect of a one-day training program on goal setting.

Experiments assess the effects of independent variables on the dependent variable. The dependent variable is the object of the researcher's interest. It is usually some aspect of behavior (or, in some cases, attitudes). In the Hegarty and Sims study, the dependent variable was the subjects' willingness to engage in unethical behavior—that is, accept kickbacks. In the Latham and Kinne study, the dependent variable was the number of cords of wood harvested by the lumber crews. The same variable can be selected as the dependent or independent variable depending upon the goals of the study. Figure 2–2 shows how a variable (employee performance) can be used as either one. In the former case, the researcher wants to study the effect of various leadership styles (independent variable) on employee performance (dependent variable). The researcher might select two types of leadership styles (a stern, taskmaster approach versus a relaxed easygoing one) and then assess their effects on job performance. In the latter case, the researcher might want to know what effect employee performance (independent variable) has on the ability to be trained (dependent variable). The employees are divided into "high-performer" and "low-performer" groups. Both groups then attend a training program to assess whether the high performers learn faster than the low performers. Note that variables are never *inherently* independent or dependent. Whether they are one or the other is up to the researcher's discretion.

Predictor and *criterion* variables are used often in I/O psychology. When scores on one variable are used to predict scores on a second, the variables are called predictor and criterion variables, respectively. For example, a student's high school grade-point average might be used to predict his or her college grade-point average. High school grades are the predictor variable; college grades are the criterion variable.

As a rule, criterion variables are the focal point of our study. Predictor variables may or may not be successful in predicting what we want to know (the criterion). Predictor variables are similar to independent variables; criterion variables are similar to dependent variables. The distinction between the two is a function of the research strategy. Independent and dependent variables are used in the context of experimentation. Predictor and criterion variables are used in any research strategy where the goal is to determine the status of subjects on one variable (the criterion) as a function of their status on another variable (the predictor).

Levels of Measurement

Variables must be measured as accurately as possible. Some variables can be measured very precisely, but others can be measured in only a coarse way. A *scale* is a measuring device to assess a person's score or status on some variable. While there are many scales, there are only four basic types: (1) nominal, (2) ordinal, (3) interval, and (4) ratio (Stevens, 1958).

Nominal Scale. A nominal scale, the crudest type of scale, classifies objects or people into categories. It simply shows that a person (or object) is a member of one of these categories. For example, a nominal scale could classify people by sex into one of two categories (male or female). Racial groups (Caucasian, Oriental, and the like) can also be categorized on a nominal scale. Note that a nominal scale does not arrange people or objects in some order or sequence.

Ordinal Scale. An ordinal scale orders objects along some dimension. The most common type of ordinal scale is a rank order. If you were asked to rank order three foods—pizza, chicken, and steak—along a dimension of taste preference, you might rank them steak, pizza, and chicken. We know you like pizza better than chicken and steak better than both pizza or chicken. But we don't know *how much* you like these foods. You may like all three or despise all three, or you may like only one. So an ordinal scale shows how things are ranked along a dimension but not the distance between the ranked items.

Interval Scale. An interval scale measures how much of a variable is present (using equal distances between scale units.) A thermometer represents an interval scale. The distance between 10° and 15° (5°) is the same as the difference between 87° and 92° (5°). An interval scale is more precise than an ordinal scale, because it shows not only relative preference (that is, rank order) but also how much the objects are preferred. Suppose you rated the three foods on a 10-point scale (where a rating of 10 is high and 1 is low) and the results were steak 9, pizza 2, and chicken 1. The scale shows that you like steak a lot but not pizza or chicken. A person who had the same rank order but rated the foods as steak 10, pizza 9, and chicken 8 would obviously feel differently.

Ratio Scale.   A ratio scale is the most precise type of scale. It has all the properties of the other three scales and one more: a true zero-point. Measures such as length, weight, and age are all ratio scales. The true zero-point in the scale means that nothing can be shorter than 0 inches (or centimeters), lighter than 0 ounces (or grams), or younger than 0 seconds. A thermometer is not a ratio scale because it has no true zero-point (−5° is a negative temperature). The term *ratio* means that a ratio can be formed between two objects; for example, a 20-year-old is *twice* as old as a 10-year-old. But we cannot say that 20° is *twice* as warm as 10°.

Analysis of Data

After the data have been collected, the researcher has to make some sense out of them. Here's where statistics come in. Many students get anxious over the topic of statistics. While some statistical analytic methods are quite complex, most are reasonably straightforward. I like to think of statistical methods as golf clubs—tools for helping do a job better. Just as some golf shots call for different clubs, different research problems require different statistical analyses. Knowing a full range of statistical methods will help you better understand the research problem. It's also impossible to understand the research process without some knowledge of statistics. The following is a brief exposure to statistics.

TABLE 2–2   *One Hundred IQ Scores*

133	141	108	124	117
110	92	88	110	79
143	101	120	104	94
117	128	102	126	84
105	143	114	70	103
151	114	87	134	81
87	120	145	98	95
97	157	99	79	107
108	107	147	156	144
118	127	96	138	102
141	113	112	94	114
133	122	89	128	112
119	99	110	118	142
123	67	120	89	118
90	114	121	146	94
128	125	114	91	124
121	125	83	99	76
120	102	129	108	98
110	144	89	122	119
117	127	134	127	112

Descriptive statistics simply describe data. They are the starting point in the data analysis process; they give the researcher a general idea of what the data are like. Descriptive statistics can show the shape of a distribution of numbers, measure the central tendency of the distribution, and measure the spread or variability in the numbers.

Distributions and Their Shape

Suppose a researcher measures the intelligence of 100 people with a traditional IQ test. Table 2–2 shows those 100 scores. To make some sense out of all these numbers, the researcher arranges the numbers according to size and then plots them in a scatter diagram. Figure 2–3 shows what those 100 test scores would look like. This is called a *frequency distribution*. Because so many scores are involved, they are grouped into categories of equal size with each interval containing ten possible scores.

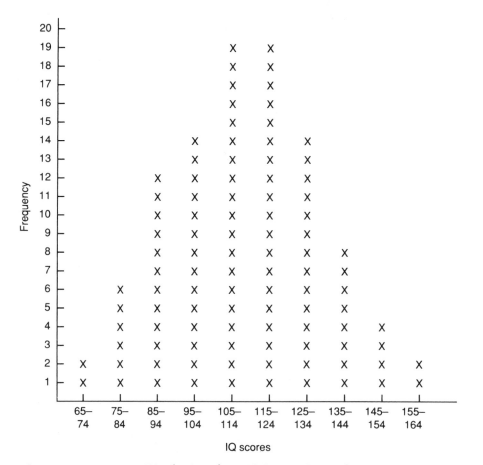

Figure 2–3   Frequency Distribution of 100 IQ Scores (Grouped Data)

The figure tells something about the IQ data. We can see that the most frequently occurring scores are in the middle of the distribution; extreme scores (both high and low) taper off as we move away from that point. The general shape of the distribution in Figure 2–3 is called a *normal* or *bell-shaped* distribution. Many variables in psychological research are distributed normally; that is, with the most frequently occurring scores in the middle of the distribution and progressively fewer scores at the extreme ends. Figure 2–4a shows a classic normal distribution. The smoothness of the curve in Figure 2–4a compared to that in Figure 2–3 is due to the fact that the occurrence of many test scores would take the "kinks" out of the distribution.

Not all distributions of scores are normal in shape—some are lopsided or pointed. If a professor gives an easy test, there will be a larger proportion of high scores. This would result in a pointed or *skewed* distribution. Figure 2–4b shows a *negatively* skewed distribution (the tail of the distribution is in the negative direction). The opposite would occur if the professor gives a difficult test; the result would be a *positively* skewed distribution (the tail points in the positive direction), as in Figure 2–4c.

Thus, plotting the distribution of data is one way to understand it. We can make inferences based on the shape of the distribution. (In the case of the negatively skewed distribution of test scores, we infer that the test was easy.)

Measures of Central Tendency

After we learn the shape of the distribution, the next step is to find the typical score. One of three measures of *central tendency* is usually used for this depending on the shape of the distribution. The *mean* is the most common measure of central tendency. The mean is the arithmetic average score in the distribution. It is computed by adding all of the individual scores and dividing by the total number of scores in the distribution. The formula for computing the mean is:

Formula 2–1

$$\overline{X} = \frac{\Sigma X}{N}$$

where $\overline{X}$ is the symbol for the mean, Σ is the symbol for summation, X is the symbol for each individual score, and N is the total number of scores in the distribution. The mean for the data in Table 2–2 is:

Formula 2–2

$$\overline{X} = \frac{11,322}{100} = 113.22$$

The average IQ in the sample of people tested is 113.22 (or 113 rounded off). The entire distribution of 100 scores can be described by one number: the mean. The

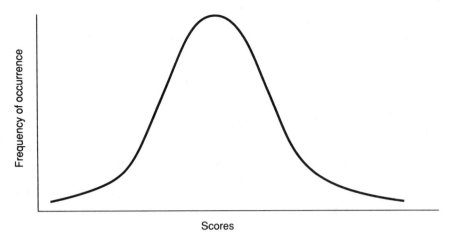

Figure 2–4a   A Normal or Bell-Shaped Distribution of Scores

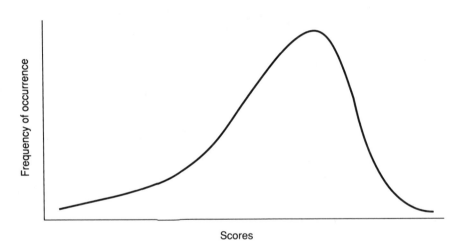

Figure 2–4b   A Negatively Skewed Distribution of Scores

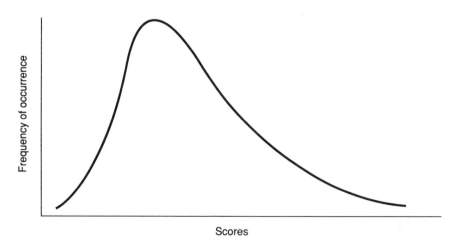

Figure 2–4c   A Positively Skewed Distribution of Scores

mean is a useful measure of central tendency and is most appropriately used with normally distributed variables.

The *median* is the midpoint of all the scores in the distribution. So 50% of all scores are above the median and 50% below. If we have a distribution of four scores and they are 1, 2, 3, and 4, the median would be 2.5; that is, half the scores (3 and 4) will be above this point, and half (1 and 2) will be below it. (The statistical procedure used to compute the median for graphed data is quite lengthy and will not be presented here. For information purposes, the median for the data presented in Table 2–2 is 112.9). The median is the best measure of central tendency for skewed distributions, because these always contain some extreme scores. The median would be relatively insensitive to these scores, but the mean would be affected by them.

The mode is the least common measure of central tendency. The *mode* is the most frequently occurring score in a distribution. The mode is not used for very many statistical analyses, but it may have a practical purpose. Some concepts are best understood in whole numbers (that is, integers), not fractions or decimals. For example, it makes more sense to say "The modal number of children in a family is 3" rather than "The mean number of children in a family is 2.75." It is difficult to imagine what three-fourths of a child would be. In cases as this the mode is the preferred measure of central tendency. Although the mean would be more appropriate than the mode for describing the data in Table 2–2, the mode is 114.

In the normal distribution, the mean ($\overline{X}$), median (Md), and mode (Mo) are equal to each other as shown in Figure 2–5a. In a skewed distribution, the mean is pulled out the farthest toward the tail of the distribution, as shown in Figure 2–5b.

Thus, one of the three measures of central tendency can be used to describe a typical score in a distribution.

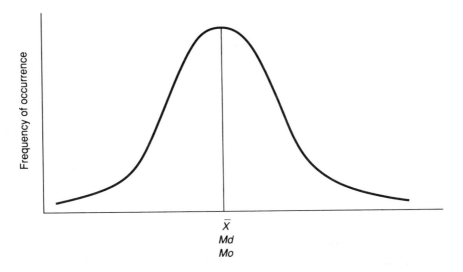

Figure 2–5a   Position of the Mean, Median, and Mode in a Normal Distribution

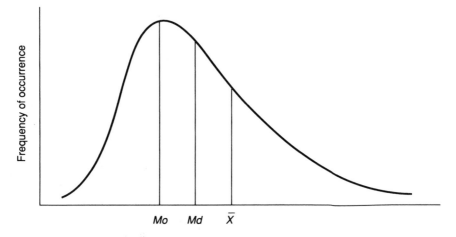

Figure 2–5b   Position of the Mean, Median, and Mode in a Skewed Distribution

Measures of Variability

In addition to describing a set of scores by the shape of their distribution and central tendency, we can also talk about the spread of the scores or their *variability*. The scores' variability is an indication of how *representative* the mean is as a measure of central tendency. There are several numerical indices to describe variability in scores. The simplest index is called the *range*, obtained by subtracting the lowest score from highest. The range of the data in Table 2–2 would be 157−67 = 90.

Consider Figure 2–6. Here there are two normal distributions with equal means but unequal variability. One distribution is very peaked with a small range; the other is quite flat with a big range. In addition to having different ranges, these distributions also differ with regard to another measure of variability, the *standard deviation*. The standard deviation is a measure of the spread of scores around the mean. The formula for the standard deviation is:

Formula 2–3
$$s = \sqrt{\frac{\Sigma(X - \bar{X})^2}{N}}$$

where s is the standard deviation, X is each individual score, Σ is the symbol for summation, $\bar{X}$ is the mean of the distribution, and N is the total number of scores in the distribution. To compute the standard deviation, subtract the mean ($\bar{X}$) from each individual score (X) in the distribution, square that number, add up all the numbers, divide that total by the number of scores in the distribution, and then take the square root of the figure. By applying this formula to the data in Table 2–2, the standard deviation for that distribution is 19.96 (or 20 rounded off).

The standard deviation is particularly important in conjunction with the normal distribution. Given the mathematical properties of the normal curve, we know that

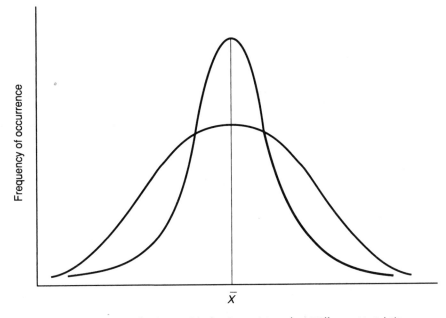

Figure 2–6 Two Distributions with the Same Mean but Different Variability

theoretically 68% of all scores fall within ±1 standard deviation of the mean. So from the data in Table 2–2 (which has a mean of 113 and a standard deviation of 20) we know that theoretically 68% of all the scores should fall between 93 (113−20) and 133 (113 + 20). Furthermore, the mathematical derivation of the normal curve indicates that theoretically 95% of all the scores should fall within ±2 standard deviations from the mean, that is between 73 (113−40) and 153 (113 + 40). Finally, theoretically 99% of all the scores should fall within ±3 standard deviations from the mean, between 53 (113−60) and 173 (113 + 60). The actual percent of scores from the data in Table 2–2 is very close to the theoretical values; 69% of the scores fell within 1 standard deviation, 96% fell within 2 standard deviations, and 100% fell within 3 standard deviations.

Although other measures of variability besides the range and standard deviation are also used, these two measures will suffice for the purposes of this book. Variability is important because it tells about the spread of scores in a distribution. And this can be just as important as knowing the most typical score in a distribution.

The Concept of Correlation

So far we have been concerned only with the statistical analysis of one variable: its shape, typical score, and dispersion. But in most I/O psychological research, we are concerned with the relationship between two (or more) variables. In particular, we are usually interested in the extent that we can understand one variable (the criterion or dependent variable) on the basis of our knowledge about another (the predictor or independent variable). A statistical procedure useful in determining this relationship is called the *correlation coefficient*.

A correlation coefficient reflects the *degree of linear relationship* between two variables, which we shall refer to as X and Y. The symbol for a correlation is r, and its range is from -1.00 to $+1.00$. A correlation coefficient tells two things about the relationship between two variables: (1) the direction of the relationship, and (2) its magnitude.

The *direction* of the relationship is either positive or negative. A positive relationship means that as one variable increases in magnitude, so does the other. An example of a positive correlation would be that between height and weight. As a rule, the taller a person is, the more he or she weighs; increasing height is associated with increasing weight. A negative relationship means that as one variable increases in magnitude, the other gets smaller. An example of a negative correlation would be the correlation between production workers' efficiency and scrap rate. The more efficient workers are, the less scrap is left. The less efficient they are, the more scrap is left.

The *magnitude* of the correlation is an index of the strength of relationship. Large correlations indicate greater strength than small correlations. A correlation of .80 indicates a very strong relationship between the variables; while a correlation of .10 indicates a very weak relationship. Also, magnitude and direction are independent. A correlation of $-.80$ is just as strong as one of $+.80$.

Figures 2–7a, b, c, and d show graphic portrayals of correlation coefficients. The first step in illustrating a correlation is to plot all pairs of variables in the study. For a sample of 100 people, record the height and weight of each person. Then plot the pairs of data points (height and weight) for each person. The stronger the relationship between the two variables, the tighter is the spread of data points around the line of best fit that runs through the scatterplot. Figure 2–7a shows a scatterplot for two variables that have a *high positive* correlation. Notice the slope of the line through the data points slants in the positive direction, and most of the data points are packed tightly around the line.

Figure 2–7b shows a scatter plot for two variables that have a *high negative* correlation. Again notice the data points are packed tightly around the line. But in this case, the line slants in the negative direction.

Figure 2–7c shows a scatterplot between two variables that have a *low positive* correlation. While the line slants in the positive direction, the data points are spread quite widely throughout the scatterplot.

Finally, Figure 2–7d shows a scatterplot between two variables that have a *low negative* correlation. The line of best fit slants in the negative direction, and the data points are not packed tightly around the line.

The stronger the correlation between two variables (either positive or negative), the more accurately we can predict one variable from the other. The statistical formula used to compute a correlation will not be presented in this book since it is available in statistics books. Also, it will not be necessary for the reader to compute any correlations. What is important is knowing what a correlation is and how to interpret one. However, the reader should realize that the only way to derive the exact numerical value of a correlation is to apply the statistical formula. The eyeball-inspection method of looking at a scatterplot will yield some idea of what the correlation is, though research has shown that people are generally not very good at inferring the magnitude of correlations by using just this method (Bobko & Karren, 1979).

A few other issues are important to remember. A correlation is useful for describing the relationship between two variables when those variables are related in a linear or straight-line relationship. But not all variables are linearly related to each other. Figure 2–8 shows the relationship between two variables, arousal and performance. It shows that when a person is not aroused or motivated to work, performance is very low. As motivation increases to a moderate amount, performance increases accordingly. However, when a person's motivation level is too high, he or she gets too anxious and performance suffers. There is a strong and clear relationship between these two variables, but it is not a linear one—it is *curvilinear*. When there is a curvilinear relationship between two variables, a typical correlation coefficient is an inappropriate statistic for measuring the degree of association between them. If a researcher were to compute a correlation between two variables that were curvilinearly related, the calculated correlation would be very small, leading the researcher to conclude there is no relationship between the two variables. But this is wrong. There *is* a relationship between the variables, but not a linear one. So the researcher would have to use another statistical technique.

Calculation of a correlation coefficient does not permit any inferences about causality; that is, whether one variable caused the other to occur. While a causal relationship may exist between two variables, just computing a correlation will not reveal this fact. Causality can be ascertained only through experimental research.

Suppose you wish to compute the correlation between (1) the amount of alcohol consumed in a town, and (2) the number of people who attend church there. You collect data on each of these variables in many towns in your area. The correlation turns out to be .85. On the basis of this high correlation, you conclude that because people drink all week, they go to church to repent (alcohol consumption causes church attendance). Your friends take the opposite point of view. They say that because people have to sit cramped together on hard wooden pews, after church they "unwind" by drinking (church attendance causes alcohol consumption). Who is correct? On the basis of the existing data, no one is correct because causality cannot be inferred from correlation. One opinion may be correct, but proof of causality must await experimental research. (In point of fact, the causal basis of this correlation is undoubtedly neither of the above opinions. It is due to the fact that the various towns in the study have different populations, which produces a systematic relationship between these two variables along with many others, such as the number of people who eat out in restaurants or attend movies).

Because correlation is a common analytic technique in I/O psychological research, many of the empirical findings in this book will be expressed in those terms.

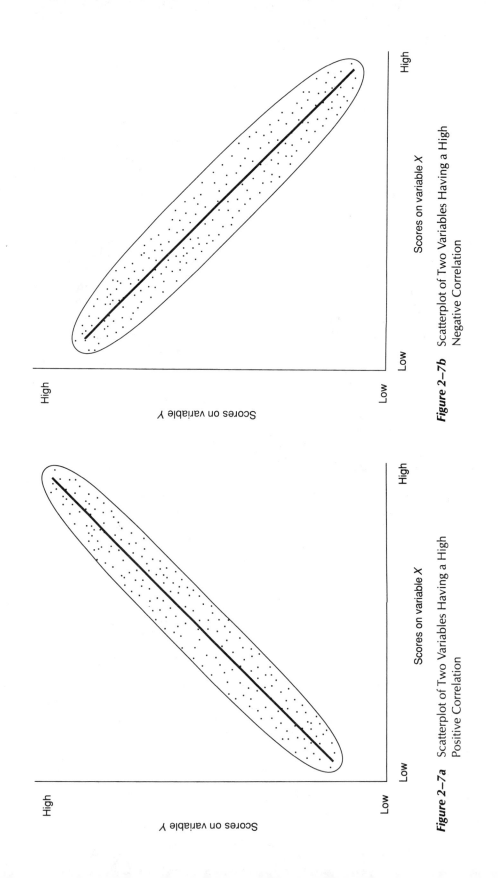

Figure 2–7a Scatterplot of Two Variables Having a High Positive Correlation

Figure 2–7b Scatterplot of Two Variables Having a High Negative Correlation

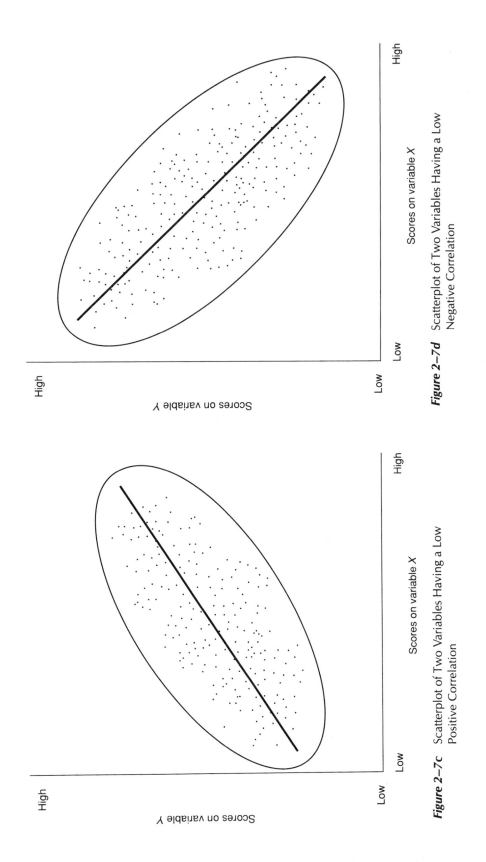

Figure 2–7c Scatterplot of Two Variables Having a Low
Positive Correlation

Scores on variable X

Scores on variable Y

High

Low

Low

High

Figure 2–7d Scatterplot of Two Variables Having a Low
Negative Correlation

Scores on variable X

Scores on variable Y

High

Low

Low

High

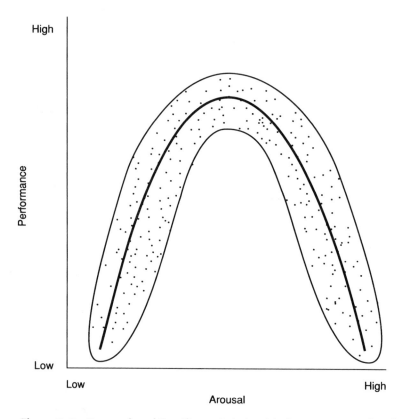

Figure 2–8   Scatterplot of Curvilinear Relationship Between Arousal and Performance

However, the concept of correlation will not magically yield accurate inferences in I/O psychological research. As Mitchell (1985) notes, a poorly designed research study cannot be "saved" by the use of correlation to draw valid conclusions. Researchers must carefully plan studies, use sound methodological procedures, *and* use appropriate statistical analyses to arrive at meaningful conclusions.

Conclusions from Research

After the data have been analyzed, the researcher draws conclusions. A conclusion may be that certain factors do indeed contribute to unethical behavior on the part of managers (Hegarty & Sims, 1978). If a company wants to diminish the likelihood of unethical behavior, it might remove any rewards associated with it. The study by Latham and Kinne (1974) concluded that goal setting increased the rate of wood harvesting. So a company might decide to implement the goal-setting procedure throughout the firm. Generally, it is unwise to implement any major changes based on the results of only *one* study. As a rule, we prefer to know the results from several studies. We want to be as certain as possible that any organizational changes are grounded in repeatable, generalizable results.

Sometimes the conclusions drawn from a study modify beliefs about a problem. Note in Figure 2-1 that a feedback loop extends from "Conclusions from Research" to "Statement of the Problem." The findings from one study influence research problems in future studies. Theories may be altered if empirical research fails to confirm some of the hypotheses put forth. While I/O psychology is not heavily dominated by theory, Ghiselli (1974) reports that most theories eventually fall out of favor rather than being *unequivocally* rejected. But the major reason they do is that they repeatedly are unsupported by data. Research is a cumulative process. Researchers build on one another's work in formulating new research questions. They communicate their results by publishing articles in journals. A competent researcher must keep up to date in his or her area of expertise to avoid repeating someone else's study. The conclusions drawn from research can affect many aspects of our lives. Research is a vital part of industry; it is the basis for changes in products and services.

Research can truly be an exciting activity, although seemingly tedious if you approach it only from the perspective of testing stuffy theories, using sterile statistics, and inevitably reaching dry conclusions. Daft (1983) has suggested research is a *craft*, and a researcher, like an artist or craftsperson, has to pull together a wide variety of human experiences to produce a superior product. Daft suggests we make better use of surprise reactions, firsthand experiences, common sense, and emotions in helping us to design research studies. Being a researcher is more like unraveling a mystery than following a cookbook (see Field Note 1). However, research is not flash-in-the-pan thrill-seeking; it involves perseverance, mental discipline, and patience. There is also no substitute for hard work. I can recall many times when I anxiously anticipated seeing computer analyses that would foretell the results of a lengthy research study. It is this sense of anticipation that is the fun of doing research—and research, in the spirit of Daft's view of researchers being craftspersons, is a craft I try to pass on to my students.

Field Note 1

Being a good researcher is a lot like being a good detective. You have to use all of your senses to buttress information collected by traditional research methods. I often administer and interpret attitude surveys for my industrial clients. The results of these surveys reveal a wealth of information about the companies. However, this information can often seem somewhat dry and bland if judged only in statistical terms. Therefore, I have taken it upon myself to understand and appreciate the statistical results better by personally experiencing the organization. I have smelled acid fumes in a metal fabricating company that burned my nose and eyes after only a few minutes' exposure. I have tasted a rancid bologna sandwich from a vending machine situated by a big window in the company cafeteria (the sun shining through the window would heat the vending machine and spoil the food). I have walked (and slipped) across a company parking lot that was a solid two-to-three-inch sheet of ice for the months of January and February. I have been in a "sound-sensitive" room that was so quiet I could hear my heartbeat. And in one status-conscious organization I have seen in the president's office a white llama-wool carpet thick enough to swallow most of your shoes as you walked across it. In and of themselves these events have little meaning, but when considered as part of the total organizational fabric, they provide a rich texture to I/O research findings.

Ethical Problems in Research

Research subjects have certain legal rights (Kelman, 1972). These rights pertain to their physical treatment during a study, confidentiality of information, privacy, and voluntary consent (no one can be forced to take part in a study). Researchers who violate these rights, particularly in studies that involve physical or psychological risk, can be subject to professional censure and possible litigation. The American Psychological Association (1981) has a code of ethics that must be honored by all APA members who conduct research. Among the researcher responsibilities covered by the code of ethics are the accurate advertising of psychological services, confidentiality of information collected during the research, and the rights of human subjects participating in it. The code of ethics was created to protect the rights of subjects and to avoid the possibility of having research conducted by unqualified people.

The researcher is faced with additional problems with employees of companies. Argyris (1968) reports that while managers generally favor research, it can cause its own share of problems in an industrial context. Employees who are naive about the purpose of research often are suspicious when asked to participate. They wonder how they were "picked" for inclusion in the study and if they will be asked difficult questions. Some people even think a psychologist can read their minds and thus discover all sorts of private thoughts. Research projects that arouse emotional responses place managers in an uncomfortable interpersonal situation.

Mirvis and Seashore (1979) have described some of the problems facing those who conduct research with employees. Most of the problems involve *role conflict*, the dilemma of being trained to be a good researcher yet having to comply with both company and professional standards (London & Bray, 1980). For example, consider a role-conflict problem I faced in doing research with industrial employees. I used a sample survey to assess the employees' opinions and morale. The management of the company commissioned the research. As part of the research design, all employees were told that their responses would be confidential. One survey response revealed the existence of employee theft. Though I did not know who the employee was, with the information given and a little help from management, that person could have been identified. Was I to violate my promise and turn over the information to management? Should I tell management that some theft has occurred, but I had no way to find out who had done it (which would not have been true)? Or was I to ignore what I knew and fail to tell management about a serious problem in the company? What I did in this case was to inform the company of the occurrence of theft but refuse to supply any information regarding the personal identity of the thief. This was an uneasy compromise between serving the needs of my client yet not betraying the confidentiality of the information source. These types of problems are not unique to my study (Williams, Seybolt, & Pinder, 1975). Lowman (1985) has presented a series of cases on ethical problems for I/O psychologists. Taken from real-life experiences, the book reveals the multitude of ethical dilemmas covering such issues as conflict of interest, plagiarizing, and "overselling" research results. The pressures to conduct high-quality research, the need to be ethical, and the reality of organizational life sometimes place the researcher in a difficult situation (see Field Note 2). These demands place constraints on the I/O psychologist that researchers in other areas do not always face.

Field Note 2

Most ethical problems do not have clear-cut solutions. Here is one I ran into. I was trying to identify some psychological tests that would be useful in selecting future sales people for a company. As part of my research, I administered the tests in question to all the employees in the sales department of the company. With the company's consent, I assured the employees that the test results would be confidential. I explained my purpose in giving the tests was to test the tests— that is, assess the value of the tests, and no one in the company would ever use the test results to evaluate the employees. In fact, no one in the company would even know the test scores. The results of my research were highly successful. I was able to identify which tests were useful in selecting potentially successful salespeople.

A few weeks later the same company approached me and said it now wanted to look into the value of using psychological tests to promote salespeople to the next highest job in the department, that of sales man-

ager. In fact, it was so impressed with the test results for selecting new salespeople, it wanted to assess the value of these very same tests for identifying good sales managers. And since I had already given the tests to their salespeople and had the scores, all I would have to do is turn over the scores to the company and it would determine if there was any relationship between scores on the tests and promotability to sales manager. I said I couldn't turn over the test results to the company, because that would violate my statement that the test results were confidential, and that no one in the company would ever know how well the employees did on the tests. I offered two alternatives. One would be to readminister the same tests to the employees under a different set of test conditions; namely, that the company *would* see the test results, and in fact the results could be used to make promotion decisions. The second alternative would be for me (not the company) to determine the value of these tests to make promotion decisions. In that way I would maintain the confidentiality of the test scores.

The company totally rejected the first alternative, saying it made no sense to readminister the same tests to the same people. I already had the test results, so why go back and get them a second time? The second alternative was also not approved. The company said I was deliberately creating a need for the company to pay me for a second consulting project when it (the company) was perfectly capable of doing the work itself, with no outside help and at no extra cost. It said, in effect, I was holding the test results as "hostage" and would not release them. In my opinion the company was asking me to compromise my professional integrity by using the test results in a way that violated the principles under which the tests were originally administered.

The issue was never really resolved. The company soon faced some major sales problems caused by competitors, and lost interest in the idea of using psychological tests for identifying sales managers. The company is still angered by my decision, asserting I am assuming ownership of "its" test results. I have not been asked to do any more consulting work for the company, but it is also quite possible it would no longer have needed my services even if I had turned the test results over to it.

Research in Industry

While the empirical research process shown in Figure 2–1 portrays the conduct of most I/O psychological research, research conducted in industry (as opposed to universities or research centers) often has some additional distinguishing features. Boehm (1980) has observed that in industry, research questions arise inevitably from organizational problems. For example, problems of excessive employee absenteeism, turnover, job dissatisfaction, and so on may be the genesis for a research study designed to reduce their severity. Rarely in industry will research questions be posed just to "test a theory." In fact, a study by Flanagan and Dipboye (1981) revealed that psychologists who view organizations simply as laboratories to test theories are not looked on favorably.

A second major difference involves how the results will be used. In industry, if the results of the study turn out to be positive and useful, the research unit of the organization will then try to "sell" (that is, gain acceptance of) the findings throughout the rest of the organization. For example, if providing job applicants with a very candid and realistic preview of the organization reduces turnover, the researchers will try to persuade the rest of the organization to use such procedures in recruiting new employees. If the results of a study turn out negative, the organization will look for side products or secondary ideas that will be of value. In research outside of industry, less attention is given to implementing the findings and convincing other people of their utility.

A third common difference between academic and industrial research is the type of individual who participates in a research study. Research conducted in industry invariably utilizes employees or job applicants as study participants. Research conducted in academia often utilizes college students as subjects. There is a long-standing debate regarding the generalizability research findings based upon college student subjects. Gordon, Slade, and Schmitt (1986) reported research studies which have utilized both students and nonstudents as subjects often obtain different results for the two types of subjects. Other researchers (for example, Greenberg, 1987) support the use of college students as subjects in research and believe results produced from such studies are highly generalizable.

Finally, there are different motives for conducting research in industry as opposed to universities. Industrial research is conducted to enhance the efficiency of the organization. Among private-sector employers this usually translates into greater profitability. For example, research can be of vital importance in finding out consumer responses to new products and services, identifying ways to reduce waste, and making better use of the human talent within an organization. In university settings research may not have such an *instrumental* purpose. Research questions are posed that have relevance to industry, but the link between the findings and their implementation may not be as direct (see Field Note 3).

I am reminded of a student who approached an organization with a research idea. The student needed a sample of managers to test a particular hypothesis. After patiently listening to the student's request, the organizational representative asked, "Why should we participate in this study? How can this study help us?" Industries that sponsor and participate in research do so for a reason: to enhance their welfare. Universities also conduct research for a reason, but that reason may be nothing more than intellectual curiosity.

Field Note 3

Industrial research is always embedded in a larger context, that is, it is conducted for a specific reason. Sometimes the research is successful, sometimes it isn't, and sometimes you can win the battle but lose the war. A client of mine gave promotional tests, tests that current employees would take to be advanced to higher positions in the company at higher rates of pay. These tests were important to the employees, for only through the tests could they be promoted. The company gave an attitude survey and discovered many employees did not like the tests. They said many test questions were outdated, there were no correct answers to some questions, and most questions were poorly worded. As a result of all these "bad" questions, employ-

ees were failing the tests and not getting promoted.

The company hired me to update and improve their promotional tests (there were 75 of them). Using the full complement of psychological research procedures, I analyzed every question on every test, eliminated the poor questions, had new questions developed, and in general "cleaned up" each of the tests. By every known standard the tests were now of very high quality. Both the company and I felt confident the employees would be delighted with these revised tests. We were wrong. In the next attitude survey given by the company, the employees continued to think poorly of the (new) tests, but their reasons were different than before.

Now they complained the tests were too hard, too technical, and required too much expertise to pass them. The employees failed the new tests with the same frequency as they had failed the old tests, and were just as unhappy. In fact, they may have been even more unhappy since their expectations about the tests had been elevated because the company had hired me to revise them. I felt I had done as good a job in revising the tests as I possibly could have, but in the final analysis I didn't really solve the company's problem. The company hired me to revise the tests, but what it really wanted was to have the employees be satisfied with the tests, which didn't occur.

While academic and industrial research may be guided by somewhat different factors, both have contributed heavily to the I/O psychological literature. The infusion of research from both sectors has in fact been very healthy and stimulating for the profession. Jahoda (1981) has commented that more psychological research needs to be done in *anticipation* of future work problems as opposed to being a reaction to current problems. Industrial researchers seem to be in the best position to forecast future organizational concerns. Thus, they may be able to find answers to problems before they become crises.

Future Research in I/O Psychology

It is difficult to predict the future of I/O psychological research. Research topics can and do boom into existence for many reasons, and others fade.

Dipboye and Flanagan (1979) argue that research topics get studied in either laboratory *or* field settings. They feel that laboratory and field research strategies should be used in coordination rather than in competition with each other. The authors believe that each basic strategy has something to offer and that researchers can gain understanding by studying the problem with both methods. Laboratory research has traditionally been regarded as more scientifically rigorous, while field research findings are regarded as being more representative of real-world conditions. Locke (1985) reached the conclusion that most findings from laboratory experiments can be generalized beyond the lab, while other individuals (for example, Mook, 1983) are more skeptical.

Gordon, Kleiman, and Hanie (1978) are quite critical of I/O psychological research as a whole, asserting that many of the findings from I/O psychological research are "commonsensical" (that is, could be predicted in advance by nonpsychologists). Gordon and associates (1978) argue for the development of more theory as a means of advancing the discipline beyond the investigation of common-sense problems. Dunnette (1966) voiced similar concerns. He argued that psychologists are too easily influenced by fads and fashions in their research, and let their research methods dictate what problems get studied. ("I have a research method that is handy. Now what can I study with it?")

Is there any relationship between what topics I/O psychologists study and the overall importance of those topics to society? Campbell, Daft, and Hulin (1982) feel there is little relationship, as some trivial research topics seem to be popular because they permit ease in asking questions and obtaining data. What *should* I/O psychologists study? Strasser and Bateman (1984) surveyed both managers and nonmanagers as to what they would like to see researched. The predominant answer from both groups related to how people can learn to get along with one another in a work context. As one respondent in their survey said, "People all have different personalities and some people we just can't get along with. How can we avoid personality conflicts and still have a good working relationship" (p. 87)? The second-most-pressing research need was on communication among people.

Thomas and Tymon (1982) believe there is an unhealthy split between academicians who research topics (the "knowledge producers") and practitioners who desire to implement research findings (the "knowledge users"). Those authors feel that individuals tend to fall into one of the camps, and we need closer interplay between producing knowledge and using it. While it may be tempting to say that researchers should tackle big, socially important problems, such problems are usually very complex and difficult to research. However, the contributions that I/O psychologists have made to such areas are among our profession's proudest achievements. I/O psychological research has been instrumental in enhancing our nation's productivity (Guzzo, Jette, & Katzell, 1985) and the quality of our work life (Lawler, 1982). An understanding of research methods is vital for psychologists to resolve problems confronting humankind in a world growing in complexity.

MAJOR CHAPTER OBJECTIVES IN REVIEW

After having read this chapter, you should know:

1. The empirical research cycle.

2. The advantages and disadvantages of laboratory experiments, field experiments, field studies, and sample surveys.

3. The four basic types of measurement scales.

4. Statistical concepts of central tendency and variability.

5. The concept of correlation and its interpretation.

6. Ethical issues associated with research.

CASE STUDY—How Should I Study This?

Robin Mosier had just returned from her psychology class and was anxious to tell her roommate about an idea she had. Julie Hansen had taken the same class the previous semester, so Robin was hopeful that Julie could help her out. The psychology professor gave the class an assignment to come up with a research design to test some hypothesis. The basis for Robin's idea stemmed from the job she held the past summer.

Robin began to describe her idea. "Last summer I worked as a clerk in the bookkeeping department of a bank. Sometimes it wasn't always clear how we should fill out certain reports and forms. I was always pretty reluctant to go to my supervisor, Mr. Kast, and ask for help. So were the other female workers. But I noticed the guys didn't seem to be reluctant at all to ask him for help. So I got this idea, see, I think females are more reluctant than males to ask a male superior for help."

"Okay," replied Julie. "So now you have to come up with a way to test that idea?"

"Right", said Robin. "I was thinking maybe I could make up a questionnaire and ask students in my class about it. I think people would know if they felt that way or not."

"Maybe so." Julie said, "but maybe they wouldn't want to admit it. You know, it could be one of those things that you either don't realize about yourself, or if you do, you just don't want to say so."

"Well, if I can't just ask people about it, maybe I could do some sort of experiment," Robin commented. "What if I gave students some tasks to do but the instructions weren't too clear? If I'm right, more males than females will ask a male experimenter for help."

"Do you think you'd get the opposite effect with a female experimenter?" asked Julie.

"You mean, would more females than males ask a female experimenter for help? I don't know. Maybe," answered Robin.

"If that's the case," said Julie, "you might want to test both male and female experimenters with both male and female subjects."

Robin scratched some notes on a pad. Then she said, "Do you think an experimenter in a study is the same thing as a boss on a job? You see your boss every day, but you may only be in an experiment for about an hour. Maybe that would make a difference in whether or not you sought help."

"I'm sure it could," replied Julie. "I know I would act differently toward someone I might not see again than someone I'd have to work with a long time."

"I know what I'll do," Robin responded. "I won't do the experiment in a lab setting, but I'll go back to the company where I worked last summer. I'll ask the male and female office workers how they feel about asking Mr. Kast for help. I saw the way they acted last summer, and I'd bet they tell me the truth."

"Wait a minute," cautioned Julie. "Just because some females may be intimidated by Mr. Kast doesn't mean that effect holds for all male supervisors. Mr. Kast is just one man. How do you know it holds for all men? That's what you want to test, right?"

Robin looked disconsolate. "There's got to be a good way to test this, although I guess its more complicated than I thought."

Questions

1. What research method should Robin use to test her idea? How would you design the study?

2. What other variables might explain the employees' attitude toward Mr. Kast?

3. If this idea were tested with a questionnaire or sample survey, what questions should be asked?

4. If this idea were tested in a laboratory or field experiment, what variables should be eliminated or controlled for in the research design?

2

Personnel Psychology

3

Criteria

Each time you evaluate someone or something, you use criteria. *Criteria* (the plural of *criterion*) are best defined as evaluative standards; they are used as reference points in making judgments. We may not be consciously aware of the criteria that affect our judgments, but they do exist. We use different criteria to evaluate different kinds of objects or people. That is, we use different standards to determine what makes a good (or bad) movie, dinner, ball game, friend, spouse, or teacher. In the context of I/O psychology, criteria are most important for defining the "goodness" of employees, programs, and units in the organization, as well as the organization itself.

Disagreement Among People in Making Evaluations

When you and some of your associates disagree in your evaluation of something, what is the cause? Chances are good the disagreement is caused by one of two types of criterion-related problems. For example, take the case of rating Professor Jones as a teacher. One student thinks he is a good teacher; another disagrees. The first student defines "goodness in teaching" as (1) preparedness, (2) course relevance, and (3) clarity of instruction. In the eyes of the first student, Jones scores very high on these criteria and receives a positive evaluation. The second student defines goodness as (1) enthusiasm, (2) capacity to inspire students, and (3) ability to relate to students on a personal basis. This student scores Jones low on these criteria and thus gives him a negative evaluation. Why the disagreement? Because the two students have different criteria for defining teaching effectiveness.

Disagreements over the proper criteria in decision making are quite common. Values and tastes often dictate people's choice of criteria. For someone with limited funds, a good car may be one that gets high gas mileage. But for a wealthy person, the main criterion may be physical comfort. Dyer, Schwab, and Theriault (1976) describe how managers and their bosses disagree on the criteria used in giving raises. Managers feel their performance is not given enough weight and that budgets are given too much weight. The authors feel that such disagreements over the right criteria can adversely affect employee motivation and satisfaction.

Not all disagreements are caused by using different criteria. Suppose that both students in our teaching example define teaching effectiveness as preparedness, course relevance, and clarity of instruction. The first student thinks Professor Jones is ill-prepared, teaches an irrelevant course, and gives unclear instruction. But the second student thinks he is well-prepared, teaches a relevant course, and gives clear instruction. Both students are using the same evaluative standards, but they do not reach the same judgment. The difference of opinion in this case is due to the discrepancies in the meaning attached to Professor Jones's behavior. These discrepancies may be due to perceptual biases, differential expectations, or operational definitions associated with the criteria that cause them. Thus, people who use the same standards in making judgments do not always reach the same conclusion.

The profession of I/O psychology does not have a monopoly on criterion-related issues and problems. They occur in all walks of life, ranging from the criteria used to judge interpersonal relationships (for example, communication, trust, respect) to the welfare of nations (for example, literacy rates, per capita income, infant mortality rates). Differences of opinion about criteria even extend to how national industries evaluate themselves. Garvin (1986) reported that Japanese companies regard issues of product quality as their primary concern, and that U.S. companies feel quality is of secondary importance to the primary goal of meeting production schedules. Since many important decisions are made on the basis of criteria, it would be difficult to overstate their significance in the decision-making process. Because criteria are used to render a wide range of judgments, I define them as the "evaluative standards by which objects, individuals, procedures, or collectivities are assessed for the purpose of ascertaining their quality." Criterion issues have major significance in the field of I/O psychology.

Conceptual Versus Actual Criteria

Psychologists have not always felt that criteria are of prime importance. Prior to World War II, they were inclined to believe that "criteria were either given of God or just to be found lying about" (Jenkins, 1946, p. 93). Unfortunately, this is not so. We must carefully consider what is meant by a "successful" worker, student, parent, and so forth. We cannot plunge headlong into measuring success, goodness, or quality until we have a fairly good idea as to what (in theory, at least) we should be looking for.

A good beginning point is the notion of a conceptual criterion. The *conceptual criterion* is a theoretical construct, an abstract idea that can never actually be measured. It is an ideal set of factors that constitute a successful person (or object or collectivity) as conceived in the psychologist's mind. Let's say we want to define a successful college student. We might start off with *intellectual growth;* that is, better students should experience more intellectual growth than lesser-quality students. Another dimension might be *emotional growth.* A college education should help students clarify their own values and beliefs, and this should aid in emotional development and stability. Finally, we might say that a good college student should want to have some voice in civic activities, to be a "good citizen," and to contribute to the well-being of his or her community. As an educated person, the good college student will assume an active role in helping to make society a better place in which to live. We might call this dimension a *citizenship* factor.

These three factors thus become the conceptual criteria for defining a "good college student." We could apply this same type of process to defining a "good worker," "good parent," or "good organization." However, because conceptual criteria are theoretical abstractions, we have to find some way to turn them into measurable, real factors. That is, we have to obtain *actual criteria* to serve as measures of the conceptual criteria that we would prefer to (but cannot) assess. The decision then becomes which variables to select as the actual criteria.

A psychologist might choose grade-point average as a measure of intellectual growth. Of course, a grade-point average is not *equivalent* to intellectual growth, but it probably reflects some degree of growth. To measure emotional growth, a psychologist might ask the student's advisor to judge how much the student has matured over his or her college career. Again, maturation is not exactly the same as emotional growth, but it is probably an easier concept to grasp and evaluate than the more abstract notion of emotional growth. Finally, as a measure of citizenship, a psychologist might count the number of volunteer organizations (student government, charitable clubs, and so on) the student has joined over his or her college career. It could again be argued that the sheer number (quantity) of joined organizations is not equivalent to the quality of participation in these activities, and that "good citizenship" is more appropriately defined by quality rather than quantity of participation. Nevertheless, because the difficulties inherent in measuring quality of participation, plus the fact that one cannot speak of quality unless there is some quantity, the psychologist decides to use this measure. Table 3–1 shows the relationship between the conceptual criteria and actual criteria of success as a college student.

How do we define a "good" college student in theory? Using the conceptual criteria as the evaluative standard, a good college student should display a high degree of intellectual and emotional growth and should be a responsible citizen in the community. How do we operationalize a good college student in practice? Using the actual criteria as the evaluative standard, we say a good college student has earned high grades, is judged by an academic advisor to be emotionally mature, and has joined many volunteer organizations throughout his or her college career. In review-

TABLE 3–1 *Conceptual Criteria and Actual Criteria of a Successful College Student*

Conceptual Criteria	Actual Criteria
1. Intellectual growth	Grade point average
2. Emotional growth	Advisor rating of emotional maturity
3. Citizenship	Number of volunteer organizations joined in college

ing the relationship between the two sets of criteria (conceptual and actual), remember "the goal is to obtain an approximate estimate of the (conceptual) criterion by selecting one or more actual criteria which we think are appropriate" (Blum & Naylor, 1968, p. 176).

Criterion Deficiency, Relevance, and Contamination

The relationship between the conceptual and actual criteria can be expressed in terms of three concepts: deficiency, relevance, and contamination. Figure 3–1 shows the degree of overlap between the conceptual and actual criteria. The circle represents the content of each type of criterion. Because the conceptual criterion is a theoretical abstraction, we can never know exactly how much overlap occurs. The actual criteria selected are never totally equivalent to the conceptual criteria we have in mind, so there will always be a certain amount (although unspecified) of deficiency, relevance, and contamination.

Criterion Deficiency.   Criterion deficiency is the degree to which the actual criteria fail to overlap the conceptual criteria; that is, how deficient the actual criteria are in representing the conceptual ones. There is always some degree of deficiency in the actual criteria. By careful selection of the actual criteria, we can reduce (but never eliminate) criterion deficiency. Conversely, criteria that are selected because they are simply expedient, without much thought given to their match to conceptual criteria, will be grossly deficient.

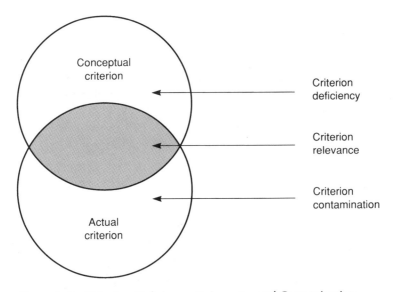

Figure 3–1   Criterion Deficiency, Relevance, and Contamination

Criterion Relevance. Criterion relevance is the degree to which the actual criteria and conceptual criteria coincide. The greater the match between the conceptual and actual criteria, the greater is the criterion relevance. Again, because the conceptual criteria are theoretical abstractions, we cannot know the exact amount of relevance.

Criterion Contamination. Criterion contamination is that part of the actual criteria that is unrelated to the conceptual criteria. It is the extent to which the actual criteria measure something other than the conceptual criteria. Contamination consists of two parts. One part, called *bias*, is the extent to which the actual criteria systematically or consistently measure something other than the conceptual criteria. The second part, called *error*, is the extent to which the actual criteria are not related to anything at all.

Both contamination and deficiency are undesirable in the actual criterion, and together they distort the conceptual criterion. This prompted Brogden and Taylor (1950b) to refer to them as *criterion distortion.* Criterion contamination distorts the actual criterion because certain factors are included that don't belong (that is, they are not present in the conceptual criterion). Criterion deficiency distorts the actual criterion because certain important dimensions of the conceptual criterion are not included in the actual criterion.

Let us consider criterion deficiency and contamination in the example of setting criteria for a good college student. How might the actual criteria we chose be *deficient* in representing the conceptual criteria?

Students typically begin a class with differing degrees of prior knowledge of the subject matter. One student may know nothing of the material, while another student may be very familiar with it. At the end of the term the former student might have grown more intellectually than the latter student, but the latter student might get a higher grade in the course. However, by using the grade-point average as our criterion, we would (falsely) conclude the latter student grew more intellectually. So the relationship between grades and intellectual growth is not perfect (that is, it is deficient). A rating of emotional maturity by an academic advisor might be deficient because the advisor is not an ideal judge. He or she might have only a limited perspective of the student. Finally, it is not enough to just count how many volunteer groups a student belongs to. Quality of participation is as important (if not more so) than quantity.

How might these actual criteria be *contaminated*? If some academic majors are more difficult than others, grades will be a contaminated measure of intellectual growth; students in "easy" majors will be judged to have experienced more intellectual growth than students in difficult majors. This is a bias between earned grade-point averages and the difficulty of the student's academic major. The source of the bias affects the actual criterion (grades) but not the conceptual criterion (intellectual growth). A rating of emotional maturity by the student's advisor could be contaminated by the student's grades. The advisor might believe that students with higher grades have greater emotional maturity than students with low grades. Thus, the grade-point average might bias an advisor's rating even though it probably has no relationship to the conceptual criterion of emotional growth. Finally, counting the number of organizations a student joins might be contaminated by the student's popularity. Students who join many organizations may simply be more popular rather than better citizens (which is what we wanted to measure.)

If we know that these criterion measures are contaminated in this way, why would we use them? In fact, when a researcher *knows* a certain form of contamination is present, its influence can be controlled through experimental or statistical procedures. The real problem lies in anticipating the occurrence of contaminating factors.

As Wallace (1965) has observed, psychologists have spent a great deal of time trying to discover new and better ways to measure actual criteria. They have used various analytical and computational procedures to get more precise assessments. Wallace has recommended that rather than dwelling on finding new ways to measure actual criteria, psychologists should spend more time choosing actual criteria that will be adequate measures of the conceptual criteria, which are what they really seek to understand. The adequacy of the actual criterion as a measure of the conceptual criterion is always a matter of professional judgment—no equation or formula will determine it. As Wherry (1957) has said, "If we are measuring the wrong thing, it will not help us to measure it better" (p. 5).

Criterion Development

I/O psychologists use several different means to identify or develop criteria. It is vital to determine the appropriate evaluative standards for making judgments. The adequacy and appropriateness of criteria set the limits for the quality of the judgments. Poor criteria beget poor judgments. But the issue of appropriate criteria is made more difficult by a time dimension. Short-term criteria for defining the goodness or quality of something may not be the same as long-term criteria. In deciding to buy a car, a short-term criterion may be initial cost, and a long-term standard, its resale value. Standards used to make short-term decisions about quality are *proximal* criteria. Standards used to make long-term decisions about quality are *distal* criteria. The following three studies of criterion development show different approaches to this topic.

Criteria may be developed *deductively* (from theory to data) or *inductively* (from data to theory). An example of the deductive approach was reported by Freeberg (1976). Freeberg wanted to define relevant criteria for judging the quality of

FRANK AND ERNEST ®by Bob Thaves

WHAT A PREACHER!... HE HAD THE CONGREGATION DOING "THE WAVE"!

11-15 THAVES

a certain youth work-training program. The program's purpose was to train hard-to-employ teenagers in certain skills so they could get full-time jobs. Freeberg carefully examined the existing literature on training programs and arrived at 32 variables indicative of performance in the training program (proximal criteria). He found 40 variables to indicate postprogram job performance (distal criteria). Trainees rated themselves on the 32 program-completion variables (for example, their degree of vocational awareness and confidence, personal adjustment, and motivation). Former trainees who now held jobs rated themselves on the 40 postprogram variables (for example, their level of job performance, extent and level of employment, and vocational planning). Freeberg used a statistical procedure called *factor analysis* to identify the major dimensions of training and posttraining success based on these ratings. The results showed that the 32 program-completion variables could be reduced to four major criteria of success in the training program: work motivation and social attitudes; social-community adjustment; training-program adjustment; and competence in vocational planning. The 40 postprogram variables were reduced to five major criteria of success on the job: overall social and vocational adjustment; on-the-job success and satisfaction; job-search motivation; competence in job planning; and short-range job orientation. This study is a good example of the deductive approach to criterion development. It starts with a careful and rational identification of possible criterion variables, followed by an empirical assessment of their value.

Another example of using deduction to develop criteria was reported by Taber and Hackman (1976). These authors were interested in establishing criteria of undergraduate college performance. Like Freeberg, they began their research with a rationally derived list of 67 aspects of student performance in college. The list covered both academic (for example, general intelligence, analysis of ideas) and nonacademic (for example, athletic involvement, participation in student organizations) areas. Faculty members and college students were asked to rate samples of "most successful" and "least successful" students on these variables. The purpose of the study was to determine what specific variables differentiate these two groups. Results showed that the criteria for success in college consisted of five academic factors (including communication proficiency and career goals) and eight nonacademic factors (such as ethical behavior, interpersonal sociability, and personal growth). The authors were able to establish that a "good" college student performs successfully in a number of specific academic and nonacademic domains. In addition, both faculty members and students had similar views regarding the criteria of college success.

One of my own studies (Muchinsky, 1975b) is a final example of criterion development (in this case, the inductive approach). I was interested in establishing the criteria of consumer credit risk. I wanted to learn how people were judged to be good or poor credit risks. Unlike the authors of the two previous studies, I had no prior theoretical notions as to what constitutes credit risk. I used the inductive approach, starting with data and culminating with some conceptual ideas, to establish the criteria of credit risk. I obtained the financial records of 500 people who had borrowed money from loan companies. Half of them were judged poor credit risks on the basis of how they repaid their loans, and had been denied further credit. The other half were judged good credit risks and would be granted another loan by the company. I wanted to find out which aspects of loan repayment affect people's credit ratings. After comparing the two groups of people on several variables associated with loan repayment, I found two critical dimensions: how delinquent the people were in making their monthly loan payments and whether they missed payments. The poor credit risks either missed several payments or were often late making them. So I determined the concept of credit risk is defined by two criteria: missed payments and delinquency of payments. Working inductively, I then proposed an explanation of consumer credit risk (Muchinsky, 1975a).

What do we "do" with criteria once we have established them? They serve many purposes, both theoretical and applied. From a theoretical viewpoint, criteria are the basis for understanding a concept. In fact, the concept is best defined by the interrelationships among the criteria used to assess it. I was able to define the concept of credit risk after identifying its criterion dimensions. This procedure, called *construct validation,* will be discussed in more detail in a later chapter.

From a practical standpoint, the identification of criteria provides a rational basis for "treating" people, programs, or social collectivities. For example, as a loan company official, you would not give a loan to someone who has a history of missing payments or being delinquent. As a training program director, you would want the program to enhance trainee motivation and increase competence in vocational planning. As the director of a welfare agency, you would want to extend financial or medical aid to those communities at certain poverty or illness levels. Identifying criteria is the first step in initiating action (for example, selecting, training, assisting) that is part of an organization's goals.

Job Analysis

I/O psychologists often must identify the criteria of effective job performance. These criteria then become the basis for hiring people (choose them on the basis of ability to meet the criteria of job performance), training them (to perform those aspects of the job that are important), paying them (high levels of performance should warrant higher pay), and classifying jobs (jobs with similar performance criteria would be grouped together). A procedure useful in identifying the criteria or performance dimensions of a job is called *job analysis,* and is conducted by a *job analyst.*

Several authors (for example, Nagle, 1953, Guion, 1961) have described how job analytic procedures may be used to develop criteria. After identifying the jobs to be analyzed, a job analysis dissects the work performed into component parts. A thorough job analysis will document the tasks that are performed on the job, the situation in which the work is performed (for example, tools and equipment present, working conditions), and the human qualities needed to perform the work. These data then provide the basic building blocks needed for many personnel decisions.

Methods of Job Analysis

There are four major types of methods for analyzing jobs. The first is a variation of the interview. Employees are asked questions about the nature of their work. They may be interviewed individually, in small groups, or through a series of panel discussions. A trained interviewer asks employees questions to get an understanding of the activities performed on the job and the skills needed to perform them. The interview method is probably the most commonly used job analytic method because it is adaptable to a wide variety of jobs. However, it is critical the employees understand the purpose of the interview, otherwise they will often exaggerate the importance of what they do and thus supply misleading information (see Field Note 1).

Field Note 1

Job analysts should explain what they are doing (and why they are doing it) when interviewing employees about their jobs. If they do not fully explain their role, employees may feel threatened, fearing the analysts may somehow jeopardize them by giving a negative evaluation of their performance, lowering their wages, firing them, and so on. While job analysts do not have the power to do these things, some employees assume the worst. When employees feel threatened, they will usually magnify the importance or difficulty of their contributions to the organization in an attempt to protect themselves. Therefore, to ensure accurate and honest responses from employees, all job analysts should go out of their way to disarm any possible suspicions or fears.

I learned the importance of this point early in my career. One of my first job analyses was for the job of sewer cleaner. I had arranged to interview three sewer cleaners about their work. However, I had neglected to provide much advance notice about myself, why I would be talking to them, or what I was trying to do. I simply arrived at the work site, introduced myself, and told the sewer cleaners that I wanted to talk to them about their jobs. Smelling trouble, the sewer cleaners proceeded to give me a memorable lesson on the importance of first establishing a nonthreatening atmosphere. One sewer cleaner turned to me and said, "Let me tell you what happens if we *don't* do our job. If we don't clean out the sewers of stuff like tree limbs, rusted hubcaps, and old tires, the sewers get clogged up. If they get clogged up, the sewage won't flow. If the sewage won't flow, it backs up. People will have sewage backed up into the basements of their homes. Manhole covers will pop open, flooding the streets with sewage. Sewage will eventually cover the highways, airport runways, and train tracks. People will be trapped in their homes surrounded by sewage. The entire city will be covered with sewage, with nobody being able to get in or out of the city. And that's what happens if we don't do our job of cleaning the sewers."

Sadder but wiser, I learned the importance of not giving employees any reason to overstate their case.

A second method uses structured questionnaires or inventories. The questionnaire would typically list many activities that could be performed on a job (several hundred questions would not be unusual). The employee would rate these activities on several scales, as how often they are performed, how important they are, and so on. The answers to these questions would be statistically analyzed to arrive at an understanding of job content. The questionnaire method is most useful for drawing comparisons among different jobs.

The third method is called direct observation. In this method employees are observed as they perform their jobs. Observers try to be as unobtrusive as possible, observing the jobs but trying not to get in the employees' way (see Field Note 2). Observers should not talk to the employees they are observing because it interferes with the conduct of work. Sometimes cameras or videotape equipment are used to facilitate the observation. Direct observation is an excellent method for appreciating and understanding the adverse conditions (for example, noise, heat) under which some jobs are performed. However, it is a poor method for understanding "why" certain behaviors occur on the job. Answers about why the job behavior occurs would be ascertained with another method, such as the interview.

Field Note 2

Although logically it may not seem so, it takes talent to watch people at work. Observation is one of the methods job analysts use to study jobs. The object is to observe the employee at work without your presence being intrusive. This requires that the analyst not *hide* from the employee but only to be as unobtrusive as possible. In attempts to avoid interfering with employees I have inadvertently positioned myself too far away to see really what was happening. I have also learned to bring earplugs and goggles to work sites, because when watching people at work you are exposed to the same environmental conditions as they are. While you can be "too far" from a worker to make accurate observations, you can also get "too close." Cascio (1982) describes this true story:

> While riding along in a police patrol car as part of a job analysis of police officers, an analyst and an officer were chatting away when a call came over the radio regarding a robbery in progress. Upon arriving at the scene the analyst and the officer both jumped out of the patrol car, but in the process the overzealous analyst managed to position himself between the robbers and the police. Although the robbers were later apprehended, they used the analyst as a decoy to make their getaway from the scene of the crime [p. 56].

The final method has workers record their own activities in logbooks or work diaries. The analyst then studies these books to infer the nature of the work performed. This is the least common and least desirable method of job analysis, primarily because individuals differ markedly in their written communication skills. Some people can clearly and concisely describe in writing what they do on the job. Other people have a difficult time writing a simple sentence. Consequently, the quality of information gleaned from this method can be questionable.

In practice a job analyst may use more than one method to study a job. I often use three methods in my job-analytic work. First, I observe the people at the work site to get a general feel for the jobs. Next I interview the workers, asking questions about what I observed. Finally, I follow up with the questionnaire, which I have found to be the most thorough method of job analysis. Although all four methods differ somewhat in the type of job-related information they provide (Prien & Ronan, 1971), each method can be useful in establishing the criteria of job performance.

Job-Oriented and Worker-Oriented Procedures

It is also possible to differentiate job-analytic questionnaires into "job-oriented" versus "worker-oriented" procedures. *Job-oriented* procedures are geared to the work that gets performed on the job. The emphasis is on the nature of the work activities that are conducted. Some job-oriented procedures break down a job into all the tasks that are performed, and the list may include as many as 400 to 500 tasks. Such analyses are sometimes called *task analyses*. Jobs are expressed in terms of the tasks that are performed through the use of such job terminology as *inspecting*, *repairing*, *hammering*, and so forth. Figure 3–2 shows part of a task analysis inventory used in the U.S. Air Force.

In contrast, a *worker-oriented* procedure is geared to the human talents needed to perform the job, and jobs are typically expressed in terms of knowledges, skills, abilities, and personal characteristics. A worker-oriented job analysis would express the job in terms of the required human characteristics, such as visual acuity, intelligence, depth perception, physical stamina, and so forth. An example of a worker-oriented procedure is the Position Analysis Questionnaire (PAQ) (McCormick, Jeanneret, & Mecham, 1972). The PAQ consists of 194 statements used to describe the human attributes needed to perform a job. The statements are organized into six major categories: information input; mental processes; work output; relationships with other persons; job context; and other job requirements. Some sample statements from the relationships with other persons category are shown in Figure 3–3. The statements shown here reflect the emphasis the PAQ places on the importance of human attributes needed to perform the job.

Both the job-oriented and worker-oriented procedures can be used to develop criteria. Job-oriented procedures define job success in terms of tasks performed; worker-oriented procedures define job success in terms of human characteristics. Most job-oriented procedures have to be handmade for each job to be analyzed because of the wide variation in jobs (McCormick, 1976). Worker-oriented procedures are more likely to be standardized, thus applicable across a broad array of jobs.

It is also possible to have a "hybrid" job-analysis procedure that looks at both the job functions performed and the human attributes required. An example of such a procedure is the Threshold Traits Analysis developed by Lopez, Kesselman, and Lopez (1981). Lopez and associates identified 33 human traits (for example, strength, problem solving, oral expression) that represent the domain of traits used in performing jobs. They further studied jobs in terms of the tasks and activities performed. Knowing what jobs consisted of in terms of tasks or functions performed, they then sought to identify the human traits needed to perform them. Figure 3–4 illustrates the authors' strategy for addressing a job from both the work-function and human-attribute perspectives. The figure identifies one human attribute, problem solving, presented in the context of a job demand and human trait. The object is to get a "fit"

Listed below is a duty and the tasks which it includes. Check all tasks which you perform. Add any tasks you do which are not listed. Then rate the tasks you have checked. A. Installing and removing aerial cable systems	Check ✔ If Done	Time Spent 1. Very much below average 2. Below average 3. Slightly below average 4. About average 5. Slightly above average 6. Above average 7. Very much above average	Importance 1. Extremely unimportant 2. Very unimportant 3. Unimportant 4. About medium importance 5. Important 6. Very important 7. Extremely important
1. Attach suspension strand to pole.			
2. Change and splice lasher wire.			
3. Deliver materials to lineman with snatch block and handline.			
4. Drill through-bolt holes and secure suspension clamps on poles.			
5. Install cable pressurization systems.			
6. Install distribution terminals.			
7. Install pulling-in line through cable rings.			
8. Load and unload cable reels.			
9. Load lashing machine with lashing wire.			

Figure 3–2   Portion of a Task Analysis Inventory for the Air Force

SOURCE: J. E. Morsh and W. B. Archer, *Procedural Guide for Conducting Occupational Surveys in the United States Air Force* (Lackland Air Force Base, TX: Personnel Research Laboratory, Aerospace Medical Division, September 1967).

between task requirements and human attributes as a means of understanding the content of jobs.

Evaluating Job-Analysis Methods

It should be evident that there are multiple ways of analyzing jobs. Are some methods better than others? Most of what we know about the relative merits of job-analysis methods is limited to the questionnaire procedure. For example, Arvey,

Relationships with Other Persons

This section deals with different aspects of interaction between people involved in various kinds of work.

Code	Importance to This Job (1)
DNA	Does not apply
1	Very minor
2	Low
3	Average
4	High
5	Extreme

4.1 Communications

Rate the following in terms of how *important* the activity is to the completion of the job. Some jobs may involve several or all of the items in this section.

4.1.1 Oral (communicating by speaking)

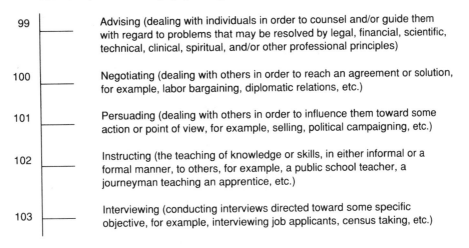

99 — Advising (dealing with individuals in order to counsel and/or guide them with regard to problems that may be resolved by legal, financial, scientific, technical, clinical, spiritual, and/or other professional principles)

100 — Negotiating (dealing with others in order to reach an agreement or solution, for example, labor bargaining, diplomatic relations, etc.)

101 — Persuading (dealing with others in order to influence them toward some action or point of view, for example, selling, political campaigning, etc.)

102 — Instructing (the teaching of knowledge or skills, in either informal or a formal manner, to others, for example, a public school teacher, a journeyman teaching an apprentice, etc.)

103 — Interviewing (conducting interviews directed toward some specific objective, for example, interviewing job applicants, census taking, etc.)

Figure 3–3 Sample Items from the PAQ

SOURCE: Reprinted by permission from Position Analysis Questionnaire. Copyright © 1969 by Purdue Research Foundation. All rights reserved.

Passino, and Lounsbury (1977) showed that the PAQ gave job analytic information that was not strongly biased either by the sex of the employee or of the analyst. Conley and Sackett (1987) demonstrated that high-performing and low-performing job incumbents gave equivalent descriptions of their job. That is, job-analytic information is not biased by the performance level of the incumbent. Cornelius, DeNisi, and Blencoe (1984) reported differences between the conclusions reached by expert job analysts versus those of college students in using the PAQ. As with most sophisticated measuring instruments, the qualifications of the user do influence the conclusions reached when utilizing the questionnaire. The PAQ does have some general and a few specific limitations applicable to many job-analysis questionnaires, mostly involving user reactions. Ash and Edgell (1975) reported the PAQ requires reading ability between high school and college graduate level. This limits the type of people who could accurately use the procedure.

Problem Solving			
The Job Functions Include		The Incumbent Must	
Processing information to reach specific conclusions, answers to problems, to adapt and assess ideas of others, to revise into workable form.		Analyze information and, by inductive reasoning, arrive at a specific conclusion or solution. (This trait also referred to as *Convergent Thinking, Reasoning.*)	
This Level Means	That the Job Activities Require Solving	At This Level	The Incumbent Must Solve
0	Very minor problems with fairly simple solutions (running out of supplies or giving directions).	0	Very minor problems with fairly simple solutions.
1	Problems with known and limited variables (diagnosing mechanical disorders or customer complaints).	1	Problems with known and limited variables.
2	More complex problems with many known variables (programming or investment analysis).	2	Problems with many known and complex variables.
3	Very complex and abstract problems with many unknown variables (advanced systems design or research).	3	Very complex and abstract problems with many unknown variables.

Figure 3–4 Sample Item from the Threshold Traits Analysis Method of Job Analysis

SOURCE: F. M. Lopez, G. A. Kesselman, and F. E. Lopez, "An Empirical Test of a Trait-Oriented Job Analysis Technique," *Personnel Psychology, 34* (1981) pp. 479–502.

The PAQ has aided our understanding of jobs more than any other single job-analytic method. The results of a study by Levine, Ash, Hall, and Sistrunk (1983) comparing seven major questionnaire methods of job analysis reflect what the I/O profession as a whole has come to understand about job analytic methods. Those authors found that different job-analytic methods are regarded as differentially effective and practical depending upon the various purposes for which they may be used. No one method consistently surfaces across the board as the best. I am of the opinion that a well-trained job analyst could draw accurate inferences and conclusions about jobs using any one of several questionnaire methods. However, the converse is also true. No method can ensure accurate results when used by someone who is inexperienced with job analysis.

One of the many uses of job-analysis results is the capacity to compare and contrast different jobs. It also permits grouping of jobs into similar clusters. Having clusters of like jobs helps determine wage rates, training needs, and other administrative functions. Indeed, Taylor (1978) reported that the PAQ helped reduce 76 insurance company jobs into six clusters based on similar performance criteria.

Another illustration of the value of job-analysis results was reported by Arvey and Begalla (1975). On the surface it may appear that two jobs are very different, or that several different jobs seemingly have little in common. However, a carefully conducted job analysis can reveal similarities (and differences) among jobs based upon actual tasks performed and skills needed rather than on mere surface impressions. Arvey and Begalla analyzed the job of a homemaker with the PAQ, and compared it to 20 other jobs. Using a statistic called D^2 (a measure of similarity between jobs), the authors were able to show that the job of a homemaker is most similar to that of patrol officer. Table 3–2 shows the results comparing the homemaker job to the 20 others (the smaller the D^2 value, the more similar the jobs). This is an example of how job analysis provides accurate insights into jobs that casual inspection will not provide.

TABLE 3–2 *Jobs Most Similar to Homemaker's Job, Based on Similarity (D^2) Scores*

Job	D^2
1. Patrolman	6.69
2. Home economist	7.95
3. Airport maintenance chief	9.96
4. Kitchen helper	9.99
5. Fire fighter	10.21
6. Trouble man	10.23
7. Instrument-maker helper	10.67
8. Electrician, foreman	10.91
9. Maintenance foreman, gas plant	11.12
10. Hydroelectric-machinery mechanic	11.17
11. Transmission mechanic	11.55
12. Lineman, repair	12.25
13. Electric-meter repairman	12.36
14. Instructor, vocational training	12.43
15. Gas serviceman	12.75
16. Inspector, motors and generators	12.84
17. Lifeguard	12.93
18. Fire captain	13.05
19. Repairman, switch gear	13.22
20. Home economist, consumer service	13.47

SOURCE: R. D. Arvey and M. E. Begalla, "Analyzing the Homemaker Job Using the PAQ," *Journal of Applied Psychology 60* (1975), p. 516.

If there is a final common point of confusion about job analysis, it pertains to what job analysis is sometimes *misperceived* to be. Job analysis is *not* a way to determine how well employees are performing their jobs (that procedure is called *performance appraisal* and is the topic of Chapter 7). Nor is job analysis a way to determine the value or worth of a job (that procedure is called *job evaluation,* and will be discussed in the next section). Perhaps the source of the confusion surrounds the fact that *criteria,* which job analyses identify, are involved in both performance appraisal and job evaluation. Job analysis results are used in performance appraisal and job evaluation, but job analysis, performance appraisal, and job evaluation are not equivalent personnel functions.

Another application of job analysis can be seen in the *Dictionary of Occupational Titles* (*DOT*) (1977). The *DOT* describes many jobs, each defined in terms of worker traits needed to perform the job. Eleven worker traits are given, including intelligence, verbal ability, numerical ability, finger dexterity, and motor coordination. The trait requirement ratings were made by job analysts who estimated how much of each of the 11 traits were needed on the job. The ratings were made on a 5-point scale and showed the amount of each trait possessed by various segments of the working population, ranging from 1 (the top 10% of the population) to 5 (the lowest 10%). The jobs in the *DOT* are also described in terms of occupational groups based on similarity of job content. A study by Cain and Green (1983) revealed that these trait ratings were very stable, indicating they are a sensitive and useful way for understanding jobs.

The actual process of distilling criteria from job-analysis data thus involves clustering similar work duties or attributes into criterion dimensions. Each cluster or group of work elements becomes the criteria for defining success in that job. Using a job-oriented procedure, I studied an auto mechanic's job. I identified four criteria of job success—competence in electrical, engine, transmission, and brake-repair work—and used them to judge the auto mechanic's performance. Following Nagle's strategy of criterion development (1953), I then collected actual behavioral measures of the mechanic's performance on each of these four criteria, which included such variables as diagnosing mechanical problems, replacing damaged parts, and using tools. The criteria were later used (1) as a standard to hire future mechanics, (2) to appraise how well each mechanic was performing, and (3) to train apprentice mechanics. Note that there are many uses for the criteria developed from a job analysis.

Job Evaluation

Different jobs have different degrees of importance or value to organizations. Some jobs are critically important, such as company president, and typically command the highest salary in the organization. Other jobs are less important to the organization's success and thus pay lower salaries. *Job evaluation* is a procedure that is useful for determining the relative value of jobs in the organization, which in turn helps to determine the level of compensation paid. It is beyond the scope of this book to present a complete discourse on compensation. The interested reader should refer to

Belcher (1974) or Milkovich and Newman (1984) for a thorough discussion of the area. For our purposes, we will simply review one component of the compensation process: job evaluation.

Organizations that wish to attract and retain competent employees have to pay competitive wages. Wages should not be set too low; otherwise competent people will obtain better-paying jobs elsewhere. Similarly, wages should not be set too high because the organization would be paying more than is necessary to staff itself. How, then, does an organization determine what is a fair and appropriate wage? Basically, two different operations are required. One is to determine *external equity. Equity* means fairness, so external equity relates to what is a fair wage in comparison to what other employers are paying. A wage survey (that is, a survey that reveals what other companies pay employees for performing their jobs) would be used to determine the "going rate" for jobs in the business community. The second operation is to determine *internal equity,* or the fairness of compensation rates within or internal to the organization. Job evaluation is used to determine the relative position (from highest paid to lowest paid) of the jobs in the organization; thus, it is used to assess internal equity.

Methods of Job Evaluation

There are several methods of job evaluation. Their common basis is their heavy reliance, implicitly or explicitly, on *criteria* to assess the relative worth of jobs. Their differences rest primarily on the degree of specificity involved in the comparison process; that is, jobs may be compared either in some global fashion (as their overall value to the company's success), or along certain specific dimensions (as how much effort they require, and the working conditions under which they are performed).

In practice, most organizations use job-evaluation methods that examine several dimensions or factors of work. These dimensions are called *compensable* factors, and refer to those factors for which employers pay compensation; that is, various levels of compensation are paid for jobs depending upon "how much" of these compensable factors are present in each. Please note a fine distinction here that people often confuse. With a few notable exceptions, organizations do not pay individuals; organizations pay jobs, which individuals fill. It is the *jobs* that determine the level of compensation, not the people in them.

There is no one fixed set of compensable factors. In theory, organizations can pay jobs for whatever reasons they want. In practice, however, effort, skill, responsibility, problem solving, and working conditions are typical compensable factors. Here is one way in which job evaluation works. Let us say the organization has selected the following four compensable factors: effort, skill, responsibility, and working conditions. While most or all the jobs in the organization would be evaluated, we will limit our discussion to two jobs: office secretary and security officer. Results of a job analysis might reveal the major criteria for a secretary's performance are typing, filing, and supervising a clerk. For the security officer, the criteria of job performance might be physically patrolling the office building, remaining vigilant, and maintaining security records. The criteria for both jobs would be evaluated or scored in terms of the degree to which the compensable factors are present. For example, the secretary's job might be evaluated as requiring considerable skill, little effort, modest responsibility, and performance under temperate working conditions. The security officer's job might be evaluated as requiring little skill, modest effort, considerable responsibility, and performance under potentially hazardous working conditions.

Thus, the level of compensation paid for jobs is a function of their status on the compensable factors. Jobs containing high levels of the compensable factors (for example, high effort, great skill) would receive higher rates of pay than jobs that contain low levels of these factors. All the jobs in the company would be evaluated in this fashion and then arranged in a hierarchy from high to low.

There are other methods of job evaluation that do not require the use of compensable factors. However, all methods do require that jobs be evaluated along one or more criteria. A (dollar) value is then ultimately attached to the relative position of every job in the hierarchy. Job evaluation attempts to ensure some correspondence between the compensation paid for the job and the value of the job to the organization.

Obviously a key to any job-evaluation system is whether the "right factors" are being considered. The evaluations should be made on the basis of factors that truly reflect the worth, importance, or value of the jobs. It should also be clear that unlike job analysis, which is basically a value-free operation (that is, an *analysis*), job evaluation is heavily laden with values (that is, an *evaluation*). Values are evidenced in terms of the selection of job factors to be evaluated and whether certain factors are considered more important than others. Therefore, job evaluation is an extension of job analysis applied to determining the relative worth of jobs in an organization for the purpose of providing equitable pay.

Research on Job Evaluation

I/O psychological research on job evaluation is not as extensive as that on job analysis. However, a few studies have been conducted. Gomez-Mejia, Page, and Tornow (1982) compared the relative accuracy and practical utility of seven different job-evaluation approaches. Their results indicated that while several job-evaluation methods provided useful information, a critical factor was the *job-analysis* data on which the job evaluation system was based. If the job-analytic data are of poor quality, their resulting use in job evaluation will also suffer. Doverspike, Carlisi, Barrett, and Alexander (1983) found that well-trained job evaluators can arrive at consistent evaluations of jobs, suggesting a common and stable basis for determining the worth of jobs. Schwab and Grams (1985) found that job-evaluation ratings were not influenced by the sex of the evaluator.

I/O psychologists typically regard *agreement* among people in describing work-related issues as being evidence of the "correctness" of their opinions. However, research on job evaluation reveals the potential fallibility of this perspective. Schwab and Wichern (1983) have suggested that *systematic bias* may be operating in the determination of compensation. For example, let us assume that most secretaries are women, and further assume that society as a whole does not highly value the work that women typically perform. Therefore, the wages paid to female secretaries are lower than they "should" be. Additionally, the same bias that operates against female wages also operates to uniformly suppress the judged value of a secretarial job vis-à-vis the compensable factors; that is, secretarial jobs are judged to be relatively low in required effort, skill, and responsibility. Therefore, what looks like a "fair" relationship between the value of the job and the wages paid for it is actually the product of linking biased job-evaluation results with biased wages. In other words, as Schwab and Wichern indicate, agreement may masquerade as truth or fairness when it is actually indicative of systematic bias. Rynes and Milkovich (1986) concluded that market wages, which often serve as criteria in job evaluation, can be biased by many factors. For example, geographical differences and company pay practices influence market wages, thus dispelling the myth that market wages reflect the true worth of a job.

The issue of systematic bias in job evaluation also relates to the doctrine of *comparable worth*. It is called a "doctrine" because it represents a philosophy of how jobs should be paid. Comparable worth refers to giving people equal pay for performing comparable work (Mahoney, 1983). This is in contrast to giving equal pay for equal work, which is the doctrine underlying the Equal Pay Act, a federal law regarding compensation. The Equal Pay Act states that men and women who perform equal work are to receive equal pay. Proponents of comparable worth believe that rarely are two jobs ever truly equal. They believe it is more reasonable to speak of jobs having *comparable* or *equivalent* worth. Jobs that are of comparable worth should be paid the same.

To determine the worth of all jobs, you would need to have a common measuring device, such as job evaluation. However, comparable worth proponents believe that many current job-evaluation methods are inherently biased against the work typically performed by females. These people point to labor statistics indicating that females on the average earn about 60 cents for every $1 earned by males. This, they assert, is *de facto* evidence that women are the victims of discrimination caused by job evaluation methods that unfairly undervalue the work they perform. Indeed, Arvey (1986) suggested that the factors selected for consideration in job evaluation may be biased against females. For example, how much physical strength exerted in a job is often used as one factor in job evaluation. Since most males are physically stronger than most females, the rated value of female-dominated jobs may suffer on this factor. Alternatively, many females work in jobs in which eyestrain is a problem, yet amount of eyestrain is typically not a factor included in job evaluation (see Field Note 3). The proponents propose the need for a bias-free system to evaluate jobs that, when applied, would serve to reduce the male/female pay differential by increasing the wages paid to women.

Field Note 3

At the core of the comparable worth debate is the question of how the worth of a job is determined. A traditional way of determining job worth is through job evaluation. It is common to rate jobs on certain factors (such as effort and working conditions), with each rating being worth a certain number of points. The points are then summed, with the total point value of the job being the measure of the relative worth of a job. People who are advocates of comparable worth believe that the very factors upon which jobs are evaluated often serve to slant the final results in favor of jobs traditionally held by men. For example, on the effort factor, jobs that involve heavy lifting are worth more than jobs that involve light lifting. On the working-conditions factor, jobs that are performed under adverse physical conditions (such as outdoor work) are worth more than jobs performed under temperate conditions (as an air-conditioned or heated office). Who is more likely to fill a job requiring heavy lifting—men or women? Typically men. Who is more likely to work outdoors? Typically men. Therefore, men's jobs are more likely to be worth more points, thus receive higher wages, than jobs traditionally filled by women. But what if we changed the very factors upon which jobs are rated? Two possible factors would be mental stress and the handling of sensitive/confidential information. Jobs that subject people to high mental stress and the handling of confidential information would be worth more than jobs that don't. Secretaries often work under mentally stressful conditions (that is, a hectic work pace and continual deadlines), and often deal with confidential information. Most secretarial jobs are held by women. Therefore, depending upon which job factors you wish to consider (effort and working conditions versus mental stress and confidential information), you could arrive at two quite different conclusions regarding the worth of a secretary's job. Job factors are nothing more than criteria, the criteria by which the worth of a job is to be determined. As stated earlier in this chapter, differences of opinion about criteria are often at the heart of many disputes. Such is certainly the case regarding comparable worth.

Opponents of comparable worth believe there is no systematic bias operating against "female" jobs. They believe that females are as free to choose whatever jobs they want as are males; they simply settle for lower paying jobs that allow them more latitude for other obligations, as family duties. In short, the opponents believe the job-evaluation system is not at fault, rather, society has socialized men and women to pursue different types of jobs. They further believe there is no way one can ever measure jobs totally free of any values, that is, to have a totally bias-free assessment.

There are currently no correct answers to this heated debate. At its core is the issue of values applied to job evaluation. It will be interesting to observe the legal and social status of comparable worth in the future, as currently it rests in limbo.

Standards for Criteria

What should criteria be like? This listing by Blum and Naylor (1968) is most representative:

1. Reliable

2. Realistic

3. Representative

4. Related to other criteria

5. Acceptable to the job analyst

6. Acceptable to management

7. Consistent from one situation to another

8. Predictable

9. Inexpensive

10. Understandable

11. Measurable

12. Relevant

13. Uncontaminated and bias-free

14. Sensitive

This list might be reduced to three general factors; criteria must be appropriate, stable, and practical. The criteria should be relevant and representative of the job. They must endure over time or across situations. Finally, they should not be too expensive or hard to measure.

Other authors (for example, Weitz, 1961) think other issues are important; for example, the *time* at which criterion measures are taken (after one month, six months on the job, and so on); the *type* of criterion measure taken (performance, errors, accidents, and so on); and the *level* of performance chosen to represent success or failure on the job (college students must perform at a "C" level before they can graduate). Weitz says the choice of criteria is usually determined either by history or precedent; unfortunately, sometimes criteria are chosen because they are merely expedient or available.

Types of Criteria

Smith (1976) has documented several types of criteria that are used in I/O psychological research. She classified criteria on the basis of whether they are "hard" or "soft." *Hard* criteria are taken from organizational records (payroll or personnel) and supposedly do not involve any type of subjective evaluation. *Soft* criteria are subjective evaluations of a person's performance (such as a supervisor might render). While hard criteria may be devoid of subjective judgment, some degree of assessment must be applied to them to give them meaning. Just knowing that an employee produced 18 units a day is not informative; this output must be compared with what other workers produce. If the average is 10 units a day, 18 units would clearly represent "good" performance. If the average is 25 units a day, 18 units is not good. Hard criteria appear to be objective, but some judgment is always involved. Soft criteria are judgmental.

Hard Criteria

Production.   Using units of production as criteria is most common in manufacturing jobs. If there is only one type of job in a whole organization, setting production criteria is easy. But in most companies, there are many types of production jobs, so productivity must be compared fairly. That is, if average productivity in one job is 6 units a day and in another job it's 300 units a day, productivity must be equated to compensate for these differences. Statistical procedures are usually used for this. The research of one psychologist, Harold Rothe, has focused on the production of various types of workers. Over the years, he has studied the work output of butter wrappers (Rothe, 1946), machine operators (Rothe, 1947), chocolate dippers (Rothe, 1951), coil winders (Rothe & Nye, 1958), welders (Rothe, 1970), and industrial employees (Rothe, 1978). His research has probably done more to increase under-standing of production as a criterion of job performance than any other set of studies.

Other factors can diminish the value of production as a criterion of performance. In an assembly-line job, the speed of the line determines how many units get pro-duced per day. Increasing the speed of the line increases production. Furthermore, everyone working on the line will have the same level of production. In a case like this, units of production are determined by factors outside the individual worker. So errors that *are* under the worker's control may be measured as the criterion of job performance. However, this is no cure-all for the criterion problem either. Errors are not fair criteria if they are more likely in some jobs than others. Due to automation and work simplification, some jobs are almost "goof-proof." In such jobs, error-free work has nothing to do with the human factor.

Salary.   Salary has been used as a criterion of an employee's worth, but it is not a particularly "clean" measure of job performance. Salaries are based not only on job performance but also on the value of the job to the organization. An efficient secretary earns less money than a poorly performing manager because managers as a group are paid more than secretaries as a group.

One alternative is to make within-job comparisons, that is, compare secretaries with one another, managers with one another, and so on. The better performers should earn more money. But this approach also has its share of problems. While performance is a part of salary, it is not the only part. Seniority or tenure also affects salaries. Two equally performing managers may have different salaries if one has been on the job longer. Also some jobs have salary limits; no matter how well people perform or how long they have been on the job, their salaries cannot exceed a certain level. These problems limit the usefulness of salary as a criterion. But it can be used if statistical controls or corrections account for some of the non-performance-based variations (for example, Hulin, 1962).

Job Level and Promotions.   Supposedly, the more promotions people have, the better they are performing. But people get promoted for reasons other than good performance, and not all good performers get promoted. There may be "political" reasons (the worker is the son or daughter of the company president), seniority reasons (everyone gets advanced after four years in the same job), as well as reasons relating to the organization's structure. Some organizations have "tall" structures; that is, there are many different jobs between the lowest and highest levels and thus many possibilities for promotion. Other organizations have a "flat" structure, with few jobs between the top and bottom. Most college professors can be promoted only twice in their careers because there are only three job levels for them to be in: assistant, associate, and full professor. Promotions are best used as a criterion of job performance in companies where there is ample opportunity for advancement. Promotions are most often used as criteria for managerial and administrative personnel.

Sales. Sales is a commonly used performance criterion for wholesale and retail sales work. But there are a number of variations that must be considered. Using the sheer *number* of sales as a criterion is appropriate only if everyone is selling the same product(s) in comparable territories. A person who sells toothbrushes should sell more units than a person who sells houses. Also, someone selling tractors in Iowa should sell more than a person whose sales territory is Rhode Island. Not only is Iowa bigger than Rhode Island but more farming is done proportionately in Iowa than in Rhode Island.

Total sales volume is equally fallible as a criterion. A real estate salesperson can sell a $100,000 house in one afternoon, but how long would it take to sell $100,000 worth of toothbrushes?

The solution to these types of problems is to use norm groups for judging success. A real estate salesperson should be compared to other real estate salespersons in the same sales territory. The same holds for other sales work. If comparisons have to be drawn across sales territories or across product lines, statistical adjustments are needed. Ideally, any differences in sales performance would then be due to the ability of the salesperson, which is the basis for using sales as a criterion of job performance.

Tenure or Turnover. Length of service is a very popular criterion in I/O psychological research. Turnover not only has a theoretical appeal (for example, Mobley, Griffeth, Hand, & Meglino, 1979) but is also a practical concern. Employers want to hire people who will stay with the company. Muchinsky and Tuttle (1979) reviewed over 100 studies that tried to predict (by a variety of means) what types of people are likely to quit. Voluntary employee turnover is related to individual personality as well as characteristics of the organization. But it is even more related to such economic factors as the availability of other jobs (Muchinsky & Morrow, 1980). For obvious, practical reasons, employers don't want to hire the chronic job-hoppers. The costs of recruiting, selecting, and training new hires can be extremely high. Turnover is perhaps the most frequently used nonperformance criterion in the psychological literature. There appears to be no consistent relationship between people who quit and their job performance (that is, good performers quit as often as poor ones). But turnover is a valuable and useful criterion because it measures stability, and this can be as important to the company as performance.

Absenteeism. Absence from work, like turnover, is an index of employee stability. While some degree of employee turnover is good for organizations, employee absenteeism always has bad consequences (Muchinsky, 1979). There is no established relationship between absenteeism and productivity, but absenteeism is often used as a criterion of job performance; indeed, excessive absenteeism can be grounds for dismissal. Many companies try absence-reduction techniques (Pedalino & Gamboa, 1974) before taking the more drastic step of firing an employee. Also, since drug and alcohol abuse are frequent causes of absenteeism (Gomez-Mejia & Balkin, 1983), some companies sponsor counseling programs to help employees deal with their addiction.

Muchinsky (1977) and Steers and Rhodes (1978) have reviewed many studies on why people are absent from work. A consistent predictor of absenteeism was the extent to which people liked their work. Feelings of job satisfaction were negatively correlated with absenteeism (typical correlations being around $-.30$). Companies that provide more interesting and stimulating jobs reap the benefits of reduced absenteeism.

Absenteeism is a pervasive problem in industry; it costs employers billions of dollars a year in decreased efficiency and increased benefit payments (for example, sick leave) and payroll costs. A British psychologist, Nigel Nicholson, has conducted some of the best research on the causes of absenteeism and has proposed a theory to explain it (Nicholson, 1977). Absenteeism has social, individual, and organizational causes, and the results of absenteeism affect individuals, companies, and even entire industrial societies. Since absenteeism is increasing both nationally and internationally, its importance as a criterion of job performance will increase in the years to come.

Accidents. Accidents are sometimes used as a criterion of job performance, though they have a number of limitations. First, accidents are used as a measure mainly for blue-collar jobs. (While white-collar workers can be injured at work, the frequency of such accidents is small.) So accidents are a measure of job performance for only a limited sample of employees. Second, accidents are hard to predict, and there is little stability or consistency in their occurrence. Third, accidents can be measured in many ways: number of accidents per hours worked, miles driven, trips taken, and so on. Different conclusions can be drawn, depending upon how accident statistics are calculated. Employers do not want to hire people who, for whatever reason, would incur job-related accidents. But in the total picture of job performance, accidents are not used as a criterion as often as production, turnover, or absence.

Theft. Employee theft is a major problem facing organizations, with annual losses estimated at $10 billion (Sackett & Harris, 1985). Hollinger and Clark (1983) administered an anonymous questionnaire regarding theft to employees at three types of organizations. The percentage of employees who admitted to stealing from their employer was 42% in retail stores, 32% in hospitals, and 26% in manufacturing firms. Thus, employee theft is a pervasive and serious problem.

From an I/O psychologist's perspective, the goal is to hire people who are unlikely to steal from the company, just as it would be desirable to hire people who have a low probability of having accidents. The problem with theft as a criterion is that we know very little about the individual identity of employees who do steal. Hollinger and Clark based their survey results on *anonymous* responses. Furthermore, those responses came from people who were willing to admit they stole from the company. Those employees who were stealing but chose not to respond to the survey or who did not admit they stole were not included in the theft results.

Another drawback of using theft as a criterion is that only a small percentage of employees are ever caught stealing. The occurrence of theft often has to be deduced on the basis of calculated shortages from company inventories of supplies and products. Further compounding the problem of studying theft as a criterion, many companies will not divulge any information about theft to outside individuals. That is, while companies will often share information on such criteria as absenteeism and turnover, theft records are too sensitive to reveal. Despite these limitations, I/O psychologists regard theft as an index of employment suitability, and we will probably witness much more research on theft in the years ahead.

Soft Criteria

Soft criteria refer to judgments made of an employee's performance. The judgment is usually a rating or ranking. For example, a supervisor might rate the employees in a department on the basis of overall effectiveness. This rating would then be the standard of job performance. Supervisor ratings are by far the most frequently used judgmental criteria. A study by Lent, Aurbach, and Levin (1971) reported that of the 1,505 criteria used in over 400 studies, 897 (60%) were supervisory ratings. But ratings may also be supplied by peers, subordinates, and the workers themselves. The ratings may be on a general factor, such as overall effectiveness, or specific factors, such as quantity of work, quality of work, creativity, practical judgment, and so forth. Some studies have even compared judgments made by two or more sets of raters (for example, supervisors and peers) who evaluate several dimensions of behavior (Lawler, 1967). Such studies normally show that certain raters are more consistent in rating certain aspects of job performance. (Supervisors may agree in rating quality of work; peers agree in rating interpersonal relations.) Chapter 7 will discuss this issue in greater detail.

Because judgmental criteria are used so often, a great deal of attention has been given to improving the quality of these judgments. If the people doing the judging don't know how to make such decisions, the quality of their decisions will be very low. Spool (1978) reviewed the research on training people to make more accurate judgments of behavior. He found that people can indeed learn to be accurate evaluators. People who are more involved and interested in evaluating behavior make more careful and accurate judgments. Research (for example, Pursell, Dossett, & Latham, 1980) has revealed that a one-day training program can greatly enhance people's skills in observing and interpreting behavior.

What are the criteria for judging wine? Wine tasters at a California vineyard.   Courtesy Wine Institute

From this discussion, it is clear that no single measure of job performance is totally adequate. While each criterion may have merit, each can also suffer from weakness along other dimensions. For instance, few people would say that an employee's absence has *no* bearing on overall job performance, but no one would say that absence is a *complete* measure of job performance. Absence, like production or job level, is but one piece of the broader picture. Readers should not be discouraged that no one criterion meets all our standards. It is precisely because job performance is multidimensional (and each single dimension is a fallible index of overall performance) that we are compelled to include many relevant aspects of work in establishing criteria.

Relationship Among Job-Performance Criteria

While several job-performance criteria can be identified for many jobs, each criterion frequently assesses a different aspect of performance on the job. Job-performance criteria are usually independent of one another. If they were all highly positively intercorrelated, say, $r = .80$ or $r = .90$, there would be no point in measuring them all. Knowing an employee's status on one criterion would give his or her status on the others. Several studies have tried to identify interrelationships among criteria.

Studies by Turner (1960), Seashore, Indik, and Georgopoulos (1960), and Ronan (1963) revealed multiple job-performance criteria and also showed that the criteria were relatively independent of one another. For example, Seashore and associates studied 975 delivery men on whom five job-performance criteria were available: productivity (objectively measured by time standards), effectiveness (subjective ratings based on quality of performance), accidents, unexcused absences, and errors (based on the number of packages not delivered). The correlations among these five criteria appear in Table 3–3. The data show that the five criteria were relatively independent of one another. The largest correlations were found among the variables of productivity, effectiveness, and errors (.28, $-.26$ and $-.32$). These results demonstrate that there really is no single measure of overall performance on the job; each criterion measures a different facet.

Heneman (1986) conducted a major study examining the relationship between supervisor ratings of job performance and objective measures of job performance. He reported an average correlation of only .27 between these two types of assessment. Quite clearly, you can arrive at different conclusions about a person's job performance depending upon how you choose to assess it.

There is also a relationship between job level and the number of criteria needed to define job performance. Lower-level, relatively simple jobs do not have many dimensions of performance; more complex jobs have many. In fact, the number of job-performance criteria can separate simple jobs from complex ones. Manual laborers who unload trucks might be measured by only three criteria: attendance (they have to show up for work), errors (they have to know how to stack the material), and speed. More complex jobs, as in the medical field (for example, Taylor, Price,

TABLE 3–3 *Intercorrelations Among Five Criterion Variables*

	Productivity	**Accidents**	**Absences**	**Errors**
Effectiveness	.28	$-.02$	$-.08$	$-.32$
Productivity		.12	$-.01$	$-.26$
Accidents			.03	$-.18$
Absences				.15

SOURCE: Adapted from S. E. Seashore, B. P. Indik, and B. S. Georgopoulos, "Relationship among Criteria of Job Performance," *Journal of Applied Psychology, 44* (1960), pp. 195–202.

Richards, & Jacobsen, 1964, 1965), might be defined by as many as 15 independent criteria. The more complex the job, the more criteria are needed to define it and the more skill or talent a person has to have to be successful.

Composite Versus Multiple Criteria

There has been a long-running controversy in I/O psychology. Should criteria of job performance somehow be added together to yield a single performance score? Or should they remain as separate indicators of performance? Backers of the former believe in the *composite criterion* approach. Those who advocate the latter follow the *multiple criteria* approach. Each approach has merit, and a resolution to the controversy has been proposed.

Composite Criterion

The composite criterion is the oldest approach to criterion conceptualization. Its premise is that the criterion should measure a person's "overall success" or "value to the organization." Advocates of the composite criterion argue that a single index or number is needed to compare and make decisions about individuals (Toops, 1944; Thorndike, 1949). They argue the criteria that define job performance (however many there are) must be combined in some way. Also, the various criterion elements should be weighted so that their difference in importance can be recognized.

A student's grade-point average is a good example of a weighted composite criterion. The criterion elements for a student are the courses he or she is taking. Performance on these dimensions is measured by grades ("A" = 4.0, "B" = 3.0, and so on). The courses are "weighted" according to the number of credit hours each is worth. Let us say a student has taken four courses: economics, psychology, art, and physical education. The credit hours for these courses are 4, 3, 3, and 1, respectively. The grades received are "A," "B," "C," and "D," respectively. The student's grade-point average (GPA) is:

GPA = [credit hours (economics grade) + credit hours (psychology grade) + credit hours (art grade) + credit hours (physical education grade)]/total credit hours

GPA = [4(4.0) + 3(3.0) + 3(2.0) + 1(1.0)]/11 = 2.91

The GPA of 2.91 would then be used to assess this person's "success" as a student. It may also be used as a basis for considering membership in an academic society, receipt of a scholarship, admission to graduate school, and so forth.

Weighting courses according to credit hours is relatively straightforward. However, in industry the weighting issue is not so clear-cut. If all the elements are equally important for job success, they all get the same weight, called *unit* weights. If the elements have different importance, they are weighted differentially. Various statistical procedures have been proposed to determine what the weights should be. The most elegant and sophisticated procedure has been proposed by Brogden and Taylor

(1950a). They state that since employees work to enhance the economic standing of the organization, "the criterion should measure the contribution of the individual to the overall efficiency of the organization." They recommend that such contributions be measured in terms of dollars and cents by applying cost-accounting procedures to the employee's job behaviors. Thus, the weights for the criterion elements are dollar values; the more valuable elements (to the organization) receive a higher dollar weight. While such a procedure is workable in theory, it is extremely difficult to calculate the dollar value of some criterion elements.

So the advocates of the composite criterion favor it for practical purposes in making decisions about employees. The issue about weighting is concerned with making more accurate decisions on the basis of having more precise information.

Multiple Criteria

The advocates of the multiple criteria approach base their arguments on two points. First, they argue that if the dimensions of job performance are relatively independent, they cannot be added to form a composite (Ghiselli, 1956; Dunnette, 1963). A worker who has perfect attendance but makes a tremendous amount of errors in production cannot fairly be called an "average" worker. Proponents say that a composite can be formed only when there are high positive intercorrelations among the criterion elements (thus indicating that a single dimension underlies performance). But the bulk of research shows that criteria rarely have a stable, unidimensional basis (Ghiselli & Haire, 1960; Bass, 1962). In response to this position, composite criterion advocates argue that despite the lack of statistical similarity among the criterion elements, when the elements are all relevant measures of economic variables, they can be coded into a composite without regard to their intercorrelations (Brogden & Taylor, 1950a).

The second argument in favor of multiple criteria is that when you lump all the criterion elements into a composite score, you lose understanding of the factors that contribute to job success. Since there are many ways a person can achieve a certain level of job proficiency (for example, a "C"-average student can earn all "C's" or half "A's" and half "F's"), it is hard to separate a composite criterion into its various parts. Therefore, the best way to understand the ingredients of successful job performance is to keep the criteria separate to begin with.

Resolution of the Controversy

Schmidt and Kaplan (1971) proposed a resolution (of sorts) to the problem of composite versus multiple criteria. They argue that the selection of composite or multiple criteria should depend on their intended use. If the goal is a practical one (as in making personnel decisions), Schmidt and Kaplan advocate a weighted composite criterion. The criterion elements are weighted and added together to derive a composite value representing the overall value of the worker. However, if the goal is to *understand* the dimensions of job performance and how they contribute to job success, then multiple criteria should be used.

The basis for the resolution is in how the criteria will be used, and in many cases, both forms are helpful. If we want to promote the employee who is performing "best" on the job, a composite criterion will assess who is the "best." If we want to train people to improve their job performance in deficient areas, multiple criteria will help spot those areas. But the composite criterion approach is not without problems, even in cases of making personnel decisions. There can be the problem of compensating criteria. If two criteria of success as a brain surgeon are visual acuity and finger dexterity, a person with the eyes of a hawk who is all thumbs just will not do. In statistically computing a composite criterion, superior visual acuity may compensate for a lack of finger dexterity. But in actual practice, a high score on one cannot make up for a deficiency in the other. In such a case, an alternative procedure would be needed to set minimal levels of performance on *each* criterion dimension. This point will be discussed again in Chapter 5.

Concluding Comments

The issue of criteria in I/O psychology is complex and important. Nagle (1953) feels that the quality of research is only as good as the criteria. I agree. The perceptive reader will note that many of the references in this chapter are from the 1950s and 1960s. The criterion problems and issues that confronted psychologists then continue to do so today. The quality of our judgments is only as good as the evaluative standards we use to make them. If our goal were to improve the quality of the educational process as shown by the number of students elected to Phi Beta Kappa (a scholastic honorary), we could lower admission standards to this honorary. However, we would be deluding only ourselves.

While new ways of thinking about criterion problems occasionally come along (for example, Barrett, Caldwell, & Alexander, 1985), students today still must understand the same criterion issues as their counterparts did many years ago. An understanding of criteria and their related problems is basic to I/O psychology.

MAJOR CHAPTER OBJECTIVES IN REVIEW

After having read this chapter, you should:

1. Understand the distinction between conceptual and actual criteria.

2. Understand the meaning of criterion deficiency, relevance, and contamination.

3. Understand the purpose of job analysis and the various methods of conducting one.

4. Understand the purpose of job evaluation and related issues associated with determining the worth of a job.

5. Understand the major types of criteria examined by I/O psychologists.

6. Understand the typical interrelationships among job performance criteria.

7. Understand the difference between multiple and composite criteria.

CASE STUDY—*Who Gets the Scholarship?*

A panel of three high school teachers at Rippowam High School had been convened by the principal to make a most important decision. A local company was willing to award a $10,000 college scholarship to "the most outstanding senior" in the class, with the recipient to be determined by the high school. Walter Plant, Sandra Meltzer, and Jerry Driscoll were given the assignment to select the scholarship recipient. They agreed to meet at 2:30 to discuss their assignment.

Driscoll opened the meeting: "I wish we had more to go on than what they gave us. A student can be *outstanding* in many ways."

"Well, I assume grades are the most important factor," said Meltzer. "Why don't we start out with the ranking of all students based upon their grade-point averages? I'd be hard pressed to award $10,000 to any student other than the class valedictorian."

"I don't think its that easy," said Plant. "I am far more impressed with a student who gets a B+ in honors physics than someone who gets an A in basket weaving. While a student's grade-point average is certainly a good measure of academic accomplishments, it's tainted by the difficulty of the courses taken."

"That's not the only problem with the grade-point average," Driscoll warned. "I've got some students in my homeroom who will graduate with the minimum number of hours, and I've got some others who branched out and took more than the minimum. I think we should give some consideration to the total number of hours taken in the curriculum."

A deep frown appeared on Plant's face. "I don't see why we should penalize the student who did only what was required by the school. We specify what is needed for graduation, and the students have to comply. While I never discourage a student from sticking to the minimum, I don't think we should devalue their performance for having done so."

"Maybe we're getting too hung up with grades and hours," said Meltzer. "Suzanne Millord won first prize in the regional science fair competition. Shouldn't something like that count too? I'm more impressed with that than an "A" in any class."

"You know," Plant commented, "we are forgetting about some other things too. How about civic activities, as participation in student government or interest clubs? We encourage student involvement in these activities to make for a more well-rounded education. I don't feel we should ignore them when it comes time to make an award."

"I feel those activities have their own rewards," said Driscoll. "We want to give this scholarship to the best student, not the most socially active one."

"While we're at it," mused Plant, "how about athletic participation? We also stress physical education as well as social and intellectual development. Maybe we should also include interscholastic athletics. We've got some outstanding athletes in this school, and who's to say that 'most outstanding' can't be defined in terms of athletics?"

"I hardly think this was designed to be an athletic scholarship," Meltzer grumbled. "If you want to make it more complicated, why not throw in financial need; $10,000 is a lot of money, and some families could use it more than others."

Driscoll stared out the window. He knew it would be a long afternoon.

Questions

1. What do you think the conceptual criteria should be in making a scholarship determination?

2. What are some sources of criterion deficiency and contamination in the actual criteria being discussed by the teachers?

3. Would the criteria for selecting the "most outstanding student" be more biased or less biased by inclusion of financial need? Why?

4. Do you think it's more difficult to identify what the appropriate criteria are, or to determine how to weight the criteria once they have been identified? Why?

5. If you had been invited to this meeting, what suggestions would you make to help the teachers reach a decision?

4

Predictors

A *predictor* is any variable used to forecast a criterion. In weather prediction, baro-metric pressure can be used to forecast rainfall. In medical prediction, body tempera-ture may be used to predict (or diagnose) illness. In I/O psychology, we seek predictors of job-performance criteria as indexed by productivity, absenteeism, turn-over, and so forth. There is no limit to the variables we may use for this purpose. While we do not use tea leaves and astrological signs as fortune-tellers do, we have explored a multitude of devices as potential predictors of job performance criteria. This chapter reviews those variables traditionally used, examines their success, and discusses some professional problems inherent in their application.

Before discussing predictor variables, we must remember that while their identification is valuable, they are always secondary in importance to criteria. If you think of criteria as being the objective or end point of an empirical journey, predictors are the roads by which we reach the criteria. Predictors are merely means to an end. Nagle (1953) described the relationship between these two sets of variables:

> . . . predictors themselves can never be anything but subsidiary to the criterion, for it is from the criterion that the predictors derive their significance. If the criterion changes, the predictors' validity is necessarily affected. If the predictors change, the criterion does not change for that reason. Likewise, it can be seen that if no criteria are used, one would never know whether or not the predictors were selecting those individuals likely to succeed. Research can be no better than the criteria used. One must, therefore, approach the prediction process in a logical fashion, developing criteria first, analyzing them, and then constructing or selecting variables to predict the criteria. When one or more variables show a satisfactory relationship to criteria, such variables may then be used as selection instruments [p. 273].

Assessing the Quality of Predictors

All predictor variables, like other measuring devices, can be assessed in terms of their quality or goodness. We can think of several features of a good measuring device. We would like it to be *accurate* and *consistent*; that is, it should repeatedly yield precise measurements. In psychology, we judge the goodness of our measuring devices by two psychometric criteria: reliability and validity. If a predictor is not both reliable and valid, it is useless.

Reliability

Reliability is the consistency or stability of a measure. A measure should yield the same estimate on repeated use. While that estimate can be inaccurate, a reliable measure will always be consistent. Three major types of reliability are used in psychology to assess the consistency or stability of the measuring device.

Test-Retest Reliability.   Perhaps the simplest way to assess a measuring device's reliability is to measure something at two points in time and compare the scores. We can give an IQ test to the same group of people at two different times and then correlate the two sets of scores. This correlation is called a *coefficient of stability* because it reflects the stability of the test over time. If the test is reliable, those who scored high the first time would also score high the second time, and vice versa. If the test is unreliable, the scores will "bounce around" between administrations in such a way that there will be no similarity in the scores for individuals between the two trials.

When we say a test (or any measure) is reliable, how high should the reliability coefficient be? The answer is "the higher the better." A test cannot be too reliable. As a rule, reliability coefficients around +.70 are professionally acceptable, though some frequently used tests have test-retest reliabilities only in the +.50 range. "Acceptable" reliability is also a function of the test's use. A test used for *individual* prediction (to diagnose brain impairment) should be much more reliable than a test used for *group* prediction (to measure the attitudes of a work group).

Equivalent-Form Reliability.   A second type of reliability is *parallel* or *equivalent form* reliability. Here a psychologist would develop two forms of a test to measure the same thing and give both to a group of people. The two scores for each person are then correlated. The resulting correlation, called a *coefficient of equivalence*, reflects the extent to which the two forms are equivalent measures of the same concept. Of the three major types of reliability, this is the least popular. The reason is that it is usually challenging to come up with *one* good test, let alone two. Many tests do not have a "parallel form." However, in the areas of intelligence and achievement testing (to be discussed shortly), equivalent forms of the same test are sometimes found. If the resulting coefficient of equivalence is high, the tests are equivalent and reliable measures of the same concept. If it is low, they are not.

Internal Consistency Reliability. The third major type of reliability is the *internal consistency* of the test—the extent to which it has homogeneous content. Two types of internal consistency reliability are typically computed. One is called *split-half* reliability. Here a test is given to a group of people, but in scoring (though not administering) it, the items are divided in half, into odd and even-numbered items. Each person thus gets two sets of scores (one for each half), and these are correlated. If the test is internally consistent, there should be a high degree of similarity in the responses (that is, right or wrong) to the odd- and even-numbered items. Because this method of computing reliability divides a test in half (that is, a 100-item test is reduced to two 50-item tests), we have really computed the reliability of only half the test. We must apply a statistical correction procedure to the resulting correlation to estimate the reliability of the entire (100-item) test. All other things being equal, the longer a test is, the greater its reliability.

A second technique for assessing internal-consistency reliability is to compute one of two coefficients, Cronbach's alpha or Kuder-Richardson 20 (KR20). Both of these procedures are similar, although not quite identical statistically. Conceptually, each item of a test is treated as a minitest in itself. Thus, a 100-item test is thought to consist of 100 minitests. The response to each item is correlated with the response to every other item. We thus have a matrix of interitem correlations whose average is related to the homogeneity of the test. If the test is homogeneous (the item content is similar), the test will have a high internal-consistency reliability. If it is heterogeneous (the test items cover a wide variety of concepts), the test is not internally consistent; the resulting coefficient will be low. Although there is some evidence that internal consistency reliability may not accurately assess a test's homogeneity (Green, Lissitz, & Mulaik, 1977), it is popular in I/O psychology.

It is possible to assess the reliability of a *single* test by using two of the methods; if a parallel form exists, all three methods can be used. We can assess the reliability of a single test via the test-retest method as well as by internal consistency. Note that a test can be differentially reliable across the methods. For example, we may design a test to measure a wide variety of abilities: quantitative ability, verbal ability, spatial ability, and so forth. In assessing the internal consistency reliability of the test, we might find it to be quite heterogeneous in content (which indeed it would be), thus having low internal-consistency reliability. However, the test may have very high test-retest reliability, meaning that it consistently measures the various abilities. The point is the various methods are not interchangeable. The test-retest method is perhaps the most generic; internal consistency should be used only with a test designed to measure similar or homogeneous content. A test might not have homogeneous content but still be a stable measure.

Validity

Reliability refers to consistency and stability of measurement; *validity* refers to accuracy and precision. A valid measure is one that yields "correct" estimates of what is being assessed. However, there is another factor that distinguishes validity from reliability. Reliability is inherent in a measuring device. Validity, on the other hand, depends on the use of a test. It refers to the *appropriateness* for predicting or drawing inferences about criteria. A given test may be highly valid for predicting employee productivity but totally invalid for predicting employee absenteeism. In other words, it would be appropriate to draw inferences about employee productivity from the test but inappropriate to draw inferences about absenteeism from it.

There are several different ways of assessing validity. They all involve determining the appropriateness of a measure (test) for drawing inferences.

Criterion-Related Validity.   *Criterion-related validity* refers, as its name suggests, to how much a predictor relates to a criterion. It is a frequently used and important type of validity in I/O psychology. The two major kinds of criterion-related validity are concurrent and predictive.

Concurrent Criterion-Related Validity.   In measuring concurrent validity, we are concerned with how well a predictor can predict a criterion at the same time, or concurrently. Many examples abound. We may wish to predict a student's grade-point average on the basis of a test score. We collect data on the grade-point averages of many students, and then we give them a predictor test. If the predictor test is a valid measure of grades, there will be a substantial correlation between test scores and school grades. We can use the same method in an industrial setting. We can predict a worker's level of productivity (the criterion) on the basis of a test (the predictor). We collect productivity data on a current group of workers, give them a test, and then correlate their scores with their productivity records. If the test is of value, we can draw an inference about a worker's productivity on the basis of the test score. In measuring concurrent validity, there is no time interval between collecting the predictor and criterion data. The two variables are assessed *concurrently,* which is how the method gets it name.

Because the criterion for concurrent validity is always available at the time of using the predictor, why bother to collect predictor data at all? The answer is that predictors usually provide a simpler, quicker, or less-expensive substitute for criterion data (Anastasi, 1976). For example, say the criterion is a salesperson's yearly dollar volume. A predictor that could predict a certain level of sales volume would be much more efficient than having all job applicants serve as salespeople for a year.

Predictive Criterion-Related Validity.   In measuring *predictive* validity, predictor information is collected and used to forecast criterion performance. A college might use a student's high school class rank to predict the criterion of overall college grade-point average four years later. A company could use a test to predict whether job applicants will pass a six-month training program.

While concurrent validity is used to diagnose existing status on some criterion, predictive validity is used to forecast future status. The only major distinction between the two is the time interval between collecting the predictor and criterion data. However, predictive validity is usually preferable to concurrent validity. In personnel selection, though, concurrent validity is used primarily as a substitute for predictive validity because of the practical constraints of obtaining criterion data for an entire set of job applicants. The conceptual significance between predictive and concurrent validity in the context of personnel selection will be discussed in the next chapter.

The logic of criterion-related validity is straightforward. You determine if there is a relationship between predictor scores and criterion scores based on a sample of employees on whom you have both sets of scores. If there is a relationship, you use scores on those predictor variables to select applicants on whom there are no criterion scores. Therefore, you predict the applicants' future (and thus unknown) criterion performance from their known test scores based upon the relationship established through criterion-related validity.

In both concurrent and predictive validity, predictor scores are correlated with criterion data. The resulting correlation is called a *validity coefficient*. While an acceptable reliability coefficient is in the .70 to .80 range, a desirable validity coefficient is in the .30 to .40 range. Validity coefficients less than .30 are not uncommon, but those over .50 are rare. Just as a predictor cannot be too reliable, it cannot be too valid. The greater the correlation between the predictor and the criterion, the more we know about the criterion on the basis of the predictor. By squaring the size of the correlation coefficient (r), we can calculate how much variance in the criterion we can account for by using the predictor. For example, if a predictor correlates .40 with a criterion, we can explain 16 percent (r^2) of the variance in the criterion by knowing the predictor. A correlation of 1.0 indicates perfect prediction (and complete knowledge).

Some criteria are difficult to predict no matter what predictors are used, and others are fairly predictable. Similarly, some predictors are consistently valid and are thus used quite often. Other predictors do not seem to be of much predictive value no matter what the criteria are and thus they fall out of use. Usually however, certain predictors are valid for predicting only certain criteria. Shortly, we will review the predictors typically used in I/O psychology and examine how valid they are for predicting criteria.

Content Validity. *Content validity* involves the degree to which a predictor covers a *representative sample* of the behavior being assessed. It is limited mainly to psychological tests, but it could also be extended to interviews or other predictors. Historically, content validity was most relevant in achievement testing. Achievement tests are designed to indicate how well a person has mastered a specific skill or area of content. In order to be "content valid," an achievement test on Civil War history, for example, must contain a representative sample or mix of test items covering the domain of Civil War history, such as battles, military and political figures, and so on. If all of the questions were about the dates of famous battles, the test would not be a balanced representation of the content of Civil War history. If a person scored high on a content-valid test of Civil War history, we would infer that he or she is very knowledgeable about the Civil War.

How do you assess content validity? Unlike criterion-related validity, you do *not* compute a correlation coefficient. Content validity is assessed by experts in the field the test covers. Civil War history experts would first define the domain of the Civil War and then write test questions covering it. These experts would then decide how content valid the test is. Their judgments could range from "not at all" to "highly valid." Presumably, the test would be revised until it showed a high degree of content validity.

A similar type of validity based on the judgments of people is called *face validity*. This is concerned with the appearance of the test items: do they look appropriate for such a test? Estimates of content validity are given by test developers; estimates of face validity are given by test takers. Because test developers are more knowledgeable, content validity is far more important than face validity. It is possible for a test item to be content valid but not face valid, and vice versa. In such a case, the test developers and test takers would disagree over the relevance or appropriateness of the item for the domain being assessed.

Recently, content validity has increased in importance for I/O psychology. While it once was used mainly for academic achievement testing, it is also relevant for employment testing. Employers develop tests that assess the knowledges, skills, and abilities needed to perform a job. How much the content of these tests is job related is assessed by content-validation procedures. First the domain of job behavior is specified by employees and supervisors. Then test items are developed to assess the factors needed for success on the job. The content validity of employment tests is thus a function of the extent to which the content of the job is reflected in the content of the test. A procedure has been developed (Lawshe, 1975) to *quantify* the content validity of an employment test, a feature previously unavailable in assessing content validity of achievement tests.

Construct Validity.   *Construct validity* is the most theoretical and complex type of validity. Examples of theoretical constructs are intelligence, motivation, anxiety, and mechanical comprehension. The construct validation process entails the following procedures. If we wish to assess whether a test measures a theoretical construct, such as intelligence, we start out with known measures of intelligence, such as numerical ability, verbal ability, and abstract reasoning. People take these tests along with the test we are developing. We then correlate scores on the new test with scores from the established tests. If the new test correlates highly with the other tests, we have a basis to believe that something in common is being measured by all of them: the construct of intelligence. We would also correlate scores on the new test with other measures that we know do *not* assess intelligence, such as physical strength. There should be no correlation between the new test and these measures. That is, we can say that scores on the new test should *converge*—show *convergent validity*—with known measures of the construct in question. They should also *diverge*—show *discriminant* or *divergent validity*—with measures that do not assess the construct. Other statistical procedures may also be used to establish the construct validity of a test (for example, Kalleberg & Kluegel, 1975). After collecting much data over a long period of time, we accumulate a body of evidence supporting the notion that the test measures a psychological construct. In turn, we would say the test manifests construct validity.

Construct validity is extremely important in I/O psychology. Many theoretical constructs have been proposed to explain human behavior in the workplace. Among them are job involvement, organizational commitment, self-esteem, organizational climate, and role clarity (these constructs will all be explained at length in Chapter 8). Through this process, we identify the variables that define the construct. Just as we know that the construct of intelligence has both a verbal and mathematical component, we have also learned the "ingredients" of such work-related constructs as morale. We further establish that work groups with high morale feel and behave differently than work groups with low morale. When we say that a test or other measuring device has construct validity, we mean the items making up the test are conceptually interrelated. Test scores also relate to attitudes or behaviors external to the test.

Construct validity is difficult to establish and is one of the highest accolades one can bestow upon a test. Tests having high construct validity are among the most widely respected and frequently used assessment devices in I/O psychology. For instance, the Job Descriptive Index (a measure of job satisfaction) has such a reputation after many years of development and use. (It will be discussed in Chapter 9.)

Some psychologists have reexamined their thinking about validity and now believe all kinds of evidence support construct validity (Landy, 1986). That is, content and criterion-related validity are actually two kinds of *validity analysis strategies* related to assessing construct validity (Lawshe, 1985). Thus, criterion-related validity can be used in part to demonstrate the construct validity of a test. That is, scores on a job satisfaction measure may well be related to a criterion, such as absenteeism. Similarly, content validity is one way to index the items constituting a construct. There is also some concern (for example, Guion, 1978) that content validity is a *procedure* more for ensuring relevance of test content than for assessing the accuracy of inferences. The fact that the different types of validity are related to one another can create confusion (for example, Tenopyr, 1977), but we must not lose sight of their common meaning. They all involve the appropriateness of making inferences (about someone's intelligence, mechanical ability, capacity to succeed on a job, personality) based on a test score. If a test is highly valid, such inferences are warranted; conversely, it would be inappropriate to draw inferences from a test that lacks validity.

Criterion Reliability and Validity

Before we leave this section on reliability and validity, note that they are as important to criteria as they are to predictors. The criteria we wish to predict must be stable measures of behavior, not will-o'-the-wisp variables that lack consistency. Similarly, the criteria must be appropriate and relevant. Shoe size is an invalid criterion of intelligence; that is, it would be inappropriate to make inferences about people's intelligence by measuring the size of their feet. However, it may be appropriate to make inferences about a person's height by measuring his or her shoe size. While the concepts of reliability and validity were deferred until this chapter on predictors, they are equally relevant to criteria.

FRANK AND ERNEST by Bob Thaves

HOW CAN A WOMAN BE SUING US FOR SEX DISCRIMINATION?... WE'VE NEVER EVEN HAD ONE WORK HERE!

©1982 Newspaper Enterprise Association, Inc.

Psychological Assessment and the Law

It is beyond the scope of this book to give a complete discourse on the relationship between the legal and psychological professions. The interested reader should refer to Bersoff (1981) or Cascio (1982). What follows is a brief synopsis of how the link between psychological assessment and the law came to be and its implications.

For the first 60 or so years of I/O psychology, there was virtually no connection between psychologists and the legal community. Psychological tests were developed, administered, and interpreted by psychologists, and as a profession psychologists governed themselves. However, during the late 1950s and early 1960s, the nation was swept up in the civil rights movement. At that time *civil rights* concerned primarily the conditions under which blacks lived and worked in this country. Blacks were denied access to colleges, restaurants, and jobs—in short, their civil rights were being denied. Presidents Kennedy and Johnson were interested in changing this aspect of American society. In 1964 the Civil Rights Act was passed, a major piece of federal legislation aimed at reducing discrimination in all walks of life. The section of the law pertaining to discrimination in employment is Title VII and is the section most relevant to I/O psychology. In essence, the message of the law was as follows: Blacks were grossly underemployed throughout the country in both private- and public-sector jobs, particularly in jobs above the lower levels of organizations. Since I/O psychologists were the ones who had developed personnel-selection methods, and these methods seemingly had produced this great underemployment of Blacks, the profession held some responsibility for this apparent employment discrimination. To reduce discrimination in employment (which was one of the mandates of the Civil Rights Act), the federal government was now going to intervene in the process of employment hiring, in essence monitor the entire procedure to ensure fairness in selection. Thus began in the 1960s the interface between I/O psychology and the law.

The Civil Rights Act was expanded to cover other people besides Blacks. In fact, five groups were identified for protection under this law: race, sex, religion, color, and national origin. These are referred to as the *protected groups*. The Civil Rights Act was also expanded to include *all* personnel functions—training, promotion, retention, and performance appraisal—in addition to selection. Further, it was no longer limited to psychological tests in personnel selection but expanded to pertain to *any* method used for making personnel decisions.

What exactly did the law say? It established a concept called *adverse impact.* Adverse impact refers to the results of any selection method that causes a disproportionate percentage of people of a given category to be hired compared to another group. Adverse impact is determined by what is known as the "4/5ths rule." The rule states that adverse impact occurs if the selection ratio (that is, the number of people hired divided by the number of people who apply) for any subgroup of people (as Blacks) is less than 4/5ths of the selection ratio for the largest group. Suppose 100 Whites apply for a job and 20 are selected. The selection ratio is 20/100, or .20. By multiplying .20 by 4/5, we get .16. This means that if fewer than 16 percent of the Black applicants are hired, the selection test has adverse impact. So if 50 Blacks applied for the job, at least 8 (50 × .16) would have to be hired.

If adverse impact is found to exist, the employer is obligated to validate the selection procedure to prove that the resulting personnel decisions were indeed based on a correct (that is, valid) method. If adverse impact does not result from the selection method, the employer is not obligated to validate it. Obviously, it is a sound business decision to validate any selection method at any time. You would always want to know if your method is identifying the best candidates for hire. However, the law requires validation of a method *only* if it results in adverse impact.

As part of the Civil Rights Act, a federal agency was created called the Equal Employment Opportunity Commission (EEOC). The mandate of the EEOC was to reduce employment discrimination by ensuring compliance with the law. The agency created a set of employment guidelines (called the EEOC Guidelines) that served as the standard for compliance with the law. The first version of these guidelines, published in 1970, was somewhat vague in specifying standards and was in fact one of four employment guidelines issued by the federal government. Other federal agencies had their own sets of employment guidelines, including the Department of Justice, the Department of Labor, and the Civil Service Commission. It was very difficult for employers to be in compliance with the law during this time because there were in essence four versions of it. Finally, in 1978 the four agencies got together and drafted a single, *uniform* set of employment guidelines for all employers to follow.

There were several landmark court cases based upon these employment guidelines. In *Griggs v. Duke Power Company,* the court ruled that individuals who bring suit against a company do not have to prove that the company's employment test was *unfair*; rather, the company has to prove its test is *fair.* Thus, the burden of proving the quality of the test rests with the employer. This finding has subsequently been referred to as "Griggs' Burden." In the case of *Albemarle v. Moody,* the court ruled on just how much judicial power the employment guidelines really have. Although they were called "guidelines," the court ruled that they be granted the "deference of law," meaning they were in effect *the* law on employment testing. Finally, in *Bakke v. University of California,* the court ruled that Whites can be the victim of discrimination as well as Blacks. Bakke (a White male) sued the University of California on the grounds that his race had been a factor in his being denied admission to their medical school. The court ruled in Bakke's favor and required the University of California to admit Bakke to the medical college. This case was heralded as a classic case of "reverse discrimination," which technically is incorrect. First, it connotes that only Blacks can be discriminated against, which obviously is not true. Second, reversal of the process of discrimination results in nondiscrimination. There have been literally thousands of cases adjudicated in the district, appellate, and state and federal supreme courts based on litigation spawned by employment law. The above three cases represent but a very small sampling.

In 1967 the government passed a separate law covering *age* discrimination called the Age Discrimination in Employment Act. It extends to people aged 40 and over the same type of legal protection granted to the five protected groups under the Civil Rights Act. There has also been a series of presidential orders of a lesser scope that have modified or amended the major laws. The employment guidelines that evolved from the Civil Rights Act are clearly regarded as the "law of the land," although many I/O psychologists feel that a set of testing principles developed by the Division of Industrial-Organizational Psychology (1987) are more technically precise. As an initial reaction to these guidelines many employers curtailed the use of psychological tests. But this was no way to avoid compliance with the guidelines, because they dealt with *any* predictor used for selection, not just psychological tests.

Here is how the federal government would become involved procedurally in employment litigation. If a company's selection procedure systematically results in the rejection of a disproportionate number of members of a certain group (for example, race, religion, sex), a rejected applicant can file a complaint against the company with the EEOC. The EEOC then investigates the complaint and tries to reach an agreement with the company regarding use of the test. If the two parties cannot agree, the company can be sued for using unfair selection procedures. The company then has to prove in court that its tests are not unfair and its selection system is valid. Companies that lose such cases have been obligated to pay multi-million-dollar sums. The money is often used to pay the victims of their unfair tests. The financial awards in such cases can be *class-action* settlements (the person who is suing represents a class of similar people) or *back-pay* settlements (the company has to pay a portion of what victims would have earned had they been hired). Awards in single lawsuits have reached $20 to $30 million. Needless to say, not everyone who fails an employment test has his or her day in court. A lawsuit must be predicated on "just cause" and not simply on the complaints of one disgruntled applicant who failed a test. Also, large employers who affect the lives of many people are more likely to be sued than small employers.

The EEOC Guidelines did more to change personnel testing in this country than any other single event. If World War II was the stimulus for the boom in psychological testing, the EEOC Guidelines were the stimulus for the reevaluation and reformulation of personnel selection procedures. The federal government is now involved in an area that used to be governed solely by the psychological profession. While many psychologists have commented on the difficulty of complying with federal law on personnel testing, they generally acknowledge that there is less unfair discrimination in employment today than before the Civil Rights Act was passed. To the extent that the EEOC Guidelines were devised to reduce discrimination in employment, they can be considered successful in meeting this important goal.

Psychological Tests and Inventories

Psychological tests and inventories have been the most frequently used predictors in I/O psychology. The difference between the two is that in a test, the answers are either right or wrong; in an inventory, there are no right or wrong answers. Usually, though, the term *tests* or *psychological testing* represents the family of tests and inventories. Testing has a long multinational history in the field of psychology. Sir Francis Galton, an English biologist, had an interest in human heredity. In the course of his research he realized the need for measuring the characteristics of biologically related and unrelated persons. He began to keep records of people on such factors as keenness of vision and hearing, muscular strength, and reaction time. By 1880, he had accumulated the first large-scale body of information on individual differences. He was probably the first scientist to devise systematic ways of measuring people. In 1890, the American psychologist Cattell introduced the term *mental test*. He devised an early test of intelligence based on sensory discrimination and reaction time. Ebbinghaus, a German psychologist, developed math and sentence-completion tests and gave them to school children. In 1897, he reported that the sentence-completion test was related to the children's scholastic achievement.

The biggest advances in the early years of testing were made by the French psychologist Binet. In 1904, the French government appointed Binet to study procedures for the education of retarded children. In order to assess mental retardation, Binet (in collaboration with Simon) developed a test of intelligence. It consisted of 30 problems covering such areas as judgment, comprehension, and reasoning, which Binet regarded as essential components of intelligence. Later revisions of this test had a greater sampling of items from different areas. Binet's research on intelligence testing was continued by the American psychologist Terman, who in 1916 developed the concept of IQ (intelligence quotient). These early pioneers paved the way for a wide variety of tests that would be developed in the years to come, many of which were used by industrial psychologists to predict job performance. While most of the early work in testing was directed as assessing intellect, testing horizons expanded to include aptitude, ability, interest, and personality.

Types of Tests

Tests can be classified by either their administrative aspects or by their content. We will use both methods.

Speed Versus Power Tests. Speed tests have a large number of easy questions—so easy that you will always get them right. The test is timed (for example, 5-minute limit), and has more items than can possibly be answered in the allotted time period. The total score on such a test is the number of items answered and reflects your speed of work.

Power tests have questions that are fairly difficult; that is, you cannot get them right just by trying. Usually, you have as much time as you need to answer all the

You don't need to give paper-and-pencil tests to assess the ability of some people. Bill Smith Photography

questions. The total score on such a test is the number of items answered correctly. Most tests given in college are power tests. If time limits are imposed, they are done mostly for the convenience of the test administrator.

Individual Versus Group Tests.   Individual tests are given to only one person at a time. Such tests are not common because of the amount of time needed to administer them to all applicants. For example, if a test takes one hour and ten people are to take it, ten hours of administration time will be required. The benefits of giving such a test must be judged against the costs. Certain types of IQ tests are individually administered, as are certain tests for evaluating high-level executives. In these tests, the administrator has to play an active part (for example, asking questions, demonstrating an object) as opposed to just monitoring them.

Group tests are administered to several people simultaneously and are the most common type of test. They do not involve the active participation of an administrator. The Army Alpha and Beta tests were early group intelligence tests used in World War I. Most tests used in educational and industrial organizations are group tests, because they are efficient in terms of time and cost.

Paper-and-Pencil Versus Performance Tests. Paper-and-pencil tests are the most common type of test used in industrial and educational organizations. Such tests do not involve the physical manipulation of objects or pieces of equipment. The questions asked in a paper-and-pencil test may require answers in either multiple choice or essay form. The physical ability of individuals to handle a pencil should not influence their score on the test. The pencil is just the means by which their response is recorded on a sheet of paper.

In a performance test, the individual has to manipulate an object or a piece of equipment. The score is a measure of the person's ability to perform the manipulation. A typing test is an example of a performance test, as is a test of finger dexterity. Sometimes both paper-and-pencil and performance tests are used jointly. To get a driver's license, most people have to pass both a written and a behind-the-wheel performance test.

Ethical Standards in Testing

To prevent misuse of psychological tests, the American Psychological Association has developed guidelines for their use. The ethics of psychological testing are a major responsibility of psychologists, as seen in the APA code of professional ethics (*Standards for Educational and Psychological Tests,* 1985). Maintaining ethical standards in testing is one of the more important ethical issues confronting the entire profession of psychology (APA, 1981).

Tests users must have certain qualifications depending on the purpose of the testing. Sometimes the test user must be a licensed professional psychologist. This is particularly true in the area of clinical psychology. But in industry, lesser qualifications are needed to administer employment tests. To prevent their misuse and to maintain test security, restrictions are also placed on who can buy the tests. Test publishers are discouraged from giving away free samples or printing detailed examples of test questions as sales promotions, which could invalidate future test results.

Other ethical issues involve the invasion of privacy and confidentiality (Anastasi, 1976). Invasion of privacy occurs when a psychological test reveals more information about a person than he or she would want. Tests should be used for precise purposes.

They should not be used to learn everything about a person, whether or not it is related to the issue at hand. If a company uses a mechanical comprehension test to hire mechanics, it should not also use a personality inventory just to learn about potential employees' personal lives. Using a personality inventory, which has no relationship to job performance, could be an invasion of the applicant's privacy.

Confidentiality refers to who should have access to test results. When a person takes an employment test, he or she should be told the purpose of the test, how the results will be used, and which people in the company will need to see the results. Problems arise if a third party (another prospective employer, for example) wants to know the test results. The scores should be kept confidential except in the case of a written release from the test taker.

Another problem in this area is the retention of records. Advances in computer technology have made it possible to store large quantities of information about people. Who should have access to this information, and what guarantees are there that it will not be misused? The results of an IQ test taken in sixth grade may become part of a student's permanent academic record. Should a potential employer get the results of this grammar school test? Furthermore, the test probably couldn't predict job performance, so why would anyone want the results? These types of questions are central to problems of confidentiality.

Sources of Information About Testing

Because testing is a rapidly changing area, it is important to keep up with current developments in the field. Old tests get revised, new tests are introduced, and some tests are discontinued.

Fortunately, several key references are available. Perhaps the most important source is the series of *Mental Measurement Yearbooks* (MMY). The *MMY* was first published in 1938 and has been revised in roughly a six-year cycle. Each yearbook includes tests published during a specified period, thus supplementing the tests reported in previous yearbooks. The *Ninth Mental Measurements Yearbook* (1985), for example, deals mainly with tests that appeared between 1978 and 1983. Tests may be reviewed again in later yearbooks as new information becomes available. Each test is critically reviewed by an expert in the field and documented with a complete list of references. Information about price, publisher, and versions of the test is also given. The *MMY* series is the most comprehensive review of psychological tests available in the field.

Other, less detailed books have been prepared by Buros. They are *Tests in Print* (1974) and *Personality Tests and Reviews* (1970). Both of these books resemble bibliographies and help locate tests in the *MMY*. Some psychological journals also review specific tests. Various professional test developers also publish test manuals. The test manual should give the information needed to administer, score, and evaluate a particular test, as well as data on the test's reliability and validity. While these manuals are useful, they are usually not as complete and critical as reviews in the *MMY*.

The test user has an obligation to use the test in a professional and competent manner. Tests should be chosen with extreme care and concern for the consequences of using the tests. Important decisions are based on test scores, and the choice of test is equally important. Cronbach (1970) recommends that a test be thoroughly analyzed before it is considered for use.

Test Content

Tests can be classified according to their content. While there are other types, the following sections discuss the major tests used in industry. Also presented is information on how valid the various types of tests have been in personnel selection as documented from their use in the psychological literature.

Intelligence Tests

Tests of mental ability or intelligence have long been used for personnel selection. Part of the reason for this is the belief that intelligence correlates with job performance. That is, all things considered, it is usually believed that if the worker is more intelligent, productivity will be higher, turnover will be lower, and so forth. While there is evidence that intelligence is correlated with performance, the relationship does not always hold. Research shows that some employees can be *too* intelligent for a job, particularly lower-level ones. The employees want more stimulation than the job can provide, so they become bored and then quit. In such a case, it's better to hire less-intelligent workers.

Among the mental ability tests commonly used in industry are the Otis Self-Administering Tests of Mental Ability (1922–1929), the Wonderlic Personnel Test (Wonderlic & Hovland, 1939), and the Adaptability Test (Tiffin & Lawshe, 1942). Wonderlic chose the term *personnel* for the test title because it is less threatening than the term *intelligence*. All of these tests are quite short; they take only 12 to 15 minutes to administer. Reliabilities in the .90 range have been reported for all the tests. The tests seem to be most valid for selecting clerical workers and, to a lesser extent, first-line supervisors. Figure 4–1 shows some sample test questions from a typical intelligence test.

Ghiselli (1973) reported a median correlation of about .25 between tests of intelligence and measures of job proficiency across seven occupational groups. A similar finding was reported by Schmitt, Gooding, Noe, and Kirsch (1984) in an

---

1. What number is missing in this series?
   3–8–14–21–29–(?)

2. SHOVEL is to DITCHDIGGER as SCALPEL is to:
   (a) knife   (b) sharp   (c) butcher   (d) surgeon   (e) cut

---

Figure 4–1   Sample Test Questions from a Typical Intelligence Test

investigation of validity studies published over a 20-year period. A validity coefficient (r) of .30 means that 9% (r^2) of the variance in job performance can be predicted by knowledge of intellectual ability. Worded in reverse, 91% of the variance in job performance is unrelated to how intelligent the jobholder is. The implication is that intelligence plays a relatively small role in job performance. There is even less of a relationship between measures of intelligence and such hard criteria as promotions, accidents, and sales volume. However, when the criterion is a supervisory rating, there appears to be a modest and consistent relationship between intelligence and job performance (see Field Note 1).

Field Note 1

During the Vietnam War there was an elite military unit called Special Forces. This unit was called upon for assignments that were very important to the military and usually very dangerous. The military was extremely selective in terms of admittance to Special Forces, typically selecting only one out of every 100 candidates. While several types of tests were used in the selection battery, one in particular was unique. I have never heard anything like it before or since.

The candidate was given a plain piece of paper with numbered blanks to record answers, and a pencil. The test was recorded on a cassette tape, and the test began when the administrator started the tape. The voice on the tape said, "Question number one. A flag pole is 40 feet tall, and casts a shadow 40 feet in length on the ground. What is the distance from the top of the flagpole to the top of the flagpole's shadow on the ground?" Eight seconds of silence followed. Then the voice said, "Question number two. What number comes next in this sequence: 4-7-13-25- ?" Eight seconds of silence followed. This procedure was repeated for the 100 questions that made up the test.

The questions consisted of basic reasoning and intelligence items, but what made the test so difficult was its manner of presentation. The questions were spoken once, the candidate had eight seconds to figure out the answer, and never got to go back and check the answers or rethink hard questions. There was one chance to get it correct when it was said, and that was it. *Your* own chances of getting these two questions correct are greater than the military candidate's because you are *reading* this, and can reread it as often as you like. How would you do if you *heard* the questions only once, and had but eight seconds to figure out each answer?

How was this test constructed and what does it measure? When in combat, members of the Special Forces have to think quickly, correctly, and under pressure. Given these conditions, the test constructors "worked backward" to develop a test that measured these characteristics. The actual content of the questions is almost incidental to the intent of the test. If you think you would be working under stress to take a test such as this, that is exactly what the test developers had in mind. This test was designed to identify who could function effectively under stress and who could not.

Mechanical Aptitude Tests

There are two types of tests dealing with mechanical aptitude: those involving mechanical reasoning and those involving spatial relations. Mechanical aptitude tests generally require a person to recognize which mechanical principle is suggested by a test item. Tests of spatial relations are included because it is assumed that the ability to perceive geometric relationships between physical objects and to manipulate those objects are both parts of the larger construct of mechanical aptitude. One of the most popular tests of mechanical reasoning is the Bennett Test of Mechanical Comprehension (Bennett, 1940). The test is a series of pictures reflecting various issues about mechanical facts and principles. Sample questions from the Bennett Test are shown in Figure 4–2.

Some of the more widely used tests of spatial relations include the Minnesota Spatial Relations Test (Paterson, 1930) and the Minnesota Paper Form Board Test

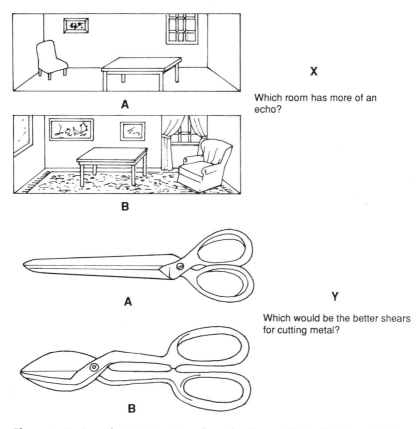

X

Which room has more of an echo?

Y

Which would be the better shears for cutting metal?

Figure 4–2   Sample Test Questions from the Bennett Test of Mechanical Comprehension

(Likert & Quasha, 1941–1948). The Minnesota Spatial Relations Test measures both dexterity and spatial relations. A picture of the test is shown in Figure 4–3. In this test, 58 geometric shapes cut from a large board have to be placed into their appropriate slots as quickly as possible. Both length of time and number of errors are counted.

The Revised Minnesota Paper Form Board Test does not involve dexterity as a variable in performance. It consists of 64 multiple-choice items. Each item shows the

Figure 4–3 The Minnesota Spatial Relations Test

parts of a geometric figure that has been cut into pieces, followed by five assembled geometric forms. The test taker must pick which geometric form is the assembled version of the parts.

Ghiselli (1973) reviewed the validity of three sets of mechanical aptitude tests for predicting job proficiency. In addition to tests of spatial relations and mechanical reasoning, he also included location tests. In location tests, test takers must identify the location of a series of points and judge the distance between them.

Ghiselli (1973) reported average validity coefficients for aptitude tests around .25 to .30 for vehicle operators, trades and craft employees, and clerical personnel, with appreciably lower coefficients for sales and service occupations. Similar findings were reported by Schmitt and associates (1984), who found an average validity coefficient of .27 for aptitude tests. It seems that the possession of certain aptitudes is needed for success in selected jobs, and that these types of tests have exhibited a modest degree of predictive accuracy.

Ability Tests

Ability tests usually cover two broad classes of tests: sensory ability and motor ability. These abilities are related to success in certain types of jobs. Sensory-ability tests assess visual acuity, color vision, and hearing sensitivity. These abilities, too, are related to success in certain types of jobs. Perhaps the best known test of visual acuity is the *Snellen Eye Chart*, a display with rows of letters that get increasingly smaller. The test taker stands 20 feet away from the chart and reads each row until the letters are indistinguishable. A ratio is then computed to express acuity:

$$\text{Acuity} = \frac{\text{Distance at which a person can read a certain line of print (usually 20 feet)}}{\text{Distance at which the average person can read the same line of print}}$$

For example, if the smallest line of print a person can read at 20 feet is a line most people can read from 40 feet, the person's score would be 20/40. Each eye is tested separately, and normal vision is 20/20. The most common way to measure hearing sensitivity is with an instrument called an *audiometer*. An audiometer produces tones of different frequencies and loudness. The tone is gradually raised in intensity. When the test taker signals that the note has been heard, the examiner records the level of intensity on an *audiogram*, which shows the intensity of sound needed to hear tones of different frequency. An audiogram is prepared for each ear. Hearing loss is detected by comparing one person's audiogram with the results from a tested population.

Researchers have also devised paper-and-pencil tests of perceptual accuracy. In these tests, two stimuli are presented, and the test taker must judge whether they are the same or different. The stimuli may be numbers or names (both are used in the

Which pairs of items are identical?
17345290—17342590
2033220638—2033220638
WPBRAEGGER—WPBREAGGER
CLAFDAPKA26—CLAPDAFKA26

Figure 4–4 Sample Test Question from a Typical Perceptual Accuracy Test

Minnesota Clerical Test). Figure 4–4 shows the types of items in a perceptual accuracy test.

Tests of motor ability assess fine or gross motor coordination. Frequently used motor-ability tests include the Purdue Pegboard (Tiffin, 1941) and the Crawford Small Parts Dexterity Test (Crawford & Crawford, 1946). In the first part of the Purdue Pegboard, pins are placed into small holes in a pegboard, using the right hand first, then the left hand, and then both hands together. In the second part, the pins are again placed in the holes but with the addition of collars and washers. The first part of the test measures manual dexterity; the second part measures finger dexterity. In the Crawford Small Parts Dexterity Test, pins are first placed in holes in the board and then metal collars are placed over the pins. In the second part of the test, a screwdriver is used to insert small screws after they have been placed by hand into threaded holes.

Ghiselli's (1973) review of test validities reveal that ability tests have an average validity between .20 and .25. They were most predictive of job success in clerical occupations and least predictive in sales occupations. On par however, the validity of ability tests is in the same general range of intelligence and aptitude tests.

Personality and Interest Inventories

Unlike the previously cited tests, which have objective answers, in personality and interest inventories the individual's responses are neither right nor wrong. Test takers answer questions about their personal likes ("I like to go swimming") or how much they agree with certain statements ("People who work hard get ahead"). In interest inventories, similar types of questions normally make up such a scale, such as an "Interest in Outdoor Activity." Responses are tallied, and scores show the degree of interest in the activity. Similar procedures are used in personality inventories, which reflect a person's introversion, dominance, confidence, and so on. These scale scores are then used to predict job success. The basic rationale is that successful employees have certain interests or personality patterns, and these patterns become the basis for selecting new employees.

Two of the commonly used interest inventories are the Strong-Campbell Interest Inventory (Campbell, 1977) and the Vocational Preference Inventory (Holland, 1965). Both of these interest inventories have series of questions about vocational interests. A person's responses are then compared with the interests of members of various occupational groups. People can then know if their interests are more like certain groups (for example, engineers) than others (for example, pilots). It is assumed that the more similar the interest pattern, the more likely one is to succeed in that occupation. Ghiselli (1973) reported an average validity coefficient of .19 for interest inventories. The research results indicate that interest inventories are useful for predicting *membership* in an occupation (for example, differentiating people in sales versus clerical occupations) but not useful for predicting success *within* it.

The use of personality inventories for predicting job success has undergone a complete cycle. Originally, psychologists thought personality variables were related to job performance. At least on logical grounds this perspective makes a lot of sense because some people seemingly have the "wrong personality" for a job. Psychologists would use large omnibus personality inventories developed by clinical psychologists to forecast job success. The classic personality inventory of this type is the Minnesota Multiphasic Personality Inventory (MMPI) developed by Hathaway and McKinley (1943). The MMPI consists of 550 statements that must be answered "true," "false," or "cannot say." The inventory is scored in terms of ten clinical scales (for example, Depression, Schizophrenia).

Personality inventories such as the MMPI were used for many years for personnel selection—in fact, overused or misused. They were used indiscriminately to assess a candidate's personality, even when there was no established relationship between test scores and job success. Soon personality inventories came under attack. They were criticized for invading a person's privacy. Some scales of a personality inventory may be useful for personnel selection decisions, but information unrelated to employment success may be revealed in the other scales. Furthermore, personality inventories were criticized for lacking empirical validity. Guion and Gottier (1965) concluded the evidence on personality inventories did not support their use for making personnel selection decisions. The upshot of these criticisms of personality inventories led to a marked curtailment in their use.

However, psychologists continued to discover that personality variables were influential in job performance. Previously, they had relied on conventional personality inventories for making predictions about job performance that were never really intended for industrial usage with "normal" adults. Personality inventories like the MMPI were developed to make clinical diagnoses, differentiating normal from abnormal personalities. Consequently their scales weren't refined enough to make accurate predictions among job candidates. Accordingly, I/O psychologists have recently begun developing new personality inventories designed exclusively for use with working populations. The results have been far more impressive than the previous research on clinical personality inventories. For example, Gough (1984) has successfully developed a personality scale to measure managerial potential, as defined by such factors as being organized, capable, mature, and self-confident. Hogan, Hogan, and Busch (1984) created a personality scale designed to measure the disposition to be helpful in dealing with other people, as indexed by such factors as being thoughtful, considerate, and cooperative. Finally, Bentz (1985) described his success in using personality measures to predict executive success at Sears Roebuck. While the "rebirth" of personality testing in industry is still unfolding, it seems psychologists are developing new personality inventories that are more sensitive and appropriate than the classic clinical personality measures.

Multiple-Aptitude Test Batteries

A final category of tests is based on their structural composition rather than item content. Test "batteries" consist of many of the types of tests already discussed: intelligence, mechanical aptitude, personality, and so on. These tests are usually quite long; they may take several hours to complete. Each part of the test measures such factors as intellectual ability and mechanical reasoning. The tests are useful because they yield a great deal of information that can later be used for hiring, placement, training, and so forth. The major disadvantages of the test are the cost and time involved. The two most widely known multiple aptitude batteries are the General Aptitude Test Battery (GATB) and the Differential Aptitude Test (DAT).

Computerized Adaptive Testing

One of the truly major advances in psychological testing is called Computerized Adaptive Testing (CAT). It is sometimes called "tailored testing." Here is how it works. CAT is an automated test administration system using a computer. The test items appear on the video display screen of the computer terminal, and the examinee answers using the keyboard. Each test question presented is prompted by the response to the previous question. The test is sequentially scored via computer software. The first question given to the examinee is of medium difficulty. If the answer given is correct, the next question selected from the item bank of questions has been precalibrated to be slightly more difficult. If the answer given to that question is wrong, the next question selected by the computer will be somewhat easier. And so on.

The purpose of the CAT system is to get as close a match as possible between the question-difficulty level and the examinee's demonstrated ability level. In fact, by the careful calibration of question difficulty, one can infer ability level on the basis of the difficulty level of the questions answered correctly. CAT systems are based upon very complex mathematical models. Proponents of CAT systems believe that tests can be of shorter length (because of higher precision of measurement), be less expensive, and have greater security than traditional paper-and-pencil tests. The military is the largest user of CAT systems, as it tests thousands of examinees monthly.

While CAT systems represent the "high-tech" approach to psychological assessment, I doubt if they will soon make all paper-and-pencil tests obsolete. First, CAT systems were designed for the assessment of abilities and aptitudes. They typically are not used for personality or interest measurement. Second, they obviously require elaborate computer programs (as well as a computer), which all organizations don't possess. Third, they are most cost efficient for very large employers, like the military. And fourth, the mathematical foundations of such systems (called "Item Response Theory") is still a matter of professional debate. While CAT systems will never completely replace traditional testing, they do represent the cutting edge of psychological assessment. Computers have made possible great advances in science, as evidenced in I/O psychology by this major breakthrough in testing.

Testing in Retrospect

As Haney (1981) has observed, society has tended to imbue psychological tests with some arcane mystical powers, which as the evidence reviewed in this chapter indicates, is totally unwarranted. There is nothing mysterious about psychological tests; they are merely tools to help make better decisions than could be made without them. The psychological testing profession has a large share of critics. Rather than a criticism of poor quality, a more accurate criticism relates to the inappropriate use of good tests. For example, since the MMPI was never originally intended to predict managerial success, we really shouldn't be too surprised or too unhappy when we find it does not. Testing has been oversold as a solution to problems. Many people have decried the "tyranny of testing"—the fact that major, critical decisions (say, entrance into a college or professional school) that affect an entire lifetime are based upon a single test. Testing has its place in our repertoire of diagnostic instruments; tests should help us meet our needs and not be the master of our decisions. This is sound advice that psychologists have long advocated. However, it is advice that both the developers and users of psychological tests have occasionally ignored or forgotten.

What we have learned about psychological tests from an I/O perspective is that some tests are useful in forecasting job success and others are not. As an entire class of predictors, psychological tests have been modestly predictive of job performance. Yet, some authors (for example, Hunter & Hunter, 1984) believe that, all things considered, psychological tests have outperformed all other types of predictors across the full spectrum of jobs. Single-validity coefficients in excess of .50 are as unusual today as they were in the early years of testing. The modal range for psychological-test validity coefficients is in the .20s; that is, between 4% and 8% of the variance in job performance across a broad range of many jobs is predictable with psychological tests. While these coefficients are not as high as we would like, it is unfair to condemn the tests as useless. Some tests are very useful for predicting success in certain jobs. Also, keep in mind that validity coefficients are a function of both the predictor and the criterion. A poorly defined and constructed criterion will produce low validity coefficients no matter what the predictor is like. But because of the limited predictive power of tests, psychologists have had to look elsewhere for forecasters of job performance. The balance of this chapter examines what other predictors psychologists have investigated.

Interviews

In terms of sheer frequency, interviews are the most popular method of selecting employees. The popularity of the employment interview may also be due to increased legal problems with paper-and-pencil tests. While most court cases regarding discrimination have involved paper-and-pencil tests, interviews along with other predictors are still regarded as a *test* by the EEOC, and as such, are subject to the same judicial review. Unlike tests, interviews are highly subjective, so *chances* for unfair discrimination seem to be greater. Because interviews are used so often in employment decisions, many research studies have been conducted. Some of the major issues inherent in the employment interview are discussed in the following sections.

Format of the Selection Interview

The interviewer's purpose is twofold: (1) to gather relevant data and (2) to evaluate the data and decide to select or reject the applicant (Blum & Naylor, 1968). The nature and amount of information an interview generates is due to the type of interview and to the characteristics of the applicant and the interviewer.

There are several types of interviews, ranging from highly structured to highly unstructured. In a highly structured interview, the interviewer asks predetermined questions of all applicants in the same way. The interviewer then records each response question by question. In an unstructured interview, the interviewer proceeds on the basis of the applicant's response to previous questions. The interviewer probes and explores the applicant's qualifications in a "play-by-ear" fashion. In theory, no two applicants would be asked the same question. In practice, most interviews are halfway between structured and unstructured. That is, the applicants get asked the same general questions, but their responses may cause the interviewer to question them more intensely.

Interviews can also be described in terms of the number of participants or trials. In most cases one applicant and one interviewer have one interview. The interviewer evaluates the applicant and makes a decision. An alternative is to have the applicant interviewed by several interviewers separately. This type of interview is usually conducted for individuals applying for higher-level jobs. The interviewers pool their separate opinions and reach a decision. A final format is for an applicant to be interviewed by a panel of perhaps as many as six or seven interviewers. Again, the interviewers pool their opinions and make a decision. This procedure is typical in government jobs where applicants are often interviewed by a Civil Service evaluation board.

Unlike a paper-and-pencil test, an interview is a dynamic selection device. Interviewers affect the behavior of applicants, and vice versa. While applicants try to impress interviewers and thereby effect a favorable decision, it is also true that interviewers can affect applicants. The interviewer can knowingly or unknowingly alter the applicant's responses by saying such things as "You're right," "I agree," or "I disagree" (Verplank, 1955). Nonverbal responses (yawning, smiling, frowning, and degree of eye contact) can alter the applicant's behavior, too. Furthermore, the outcome of an interview can be affected by the interviewer's behavior. Thus, an interviewer's own behavior during the interview may be a determining factor as to whether the applicant is hired! Experienced interviewers learn a standardized interview style to minimize the impact of their own behavior on the outcome of the interview.

Schmitt (1976) has developed a graphic model of the determinants of interview decisions. As can be seen in Figure 4–5, the interaction of the applicant and the interviewer determines the outcome. We will explore some of these factors in greater detail shortly. For the moment, note that many variables that affect the outcomes of interviews do not influence tests. For example, the interviewer's sex may influence who gets offered a job, but the sex of the test scorer would not influence the applicant's score.

Evaluation of the Interview

Interviews have been called "conversations with a purpose" (Bingham & Moore, 1941). The "goodness" of these conversations as predictors of job performance can be judged by the same criteria used to judge any predictor: reliability and validity.

Reliability. The reliability of an interview refers to the similarity of judgments made by the same interviewer over time (*intra*interviewer reliability) or the similarity of judgments made by different interviewers about the same job applicant (*inter*-interviewer reliability). The two types of reliability address different issues.

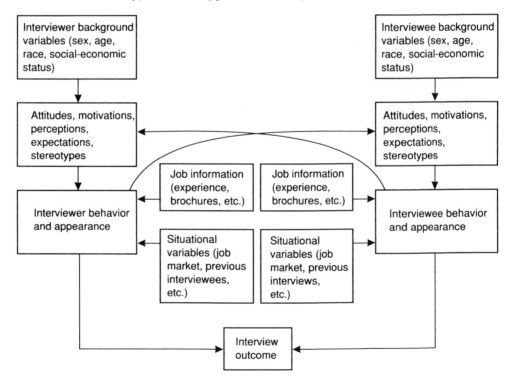

Figure 4–5 Determinants of Interview Outcome

SOURCE: N. Schmitt, "Social and Situational Determinants of Interview Decisions; Implications for the Employment Interview," *Personnel Psychology 29* (1976), pp. 79–101.

Most of the research on *intra*interviewer reliability indicates that interviewers are quite consistent in their evaluations. Whatever they like or dislike about applicants appears stable, so they make consistent evaluations. Carlson (1968) has shown that interviewer self-consistency increases when (1) the interviewer has a relative standard (that is, a hypothetical ideal person) that can be used for comparisons, and (2) the applicants are quite diverse (that is, some are good, some are bad).

While *intra*interviewer reliability is typically high, this is not always true for *inter*interviewer reliability. *Inter*interviewer reliability assesses the extent to which different interviewers reach the same decision in evaluating applicants. A lot of research can be summarized by saying sometimes they agree, and sometimes they don't. Some studies report *inter*interviewer reliabilities in the 80s; other studies report *inter*interviewer reliabilities as low as .15. A crucial determinant of agreement among interviewers is what specifically they are being asked to evaluate. If the applicants are being judged in terms of how appropriate their work history is for a given job, most interviewers should agree (*inter*interviewer reliability would be high). If the applicants are judged on their personality and how it relates to the job, most interviewers would probably disagree (*inter*interviewer reliability would be low). This occurs because interviewers have different ideas as to what the personality constructs mean and how they get translated into job performance. For example, if interviewers were asked if an applicant were "aggressive" enough to succeed in the job, each might have a different view on what aggressiveness is and how much of it is needed on the job.

Validity. Care must be exercised in evaluating the validity of the interview process as a whole versus the validity of the interviewer. The validity of *interviewers* refers to the capacity of individuals to be accurate, sensitive judges of human talent. Research (for example, Zedeck, Tziner, & Middlestadt, 1983) indicates that some interviewers are very good at what they do and that others are poor. The validity of the *interview* process refers to the extent that all of the information about an applicant brought to the attention of the interviewer is predictive of job performance. This would include not only the content of the interview itself but also test scores, letters of reference, and records of past work.

The validity of an interviewer is often tangled up in the validity of these other sources. It's hard to tell how much of the hiring decision was due solely to the interviewer's judgment and how much was due to the other information. Carlson (1972) reported that in reviewing 13 studies where the interviewer was the only source of information, 9 studies had validity coefficients in the .15 to .25 range. Reilly and Chao (1982) estimate the validity of the interview at .19, less than the validity of psychological tests. On par the validity of interviews to predict job success does not warrant their extensive frequency of use. Given the mediocre validity of the interview, exactly what is the basis for most employers' infatuation with the interview as a means of evaluating job candidates? Arvey and Campion (1982) have postulated several reasons for its persistent use. First, the interview really *is* more valid than our research studies indicate. However, due to methodological problems and limitations in our research, we can't demonstrate *how* valid it actually is. Second, people generally are prone to place confidence in highly fallible interview judgments, that is, we are not good judges of people, but we think we are, a phenomenon called the "illusion of validity." Finally, although the interview may not be highly valid for selection, it serves other personnel functions unrelated to employee selection, for example, selling candidates on the value of the job and of the organization as an attractive employer. Whatever the reasons for the interview's popularity, few companies are willing to do something as important as extending a job offer without first seeing a person "in the flesh." While there may be several desirable reasons to conduct employment interviews, their capacity to predict job success accurately is most certainly not one of them.

Factors Influencing Interview Outcomes

Through extensive research involving hundreds of studies, psychologists now know that many factors can influence the outcome of an interview. Schmitt (1976) reviewed the literature on interviews and found a dozen factors (apart from the applicant's qualifications) that affect an interviewer's decision. (The criterion in this research is whether or not applicants are offered jobs, not whether they turn out to be successful employees.) We will examine some of the major findings from Schmitt's study.

Negative-Positive Nature of the Information.   Is it something positive that applicants have said that results in being hired, or is it something negative they have said that causes their rejection? Research shows that negative information is more important than positive information. Many interviewers look for reasons (information) *not* to hire an applicant, and when they find it, the applicant is rejected. Suppose a high school graduate said she was on the honor roll for two years. This positive piece of information could be outweighed if she also said that she was expelled from school for two weeks for disciplinary reasons.

Temporal Placement of Information.   Does it make a difference *when* certain information is presented to the interviewer? If interviewers are most influenced by information given early in the interview, this is called a *primacy* effect. If they are most influenced by information given late in the interview, this is called a *recency* effect. The evidence for either is not clear-cut. Some interviewers are influenced by primacy effects, others by recency effects. But *what* gets said can interact with *when* it is said. In particular, a negative information-primacy effect results in unfavorable ratings. That is, if you start off the interview with something negative about yourself, you will more likely get rejected than if you "bury" it in the middle of the interview.

Interviewer Stereotypes.   Do interviewers have an "ideal" candidate in mind when they interview applicants? The answer seems to be yes. But not all interviewers have the same ideal candidate in mind, even if they are interviewing for the same job. The "ideal candidate" probably contributes to high *intra*interviewer reliability since interviewers are very consistent in evaluating applicants in comparison to their ideal applicant. Whether their conception of the ideal applicant is valid (would result in the best job performance) is another question.

Contrast Effects.   Is one applicant's evaluation influenced by preceding applicants? Will an applicant of average credentials appear worse if he or she was preceded by someone with superior credentials? Research indicates that contrast effects do occur. Applicants with average credentials appear better to the interviewer if they follow someone with poor credentials and they appear worse if they follow someone with superior credentials. A more controversial question is *how much* contrast effects influence interviewers. Some researchers think they exert substantial influence; others think their effects are minimal. It has been suggested that the interviewer's experience controls the impact of contrast effects; that is, more experienced interviewers are less influenced by contrast effects.

Similarity of Sex.   Do interviewers prefer applicants of their own sex? The answer seems to be no. But what does appear to matter is whether male and female applicants are applying for traditional male and female jobs. Interviewers seem more likely to hire females for traditional female jobs than for traditional male jobs, and vice versa. The *congruence* between the sex of the applicant and the traditional sex-orientation of the job is more influential than whether the applicant and interviewer are the same sex.

Some of the other factors reviewed by Schmitt include the experience of the interviewer, the effect of information about the job, and the degree of structure of the interview. Interviews are far more psychologically complex than many other predictors of job performance. With paper-and-pencil tests, what counts is whether the applicant got a passing score. The determinants of the passing score include such factors as knowledge of the test material, the applicant's motivation to pass, and the applicant's anxiety level. Interviews, on the other hand, are influenced by a far greater number of factors. Some factors are more important than others, but they all influence the final decision. Their complexity aside, interviews must still conform to the same psychometric and legal standards as any other predictor of job performance. I concur with Arvey (1979), who said that a lot more research needs to be done on the interview as a selection device in I/O psychology.

Work Samples and Situational Exercises

Work Samples

Work samples are a relatively new and exciting approach to personnel selection. Their rationale is simple. Rather than trying to identify predictors of job success that are usually quite different in nature from the criterion they are supposed to predict, why don't we create a "miniature criterion" and use that as the predictor? In other words, our goal is to take the content of a person's job, shrink it down to a manageable time period, and let applicants demonstrate their ability in performing this replica of the job. This rationale was presented in an article by Wernimont and Campbell (1968), and has served as the blueprint for later empirical studies.

An excellent example of a work sample was reported by Campion (1972).

Campion wanted to develop a predictor of job success for mechanics. Using job analytic techniques, he learned that the mechanic's job was defined by success in the use of tools, accuracy of work, and overall mechanical ability. He then designed tasks that would show an applicant's performance in these three areas. Through the cooperation of job incumbents, he designed a work sample that involved such typical tasks as installing pulleys and belts, taking apart and repairing a gearbox, and so on. The proper steps necessary to perform these tasks were identified and given numerical values according to their appropriateness (for example, 10 points for aligning a motor with a dial indicator, 1 point for aligning it by feeling the motor, 0 points for just looking at the motor). Using a concurrent, criterion-related validity design, each mechanic in the shop took the work sample. Their scores were correlated with the criterion of supervisor ratings of their job performance. The validity of the work sample was excellent: it correlated .66 with use of tools, .42 with accuracy of work, and .46 with overall mechanical ability. Campion showed that there was a substantial relationship between how well mechanics did on the work sample and how well they did on the job.

Subsequent research on work samples has been very positive and encouraging. Muchinsky (1975) and Schmidt, Greenthal, Berner, Hunter, and Seaton (1977) reported that work samples were the type of predictor device that readily conformed to EEOC standards for test fairness and lack of adverse impact. Mount, Muchinsky, and Hanser (1977) found that work samples gave highly desirable validity coefficients in both predictive and concurrent validity designs. Brugnoli, Campion, and Basen (1979) reported that work samples were relatively free of bias in the testing of black and white applicants. Finally, and perhaps most important, work samples repeatedly have been shown to be highly valid. Validity coefficients in the .40 to .60 range are not uncommon.

But work samples do have limitations. First, they work primarily in blue-collar jobs that involve either the mechanical trades (for example, mechanics, carpenters, electricians) or the manipulation of objects. They do not work very well when the job involves working with people as opposed to things. Second, work samples assess what a person *can* do; they don't assess potential. They seem best suited to hiring experienced workers rather than trainees. Finally, work samples are time-consuming and costly to administer. Because they are individual tests, they require a lot of supervision and monitoring. Few work samples are designed to be completed in less than one hour. If there are 100 applicants to fill five jobs, it may not be worth it to give a work sample to all applicants. Perhaps the applicant pool could be reduced with some other selection instrument (for example, a review of previous work history). Yet, despite their limitations, work samples are quite useful in personnel selection.

Robertson and Kandola (1982) report another advantage of work samples: applicants respond to them very favorably. Work samples engender a positive reaction from applicants because of their high face validity. Applicants perceive a direct link between how well they do on a work-sample and how well they would do on the job (that is, the concept of criterion-related validity). Indeed, Cascio and Phillips (1979) reported that one major U.S. city has instituted work sample selection tests for many city jobs, in part because of the high appeal of the method to applicants.

Situational Exercises

Situational exercises are roughly the white-collar counterpart of work samples; that is, they are used mainly to select people for managerial and professional jobs. Unlike work samples, which are designed to be replicas of the job, situational exercises only mirror *part* of the job.

Situational exercises involve a whole family of tests that in one way or another assess problem-solving ability. Two good examples of situational exercises are the In-Basket Test (Frederiksen, 1968) and the Leaderless Group Discussion (Bass, 1954). The In-Basket Test involves having applicants sort through an in-basket (of things to do). The contents of the in-basket are carefully designed letters, memos, brief reports, and the like that require the applicant's immediate attention and response. The applicant goes through the contents and takes the appropriate action to solve the problems presented, such as making a phone call, writing a letter, or calling a meeting. A number of observers score the applicant in terms of such factors as productivity (how much work got done) and problem-solving effectiveness (versatility in resolving problems). The In-Basket Test is predictive of job performance of managers and executives, a traditionally difficult group of employees to select. But a major problem with the test is that it takes up to three hours and, like a work sample, is an individual test. Time needed to administer the In-Basket Test is prohibitive if there are many applicants.

The Leaderless Group Discussion (LGD) involves having a group of applicants (normally, two to eight) engage in a job-related discussion in which no spokesperson or group leader has been named. Raters observe and then assess each applicant on such factors as "individual prominence," "group goal facilitation," and "sociability." Scores on these factors are then used as a hiring basis. The reliability of the LGD increases with the number of people in the group. The typical validity coefficient for the LGD is in the .15 to.35 range.

Although neither the In-Basket Test nor the LGD has the validity of a typical work sample, remember that the criterion of success for a manager is usually more difficult to define. If a mechanic installs a motor upside down, people know about it right away. If a manager picks the wrong people to do a job, it can be some time before the source of the problem is ascertained. Thus, the lower validities usually found in the selection of managerial personnel are as attributable to problems with the criterion and its proper articulation as anything else.

Biographical Information

If an Academy Award were given for the "most consistently valid predictor," biographical information would be the winner. Of all the predictors used to forecast job performance, biographical information (as a general class) has consistently shown the greatest validity. What is more remarkable about this finding is that it occurs across wide differences in people, jobs, and criteria. Though in some cases, certain tests, interviews, work samples, and so on outperform biographical information, it has the best overall track record as a general type of predictor.

Biographical information is frequently recorded on an application blank. The application blank, in turn, can be used as a selection device, on the basis of the information presented. However, application blanks need not be used for personnel selection purposes. Sometimes the information is used just to facilitate record keeping; for example, the applicant's home telephone number, and home address.

One issue in developing application blanks is to decide which questions to ask. The answer is not too difficult. If the application blank is being used only for record-keeping purposes, ask only questions that are useful or meaningful for the company, such as home address, and home telephone number. Questions like "How many older brothers do you have?" would have no practical value and should not be asked. However, if the application blank is being used for selection purposes, items that are predictive of job performance should be retained for making hiring decisions. While the maintenance of personnel record keeping is important, we will focus on the latter use of application blanks—as a predictor of job success.

Application blanks (or personnel data forms, as they are sometimes called) are quite varied. Some ask as few as 15 to 20 questions; others, which are used for research purposes, may have as many as 800 items. Some questions can be verified: "Did you graduate from high school?" "What did your father do for a living?" Other questions are self-reports that cannot be verified: "Did you enjoy high school?" "Did you get along well with your father?" Most traditional application blanks contain only the former types. But some companies ask both types of questions (called "biodata," a contraction for biographical data) for selection purposes.

In using biographical information for selection purposes, the following procedure is used. A criterion of interest is chosen, usually productivity, turnover, or absenteeism. The sample of current employees may be divided into two groups (high productivity and low productivity, high turnover and low turnover, or high absenteeism and low absenteeism). Management usually decides what constitutes "high" and "low" performance. The next step is to see if the high- and low-criterion groups differ in terms of the characteristics of the members. If the responses to some biographical questions occur far more often in one group, that question is predictive of job performance. For instance, suppose 80% of the high-productivity group graduated from high school and only 30% of the low-productivity group did. The item "Did you graduate from high school?" would be predictive of productivity and could be used to hire employees. Items that do not differentiate criterion groups would not be used for selection purposes.

The literature is filled with examples of useful applications of biographical information. Cascio (1976) reported validity coefficients of .77 and .79 for predicting the turnover of white and black workers, respectively. While the magnitude of these validity coefficients is extremely impressive, what is also desirable is that the application-blank method was fair to members of both racial groups. Childs and Klimoski (1986) demonstrated that selected early life experiences not only predicted later success in a job but also were predictive of feelings of personal and career accomplishments throughout a lifetime. Other researchers have reported the success of application blanks in predicting salary earnings, absenteeism, and productivity. Lee and Booth (1974) showed that the proper use of an application blank resulted in a cost savings of $250,000 over a 25-month period. Also, the method is not complicated or too costly to develop. It takes time to identify the valid items (which is an ongoing process), but after that the method is quite efficient.

Four other issues are relevant to this type of predictor. One deals with how truthful people are. What little information we have on this topic is that most people do not lie. Cascio (1975) reported a correlation of .94 between self-reported information on an application blank and subsequently verified answers to the same questions. He took this as evidence of the truthfulness of such answers. Other researchers have reported less positive-results. People seem to be more honest when they think their answers will be verified.

A second issue is the stability of the validity coefficients over time. Most studies show varying degrees of validity decay. One application blank used to predict turnover had an initial validity of .74. Two years later, the validity fell to .61; three years later, it was .38; and five years later, it was .07. When the scoring key was revised, only three of the original fifteen valid items were retained, so application blanks should be revalidated on a systematic, short-term basis. Changes in applicant pools, job-market conditions, and the jobs themselves cause the validity coefficients to be unstable. Continually reassessing items is cumbersome, but given the spectacular validity coefficients reported as well as the relative freedom from discrimination charges, the gains seem to far outweigh the problems.

A third issue deals with the way biographical items are identified as being valid. The method is purely empirical; that is, responses to questions are correlated with a criterion of job success. The items that are predictive are retained for selection purposes. There is little in the way of theory or rationale that guides the selection of items; that being so, some statistically valid biographical items may appear to have no logical connection to job success. This has prompted some authors (for example, Pace & Schoenfeldt, 1977) to question the legal defensibility of a selection method that has little or no apparent relevance to job performance. They advocate selecting biographical items that are logically or conceptually related as well as empirically related to the criterion. One study (Mitchell & Klimoski, 1982) examined the comparative validity of a purely empirically derived biographical inventory versus one that had been constructed rationally. The results indicated the empirical approach to item selection accounted for 8.2% more criterion variance than did the rational selection method. The implication of this finding does not bode well for I/O psychologists. One option is to accept lowered predictive accuracy in a selection method that does have perceived relevance to the job in question. The other option is to have greater predictive accuracy but also accept a method that may lack relevance. Asking a question on a biographical selection test like "Did you operate a paper route as a child?" may lead to enhanced prediction of the criterion but at the expense of having candidates question the appropriateness of such an item on the test (see Field Note 2).

A fourth issue serves to temper our enthusiasm for this method. Typically, it takes a very large sample size to identify biographical items that will be stable and valid predictors of job success. From a methodological standpoint, researchers should *cross-validate* their findings with biographical data. (Cross-validation is an analytic procedure used to evaluate the stability of valid predictors and will be described in greater detail in Chapter 5.) A further consideration is that biographical-items data are not always generalizable across jobs or applicants; that is, valid items may be unique to a given sample or job. The implication of these issues is that it takes a lot of research time and effort to identify valid biographical items. The results are frequently worth the time invested in the method, but it is by no means a "quick-and-easy" solution to personnel selection.

As a final note, one might ask *why* biographical information is so valid. There is little in the way of theory to suggest an answer. I propose two answers. A detailed biographical form samples a large domain of activities and interests in a person's life. There is frequently a fair degree of consistency in the lives of people; individuals who played with mechanical toys as children often retain interest in manipulating mechanical objects as adults. The oft-used axiom in I/O psychology that "the best predictor of future behavior is past behavior of a similar kind" is perhaps the core of the validity of biographical information. Owens and Schoenfeldt (1979) have documented the validity of biographical information for a host of criterion variables ranging from selecting a major in college to performance on the job.

A second explanation is psychometric in nature. Biographical information is very reliable. Since validity is limited by reliability, the high reliability of biographical information does not put any "ceiling" on its potential validity.

Field Note 2

Biographical items sometimes lack content validity to the job in question even though they manifest empirical criterion-related validity. The potential irrelevance of biographical questions is always a concern in personnel selection. Here is a case in point.

A city had developed a biographical inventory that was to be used along with some psychological tests to evaluate police officers for promotion to police detectives. All the questions included on the biographical inventory were predictive of job performance as a detective, as determined by a criterion-related validity study. One of the questions on the inventory was this one: "Did you have sexual intercourse for the first time before the age of 16?" Some police officers who took this promotional exam and who failed it sued the city for asking such a question in an em-

ployment test. The officers said the question had absolutely no relevance to the conduct of a detective's job, and furthermore it was an invasion of their privacy. They had been denied a detective's job because of a totally inappropriate question and therefore they wanted the entire test results thrown out.

The case was heard at the district court. The judge ruled in favor of the officers, saying that question was totally lacking in content validity and job relevance and therefore the officers should be reconsidered for promotion to detective. The city appealed the verdict to the state supreme court. The judge there reversed the lower court ruling and allowed the test results to stand, meaning the officers would not get promoted. The state supreme court judge based his decision on the grounds that the answer to that question did correlate with job performance as a detective. No matter how irrelevant a test question might seem, if scores on that question are predictive of future job performance, the soundness of its conclusion in the test is unassailable.

This case reveals how different judges place varying degrees of importance on content versus criterion-related validity in assessing the suitability of a test. It also illustrates how items may be predictive of job success even though they have no apparent relevance to the job.

Peer Assessment

Rather than having supervisors evaluate employees, an alternative is to have employees evaluate one another. This is the basis of *peer assessment* (Kane & Lawler, 1978). Though the peer-assessment technique has some peculiar limitations, the method has yielded encouraging results when applicable.

Peer assessments are best used when the applicants for a job have known one another for some time. The method is not employed for initial entry into an organization but for selection to advanced positions. It has been used in the military to predict success as an officer and in industry to predict success after training. Applicants answer such questions as "Which of you do you think will make the best officer?" and "Who do you think will score the highest on the final exam in this course?" Responses are tabulated and then correlated with a criterion of performance. Hollander (1965) reported that peer ratings made in the third week of officer training correlated .40 with ratings of success as an officer three years later. Mayfield (1972) found that peer assessments made by life insurance salesmen in a training program correlated .29 with tenure and .30 with production. These ratings, made 18 days after the start of the training program, were predictive of those two criteria one year later.

By far the biggest limitation of peer assessments is that they cannot be used prior to hiring. Despite this practical limitation, it is apparent that candidates themselves, after a brief exposure to one another have a fairly accurate sense of each other's ability. It is likely that industry will continue to use peer assessments on a limited basis because of their validity and ease of administration.

Letters of Recommendation

One of the most commonly used and least valid of all predictors is the letter of recommendation. Letters of recommendation and reference checks are as widespread in personnel selection as the interview and the application blank. Unfortunately, they usually lack the same validity. Letters of recommendation are usually written in behalf of an applicant by a current employer, professional associate, or personal friend. The respondent rates the applicant on such dimensions as leadership ability and written and oral communication skills. The responses are then used as a basis for hiring. When validating the letter of recommendation as a predictor, the two most frequently used criteria are tenure and supervisory ratings.

One review of letters of recommendation (Muchinsky, 1979) reported an *average* validity of .13. Some people even make recommendations that have an *inverse* relationship with the criterion; that is, if the applicant is recommended for hire, the company would do best to reject him or her! One of the biggest problems with letters of recommendation is their restricted range. As you might expect, almost all letters of recommendation are positive. Most often, the applicants themselves choose who will write the letters, so it isn't surprising that they pick people who will make them look good. Because of this restriction (that is, that almost all applicants are described positively), the lack of predictive ability of the letter of recommendation is not unexpected.

While a few studies using specially constructed evaluation forms have reported moderate validity coefficients, the typical validity coefficient is close to zero. Because of their limited validity, letters of recommendation should not be taken too seriously in making personnel selection decisions. The only major exception to this statement would be the following condition: when applicants are described in positive terms, you will not know if they will be successful on the job. However, on those rare occasions when the applicant is described in negative terms (even if only mildly), such an assessment is usually indicative of future problems on the job. Those types of letters should be taken seriously. On par though, the percentage of letters of recommendation that contain nonsupportive information about an applicant is very small (see Field Note 3.)

More recent research on the value of letters of recommendation has added to our understanding of the method. Knouse (1983) discovered that letter writers who buttress their overall evaluation of a candidate with information specific to the evaluation are perceived as more credible information sources. Ceci and Peters (1984) examined the effect on letter writers of the accessibility of their letters to applicants, that is, of the letters' confidentiality. When an applicant indicates to a letter writer that the letter will *not* be confidential (that is, he or she will have access to it), the letter writer will tend to compose a very bland letter devoid of any negative evaluations. On the other hand, confidential letters tend to elicit a greater proportion of negative evaluations. This finding has several implications. One is that letters of recommendation that are not confidential are probably worthless. Second, recipients of these letters will probably come to regard them as containing very little accurate information, and thus will tend to ignore them in evaluating the candidate.

Why did Ceci and Peters obtain these findings? Two reasons seem likely. One is that people do not like to be confronted by individuals over negative evaluations made about them. It is simply easier from a social standpoint to avoid confrontation by omitting any negative comments. Second, the applicant could potentially sue the letter writer for defamation of character and make the writer prove in court that what he or she said was in fact correct. This is especially possible if the writer's letter prevented the applicant from getting a job. These recent developments about letters of recommendation cast even more doubt on the value of an already questionable selection method.

I was the director of a graduate program to which about 100 students per year seek admission. One of the requirements for admission is for the applicant to submit letters of recommendation in his or her behalf. Over the years I have received several memorable letters of recommendation, but on one occasion I received a letter (actually, two) that beautifully illustrates why such letters have little predictive value. This letter came from the president of a foreign university where the student was enrolled. It made the student sound incredibly strong academically: the class valedictorian, the only recipient of the native king's fellowship program, the only student who received a special citation from the university, and so forth. Needless to say, I was most impressed by this letter.

About two weeks later I got another application for admission from a second student from that same university. Accompanying this application was another letter supposedly written by the university president. This letter was identical in content to the first. The only difference was the name of the student typed at the top of the letter. Thus, both students had been the class valedictorian, both were the only recipient of the fellowship, and so on.

I then called a different academic department and discovered *it, too,* had received the identical letter on yet a third student from that university who was applying for graduate work in that department. What we had was literally a form letter in which every student in the university was being described, word for word, as the best. The university apparently provided this "service" to its students seeking admission to graduate schools in the United States. Needless to say, such attempts at deception do nothing to portray fairly a candidate's strengths and weaknesses—and most certainly do not enhance the validity of the letter of recommendation as a personnel selection method.

New and Controversial Methods

The final category is reserved for new and controversial methods of assessing job applicants. Four such methods will be presented.

Drug Testing. Drug testing is the popular term for the detection of substance abuse, which refers to the use of illegal drugs and the improper and illegal use of prescription and over-the-counter medications, alcohol, and other chemical compounds. Substance abuse is a major global problem with far-reaching societal, moral, and economic consequences. The role that I/O psychology plays in this vast and complex picture is the detection of substance abuse in the workplace. Employees who engage in substance abuse jeopardize not only their own welfare but also potentially the welfare of fellow employees and other individuals. I/O psychologists are involved in screening out substance abusers among both job applicants and current employees.

Unlike other forms of assessment utilized by I/O psychologists that involve estimates of cognitive or motor abilities, drug testing embraces chemical assessments. The method of assessment is based upon a urine sample. The rationale of the assessment is that the presence of drugs will be revealed in a person's urine. Therefore, a sample of urine is treated with chemicals that will reveal the presence of drugs if they have been ingested by the person. There are two basic types of assessments. A *screening* test assures the potential presence of a wide variety of chemicals. A *confirmation* test on the same sample identifies the presence of chemicals suggested by the initial screening test. I/O psychologists would not be directly involved with these tests, because they are performed in chemical laboratories by individuals with special technical training. The profession of I/O psychology does become involved in drug testing because it assesses suitability for employment, with concomitant concern about the reliability, validity, legality, and cost of these tests.

Although the issues are very complex, I will briefly describe some concerns. The reliability of the chemical tests is much higher than the reliability of traditional paper-and-pencil psychological assessments. However, the reliability is not perfect, which means that different conclusions can be drawn about substance abuse as a function of the laboratory conducting the testing. Questions of validity are much more problematic. The accurate detection of drug usage varies as a function of the type of drug involved, because some drugs remain in our systems for days and others remain for weeks. Thus, the timing of the urine sample is critical. It is also possible that diet can falsely contribute to the results of a drug test. For example, eating poppy-seed cake may trigger a confirmatory response to heroin usage because heroin is derived from poppy seeds. The legality of drug testing is also highly controversial. Critics of drug testing contend it violates the U.S. Constitution with regard to unreasonable search and seizure, self-incrimination, and the right to privacy. It is also a matter of debate as to which jobs should be subject to drug testing. Some people argue for routine drug testing; others say drug testing should be limited to jobs that potentially impact the lives of others (for example, transportation). Yet another issue involves the criteria for intoxication and performance impairment. What dosage of a drug constitutes a level that would impair job performance? Finally, there is the matter of cost. Screening tests cost about $10 per specimen, but confirmatory tests can cost up to $100 per specimen. These costs will eventually have to get passed on to consumers as part of the price they pay for having their goods and services rendered by a drug-free work force.

As can be seen, drug testing is an exceedingly complex and controversial issue. While the analysis of urine is beyond the purview of I/O psychology, making decisions about an applicant's suitability for employment is not. I/O psychology is finding itself drawn into a complicated web of issues that affects all of society. Our profession may be asked to provide solutions to problems we couldn't even have imagined 20 years ago.

Polygraphy or Lie Detection.   A polygraph is an instrument that measures aspects of the autonomic system: physiological reactions of the body such as heart rate and perspiration. In theory these autonomic responses will "give you away" when you are telling a lie. The polygraph is attached to the body with electronic sensors for detecting the physiological reactions. Polygraphs are used more to evaluate people charged with criminal activity in a post hoc fashion (for example, after a robbery within a company has occurred) than to select people into a job, although it has been used to some degree in the latter capacity.

Is a polygraph foolproof? No. People can appear to be innocent of any wrong-doing according to the polygraph but in fact be guilty of misconduct. Is a polygraph at all valid? Yes. Lykken (1974) estimated that polygraphs are 14 to 21% better than chance at detecting lies. However, Ginton, Daie, Elaad, and Ben-Shakhar (1982) found that a polygraph was no more accurate in identifying thieves than were behavioral observations (for example, eyewitnesses). Perhaps more disturbing from a personnel standpoint, Waid and Orne (1980) found that more innocent people will be falsely judged guilty than will guilty people be falsely judged innocent with a polygraph. In short, the method produces both types of errors, with one being more critical to the individual and the other more critical to the company. In 1988 President Reagan signed into law a bill banning the widespread use of polygraphs for preemployment screening. Some exceptions were made, permitting the use of polygraphy tests for cases involving theft, embezzlement, or sabotage. However, the new law requires the employer to request the employee submit to a polygraph examination, and no reprisals can follow an employee's refusal to take a polygraph test. Given these limitations, I doubt if polygraphy will ever be used as a major method of personnel selection.

Graphology. Graphology or handwriting analysis is very popular in Europe as a selection method (Levy, 1979). Here is how it works. A person trained in handwriting analysis (called a *graphologist*) examines a sample of a candidate's handwriting. Based on such factors as the specific formation of letters, the slant and size of the writing, and how hard the person presses the pen or pencil on the paper, the graphologist makes an assessment of the candidate's personality. This personality assessment is then correlated with criteria of job success.

Rafaeli and Klimoski (1983) had twenty graphologists analyze handwriting and correlated their assessments with three types of criteria: supervisory ratings, self-ratings, and sales production. While the authors found some evidence of interrater agreement (meaning the graphologists tended to base their assessments on the same facets of handwriting), the handwriting assessments did not correlate with any criteria. Ben-Shakhar and associates (1986) reported graphologists did not perform significantly better than chance in predicting the job performance of bank employees. In summary, graphology is a method of personnel selection occasionally used in practice, but it has yet to be empirically supported by scientific research.

Genetic Screening. Research in the area of genetics indicates that individuals with various genetic makeups are highly susceptible to toxic effects in the work environment. These types of people are much more likely than the average person to develop occupational diseases. Genetic screening in the workplace involves the identification of such hypersusceptible individuals for the purposes of minimizing their exposure to these toxic conditions. According to Olian (1984), the value of genetic screening for controlling the frequency of occupational diseases depends on the existence of valid tests capable of detecting genetic predispositions that increase the individual's susceptibility to disease, once toxic exposure occurs. "Such individuals could be screened out of chemically dangerous jobs and placed only in positions where environmental toxins do not present special hazards" (p. 424). For example, if a factory uses a certain chemical (such as naphthalene) as part of its manufacturing process, and a job applicant was identified as having a genetic structure that when exposed to this chemical greatly increased the likelihood of disease, the applicant would most likely not be hired for the job. The applicant would have to seek employment elsewhere, or would have to be assigned to a job where the degree of exposure was greatly reduced.

Because there is very little research on this subject, I/O psychologists are just beginning to understand how complex the problem is, let alone the answers. One aspect of the problem is the long latency period of diseases caused by the interaction between genetic material and toxic substances found in the environment. Latency periods of 20 years are common for some diseases, like cancer. Additionally, current federal law prohibits personnel decisions from producing adverse impacts on protected group members. Yet these genetic conditions have been found to fall heavily along gender and racial lines. For example, blacks are over 150 times more likely than whites to develop a form of anemia if they possess a certain genetic condition. Certain chemicals are likely to cause fetal damage, yet only females can be pregnant. Thus, these genetic screens would have a very strong adverse impact, resulting (in these two examples) of a much higher percentage of blacks (than whites) and females (than males) being rejected for employment in such jobs. It is not yet clear from a legal standpoint how much validational evidence would have to be provided to substantiate such decisions.

Most certainly, I/O psychologists are not chemists or geneticists, nor do we pretend to have such expertise. Yet we are being called upon to render opinions about suitability for employment, which is our area of expertise, and which is now taking us into new arenas of knowledge. While I/O psychologists will continue to rely heavily on paper-and-pencil means of psychological assessment, we are on the threshold of some frontiers of assessment for which we have no legacy.

Overview and Evaluation of Predictors

Personnel selection methods can be evaluated by many standards. I have identified four major standards that I feel are useful in organizing all the information we have gathered about predictors.

The first is *validity,* and as defined in this book, it refers it to the capacity of the predictor to forecast criterion performance accurately. Many authorities would argue that validity is the predominant evaluative standard in judging selection methods; however, the relevance of the other three standards is also substantial.

The second standard is *fairness,* and refers to the capacity of the predictor to render unbiased predictions of job success across applicants in various subgroups of sex, race, age, and so on. We will discuss the issue of fairness in greater detail in Chapter 5.

Applicability, the third standard, refers to whether the selection method can be applied across the full range of job and applicant types. Some predictors have wide applicability in that they appear well suited for a diverse range of people and jobs. Other methods have peculiar limitations that affect their applicability.

The final standard refers to the *cost* of implementing the method. The various personnel selection methods differ markedly in their cost, which has a direct bearing on their overall value.

Table 4–1 presents a summary of the nine personnel selection methods appraised on each of the four evaluative standards. I have partitioned each standard into three levels, which are labeled low, moderate, and high. This classification scheme is admittedly oversimplified, and in some cases the evaluation of a selection method did not readily lend itself to a uniform rating. Nevertheless, this method should be useful in providing a broadbrush view of all the personnel selection methods.

Average validities in the .00-to-.20, .21-to-.40, and over-.40 ranges were labeled low, moderate, and high, respectively. Selection methods having great, some, and few problems of fairness were labeled low, moderate, and high, respectively. The applicability standard, the most difficult one to appraise on a single dimension, was classified according to the ease of using the method in terms of feasibility and generalizability across jobs. Finally direct-cost estimates were made for each selection method. Methods estimated as costing less than $20 per applicant were labeled low; $20 to $50, moderate; and over $50, high. The ideal personnel selection method would be high in validity, fairness, and applicability, and low in cost. Inspection of Table 4–1 reveals that no method has an ideal profile. The nine methods produce a series of trade-offs among validity, fairness, applicability, and cost. This shouldn't be surprising, for if there were one uniformly ideal personnel selection method, there probably would be little need to consider eight others.

In terms of validity, our best methods are work samples, biographical information, and peer assessments. However, each of these methods is limited by some problems with fairness, applicability, or cost. Ironically, two of our worst selection methods in terms of validity, interviews and letters of recommendation, are among

TABLE 4–1   *Assessment of Nine Personnel Selection Methods Along Four Evaluative Standards*

Selection Method	Evaluative Standards			
	Validity	Fairness	Applicability	Cost
Intelligence tests	Moderate	Moderate	High	Low
Aptitude and ability tests	Moderate	High	Moderate	Low
Personality and interest tests	Moderate	High	Low	Moderate
Interviews	Low	Moderate	High	Moderate
Work samples	High	High	Low	High
Situational exercises	Moderate	(Unknown)	Low	Moderate
Biographical information	High	Moderate	High	Low
Peer assessments	High	Moderate	Low	Low
Letters of recommendation	Low	(Unknown)	High	Low

the most frequently used. However, both of these methods are characterized by high applicability and low or moderate cost, which no doubt accounts for their popularity.

While the issue of fairness has generated a great deal of controversy, no method is classified in Table 4–1 as having low fairness. Insufficient information is available on two of the methods (situational exercises and letters of recommendation) to render an evaluation of their fairness, but it seems unlikely they would be judged as grossly unfair. While several of the methods have exhibited some problems of fairness (thus warranting caution in their use), the problems are not so severe as to reject the method as a means of selecting personnel.

The applicability dimension was the most difficult to assess, and is also the one whose evaluation is most subject to qualification. For example, work samples are characterized by low applicability, for they are highly limited to certain types of jobs (that is, jobs involving the mechanical manipulation of objects). However, this limitation appears to be more than offset by the method's high validity and fairness. Simply put, the problem with this method is its feasibility for only a selected range of jobs. Such a limitation seems far more palatable than the problems of low applicability experienced with peer assessments, for example. Peer assessments are limited by their exclusive use as a selection device for entry into secondary or advanced positions, positions that not all organizations have. Alternatively, other methods have high applicability (such as the interview), and qualify as an almost universal means of selection.

The cost dimension is perhaps the most arbitrary. There may be indirect or hidden costs associated with selection methods that were not included in their evaluation but perhaps could have been. The break points in the classification scheme are also highly subjective. For example, I consider a $40 per applicant cost to be moderate; others might say it is low or high. These issues notwithstanding, one can see a full range of cost estimates in Table 4–1. The most expensive selection method (work samples) is also the only one that is classified high in both validity and fairness. Some methods do not cost much (for example, letters of recommendation), but they do not appear to be worth much either.

Which personnel selection method is, all things considered, the "best"? On the basis of my evaluation scheme, biographical information is the winner. It has high validity, high applicability, and low cost, and is "marred" by having only *moderate* fairness. The validity of biographical information is legion. Ghiselli (1966) found it to be the most valid predictor of job success. It has high applicability in that there are no reported cases of jobs for which biographical data do not predict success (at least to some degree). The cost of collecting biographical information is low, typically involving only a paper-and-pencil format. However, there are some problems with biographical information in terms of the content of the information requested of applicants. Exclusion of the "sensitive" questions (to reduce chances of unfair discrimination) may also produce a decrement in validity.

Given the apparent superiority of biographical information as a personnel selection method, one may ask why we use other methods. While there are probably several appropriate answers to such a question, a major one is psychometric in nature. Even our best single selection methods (that is, those having a validity of .50) leave 75% of the criterion variance unaccounted for. By using a combination of methods, we hope to make incremental gains in our understanding of a candidate's predicted job success. Thus, the candidate's interview performance may explain a portion of the criterion variance that biographical information does not. The real issue in personnel selection is knowing which of the many possible methods to include in an assessment battery.

Summary

In this chapter, we have examined six major types of predictors used in personnel selection: psychological tests (intelligence, aptitude, ability, personality, and interest), interviews, work samples and situational exercises, biographical information, peer assessments, and letters of recommendation. These predictors have been validated against a number of different criteria for a variety of occupational groups. Some predictors have been used more extensively than others. Furthermore, certain predictors have historically shown more validity than others. Figure 4–6 shows the results of Ghiselli's (1966) study. He tablulated the proportion of validity coefficients of .50 or higher using job proficiency as the criterion. Not all of the predictors in this chapter were included in his review. But note that the most consistently good predictors are biographical information and work samples. Over half (55%) of all studies using

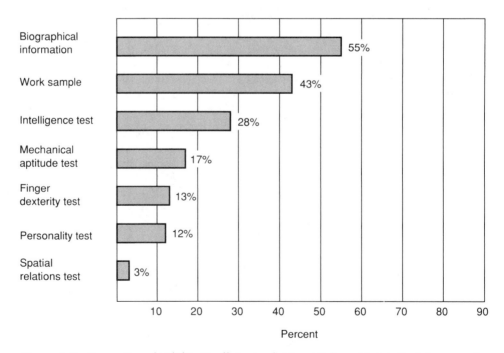

Figure 4–6 Proportion of Validity Coefficients of .50 or Higher with Job Proficiency as the Criterion

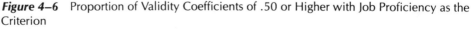

SOURCE: E. E. Ghiselli, *The Validity of Occupational Aptitude Tests* (New York: John Wiley & Sons, 1966).

biographical information report validity coefficients over .50. Some predictors rarely demonstrate this degree of validity (only 3% of spatial ability tests do so). However, as the data indicate, all selection methods have reached that level of predictability in various proportions.

In Chapter 3, we listed the attributes of good criteria. A similar list can be derived for predictors.

1. Reliable

2. Valid

3. Bias-free

4. Consistent from one sample to another

5. Inexpensive

6. Not time consuming

The ideal predictor would be an accurate forecaster of the criterion, equally applicable across different groups of people, and not too lengthy or costly to administer. But predictors rarely meet all these standards in practice.

Table 4–2 shows an integration of the content of Chapters 3 and 4. Across the top are the criteria of interest to I/O psychologists as discussed in Chapter 3. Down the column are the predictors that have been used to predict the criteria. Nine criteria and 11 predictors are listed. While other criterion and predictor variables occasionally have been used, the validation of personnel selection methods normally involves establishing these 99 (9 × 11) predictor-criterion relationships. The entries L, M, and S in the table reflect whether a large (L), moderate (M), or small (S) amount of research has been devoted to the particular predictor-criterion relationship. Certain relationships have been studied far more extensively than others; others may never have been established at all. The criterion of ratings has been used extensively in the psychological literature, as has the predictor of biographical information. Much less is known about the predictor of situational exercises with respect to the criterion of accidents. Finally, to the best of my knowledge, some predictor-criterion relationships have never been examined, such as using peer assessments to predict the criterion of absence. Table 4–2 provides an overview of the principal participants in the personnel selection process. The mechanics of that process and related issues are discussed in Chapter 5.

MAJOR CHAPTER OBJECTIVES IN REVIEW

After having read this chapter, you should know:

1. Major types of reliability and what they measure.

2. Major representations of validity and what they measure.

3. Major types of psychological tests categorized by administration and content.

TABLE 4–2 *Job Performance Criteria and Predictors Used in Personnel Selection and the Frequency of Their Investigation*

Predictors	Job Performance Criteria								
	Production	Absence	Turnover	Accidents	Salary	Promotions	Theft	Sales	Ratings
Intelligence tests	L	S	M	S	S	M	S	S	L
Aptitude tests	L	M	S	S	S	S	S	S	L
Ability tests	L	M	M	M	S	S	S	S	M
Interest inventories	S	S	M	S	S	M	S	S	M
Personality inventories	M	M	S	M	M	M	M	L	M
Interviews	S	S	M	S	M	M	S	M	L
Work samples	M	S	S	S	S	S	S	S	M
Situational exercises	S	S	S	S	L	L	S	M	L
Biographical information	M	L	L	L	M	M	M	M	L
Peer assessments	S	S	L	S	M	L	S	M	L
Letters of recommendation	S	S	M	S	S	S	S	S	M

Note: L, M, and S indicate a large, moderate, or small amount of research directed toward a predictor-criterion relationship.

4. Legal influence on psychological assessment.

5. Non-test predictors as interviews, work samples, biographical information, peer assessment, and letters of recommendation.

6. Role of psychological testing in making assessments of people, including ethical issues and predictive accuracy.

CASE STUDY—How Do We Hire Police Officers?

Bay Ridge, a city with a population of about 125,000 people, experienced remarkable growth over a short period of time for two major reasons. First, several large industries had been attracted to the area, and with more jobs, there were more people. Second, due to a rezoning plan, several small townships were incorporated into Bay Ridge, and this caused a sudden burgeoning in the city's official population.

As a consequence of this growth, the city needed to expand its police force. For many years, the city had only a relatively small force and used only a brief interview to select the officers. Recently, however, there had been several complaints against the city's selection interview. Due to the complaints and the need to hire many more officers, the city council decided to abandon the old method of hiring. The city commissioned a job analysis for police officers and determined that three major factors contributed to success on the job. The next step was to develop selection measures to assess each of the three factors. The city council called a meeting with the city personnel director to get a progress report on the selection measures being proposed. Four city council members and Ron Davenport, the city personnel director, attended.

Davenport: I'm pleased to report to you that we have made substantial progress in our study. The job analysis revealed that the following factors determine success on the police force: (1) physical agility, (2) sensitivity to community relations, and (3) practical judgment. We are fairly pleased with the tests developed to assess two of the factors, although one of them is causing us some problems.

Councilmember DeRosa: Would you kindly elaborate on what these factors mean?

Davenport: Certainly. Physical agility is important in being able to apprehend and possibly disarm a suspect. It is also important in being able to carry a wounded officer out of the line of hostile fire. Sensitivity to community relations involves knowledge of racial and ethnic problems in the city, plus an ability to work with the community in preventing crime. Practical judgment reflects knowing when it is advisable to pursue a criminal suspect and what methods of action to use in uncertain situations.

Councilmember Flory: How do you propose to measure physical agility?

Davenport: It looks like we'll go with some physical standard—being able to carry a 150-pound dummy 25 yards, or something similar. We might also use some height and weight requirements. We could have some problems with sex differences in that females are not as strong as males, but I think we can work it out.

Councilmember Reddinger: Are all of these tests going to be performance tests?

Davenport: No, that's the only one so far. For the community relations factor, we're going to use a group interview. We'll ask the candidates how they would go about dealing with some hypothetical but realistic problem, like handling a domestic argument. The interviewers will grade their answers and give them a total score.

Councilmember Hamilton: What will be a passing score in this interview?

Davenport: We haven't determined that yet. We're still trying to determine if this is the best way to measure the factor.

Councilmember Flory: How do you plan to measure practical judgment?

Davenport: That's the problem case. We really haven't figured out a good test of that yet.

Councilmember DeRosa: How about a test of general intelligence?

Davenport: It appears that practical judgment is related to intelligence, but it's not the same thing. A person can be very intelligent in terms of verbal and numerical ability but not possess a great deal of practical judgment.

Councilmember Reddinger: Hasn't some psychologist developed a test of practical judgment?

Davenport: Not that we know of. You also have to remember that the type of judgment a police officer has to demonstrate is not the same thing as the type of judgment, say, a banker has to show. I guess I'm saying there appear to be different kinds of practical judgment.

Councilmember Hamilton: Could you use some personality inventory to measure it?

Davenport: I don't think so. I doubt that practical judgment is a personality trait. At least I'm not aware of any direct measures of it.

Councilmember Flory: How about using the interview again? A police officer has to demonstrate practical judgment in handling community relations. Can't you just expand the interview a bit?

Davenport: That's a possibility we're considering. Another possibility is to put candidates in a test situation where they have to demonstrate their practical judgment. It could be a pretty expensive method, all things considered, but it may be the best way to go.

Councilmember DeRosa: I have a feeling, Mr. Davenport, that your success in measuring practical judgment will determine just how many good officers we get on the force.

Questions

1. The city would have to validate whatever predictors it developed to select police officers. What method or methods of validation do you think it would use?

2. Do you think that biographical information might be useful in predicting success as a police officer? If so, what types of items might be useful?

3. Describe a work sample or situational exercise that might measure practical judgment.

4. What would be a problem in using peer assessments to select police officers?

5. Imagine the personnel department asked you to assist in developing or selecting predictors of police officer performance. What advice would you give?

5

Personnel Decisions

Personnel decisions are decisions that affect people's work lives. They include hiring, promotions, training, placement, and termination of employment. These decisions can be evaluated in terms of *institutional* or *individual* criteria. Institutional criteria refer to the extent to which the decision ultimately benefits the company or institution as indexed by greater productivity and reduced costs. Individual criteria refer to the extent to which the decision ultimately benefits the individual, as indexed by personal satisfaction and feelings of accomplishment.

Institutional decisions aim to enhance the attainment of institutional goals and are usually made on the basis of some objective standards. These objective standards reflect a person's predicted probability of success based on test scores, performance in an interview, or some other measure. Most companies do not offer a job unless there is a high probability that the person would succeed.

Individual decisions are designed to enhance the attainment of individual goals and usually are made on the basis of both subjective and objective standards. Subjective standards involve individual preferences, likes, and tastes. A person might seek a career as a psychologist because he or she likes (or believes he or she would like) the work psychologists perform. An objective standard used to aid in vocational choices is a vocational interest inventory, such as the Strong-Campbell Interest Inventory discussed in the previous chapter. By taking the interest inventory, people can see if their vocational interests and values are similar to those of people already in a given profession. A vocational counselor might advise a person to pursue a career that is a good match between what he or she would like to do and what he or she seems to be most suited for on the basis of aptitudes and abilities.

In almost all cases, there are limitations on both institutions and individuals with regard to personnel decisions; that is, a company cannot hire all applicants in order to discover which ones will succeed on the job. Likewise, individuals cannot try out 10 or 20 careers. Choices or decisions have to be made; some people are hired (or trained or promoted), and others are rejected. Likewise, some career is eventually selected, and others are ruled out. No one likes to make mistakes. Companies prefer to have the "right people," and people prefer to choose the "right careers." This chapter examines the personnel decision process and explores the issues inherent in making good decisions.

Fortunately, there is a fair degree of overlap between personnel decisions that are "good" for the institution and those that are "good" for the individual. Decisions that benefit or hurt the company usually benefit or hurt the individual. A good match between a person's talents and a company's needs enhances the attainment of both individual and institutional goals.

Sometimes, however, legitimate conflict between individual and institutional goals does occur. A company may wish to promote an employee based on his or her abilities. It would benefit the company to have this person in that job. The employee, on the other hand, may not want the added responsibilities and pressures of the new job (especially if it entails a move to another city). So it would benefit the individual, all things considered, not to take the position. Here is a case of conflicting goals. Another more frequent case involves having too many qualified applicants competing for a few job openings. The company is in a "sweet" position; it can choose whomever it wants, knowing that its needs will be met. The rejected applicants, however, would not have their needs met. In such a case, the company must have legitimate and professionally sound reasons for hiring the people it does. The selection process must be valid and fair. This chapter, therefore, examines the process of making personnel decisions and the factors that help assess the degree of fit between the person and the job.

Recruitment

The personnel function of *recruitment* refers to the process of attracting people to apply for a job. You can select from only those people who apply. If few people apply for a job, the odds of finding a strong candidate are less than if you have many applicants to choose from.

There is more to recruiting than you might think. Hawk (1967) described the "recruiting yield pyramid" procedure for hiring candidates. A diagram of that pyramid is shown in Figure 5–1. Let us say that the goal is to hire 5 managers. The company has learned from past experience that for every 2 managers who are offered jobs, only 1 will accept. Therefore, the company will need to make 10 offers. Furthermore, the company has learned that to find 10 managers who are good enough to receive an offer, it has to interview 40 candidates; that is, only 1 manager out of 4 is usually judged acceptable. However, to get 40 managers to travel to the company for an interview, the company has to invite 60 people; that is, only 2 out of 3 candidates typically are interested enough in the job to agree to be interviewed. Finally, in order to find 60 potentially interested managers, the company needs to get four times as many contacts or leads. Some people will not want to change jobs, others will not want to move, and still others will simply be unsuitable for further consideration. Therefore, the company has to make initial contact with about 240 managerial candidates. Note the mushrooming effect in trying to recruit applicants. Stated in reverse order, you contact 240 people to find 60 who are interested, to find

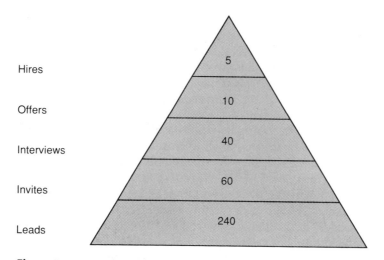

Figure 5–1   Recruiting Yield Pyramid

40 who agree to be interviewed, to find 10 who are acceptable, to get the 5 people who will accept the offer.

Obviously these yield ratios (that is, 240:5) will differ, depending on the organization and the job in question. Highly attractive employers will have fewer people decline their offers, and less-demanding jobs will be filled with less selectivity. Also, economic conditions play a big role in whether the company must pursue the applicant or vice versa. Nevertheless, a poor job of recruiting will greatly limit the calibre of people available for hire. Also, from the time a company realizes it needs new employees until the time the employees show up for work is typically measured in weeks or months rather than days.

I/O psychologists have investigated several aspects of the recruitment process. One area has to do with the means by which applicants are recruited, and the resulting quality of the people hired. In other words, is there any difference in the types of people hired as a function of their recruitment through newspaper advertisements, television commercials, employment agencies, or other means? Several studies have investigated this issue, but relatively few consistent findings have emerged. For example, Taylor and Schmidt (1983) found that rehires (that is, people who formerly worked for the company) made the best employees as indexed by job performance and absenteeism. Breaugh (1981) found that newspaper ads and college placement offices were poor sources of good recruits. Gannon (1971) reported that seven recruiting sources used by a bank yielded quit rates within a year after hire that varied from 21% to 40%. If the bank had limited its recruiting to the four best sources and neglected the worst three, it would have reduced its quit rate by 9% with a cost savings of $180,000. In general, this line of research indicates that rehires typically make for good employees, while responders to newspaper want ads are typically unacceptable.

A second area of recruiting research addresses what is called the *realistic job preview* (RJP). The realistic job preview is the opposite of slick promotional advertising that overemphasizes the job's good points and ignores its bad points. Rather, RJPs attempt to portray jobs realistically. The RJP may be in the form of a booklet, a videotape, or an on-site visit. The rationale behind RJPs is that one reason people quit their jobs is due to disillusionment. They were initially led to believe the jobs were going to be highly attractive, but over time reality set in, and the jobs were not so great after all. However, if people can see for themselves from the beginning what the jobs are really like, they will not have such false expectations. In fact, Dugoni and Ilgen (1981) proposed three reasons that RJPs might be effective. First, they lower initial expectations, which in turn increases ultimate job satisfaction. Second, they enhance employees' ability to cope with unpleasant job circumstances. Third, applicants perceive greater openness and honesty with a company that candidly reveals to them what their jobs will really be like.

Are realistic job previews effective in reducing turnover? The results indicate their effect is modest at best. Zaharia and Baumeister (1981) studied the effect of two types of RJPs (a written description and a videotape) on the turnover of attendants in a facility for the retarded. The RJPs had no effect on turnover. Reilly, Brown, Blood, and Malatesta (1981) reported that a realistic film and a job visit had no effect on job acceptance rates, employee commitment, or eventual turnover. Dean and Wanous (1984) found that bank tellers who were given an RJP tended to quit their jobs sooner than control-group tellers. However, in the course of a year there was no difference in the overall turnover of the two groups. Reilly and associates estimated that if RJPs had any effect in reducing turnover, it would be no more than 6%. Breaugh (1983) felt the value of RJPs is questionable and speculates that some of the inconsistency in the research findings is due to differences in the times at which RJPs are administered. Some companies administer RJPs after a job offer has been extended but before the applicant has accepted it. Other companies give RJPs *after* a job offer has been accepted. Whatever the reasons, RJPs in total have not been as successful in reducing turnover as I/O psychologists have hoped.

In Chapter 4 we discussed how EEO legislation influences a variety of employment functions. The recruitment function is not governed by EEO, but by a social policy called *Affirmative Action*. Affirmative Action programs are designed to promote active recruiting of all qualified members of the work force, and to correct previous wrongs in the composition of the work force. Employers are expected to recruit minority group members as they do others. Recruiters may (1) visit colleges with mainly Black or female students, or (2) advertise job openings in magazines or newspapers read by minority groups or on radio or TV programs favored by minorities. Affirmative Action programs require employers to recruit minority applicants who might not otherwise seek employment with the companies. Also, companies must prepare affirmative action goals and timetables for employing a certain percentage of minority employees. This is required because many employers have a disproportionately small percentage of minorities in their work forces compared to the population at large. Since affirmative action is not law, a company cannot be sued for not having an affirmative action program. But economic pressures can be brought to bear against the company for lack of participation. If a company receives a portion of its business from government contracts, the government can withhold funds until the company develops an affirmative action program. Companies that rely heavily on federal contracts can be driven out of business for not having such a program.

Research related to affirmative action issues has revealed some interesting psychological correlates to this recruitment philosophy. Heilman and Herlihy (1984) investigated the reactions of individuals to women who got their jobs on the basis of merit or because of preferential treatment based on gender. Neither men nor women were attracted to jobs when it was believed that women in those jobs had acquired them because of their sex. Chacko (1982) reported that women who believed they got their jobs just because they were women felt less organizational commitment, were less satisfied with their work, and experienced more role conflict than women who felt sex was not an important factor in their selection. A study by Heilman, Simon, and Repper (1987) also examined the effects of sex-based selection. In a lab study the authors led females to believe they were selected for a group leader position either because of their sex or their ability. When selected on the basis of sex, women devalued their leadership performance, took less credit for successful outcomes, and reported less interest in persisting as leaders. The findings suggest that when individuals have doubts about their competence to perform a job effectively, sex-based preferential selection is likely to have adverse consequences on how they view themselves and their performance.

In summary, recruitment deals with the process of making applicants available for selection. The ease or difficulty of recruiting depends upon such factors as economic conditions, the job in question, the reputation of the organization, and the urgency of filling the job opening. Organizations that have the luxury of a leisurely, deliberate recruiting process will most likely be more successful than those that are rushed into filling a position. Thorough recruiting does not guarantee that the best candidates will be selected; however, haphazard or casual recruiting frequently results in few good candidates to choose from (see Field Note 1).

Field Note 1

One of the more unusual personnel selection consulting projects I've worked on involved the hiring of a dentist. A dentist in my town had just experienced an unpleasant breakup with his partner. They disagreed on many major issues surrounding dentistry, including the relative importance of preventive dental maintenance versus treatment, pain management for patients, and so on. Their parting was not amicable. The dentist who remained solicited my help in getting a new partner. He described for me at great length the characteristics he was looking for in a new partner. Some of the characteristics were more along the lines of possessing certain dentistry skills, others dealt more with attitudinal or philosophical orientations toward dentistry.

I didn't envision any major problems in picking a new partner because the characteristics desired in the person seemed reasonable to me, plus I knew dental schools turned out many graduates per year (thus I would have a large applicant pool). Then came a curve ball I neither anticipated nor understood initially. The dentist then said to me, "And, of course, my new partner must be left-handed." The dumb look on my face must have told the dentist I didn't quite catch the significance of left-handedness. The dentist then explained to me something I never realized despite all the years I have gone to dentists. Dental partners often share instruments in their practice, and there are both left-handed and right-handed dental instruments. The dentist was left-handed himself, therefore his new partner would also have to be left-handed. I then asked the dentist what proportion of dentists were left-handed. He said he didn't know for sure, but knew it was a small percentage.

Suddenly, my task had become much more difficult.

It was one thing to find a new dentist who met the specifications for the job and who would like to set up a practice in a small Iowa town. It was another thing to have the size of the potential applicant pool be greatly reduced by such a limiting factor as left-handedness. There is a technical term for left-handedness in this case: "bona fide occupational qualification" (BFOQ). For a qualification to be a BFOQ it must be "reasonably necessary to the operation of that particular business or enterprise." Thus, an employer could use left-handedness as a BFOQ in dentistry, but left-handedness would not be a BFOQ in accounting, for example. I am happy to tell you I found a dentist who met all the qualifications. The two dentists have been partners for over twelve years now, and their practice continues to grow (including left-handed patients).

Selection

Selection is the process of choosing for employment a subset of applicants available for hire. Selection implies that some applicants will get hired, others will not. If *all* the applicants will be hired, and it is just a case of which jobs they will fill, then there is no selection. What you have in this context is more appropriately called *placement* or *classification*, topics that will be discussed later in the chapter. Selection is predicated on the premise that some applicants are better suited for a job than others, and its purpose is to identify these "better" applicants. If all the applicants are equally suited or can be thought of as interchangeable, then it makes no difference who gets selected. In the vast majority of cases, however, all applicants are *not* equally suited, so it does matter who gets selected.

It is important to understand on what basis applicants are selected for hire. Selected applicants are predicted to have a higher probability of job success than the rejected applicants. The basis for this prediction may be a test score, the results of an interview, or any other predictor discussed in Chapter 4. For example, a passing score on a test may be set at 8 because it is predicted (via statistical techniques) that those applicants who score 8 or above will succeed on the job. It is important to understand how that passing score is determined.

Regression Analysis

The statistical technique used to predict criterion performance on the basis of a predictor score is called *regression analysis*. While a correlation coefficient is useful for showing the degree of relationship between two variables, it is not useful for predicting one variable from the other. Regression analysis, however, does permit prediction of a person's status on one variable (the criterion) based on his or her status on another variable (the predictor). If we assume that the relationship between the two variables is linear (as it usually is), it can be described mathematically with a regression equation:

Formula 5–1

$$\hat{Y} = a + bX$$

where $\hat{Y}$ = the predicted criterion score
$\quad\quad a$ = a mathematical constant reflecting where the regression line intercepts the ordinate (or Y axis),
$\quad\quad b$ = a mathematical constant reflecting the slope of the regression line, and
$\quad\quad X$ = the predictor scores for a given individual.

The values of a and b are derived through mathematical procedures that minimize the distance between the regression line (that is, a line useful for making predictions) and the pairs of predictor-criterion data points. To develop a regression equation, you need predictor and criterion data on a sample of people. Let us say we have a sample of 100 employees. Supervisor ratings of job performance are the criterion, while the predictor test we wish to investigate is an intelligence test. We administer the intelligence test to the workers, collect the criterion data, and then see if we can predict the criterion scores on the basis of the intelligence test. On the basis of the predictor-criterion data, we derive the following regression equation:

Formula 5–2

$$\hat{Y} = 1 + .5X$$

The relationship between the two variables is shown in Figure 5–2. Note that the regression line crosses the Y axis at a value of 1 (that is, $a = 1$). Also, for every two-unit increase in X, there is a corresponding one-unit increase in Y. Thus, the slope of the regression line, defined as the change in Y divided by the change in X, equals 1/2 or .5 (that is, $b = .5$).

For any value of X, we can now predict a corresponding Y score. For example, if someone scores 12 on the intelligence test, the predicted criterion rating would be:

Formula 5–3

$$\hat{Y} = 1 + .5(12)$$
$$\hat{Y} = 7$$

If a supervisor rating of 5 represented adequate job performance (and we did not want anyone with a lower rating), the regression equation can be worked backward to get the minimum passing score:

$$5 = 1 + .5X$$
$$X = 8$$

So, if we use the intelligence test to hire, we would not accept any applicants who scored less than 8. Scores less than 8 would result in a predicted level of job performance lower than we wanted. There is also another way to find the passing score. In Figure 5-2, locate the value of 5 on the Y axis (the criterion). Move horizontally to the regression line, and then drop down to the corresponding point of the X axis (the predictor). The score is 8.

In addition to thinking about b as the slope of the regression line, one can think about b in a way that shows the relationship between correlation and regression. Regression is based on correlation. That should make sense because if you can predict one variable from another, those two variables should be related. An alternative conceptualization for b is the correlation between X and Y, times the ratio of the standard deviation of Y, divided by the standard deviation of X; that is,

Formula 5–4

$$b = r_{xy}\left(\frac{S_y}{S_x}\right)$$

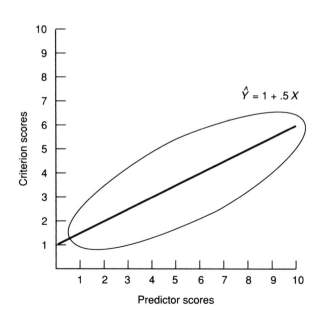

Figure 5–2 Predictor-Criterion Scatterplot and Regression Line of Best Fit

If the correlation between the intelligence test and the supervisor rating was .60, the standard deviation of the supervisor rating (S_y) 2.5, and the standard deviation of the intelligence test (S_x) 3, we would have

Formula 5–5

$$b = .60\left(\frac{2.5}{3.0}\right)$$

$$= .5$$

In thinking about b this way, you can see that if there were no correlation between the two variables, you could not predict one from the other. If $r_{xy} = .00$, then $b = 0$. If $b = 0$, the regression line would have no slope (it would be parallel to the X axis), and every value of X would yield the same predicted value of Y, thus making prediction of Y pointless. Also, if the standard deviation of the criterion and predictor were equal, then the slope of the regression line would equal the correlation coefficient, or $b = r$. Figure 5–3 shows three different regression lines that demonstrate this relationship. Note that the intercept and slope in the graph correspond to their expression in the equation.

Multiple Predictors

Many better personnel decisions are made on the basis of more than one piece of information. How well two or more predictors combined improve the predictability of the criterion depends on their individual relationships to the criterion and their

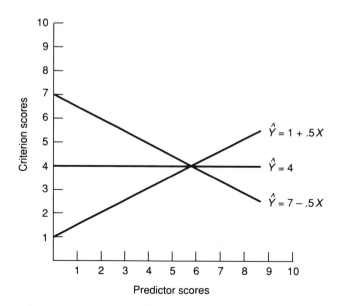

Figure 5–3   Three Regression Equations with Their Mathematical Statements

relationship to each other. Suppose two predictors both correlate with the criterion but do not correlate with each other. This relationship is expressed in Figure 5–4.

The shaded area on the left shows how much the first predictor overlaps with the criterion. The overlap area is the validity of the first predictor, symbolized by the notation r_{1c}, where the subscript 1 stands for the first predictor and the subscript c stands for the criterion. The shaded area on the right shows the extent to which the second predictor overlaps with the criterion; its validity can be expressed as r_{2c}. As can be seen, a lot more of the criterion can be explained by using two predictors instead of one. Also note that the two predictors are unrelated to each other, meaning that they predict different aspects of the criterion. The combined relationship between two or more predictors and the criterion is referred to as a *multiple correlation* (*R*). The only conceptual difference between r and R is that the range of R is from 0 to 1.0, while r ranges from -1.0 to 1.0. When R is squared, the resulting R^2 value represents the total amount of variance in the criterion that can be explained by two or more predictors. When predictors 1 and 2 are not correlated with each other, the squared multiple correlation (R^2) is equal to the sum of the squared individual validity coefficients, or

Formula 5–6

$$R^2_{c.12} = r^2_{1c} + r^2_{2c}$$

For example, if $r_{1c} = .60$ and $r_{2c} = .50$, then

Formula 5–7

$$R^2_{c.12} = (.60)^2 + (.50)^2$$

$$= .36 + .25$$

$$= .61$$

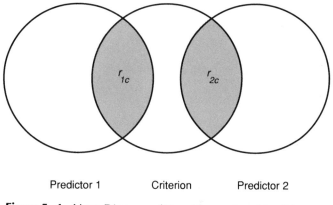

Predictor 1   Criterion   Predictor 2

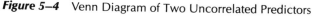

Figure 5–4   Venn Diagram of Two Uncorrelated Predictors

The notation $R^2_{c.12}$ is "the squared multiple correlation between the criterion and two predictors." In this condition (when the two predictors are unrelated to each other), 61% of the variance in the criterion can be explained by two predictors.

In most cases, however, it is rare that two predictors relating to the same criterion are unrelated to each other. Usually, all three variables share some variance with one another; that is, the intercorrelation between the two predictors (r_{12}) is not zero. Such a relationship is presented graphically in Figure 5.5.

In Figure 5–5 each predictor correlates substantially with the criterion (r_{1c} and r_{2c}), but the two predictors also overlap each other (r_{12}). The addition of the second predictor adds more criterion variance than can be accounted for by one predictor alone. Yet all of the criterion variance accounted for by the second predictor is not new variance; part of it was explained by the first predictor. When there is a correlation between the two predictors (r_{12}), the equation for calculating the squared multiple correlation must be expanded to

Formula 5–8

$$R^2_{c.12} = \frac{r^2_{1c} + r^2_{2c} - 2r_{12}r_{1c}r_{2c}}{1 - r^2_{12}}$$

For example, if the two predictors intercorrelated .30, given the validity coefficients from the previous example and $r_{12} = .30$, we will have:

Formula 5–9

$$R^2_{c.12} = \frac{(.60)^2 + (.50)^2 - 2(.30)(.60)(.50)}{1 - (.30)^2}$$

$$= .47$$

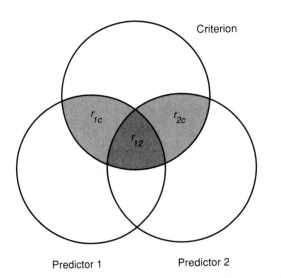

Criterion

r_{1c} r_{2c}

r_{12}

Predictor 1   Predictor 2

Figure 5–5 Venn Diagram of Two Correlated Predictors

As can be seen, the explanatory power of two intercorrelated predictor variables is diminished compared to the explanatory power when they are uncorrelated (.47 versus .61). This example provides a rule about multiple predictors: It is generally advisable to seek predictors that are related to the criterion but are uncorrelated with each other.[1] However, in practice, it is very difficult to find multiple variables that are statistically related to another variable (the criterion) but at the same time statistically unrelated to each other. Usually variables that are predictive of a criterion are also predictive of each other. Also note that the abbreviated version of the equation used to compute the squared multiple correlation with independent predictors is just a special case of the expanded equation, caused by r_{12} being equal to zero.

Multiple Regression Analysis

The relationship between correlation and regression is the foundation for the relationship between multiple correlation and multiple regression. Just as regression permits prediction on the basis of one predictor, *multiple regression* permits prediction on the basis of multiple predictors. The logic for using multiple regression is the same as the logic for using multiple correlation: It usually enhances prediction of the criterion.

As we noted before, the formula for a regression equation with one predictor is

Formula 5–10

$$\hat{Y} = a + bX$$

When we expand this to the case of two predictors, we have

Formula 5–11

$$\hat{Y} = a + b_1 X_1 + b_2 X_2$$

where X_1 and X_2 are the two predictors and b_1 and b_2 are the regression weights associated with the two predictors. As before, the b values are based in part upon the correlation between the predictors and the criterion. In addition, in multiple regression the b values are also influenced by the correlations among the predictors. However, the procedure for making predictions in multiple regression is similar to that used in one-predictor (or simple) regression.

Suppose we have criterion data on a sample of industrial workers who take two tests we think may be useful for hiring future workers. We analyze the data to derive the values of a, b_1, and b_2 and we arrive at the following regression equation:

---

[1] In point of fact, the statistical relationship between the predictor intercorrelation (r_{12}) and the total predictability of a criterion (R^2) is very complex. Dudycha, Dudycha, and Schmitt (1974) have shown that negative intercorrelations and extreme positive intercorrelations (.95 and greater) enhance the predictability of the criterion beyond what would have been attained with independent ($r_{12} = .00$) predictors. Of course, in reality, the likelihood of finding variables with such statistical properties is extremely small.

Formula 5–12

$$\hat{Y} = 2 + .4X_1 + .7X_2$$

If a person scores 30 on test 1 and 40 on test 2, his or her predicted criterion performance would be

Formula 5–13

$$\hat{Y} = 2 + .4(30) + .7(40)$$
$$\hat{Y} = 42$$

The degree of predictability afforded by the two predictors is measured by the multiple correlation between the predictors and the criterion. If the multiple correlation is large enough to be of some value for prediction purposes, we might use the two tests to hire future workers. The company would undoubtedly set a minimum predicted criterion score at a certain value, say, 40. In this example, the person's predicted job-performance score (42) was above the minimum score set by the company (40), so the person would be hired.

Multiple regression is not limited to just two predictors; predictors can be added to the regression equation until they no longer enhance prediction of the criterion. The k-predictor regression equation is simply an extension of the two-predictor regression equation, and all terms are interpreted as before. Such an equation would look like

Formula 5–14

$$\hat{Y} = a + b_1X_1 + b_2X_2 + b_3X_3 + \ldots + b_kX_k$$

Usually, there comes a point at which adding more predictors will not enhance the prediction of the criterion. Regression equations with four or five predictors usually do as good a job as those with more. The reason is that the shared variance among the predictors becomes very large after four to five predictors, so adding more will not add unique variance in the criterion. If we could find another predictor that was (1) uncorrelated with the other predictors, and (2) correlated with the criterion, it would be a useful addition to the equation. Multiple regression is a very popular prediction strategy in I/O psychology, and is used extensively for a wide variety of research problems.

Cross-Validation

Cross-validation is a statistical technique involving regression analysis in general but more commonly used with multiple regression (Mosier, 1951). Its purpose is to examine the stability of the regression weights to determine whether the predictive power of a regression equation is enduring or, alternatively, is not due to sample-specific characteristics of the data (Cattin, 1980).

Let us say that a company is interested in testing the validity of two tests that may be useful in hiring production workers. It employs 200 production workers who can be used to test the tests in a concurrent criterion-related validity study. The company gives the two tests to all the workers and then obtains criterion data on them that reflect their job performance. It then randomly divides the total sample into two groups of 100 workers each. It takes the first sample of workers and develops a multiple regression equation examining the extent to which the two tests are predictive of job performance. The resulting multiple regression equation might look like this:

Formula 5–15

$$\hat{Y} = 2 + .5X_1 + .6X_2$$

Let us assume that the multiple correlation coefficient is .65. Using this regression equation, we then predict what the criterion scores will be for the second sample of workers based on the regression weights from the first. The first sample is the *validation* or *developmental* sample; the second sample is the *cross-validation* or *hold-out* sample. In other words, the multiple regression equation is *developed* on the first sample, while the second sample is *held out* from the original analysis to test the stability of the regression weights.

If the regression equation is equally valid in making predictions in the second sample, the degree of predictability in the two samples should be equal. Applying the regression equation to the second sample, we discover that the multiple correlation is .61. While .61 is quite good, it is not as good as the .65 in the first sample. We would conclude that the multiple regression equation did cross-validate fairly well because the two multiple correlation values were quite close to each other. A successful cross-validation means that the *a* and *b* values in the developmental sample are appropriate for making predictions in the hold-out sample. In other words, the *a* and *b* values are stable and can be used for prediction in another sample. Successful cross-validation adds confidence to our conclusions about the predictability of the criterion.

The ultimate test of the goodness of cross-validation is a comparison of the multiple correlation coefficients. If the *a* and *b* values in the second sample were very different from those of the first sample (meaning the tests do not predict the criterion in the same manner), the resulting multiple correlation in the second sample would be very different. This would imply that the *a* and *b* values are specific only to the developmental sample at the time the study was conducted. Therefore, we should be wary of the conclusions we would draw regarding predictability and stability.

Shrinkage is the difference between the multiple correlation derived in the developmental sample and the multiple correlation derived in the hold-out sample. The amount of shrinkage in our problem was .65 − .61 = .04. The smaller the shrinkage, the more successful was the cross-validation. If the multiple correlation in the second sample had been .10 instead of .61, the shrinkage would have been .65 − .10 = .55, and our cross-validation would have been unsuccessful. Shrinkage is influenced by the similarity of the two samples, the number of predictors in the multiple regression equation, and the sample size. Large shrinkage is most likely when the two samples are quite different (for example, the developmental sample had workers with a lot of experience, the hold-out sample had mostly new employees) and when many predictors and few subjects are used. Little shrinkage is most likely when the two samples are comparable, few predictors are used, and many subjects are involved in the study. The proper ratio between the number of subjects and the number of predictors has been estimated around 10:1; that is, there should be 10 subjects for every predictor in the equation. In our example, we had 100 subjects and 2 predictors (a ratio of 50:1), well within the proper bounds for cross-validation.

Development of Test Batteries

Because the predictability of a criterion is almost always enhanced by using multiple predictors, psychologists often employ several tests as predictors. They begin with several tests that they think may be predictive of the criterion. The tests that are used are referred to collectively as a *test battery*.

The initial test battery is experimental because the psychologist does not know which tests will be predictive. Perhaps as many as ten or 15 tests are included in the initial battery. The next step is to identify a subset of those tests that are predictive of the criterion. Several procedures have been proposed for creating an "optimal" test battery. One procedure is to start with the one test that is most predictive of the criterion. The next step is successively to add predictors that will most increase the multiple correlation based on their individual validities as well as their correlations with the other tests. At some point, adding more predictors will not appreciably increase the predictability of the criterion. It is at that point where the final test battery is identified.

Table 5–1 is a list of ten tests that might constitute a test battery, their individual correlation with the criterion, and the extent to which they add to the multiple

TABLE 5–1 *Sequential Ordering of Tests into a Battery Based on Incremental Gain in the Multiple Correlation*

Order of Entry into Battery	Test	Individual r	Cumulative R^2
1	Intelligence	.50	.25
2	Mechanical aptitude	.31	.32
3	Spatial relations	.24	.36
4	Numerical ability	.45	.39
5	Verbal ability	.19	.41
6	Visual acuity	.21	.43
7	Abstract reasoning	.14	.43
8	Creative thinking	.09	.43
9	Finger dexterity	.26	.43
10	Eye-hand coordination	.22	.43

correlation when added to the test battery. The tests are listed in order of their value to the battery. The intelligence test has the largest single correlation with the criterion, so it is the first test in the battery. The test of mechanical aptitude, although *not* having the second-largest correlation with the criterion, is added second to the battery because its incremental gain in the multiple correlation is greater than that of any other test. The remaining tests are added to the battery in order of their incremental increase in the multiple correlation.

The value of the multiple correlation achieved through adding new predictors is determined sequentially with multiple regression analysis. The final test battery would consist of the first six tests since the remaining tests do not add to the overall predictability of the criterion. While each of those four tests does correlate with the criterion, its intercorrelation with the other predictors is such that the variance in the criterion it accounts for has already been represented by the other tests; that is, the criterion variance accounted for is not unique. If the psychologists had been clairvoyant, they would have "known" from the start that these six tests would compose the final battery. Because they do not, it is only through the sequential testing of predictors that the psychologists arrive at the final battery.

Some other procedures (basically modifications of the above) have been proposed for developing test batteries. One such procedure is based on testing time; another is based on cost. All other things being equal, the one preferred test out of several with equal validity is the one that (1) takes the least time to complete, and (2) costs the least. These procedures attempt to arrive at a test battery that is both predictive and efficient in terms of time and money. These constraints add to the complexity of creating a test battery.

The final step in developing a test battery is to examine it for shrinkage with cross-validation; a good test battery will not incur much shrinkage. Recall that one determinant of shrinkage is the number of predictors, so large test batteries are more likely to incur shrinkage, all other things being equal. We can place a lot of confidence in the generalizability of our test battery when shrinkage is small. Therefore, we could use the battery with different samples of employees as opposed to coming up with a new battery for each group.

Assessing the Utility of a Predictor

The *utility* of a predictor is the degree to which its use improves the quality of the people being selected beyond what it would have been had that predictor not been used (Blum & Naylor, 1968). Several factors contribute to the utility of a predictor, some of which we will examine in close detail.

Criterion Reliability. As we saw in the previous chapter, the measure of job performance against which a predictor is validated must be stable. Stability in the criterion is imperative; without it we cannot draw any accurate conclusions about predicted employee performance because that performance is too variable. It means little to talk about "average" job performance when performance fluctuates wildly. As was the case with predictor reliability, adequate criterion reliability should be in excess of .70.

Criterion Relevance.   Criterion relevance is analogous to predictor validity. It is important that the actual criterion that is selected to represent the conceptual criterion of job performance be an appropriate (that is, *valid*) measure. The utility of a predictor is gauged by the improvement in the *quality* of the people being hired, so the criterion must be an accurate indicator of quality. If the criterion that is selected to represent job performance is lacking in relevance, it is highly unlikely that *any* predictor will systematically result in the hiring of better-quality people. While criterion relevance cannot be expressed in a quantitative way (and thus is somewhat elusive), it is necessary to have a "good" (relevant) criterion against which to validate a predictor.

Predictor Reliability.   As was stated earlier, a predictor must be reliable if it is going to have any value. But high reliability alone is no guarantee that the predictor will be useful. It is possible for a predictor to have *high reliability* but *low validity*. Recall that validity is not an inherent property of a test; rather, it involves the appropriateness of inferences drawn from the test. A highly reliable clerical test may have no validity at all for supervisors. However, the converse is not true. If a test has high validity, it must also have high reliability. The estimated upper limit of a test's validity is the square root of its reliability; that is, a test with a reliability of .64 would have as an upper limit a validity of .80. A test that has no reliability would, of course, also have no validity. Therefore, predictor reliability, like criterion reliability, is a necessary but not sufficient condition for predictor utility.

Predictor Validity.   While the first three factors are necessary for a predictor to have any utility, *predictor validity* is a factor that has a direct and highly visible effect. In fact, predictor utility is influenced more by predictor validity than any other factor.

To illustrate, consider Figure 5–6. It shows a predictor-criterion correlation of .80. Along the predictor axis is a line, the *predictor cutoff*, that separates passing from failing applicants. People above the cutoff were accepted for hire; those below it were rejected. Also, observe the three horizontal lines. The solid line represents the criterion performance of the entire group, and it cuts the entire distribution of scores in half. The dotted line, the criterion performance of the rejected group, is *below* the performance of the total group. Finally, the dashed line, the criterion performance of the accepted group, is *above* the performance of the total group. The people who would be expected to perform the best on the job are those above the predictor cutoff. In a simple and straightforward sense, that is what a valid predictor does in personnel selection: it identifies the more capable people from the total pool.

A different picture emerges for a predictor that has no correlation with the criterion, as shown in Figure 5–7. Again, the predictor cutoff separates those accepted from those rejected. This time however, the three horizontal lines are all superimposed; that is, the criterion performance of the accepted group is no better than that of the rejected group, and both are the same as the performance of the total group.

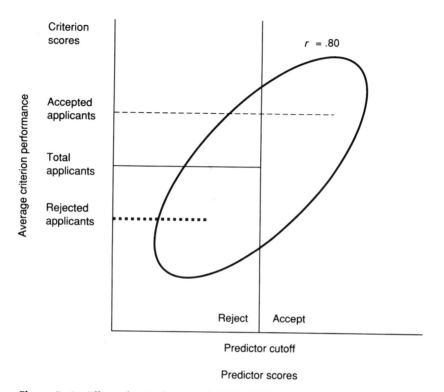

Figure 5–6   Effect of a Predictor with High Validity ($r = .80$) on Test Utility

Predictor utility is measured by the *difference* between the average performance of the accepted group and the average performance of the total group. As can be seen, these two values are the same, so their difference equals zero. In other words, predictors that have no validity also have no utility.

On the basis of this example, we see a direct relationship between predictor utility and predictor validity: The greater the validity of the predictor, the greater its utility as measured by the increase in average criterion performance for the accepted group over that for the total group.

Selection Ratio.   A fifth factor that determines the utility of a predictor is the *selection ratio* (SR). The selection ratio is defined as the number of job openings (n) divided by the number of job applicants (N), or:

Formula 5–16

$$SR = \frac{n}{N}$$

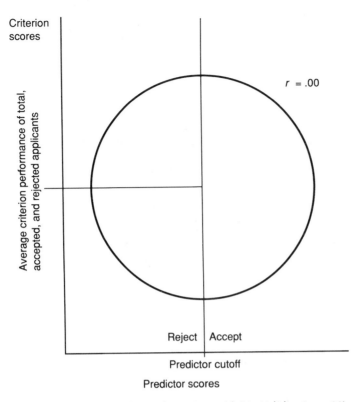

Criterion
scores

Average criterion performance of total,
accepted, and rejected applicants

$r = .00$

Reject │ Accept

Predictor cutoff

Predictor scores

Figure 5–7   Effect of a Predictor Test with No Validity ($r = .00$) on Test Utility

When the SR is equal to 1 (there are as many openings as there are applicants) or greater (there are more openings than applicants), the use of any selection device has little meaning. The company can use any applicant who walks through the door. But most often, there are more applicants than openings (the SR is somewhere between 0 and 1), and thus the SR is meaningful for personnel selection.

The effect of the SR on predictor utility can be seen in Figure 5–8 and 5–9. Let us assume we have a validity coefficient of .80 and the selection ratio is .75, meaning we will hire three out of every four applicants. Figure 5–8 shows the predictor-criterion relationship, the predictor cutoff that results in accepting the top 75% of all applicants, and the respective average criterion performance of the total group and the accepted group. By hiring the top 75%, the average criterion performance of that group is greater than that of the total group (which is weighted down by the bottom 25% of the applicants). Again, utility is measured by this difference between average criterion scores. Further, by lopping off the bottom 25% (the one applicant out of four who is not hired), the average criterion performance of the accepted group will be greater than for the total group.

In Figure 5–9 we have the same validity coefficient ($r = .80$), but this time the SR is .25; that is, out of every four applicants, we will hire only one. The figure shows the location of the predictor cutoff that results in hiring only the top 25% of all applicants and the respective average criterion performance of the total and accepted groups. The average criterion performance of the accepted group is not only above that of the total group, as before, but the difference is also much greater. In other words, when only the top 25% are hired, their average criterion performance will be

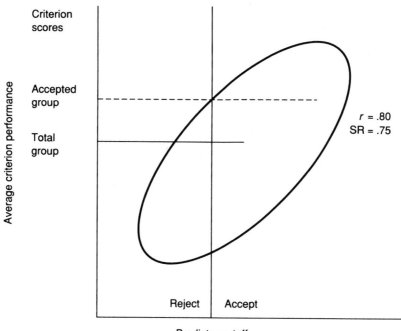

Figure 5–8 Effect of Large Selection Ratio (SR = .75) on Test Utility

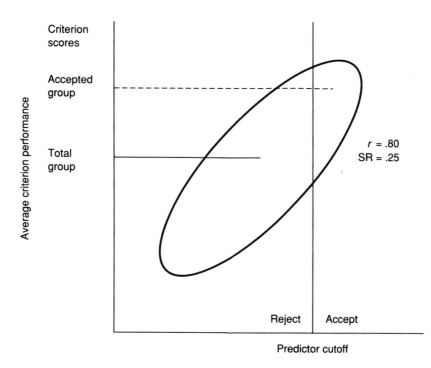

Figure 5–9 Effect of Small Selection Ratio (SR = .25) on Test Utility

greater than the performance of the top 75% of the applicants, and both of these values will be greater than the average performance of the total group.

The relationship between SR and predictor utility should be clear: The smaller the SR, the greater the predictor's utility or value. This should also make sense intuitively. The fussier we are in admitting people (that is, the smaller the selection ratio), the more likely it is that the people admitted (or hired) will be of the quality we desire.

Percentage of Present Employees Who Are Successful. The sixth factor that influences the utility of a predictor is the percentage of present employees who are successful (also called the *base rate*). Management usually decides what constitutes successful job performance. It has in mind a standard or critical value that separates successful from unsuccessful workers. This critical value is the *criterion cutoff*. For example, in most undergraduate colleges, the criterion cutoff separating successful from unsuccessful students is a "C" average (2.0/4.0).

The relationship between the base rate and predictor utility is somewhat deceptive because it depends on the way gains in average criterion performance are viewed. The possibility for the largest potential gain in criterion performance (in a *relative* sense) occurs for *low* base rates. If many people in a company are performing poorly (that is, the base rate is low), the odds are fairly good that a new predictor will elevate the average performance of the group. For example, if the base rate of a company is 5%, a particular predictor may result in improving the quality of the work force to 10%, a 5% improvement in absolute terms but a 100% (5% / 5%) improvement in relative terms. Conversely, if everyone in the company is performing successfully (that is, the base rate is 1.00), it would be impossible for a new predictor to improve on this ideal state.

Therefore, in relative terms, the lower the base rate, the larger the percentage increase in satisfactorily performing employees when a new predictor is used. However, in *absolute* terms, the largest gains in average criterion performance will occur with a base rate of .50; that is, a new predictor will produce the greatest increase in the number of people who will attain satisfactory performance if the base rate is .50. For example, given a base rate of 50%, a particular predictor may result in improving the quality of the work force to 67%, a 17% improvement in absolute terms but a 34% (17% / 50%) improvement in relative terms. As the base rate becomes more extreme (high or low), the absolute utility of the predictor decreases. In other words, it is difficult for a predictor to change the actual number of workers who are performing successfully if the current group of employees is performing extremely well or poorly. Therefore, a base rate of .50 will produce the greatest change in the *absolute* percentage, while the greatest gains on a *relative* percentage basis will occur with low base rates.

In summary, the relationship between the percentage of present employees who are performing successfully and predictor utility is as follows: The closer the base rate is to .50, the greater will be the gain in the *actual number* of new employees who will perform successfully.

TABLE 5–2 *Effects of Seven Variables on Test Utility*

Variable	Degree Required for High Utility
Criterion reliability	High
Criterion relevance	High
Predictor reliability	High
Predictor validity	High
Selection ratio	Low
Base rate	.50
Cost	Low

Cost. All other things being equal, the predictor that costs the least to administer has the greatest utility. In many cases, however, all other things are usually *not* equal. For example, sometimes the most valid predictor also costs the most money to administer or score. In this case, is the increased cost of a predictor offset by its increased validity? As we will see later, increases in validity usually compensate for any increases in cost—unless, of course, the predictor is prohibitively expensive. Predictor validity has the greatest impact on utility, so in almost all cases, a more valid predictor is worth it.

While the seven factors listed here all influence predictor utility, the last four factors have the greatest impact. Also, they are more likely to be manipulated by the company. A company can alter its selection ratio (up or down) depending on staffing needs and the job market, and it can choose predictors based on their cost. Given these four factors, when will a predictor result in the greatest utility? This will occur when the predictor is highly valid, the selection ratio is low, the base rate is .50, and the cost of the predictor is low. The relationship between all seven of the factors and test utility is summarized in Table 5–2.

Selection Decisions

As long as the predictor used for selection has less than perfect validity ($r = 1.00$), we will always make some errors in personnel selection. The object is, of course, to make as few mistakes as possible. With the aid of the scatterplot, we can examine where the mistakes occur in making selection decisions.

Part (a) of Figure 5–10 shows a predictor-criterion relationship of about .80 where the criterion scores have been separated by a criterion cutoff. The *criterion cutoff* is the point that separates successful (above) from unsuccessful (below) employees. Again, management decides what constitutes successful and unsuccessful performance.

---

[2] In some public sector organizations (e.g., state governments), the passing score for a test is determined by law. Usually a passing score is set at 70% correct.

Part (b) shows the same predictor-criterion relationship, except this time the predictor scores have been separated by a predictor cutoff. The predictor cutoff is the point that separates accepted (right) from rejected (left) applicants. The score that constitutes passing the predictor test is determined by the selection ratio, cost factors, or occasionally by law.[2]

Part (c) shows the predictor-criterion relationship intersected by both cutoffs. Each of the resulting four sections of the scatterplot is identified by a letter representing a different group of people:

Section A: Applicants who are above the predictor cutoff and above the criterion cutoff are called *true positives*. These are the people we think will succeed on the job because they passed the predictor test, and who in fact do turn out to be successful employees (vis-à-vis a predictive criterion-related validity paradigm). This group represents a correct decision: we correctly decided to hire them.

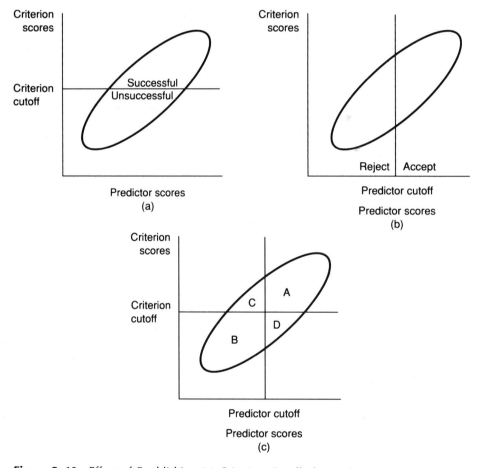

Figure 5–10   Effect of Establishing (a) Criterion Cutoff, (b) Predictor Cuttoff, and (c) Both Cutoffs on a Predictor-Criterion Scatterplot.

Section B: The people in this group are those we thought would not succeed on the job because they failed the predictor test and who, if hired anyway, would have performed unsatisfactorily. This group represents a correct decision: we correctly predicted they would not succeed on the job. These people are *true negatives*.

Section C: People who failed the predictor test (and are thus predicted not to succeed on the job) but who would have succeeded had they been given the chance are called *false negatives*. We have made a mistake in our decision-making process with these people. They would really turn out to be good employees, but we mistakenly decided they would not succeed. These are "the good ones we let get away."

Section D: The people who passed the predictor test (and are thus predicted to succeed on the job) but perform unsatisfactorily after being hired are called *false positives*. We have also erred with these people. They are really ineffective employees who should not have been hired, but we mistakenly thought they would succeed. They are "the bad ones we let in."

Positive/negative refers to the result of passing/failing the predictor test; true/false refers to the quality (good/bad) of our decision to hire the person. In personnel selection, we want to minimize the false positives and false negatives.

If there is no difference between making false positive and false negative decisions (that is, letting a bad worker in is no worse than letting a good one get away), it will do no good to "juggle" the cutoff scores. By lowering the predictor cutoff in part (c) of Figure 5–10 (moving the line to the left), we will *decrease* the size of section C, the false negatives. But by reducing the number of false negatives, we *increase* the space in part D, the false positives. The converse holds for raising the predictor cutoff (moving the line to the right). Conceivably, we could juggle the criterion cutoff (with the same result), but in practice it is unusual to "adjust" what constitutes successful job performance. However, cutoff scores cannot be established solely for the purpose of minimizing false positives or false negatives. Cascio, Alexander, and Barrett (1988) indicate there must be some rational relationship between the cutoff score and the purpose of the test. Cutoff scores should be consistent with normal expectations of acceptable performance within the work force.

For many years, employers were *not* indifferent between making false positive and false negative mistakes. Most employers preferred to let a good employee get away (in the belief that someone else who is good could be hired) rather than hire a bad worker. The cost of training, reduced efficiency, turnover, and so on made the false positive highly undesirable. While most employers still want to avoid false positives, false negatives are increasing in importance. The applicant who fails the predictor test and sues the employer on the grounds of using unfair tests can be devastatingly expensive. If people do fail an employment test, most employers want to be as sure as possible that they were not rejected due to unfair and discriminatory practices. Denying employment to a qualified applicant is tragic; denying employment to a qualified minority applicant can be both tragic and expensive. Equal-employment-opportunity legislation has accentuated the impact of this type of selection mistake. Both types of selection errors can be reduced by increasing the validity of the predictor test. The greater the validity of the predictor, the smaller the chance that people will be mistakenly classified.

Expectancy Charts

Expectancy charts are an alternative to the correlation coefficient as a means of showing a test's validity. An expectancy chart shows what percentage of employees in each test score category will meet a certain level of job performance. Job performance may be based on productivity, length of service, or any other criterion relevant to the company. The method works this way. First, we evaluate all employees on the criterion—let us say, a rating of work quality. We want to hire people who will produce superior-quality work. Next, we administer a test, a scored application blank, or some other predictor to all employees. We then classify all the predictor scores into certain categories, such as 0 to 20, 21 to 40, 41 to 60, 61 to 80, and 81 to 100. We then compute the probability or odds that a person with a predictor score in a given category (say, in the 41 to 60 category) will be a superior performer on the job.

By tabulating the frequency with which certain predictor test scores are paired with the criterion of a superior rating, we can establish the likelihood of a person's being a superior worker as a function of a given test score. Such an *individual* expectancy chart is shown in Figure 5–11. If an individual applicant scores in the

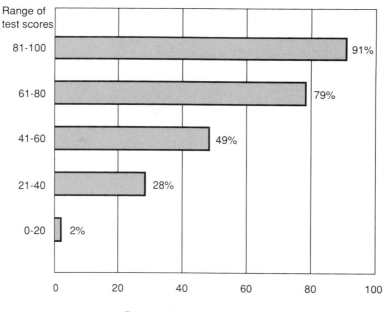

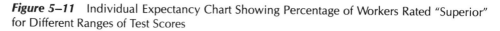

Figure 5–11 Individual Expectancy Chart Showing Percentage of Workers Rated "Superior" for Different Ranges of Test Scores

81-to-100 range, the odds are 91 chances out of 100 he or she will become a superior worker. As we can infer, there is a sizable relationship between test score and job performance. Applicants in the 0-to-20 test score range have virtually no chance (2%) of becoming a superior worker. An *individual* expectancy chart permits predictions about a person's likelihood of reaching a certain level of criterion performance given a certain test score. A second type of expectancy chart, called an *institutional* chart, deals with the prediction of group performance. The logic and rationale of both types of charts are the same.

Expectancy charts have two major advantages over the correlation coefficient as a means of expressing test validity. First, they are not limited to linear predictor-criterion relationships. If both high- and low-scoring applicants are likely to be successful on the job while middle-scoring applicants are not, the individual expectancy chart will clearly show the relationship. Such nonlinearity, on the other hand, would cause the correlation coefficient to yield an inaccurate assessment of the test's validity. Second, I have found it easier to explain to lay people the concept of prediction via an expectancy table than via a correlation coefficient. The ability to understand a correlation coefficient requires some degree of statistical knowledge; an expectancy table conveys the same message but through a graphical display of information.

Classic Selection Model

The *classic selection model*, like all selection models, is based on individual differences. It tries to select people who have the greatest amount of the attribute deemed important for job success. Figure 5–12 shows the six-step process of the classic selection model.

Step 1: Analysis of the Vacant Job(s). Using job-analytic procedures, the vacant job is studied to find the knowledge, skills, and abilities needed for job success. Many problems in personnel selection stem from the fact that there is often inadequate understanding of the job and its requirements. The "best" person is best only insofar as he or she optimally meets these requirements. A person who is best for one job may not be best for another.

Step 2: Selection of Criterion and Predictor. This step involves two procedures. First, on the basis of the job analysis, a criterion of job success is chosen. As always, the criterion must be a sensitive indicator of work quality.

Similarly, a predictor must be chosen. However, the choice of a predictor need not be as carefully considered as the choice of a criterion. If one predictor does not turn out to be useful, another one can always be selected. A psychologist could choose any of the predictors presented in Chapter 4. Predictors are chosen on the basis of an educated hunch. However, the actual verification of the predictor's value is done empirically.

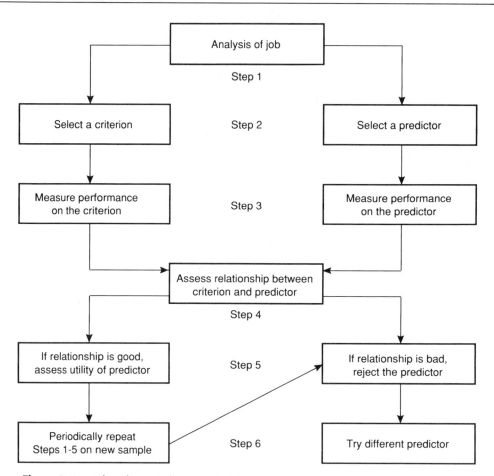

Figure 5–12   The Classic Selection Model

Step 3: Measuring Performance.   After the criterion and predictor have been chosen, the worker's performance is measured on both variables. This can be done in one of two ways. One way is to record the current employees' job performances and then give them the predictor test (for the purpose of testing the test). The second way is to give the predictor to all job applicants, hire all the applicants, and some time later collect criterion data on them. This is the difference between concurrent and predictive criterion-related validity. The significance of the difference between the two methods will be discussed shortly.

Step 4: Assessing the Predictor's Validity.   The fourth step is to determine if differences in predictor scores correspond with differences in criterion scores; that is, does the predictor have validity? This procedure is done with statistical analysis, in most cases by computing a correlation coefficient. If the predictor has validity, there will be some appreciable relationship between predictor scores and criterion scores. If the predictor is lacking in validity, there will be no correspondence between the two sets of scores.

Step 5: Determining the Predictor's Utility. If the predictor has statistical validity, the next step is to determine just how useful it will be in improving the quality of the work force. Remember that the utility of a predictor is determined primarily by its validity, the selection ratio, the base rate, and cost. If the predictor has no validity, there is no point in analyzing its utility since utility is most directly influenced by validity.

Step 6: Reanalysis. Over time, jobs can be changed, applicant pools can be altered, predictors can lose validity, invalid predictors can become valid, and so on. Any personnel selection program should be periodically reevaluated to see if changing employment conditions have altered the predictor-criterion relationship. This should be done at least every five to ten years.

Concurrent Versus Predictive Validity

Criterion or job performance data can be collected in either a concurrent or predictive validity design. The difference between these two research designs has been the topic of much discussion in personnel selection research. The major distinction between concurrent and predictive criterion-related validity is the time interval between collection of the predictor and criterion data. While this distinction is technically correct, within the context of personnel selection and test validation there are many significant implications. The concurrent validity of a test is frequently established for practical reasons, but some authors (for example, Guion, 1965) believe that concurrent validity should not be thought of as a substitute for, or even an approximation of, predictive validity. Guion feels the two methods are not even equivalent. Here are some of the reasons.

When a concurrent validity study is undertaken, the present workers take a predictor test for the sake of testing the test. Their scores are correlated with their job performance to obtain an estimate of the (concurrent) validity of the test. There are several problems with this method. First, employees who are secure in their jobs are less motivated to do well on the test than ambitious applicants who need work. Applicants' scores can be higher than employees' scores. Rothe (1947) found that a predictor cutoff for a test that resulted in rejecting 15% of the actual applicants would have also resulted in rejecting 40% of the present employees had they been applying for their own jobs.

A second problem is one of experience. What an employee learns on the job may influence how he or she responds to a test item. The experience may increase the employee's test score, or it may decrease it if the employee reads too much into the question and thus gets the item wrong.

Finally, range in ability among present employees is restricted. Present employees are the "survivors" of some previous applicant pool. They are more homogeneous (and better) than the original pool of applicants from which they were drawn. The restriction in range causes a reduction in the variability of test scores, which serves to underestimate the validity of the test.

Some researchers have tried to establish the validity of a new predictor by giving the test to a group of selected applicants who were hired on the basis of some other predictor. No selection decisions are made on the basis of the new predictor score; they are just recorded for later use in a predictive validity study. This procedure has one major flaw. If scores on the new predictor (that is being tested) and scores on the other predictor (on which selection decisions were made) are substantially correlated, there will be the same restriction in range. Only if the two predictors are uncorrelated will there be no restriction in range.

For many years, the doctrine of the superiority of predictive validity over concurrent validity (for the reasons cited by Guion, 1965) has been accepted by I/O psychologists. Recently, however, this doctrine has been challenged. Barrett, Phillips, and Alexander (1981) feel the conceptual distinction between predictive and concurrent validity has been exaggerated. The ultimate test of the relative superiority of the two methods involves examining the quality of new employees hired with each method. If better-quality workers are hired with tests validated predictively than with tests validated concurrently, the former method can be considered superior. However, if both methods result in the same quality of new hires, neither method can be declared "better" than the other.[3]

While Barrett and associates do not present any data on the comparability of the two methods, they correctly comment that rarely have any data been presented showing the superiority of predictive validity. While predictive validity seems to be preferable on logical or conceptual grounds, the authors point out that it has little *empirical* support. They also comment that predictive validity designs have problems as well. It remains to be seen whether I/O psychologists will revise their opinions of the long-held doctrine of the deficiency of the concurrent method. Because many validation studies rely on the concurrent method, it would be encouraging to know that the findings from such a design are not "poor substitutes" for or an "approximation" of results from the predictive validity designs. Concurrent validity designs have long been used out of expedience. Predictive validity designs have many practical problems for the employer, such as the hiring of all job applicants. If concurrent validity designs provide an accurate estimate of predictive validity, then they will be an extremely useful tool in personnel selection.

Selection Strategies

The problem facing a psychologist in making a personnel selection decision is, should this person be hired? Several selection strategies can be used to help with the decision. These strategies differ in complexity as well as in their assumptions about predictor-criterion relationships. Each strategy has its own strengths and weaknesses, and each presents a rationale for selecting the "best" person for the job. Four such strategies are

---

[3] However, other factors, such as cost, may also enter into the decision. If two methods result in the hiring of equally competent workers, the preferred method will be the one that costs less.

used: (1) multiple regression, (2) multiple cutoff, (3) multiple hurdle, and (4) profile matching.

Multiple Regression

The *multiple-regression* selection strategy is based on the statistical procedure of multiple regression analysis. Recall that the method involves the use of two or more predictors weighted and added together to enhance the prediction of a criterion. Using a two-predictor model and assuming $a = 0$, the multiple regression equation would be

Formula 5–17

$$\hat{Y} = b_1 X_1 + b_2 X_2$$

This approach assumes that (1) there is a linear relationship between the predictors and the criterion (that is, higher scores on the predictors will lead to higher scores on the criterion), and (2) having a lot of the attribute measured by one predictor compensates for having only a little of the attribute measured by the second predictor. While the former assumption (linearity) is usually met, the latter assumption (compensating predictors) is a more serious limitation.

Given a two-predictor regression equation where $a = 0$, $b_1 = 4$, and $b_2 = 2$, the following equation would be used to select job applicants:

Formula 5–18

$$\hat{Y} = 4X_1 + 2X_2$$

Let us say that a predicted criterion score ($\hat{Y}$) of 100 is considered necessary for hiring. Scores on the two predictors that would result in a passing score for four hypothetical applicants are presented in Table 5–3. Applicant A has none of the attribute measured by X_2, but because of the high score on X_1, he or she meets the minimum passing score of 100. Applicant B is just the reverse, having none of the attribute measured by X_1 but a lot of that measured by X_2. Applicants C and D have differing amounts of X_1 and X_2, which compensate for each other in reaching a score of 100.

TABLE 5–3   *How Four Job Applicants with Different Predictor Scores Can Have the Same Predicted Criterion Score Using Multiple Regression Analysis*

Applicant	Score on X_1	Score on X_2	Predicted Criterion Score
A	25	0	100
B	0	50	100
C	20	10	100
D	15	20	100

Note: Based on the equation $\hat{Y} = 4X_1 + 2X_2$.

As can be seen, there are many combinations of predictor scores that result in a passing score on the criterion. Is this notion of "compensating predictors" acceptable for predicting job success? Sometimes it is, and sometimes it is not. For instance, in the case of a surgeon, a low score on one attribute (finger dexterity) cannot be compensated for by a high score on a second attribute (visual acuity). But for other jobs, it may be acceptable to trade off low levels of one attribute with high levels of another. Keep in mind that it is rare for a person to have absolutely *no* amount of any attribute, so the degree of compensation is usually not as extreme in practice as it could be in theory. An interesting discussion of compensating and noncompensating predictors has been presented by Einhorn (1970). Despite this limitation, the multiple regression strategy is a powerful and popular technique in personnel selection.

Multiple Cutoff

The *multiple-cutoff* selection strategy is an alternative to the multiple-regression selection strategy. The multiple-cutoff method is limited by neither a linear relationship between predictors and criterion or the problem of compensating predictors. This straightforward and uncomplicated method assumes that a *minimal* amount of ability on *all* predictors is needed for job success. Minimal passing-score cutoffs are set for *each* predictor. If an applicant is below the cutoff on *any* predictor, he or she is rejected. All applicants who have scores at or above the cutoffs are hired. Having a high score on one predictor cannot compensate for having a low score on another.

The advantages of the multiple-cutoff technique are that there are no limiting assumptions and the method is easy to use. No formulas are involved in determining who passes and who fails. The major disadvantage involves determining the cutting scores. Cutting scores are generally set by trial and error, with different ones set for each predictor. However, it is quite difficult to establish the *validity* of a cutting score with concurrent validation procedures when no one in the company hired with the method would have any scores *below* it. (If they did, they would not have been hired.) Thus, if it were felt that the cutoffs were set too high, it would be difficult to assess what effect lowering them would have on job performance. This restriction-in-range problem is not limited to just the multiple-cutoff method, however; it affects all concurrent validity studies (see Field Note 2).

Field Note 2

The multiple-cutoff method of personnel selection is used when the applicants need a minimal amount of ability on two or more factors and thus high scores on one factor cannot make up for low scores on another. I recently completed a validation study for a client in which I used the multiple-cutoff method. The job under investigation was that of retail salesperson. Salespeople must possess some special talents to be successful, and there is no way around not having them.

The results of my study revealed that

salespeople had four characteristics that contributed to their success: a very high energy level; a high need for organization; a responsible, take-charge attitude; and high self-esteem. The high energy level means always being on the go, traveling to customers, making calls, and, ultimately, making sales. The organization factor relates to the importance of having a plan, a strategy to selling. It is not just an uncontrolled burst of energy but energy channeled in a carefully mapped out sequence of customer calls and sales tactics. The high level of responsibility refers to the salespeople's being independent of one another. If they do not make the sale, no other employee will. They are responsible for the sales volume in their sales territory. When sales are good, they share the credit with no one. But when sales are bad, they cannot point the finger at anyone else. The self-esteem factor means that salespeople must inwardly feel good about themselves. They have to be positive, resilient, "up-beat," and undeterred. They will encounter a lot of rejection in their work; customers will often not buy their products. They cannot internalize these rejections.

The multiple-cutoff method provided a way to identify applicants who would be successful. Applicants who did not meet all four standards would get flushed. It is difficult to find people who can meet all four—but then, being a successful salesperson is not something just anyone can do.

The multiple regression and multiple-cutoff methods can be used in combination. This can take the form of not hiring some people unless their predicted criterion score was above a certain level (from the multiple regression strategy) *and* they were above some cutoff on each predictor (from the multiple cutoff strategy). These techniques work best when the selection ratio is low and there are many job applicants. Large numbers of applicants are needed because many will be rejected for one of two reasons: (1) they fell below the cutoff on one or more predictors, or (2) even though they were above each individual cutoff, their predicted criterion performance was not high enough. This combined approach is often used in selecting students for graduate school. Applicants usually must have minimally acceptable quantitative and verbal ability as well as an acceptable predicted grade-point average in graduate school (a frequently used criterion of success in academia).

Multiple Hurdle

In the *multiple hurdle* strategy, applicants must get satisfactory scores on a number of predictor variables (or hurdles) that are administered over time. The successful applicant is one who passes each hurdle and is thus ultimately hired. The multiple hurdle approach is not used very often, but when it is used, it is found most frequently in management training programs and in the military. First, people who meet certain basic requirements (perhaps nothing more than interest in the job) are chosen to make up a pool of applicants. The first hurdle is designed to eliminate the least-qualified applicants. In an industrial training program, the first hurdle may be a knowledge test covering the first few weeks of specialized instruction. In the military, the first hurdle for prospective paratroopers may be some test of physical fitness. At various points in time, additional hurdles (that is, evaluations) are presented. To survive in the program, applicants must pass each hurdle; those who do not are dropped along the way. Eventually, a certain number pass all the hurdles, and these people become industrial managers, paratroopers, and so on.

The advantage of the program is that unqualified people do not have to endure an entire evaluation program before they are rejected. It is best for the company and the applicant to discover as soon as possible if he or she will not make it on the job. Because many evaluations are made, the company can be more confident in the quality of its final decision. The odds of a false positive's surviving multiple evaluations are much lower than those of surviving one test. The method is used primarily

People selected to be astronauts are the survivors of a very rigorous multiple hurdle evaluation process. Courtesy NASA

for jobs whose significance to the company warrants such an extensive selection program. Lower-level jobs are rarely so critical to the company.

The disadvantages of the method are the time and cost involved. Again, the job's value to the company should be a major factor in deciding whether to use this type of program. A problem (although not necessarily a disadvantage) is that the final survivors are extremely similar to one another so there is a major restriction in range in all their predictor scores. If their predictor scores were correlated with some criterion of job success taken later, the correlation would be very low. One interpretation is that the predictors lack validity. A more likely explanation is that because the survivors are so homogeneous, the similarity of their predictor scores rules out a high correlation with any criterion.

Profile Matching

The last major selection strategy is called *profile* (or *pattern*) *matching*. In this method, all the current employees take a number (k) of predictor tests. Test scores are correlated with measures of job performance. Of the k tests that were administered, a subset of them (n) would probably show some relationship to job success, or be valid predictors. These n valid predictors are plotted on a graph that would look something like Figure 5–13. In this example, six predictors are listed along the X axis, while the average score for each is plotted on the Y axis. Connecting the points creates a profile or pattern of the average successful employee. In using the method to hire future employees, we would administer the six valid predictors to the applicants, plot their scores, and then select the person whose profile best matched the standard profile. But finding which applicant best matches the standard is not as simple as it may seem.

Two analyses are used to determine the degree of match between the applicant's

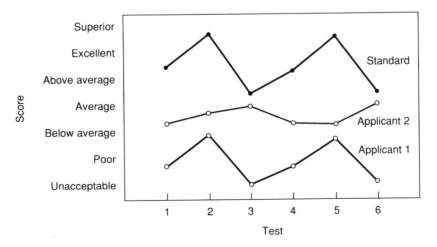

Figure 5–13 A Hypothetical Standard Profile and Profiles of Two Job Applicants

profile and the standard profile. What complicates the picture is that sometimes the two analyses yield different conclusions about whom to hire. One approach is to simply correlate the applicant's scores on the predictors with the average company scores and then hire the person whose scores correlate the highest. While this may seem sensible, there is one problem. Correlation is a measure of the degree of relationship between two variables. While two sets of scores may correlate highly, there may be vast differences in their *magnitude*. An applicant whose profile is similar to the standard but whose scores are well below it in terms of magnitude would appear to be a good candidate. Correlation reflects similarity of the *shape* of the two profiles but not the degree of closeness. Using correlation as a measure of fit, applicant 1 in Figure 5–13 would be hired because her profile is more similar to the standard.

The second analytical procedure is to compute a measure of the differences between the applicant's scores and the standard scores. The difference (d) is computed between each predictor and the standard. The differences are squared (d^2) so that the positive and negative differences will not cancel each other out, and then all the difference scores (six in our example) are added together. Because of this figure, symbolized by d^2 as a measure of fit, applicant 2 in Figure 5–13 would be hired because of the lesser distance between her test scores and the standard.

Which method is better? The only way to answer that question is to compare the two methods empirically. The best method is the one that results in the hiring of better-quality people. In practice, some people use a combination of the two methods. First, they consider only applicants whose scores are *above* the standard (on the grounds that new applicants should be no worse on these predictors than current employees). Second, they select the applicant whose profile is most similar in shape to the standard. This combination approach overcomes the deficiencies of either method alone. But it creates another problem: Many applicants will be needed to find a few people who will meet these criteria. In short, this combination of the methods works only when the selection ratio is small and there are many applicants (see Field Note 3).

Field Note 3

This chapter is devoted to explaining how personnel decisions are made. Many factors have been identified and explained, but one has been left out. I've never seen it discussed in any book or article on personnel selection, but (unfortunately) it is sometimes a critical, if not deciding, factor. It is called *politics*. Consider this experience I had.

I was hired for a very important consulting project: to pick the chief of police for a large city. The job has tremendous visibility, high influence, and great responsibility. I didn't want to "blow it" as the consultant. The city recruited applicants for the opening, and a total of 50 applicants met the minimal qualifications for consideration set by the city. I was handed the 50 applications and told to identify the best candidates in the applicant pool.

My first step was to evaluate each candidate in terms of education and experience using a weighted application blank procedure. That got the applicant pool down to 25. These 25 quarterfinalists then had to submit written answers to three essay test questions about how they would handle some difficult police problems. These answers were evaluated, and the 15 best applicants proceeded to the semifinalist stage. Here the candidates took a series of personality inventories and intelligence tests. Based upon those results, ten finalists were selected. These in turn were subjected to a lengthy oral interview. Based on all the assessment results, I rank ordered the ten finalists and submitted the list to the city council, which had the judicial authority to approve the new chief of police. The candidate ranked first was from a different state, the candidate ranked second was currently the assistant chief of police, the second in command. The candidate ranked first was clearly the best person for the job, being far and away better than anyone else. I thought the city council (composed of seven people) had an easy job: to approve the top candidate as the new chief of police. It is here that politics came in, and it got rather dirty.

The assistant chief of police was a close personal friend of three of the city council members. They played cards together, as did their wives. From the very beginning, the three city council members had known the assistant chief of police would come out favorably in the selection process. In fact, nearly everyone had thought he would be the next chief of police. When I presented the city council with my list of the ten candidates, things got very awkward: "their man" was not first on the list. The press followed the selection process carefully, because it was a hot news item. The media announced the rank order of the ten finalists. The public's general reaction was to have the city council approve the candidate who had been ranked first. But the head of the city council was not

about to sell out his old friend, the assistant police chief.

The head of the city council (one of the three friends on the council) then made this startling announcement. Because every rookie cop on the force dreams about one day rising to be the chief; to award the chief's job to an "outsider" (that is, a candidate not native to the city) would destroy the morale of the police force and take away every rookie's dream forever. Therefore, he was going to advise the city council to select as the next chief of police not the person ranked first (the outsider) but the person ranked second (the assistant chief—and his friend). This was the first time anyone had made any reference at all to the insider/outsider distinction. It was a new hurdle imposed at the eleventh hour as a means of bumping the top-ranked candidate from the list. Some members of the community howled in protest at this announcement, as did the media, declaring it was a "fix" to install the council's personal choice. All the three city council members had to do was convince a fourth member to vote for the second-ranked person, and he would be in. In a highly electrified meeting of the city council in a council chamber jampacked with reporters and camera crews, the city council members publicly cast their votes. By a vote of 4-3, the number-one-ranked candidate (the outsider) was approved and became the new chief of police.

I would like to believe the four "yes" votes came from people who recognized the quality of the top candidate, but I know better. Politics being what it is, strange things can happen. They voted the way they did not simply because they supported the stronger candidate but because they wanted to get even with the three council members against whom they had held a grudge from a previous political episode. In short, the right decision was made, but for the wrong reason.

I wish to emphasize that there was absolutely nothing in my graduate training to prepare me for this experience. Similarly, there is no section of this book entitled "How to Cope with Political Intrigue." But politics is a driving force in all organizations at all levels. Given this fact, sometimes I wonder how I/O psychologists accomplish as much as they do.

Validity Generalization

The concept of *validity generalization* refers to a predictor's validity spreading or generalizing to other jobs or contexts beyond the one in which it was validated. For example, let us say that a test is found valid for hiring secretaries in a company. If that same test were found useful in hiring secretaries in another company, we would say its validity had generalized. That same test could also be found useful in selecting people for a different job, such as clerks. Here is another case of the test's validity generalizing. The concept of validity generalization has long been a goal of I/O psychologists because its implication would certainly make our jobs easier. However, the problem with the concept is that when we did examine whether a test's validity would generalize across either companies or jobs, we often found that it did not; that is, we often found that a test's validity was specific to the situation in which it was originally validated. The implication of this finding was, of course, that we had

"Let's put it this way—if you can find a village without an idiot, you've got yourself a job."

Reprinted from *The Industrial-Organizational Psychologist*

to validate every test in every situation in which it was used. We could not assume that its validity would generalize.

Schmidt and Hunter (1978, 1980) are proponents of validity generalization as a means of selecting personnel. They argue that the problem of situational specificity of test validity is based on psychologists' erroneous belief in the "law of small numbers." The law of small numbers is the belief that whatever results hold for large samples will also hold for small samples. They think this belief is incorrect—that in small samples results are highly unstable, resulting in highly variable test validities. Schmidt and Hunter believe that in most cases psychologists settle for small samples (40 to 50) with which to validate tests. Indeed, Monahan and Muchinsky (1983) found that in fewer than 10% of the personnel selection validation studies conducted over a 30-year period did the researchers use a sufficiently large sample size, according to the standards Schmidt and Hunter recommend. So situation-specific test validities are obtained. Schmidt and Hunter argue that if tests were validated in large samples, the results would generalize (not be situation specific).

Validity generalization means that there is a single "true" relationship between a test and job performance, as for a secretary. Let us say that relationship is a correlation of .40 as based upon validity studies involving thousands of subjects each. In theory, we could generalize the validity of these findings from huge sample sizes to more typical employment situations with small samples. So companies with immense sample sizes would validate certain tests; the rest of the business world would simply "borrow" these validities as a basis for using the tests for hiring in their own companies.

In support of their position, Schmidt and Hunter (1978) present data based on a sample size of over 10,000 individuals. The sample was drawn from the army. Data were reported on ten predictors that were used to forecast success in 35 jobs. The results indicated highly similar validity coefficients across different jobs, meaning that differences among jobs did *not* moderate predictor-criterion relationships. Subsequent validity generalization research on computer programmers (Schmidt, Gast-Rosenberg, & Hunter, 1980), oil industry employees (Schmidt, Hunter, & Caplan, 1981), and clerical employees (Pearlman, Schmidt, & Hunter, 1980) have all yielded consistent and similar findings. The researchers concluded that the effects of situational moderators disappear with appropriately large sample sizes.

Few I/O psychologists reject the concept of validity generalization in total. Rather, it is a question of just how far they believe validity can be generalized. At one end of the continuum there is the doctrine of situational specificity of validity—meaning there is no validity generalization at all. At the other extreme there is validity generalization in its complete form—meaning that the validity of a single test can generalize across all jobs. Thus, an intelligence test valid for hiring secretaries would also be valid for hiring everyone from plumbers to executives and all jobs in between.

The research of Schmidt and Hunter and their associates compellingly demonstrates that validity is not situation specific. However, going to the other extreme and believing that validity can generalize across all jobs is currently meeting with professional skepticism. In other words, within-job validity generalization (for example, a test valid for predicting success across clerical jobs) seems highly tenable, but across-job validity generalization is much less so. Tenopyr (1981) rejects the notion of validity generalization in the extreme form, saying that it implies one can use any test to predict success in any job. She believes that I/O psychologists will never resort to having but one test in their assessment repertoire, for it was precisely that practice 70 years ago that led them to develop different tests; that is, no one test was found that could predict success across all jobs. We still do not have a firm understanding of the limits of validity generalization, it is a matter of professional debate even among I/O psychologists (Schmidt, Pearlman, Hunter, & Hirsh, 1985). While research is being conducted in support of validity generalization (for example, Brown, 1981), it is doubtful that the profession of I/O psychology will ever embrace validity generalization as a panacea for all our selection problems. As Burke (1984) states, "Especially in the area of test validity, let us not overcompensate for past excesses (e.g., maintaining that every test must have a local validation study performed) by committing similar excesses in the opposite direction" (p. 113).

Test Utility and Organizational Efficiency

It is important to remember always that a personnel office is only one part of an organization. Each part must contribute to the overall success of the organization. If the company is a profit-making firm (as many are) or just wants to improve operating efficiency (as all organizations should), a basic question involves how much improved personnel selection techniques contribute to its overall profitability or efficiency. If we hire more productive workers as a result of a new selection technique, how much value or *utility* will they have to the company? Several studies have shown just how much utility a valid testing program can provide.

Schmidt, Hunter, McKenzie, and Muldrow (1979) tried to find the dollar value to the company of using a valid employee-selection program. The authors analyzed the job of a computer programmer. They asked supervisors to estimate the "worth" (in dollars) of a good, average, and poor-quality computer programmer to the company. Supervisors considered such factors as work speed, number of errors, and so on. The authors used the responses along with the following information they had collected: (1) a certain test useful in hiring computer programmers had a validity of .76; (2) it cost $10 to administer the test to each applicant; (3) over 4,000 computer programmers were employed by the company (which was, in this case, the federal government); (4) over 600 new programmers were hired each year; and (5) once on the job, the average programmer lasted about ten years.

Using all this information, the authors compared the expected utility of the test (which had a validity of .76) to other tests that had been used in the past and that had validities ranging from .00 to .50. They also examined the effect of various selection ratios ranging from .05 to .80. The dollar value to the government of using the more valid test was astonishing. When the previously used test was assumed to have a validity of .50 and the selection ratio was .80, the incremental gains in efficiency (that is, the result of hiring better-quality people) was $5.6 *million* in one year. This was the *smallest* dollar gain because the previous testing conditions were quite favorable ($r = .50$). Given the poorest testing condition (a previous test with no validity) and a selection ratio of .05, the dollar gain was $97.2 *million* in one year. That is an amazing return on an investment of only $6,000 per year (600 applicants, $10 cost per applicant).

Keep in mind that these dollar values pertain to using just one test to hire people in one job in one organization for just one year. If you extend these principles to testing in general across many jobs and many companies (and also across time), the dollar value extends into the *billions*. Other studies have shown that the utility of valid tests enhances efficiency by reducing turnover, training time, and accidents. The key element in improved utility is test validity. The impact of test validity on subsequent job performance is dramatic; there is no substitute for using "good" selection techniques.

There have been other advances in the area of utility assessment. Schmidt, Mack, and Hunter (1984) applied their utility calculations to a service job, that of a federal park ranger. By using valid tests to hire the rangers, Schmidt and associates estimated there would be a 13% increase in their productivity, worth approximately $1.3 million per year. Furthermore, by using valid tests to identify the most productive applicants, organizations can reduce their payroll costs by hiring fewer (but more productive) people. This is an especially important consideration when organizations are being forced to cut back on their personnel staffs. Schmidt, Hunter, Outerbridge, and Trattner (1986) also showed the economic gains to be made by deterring the turnover of successful employees. Hiring good people from the start and retaining them means you don't have to hire so many replacements.

However, while some authors believe the economic gains attributable to any valid tests are impressive, there are additional cost issues to consider. For example, Boudreau (1983) identified several cost factors as increased taxes that must be paid by more productive corporations. However, these additional costs do not outweigh the benefits of using valid tests. It seems clear to me that the ability of I/O psychologists to translate what they do into a universally understood metric—dollars and cents— can only strengthen our credibility as contributors to organizational success. The utility concept has even been applied to other personnel functions, such as training and performance appraisal (that is, Landy, Farr, & Jacobs, 1982), demonstrating the value of those activities to the organization. Cascio (1987) was even able to demonstrate the economic gains from instituting nonsmoking programs within organizations. I believe that the profession of I/O psychology has substantially enhanced its stature as a result of such utility research. We are now capable of demonstrating to key organizational decision makers how much our efforts contribute to the financial welfare of the organizations we serve.

Placement and Classification

The vast majority of research in personnel psychology is on selection, the process by which applicants are hired. Another personnel function (albeit less popular) involves deciding *which* jobs people should be assigned to after they have been hired. This personnel function is called either *placement* or *classification*, depending on the basis for the assignment. In many cases, selection and placement are not separate procedures. Usually, people apply for certain, fixed jobs. If they are hired, they fill the jobs they were applying for. However, in some organizations (and at certain times in our nation's history) decisions about selection and placement have to be made separately.

Placement and classification decisions are usually limited to large organizations having two or more jobs an applicant could fill. It must be decided *which* job would best match the person's talents and abilities. A classic example is the military. Thousands of applicants used to be selected each year, either voluntarily or through the draft. Once "in," the next question was where to assign them. Placement and classification procedures are designed to get the best match between people and jobs.

Placement differs from classification on the basis of the number of predictors used to make the job assignment. *Placement* involves allocating people to two or more groups (or jobs) on the basis of a single predictor score. Many junior high school students are placed in math classes on the basis of a math aptitude test. The aptitude test is usually given during seventh grade. Students with high math aptitude are placed in an algebra class in eighth grade; students with average aptitude do not take algebra until ninth grade; students with low math aptitude do not take algebra until tenth grade, if at all. Applicants for secretarial positions may be placed into job grades (for example, secretary I, secretary II) on the basis of a typing test. The point is that placement decisions are made on the basis of one predictor factor (math aptitude, typing speed, and so on).

Classification involves allocating people to jobs on the basis of two or more valid predictor factors. For this reason, classification is more complex. However, it results in a better assignment of people to jobs than placement. Classification uses smaller selection ratios than placement, which accounts for its greater utility. The reason that classification is not always used instead of placement is that it is often difficult to find more than one valid predictor to use in assigning people to jobs. The military has been the basis of most classification research. Military recruits would take a battery of different tests covering such areas as intelligence, ability, and aptitude. On the basis of these test scores, recruits would be assigned to jobs in the infantry, medical corps, military intelligence, and so on. The procedure is also used by other organizations that have to assign large numbers of people to large numbers of jobs. Given this constraint, relatively few companies need to use classification procedures. Nevertheless, Brogden (1951) has shown that the proper classification is just as important for organizational efficiency as the use of proper selection techniques.

Two sets of issues are particularly important in the areas of placement and classification. One has to do with the nature of the jobs that need to be filled. Placement and classification decisions are easier when the jobs are very different. It is easier to decide whether a person should be assigned to the job of a janitor or a clerk than to decide between the job of a secretary or a clerk. The janitor and clerk jobs require very different types of skills, while the secretarial and clerk jobs have many similar job requirements. These decisions become more complex if the jobs in question require successive operations (such as on an assembly line) or if they involve coordination among work units. In these cases, we are also concerned about how well all of the people in the work unit will fit together to form a cohesive team (Cronbach & Gleser, 1965).

A second issue involved in placement and classification is the question of values.

What is best in terms of satisfaction and productivity for the individual may not be the best for the company, and vice versa (Cascio, 1978). There can be conflicts between individuals and organizations as to which values underlie manpower allocation decisions. Basically three strategies are possible, each reflecting different values.

The *vocational guidance* strategy aims toward maximizing the values of the individual in terms of his or her wants or preferences. College students select their own majors based on the careers they wish to pursue. In other words, no college ever states that a student "must" major in a certain area; the decision is strictly an individual one.

The *pure selection* strategy maximizes organizational values. In this case, only the best-qualified people are placed in a job. While the placed people are indeed very good, the method is somewhat impractical. Large numbers of people might not get placed into *any* job because they are not the "best" of the applicants. The method is inherently wasteful because many applicants remain unemployed. Both the vocational guidance and pure selection strategies have weaknesses. While the vocational guidance method may work well in educational institutions, it does not work well in industry. If all the applicants wanted to be the company president, large numbers of jobs would go unfilled.

The *successive selection* strategy is a compromise between the first two extremes. In this method, (1) all jobs are filled by at least minimally qualified people, and (2) given available jobs, people are placed in those that will make the best use of their talents. Successive selection is a good compromise because the jobs get filled (the organization's needs are met) and the individuals get assigned to jobs for which they are suited (the individual's needs are met).

At one time, placement and classification were more important than selection. During World War II, industry needed large numbers of people to produce war material. The question was not whether people would get a job but what kind of job they would fill. A similar situation occurred in the military as thousands of recruits were being inducted every month. It was of paramount importance to get the right people in the right jobs. Today, selection decisions are more numerous (Ghiselli, 1956). While some research continues to be done on classification (for example, Schoenfeldt, 1974), the volume on selection is much greater. However, the rationale behind placement and classification is still the same as before: that certain people will perform better in certain jobs than others. To this end, placement and classification are aimed at assigning people to jobs in which their predicted job performance will be the greatest.

MAJOR CHAPTER OBJECTIVES IN REVIEW

After having read this chapter, you should know:

1. Personnel function of recruitment and associated issues of attracting desirable job candidates.

2. Statistical concept of regression analysis.

3. Value of using multiple predictors and the statistical concept of multiple regression analysis.

4. Factors that contribute to assessing the quality of predictor variables.

5. Four possible selection decisions that result from assessing job applicants.

6. Personnel selection strategies of multiple regression, multiple cutoff, multiple hurdle, and profile matching.

7. Concept and significance of validity generalization.

8. Concept and significance of utility.

9. Personnel functions of placement and classification.

CASE STUDY—Whom Should I Hire?

Todd Costanza intently examined the two personnel folders on his desk. As the credit manager of the company he was faced with replacing two employees who had just left the company from his department. One was for a verifier position, the other was an account executive. A verifier was someone who would verify the accuracy of information presented on a credit application form. Prospective customers seeking an approved line of credit (meaning they wouldn't have to pay cash for all their orders) would fill out an application, and the verifier's job was to ensure the information was accurate. It was an entry clerical position, and most verifiers didn't stay in their jobs for much over two years. Most were either promoted or they quit (after citing boredom as their reason for leaving). The account executive position was a much higher level position. An account executive authorized large amounts of credit, some as high as $50,000 per month. The position entailed staying on top of all accounts, being sure each account paid invoices on time, and regulating the amount of credit each account could handle financially. These positions made or cost the company a great deal of money because the account executive's judgment in appraising accounts was critical to the success of the Credit Department. Accounts that were delinquent or that forfeited their payments were a direct loss to the company. Accounts that weren't extended enough credit to run their business would go to a competitor for a larger line of credit. Either way represented a loss of income for the company. Thus, the account executive walked a fine line between extending the accounts too much or not giving enough credit.

The two folders contained the results of assessments by the Personnel Office of the most-recommended candidates for the two positions. Neither candidate looked very inspiring. Carl Worrell was the best applicant for the verifier's position. However, his test score was only average, and his performance in the interview had been adequate, but nothing more. Cheryl Catrell emerged as the best possible account executive, but she too appeared as a marginal case. Her previous experience was limited, her test scores were acceptable, but her interview was fairly weak. Yet she received a favorable evaluation from her previous employer. Costanza wished there had been better applicants to select from, but these two people represented the best of their respective applicant pools.

After examining the candidates' credentials one last time, Costanza decided to hire Worrell as the verifier. He reasoned the job was not that critical to the success of his department, and it was a high turnover job. While Worrell didn't appear to be a surefire hit, Costanza figured Worrell wouldn't hurt the company too badly if he bombed. However, Catrell seemed to be a different story. Although her respective qualifications were no worse than Worrell's, the consequences of Catrell's failing in the account executive job were far greater than Worrell's potential failure as a verifier. Costanza believed he really had to feel confident about hiring a new account executive, and Catrell didn't inspire that confidence. Therefore, Costanza would elect not to fill the account executive position at this time but would reopen the recruiting process to find a better-qualified applicant.

Costanza knew what awaited him. The Personnel Office would want to know why he decided to hire the male but not the female. It would be particularly concerned because Catrell's respective qualifications were no worse than Worrell's. Costanza was worried about how people would react to his decision. He appeared to be giving the benefit of the doubt to the male but not the female. Costanza saw it as a question of two different jobs, not a male and a female. However, Costanza had been around long enough to know that not everyone saw things the way he did.

Questions

1. To what extent were Costanza's decisions influenced by the more extensive assessment procedure's having been applied to the account executive position?

2. Could you accept Costanza's decision based solely on the difference in importance between the two jobs? Why or why not?

3. What other information would you like to have besides what is presented in the case to address the concerns of the Personnel Office?

4. What are the potential costs and benefits of other decisions besides the two reached by Costanza?

5. In your opinion is the sex of the applicants an important variable in making selection decisions? Why or why not?

6

Personnel Training

Personnel training is somewhat of a paradox. On the one hand, it is an extremely important and popular activity in industry and a $100 billion-a-year expenditure for businesses (Baldwin & Ford, 1988). On the other hand, the training literature has been described as "nonempirical, nontheoretical, poorly written, and dull" (Campbell, 1971, p. 565). I think that personnel training in general lacks the empirical precision found in personnel selection; that is, it is not nearly as well guided by an established array of scientific methodologies and paradigms as some other areas of I/O psychology. This is not a criticism but, rather, an observation that many of the factors that contribute to the scientific rigor in other areas are not as manifest in personnel training. Among these factors are the following:

1. The field of personnel training is dominated by practitioners, most of whom are not psychologists (Hinrichs, 1976), so there is little creative interplay between scientists and practitioners. Without science's steady influx of new ideas, it is not surprising that personnel training is quite static. Training programs are designed and implemented today in almost the same way they were 30 or 40 years ago.

2. Many industrial training programs are born out of an emergency. A company suddenly realizes that a portion of its work force lacks some skill it needs to work effectively. Management then orders the personnel office to develop a training program to correct this problem. Under pressure to "do something," the personnel office may not have the time to analyze the problem carefully and develop an empirical rationale for the training program.

3. Training programs are, and have always been, dominated by fads and fashions. Some techniques are mere gimmicks, some are indeed valuable, but few deliver on all of the sponsor's claims or user's expectations.

4. Despite the extensive amount of training conducted in industry, only a small amount of theory has evolved. One of the benefits of theory is that it permits us to build on our existing knowledge; we need not start at square one with every new

study. Car manufacturers use existing knowledge of combustion, chemical bonding, aerodynamics, and so forth in designing and building cars. We get new styles in cars every year only because the greatest part of a car's structure is carried over from preceding years. But training program designers rarely use such an *incremental* or *additive* strategy; often they do, in fact, begin each time at square one.

5. Finally, personnel training is complex and multifaceted. There are many forces that shape people's behavior. Personnel trainers have to earmark a few of these forces, modify them in some way, and then assess their effects on certain aspects of subsequent behavior. It is not easy to unravel a few strands from a skein, "treat" them, and then determine the effects of the treatment on the total skein. Many factors contribute to success in training. For example, Eden and Shani (1982) reported that just the trainer's expectations for the trainees' performance had a profound impact on training success. The trainer's expectations explained 73% of the variance in trainee performance and 66% in trainee attitude. Note the trainer's expectations have nothing to do with the calibre of the trainees or the specific content of the training programs, two factors that normally account for success in training. While more research would help, the problems in conducting systematic, high-quality research in such a multifaceted area are tremendous. The problems and limitations encountered in personnel training should not be attributed solely to trainers' weaknesses. While as professionals we could do better work in personnel training, many of the problems stem from the inherent complexity of the issues that we must confront.

Training and Learning

In theory, the principles of learning make training work; that is, the factors that contribute to how a person *learns* should be the guiding principles in explaining how a person is *trained*. Such principles as practice, feedback, motivation to learn, and similarity between the learning task and the final task have long been identified as instrumental for learning. But, in fact, training practitioners usually ignore these classic principles in designing training programs. And if they are incorporated, it is not necessarily on some theoretical basis.

Why are these learning principles not formally incorporated into training? As Hinrichs (1976) has said, it's either because (1) the personnel trainer foolishly ignores them, or (2) the principles do not work outside a learning laboratory. Hinrichs feels there is some truth to both of these positions. A common finding is that new behaviors acquired in training do not persist on the job (that is, people resort to their old ways of doing things). Perhaps a more complete study of the factors that contribute to learning persistence will help alleviate this problem. However, it is also true that many learning principles derived in sterile laboratory conditions cannot be generalized to complex field conditions. It is one thing to assess in a laboratory the effects of one variable (for example, practice) when all other variables are controlled for; it is quite another to assess that variable in a field setting in the presence of many other variables. This is a prime example of laboratory and field methods not producing the same conclusions.

Classic learning principles seem to have only marginal relevance for personnel training, but because they are relevant in some situations, they should not be ignored. We will examine these situations and discuss how successful training programs have been enacted.

Training Defined

Training in industry has been defined as "the formal procedures which a company utilizes to facilitate learning so that the resultant behavior contributes to the attainment of the company's goals and objectives" (McGehee & Thayer, 1961, p. 3). This definition has four noteworthy components. By "formal procedures" we mean that training is a systematic and intentional process, not random or haphazard. The "facilitation of learning" is the key psychological principle that accounts for the persistence of activity—that is, it is *learned* skill. "Resultant behavior" means that training is designed to alter *behavior* (directly or indirectly). People should *do* things differently after training. Finally, "the attainment of the company's goals and objectives" refers to why training is conducted in the first place: its purpose is to alter people's behavior in a way that will contribute to organizational effectiveness. Fortunately, in most cases the change in behavior also contributes to the *individual's* effectiveness at work, so people are rarely trained against their will.

Any behavior that has been learned is a *skill.* Within the area of training, the learning process is task oriented; it enhances skills (Hinrichs, 1976). Training, therefore, is directed toward enhancing a specific skill, which in turn enhances a person's proficiency in performing a certain task. For example, students in a driver education class are trained to shift gears, accelerate, brake, and so on to enhance their driving proficiency. Skills become the "target areas" of training, especially personnel training. In industry, training enhances three broad classes of skills. *Motor skills* refer to the manipulation of the physical environment based on certain patterns of bodily movements. *Cognitive skills* relate to the acquisition of mental or attitudinal factors. *Interpersonal skills* refer to enhancing interactions with other people. Though all three types of skills are the object of personnel training, their relative importance depends on the nature of the job. Machine operators need motor skills, managers need cognitive and interpersonal skills.

Relationship to Organizational and Individual Goals

Personnel training should contribute to the goals of both the organization and the individual. Training is a management tool designed to enhance the organization's efficiency. However, in the process of attaining organizational goals, many individual goals can also be attained. McGehee (1979) describes two issues that must be addressed when contemplating a training program.

The first issue involves why the company should provide training—what *specific goals* are to be met as a result. If there are no apparent organizational goals that a training program can influence, there is no reason for the program. McGehee and Thayer (1961) list several specific ways in which training can contribute to organizational goals:

1. Reducing labor costs by decreasing the amount of time it takes to perform the operations involved in producing goods or services; also, reducing the time needed to bring the inexperienced employee to an acceptable level of job proficiency.

2. Reducing the costs of materials and supplies by reducing losses due to excess waste and the production of defective products.

3. Reducing the costs of managing personnel activities as reflected in turnover, absenteeism, accidents, grievances, and complaints.

4. Reducing the costs of efficiently servicing customers by improving the flow of goods or services from the company to the consumer.

The second issue raised by McGehee is one of cost effectiveness. *Cost effectiveness* refers to the amount of money spent to attain organizational goals versus that spent on other activities in pursuit of those same goals. A cost-effective program permits the attainment of organizational goals within a "reasonable" budget. Within the area of personnel training, an organization has to decide if the goal of increased productivity could most economically be reached by training employees to be more productive, by redesigning the task so that it is easier to perform, or by automating it. (This issue will be discussed in more detail later in this chapter.)

Obviously, employees must get some benefit from training or they would not participate. The first benefit is that training provides an adequate opportunity to learn the job's duties and responsibilities. A structured approach is always preferable to a haphazard one. Adequate training gives the employee a chance to be successful at work and helps him or her avoid the psychological problems of failure or incompetence (or outright dismissal). However, research by Noe (1986) and Noe and Schmitt (1986) underscores the importance of trainee attitudes toward training. If employees do not understand why and how their strengths and weaknesses were diagnosed or doubt the accuracy of the information, they likely will be resistant to change. As a result, motivation to learn in the training program will be low, less learning will occur, and evaluation of the training will find fewer effects than expected.

A second benefit involves pay. Employees paid on a piece-rate system (that is, X amount per object produced) can earn more if they are well trained. This benefit, though less obvious, still holds for hourly or salaried personnel. Merit pay increases are more likely for people who know their work (as a result of training).

Finally, trained employees are more marketable for higher-level jobs. Promotions are usually given to those who perform their current jobs the best. People can also become more marketable for other employers by enhancing their skills through training. Many organizations try to keep training "company specific" so they will not be training people for their competitors. (Some years ago, one company developed such an excellent management training program that other companies "raided" it for their own managerial talent. To reduce the turnover of young managers, the program had to be made more specific to the company.)

Stating Training Objectives in Behavioral Terms

Training objectives should always be expressed in behavioral terms, though it is not always easy to do so. If training objectives are stated in vague and general terms, two problems ensue. First, the objective or goal of the training may be ill defined; neither the trainers nor the participants fully understand what they are trying to accomplish. Second, assessing training effectiveness depends on the extent to which the *criteria* of effectiveness have been met. If the criteria are "fuzzy," the assessment will be ambiguous. As in personnel selection, success depends on a clear and comprehensive understanding of criteria. The success of any training program is a function of the degree to which it has enhanced employee performance on job-related criteria.

The following pairs of training objectives are stated first in vague terms and next in behavioral terms.

1. To have more productive workers.
   To increase output by 10% over current levels of production.

2. To get more employees to show up for work.
   To decrease the amount of employee absenteeism to less than 5% for the total work force.

3. To give our managers a better understanding of financial matters.
   To enable our managers to complete a profit-and-loss report independently.

The behaviorally specified objectives are far more precise. Furthermore, they are not just another way of stating the more general objective. There could be *many* ways, for example, to increase a manager's knowledge of financial matters. Completing a profit-and-loss report is one way; developing a long-range budget proposal is another.

Behaviorally specified objectives represent *training outcomes.* By using behavioral terms, differences in opinion about the overall goal of training can be identified and ironed out. Admittedly, some training results are more difficult to specify behaviorally than others. Some managers participate in training designed to enhance their understanding of the problems of black and female employees—growing components of the work force. How do you translate "enhance the understanding" into more concrete behavioral terms? Training programs designed to enhance sensitivity and awareness are not nearly as grounded in their objectives. One way to operationalize such an objective might be "to decrease the number of voluntary resignations of Blacks and females due to their perceived inability to fit into a predominately White male work force."

Deterrents to Effective Training

Several factors can block the effectiveness of training (McGehee & Thayer, 1961), and management must make a conscious effort to minimize their effect. First, training must be viewed as a means to an end rather than an end in itself. McGehee (1979) describes a hypothetical company vice president who is asked why his company has a training department. His answer is, "Of course, to train employees." But, when asked why his company has a research and development department, his answer deals with the need to keep up with competition, to develop better and more attractive products, and so forth. Yet, both departments have the same general goal—to improve corporate efficiency—though each does it in its own way. The training department does it by enhancing employees' skills; R&D does it by creating new products. Not until company executives view training as they do any other function (as a means to increased effectiveness), will it be considered more than a necessary nuisance.

Second, management must be responsible for training. Employees learn in many ways. They learn something about their work (work flow, operating procedures, and the like) simply by being on the job. They pick up this information just by watching or asking a few questions. The effectiveness of this kind of learning can be contrasted with the more formal and structured approach a personnel training program would provide. The opposite of formal training is not the complete absence of training but, rather, the acquisition of skills on an unstructured basis. While not all companies have formal training, all employees do indeed learn on the job. The question is, would they learn better, more, faster, and sooner as a result of a formal training program? If the answer is yes (as it invariably is), management must develop and staff such a program.

Third, management must have the knowledge and skill to develop and implement personnel training. If it does not, it should hire trainers who do. Training is a profession, and the trainer is an authority. Personnel training should not be turned over to someone who flunked out of the accounting department. Training is not something that just anyone can do.

Last, the general climate of an organization should be one that favors (that is, recognizes the benefits of) personnel training. Employees will be reluctant to participate in a training program if more productive employees (1) are not paid more, and (2) have no opportunity for advancement. If poor performers are treated the same in all respects as good performers (including job retention), the results of training will seem to count for nothing. In short, management must structure the organization so that personnel training will have some meaning for employees.

Out of these four deterrents to training effectiveness a consistent theme emerges: the role of management. Training is a management tool. Management can make personnel training a viable corporate activity, but through benign neglect, it can also relegate personnel training to the back burner of the organization's priorities. One key to an organization's success is the quality of its employees. Personnel training can enhance that quality. To a large extent, the attitudes and actions of management determine the success of any training program.

The Design of Personnel Training

The entire personnel training process is predicated on a rational, cyclical design (see Figure 6–1). It consists of seven steps or stages (Parker, 1976). The design of personnel training begins with an analysis of training needs and culminates in the assessment of training results. Important steps in between involve developing objectives, choosing methods, and designing an evaluation. Training directors must keep up with the current literature on training methods because previous successes or failures can help shape the selection or design of a training program. It is equally important to determine a means of evaluating the program before it is implemented; that is,

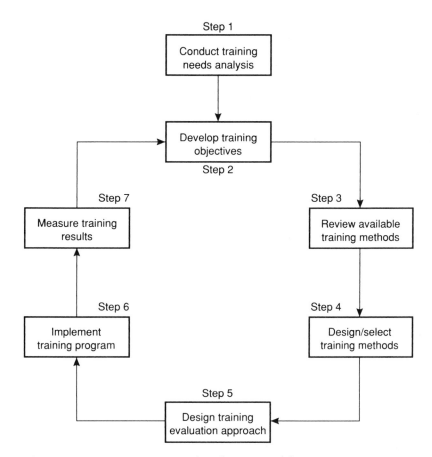

Figure 6–1 Training Design and Evaluation Model

SOURCE: Adapted from T. C. Parker, "Statistical Methods for Measuring Training Results," in *Training and Development Handbook,* 2nd ed., ed. R. L. Craig (New York: McGraw-Hill, 1976). Copyright ©1976. Used by permission.

evaluative criteria must be selected to serve as the program's scorecard. The bulk of this chapter will discuss the major steps in the design of personnel training.

Assessing Training Needs

If an organization uses training to achieve its goals, it must first assess its training needs. Which goals can it attain through personnel training? Which people need training, and for what purpose? Finally, what will the training cover? Goldstein (1980a) believes that assessing training needs is far more important than choosing particular training techniques (though trainers seem to have more interest in the latter). Assessing training needs usually involves a three-step process (McGehee & Thayer, 1961):

1. *Organization analysis*—determining where training emphasis can and should be placed within the organization.

2. *Operations analysis*—determining the content of training in terms of what an employee must do to perform a task, job, or assignment effectively.

3. *Person analysis*—determining what skills, knowledges, or attitudes an employee must develop to perform the tasks involved in his or her job.

Organization Analysis

Organization analysis is the study of an entire organization: its objectives, resources, and the ways in which it allocates resources to attain its goals. At this level of analysis, we are not concerned with people's specific training needs; that function is addressed in operations and person analysis. Rather, we are concerned here with the global problems confronting the organization, which training may in some way help resolve.

Organization analysis can take several forms. One form is that of a personnel audit for manpower planning. A *personnel audit* is an inventory of the personnel assets of an organization and a projection of the kinds and numbers of employees that will be required in the future. Figure 6–2 shows a personnel audit for one division of a company.

Information is usually collected by job and includes demographic data regarding age and turnover rates. A personnel audit might show that many of a company's managers are in their late 50s and 60s. To this information is added the fact that most managers retire by 65, plus there are a certain number of deaths, resignations, and early retirements each year. So in five to seven years, many new managers will be needed. Based on these projections, the company decides to train current supervisors to fill these future positions. Such a personnel audit shows an organizational need and provides enough lead time for the company to plan a rational and orderly solution (see Field Note 1).

These kinds of analyses are routine in large organizations and are the basis for

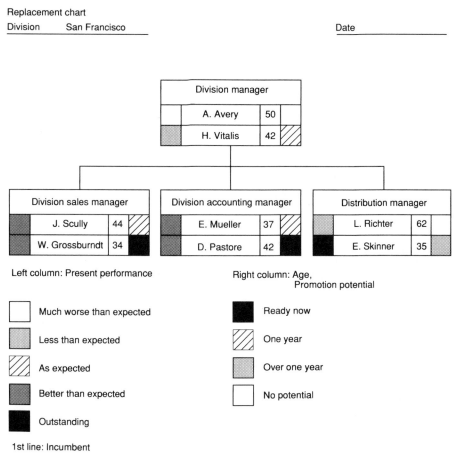

Replacement chart
Division   San Francisco   Date

Left column: Present performance   Right column: Age,
                                                              Promotion potential

Much worse than expected   Ready now

Less than expected   One year

As expected   Over one year

Better than expected   No potential

Outstanding

1st line: Incumbent
2nd line: Replacement

Figure 6–2 Organization Analysis Personnel Replacement Chart
SOURCE: Adapted from J. H. Morrison, "Determining Training Needs," in *Training and Development Handbook*, 2nd ed., ed. R. L. Craig (New York: McGraw-Hill, 1976). Copyright ©1976. Used by permission.

many staffing decisions. However, organization analysis does not necessarily lead to a personnel training decision. New managers could be hired rather than promoted from the supervisors' ranks. Again, training is but one way to meet organizational goals—in this case, the goal of staffing the organization with capable people.[1]

---

[1] Some research has involved combining both the personnel selection and training approaches to organizational staffing problems. Robertson and Downs (1979), for example, have described the development of *trainability testing*—the concept of selecting people into the organization on the basis of their ability to be trained to meet certain job requirements. Traditional personnel selection is usually based on the applicant already being competent to perform the job, while traditional personnel training often assumes no prior competence. Trainability testing is a cross between these two approaches. It assumes that those people who will succeed in training can be rationally selected with a test.

Field Note 1

Personnel audits can be very helpful in planning for the future. One organizational client of mine is a very traditional and conservative company in the financial industry. It has been in existence for over 100 years, and the secret for getting ahead in the company has remained unchanged: be patient. The company promotes people slowly but continually. By the time you are between 50 and 55, you most likely will become a senior officer. You will remain there until age 65 to 70, at which time you retire, and some other 50-to-55-year-old person will take your place. This succession strategy had been effective for many years. There was a continuous supply of new officer material to replace those who retired. Nobody jumped ranks, and if you were good and patient, it would just be a matter of time until you got your promotion.

But then some problems began to emerge. The young junior managers in the 25-to-35 age group were not as patient as their predecessors. They wanted more challenge and a much faster track to the top. They were not willing to wait 20 to 30 years to become a senior officer. Because the company had no intention of moving them along any faster than it had always made its promotions, the young managers began to quit. They joined other companies that had more rapid career paths. A personnel audit I conducted revealed a big gap in the company's personnel. It had young people in the 25-to-35 age group and people 50 to 65, but relatively few people in between. The company realized it had a problem, but as of yet it has not agreed on a solution. It dislikes the idea of having 35-year-old senior officers; it does not want to bring in senior officers from outside the company; and it is reluctant to accelerate the career advancement process. It thinks it would be unfair to all the people who did patiently "wait their turn" and did not quit. The personnel audit identified the problem and its scope. It did not, however, provide built-in solutions to the problems it identified.

A second approach to organization analysis involves indicators of organizational effectiveness. These are examined to see if training could improve the company's performance. Most companies measure effectiveness through a variety of indicators, including labor costs, accidents, turnover, absenteeism, and quality of products or services. These indicators are not recorded just to identify training needs. Indeed, training alone may not be able to alter the company's status on a given indicator. But training may be one means to the end, and indicators do provide target objectives. For example, due to the rising costs of raw materials, the dollar value of scrap and waste is threatening to reach a critical level. Management thus decides that something has to be done to reduce the amount of material waste. One approach might be a training program to teach employees to be more careful. Another approach might be to redesign the work (that is, with new equipment or a different production process). So the goal of reducing scrap might be met by either personnel training or work redesign.

Note that in both examples of organization analysis, the level of analysis is quite general. The analysis revealed problems (material scrap) or potential problems (personnel planning). These are not once-in-a-lifetime activities in the organization but activities that are performed on an ongoing basis. In a general sense, an organization analysis is an attempt to take the pulse of an entire organization. If the organization is "ill" in some regard, personnel training may be one type of remedy.

Operations Analysis

Operations analysis examines the task or job requirements regardless of the person holding the job. It determines what an employee must do to perform the job properly. Operations analysis is most directly concerned with what training should cover. As Goldstein (1974) has observed, machinists do not choose their tools before they have examined their job; builders do not order materials or plan schedules until they have blueprints. So why do trainers argue over training techniques without specifying what the techniques are supposed to accomplish? Operations analysis should identify their purposes.

Operations analysis is the orderly and systematic collection of data about an existing or potential task or a cluster of tasks that define a job (McGehee & Thayer, 1961). Its goal is to identify what an employee must be taught in order to perform the task or job. An operations analysis results in the following information:

1. The standards of performance for the task or job.

2. The identification of what tasks constitute a job.

3. Determination of how these tasks are to be performed.

4. Determination of the behavior required of an employee in order to perform the tasks.

Standards of Performance. Standards of performance are statements regarding work output. They are usually given in units of output of a specific quality in a specified amount of time. Management normally decides what level of performance constitutes a standard. So standards of performance are the measures that define job success. For example, typing 60 words per minute and selling $1 million's worth of products per year might be the standard of performance for a typist and salesperson, respectively. These company-set values represent the level of job performance considered acceptable or standard. In some automated tasks, the standard of performance is determined by the machine. An example is an auto assembly line, on which a new car passes by a worker every few minutes. Without standards of performance, we would not know whether training is successful, that is, whether it raises an employee's performance to an "acceptable" level.

Identification of Tasks. To train an employee for a job, we must know what tasks are involved. We also need to know the relationship between these tasks and the job's standard of performance; that is, some tasks may be more closely related to overall job success than others. An operations analysis lists each task and then indicates its significance to total job performance. For example, a secretary's tasks might include typing, filing, shorthand, and answering the phone. These tasks, in turn, can be broken down into more refined units (setting margins, centering the paper, and so on). Tasks can be identified through established job- and task-analysis procedures. These involve observing incumbents perform a job, asking them questions about their work duties, and perhaps recording job activities in some systematic way. The tasks are then related to overall performance by assessing the proportionate amount of time devoted to each, the importance of each to the job, and so forth.

How Each Task Is to Be Performed. The previous stage identified *what* is done; this stage identifies *how* it is done. Time-and-motion studies are often used to determine the "best way" to perform a task. Time-and-motion studies examine the amount of time it takes to perform a certain body motion and relate that activity to job performance. For example, one worker's job on an assembly line is to bolt a bumper to a car. If the worker drops a bolt on the floor while performing this task, should she or he pick it up or grab a new one? A time-and-motion study might show that it is more efficient to grab a new bolt rather than to scurry around looking for the dropped one. Thus, the "best" method is determined by efficiency criteria.

Typing is one task in a secretary's job. But the amount of typing to be done, speed of work, importance of neatness, and so on determine whether a word processor or electric typewriter should be used. A secretary who does little typing needs only an electric typewriter. For a secretarial job involving heavy typing, a word processor might be better; that is, it would help in meeting the job's standards of performance.

Yet in other situations, workers have some latitude in developing their own methods for performing tasks. My work style is a case in point. Part of my job is to compose many letters. Part of my secretary's job is to type the letters. I prefer to write out the letters, and my secretary prefers to type from a rough draft. We have developed a work method that is mutually satisfactory and efficient. Other secretary/boss teams may use a different method. The point is that while the task (letter composing) is a fixed part of my job, the method used to produce the finished product (a typed letter) was determined by mutual preference. As long as I am proficient in my task (letter composing) and my secretary is proficient in hers (letter typing), we will continue to use this method. If we were inefficient in these tasks, it would be better for both of us to be trained to use a new work method.

Employee Behavior. The final stage of operations analysis is identifying the skills, knowledge, and attitudes that must be possessed or developed on the job. The nature of the job determines the amount of these elements. Suppose a company produces 80-pound bags of cement. If manual laborers are needed to load the cement onto trucks and freight cars, the company will have to select people who have the physical skill (that is, strength) to lift 80 pounds or train them to develop it. A secretarial job may entail a great deal of typing and speed demands of 100 words per minute. A person who could not type this fast would have to be trained to meet the standards of performance for that job. For jobs in which the skill, knowledge, or attitude levels are constant, people must be trained to reach these performance levels. For jobs where the skill, knowledge, or attitude levels are increasing, the problem is more complex. In some areas like computer science, rapidly changing technology demands increasing levels of skill. So incumbents must be continually trained to keep up with the demands of the job. A similar problem occurs in medicine, where new procedures are being developed all the time. People in this field need constant retraining or updating.

Person Analysis

The final step, *person analysis,* is directed toward learning (1) whether the individual employee needs training, and (2) what training he or she needs. It is focused directly on the individual employee. Person analysis is concerned first with ascertaining how well a specific employee is carrying out his or her other tasks. It is concerned second with determining what skills must be developed, what knowledge acquired, and what attitudes cultivated if the employee is to improve his or her job performance (McGehee & Thayer, 1961).

A large portion of person analysis involves *diagnosis.* We want to know not only how well people are performing but *why* they are performing at that level. We try to determine whether poor performance on a task is the result of insufficient skill or knowledge or of situational factors beyond the person's control. It is not easy to conduct a person analysis. The first part involves appraising an employee's performance. (Specific techniques are discussed in the next chapter.) Suffice it to say that performance appraisal can sometimes be imprecise. If a person's performance is judged to be uniformly positive, there is probably little need for "corrective" training. But, if the performance is deficient in some way, the next step is to diagnose *why.*

Information about an employee's current level of performance is usually collected by traditional performance appraisal techniques. These involve both subjective evaluations and objective records. Supervisors may judge an employee's interpersonal skills, written communication skills, various types of job knowledges, and so on. Figure 6–3 shows a person analysis based on a supervisor's evaluation (Morrison, 1976).

Objective records also supply information about an employee's performance (words typed per minute, units produced per hour, or sales made per month). These figures are then compared to the job's standards of performance, and any deficiencies are targets for improvement. But not all deficiencies in performance are due to deficiencies in skill, knowledge, or attitude. For example, substandard performance may be caused by using broken or antiquated tools or machinery. In this case, replacing worn-out equipment is a better solution than training.

Diagnostic achievement tests are another approach to person analysis. These tests determine whether the employee has the knowledge necessary to perform the assigned tasks. In many industrial jobs, an employee must know certain facts. A secretary has to know grammar and punctuation; a design engineer has to know the

TRAINING NEEDS ANALYSIS

EXPLANATION:

S = Outstanding Strength
M = Meets Requirements or
      Not Applicable to Job
D = Development Need

SUPERVISOR: Discusses strengths and weaknesses with subordinate during post-appraisal interview.
INCUMBENT: Discusses needs and goals with supervisor during post-appraisal interview.

	Management Activity	S	M	D
Planning	Promoting improvements			
	Developing original ideas			
	Applying new ideas			
	Gathering information			
	Analyzing information			
	Planning objectives			
Organizing	Organizing ability			
	Selecting people			
	Utilizing people			
	Delegation			
Directing and Coordinating	Coaching			
	Training and developing people			
	Oral expression			
	Conducting meetings			
	Written expression			
	Keeping supervisor informed			
	Keeping subordinates informed			
	Achieving results through others			
	Personal acceptance by others			
	Setting standards for others			
Controlling	Maintaining control of operations			
	Willingness to follow up			
	Measuring results of operation			
	Control of costs			
	Control of quality			
	Expanding income			
	Improving net earnings			

Signed: _____ Date: _____
Incumbent

Figure 6–3   Person Analysis Evaluation Form

SOURCE: J. H. Morrison, "Determining Training Needs," in
Training Development Handbook, 2nd ed., R. L. Craig (New
York: McGraw-Hill, 1976). Copyright©1976. Used by permission.

principles of physical stress. An achievement test can help determine if a poorly performing employee needs more job knowledge. Furthermore, a worker's wrong answers pinpoint areas for training. If an employee does well on such a test but still performs poorly on the job, the problem may be in attitude, motivation, or situational (job) factors.

When job success involves "doing" as well as "knowing," paper-and-pencil tests tell only part of the story. Having a thorough knowledge of traffic laws doesn't necessarily make a good driver. Performance tests, however, can assess an employee's motor skills in performing a certain task. They are most frequently used for carpenters, electricians, welders, plumbers, and those in other skilled trades. Both skills and knowledge are measured in performance tests, making them a valuable diagnostic tool. A person who passes a job knowledge test but fails a performance test needs training in "how to do it" (motor skills) not in "what to do" (cognitive skills).

In general, person analysis is based more on assessing actual job performance than on achievement tests. Almost all employees get evaluated, either formally or informally. This, then, is a convenient basis on which to start a person analysis to determine individual training needs. Companies that have developed diagnostic achievement tests can supplement them with performance appraisal. Both methods are designed to assess the training needs of the individual employee.

In summary, assessing training needs is a three-part process. Organization analysis identifies company-wide goals, objectives, and problems. Operations analysis is concerned with the operations performed in a job: standards of operating performance, identification of tasks, and understanding of the methods and human attributes needed to perform them. Finally, person analysis focuses on individual training needs.

Each phase involves a different level of analysis: the company as a whole, the work to be performed in jobs, and the needs of individuals. Assessing training needs has been described as "a grimy business, frustrating, and often carried on under increasing pressure to get something, just anything, going" (McGehee & Thayer, 1961, p. 25). However, it is vitally important for a training program's success. Moore and Dutton (1978) suggest that training-needs analysis should be an ongoing process within the organization. Without such an assessment, training is conducted without any clear reason, continues with no purpose, and ends with no clear-cut results.

Methods and Techniques of Training

After determining an organization's training needs and translating them into objectives, the next step is to design a training program to meet these objectives. This isn't an easy task because each training method has its strengths, weaknesses, and costs. Ideally, we seek the "best" method: the one that meets our objectives in a cost-efficient manner. There are many training methods available. They can be classified in a number of ways, though probably the best way is according to *where* the training takes place.

On-Site Training Methods

As the name suggests, *on-site* methods are conducted on the job site. On-site methods usually involve training in the total job, whereas off-site instruction often involves only part of the job (Bass & Barrett, 1981).

On-the-Job Training. On-the-job training is perhaps the oldest and most common form of instruction. Usually no special equipment or space is needed since new employees are trained at the actual job location. The instructors are usually more established workers, and the employees learn by imitation. They watch an established worker perform a task and try to imitate the behavior. One of the classic principles of training—transfer of training—is maximized by this method. *Transfer of training* refers to the extent to which the skills learned in training can be effectively transferred to the job. Since the training content and location are the same as the job content, there are usually few problems with transfer.

But on-the-job training has several limitations. It is often brief and poorly structured—often little more than "Watch me, kid, and I'll show you how to do it." Also many established workers find teaching a new recruit to be a nuisance, and the new employee may be pressured to master the task too quickly. On-the-job training is popular partly because it is so easy to administer. But since many new recruits make mistakes while training, the consequences of error must be evaluated. On-the-job training obviously is far more feasible for custodians than for brain surgeons.

Vestibule Training. Vestibule training is a type of instruction often found in production work. A *vestibule* consists of training equipment that is set up a short distance from the actual production line. Trainees can practice in the vestibule without getting in the way or slowing down the production line. These special training areas are usually used for skilled and semiskilled jobs, particularly those involving technical equipment. One limitation is that the vestibule is small, so relatively few people can be trained at the same time. The method is good for promoting *practice,* a learning principle involving the repetition of behavior.

Lefkowitz (1970) describes a study comparing vestibule training with on-the-job training for a sample of sewing machine operators. New employees were divided into four groups. The first three groups received one, two, and three days of vestibule

training, respectively. The fourth group spent the first day in vestibule training, the second day in on-the-job training, and the third day back in vestibule training before actually starting work. Results showed that the longer the people were in vestibule training, the less likely they were to quit. But their average productivity was also slightly lower. The best overall results occurred for the people in the fourth group; their productivity was at or above the other groups, and they had a relatively low quit rate. Lefkowitz concluded that a combination of the two methods was the most effective way to train sewing machine operators.

Job Rotation.   Job rotation is a method of training wherein workers rotate through a variety of jobs. They may be in the same job anywhere from a week to a year before they rotate. Job rotation is used with both blue-collar production workers and white-collar managers, and it has many organizational benefits. It acquaints workers with many jobs in a company and gives them the opportunity to learn by doing. Job rotation creates flexibility; during worker shortages, workers have the skills to step in and fill open slots. The method also provides new and different work on a systematic basis, giving employees a variety of experiences and challenges. Employees also increase their flexibility and marketability because they can perform a wide array of tasks.

Like any method, job rotation also has its limitations. If workers are paid on a piece-rate or commission basis, they can earn more money on some jobs rather than others; that is, due to individual differences, people are not equally suited for all jobs. Workers are then reluctant to rotate out of their "best" job. Another problem is that the method weakens a worker's commitment to a given job (though it may increase loyalty to the company as a whole). Job rotation also challenges one of the basic principles of personnel placement: that workers be assigned to jobs that best match their talents and interests. Some employees are wary of a training system that puts them in jobs they are not good at or do not like. Workers' willingness to learn new jobs is a key factor in the success of a job rotation system.

Apprentice Training.   The apprentice system is one of the oldest types of training programs in existence. It is particularly common in the skilled trades. A new worker is "tutored" by an established worker for a long period of time (sometimes up to five years). The apprentice serves as an assistant and learns the craft by working with a fully skilled member of the trade called a *journeyman*. Apprenticeship programs are often used in the plumbing, carpentry, and electrical trades. At the end of the apprenticeship program, the person is "promoted" to journeyman. Training is intense, lengthy, and usually on a one-to-one basis. Usually one apprentice is assigned to one journeyman.

A weakness of the method is that the amount of time an apprenticeship lasts is predetermined by the members of the trade. Individual differences in learning time are generally not allowed, so *all* apprentices have to work for a fixed time before they are upgraded. It has been argued that the apprentice program should be modified to allow more rapid rates of progression for fast learners (Franklin, 1976).

Off-Site Training Methods

There is more diversity in *off-site* training methods than on-site methods. In addition, they differ markedly in their content and approach to learning.

Lectures.   As all students know, the lecture method is a popular form of instruction in educational institutions. It is also used in industry. With the lecture method, large numbers of people can be taught at the same time. In that sense, it is quite cost efficient. However, the more diversified the audience, the more general the content usually becomes. Hence, its utility for imparting specialized knowledge is more limited. A frequent reaction after a lecture on improving sales techniques is; "That idea sounds okay in principle, but how do I put it into operation in my company?" With a more homogeneous audience, a trainer (or teacher) can direct the lecture to specific topics and techniques, which are often more beneficial than using some broad-based material. Lectures are an effective way to train large numbers of people at once, particularly if they have a specific training need.

On the negative side, lectures are usually one-way communication. There is little chance of dialogue, questions, or discussions of individual problems and special interests. Trainees themselves have to understand and personalize the content of the lecture. The lecture method is weak in such classic training principles as practice, feedback, and transfer (Bass & Vaughan, 1966). While popular, it is not the best method to use for skill acquisition.

Audio-Visual Material.   Audio-visual material covers an array of training techniques, such as films, slides, and videotapes. It allows participants to see as well as hear, and is usually quite good at capturing their interest. This underscores the importance of motivation and interest as necessary conditions for learning. After the initial expense of creating such a program, the cost of repeated use is usually minimal. Audio-visual material is particularly useful in training people in a work process or sequence. People can more readily trace the pattern of work flow when it is laid out graphically. Konz and Dickey (1969) demonstrated that a slide presentation was superior to verbal and printed instructions in training employees to complete various assembly operations.

On the negative side, it is difficult to modify these training methods. If the training content changes, a whole new film has to be made. Slide presentations are more modifiable since the outdated slides can be replaced with more current ones. The production cost of training films can be quite substantial. A half-hour, color film with a sound track can cost $75,000 to produce. However, the costs are worth it if the task or job is very important to the company. With the aid of close-up images, stop action, slow motion, and instant replay, delicate and complex tasks can be broken down into discrete and understandable units.

Videotape is particularly useful in recording employees' job behaviors. Their performance can be taped and then observed and evaluated for effective and ineffective behaviors. The method is excellent for providing feedback. Feedback is a means to let people know how they are doing, and many studies (for example, Ilgen, Fisher,

& Taylor, 1979) suggest that it is an important part of the learning process. Kidd (1961) showed that videotape instruction was useful for training people as diplomatic advisors overseas. They learned more effectively and retained more than people who only read a training manual on the same material. Seeing yourself on videotape can also be a most enlightening (and unnerving) experience. The first time I saw a videotape of one of my lectures, my reaction was "I look like *that*?" I quickly saw my weaknesses as a teacher. With new electronic recording equipment, the use of videotape as a training technique will probably increase in the future.

Conferences.   The conference method of training stresses two-way communication. It is particularly effective if the ratio of trainees to trainers is not very large. This method is useful when the material needs clarification or elaboration or where a lively discussion would facilitate understanding. Sometimes the lecture method can be followed up with a conference discussion, giving the participants a chance to share opinions about the material (Bass & Barrett, 1981). The trainer can call on people to see if they understand the material, and participants can ask questions. An effective trainer can get all the participants involved, even the less-vocal ones. The success of this method depends heavily on the skills and personality of the discussion leader. A dogmatic, abrasive leader can stifle discussion. A good leader knows when to lead the discussion and when to allow others to lead.

The conference method can draw on the learning principles of motivation and feedback. Stimulated participants readily join in the discussion and then receive feedback on their ideas from others in the group. The conference method is used to enhance knowledge or attitudinal development. The willingness of the participants to acquire new knowledge and explore attitude change (and the trainer's ability to facilitate such learning) influences the success of the conference method. Perhaps because this method does not usually involve any tangible assets other than people, the attitudes, enthusiasm, and verbal communication skills of the participants affect the outcome more than for any other training method.

Programmed Instruction.   Programmed instruction (PI) is a newer method of training, but its origin goes back to the research of learning theorist B. F. Skinner. The method of PI may involve an actual piece of equipment (usually called a teaching machine) or a specially constructed paper booklet. In either case, the method has three main characteristics. First, the participants are active in the training process. In fact, they determine their own learning pace. Second, what is to be learned involves many discrete pieces of material, and the participants get immediate feedback on whether they have learned each piece. Third, the material is divided into an organized sequence.

It takes a lot of time to develop material for PI. Each segment has to facilitate understanding of the total material covered. Thus, the sequence of material is highly integrated. It is verified to ensure that each piece contributes to understanding and that the entire process covers a unified theme.

Bass and Barrett (1981) describe the common features of PI:

1. A single piece of information is presented at each stage, or *frame*. All of the frames taken together (however many it takes to present the material) are called a program. The first frame deals with the first step in some procedure; in industrial training, this is usually a work procedure (like operating a piece of equipment). The frames may involve only one question, or they may involve examining some information given in a figure or diagram. A question is then asked about the diagram. The answer is either true/false or multiple choice.

2. The participant gives an answer to the question in the first frame. If the answer is correct, the participant proceeds to the next frame (by turning a knob on the teaching machine or turning the page in a booklet). If the answer is incorrect, the right answer is given along with an explanation of why it is correct.

3. The frames are arranged in the exact sequence that occur in the work process. This step-by-step sequence in learning matches the step-by-step sequence followed in performing the task on the job.

4. The participant goes through the program at his or her own pace. Emphasis is placed on correct answers rather than work speed. Some people learn best at a slow pace; others can learn more rapidly.

5. The participant proceeds through the entire program. After completing it, the number of correct answers is tabulated (either automatically on the machine or by hand with the booklet). A criterion of mastery has been set prior to training, usually 90% or 95% correct. If the participant reaches that level, training on that program is ended for that participant. If the percentage of correct answers falls below the criterion, the participant repeats the program.

Figure 6–4 shows a sample frame from a PI program designed to train workers on the proper way to lift heavy boxes. While PI has been used in industry, it is also used for schoolchildren.

There are many advantages to PI as a training method. Participants get immediate feedback. Because the material is presented in a precise and systematic manner, there are no gaps in the presentation. The participants are active learners; there is a constant exchange of information between themselves and program. When participants make mistakes, they suffer no embarrassment, because they are the only ones who know they erred. Fast learners do not have to wait for slow ones to catch up; slow learners do not always have to try to catch up. Finally, PI is an efficient way to train people on material that is structured and rote. It gives a trainer more time to cover unstructured and ambiguous material with a different method (usually the conference).

On the negative side, developing a PI program is time consuming. The material has to be broken down into a logical sequence. Each frame has to be checked to be sure that it is accurate and contributes to overall learning of the material. Some work procedures are hard to break down into an exact sequence since there may be several correct ways to perform the task. Also, the stability or consistency of a structured task must be considered before developing a PI program. A PI has its place in a

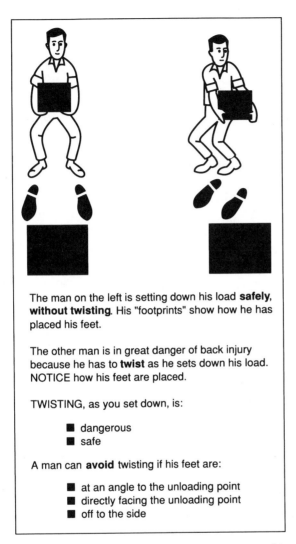

The man on the left is setting down his load **safely**, **without twisting**. His "footprints" show how he has placed his feet.

The other man is in great danger of back injury because he has to **twist** as he sets down his load. NOTICE how his feet are placed.

TWISTING, as you set down, is:

- dangerous
- safe

A man can **avoid** twisting if his feet are:

- at an angle to the unloading point
- directly facing the unloading point
- off to the side

Figure 6—4   Sample Problem from a Programmed Instruction Safety Program

SOURCE: *A New Approach to Management's Role in Back Safety* (Hicksville, N.Y.: Advanced Learning Systems, 1966).

rapidly changing technological area, but it is not a panacea for all training needs (Brethower, 1976).

Even with its limitations, PI has been a great asset to industrial training. Welsh, Antoinetti, and Thayer (1965) described the development of a 625-frame PI program designed to teach salespeople the fundamentals of selling life insurance. The authors reported that the PI method was as effective (but no more so) than more conventional training methods, but its major benefit was the amount of time (and thus money) it saved industrial trainers. Another example of the PI method was reported by Hughes and McNamara (1961). In this study, a company compared the PI and lecture methods of training people to operate large, high-speed computers. Forty-two employees were trained with the classroom method, 70 employees were trained with PI. The results of the study showed that training time with PI was 11 hours compared to 15 hours for the other method. The 90% criterion of mastery was attained by 89% of the employees trained with PI compared to only 45% of the employees who learned in the classroom. Almost all the employees who had PI training reported that it was an exciting way to learn, and most wanted it to be a part of future training programs. Additionally, the initial cost of developing the PI material constituted almost all the cost involved.

Nash, Muczyk, and Vettori (1971) conducted a survey of industrial training programs in which PI was rated "practically superior" (defined as a 10% improvement in results over conventional training methods). Three criteria of training effectiveness were assessed: training time, immediate learning, and retention. The results are shown in Figure 6–5. On the basis of this study, it appears that PI does not enhance retention or immediate learning. Its primary advantage is training time. It takes less time to train employees with PI, which reduces costs and allows the trainers time for other methods.

Computer-Assisted Instruction. The most recently developed training method is computer-assisted instruction (CAI). It is a logical extension of PI and shares many of its benefits. But it has many more limitations, and because the method is so new, we do not know as much about it as the more-established methods. CAI was born

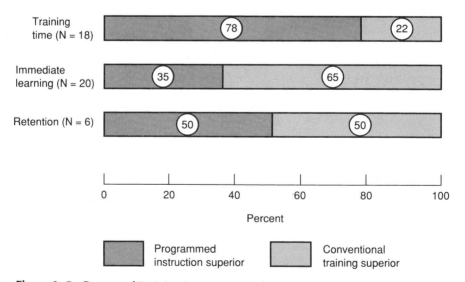

Figure 6–5 Percent of Training Programs in Industry in Which Programmed Instruction Was Rated Practically Superior to Conventional Training Methods on Three Training Criteria.

SOURCE: A. N. Nash, J. P. Muczyk, and F. L. Vettori, "The Relative Practical Effectiveness of Programmed Instruction," *Personnel Psychology*, 24 (1971), pp. 397–418.

with the advent of large, complex computers. The computer is the trainer and is programmed to teach a particular skill. As in PI, the task is broken down into its component parts. Questions are then asked about the material being covered. However, a major difference between CAI and PI is that computers can be programmed to ask questions of varying levels of difficulty. Furthermore, the computer can be programmed to "ask" why a person gave a wrong answer—for example, whether it was because he or she did not know the meaning of a term, thought the term meant something else, knew the term but did not know how to apply it, and so on. CAI is a sophisticated approach. It can teach a wide range of skills, ranging from how to speak a foreign language to how to fly a helicopter.

CAI works as follows. The trainee sits at a console, usually a video screen along with a keyboard. Both parts are connected to a computer programmed with the training material. The person communicates to the computer through the keyboard; the computer flashes its messages on the screen to the person. Questions and related information are displayed on the screen, and the person has to answer by pushing certain keys on the keyboard. One CAI program begins by flashing the words "Good Morning" on the screen. If the person fails to press a key that says "Good Morning" back to the computer in five seconds, the computer flashes a second message: "What's the matter—kind of grumpy today?" All this has been arranged (that is, programmed) to make the trainee feel that the computer is not totally impersonal. This, in turn, is designed to enhance motivation.

Needless to say, access to a computer is expensive. Not surprisingly, most CAI industrial training is done in companies that use computers for their normal business operations. The banking and airline industries are two such examples. However, with the advent of microcomputers, more companies are utilizing CAI training. Once they have computers, they can program them to perform another function: train employees.

Hickey (1976) describes several advantages to CAI, including (1) individualized instruction, (2) reduced training time, (3) elimination of travel for training, and (4) standardized training. The advantages to the trainee include being able to (1) work at his or her own pace, (2) begin and end a lesson when convenient, and (3) enter a program at his or her current level of achievement. Indeed, Dossett and Hulvershorn (1983) reported the average training time with CAI was less than with the lecture method for training military recruits in electronics.

Koerner (1973) describes the disadvantages: (1) it is very expensive, (2) program development lags far behind that of computers, and (3) programming for training purposes is still in its infancy. In other words, even if no new computers were made, we would still be challenged to develop good programs for the computers already here. But new computers are being produced all the time, so we are always behind in our ability to program them effectively.

As Suppes and Morningstar (1969) have discussed, CAI is a new and versatile approach to training. It is used in the military, in schools, and to some extent, in industry. Since it is a new training technique, we have a lot to learn. As more industrial organizations come to rely on computers to assist them in their operations, they will make greater use of CAI in the years to come. At this stage of development, CAI probably has more potential for training in complex skills than any other technique (see Field Note 2).

Field Note 2

Two of my organizational clients use computer-assisted instruction. Both companies are in the insurance business, and both make extensive use of microcomputers. One company continuously works at developing and enhancing its CAI capabilities. It writes new software training programs, conducts analyses of which types of training needs CAI might handle, has developed a CAI library and resource room, and sends some of its employees off to industry-based workshops on the use of CAI. The other company got into CAI as a fad. It purchased some canned CAI programs that it used with some departments. Now those programs are obsolete (because the nature of the insurance business has changed), but the company has not purchased any new programs or taken the time to develop its own. The company has also

decided not to purchase any advanced programs to train further those employees who went through the earlier training. CAI, originally treated like a birthday present that captured everybody's interest for a brief while, fell into disuse once the novelty wore off. For all intents and purposes, CAI is dead as a training method at the second company.

The second company has substantial CAI training material and doesn't know what to do with it. The first company however, made enough of a commitment in the method to retain its value as a training tool. Like all methods, CAI has to be maintained and adjusted over time. Training methods that are adopted as quick fixes usually wind up stored in the company attic or eventually get thrown in the trash bin.

Simulation. Coppard (1976) defines simulation as "a representation of a real-life situation which attempts to duplicate selected components of the situation along with their interrelationships in such a way that it can be manipulated by the user." Simulations are carefully developed exercises. They try to model the important parts of the situation they are supposed to replicate. Simulations usually enhance cognitive skills, particularly decision making. They are a popular training technique for higher-level jobs in which the employee must process large amounts of information.

Simulations have many forms. Some use expensive, technical equipment; others are far less costly. Some simulations need only one participant; others may involve as many as 15 to 20 people working together as a team. Simulations are a broad-based training technique that can be adapted to suit a company's needs.

One example of a simulation is a training technique for managers called the *in-basket* (Frederiksen, 1961). The in-basket simulates how managers make decisions and allocate their time. As we saw in chapter 4, the in-basket is an individual-level training technique. The manager sits at a desk in a room especially created for the training. The desk has a telephone, note pad, calendar, and so on. The most important feature is a manager's "in-basket" for incoming matters that need attention. But in this case, the contents of the in-basket are carefully developed and arranged in sequence. The manager proceeds through the in-basket and makes decisions about the matters that need attention. Usually there are 12 to 15 items in the in-basket; the entire exercise may take two to three hours to complete. One item in the in-basket may be a request for information about the cost of a product. Another item may inform the manager of the possibility of having to discipline an employee. The manager responds to these items in the same way he or she would on the job. Judges unobtrusively observe and evaluate the manager's performance along certain dimensions, such as the quantity and quality of the work accomplished. The in-basket exercise may reveal deficiencies in the manager's work style (not delegating less imporant tasks to subordinates, spending too much time on certain matters and not enough on others, and so on). The manager gets feedback from the panel with which to enhance his or her performance on the job.

Many simulations use *games*. Business games train employees in certain skills. Within the rules of the game, participants try to meet the stated objectives of the exercise. Business games can be used to train individuals or groups. Games have been developed to simulate interpersonal relations problems, financial and budgeting issues, and resource-allocation decisions. Participants are told the objective of the game (for example, to reach a certain profit level or to maximize financial return with a fixed budget). They are then evaluated on whether they have met the game's objectives. Business games are popular for training managers and executives, particularly in financial matters. Raia (1966) reports that business games were superior to the lecture and conference methods in training managers in certain problem areas.

Not all simulations have involved games; some have been built to model a work process. In this case, the goal is to acquaint the employee with what the process will be like when it is done for real. Driving and flying simulators are examples. Flying simulators are used extensively in pilot training; a complex, computerized system simulates how an airplane behaves under various operating conditions.

It is difficult to judge the utility of simulations because they cover such a broad range of training exercises. As a rule, the closer the simulation comes to modeling the job in *all* respects, the better the simulation will be as a training technique. Simulations that do not replicate crucial aspects of the job will not be very successful. A problem with simulations that have a game component is that the participants *know* it is only a game. Failing at a game is not the same as failing on the job. Participants sometimes behave differently than they would in real life. For example, in a marketing course, a business game was created to simulate marketing a product. The class was divided into work teams. The team that showed the greatest profit at the end of the semester received an award. Within the rules of the game (advertising the product, spending on research to improve the product, and so on), the "sales volume" of each work team was posted weekly. As the weeks went by, some work teams gradually fell behind in profit. So members of the losing teams began to take unnatural risks with their companies, risks they probably would not have taken on a real job. They did not care if their actions failed (the company went bankrupt) because it was only a game. And if their wild risks came through, they would receive the award. In this case, the game did not include some key components found on the job. Unlike a semester, the life span of a real company does not end on a predetermined date. The consequences of losing one's job (as well as destroying a company) are not the same as simply failing to win a class award. The best simulations are "best" because they provide for a high degree of transfer of training to the actual job. Needless to say, some simulations are easier than others to construct so as to maximize this transfer.

Role Playing.   Role playing is a training method often aimed at enhancing either human relations skills or sales techniques. As opposed to programmed instruction, which is deliberately geared to the individual, role playing involves many people. Wohlking (1976) defines role playing as "an educational or therapeutic technique in which some problems involving human interaction, real or imaginary, are presented and then spontaneously acted out." The enactment is normally followed by a discussion to determine what happened and why. Participants suggest how the problem could be handled more effectively in the future.

Role playing is less tightly structured than acting, where performers have to say set lines on cue. Participants are assigned roles in the scenario to be enacted. For example, the scenario may be a department store. One person takes the role of an irate customer who is dissatisfied with a recently purchased product. A second person might be assigned the role of the clerk who has to attend to the customer's complaint. Aside from observing some general guidelines about the product, the participants are free to act out their roles however they wish. Their performance is judged by people who do not have an active part in the role playing. In an educational setting, the observers may be other students in the class; in a business setting, they might be supervisors.

Many variations of role playing are possible. In some exercises, participants repeat the enactment several times but switch roles. In other cases, participants reverse the role they play in real life—for example, the supervisor plays a union representative. Participants are forced by their roles to adopt the position of the other side and then defend it.

Goldstein (1980b) describes some recent advances with a technique called *behavioral role modeling*, which uses role playing as one of its parts. In behavioral role modeling, some points or principles to be stressed in training are identified. The participants watch a model use the principles (often on film). The participants rehearse the principles by role playing and then get social reinforcement from the trainer and other group members. Latham and Saari (1979) reported a study of behavioral role modeling that was designed to increase interpersonal skills in dealing with employees. Forty first-line supervisors were assigned to either the modeling group or a control group (which received another form of training to meet the same objectives). Results showed that the supervisors trained with behavioral role modeling were more impressed with the training, scored higher on a learning test six months after training, and were judged to be performing better on the job a year later.

The advantages of role playing include the fact that participants are highly active. By "putting their feet in the other person's shoes," participants gain some understanding of what it is like to experience interpersonal conflict in someone else's position. Interpersonal relations skills are among the more difficult ones to enhance with any method. Despite legitimate criticism that some people put more emphasis on acting than problem solving, the method has been quite useful.

Sensitivity Training.   Sensitivity training is also called T-group (T for training) and human relations laboratory training. It is also probably the most controversial training method. Its general goal is to enhance interpersonal relations skills; specific sessions may be devoted to such themes as expressing anger, building trust, reducing conflict, and so on. As the name suggests, its overall objective is to increase human sensitivity to others and their problems. Sensitivity training has its origins in clinical psychology, where it is used as a form of psychotherapy. In the past 30 years, it has been used as an industrial training technique.

Sensitivity training involves several participants at once—usually 10 to 12. The training is quite lengthy, typically several days. Participants usually go to a retreat, a place removed from their place of work. The retreat can be held at a motel or hotel or a full-time social laboratory created for the training. Participants either know one another from work or come from different organizations. They are usually chosen by someone in their company who feels they need training in human relations. The participants (under the direction of a staff of trainers) face an ambiguous situation. The normal factors encountered at work (an agenda, structure, norms, superior/subordinate relationships) are absent. Their task is to learn about themselves as people—their values, methods of behaving, and how they perceive others and are perceived by others. As people act, their behavior becomes the subject of learning. Activities then clarify, extend, and support the overall goal of becoming more sensitive people.

There are many types of activities involved. Some situational exercises are designed to stress certain responses, such as trust. In one exercise, called a "trust walk," one person whose eyes are shut is led by another. The "leader" can lead the person around a room or out of a building and across a busy street. The "follower" can end the exercise at any time by opening his or her eyes. This exercise is observed by other people. The two participants are asked how they felt about trusting and being trusted, whether the leader "used" the follower to show off, whether the follower's trust bordered on gullibility, and so forth. They also have discussions, role play, and perhaps watch themselves on videotape.

According to Dupre (1976), the goals of sensitivity training are as follows:

1. Introspectiveness or awareness: the ability to reflect on feelings and ideas within ourselves.

2. Awareness of feelings: developing a high regard for the significance of feelings in living and working.

3. Recognition of, and concern about, feeling-behavior discrepancies: developing an ability to diagnose the relationship between how we feel and how we behave and to move toward greater congruence between the two.

4. Flexibility: developing skill in behaving in new and different ways. As can be seen by these goals, sensitivity training is aimed at the development of the entire person, not just one particular skill.

Sensitivity training can be a very traumatic experience for some people. They may learn things about themselves they do not like. There are sharply divided opinions on the value of sensitivity training. Some psychologists like the method, others do not, and still others conclude they do not know why the method produces the results it does (Smith, 1975). The mixed verdict on sensitivity training is perhaps best expressed by Cooper and Levine (1978). They say that sensitivity training can be a meaningful experience for certain people in certain circumstances. One of the problems with the method is transfer of training. Participants in sensitivity training learn new skills while in a very cloistered environment, one deliberately created so as to free them to express their feelings. Once they learn these skills (and have them reinforced by the group), participants return to the same environment that molded the very behavior they sought to change. Back on the job, they may not be reinforced by others for being more trusting, open, or sensitive. This can be a frustrating experience for some people, especially those who had positive feelings about their newfound behaviors. One person who experienced this problem summed up her reaction by saying, "My boss should have gone through that sensitivity training with me. He needs it more than I did."

Overview of Training Methods

Bass and Vaughan (1966) rated some of the off-site training methods in terms of their use of several learning principles and the types of training programs in which they are used. Their evaluation is shown in Figure 6–6. PI draws heavily on the various learning principles, while lectures and films are more limited in their use of them. Active participation of the subject is the most commonly used learning principle. Transfer of training seems to be a consistently underutilized principle. This is particularly true for off-site training methods.

The 12 training methods we have discussed are used for different purposes. No one method is best. What is important is not the method per se but the change in behavior the method is designed to bring about. People who tout certain methods as panaceas for training needs have a misplaced sense of values. I concur with Goldstein's opinion (1980a): Greater emphasis should be given to identifying training needs rather than designing new training methods (see Field Note 3).

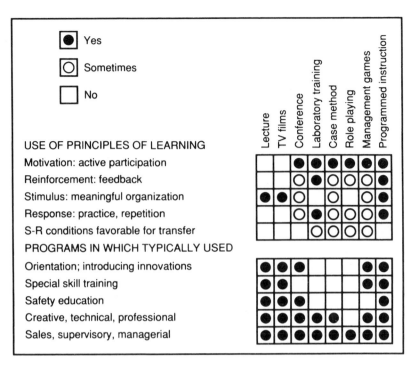

	Lecture	TV films	Conference	Laboratory training	Case method	Role playing	Management games	Programmed instruction
● Yes								
○ Sometimes								
□ No								
USE OF PRINCIPLES OF LEARNING								
Motivation: active participation			●	●	●	●	●	●
Reinforcement: feedback			○	●	○	○	○	○
Stimulus: meaningful organization	●	●	○		○		○	●
Response: practice, repetition			○	●	○	○	○	●
S-R conditions favorable for transfer				○	○	○	○	
PROGRAMS IN WHICH TYPICALLY USED								
Orientation; introducing innovations	●	●	●				●	●
Special skill training	●	●					●	●
Safety education	●	●	●					●
Creative, technical, professional	●	●	●	●	●		●	●
Sales, supervisory, managerial	●	●	●	●	●	●	●	●

Figure 6–6 Extent to Which Certain Methods Utilize Certain Learning Principles and Typical Applications of Training Methods

SOURCE: B. M. Bass and J. A. Vaughan, *Training in Industry: The Management of Learning* (Pacific Grove, Calif.: Brooks/Cole Publishing, 1966).

Sometimes in training you have to get it right the first time—a beginning skydiver (right) and a trainer. Courtesy United States Parachute Association.

When I was in graduate school, I was involved in helping a professor with a study of the coal mining industry. Coal mines were incurring many on-the-job accidents, and our assignment was to develop a safety training program to reduce them. My personal assignment was to observe and interview the coal miners about their work. While down in the mines, I noticed the miners engaged in dangerous behaviors, such as not wearing their hard hats, leaving off their masks (which filtered out coal dust), and smoking in the mine (where an open flame could trigger an explosion). In addition to being unsafe, some of these behaviors were blatant violations of safety rules.

After the miners finished their work shifts, I would interview them about their jobs. I was interested particularly in why they did such seemingly hazardous things. Since our goal was to develop a training program that would reduce accidents, I felt that eliminating these unsafe behaviors would be an obvious place to start. So I asked them why they sometimes did not wear their hard hats, masks, and other safety equipment. I did not expect their answer. They said they believed there was no relationship between what they did in the mine and what happened to them. They felt their lives were in the hands of luck, fate, or God, and it did not really matter how they conducted themselves. They all seemed to have personal anecdotes about other miners who were extremely safety conscious (that is, always wore all the safety equipment and were exceedingly cautious people in general) yet incurred serious injuries or death in accidents through no fault of their own, such as a cave-in. In short, the miners were highly fatalistic. They believed that if "your number was up," you would get hurt or killed, and there was nothing you could do about it. While a hard hat was a fine thing to wear, it would not do much good if five tons of rock fell on you. Therefore, they were not interested in engaging in safe behavior, because their behavior did not matter one way or the other.

This experience taught me many lessons about training. The major one is this: If people are not motivated to be trained, to learn some new behaviors, it is pointless to try. As every teacher who has ever taught can tell you, if students do not want to learn or just do not care, there is nothing you can do to force them to learn. The coal miners simply did not want to learn new behaviors because in their minds their lives and welfare were determined by factors beyond their control. Trainers are like chefs: They can prepare the finest meals, but they cannot make you eat if you are not hungry.

Evaluation of Training Programs

As is the case with any assessment or evaluation, some measure of performance must be obtained. Measures of performance refer to criteria, and the criteria used to evaluate training are just as important as those used in personnel selection. Relevance, reliability, freedom from bias, and so on are all important considerations. One distinction between criteria used in personnel selection and criteria used to evaluate training is that training criteria are more varied and are used to evaluate multiple aspects of a training program.

Criteria

Kirkpatrick (1976) identified four levels of criteria used to evaluate training programs: reaction, learning, behavioral, and results.

Reaction criteria are the participants' reaction to the program. They measure impressions and feelings about the training; for example, was it useful, or did it add to their knowledge? Reaction criteria are treated as a measure of the *face validity* of the training program. An evaluation form used to assess participant reactions is shown in Figure 6–7.

Learning criteria, when used, evaluate how much has been learned in the training program. A final exam given at the end of a training program would be an example of a learning criterion. With some training methods, such as programmed instruction, the learning criterion is built right into the program; the participant must reach a certain level of proficiency (for example, 90% correct) before training is complete. With other methods, such as role playing directed at improving attitudinal skills, there may be no formal evaluation of how much was learned; or participants might simply be asked if they changed their attitudes because of the training. Collectively, reaction and learning criteria are called "internal" criteria—they refer to assessments internal to the training program itself.

Behavioral criteria refer to actual changes in performance once back on the job. They address such questions as "To what extent are the desired changes in the job behaviors of the trainee realized by the training program?" (Landy & Trumbo, 1980). If the goal of the training program is to increase production, the behavioral criterion involves assessing output before and after training. Other types of behavioral criteria include absenteeism, scrap rate, accidents, and grievances. All of these are hard criteria as discussed in Chapter 3. They can be measured easily and have relatively clear meaning. But if the goal of the training program is to increase managers' sensitivity toward hiring the handicapped, "increased sensitivity" has to be translated into some objective behavioral criteria. Also, note that scores on learning criteria and on behavioral criteria do not always correspond to a great degree. Some people who perform well in training cannot transfer their new knowledge or skills back to the job. This is particularly true with training programs aimed at changing attitudes or feelings.

Results criteria refer to the ultimate value of the training program to the company. They involve comparing the costs of the training program with its benefits. Depending on the objective of the program, this can be quite difficult to do. Evaluating increased production output may not be too difficult. All the costs of the training (trainer time, employee time away from the job, training equipment and supplies, and the like) are calculated. Then the employees' level of productivity after training is calculated. The utility of the increased productivity is measured in terms of the company's greater profit as a result of having a more productive work force per the same unit of time (hour, day). If the benefits of training exceed the cost, the training program was worth it. But for some training programs aimed at improving attitudes, it is hard to quantify the value of employees with "better attitudes." Some attempts have been made to cost-account these variables (Mirvis & Lawler, 1977), but gener-

ACME TRAINING PROGRAM

Trainer _____   Subject _____

Date _____

1. Was the subject pertinent to your needs and interests?

    ☐ No   ☐ To some extent   ☐ Very much so

2. How was the ratio of lecture to discussion?

    ☐ Too much lecture   ☐ OK   ☐ Too much discussion

3. Rate the leader on the following:

	Excellent	Very Good	Good	Fair	Poor
A. How well did he state objectives?					
B. How well did he keep the session alive and interesting?					
C. How well did he use the blackboard, charts, and other aids?					
D. How well did he summarize during the session?					
E. How well did he maintain a friendly and helpful manner?					
F. How well did he illustrate and clarify the points?					
G. How was his summary at the close of the session?					

What is your overall rating of the leader?

    ☐ Excellent   ☐ Very good   ☐ Good   ☐ Fair   ☐ Poor

4. What would have made the session more effective?

_____

_____

_____
Signature (optional)

Figure 6–7   Participant Evaluation Form

SOURCE: Adapted from D. L. Kirkpatrick, "Evaluation
of Training," in *Training and Development Handbook*,
2nd ed., ed. R. L. Craig (New York: McGraw-Hill, 1976).
Copyright©1976. Used by permission.

ally they are difficult to translate into dollars and cents. Also there can be many
hidden benefits and costs. A well-trained employee is far more promotable. But that
same employee can market these newly acquired talents to a competitor—a potential
cost. In general, results criteria are the most important and the most difficult to

develop. Collectively, behavioral and results criteria are called *external* criteria; they are evaluations external to the training program itself. Consideration of these four criteria sometimes produces different conclusions about the effectiveness of training than a judgment reached by just one or two criteria. For example, Campion and Campion (1987) compared two methods for improving a person's interview skills. An experimental group received multiple instruction techniques on improving their interview skills, while a control group engaged in self-study of relevant material. The results revealed the experimental group performed better on reaction and learning criteria, but the two groups were equivalent with regard to behavioral and results criteria.

A survey conducted by Catalanello and Kirkpatrick (1968) revealed how companies evaluate their human relations training programs by four types of criteria. Out of 110 organizations responding to the survey, 78% said they attempt to measure trainee reactions and about 50% attempted to assess learning, behavior, and/or results criteria. The results of their survey are shown in Figure 6–8. A large number of the companies tried to assess *learning* before and after training, but they were less involved with measuring change in *behavior*. Results of human relations training are disappointing; 31 of 47 companies reported that they did not achieve the desired

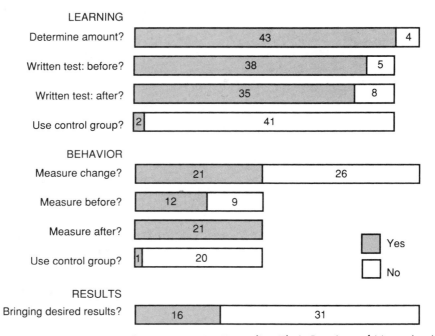

Figure 6–8 Responses from Companies Regarding Their Practices of Measuring Learning, Behavior, and Results of Human Relations Training Programs

results. But note that control groups were rarely used, which indicates that companies seldom used adequate experimental designs. More will be said about experimental designs shortly.

I/O psychologists' interest in training criteria has blossomed recently. This interest is part of a general interest in *evaluation methodology,* the technique of evaluating how well programs of all types (for example, medicine, criminal justice, social welfare) have worked. Within the area of training, Freeberg (1976) has stressed the need for multiple behavioral indices of training effectiveness, the need to have appropriate criteria for evaluating training, and the basic requirement of criterion relevance. Freeberg developed multiple criterion measures to assess the impact of job training programs created by federal manpower legislation. He defined training effectiveness in terms of how well individuals, communities, and occupations adjusted to the impact of these programs. He used these measures first at the end of the program and then six months later to show the interrelationships among the various sets of measures.

Goldstein (1978) illustrated the importance of assessing training effectiveness from multiple perspectives. He created some hypothetical complaints to show the many viewpoints by which the success of any training program can be judged:

From a trainee:
There is a conspiracy. I just finished my training program. I even completed a pretest and a posttest. My posttest score was significantly better than the scores of my friends in the on-the-job control group. However, I lost my job because I could not perform the work.

From a trainer:
There is a conspiracy. Everyone praised our training program. They said it was the best training program they ever attended. The trainees even had a chance to laugh a little. Now the trainees tell me that management will not let them perform their job the way we trained them.

From an administrative officer in the company:
There is a conspiracy. My competition used the training program, and it worked for them. They saved a million. I took it straight from their manuals, and my employees still cannot do the job.

Each of these people asserts that the program did not have the intended effect. Goldstein says that the validity of any training program can be assessed along four dimensions:

1. *Training validity.* Did the trainees match the criteria established for them in the training program? This dimension is concerned with what Kirkpatrick (1976) referred to as *internal* criteria and addresses the extent to which the trainees mastered the training.

2. *Performance validity.* Did the trainees match the criteria for success when they were back on the job? This dimension involves external criteria and addresses the extent to which employee performance on the job was enhanced by training.

3. *Intraorganizational validity.* Is the training program equally effective with different groups of trainees within the same organization? This dimension is concerned with the *internal generalizability* of the training, such as the effectiveness of sensitivity training for sales versus production workers in the same organization.

4. *Interorganizational validity.* Is the training program equally effective with different trainees in companies other than the one that developed the training program? This dimension involves the *external generalizability* of the training, such as the degree to which a training program successful for a manufacturing company would also be successful in a financial organization.

In a review of studies that examined the effectiveness of managerial training programs, Burke and Day (1986) concluded managerial training is moderately effective in improving learning and job performance, but we have relatively little knowledge about the intra- and interorganizational validity of such programs. The question of training program success is not a simple one. I think that performance validity is the ultimate test of training program effectiveness. But depending on the company's objectives, the last two types of validity can also be important.

Research Designs

The basic issue in the design of training research is whether differences in criterion behavior are indeed the result of training. A *research design* assesses whether a training program has achieved its intended objectives. There are many research designs that can be used to measure training effectiveness. The more elaborate the design, the more confidence we have that the change in job performance is due to the effects of the training program.

The simplest research design is shown in Figure 6–9. One group of people is assessed before and after training. We attribute the difference between pre- and posttraining scores to training. But such a conclusion may be wrong; the change may be due to a Hawthorne effect. Also, employees may change over time simply because they have more job experience, acquire new skills or knowledge, increase their self-confidence, and so on. These types of factors are called "history"; that is, people may become more productive or make fewer errors just because they develop on the job, which has nothing to do with training. For these reasons, simple pretest/posttest designs are usually inadequate.

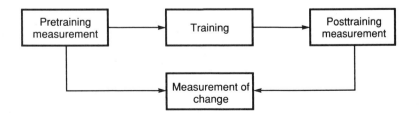

Figure 6–9 One-Group Pretest/Posttest Experimental Design

A research design that can be used to address a Hawthorne effect is shown in Figure 6–10. This is a two-group design. One group receives the experimental training, the other receives placebo training. *Placebo training* means that group receives some form of training other than that being studied. Placebo training is better than *no* training at all for that group since a Hawthorne effect is still possible. In this design, both groups experience the novelty of training. This design is preferable to the one-group design, but it too has limitations. The two groups are used as a basis for comparison, but we do not know if the groups are comparable to begin with. Perhaps one group of people was more intelligent, more motivated, or more highly skilled from the start. So we have no *premeasure* of performance to indicate the initial comparability of the two groups.

The design shown in Figure 6–11 deals with the problems of the previous design. This is also a two-group design, but both groups are assessed before training as well as after training. This is a "powerful" design. By carefully analyzing the results, we can conclude with a high degree of confidence just how much of the difference in job performance is attributable to the experimental training.

Other, more complex research designs are also available (Solomon, 1949). They

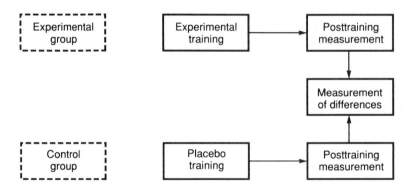

Figure 6–10   Two-Group Experimental Design with No Pretest

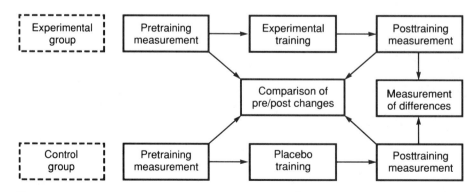

Figure 6–11   Two-Group Pretest/Posttest Experimental Design

differ mainly in the use of multiple control groups, but they are not too practical in personnel training. It is sometimes difficult to divide intact employee work units into different groups. For example, if there is a lot of interaction among people in a work group, there will be practical problems if some of the people get experimental training and others get placebo training. If employees talk among themselves about their training, this can alter motivation and otherwise contaminate the design. In fact, some evidence (Hand & Slocum, 1972) suggests that experimental groups often outperform control groups because people in the control group lose motivation; they are jealous or angry that *they* were not chosen for the experimental training.

The importance of having rigorous evaluation designs is well illustrated in a study by Bunker and Cohen (1977). The authors used a rather complex four-group design to assess the effectiveness of a basic electricity training program for telephone installers. The four groups were as follows:

1. Pretested—trained—posttested.

2. Pretested—untrained—posttested.

3. Unpretested—trained—posttested.

4. Unpretested—untrained—posttested.

Such a research design permits many comparisons: the effects of experimental training (groups 1 and 3) versus placebo training (groups 2 and 4) and the effects of using a pretest (groups 1 and 2) versus no pretest (groups 3 and 4). The findings show the importance of measurement contamination. After reviewing the results in increasing order of analytical sophistication, the authors saw that different conclusions were reached, depending on the level of evaluation design selected, that is, a simple research design (such as Figure 6–9) versus more sophisticated ones. The Bunker and Cohen study is a strong indictment against simple evaluation designs that lead to wrong conclusions and waste training and work time. The authors recommend that training researchers give as much care and thought to the evaluation of training as they do to its implementation. Sussman and Robertson (1986) concluded that no one research design is uniformly the best, and we should try to utilize more than one design to assess training.

The evaluation of training is vitally important. Without it, we do not know if the training was successful. Furthermore, as Ford and Wroten (1984) indicate, without evaluation we will not even be able to tell if there is a match between training needs and training emphasis. In an era in which more pressure is being put on departments to be *accountable* for their actions (if not their very existence), personnel departments too must prove that what they do is valuable to the company. Probably the two toughest questions that a training director has to answer are "Is the training program effective in bringing about desired changes in performance?" (behavioral criteria) and "If the training program is effective, is it worth it to the company?" (results criteria). While we are just beginning to make utility assessments of training, the preliminary results are positive. Mathieu and Leonard (1987) showed that supervisory training for bank employees produced a financial benefit of $219,000 for the bank, given an initial training cost of $12,800. While we need much more research on the utility of training, such as in the area of the utility of personnel selection, I'm confident we will be pleased with the results of our efforts.

Equal Employment Opportunity and Training

Though far more lawsuits have charged unfair discrimination in the *selection* process, personnel training is subject to the same legal scrutiny. Employers must show the fairness and validity of their training procedures as well as their selection procedures. One major case before the U.S. Supreme Court—*Kaiser Aluminum & Chemical Co. v. Weber*—involved charges of unfair discrimination in a company's training programs. Weber, a White male, alleged that he was denied the same access to Kaiser's training program as Black employees. Without the training, employees were not promoted to a higher position. Kaiser's system of admitting employees to its training program involved taking the same proportion of Black employees as White employees. Kaiser felt that it did not have enough Black employees at higher levels in the company, so it set up a racial quota system to help resolve the problem. Weber alleged that this system represented unfair discrimination. He contended that admission to the training program was in part determined by race, and as the EEOC guidelines state, race cannot be a factor in making personnel decisions.

The Supreme Court ruled in favor of Kaiser Aluminum. It said, in effect, that race can be used as a factor in personnel decisions when it is done to compensate for previous inequities in the composition of the company's work force. While the *Weber* case is best known as a test of reverse discrimination, it was based on a company's training program. It illustrates the importance of a company's having a rational and defensible policy with regard to administering a training program.

Some organizations select applicants on the basis of their predicted success in a training program as opposed to actual job performance. An example would be the use of a test to predict success in police academy training, which is required to becoming a police officer. As Russell (1984) notes, the courts have rendered mixed verdicts on the appropriateness of success in training as a criterion for validating selection tests. One interpretation indicates that training success is a sufficient criterion, while another requires that it also be validated with job performance.

Bartlett (1978) decomposed the training process into its constituent parts and showed how each part has a potential for discrimination. Possibilities exist with regard to whether training is a job prerequisite, who gets admitted to a training program, comparable treatment of individuals in the training program, who passes and who fails training, placement of employees into jobs as a result of training, and promotion, advancement, and compensation after training. Bartlett warns that a company must be prepared to defend its reasons at each stage of the training process. Personnel training, like personnel selection, must conform to fair employment practices.

Summary

Personnel training is an evolutionary process. The first step is to conduct an assessment of training needs using organization, operations, and person analysis. After this, training objectives are delineated in behavioral terms. Next, training methods are reviewed to see which method(s) seem best suited to meet the objectives. Those methods that appear to offer the most promise are then developed or selected. The best approach for evaluating the program is considered. This decision depends on the nature of the training objectives and the feasibility of using various research evaluation designs. Next, the training program is actually implemented. The results of training are then evaluated. Finally, the results from the evaluation then become the basis for developing future training objectives. The training process that a company uses should be rational and legally defensible because the same legislation that governs personnel selection also applies to personnel training.

MAJOR CHAPTER OBJECTIVES IN REVIEW

After having read this chapter, you should know:

1. How personnel training relates to organizational goals.

2. Assessment of training needs.

3. Major methods of training and their associated strengths and weaknesses.

4. Evaluation of training programs including relevant criteria and research designs.

5. Legal influence on personnel training.

CASE STUDY—What Do I Do Now?

Stan Rhodus, plant personnel director, was showing his new assistant the results of a job analysis. Rhodus was pointing to the findings from the accounting department and was in midsentence when the door to his office burst open. Andy Carey, the plant manager, was standing in the doorway with a red face and glaring eyes. While Carey was known for his quick temper, he never seemed to lose his cool as much as today.

"Stan," bellowed Carey, "I've got a problem, and you're going to solve it! Our weekly staff meeting just ended with a lot of yelling, name calling, and vicious backbiting. I can't get the people in this plant to work together as a team. They're at each other's throats all the time. If I don't have enough trouble as it is with rising interest rates, competition, and delinquent accounts, now I have to put up with running a zoo. And it just didn't start today. Internal dissension has been hurting us all along, but now it's getting out of hand."

"You're in charge of personnel," Carey continued, "and it's your responsibility to see that the staff gets along. I want you to run our people through some human relations training. I don't care if you show them a film, give them a lecture, hold a discussion, or what. Frankly, I don't care if you bash a few heads together. But one way or another, our people are going to learn to respect each other, help each other, and work together. And if we don't do it, and soon, we'll all be collecting unemployment checks together. Our competition won't have to do us in—we'll do it ourselves. I can't figure these people out. They act like they're playing survival games, and everyone is looking out for number one. Well, it's going to stop—it's got to stop, or we'll all lose."

Carey turned toward the door. He stopped only long enough to say he wanted some human relations training proposal on his desk by Monday.

Rhodus slumped in his chair. A dozen thoughts raced through his mind at once. He wondered what he would come up with for Carey. He could certainly produce something, but he didn't know if it would work in the long run. If it didn't, he knew Carey would be back in his office again, maybe only to give him his walking papers. Rhodus also wondered if he had the guts to tell Carey that *he* should be the first one to go through human relations training.

The hesitating voice of his assistant broke his concentration: "Is it always like this in personnel?"

Questions

1. Should we take it for granted that Carey is correct in his assessment of the need for human relations training? Why or why not?

2. If Rhodus wanted to corroborate the need for human relations training, what types of training needs analysis should be conducted?

3. If human relations training is needed, what training methods do you think might be effective?

4. How should Rhodus assess whether the proposed training has been effective?

5. Do you think that the personnel training approach is the most appropriate for addressing this problem? Why or why not?

7

Performance Appraisal

Employees continually have their job performance appraised, whether on a formal or informal basis. Appraisals may be made from haphazard observation, memory, hearsay, or intuition. Alternatively, a formal and rational system may be used. With the latter approach, appraisals are more accurate, fair, and useful to all concerned (Kujawski & Young, 1979). This chapter deals with formal programs, methods, and techniques for appraising employee performance.

Such appraisal can be defined as "a systematic review of an individual employee's performance on the job which is used to evaluate the effectiveness of his or her work." The purposes of appraisal programs fall into three categories (Barrett, 1966):

1. *Administrative*: Involving personnel actions, such as raises, promotions, transfers, or discharge.

2. *Performance improvement*: Using appraisal information to identify weaknesses in performance; this helps guide the employee in setting goals for improvement.

3. *Research*: Performance appraisal information is often used as a criterion to assess the validity of personnel selection and training procedures.

Just as organizations need to have a reason for conducting a training program, they must also have a rationale for conducting a performance appraisal program. The needs of the orgazization must be clearly stated so the appraisal program can be designed to meet them. Just as trainers seemingly have been more preoccupied with developing training methods than assessing training needs, it seems that many I/O psychologists have been more concerned with developing new appraisal techniques than with the more basic issue of what the appraisal program is supposed to accomplish. If the program has many purposes, care must be taken to ensure that each is met. Rarely does one technique meet all the desired objectives. Sometimes several are used at the same time or they are consolidated to meet the organization's major objectives. For example, the best appraisal technique for determining merit raises may not be the best for giving employees feedback on their performance.

Implementing a Performance Appraisal Program

McGregor (1957) commented that people dislike formally evaluating others. They therefore usually show some resistance to participating in such a program. Managers have refused to conduct appraisal sessions or else have conducted them in such a perfunctory way that they had little or no value. Some of the reasons behind this resistance are that managers do not like to criticize subordinates, dislike "playing God" in appraising performance, and lack evaluation skills. Therefore, an appraisal program should be developed that not only teaches supervisors how to evaluate but also shows employees the need for appraisal. This reduces supervisor reluctance and employee anxiety.

Training Supervisors. A comprehensive training program for supervisors who serve as appraisers is a major phase of an appraisal program. Like any skill, evaluating someone's performance and using that information can be enhanced with training. Without trained appraisers, evaluations may be invalid.

Having trained supervisors is important. But Lopez (1966) found that fewer than 50% of the organizations responding to a survey had formal training programs for supervisors on how to evaluate performance. Paradoxically, the same respondents rated ineptness of supervisors as the main obstacle to setting up an effective appraisal program. Lack of supervisor training is not due to lack of training methods. Videotapes of how to appraise performance and how to communicate the results back to employees have been used, as have CAI methods designed to help supervisors identify major aspects of job performance.

As part of the performance appraisal program, the organization should develop a manual outlining its philosophy, objectives, and standards for the program. This can serve as a text during training and later as a handy reference. We will examine the topic of rater training later in this chapter.

Orienting Employees. Organizations should explain to all employees that their performance will be evaluated. Employees should also know the goals and objectives of the program as well as how they will benefit from it. Performance evaluations can be threatening, and such explanations help ease fears. To avoid problems, employees should also understand how the appraisal will be used. If employees believe the information will be used for pay-raise and promotion decisions, they may be far more defensive about their weaknesses. On the other hand, if they believe the appraisal is a diagnostic aid to help them strengthen their weak areas, they may be far more accepting. In some organizations, appraisals are perfunctory. The company makes no use of them, so employees adopt a "who-cares" attitude about the whole system. The importance of open and honest communication about the intent of an appraisal cannot be overemphasized.

Role of Management. As in training, management plays a vital role in the success of any performance-appraisal program. Appraisal is a management tool, so management has the main responsibility for making it work. Management must strongly support the program and tie it into the organization's overall goals. Clearly, appraisal has to "count" for something, and management has the authority to give it some clout. If pay raises are based on performance but every employee gets the same raise, the appraisal program will lose credibility. The same thing will happen if promotions are supposed to be based on performance but are actually awarded on seniority. In one organization, performance appraisals were supposed to be used to determine raises, but many managers did not bother to evaluate their employees; they just gave everyone the same percentage increase. To get managers to conduct appraisals, the company stated that those managers who failed to do so would forfeit *their* annual pay increase. Not surprisingly, participation jumped to 100%. Like personnel selection and training programs, performance appraisal must be heavily backed by management in order to be effective.

Monitoring and Revising the Program.   Monitoring and revising the appraisal program is a continuous process. Even the best-designed and best-administered appraisal program is a time-consuming task for those involved. Monitoring is done by the personnel department. The first concern is that the appraisals are actually done. Appraisals are usually conducted annually. They can be tied to (1) an employee's birthday, (2) an employee's employment anniversary date, (3) a fixed period for all employees, (4) a per-month basis for alphabetical groupings, and (5) a per-month basis for a department or group.

An even more important issue is how effectively the program meets its goals. If the program's goal is to identify those worthy of promotion, did these people in fact get promoted? If the program's goal is to give larger raises to more productive workers, was this in fact accomplished? These questions and others all address the *validity* of the appraisal program. As stated earlier, assessing validity is not always easy. A performance appraisal program may be valid for identifying weaknesses in employee performance. But a different appraisal system may have to be developed for making promotion decisions (or promotions could be based on other factors, such as seniority). Appraisal systems must meet organizational goals. If they do not or if goals change, then the system must be changed too.

Using the Results of Performance Appraisal

Results of a performance appraisal program may be applied to many other management functions (see Figure 7–1). As discussed in Chapter 3, criteria are derived from job-analysis procedures; the criteria, in turn, are the basis for appraisals. The major uses of performance appraisal listed in Figure 7–1 are described in the following paragraphs.

Personnel Training.   Perhaps the main use of performance appraisal information is for employee feedback. Feedback highlights employees' strengths and weaknesses. Of course, the appraisal should pertain to *job-related* characteristics only. Deficiencies or weaknesses are then the targets for training. Training should involve only

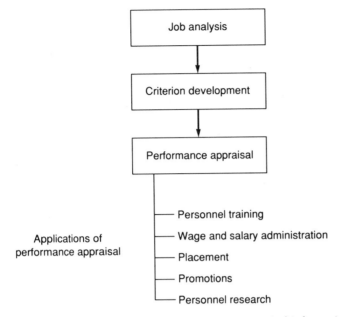

Figure 7–1 Development of Performance Appraisal Information and Its Applications

those areas where poor performance can be attributed to the individual and not to aspects of the work environment. The supervisor plays a key role in helping develop the employee's skills. Although, by definition, performance appraisals are *evaluative*, in this context they serve more as *diagnostic* aids. Since some employees will not acknowledge their weaknesses, a supportive supervisor is more effective than one who is threatening or critical. More will be said about this later in the chapter.

Wage and Salary Administration. Perhaps the second-most-common use of performance appraisals is to make raises. Pay increases are often made, in part, on job performance. Appraisal programs can be designed so that there will be a direct relationship between the evaluation and the size of the raise. For example, an employee who is judged to be performing in the top 10% of the work force might get a 12% raise. Conversely, an employee who performs in the bottom 10% might get only a 2% raise.

Unfortunately, the "personnel-development" and "salary-administration" aspects of appraisal are often uncomfortable partners. Many employees attach far more meaning to raises because they are more immediate and real than revelations about weaknesses on the job. If the two functions are combined in the same appraisal, employees can become defensive. When admitting weaknesses means getting a smaller raise, personnel development may take a back seat in importance.

In a classic article, Meyer, Kay, and French (1965) talked about the need for "split roles" for supervisors in conducting appraisals. One is that of a counselor or coach in employee development or performance improvement. The other is that of a judge in making salary decisions. Evidence shows that most supervisors cannot play both roles at the same time. The problem has been solved by having two appraisals—for example, one in January for employee development, the other in June for salary. Or the supervisor may handle development, and the personnel department, salary. While both functions are important, it has customarily been assumed that they not be conducted at the same time by the same person. However, some recent research by Prince and Lawler (1986) has challenged the view that salary discussion hinders the developmental function of performance appraisal. The authors contend that employees prefer less ambiguity in the evaluation-to-reward connection, therefore it may be advisable to combine the administrative and diagnostic functions of performance appraisal.

Placement.   Performance-appraisal information is vital for placement decisions. New employees (such as management trainees) are often exposed to many tasks or jobs at first. Over a twelve-month period, a trainee might have jobs in marketing, finance, and accounting. After being appraised in each, the trainee might be permanently assigned to that area where he or she performed best. By identifying the employee's strengths, performance appraisal indicates where the person's talents might best be used.

Promotions.   Promotion may be based on how well an employee performs on his or her current job. Appraisals identify the better-performing employees, and an employee who cannot perform well on his or her current job will not be considered for promotion. However, performance is not the sole reason for promotion. Promotions are usually granted on a combination of seniority and merit. If based strictly on seniority, there is little way to ensure that competent people get promoted. Promotions based strictly on performance are more defensible, but most experts agree that experience in a job is also worth considering.

Personnel Research.   In many criterion-related validity studies, assessments of the criterion are derived from performance appraisals. Recall that the criterion is a measure of job success, and that is what performance appraisals are supposed to measure. When the personnel department wants to validate a new predictor test, it correlates scores with criterion measures, which are often exhumed from the company's performance-appraisal files. The value of any selection device is only as good as the criterion it tries to predict. So the appraisal must be a relevant measure of job success. Research (for example, Bass & Turner, 1973; Boehm, 1977) indicates that for the purpose of personnel research, specially constructed performance-appraisal instruments are more useful than "borrowing" appraisal information originally collected for another purpose (for example, salary administration). In either case, appraisals can be used to assess job performance criteria. In turn, these are used for test validation research (see Field Note 1).

Performance appraisals are always conducted for a purpose; that is, the appraisal information is put to some use in terms of giving feedback to employees on their own job performance, in determining merit pay raises, or some other application. There should be a high degree of correspondence between the extensiveness of the appraisal process and how extensively the resulting information is used. When there is little correspondence between the two, major problems typically ensue. Here is a case in point.

One organization I am familiar with prided itself on the thoroughness of its performance-appraisal process. It used performance-appraisal information to determine merit pay raises, making the amount of the raise a function of an employee's merit. It had a highly extensive performance-appraisal program. It used a frequency count of units of production where applicable, and also considered attendance. It relied heavily on rated performance—from the supervisors, from peers, even self-evaluations. It used both behavioral and trait rating scales, and also rank-ordered employees on the basis of overall performance. In short, it judged employees along every conceivable performance dimension with a multitude of methods.

All of the information was finally brought together, and the employees were ordered from high to low. The top person typically had three times the level of perform-

ance of the bottom person. All this information was now going to be used to determine salary raises. After careful deliberation based on all the information, the company awarded a 5% pay raise to the bottom performer and a 7% pay raise to the top performer, with everyone else falling in between. Big deal! The lengthy and tedious performance appraisal process turned out to be a farce (at least insofar as the pay raise issue was concerned). The difference between a 5% and 7% pay raise was trivial and certainly not worth all the ballyhoo the company had gone through. If the top performer was truly three times better than the bottom performer (as their highly detailed evaluations indicated), then the former's raise should have been about three times greater than the latter's— that is, about 15%, not 7%. Since the company wanted to use merit pay raises to motivate the employees to perform well, it should have made superior performance "worth it" to them. Instead, the company communicated the opposite message. The employees figured, "Why bother?" If being the best performer was worth only a few dollars more than being the worst, it simply wasn't worth it to them to perform well. The merit pay system based upon a thorough performance appraisal system blew up in the company's face, and they soon thereafter abandoned the system.

Performance Appraisal and the Law

Federal law on fair employment practices also pertains to performance appraisal. Unfair discrimination can occur not only on the predictor (test) side of the equation but also in the job behavior the test is trying to predict.

Holley and Feild (1975) discussed the relationship between performance appraisal and the law, and raised concern about several possible areas for discrimination. For one, the appraisal system must be relevant to the job. As an example, security guards who were appraised on the pleasantness of their personalities could seriously question the relevance of the appraisal. Another factor is that supervisors should not evaluate aspects of an employee's performance that were not observable. This precludes the possibility of biases and misconceptions. Finally, evaluations should not be based on subjective and vague factors like "desire to succeed." This desire can take many forms for different people. The clearer the factors, the more likely the supervisor's attention will be centered on the pertinent aspects of job behavior.

Kleiman and Durham (1981) reviewed 23 court cases involving charges of discrimination in performance appraisal. They sought to determine the standards set by the courts in assessing performance appraisal systems. The authors discovered that the courts (1) have a strong interest in appraisal systems regardless of their adverse impact; (2) emphasize job-analytic procedures for identifying relevant appraisal criteria; and (3) want employers to demonstrate the *construct validity* of their performance-appraisal evaluations. These legal findings support the results from empirical research on sex and race bias in performance appraisal (Schmitt & Lappin, 1980). Schmitt and Lappin demonstrated that raters of different races evaluate members of their own racial group differently than members of other racial groups. Black raters gave higher ratings to blacks than to whites; the opposite effect was observed for white raters. With such an empirical demonstration of race-linked bias, it should be apparent that performance appraisal, like personnel selection and training, is another possible avenue for unfair discrimination in employment.

Feild and Holley (1982) examined the effects of 13 appraisal system characteristics on the verdicts rendered in 66 employment discrimination cases. They found five factors that determined whether the judgments were for the plaintiff or the defendant: (1) use of job analysis to develop the appraisal system; (2) trait versus behavioral orientation of the appraisal instrument; (3) whether evaluators were given specific written instructions; (4) whether the appraisal results were reviewed with employees; and (5) whether the defendant was an industrial or nonindustrial (for example, governmental) organization (nonindustrial defendants were more likely to win). In a review of major court cases involving performance-appraisal issues, Barrett and Kernan (1987) identified six dimensions to a professionally sound performance appraisal system.

1. Job analyses should be conducted to identify characteristics necessary for successful job performance.

2. These characteristics should be incorporated into the evaluation instrument.

3. Supervisors should be trained in how to use the evaluation instrument.

4. Formal appeal mechanisms should be created to reconsider any evaluation.

5. The performance evaluations should be clearly documented.

6. The organization should provide corrective guidance for poor performers.

In summary, organizations must justify personnel decisions based on employee-performance appraisal. EEOC guidelines state that performance appraisal must not be discriminatory (Latham & Wexley, 1981). The number of court cases involving alleged discrimination in performance appraisal is not as great as those involving personnel selection. But the number is growing, and that trend is likely to continue.

Sources of Performance-Appraisal Information

As stated in Chapter 3, job performance can be characterized by many criteria. Guion (1965) identified three different measures: *objective production data* (for example, output), *personnel data*, and *judgmental data*. Each of these job performance measures will be described, along with information about their reliability and validity.

Objective Production Data

Using *objective production data* as an index of how well an employee is performing on the job is limited in its frequency and value. For a person holding the job of a machine operator, job performance may be measured by counting the number of objects produced per day, per week, and so forth. Similarly, salespeople are appraised in terms of assessing (counting) their sales volume over a given period of time. It is even possible to evaluate the performance of firefighters by counting the number of fires they extinguish.

While each of these objective production measures has some degree of intuitive appeal, none is usually a complete measure of job performance. Two problems in particular affect each of these measures. First, we would like to assume that differences in performance across people reflect true differences in terms of how well these people perform their jobs. Unfortunately, variability in performance can be due to factors beyond the individual's control. One machine operator may produce more because he or she works with a better machine. A salesperson might have a large sales volume because his or her territory is better. Firefighters who put out few fires might be responsible for an area with relatively few buildings. This problem of variation in performance stemming from external factors should sound familiar: It represents a form of *criterion contamination*, a topic discussed in Chapter 3.

The second problem with objective performance measures is that they rarely tell the whole story. A machine operator who produced more objects per day but who also produced more defective objects would not be described as the "best." *Quality* may be as important as *quantity*, but this cannot be recorded in a simple count of objects produced. A salesperson spends a lot of time recruiting new customers, an aspect that must be weighed against simply making calls on established customers. Creating new customers can be as important as maintaining business with old ones. Sales volume might be less at first, but in the long run, the new customers will increase total sales volume. Finally, extinguishing fires is but one aspect of a firefighter's job; preventing fires is another one. The "best" firefighter conceivably might not have put out many fires at all but contributed heavily toward preventing the fires in the first place. In short, all of these actual criteria suffer from *criterion deficiency*. They are deficient measures of the conceptual criteria they seek to measure.

Validity of Objective Production Data.   When we speak of a criterion's validity, we mean its *relevance*. For the jobs mentioned, objective production data has *some* relevance. It would be silly to say that sales volume has no bearing on a salesperson's performance. The salesperson's job is indeed to sell. The issue is one of degree of relevance. It is a mistake to give too much importance to objective production data in performance appraisal. This is sometimes a great temptation because such data are usually very accessible, but the meaning of those clear-cut numbers is not always so evident. Finally, for many jobs objective performance measures do not exist, or if they do, they have little relevance to actual performance. It would be difficult to argue that a teacher's performance can be appraised by counting the number of students in a class. In fact, this "body count" approach to measuring teacher effectiveness can be argued either way. A teacher who is judged to be performing well can point to a large class enrollment as evidence of his or her skill—some students are sitting in the aisles just to partake in the learning experience. Another teacher who is judged to be performing poorly can point to a large class enrollment as being a handicap to good teaching—how can anyone teach well with students crammed wall to wall? In summary, the issue of criterion relevance is a question of judgment. For some jobs, objective performance data are partially relevant measures of success; in many others, such relevance is lacking.

Personnel Data

The second type of appraisal information is *personnel data*, data retained by a company's personnel office. The two most common indexes of performance are absenteeism and turnover, though records may also be kept on accidents, grievances, and lateness. The critical issue with these variables is criterion relevance. To what extent do they reflect differences in job performance? Absenteeism is probably the most sensitive measure of performance. In almost all jobs, employees who are often absent are judged as performing worse than others, all other factors being equal. Indeed, an employee can be fired for excessive absence.

Most organizations have policies for dealing with absenteeism, which attests to its importance as a variable in judging overall performance. However, the measurement and interpretation of absenteeism are not clear-cut (Muchinsky, 1977). Absences can be "excused" or "unexcused" depending on many factors pertaining to both the individual (for example, seniority) and the job (for example, job level). An employee who has ten days of excused absence may still be appraised as performing better than an employee with five days of unexcused absence. Whether or not the absence was allowed must be determined before performance judgments are made. Measuring absenteeism is a thorny problem, but it is seen as a highly relevant criterion variable in most organizations.

Turnover is also used to measure performance. It too involves measurement problems. Some turnover is voluntary (the employee quits); some is involuntary (the employee is fired). An employee who quit would probably be appraised "better" than an employee who was fired. Some organizations will let an employee resign to improve his or her chances of getting another job. This clouds the value of turnover as a measure of performance. The meaning attached to a chronic job-hopper has also changed over the years. Twenty years ago, job-hoppers were viewed with some suspicion at the management level; they seemed unstable and unable to hold a job for long. Today, however, job-hoppers are regarded more positively. Exposure to different jobs is taken to mean that they have more breadth of experience. This is an example of how the same behavior (turnover) acquires different interpretations over time.

Accidents can be used as a measure of job performance but only for a limited number of jobs. Frequency and severity of accidents are both used as variables, as are accidents resulting in injury or property damage. Accidents are a more relevant criterion variable for blue-collar than for white-collar jobs. People who drive delivery trucks may be evaluated in part on the number of accidents they have. This variable can be contaminated by many sources, though. Road conditions, miles driven, time of day, and condition of the truck can all contribute to accidents. While relevance is limited to certain jobs, accidents can contribute greatly to appraisal. Some companies give large raises to drivers with no accidents and fire those with a large number.

Grievances and lateness have the least relevance, but they may be of value in some situations. Grievances are formal, written complaints submitted by an employee. They seem to be related more to how well employees like their jobs than to how well they are performing. However, it is possible that the "chronic complainer" with a high grievance rate would be viewed negatively. He or she might be coaxed into seeking employment elsewhere. Lateness is often caused by external factors (for example, snowstorms, sick children). Again, however, if the same employee were repeatedly late, the conclusion would be that it was the employee's fault, and this would then affect appraisal. In general, being on time is not regarded as a virtue, but lateness (especially repeated lateness) is viewed as harmful to performance.

Validity of Personnel Data.   The validity of personnel data varies greatly. A problem common to all personnel information is inaccurate record keeping. Sloppy record keeping is not unusual and can be a source of error. Latham and Pursell (1975) found turnover recorded as extended absence. Recording of accidents likewise is notoriously poor (Blum & Naylor, 1968). Occasional lateness may not be reported until it has become a consistent problem. Though personnel data are indeed relevant in assessing job performance, their accuracy may be questionable.

Judgmental Data

Judgmental data are usually used for performance appraisal. Guion (1965) reported that in 81% of the validation studies performed over a five-year period, some form of rated or judged performance was the criterion for job success. Lent, Aurbach, and Levin (1971) reported that in 1,500 criterion measures used in I/O research, almost 900 (60%) were supervisory ratings of subordinates' performance. Judgmental data are popular in performance appraisal because finding relevant objective measures is difficult. Subjective assessments can also apply to almost all jobs. Those who do the assessments are usually supervisors, but some use has also been made of self-assessment, peer assessment, and subordinate assessment.

Performance appraisal has been addressed by researchers from several disciplines (for example, those interested in organizations, communication, and education). The contributions of I/O psychologists are particularly manifest in designing performance appraisal methods. A wide variety have been developed, all intended to provide accurate assessments of how people are performing. The major systems used in performance appraisal include:

1. Graphic rating scales

2. Employee comparison methods
    a. Rank order
    b. Paired comparison
    c. Forced distribution

3. Behavioral checklists and scales
    a. Critical incidents
    b. Weighted checklist
    c. Behaviorially anchored rating scale (BARS)
    d. Behavioral observation scale (BOS)
    e. Mixed standard rating scale

Graphic Rating Scales.   Graphic rating scales are the most commonly used system in performance appraisal. Individuals are rated on a number of traits or factors. The rater judges "how much" of each factor the individual has. Usually performance is judged on a 5- or 7-point scale, and the number of factors ranges between 5 and 20. The more common dimensions rated are quantity of work, quality of work, practical judgment, job knowledge, cooperation, and motivation. Examples of typical graphic rating scales are shown in Figure 7–2.

In reality, these aspects of performance are rarely independent of each other. In one study (Muchinsky, 1974), the performance of a sample of professional engineers was rated by their supervisor. The ratings on ten criteria were intercorrelated, and the average correlation was about .50. These ten dimensions thus assessed related aspects of performance. Using a statistical method called factor analysis, ratings on the ten criteria were condensed to identify the underlying dimensions of performance as an engineer. Successful performance was shown to be a function of two factors: interpersonal-relations ability and technical ability. The competent engineer knew the "facts and figures" and was able to relate to other people in a cordial manner.

Rating Errors.   In making appraisals with rating scales, the rater may unknowingly commit errors in judgment. These can be placed into three major categories: leniency errors, halo errors, and central tendency errors. All three stem from rater bias and misperception.

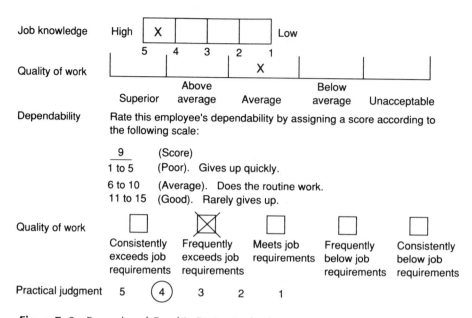

Figure 7–2 Examples of Graphic Rating Scales for Various Performance Dimensions

Leniency errors. Some teachers are "hard graders" and others "easy graders." So raters can be characterized by the leniency of their appraisals. Harsh raters give evaluations that are *lower* than the "true" level of ability (if it can be ascertained); this is called *severity* or *negative leniency.* The easy rater gives evaluations that are *higher* than the "true" level; this is called *positive leniency.* These errors usually occur because the rater has applied personal standards derived from his or her own personality or previous experience.

Halo errors. Halo errors are evaluations (good or bad) based on the rater's general feelings about an employee. Thus, the rater generally has a favorable or unfavorable attitude toward the employee that permeates all evaluations of this person. Typically, the rater has strong feelings about at least one important aspect of the employee's performance. This is then generalized to other performance factors, and the employee is judged (across many factors) as uniformly good or bad. The rater who is impressed by an employee's idea might allow feelings about this one incident to carry over to evaluation of leadership, cooperation, motivation, and so on. This occurs even though the "good idea" is not related to other factors. The converse also holds: The rater who is displeased with an employee's idea might allow this to spread to other aspects of performance.

It might be said that the employee who can do no wrong in the rater's eyes and the employee who is chronically in the "doghouse" are the victims of halo error on the part of the rater. Raters who commit halo errors do not distinguish among the many dimensions of employee performance. However, a compounding problem with halo is that there are two types. One type is truly a rating *error* and refers to the failure to differentiate an employee's performance across different dimensions. The second type refers to giving uniformly consistent ratings to an employee (either high or low) when these ratings are in fact justified; that is, the employee is truly good (or bad) across many performance dimensions. Bartlett (1983) refers to these as invalid and valid halo, respectively. In general, halo is considered to be the most serious and pervasive of all rating errors (Cooper, 1981).

Central-tendency errors. Central-tendency error refers to the rater's unwillingness to assign extreme—high or low—ratings (Landy & Trumbo, 1980). Everyone is "average," and only the middle (central) part of the scale is used. This may happen when raters are asked to evaluate unfamiliar aspects of performance. Rather than not respond, they play it safe and say the person is average in this "unknown" ability.

Despite the fact that we have long been aware of leniency, halo, and central-tendency errors, there is no clear consensus on how these errors manifest themselves in ratings. Saal, Downey, and Lahey (1980) observed that researchers define these errors in somewhat different ways. For example, leniency errors are sometimes equated with *skew* in the distribution of ratings; that is, positive skew is evidence of negative leniency and negative skew of positive leniency. Other researchers say that an average rating on a particular scale above the midpoint indicates positive leniency. The exact meaning of *central tendency* is also unclear. Central-tendency errors occur if the average rating is around the mid-point of the scale but there is not much variance in the ratings. The amount of variance that separates central tendency errors from "good" ratings has not been defined. Saal and associates feel that more precise definitions of these errors must be developed before they can be overcome.

All three errors can lead to a restriction in range, that is, to a concentration of ratings at the ends or midpoint of the rating scale. When the range of variability is restricted on the criterion, the validity coefficient for predicting this criterion will be greatly curtailed. Thus, when supervisor ratings are used in personnel research and validity coefficients are low, the conclusion that the predictor lacks validity may be wrong. Restriction in range on either the predictor or criterion (or both) can lead the researcher astray in assessing its validity. Similarly, the value of appraisal systems meant to identify an employee's strengths and weaknesses is questionable if aspects of performance are not differentiated. To help combat the errors discussed, other appraisal methods have been developed, as discussed in the following paragraphs.

Employee-Comparison Methods. Rating scales provide for evaluating employees against some defined standard. With employee comparison methods, individuals are compared with one another; variance is thereby forced into the appraisals. Thus, the concentration of ratings at one part of the scale caused by rating error is avoided. However, all methods of employee comparison involve the question of whether variation represents true differences in performance or whether it creates a false impression of large differences when they are in fact small. There are three major employee comparison methods.

Rank-Order Method.   With the rank-order method, the rater ranks employees from high to low on a given performance dimension. The person ranked first is regarded as the "best" and the person ranked last as the "worst." However, because rank-order data have only ordinal scale properties, we do not know how good the "best" is or how bad the "worst" is. We do not know the *level* of performance. For example, the Nobel Prize winners in a given year can be ranked in terms of their overall contributions to science. But we would be hard pressed to conclude that the Nobel laureate ranked last made the worst contribution to science. Rank-order data are all relative to some standard; in this case, excellence in scientific research. Another problem is that it becomes quite tedious and perhaps somewhat meaningless to rank order large numbers of people. What usually happens is that the rater can sort out the people at the top and bottom of the pile. However, for the rest with undifferentiated performance, the rankings may be somewhat arbitrary.

Paired-Comparison Method.   With the paired-comparison method, each employee is compared to every other employee in the group being evaluated. The rater's task is select which of the two is better on the dimension being rated. The method is typically used to evaluate employees on a single dimension: overall ability to perform the job. The process can also be repeated for several performance aspects (for example, Campion, 1972). The number of evaluation pairs is computed by the formula $n(n - 1)/2$, where n is the number of people to be evaluated. For example, if there are ten people in a group, the number of paired comparisons is $10(9)/2 = 45$. At the conclusion of the evaluation, the number of times each person was selected as the better of the two is tallied. The people are then ranked by the number of tallies they receive.

A major limitation of the method is that the number of comparisons made mushrooms dramatically with large numbers of employees. If 50 people are to be appraised, the number of comparisons is 1,225; this will obviously take too much time. Some procedures have been developed to reduce the number of evaluations necessary with a large sample. The original group is divided into smaller groups (Lawshe, Kephart, & McCormick, 1949), or a patterned sample of pairs is drawn (McCormick & Bachus, 1952). But the paired comparison method is still best for relatively small samples.

Forced-Distribution Method.   The forced-distribution method is most useful when the other employee-comparison methods are most limited: when the sample size is large. It is typically used when the rater must evaluate employees on a single dimension, but it can also be used when multiple dimensions are required. The procedure is based on the normal distribution and assumes that employee performance is normally distributed. The distribution is divided into five to seven categories. Using predetermined percentages (based on the normal distribution), the rater evaluates an employee by placing him or her into one of the categories. All employees are evaluated in this manner. The method "forces" the rater to distribute the employees in all categories (which is how the method gets its name). It is thus impossible for all employees to be rated excellent, average, or poor. An example of the procedure for a sample of 50 employees is shown in Figure 7–3.

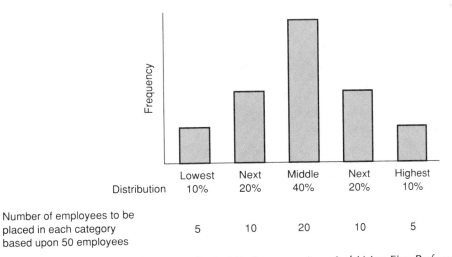

Figure 7–3 Forced Distribution Method of Performance Appraisal Using Five Performance Categories with a Sample of Fifty Employees

Some raters react negatively to the method, saying that the procedure creates artificial distinctions among employees. This is partly because they feel that performance is not normally distributed but rather negatively skewed (that is, most of their employees are performing very well) (see Field Note 2). The dissatisfaction can be partially allayed by saying that those in the lowest 10% are performing not necessarily poorly, just not as well as the others. The problem (as with all comparison methods) is that performance is not compared to a defined standard. The *meaning* of the differences among employees must be supplied from some other source.

Field Note 2

Although it is rarely discussed in performance appraisal, one of the problems regarding the evaluation of employees deals with the shape of the distribution of employee job performance. As we discussed in Chapter 2, there are statistical distributions that depart from normality, with a skewed distribution being the most common. Some performance appraisal methods are premised upon employee performances' being normally distributed, the forced-distribution method being a case in point. In fact, most psychologists probably believe that variables are normally distributed unless they have reason to believe

otherwise. However, there are some strong arguments that lead us to conclude that job performance is not normally distributed but *negatively skewed.* That is, there are far more employees who are performing their jobs successfully than those who are performing their jobs unsuccessfully. Why? Think about it. I/O psychology addresses itself to the attraction, selection, and development of successful employees. We try to recruit applicants from sources and in ways that will result in good candidates. We carefully select employees who we predict will succeed on the job. Once on the job, employees are given training to improve their job performance further. Individuals who don't perform well are often dismissed from employment. The product of all these forces is to shift the overall distribution of job performance to the high end of the scale. There are always some employees who don't perform their jobs as well as the company would like, but they typically are in the minority. Consequently, in my opinion, the distribution of job performance in most companies is far more negatively skewed than normal. One of the problems with performance-appraisal methods predicated upon a normal distribution is that one assumption of the method (normality) just doesn't fit reality in some cases. I believe I/O psychologists should give more thought to the underlying distribution of job performance and how it affects evaluation of job performance. While many variables in psychology are normally distributed, I don't believe job performance is one of them.

Behavioral Checklists and Scales.   Most recent advances in performance appraisal have involved behavioral checklists and scales. The key term is *behavior*. Behaviors are less vague than other factors. The greater the agreement on the meaning of the performance appraised, the greater the chance that the appraisal will be accurate. All

"Barkley, I perceive my role in this institution not as a judge but merely as an observer and recorder. I have observed you to be a prize boob and have so recorded it." *Reprinted by permission: Tribune Media Services*

of the methods in this group have their origin directly or indirectly in the critical-incidents method.

Critical Incidents.   Critical incidents are behaviors that result in good or poor job performance. Flanagan (1954) developed the critical-incidents method. Supervisors record behaviors of employees that greatly influence their job performance. The supervisors are either to keep a running tally of these critical incidents as they occur on the job or to recall them at a later time. Critical incidents are usually grouped by aspects of performance: job knowledge, decision-making ability, leadership, and so on. The end product is a list of behaviors (good and bad) that constitute effective and ineffective job performance.

The original method did not lend itself to quantification (that is, a score reflecting performance). It was used to guide employees in the specifics of their job performance. Each employee's performance can be described in terms of the occurrence of these critical behaviors. The supervisor can then counsel the employee to avoid the bad and continue the good behaviors. For example, a negative critical incident for a machine operator might be "leaves machine running while unattended." A positive one might be "always wears safety goggles on the job." Discussing performance in such clear terms is more understandable than such vague statements as "poor attitude" or "careless work habits."

Weighted Checklist.   A weighted checklist is simply an attempt to quantify performance using the critical-incidents technique. The procedure for developing a weighted checklist begins with a list of critical incidents. Once the list has been developed, a panel of "experts" (usually supervisors) rates each critical incident in terms of just how "good" the good ones are and just how "bad" the bad ones are. Thus, a scale value is derived for each incident reflecting its relative degree of importance to the job. The scale values are usually derived by averaging the ratings made by the supervisor. Figure 7–4 shows some examples of items from a weighted checklist for the job of secretary.

Critical Incident	Scale Value
1. Knows the difference between correcting the grammar in the boss's letter and correcting the writing style.	+6.5
2. Knows various postal rates and mails material in a cost-efficient manner.	+4.2
3. Knows what typing is to be done on plain paper versus dittos.	+3.1
4. Keeps a running count on the use of office supplies.	+2.5
5. Opens all mail whether or not it is marked "confidential."	−1.9
6. Confuses priorities on typing that need immediate attention and projects that have no established deadline.	−3.8
7. Files away correspondence so that it can rarely be found for later reference.	−5.2
8. Leaves many mistakes in typing from failing to proofread the typed copy.	−7.1

Figure 7–4   Checklist of Weighted Critical Incidents for a Secretarial Job

Supervisors then evaluate employee performance by checking off observed behaviors. The values for all behaviors checked off are added to yield the employee's score. The ideal employee would exhibit all the positive and none of the negative behaviors. The method gives information that can be used in many ways, including counseling employees on how to improve performance. Employees can be ranked on total scores, thus providing information on the range of performance. The scores can be averaged for a measure of "typical" performance, which can serve as a standard for judging individual employees.

Behaviorally Anchored Rating Scales.   Behaviorally anchored rating scales (BARS) are a combination of behavioral-incident and rating-scale methods. Performance is rated on a scale, but the scale points are anchored with behavioral incidents. The development of BARS is time consuming, but their benefits make them worthwhile. BARS are developed in a five-step process:

1.   A list of critical incidents is generated in the manner discussed previously.

2.   A group of people (usually supervisors—either the same people who generated the critical incidents initially or another group) cluster the incidents into a smaller set of performance dimensions (usually five to ten) that they typically represent. The result is a given number of performance dimensions, each containing several illustrative critical incidents.

3.   Another group of knowledgeable people are instructed to perform the following task. The critical incidents are "scrambled" in such a way that they are no longer listed under the dimensions described in step 2. The critical incidents might be written on separate note cards and presented to the people in random order. The rater's task is to reassign or retranslate all the critical incidents back to the original performance dimensions. This step is a variation of the procedure developed by Smith and Kendall (1963), wherein the goal is to have critical incidents that clearly represent the performance dimensions under consideration. A critical incident generally is said to be successfully retranslated if some percentage (usually 50 to 80%) of the raters reassign it back to the dimension from which it came. Incidents that are not retranslated successfully (that is, there is ample confusion as to which dimension they represent) are discarded.

4.   The people who retranslated the items are asked to rate each "surviving" critical incident on a scale (typically 7 or 9 points) in terms of just how effectively or ineffectively it represents performance on the appropriate dimension. This rating phase is similar to the process used to derive the scale weights in the weighted checklist. The ratings given to each incident are then averaged. The standard deviation for each item is then computed. Low standard deviations indicate high rater agreement on the value of the incident. Large standard deviations indicate low rater agreement. A standard deviation criterion is then set for deciding which incidents will be retained for inclusion in the final form of the BARS. Incidents that have a standard deviation in excess of 1.50 typically are discarded because the raters could not agree on their respective values.

5. The final form of the instrument consists of critical incidents that survived both the retranslation and standard deviation criteria. The incidents serve as behavioral anchors for the performance dimension scales. The final BARS instrument consists of a series of scales listed vertically (one for each dimension) and anchored by the retained incidents. Each incident is located along the scale according to its established rating (Schwab, Heneman, & DeCotiis, 1975). An example of a BARS for patrol officer performance is shown in Figure 7–5. As can be seen, behaviors are listed with respect to what the employee is *expected* to do at various performance levels. For this reason, BARS are sometimes referred to as "behavioral expectation scales" (BES).

One of the major advantages of the method does not involve performance appraisal. It is based on the high degree of involvement of persons developing the scale. The participants must carefully examine specific behaviors that lead to effective performance. In so doing, they may reject false stereotypes about ineffective performances. The method has face validity for both the rater and ratee. It also appears to be useful for training raters. However, a disadvantage of BARS is that they are job specific; that is, you need to develop a different behaviorally anchored rating scale for every job.

Research on reducing rating errors with BARS is mixed. Some studies (for example, Campbell, Dunnette, Arvey, & Hellervik, 1973) report fewer leniency errors with BARS. Other studies (for example, Borman & Vallon, 1974) report the reverse. Still others (for example, Kingstrom & Bass, 1981) find no difference at all between BARS and other formats in reducing rating errors. Generally, it seems that BARS are not much better than graphic rating scales in reducing rating errors. However, Landy and Trumbo (1980) commented that the scale-development process ensures understanding of performance determinants. This alone is a benefit over simple graphic rating scales.

Behavioral-Observation Scales. A recent development in appraisal is the behavioral-observation scale (BOS). Like BARS, it is based on critical incidents. With BOS the rater must rate the employee on the *frequency* of critical incidents. The rater observes the employee over a period of time, such as a month. An example of a 5-point critical incident scale used in appraising salespeople, as provided by Latham and Wexley (1977), follows:

Knows the Price of Competitive Products

Never	Seldom	Sometimes	Generally	Always
1	2	3	4	5

Raters evaluate the employees on several such critical incidents, recording how often they observed the behavior. The total score is the sum for all of the critical incidents. The final step is to correlate the response for each incident (a rating of 1, 2, 3, 4, or 5) with the total performance score. This is called *item analysis*. It is meant to detect the critical incidents that most influence overall performance. Those incidents that

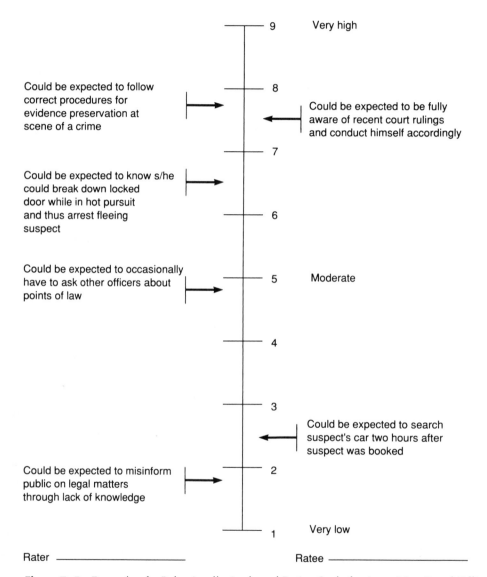

Job knowledge: Awareness of procedures, laws, and court rulings and changes in them

9 — Very high

Could be expected to follow correct procedures for evidence preservation at scene of a crime — 8

Could be expected to be fully aware of recent court rulings and conduct himself accordingly

— 7

Could be expected to know s/he could break down locked door while in hot pursuit and thus arrest fleeing suspect — 6

Could be expected to occasionally have to ask other officers about points of law — 5 Moderate

— 4

— 3

Could be expected to search suspect's car two hours after suspect was booked

Could be expected to misinform public on legal matters through lack of knowledge — 2

1 — Very low

Rater _____   Ratee _____

Figure 7–5 Example of a Behaviorally Anchored Rating Scale for Appraising Patrol Officers

SOURCE: F. J. Landy and D. A. Trumbo, *Psychology of Work Behavior*, rev. ed. (Pacific Grove, Calif.: Brooks/Cole, 1980), p. 128.

have the highest correlations with the total score are the most discriminating factors in performance. They would be retained to develop criteria for job success.

Latham, Fay, and Saari (1979) suggested advantages to performance appraisals with BOS. Like BARS, BOS are developed by those using the method for evaluation, who understand they are committed to using the scales. Second, BOS information can be used to teach new employees the behaviors most critical to the job. Finally, BOS are content valid; the aspects of performance appraised are derived directly from the job. The authors believe this satisfies the EEO requirement that appraisal methods be job relevant.

Few data are available on reducing rating errors with BOS versus BARS. There is some controversy (for example, Bernardin & Kane, 1980; Latham, Saari, & Fay, 1980) over the merits of BOS as proposed by Latham and associates (1979). Murphy, Martin, and Garcia (1982) contend that BOS are influenced by the raters' ability to recall certain behaviors observed on the job. Which behaviors they recall may be highly influenced by their mental set. Thus, the authors believe that BOS measure more complex traitlike judgments rather than simpler behavioral observations. In a finding with important legal implications, Wiersma and Latham (1986) reported that a sample of lawyers rated BOS as the most defensible method of appraising performance in employment litigation. As Kane and Bernardin (1982) comment, we need to do more research on the value of BOS as a means of appraising performance.

Mixed-Standard Rating Scales. The final method we will consider is one that is still experimental: the mixed-standard rating scale. It was developed by Blanz and Ghiselli (1972). The dimensions of performance (for example, practical judgment) to be appraised are identified. *Three* critical incidents illustrating good, average, and poor performance for each dimension are obtained as described earlier. The incidents for each performance dimension are *randomly* presented to the rater so that a sequence (good, average, poor) *cannot* be detected. The rater also does not know the value (good, average, poor) of the incidents.

The rater is asked to evaluate each employee on whether he or she is "better than," "worse than," or "the same as" each critical incident in the random list. An example of this kind of scale is shown in Figure 7–6. The scale is being used for police officer performance. Three dimensions have been identified: judgment (J), job knowledge (K), and relations with others (R). Given three performance dimensions with three critical incidents each, nine statements are presented. There are poor (P), average (A), and good (G) examples for each dimension. The rater must decide whether performance is better than, worse than, or the same as each statement.

It has been proposed that the "mixed" nature of the rating form helps to minimize leniency errors as well as cause the rater to give careful consideration to each performance dimension and thus minimize halo effects. The method is also useful for identifying careless raters who give inconsistent evaluations. Though the method has not been used very much, one study (Saal & Landy, 1977) reported that it reduced leniency and halo effects. However, the reliability of the method was not impressive. Saal (1979) developed a coding system that was useful in correcting for inconsistency. This may make the scale more reliable. However, Barnes-Farrell and Weiss (1984) discovered that the degree to which the extreme standards (that is, the good and the bad conduct) were pronounced made a difference in the rated level of performance; that is, different results occurred depending on whether the good incident was indicative of "mildly good" or "outstanding" performance. Thus, the incidents selected for inclusion can influence the validity of the scale.

		Rating
(K)	1. The officer could be expected to misinform the public on legal matters through lack of knowledge. (P)	_____
(R)	2. The officer could be expected to take the time to carefully answer a rookie's question. (G)	_____
(K)	3. This patrol officer never has to ask others about points of law. (G)	_____
(J)	4. The officer could be expected to refrain from writing tickets for traffic violations that occur at a particular intersection which is unusually confusing to motorists. (G)	_____
(J)	5. The patrol officer could be expected to call for assistance and clear the area of bystanders before confronting a barricaded, heavily armed suspect. (A)	_____
(R)	6. The officer could be expected to use racially toned language in front of minority group members. (P)	_____
(K)	7. The officer follows correct procedures for evidence preservation at the scene of a crime. (A)	_____
(J)	8. The patrol officer could be expected to continue to write a traffic violation in spite of hearing a report of a nearby robbery in progress. (P)	_____
(R)	9. This officer is considered friendly by the other officers on the shift. (A)	_____

Figure 7–6 Example of the Mixed Standard Rating Scale for Appraising the Performance of Police Officers

SOURCE: F. J. Landy and D. A. Trumbo, *Psychology of Work Behavior, rev. ed.* (Pacific Grove, Calif.: Brooks/Cole, 1980).

Dickinson and Zellinger (1980) found that the mixed-standard scale was not very popular among raters. As part of a larger study, they compared the reactions of teachers and students who used three rating scales: mixed standard, BARS, and a variation of the graphic scale. The raters were asked which scale was easiest to use, most preferred, and so on. The results are presented in Table 7–1. As shown, the mixed standard scale was not rated highest on any of the five questions asked. In particular, it was difficult to use.

TABLE 7–1 *Percentage of Preferences for Three Rating Formats*

Questions Asked of Raters	Format		
	MSS	BARS	GT
Instructions for this form were clear and easily understood.	22%	18%	60%
This form was most successful in meeting assessment goals.	24	52	24
This form was easiest to use.	13	31	56
This form would provide the best feedback to students and faculty members.	34	47	19
Which form do you prefer?	23	47	30

Note: MSS = Mixed standard scale; BARS = Behaviorally anchored rating scale; GT = Graphic type.

SOURCE: Adapted from T. L. Dickinson and P. M. Zellinger, "A Comparison of the Behaviorally Anchored Rating and Mixed Standard Scale Formats," *Journal of Applied Psychology, 65* (1980), pp. 147–154.

Validity of Judgmental Data.   The validity of judgmental data in performance appraisal, as is true of the validity of any type of performance-appraisal data, refers to the extent to which the observed data are accurate measures of the "true" variable being measured. The "true" variable can refer to a global construct, such as overall job performance, or a dimension of job performance, such as interpersonal-relations ability. One method of assessing the validity of judgmental data is to correlate them with appraisals of performance emerging with another method, such as objective production or personnel data. In studies that have conducted this type of analysis, the resulting correlations have been only moderate in magnitude. While these results may be interpreted to mean that judgmental data have only moderate validity, the key question is whether the objective production data or the personnel data can be assumed to represent "true" ability. Those types of data might be just as incomplete or remotely relevant as judgmental data. Since we never obtain measures of the conceptual criterion (that is, "true" ability), we are forced to deal with imperfect measures that, not surprisingly, yield imperfect results.

Borman (1978) had another approach to assessing the validity of judgmental data. He made videotapes of two employment situations: a manager talking with a problem employee and a recruiter interviewing a job candidate. Sixteen videotapes were made, eight of each situation. Each tape showed a different degree of performance, for example, from a highly competent recruiter to a totally inept one. Similar degrees of performance were shown of the manager/subordinate meeting. Professional actors were used in the tapes. The same actor played the recruiter in all eight tapes, but a different actor played the new employee in each tape. Thus, the performance level (the "true" ability of the manager or recruiter) was "programmed" into the scripts.

Raters were asked to rate the performance of the manager and recruiter with a series of rating scales. The evaluations were correlated with the performance levels depicted. Correlations between ratings and level of performance across several job dimensions (organizing the interview, establishing rapport, and so on) ranged from .42 to .97. The median was .69. Although this study used a simulation as opposed to actual job performance, it did show that various types of rating procedures were susceptible to differences in validity. The study also revealed that certain dimensions of performance were more accurately evaluated ("answering recruitee's questions," $r = .97$) than others ("reacting to stress," $r = .42$). Borman was led to conclude that raters are limited in their ability to appraise performance in that they could not accurately evaluate the levels of "true" performance that were acted out in the scripts. He suggested a practical upper limit to validity that is less than the theoretical limit ($r = 1.0$) (see Field Note 3).

Field Note 3

Many times there are unexpected costs associated with performance appraisal. Here is the story of one of the more unusual expenses I have ever encountered in a research study.

One of the uses of performance-appraisal information is to serve as a criterion of job performance. In turn, criteria of job performance may be used to validate selection tests, a process previously described. I had a colleague who needed to collect both performance-appraisal (criterion) data and test score (predictor) data to develop a selection test battery for a company. He traveled to the company and had all the supervisors convene in the company cafeteria. He explained the nature of the performance ratings he wanted them to make on their subordinates. Then he explained that all their subordinates would be taking a 30-minute test, the scores from which would be correlated with the supervisors' performance-appraisal ratings, as is done in a concurrent criterion-related validity study. My colleague then asked the supervisors if they wanted to take the same test their subordinates would be taking just to get a feel for what it is like. They agreed. He then passed out the tests and informed them they would have 30 minutes to complete it. He wanted the testing procedure to be very exact, giving everyone precisely 30 minutes. His watch did not have a second hand, so he was about to ask if he could borrow someone's watch that did have one, when he spied the company's microwave oven on the wall in the cafeteria. He went over to the microwave, set the timer for 30 minutes, told the supervisors to begin the test, and started the microwave.

About 20 minutes into the test, a terrible odor began to fill the cafeteria. Somebody noticed it was coming from the microwave. My colleague had failed to place anything into the microwave when he started it, so for 20 minutes the microwave cooked itself, ultimately suffering terminal meltdown. The microwave cost $800 to replace and is one of the more unusual test-validation expense items I have ever heard of. Incidentally, the test turned out to be highly predictive of the performance-appraisal ratings, so the exercise was not a complete waste.

Rater Training

Can you train raters to make better performance appraisals? The answer appears to be yes. Most rater-training studies seek to train appraisers to make fewer leniency, halo, and central-tendency errors. For example, Latham, Wexley, and Pursell (1975) randomly assigned 60 managers who appraised performance to one of the following three groups:

1. *Workshop group.* This group was shown videotapes on evaluating individuals. Members then discussed appraisal procedures and problems in making appraisals, all with the intent of reducing rating errors.

2. *Discussion group.* This group received training similar in content, but the main method was discussion.

3. *Control group.* This group received no training.

Six months later, the three groups were "tested." They were shown videotapes of several hypothetical job candidates along with job requirements. The managers were asked to evaluate the candidates' suitability for the jobs in question. There were major differences in the rating errors made by each of the groups. Those in the workshop group had no rating errors. Those in the control group performed the worst; they made three types of errors.

Other studies report less uniform findings. Pulakos (1984) found that halo errors were best reduced by one type of training, while leniency errors were best reduced of another. Fay and Latham (1982) reported success in reducing rating errors across three types of rating scales: BOS, BARS, and graphic. However, the behavioral based scales were more resistant to errors in general than the graphic scale. Zedeck and Cascio (1982) considered the purpose for which performance-appraisal ratings were made—merit raise, retention, or development—and found that training works better for some purposes than others. Training typically enhances the accuracy of performance appraisals, but also their acceptability to those appraised. Davis and Mount (1984) found that managers who were trained in performance appraisal conducted appraisal discussions that were perceived by employees as more satisfying than those of untrained managers.

However, not all of the research on rater training is positive. Bernardin and Pence (1980) reported that raters who were trained to reduce halo errors actually made *less*-accurate ratings after training. This seems due to the fact, that as Bartlett (1983) noted, there are two types of halo; reduction of invalid halo will increase accuracy, but reduction of valid halo will decrease it.

Hedge and Kavanagh (1988) found that some training methods reduce the occurrence of classical rating errors but also reduce rating accuracy. Other methods increase accuracy but do not reduce errors. Pulakos (1986) concluded that not only is there no one best appraisal instrument but there is also no one best way to train raters to provide accurate performance ratings. While ample research has been conducted on various techniques of rater training, an equally important need is to train people to be critical judges of performance. Most people do not like to be critical of others (they would rather say nice things to or about them). Therefore, the emphasis in rater training should be less on the evaluative *skills* of the raters than on their *attitudes* about making ratings.

Evaluation of Poor Performance

When an employee is judged to be performing poorly, what is the cause of the poor performance? Some recent research has addressed this question. Mitchell and Kalb (1982) found that experienced supervisors are more likely to blame the environment (for example, tools, equipment, working conditions) for poor performance and to recommend more changes in that area than are inexperienced supervisors. Podsakoff (1982) reported that supervisors punish poor performance when they perceive it as a result of lack of motivation rather than a lack of ability or task difficulty. Mitchell and Linden (1982) revealed how complex social situations can moderate a supervisor's explanation of poor performance. They found that a supervisor will rate poor performers more positively when they are high in social skills than when they are weak in this area. It also appears that supervisors may be influenced by characteristics of the work group when assessing a subordinate's poor performance. Ilgen, Mitchell,

Rater bias is a problem in judging some Olympic events. Judges often give athletes from their own country higher ratings than do judges from other countries.   Duomo Photography, Inc./Paul Sutton

and Fredrickson (1981) found that supervisors tend to hold generalized negative biases toward poor performers, even when their poor performance occurred in a specific task. What all these studies indicate is that because subordinate's poor performance is a liability for supervisors, it must somehow be accounted for. Supervisors are ultimately responsible for the performance of their groups and will rarely tolerate poor subordinate performance for very long. Green, Fairhurst, and Snavely (1986) found that there was a better resolution of problems of poor performance when more punitive control tactics (such as warnings and probation) than nonpunishing actions (such as discussion and job modification) were utilized by supervisors. The research on poor performance reveals the variety of mechanisms supervisors use to explain and react to the poor performer.

Not all of the research on poor performance involves supervisor reactions to it. Some studies examine the conditions under which poor performance is perceived to exist. Heilman and Stopeck (1985) examined the relationship between physical attractiveness, sex, and perceived performance. Physical attractiveness proved advantageous for women in nonmanagerial jobs and disadvantageous for women in managerial jobs. The image of a good-looking woman holding a high-status job was too threatening, and her job performance would more likely have been rated as poor compared to that of a less-attractive woman in a managerial job or an attractive woman in a lower-level job. However, physical appearance was found to have no effect on the judgments of male job performance. The authors concluded that attractiveness enhanced the perceived femininity of women, but did not enhance the perceived masculinity of men.

We will probably continue to witness interest in the topic of poor performance in the years ahead, particularly as it relates to differing standards for its occurrence across protected group members and reactions of supervisors. Most people enjoy being the bearers of "good news" (that is, positive evaluations). However, supervisors often feel reluctant to convey evaluations of poor performance. In fact, it is the very basis on which supervisors recoil from making evaluations, because they do not like to "play God."

Self and Peer Appraisals

Most research on judgmental performance appraisal deals with evaluations made by a superior (supervisor, manager). However, there is also information on the value of performance appraisals made by colleagues or peers. Self-evaluations have also been discussed. Our knowledge is somewhat limited, but these methods do offer added understanding of performance appraisal.

Self-Assessments

With *self-assessment,* as the term suggests, each employee appraises his or her own performance. The procedure most commonly used is some type of graphic rating scale. Meyer (1980) reported a study in which 92 engineers rated their performance against their views of the performance of other engineers in the company. On average, each engineer thought he or she was performing better than 75% of the rest of the engineers in the study. Statistically, it is quite a trick to have 75% of the work force feel that they are in the top 25% of job performers. This underscores the biggest problem with self-assessment: positive leniency. Most people have higher opinions of their own performance than do others.

Anderson, Warner, and Spencer (1984) demonstrated in a clever study just how prevalent and pervasive inflation bias is in self-assessments of ability. The authors had applicants rate their own abilities in real clerical tasks as well as bogus tasks that sounded real but were in fact nonsense. Some of the bogus tasks were "operating matriculation machine," "typing from audio-fortran reports," and "circumscribing general meeting registers." The clerical applicants rated themselves high not only in the real tasks (where their ability was not verified) but also in tasks that did not even exist! Steel and Ovalle (1984) found that there was less positive leniency in self-assessments when there was a high degree of feedback from supervisors. In other words, employees who get little feedback from their supervisors think more highly of their own abilities than employees who receive a lot. Mount (1984) found that managers evaluate themselves more leniently compared both to how they evaluate their supervisors and to how their supervisors evaluate them.

Thornton (1980) reports that despite leniency problems, there are *fewer* halo errors with self-appraisals. It appears that people recognize their strengths and weaknesses and appraise themselves accordingly. Thornton also reported little agreement in most studies comparing self-assessmemts and supervisor assessments. Superiors do not evaluate employees in the same way that employees evaluate themselves. This does not mean that one appraisal is "right" and the other "wrong." It just means that the two groups do not agree in evaluating the same performance. Thornton suggests this may be healthy because it provides a basis for discussing differences and may foster an exchange of ideas.

A study by Levine, Flory, and Ash (1977) showed that self-assessments of clerical employees in such areas as spelling, grammar, reading speed, and word meaning correlated fairly well with two criteria of job performance. There were correlations as high as .74 among self-assessments, written tests, and supervisor ratings. Furthermore, self-assessments of typing speed correlated .62 with typing test scores. However, these were *concurrent* criterion-related validity coefficients, because these people already held jobs. Among job *applicants,* there may be more incentive to distort information. While the *predictive* validity of self-assessments awaits further research, the concurrent validity coefficients reported by Levine and associates (1977) are as good as the predictions made by other types of variables. Across all types of studies, Mabe and West (1982) found self-assessments of ability had an average correlation of .29 with measures of job performance. Campbell and Lee (1988) concluded that self assessments were of greater value when used for developmental purposes rather than for administrative purposes.

Peer Assessments

In *peer assessment,* members of a group appraise the performance of their fellows. According to Kane and Lawler (1978), three techniques are commonly used. One is *peer nomination*: each person nominates a specified number of group members as being highest on the particular dimension of performance. *Peer ratings* have each group member rate the others on a set of performance dimensions using one of several kinds of rating scales. The third technique is *peer ranking*: having each member rank all others from best to worst on one or more performance dimensions.

The method's reliability is determined by assessing the degree of interrater agreement. Most studies report high reliabilities (coefficients in the .80s and .90s), indicating that peers agree about the job performance of group members. Validity of peer assessments is determined by correlating the peer assessments with criterion measures usually made later: who successfully completed a training program, who got promoted first, the size of raises, and so on. What is uncanny is that group members who have known one another a relatively short time (two to three weeks) can be quite accurate in making long-term predictions about one another. Validity coefficients are fairly impressive, commonly in the .40-to-.50 range. The peer *nomination* technique appears to be the best in identifying people with extreme levels of attributes compared to other members of the group. Peer *ratings* are the most applicable but have only marginal empirical support. It has been suggested that their use be limited to giving feedback to employees on how others perceive them. Relatively few data are available on the value of peer *rankings*, though they may be the best method for assessing overall job performance.

Love (1981) compared the three peer-assessment methods in a study of police officers. He found that the peer-ranking and nomination methods had more reliability and validity than did the peer-rating technique. However, the police officers did not like evaluating their peers' performance regardless of the method used.

There is some evidence that peer assessments are biased by friendship (that is, employees evaluate their friends most favorably). But friendships may be formed on the basis of performance. Also, many work group members do not like to evaluate one another, so part of the method's success hinges on impressing participants with its value. Indeed, a study by Cederblom and Lounsbury (1980) showed that lack of user acceptance may be a serious obstacle in using this otherwise promising method. The authors found that a sample of college professors felt peer assessments were heavily biased by friendship. They thought peers would rate and be rated by their friends more favorably than would be justified. Problems with knowing the people to be rated and fostering a "mutual admiration society" caused the professors to question the value of peer assessment. They also felt that the method should be used for feedback, not for raises and promotions. A similar conclusion regarding the user acceptance of peer appraisals was reached by McEvoy and Buller (1987).

Peer assessment, like self-assessment, is part of an overall performance-appraisal system. The information generated cannot be isolated from information gained using other methods. Holzbach (1978) showed that superior, peer, and self-assessments all contribute information about performance. But information from each source involved halo errors. Borman (1974) showed that peers, superiors, and subordinates (if any) hold unique pieces of the puzzle that portrays a person's job performance. Thus, rather than having raters at just one level of the organization perform the entire appraisal, it is better to have each level contribute the portion that it is able to perform most effectively. Each performance dimension should be defined precisely enough to obtain the information unique to the relevant source. Overlap with dimensions better assessed by other sources should be avoided. The appraisal system should include compatible and mutually supporting segments. Each segment should be assigned the role to which it is best suited (Kane & Lawler, 1978). Performance appraisal should not be seen as simply selecting the best method. What is "best" varies with the use made of the information, the complexity of the performance appraised, and the people capable of making such judgments.

Assessment Centers

Assessment centers involve appraising multiple dimensions of performance using several methods and raters. Assessment centers are a group-oriented, standardized series of activities that provide a basis for judgments or predictions of human behaviors believed or known to be relevant to work performed in an organizational setting (Finkle, 1976). They may be a physical part of some organizations, such as special rooms designed for the purpose. They can also be located in a conference center away from the normal workplace. Because these centers are expensive, they have been used mainly by large organizations that can afford them. However, some private organizations conduct assessment center appraisals for smaller companies. The centers are used to appraise management personnel. The earliest systematic approach to assessment center evaluation was developed in 1956 by AT&T and is described in detail by Bray, Campbell, and Grant (1974) and summarized by Bray (1982). Since the pioneering efforts of AT&T, hundreds of other organizations have developed centers for the appraisal of upper-level employees.

There are several characteristics of the assessment center approach:

1. Those selected to attend (the assessees) are usually management-level personnel whom the company wants to evaluate for possible promotion, transfer, or training. Occasionally organizations will send management *applicants* to the center and then use appraisal information for selection.

2. Assessees are evaluated in groups of usually 10 to 20. They may be divided into smaller groups for various exercises, but the basic strategy is to appraise individuals against the performance of others in the group.

3. Several raters (the assessors) do the evaluation. They work in teams and collectively or individually recommend personnel action (for example, selection, promotion). Raters may be psychologists, but they are usually company employees unfamiliar with the assessees. Raters are usually trained in how to appraise performance. The training may last from several hours to a few days.

4. Performance is appraised using a wide variety of methods. Many involve group interactions, for example, leaderless group discussions in which leaders "emerge" via their degree of participation in the exercise. Other methods include in-basket tests, projective personality inventories, personal history information forms, and interviews. The program typically takes from at least one day to several days.

Given the variety of tests, the person assessed provides a lot of information about his or her performance. Raters evaluate the assessees on a number of performance dimensions judged relevant for the job in question. These involve leadership, decision making, practical judgment, and interpersonal relations skills—the typical performance dimensions for managerial jobs. Based on these evaluations, a summary report is prepared for each assessee. Portions of the report are fed back to the assessee by a rater. Recommendations for personnel action are forwarded to the organization for review and consideration.

Conclusions about assessment center effectiveness are mixed, though most evidence is quite positive. Since the evaluations are mainly rater judgments, their reliability is very important. Hinrichs and Haanpera (1976) reported interrater reliability coefficients for 15 performance dimensions from .23 to .92, with an average of .52. It was clear that raters agreed more on some dimensions than others. In a similar study, Schmitt (1977) found interrater reliability coefficients for 17 dimensions from .46 to .88 based on evaluations made *before* raters discussed the candidates. *After* they "compared notes" and tried to iron out some differences of opinion, they rerated the candidates. The range then rose to .74 to .95. The practical implication is that companies should not draw conclusions about employee performance on dimensions with low reliability. Personnel actions should be based only on those aspects where there is satisfactory agreement.

The validity of assessment center evaluations is determined by comparing the judgments of performance made in the center with some criterion of performance back on the job, usually rated job performance, promotions, or salary (Huck, 1973). Validity studies on assessment center evaluations are generally quite positive. Byham (1970) reported that correlations of center evaluations of managers with subsequent job performance rated by superiors ranged from .47 to .64. Moses and Boehm (1975) analyzed center evaluations for male and female employees and concluded that assessment centers predicted the future performance for females as accurately as they did for males. Ritchie and Moses (1983) found that assessment center ratings were predictive of the career programs of women seven years later. Huck and Bray (1976) reported a similar finding regarding the fairness of assessment centers in predicting the future job performance of White and Black employees. It seems that assessment center evaluations do not have the racial or sex bias of some job performance predictors.

The long-term validity of assessment center evaluations is also encouraging. Mitchel (1975) reported an average multiple correlation of .42 between assessment center judgments and a criterion of salary growth after one, three, and five years for a sample of managers. Hinrichs (1978) examined the predictive validity of 12 assessment center evaluations in forecasting managers' positions one and eight years later. The results are shown in Table 7–2. Eleven of the 12 predictors *increased* in validity

TABLE 7–2 *Correlations of Assessment Center Characteristics with a Promotional Criterion*

	Promotional Level	
Characteristic	Year 1	Year 8
Aggressiveness	.27	.69
Persuasive and selling ability	.29	.59
Oral communication	.35	.50
Self-confidence	.46	.60
Interpersonal contact	.34	.48
Decision making	.36	.42
Resistance to stress	.41	.42
Energy level	.17	.34
Administrative ability	.20	.22
Written communications	.02	.22
Planning and organization	.11	.20
Risk taking	.16	.01

SOURCE: Adapted from J. R. Hinrichs, "An Eight-Year Follow-up of a Management Assessment Center," *Journal of Applied Psychology, 63* (1978), pp. 596–601.

between the first and eighth year. Self-confidence was the strongest predictor ($r = .46$) after one year; aggressiveness was the strongest, $r = .69$, after eight years. Some predictors were uniformly valid. Others (for example, risk taking) were not predictive of later performance. These validity coefficients are extremely impressive, not only because of their size but also because the criterion was assessed many years after collection of the assessment evaluation. In a review of 50 empirical studies on assessment center validity, Gaugler, Rosenthal, Thornton, and Bentson (1987) reported an average validity coefficient of .37 for assessment center evaluations. The authors also found that higher validities were observed when psychologists rather than managers served as assessors.

However, as a study by Cascio and Silbey (1979) indicated, one need not have very high validity coefficients in order for assessment center evaluations to have *utility*. As discussed in Chapter 5, the validity of a predictor has the most impact on utility. However, those who go through assessment centers usually hold important jobs where the consequences of making errors will be expensive to the company. Validity coefficients as low as .10 can produce significant gains in overall criterion performance compared to random ($r = .00$) selection; that is, the utility of valid evaluations is increased because of the value of the assessee's job to the organization.

Assessment centers offer promise for identifying persons with potential for success in management. Assessment centers seem to be successful in their major goal of selecting high-talent people. Nevertheless, not all of the research results are totally positive. A critical factor seems to be the criterion against which assessment center ratings are validated. For example, Borman (1982) and Tziner and Dolan (1982) found that assessment center ratings were predictive of success in military training and far superior in validity to interviews or psychological tests. We also have known for a long time that assessment center ratings predict the criterion of promotability. Thus, assessment ratings have the capacity to identify individuals who will "get ahead" in the organization. However, Turnage and Muchinsky (1984) found that assessment center ratings were *not* predictive of actual on-the-job performance measures, as indexed by 21 criteria of supervisory performance. Thus, assessment ratings predict advancement but not performance.

What is it, then, that assessment center evaluations measure? Sackett and Dreher (1982) feel they do *not* measure the different constructs they are supposed to measure. They believe the assessment ratings are highly influenced by the biases of the assessors. In fact, Turnage and Muchinsky (1982) found assessment evaluations to be heavily saturated with halo error with little differentiation across rated constructs, resulting in all assessees being rated along a single good/bad continuum. In short, while assessment center ratings are predictive of certain criteria, they are not uniformly predictive of all relevant criteria.

Assessment center evaluations are particularly susceptible to criterion *contamination* from several sources. One is that overall judgments of performance are based on many evaluation methods (tests, interviews, life history forms, and so on). The validity of the evaluations may stem from the validity of these separate appraisal methods; that is, a valid interview or test might be just as capable of forecasting later job success as the resulting evaluation. But because the incremental value of these methods is "buried" in the overall assessor judgments, it is debatable how much assessors' ratings contribute to predicting future performance beyond these separate methods (Howard, 1974). Some research attests to the predictive value of assessor judgments. Other studies find traditional predictions of job success based on test scores to be superior (for example, Wollowick & McNamara, 1969).

A second source of contamination is far more subtle and has been proposed by Klimoski and Strickland (1977). They contend that the reasons assessment center evaluations are predictive is that both assessors and company supervisors hold common stereotypes of the "effective employee." Assessors give higher evaluations to those who "look" like good management talent. Supervisors give higher evaluations to those who "look" like good "company" people. If the two sets of stereotypes were held in common, then (biased) assessment center evaluations would correlate with (biased) job performance evaluations. The danger is that organizations would hire and promote those who fit the image of the successful employee. The long-term effect would be an organization staffed with people who were mirror images of one another. Opportunity for creative people who "don't fit the mold" but might be effective if given the chance would be greatly limited.

After reviewing the literature on assessment centers, Klimoski and Brickner (1987) concluded that assessment evaluations are indeed valid but I/O psychologists still do not really know why. The authors proposed five possible explanations.

1. Actual criterion contamination. Companies use the assessment evaluations to make decisions regarding promotions, pay raises, and rated job performance, so it is hardly surprising that assessment evaluations would predict such criteria.

2. Subtle criterion contamination. As explained by Klimoski and Strickland (1977), both assessors and company supervisors hold common stereotypes of the successful employee, so biased assessment evaluations are related to biased job evaluations.

3. Self-fulfilling prophecy. Companies designate their "up-and-coming" employees to attend assessment centers, and after assessment these same people are indeed the ones who get ahead in the company.

4. Performance consistency. People who succeed in work-related activities do so in many arenas—in assessment centers, in training, on the job, and so on. They are consistently good performers, so success in assessment relates to success on the job.

5. Managerial intelligence. The skills and abilities needed to be successful in assessment centers and on the job have much in common. Such talents as verbal skills, analytic reasoning, and well-developed plans of action are acquired and cultivated by more intellectually capable people. The authors refer to this construct as "managerial intelligence."

Research on assessment centers has been evolutionary in nature. Early research addressed whether assessment evaluations were predictive of job success and found they were. More recent research addresses the limits of this method of assessment, and the reasons that assessment evaluations are predictive. As our knowledge about assessment centers continues to grow, we are beginning to address some complex and intriguing questions of both theoretical and practical significance (see Field Note 4).

Field Note 4

One of the characteristics of assessment centers is that they are highly obtrusive; that is, the assessees know they are being evaluated and, within reasonable limits, typically know what the assessors are looking for in the candidates. Most assessment exercises are group evaluations wherein the assessees discuss problems, propose solutions, try to get their own ideas endorsed by the group, and in general try to appear as "leaders," for they are typically being evaluated for some leadership position. A problem with this type of assessment paradigm is that the assessees may act differently during assessment than they do (or would) back on the job. One veteran assessee I spoke to referred to this phenomenon as "Show Time" and likened it to giving a performance on stage. Although the assessors do not hold up rating cards at the end of each performance as they do in some Olympic events, in a very real way the "Show Time" analogy is highly appropriate.

Here is what the assessee had to say:

> I know I must give a good performance to get a good rating. So I try to psych them out and give them what I think they want to see. I talk a lot, but I'm not rude to others. I sit attentively in my chair; I don't lean back. I want to give the impression I'm really into the exercise. I acknowledge the value of other people's opinions, but I never back down from my own. I always

come up with a solution or a plan to the problem being discussed. I never leave it hanging. I want them to know I'm action-oriented and a doer. I smile a lot and nod my head often. I want them to know I'm a positive, confident, and accepting person. Is this the way I normally am? No. In real life I operate much more slowly. I take more time to make decisions and to think things through. I don't normally solicit other people's opinions as a matter of course. I will do so if I truly want to know how they feel, but usually I don't care. I don't act my normal way in assessment because I'm afraid they might take me the wrong way. They might equate my being slow with being stupid and my silence with not caring about the problem. I can't risk them thinking that about me. I know I'm "on" in assessment, which is why I call it "Show Time."

How pervasive is this problem of assessees acting differently than they normally would? I don't know, but I assume all candidates are apprehensive to some degree about being appraised. This, in turn, might make them behave somewhat atypically. A well-trained assessor should not be deceived by a few cosmetic actions, but in a brief evaluation period they could significantly influence the assessor's judgment.

Feedback of Appraisal Information to Employees

In the final step of appraisal, the employee and his or her superior review and discuss the evaluation. This is usually referred to by the misnomer "performance appraisal interview." Performance was appraised before the interview; the interview is a means of giving the employee the results. Both superior and subordinate are usually very uneasy about the interview. Employees often get defensive about negative performance aspects. Superiors are often nervous about having to confront employees face to face with negative evaluations. However, for an appraisal system to be effective, interview objectives must be met with the same rigor as the other system objectives.

The interview typically has two main objectives. The first is feedback on how well the employee is performing. This often means reviewing major job responsibilities and how well the employee has met them. The second objective is future planning. This means identifying goals the employee will try to meet before the next review. Both employee and superior should provide input in setting goals.

There has been much research on factors that contribute to success in meeting the two objectives of the interview. Feedback on job performance has two properties: information and motivation. That is, feedback can tell the employee how to perform better. It can also increase the employee's desire to perform well. Ilgen, Fisher, and Taylor (1979) showed that how the employee perceives the superior can greatly influence his or her response to feedback. They feel credibility and power are the most important aspects here. *Credibility* is the extent to which the superior is seen as someone who can legitimately evaluate performance. It is enhanced when the superior is seen as having expertise about the employee's job and being in a position to evaluate performance. *Power* is the extent to which the superior can control valued rewards. Ilgen and associates believe that credibility and power influence (1) how well the employee understands feedback; (2) the extent to which the feedback is seen as correct; and (3) the willingness of the employee to alter behavior as suggested by the feedback.

Other factors can also influence employee reactions to the performance appraisal interview. Kay, Meyer, and French (1965) studied the relationship between criticism and employee defensiveness. They found that the more critical the superior, the more defensive the employee became. However, praise per se did not make employees more at ease. Most criticism was buried in a "praise sandwich" (that is, praise/criticism/praise). The superior would praise the employee ostensibly to make him or her feel more at ease, then criticize some aspect of the employee's performance, then praise the employee again so that he or she left with a "good feeling." But employees became conditioned to the fact that when they were praised, it was a signal that some criticism was just around the corner.

Another area of research—but largely untested in this context—is nonverbal communication. People give messages with a variety of nonverbal cues like frowning, smiling, eye contact, and twitching. Extensive research (for example, Vetter, 1969) has shown that people do attribute meaning to these nonverbal cues, though the meaning may not accurately reveal the affective state of the cue sender. For example, if an employee slouches in the chair during the interview, the superior can interpret the behavior to mean the employee is indifferent or bored. The superior who does not smile during the meeting may be perceived by the employee as having a rejecting feeling about him or her. Both parties could be wrong in their attributions of meaning. The slouching employee may be very nervous, not bored. The unsmiling superior may only be trying to avoid the image that the interview is a lighthearted affair that should not be taken seriously. Sometimes nonverbal cues are seen as complementing the verbal message. ("I got praised up and down, and he never quit smiling the whole time.") At other times, they may be a mixed signal. ("I can't quite figure it out—he said I was doing great, but he didn't smile at me once.") The extent to which nonverbal cues are perceived to provide feedback in an interview relative to verbal responses is a matter that awaits further research.

The most effective way to conduct the appraisal interview from the perspective of setting target performance objectives has also been the subject of considerable research. Much of the research is based on addressing the degree of employee participation in the interview. Maier (1976) proposed three interview styles: tell and sell, tell and listen, and problem solving. In the tell-and-sell style, employees have very little involvement in the interview; the superior "tells" them what to do and tries to "sell" them on how to improve performance. In the tell-and-listen style, employees are told their strengths and weaknesses, but they are allowed to express their feelings about how they can improve their performance. The problem-solving style allows employees the most participation. Job-related plans and goals are set based on the ideas of both parties. Maier's research indicates that employee satisfaction with the interview and motivation were most enhanced by the problem-solving style.

Increased satisfaction and motivation and actual improvements in performance were identified as the most important consequences of the appraisal interview (Burke & Wilcox, 1969). Furthermore Burke, Weitzel, and Weir (1978) found that different aspects of the appraisal interview were related to the outcomes of employee satisfaction and subsequent improvements in job performance. Increased employee participation in the interview resulted in greater satisfaction but not improved job performance. Discussion of problem solving and goal setting did result in subsequent job performance improvements. However, as Ivancevich (1982) has noted, while assigning goals to subordinates may increase their performance, it also increases their anxiety.

The apparent superiority of the problem-solving style of interview seems to hold regardless of the employee's personality. Wexley, Singh, and Yukl (1973) found that two personality variables—authoritarianism and need for independence—did not affect the amount of participation the employee desired in the interview. Their results indicated that it was desirable to allow employees to have substantial participation in appraisal interview decisions since it increased their satisfaction with the interview and motivation to improve subsequent job performance. While Latham and Yukl (1975) concede that attitudes, education, and cultural background may affect an employee's response to mutual goal setting, we do not know the effect of these variables on the problem-solving style.

In any case, the appraisal interview, however conducted, is a vital last link in the total performance-appraisal system. Most research has focused on methods of collecting appraisal information. But getting that information back to employees is critical. Without the interview, performance appraisal can appear to be a perfunctory operation that has no real impact on employees. Research on the performance-appraisal interview indicates that it can greatly influence the subsequent employee's behavior on the job.

Cederblom (1982) found that three factors seem consistently useful in producing effective performance-appraisal interviews: (1) the supervisor's knowledge of the subordinate's job and performance in it; (2) the supervisor's support of the subordinate; and (3) a welcoming of the subordinate's participation. However, it should also be realized that just conducting a performance-appraisal interview will not resolve all problems in evaluating subordinate performance. Ilgen, Peterson, Martin, and Boeschen (1981) found that even *after* the performance-appraisal interview, subordinates and supervisors sometimes disagreed on the level of subordinate performance, with subordinates feeling their performance was at a higher level.

In a review of performance evaluations, Greenberg (1986) identified seven characteristics that contributed to employees' accepting their evaluations and feeling they were fair:

1. Soliciting employee input prior to the evaluation and using it;

2. Having two-way communication during the appraisal interview;

3. Allowing for the opportunity to challenge/rebut the evaluation;

4. The rater's degree of familiarity with the ratee's work;

5. The use of consistent application of performance standards;

6. Ratings being based on actual performance achieved; and

7. Recommendations for salary/promotions being based on the ratings.

I fully concur with the findings from Greenberg's research. My experience with effective performance-appraisal systems underscores the importance of all of these characteristics, and clearly reveals there is a lot more to performance evaluation than making a check mark on an appraisal instrument.

Concluding Comments

As noted, the major contribution of I/O psychologists to performance appraisal is the design of methods. Although the value of such methods is great, I feel that the heavy emphasis on "technique" is somewhat misplaced. Feldman (1981) observed that the psychological aspects of appraisal are complex. Evaluators must organize and store a great deal of information about subordinates, information obtained through daily interaction. Attention and recognition are involved because certain aspects of behavior are judged to be more noteworthy than others. An evaluator must appraise an employee's performance about once a year. The information then must be recalled, categorized, integrated, and evaluated. Finally, a check mark is made on a rating sheet reflecting the entirety of all the information processed. There is clearly more to performance appraisal than deciding if the check mark is to be made on a graphic rating scale, forced distribution scale, BARS, BOS, or the mixed-standard scale. Because I/O psychologists are deeply concerned with problems of measurement, it is easy to see how their infatuation with rating scales came to be.

Despite the legitimate need to understand "technique," we should expand our horizons to other issues in performance appraisal. The cognitive processes used by raters such as those Feldman proposed are one avenue. Another larger issue is demonstration of the *utility* of performance appraisal for the organization. If we believe (as we do) that performance appraisal is a valuable tool for enhancing the welfare of both individuals and organizations, we should be able to demonstrate its actual worth, just as we did with personnel selection procedures. Another fertile area for research is how performance-appraisal information is *used* after it is collected (by whatever means). Issues regarding exactly how administrators use performance-appraisal information to make promotions, determine pay raises, and guide employees are just as important as whether the information is biased or accurate. In summary, performance appraisal covers a broad array of substantive issues, ranging from how the human brain processes information to interorganizational differences in using performance-appraisal information. We must not lose sight of the diversity of issues facing us in our pursuit of knowledge, and we should not fix most of our attention on but one part of the entire process.

Much of the research on performance appraisal conducted by I/O psychologists in recent years has been of the laboratory variety. As we discussed in Chapter 2, the generalizability of the findings from laboratory studies is sometimes questionable. Are some of the performance-appraisal research findings limited in applicability to the real world? Some authors think so. Mobley (1982) questions the validity of laboratory studies that show that sex and race are important factors in determining rated performance. Mobley estimates that in real life, race and sex effects account for less than 5% of the variance in performance appraisals. Ilgen and Favero (1985) feel that laboratory studies of performance appraisals have failed to consider the continuous nature of interactions between the appraiser and appraisees. In actual practice, formal performance appraisal is but one function performed rarely (perhaps once a year) in what is an ongoing relationship between supervisors and subordinates. Ilgen and Favero believe the findings of some laboratory studies may be biased because of the highly segmented nature of performance appraisals created in these settings.

Latham (1986) makes a similar point by noting that in many experimental studies of performance appraisal the appraiser is not accountable for the evaluations that were made. In real life, supervisors who make evaluations of their subordinates are, in turn, evaluated by their bosses. It is conceivable that the poor job performance of subordinates may be attributable to having a poor supervisor, and "corrective" action may be taken with the supervisor, not the subordinates. This type of issue is rarely considered in many experimental studies of performance appraisal. Finally, Banks and Murphy (1985) raise a critical point on which I totally agree. While findings from performance appraisal research enhance our *ability* to judge accurately, they do not necessarily address the rater's *willingness* to provide accurate ratings. If raters are truly reluctant to "play God," all that we have learned about performance appraisal will scarcely matter. I feel we should pay as much attention to our *desire* to appraise performance accurately as we do to techniques of doing so.

MAJOR CHAPTER OBJECTIVES IN REVIEW

After having read this chapter, you should know:

1. Steps followed in implementing a performance appraisal program.

2. Uses of performance-appraisal information.

3. Sources of performance-appraisal data and associated limitations of each.

4. Major types of rating errors.

5. Purpose of rater training.

6. Self-appraisal and peer appraisal.

7. Purpose of assessment centers and issues associated with their use.

8. Performance-appraisal interview.

CASE STUDY—Who Shall Survive?

Franklin Community College employed a staff of 40 teachers. It was a new college offering a two-year associate of arts degree in a variety of areas. The teachers reported to Louise Medwick, who was in charge of faculty personnel. Economic conditions at the college were not good. The college had to fight for its yearly budget from the state education association, and lately, education had not been a high-priority item. The college had been told that due to cutbacks, 20% of the teachers must be laid off.

Part of Medwick's job was to conduct an annual performance appraisal of the teachers. She did not like this part of her job, but she knew it was critical. Her evaluations would be the main basis for the layoffs. Her boss, college president Fred Schweiker, was adamant about keeping the "best" faculty, and it was her job to determine who was best. There was also the usual concern over raises, as part of a teacher's raise was based on merit. This year, though, the stakes were a lot higher. It's one thing to get a 6% raise when you felt you deserved 8%; it's quite another to get laid off. Medwick knew her decisions would directly and intimately affect the lives of eight teachers. She personally knew and liked the teaching staff, which didn't help matters either. The ax was going to fall, and it was just a case of whose heads were going to roll.

Medwick also faced a somewhat peculiar situation that made matters more easy and more difficult at the same time. The faculty at the college was not unionized. Thus, there was no formal labor contract covering layoffs. Some organizations used seniority as the basis for layoffs—the last person hired was the first laid off. While the college was not compelled to consider seniority in making lay-offs, they could always do so if they wished. The problem was Schweiker didn't want to consider seniority—he wanted those laid off to be the poorest performers, not just the newest staff members.

The other oddity was that because the college was less then 3 years old, none of the staff had tenure. Tenure could preclude the dismissal of those teachers that had it, but no one did. Medwick saw the situation as a curse and a blessing. Seniority and tenure couldn't be used to reduce the pool of teachers who could be laid off, and this made her task more difficult. At the same time, poorly performing teachers couldn't hide behind seniority and tenure as reasons for their retention. Thus, everyone was thrown in the same pot. It was her job to give them all a fair shake.

Medwick knew all about the usual methods of appraising teacher performance, but she was very aware of the limitations when so much was on the line. She had used student ratings in the past. However, many teachers felt they were little more than a popularity contest. At least that's what the teachers who got low ratings said. She also used peer ratings, but only to help teachers improve, not for administrative decisions. Just about everyone taught the same number of classes, so there was no point in simply counting classroom hours. Besides, it would be hard to convince Schweiker that the best teachers also taught the most classes. Last year she wanted to start a behavioral measure of teacher performance—critical incidents, rating scales, the whole bit—but the idea got scratched because of time and financial problems. She wished she had forced this issue, but now it was too late.

Whatever method she used, she would have to be able to explain it and defend it. She also knew she would take a lot of heat from those who got laid off. While Medwick accepted her task as part of the responsibility that comes with the job, she wished she had more solid information to go on. Picking the best from the rest was complicated and she wasn't totally sure in specific terms what the "best" was. Best lecturer, best grader, best advisor? Medwick also knew that while some appraisals simply got filed away, this one wouldn't. The lives of 40 teachers and their families were riding on her decision.

Questions

1. Do you see any relationships between the topic of criteria discussed in Chapter 3 and the issue of performance appraisal? What are some of these relationships?

2. Can you think of any objective performance indexes or personnel data that might help Medwick make her decisions? Do you feel the best teachers would be identified with these indexes

3. If the method used involves *ratings*, who do you think would best serve as raters?

4. One method Medwick could use is some type of forced-choice technique. What problems might Medwick face in ranking the teachers?

5. Suppose Medwick were allowed to use some other factors along with merit performance. What might some of those factors be?

3

Organizational Psychology

8

Organizations and Their Influence on Behavior

As I/O psychologists expanded their scope of inquiry, we gained more appreciation for the organizational context in which work occurs. The Hawthorne studies showed dramatically that employee behavior and attitudes are influenced by more than personal ability and disposition. The O in I/O psychology testifies to the influence that organizations have on behavior. While psychologists have traditionally studied *individuals*, it is obvious that they cannot understand employee behavior apart from the social or organizational context in which employees work. Thus, "organizational psychology" tends to deal with a broader range of variables than "personnel psychology." This does not mean that personnel psychology is simplistic; rather, that personnel selection, training, and performance appraisal embrace a narrower range of issues. Many of the topics addressed in personnel psychology involve techniques, such as those for hiring, training, or appraising performance, and relatively few *theories*. Conversely, there are many theories in organizational psychology, such as those concerning job satisfaction, motivation, and leadership. Because there are many influences that shape behavior in organizations, it is an imposing task to integrate them into a theory of organizational behavior. However, researchers have begun to make strides in this direction (for example, Naylor, Pritchard, & Ilgen, 1980).

Organizational Theory

We will begin this chapter with a brief examination of the theory of organizations— that is, ways that scholars have conceptualized organizations. As you will see, there are several ways to view organizations, and these views (that is, theories) are still evolving among organizational theorists. For the most part, I/O psychologists have not been the primary contributors to organizational theory. Historically, the earliest prominent developments in organizational theory came out of the discipline of sociology. More recent theories have their origins in the biological sciences. As the influence of these scholars spread, researchers from many disciplines contributed to the study of organizations. I/O psychologists have been most interested in how organizations influence the attitudes and behavior of both individuals and groups. The major part of this chapter deals with the product of this influence process.

Three Theories of Organization

It is probably easier to state why organizations exist rather than to define what they are. In their simplest form, organizations exist as a vehicle for accomplishing goals and objectives. That is, organizations are collectivities of parts, parts that cannot accomplish their goals as effectively as they can if they organize themselves in some fashion. How one chooses to examine this organizing process produces the various schools of thought or theories about organizations. In my opinion there are three major schools of thought about organizations, with many variations and emphases (a full discussion of which would take us well beyond the scope of this book). The three major schools of thought take markedly different views of the same phenomenon under consideration. These three schools of thought are called the classical, neoclassical, and modern theories of organization.

Classical Theory

Classical theory, the first of the three to emerge, is concerned mainly with structural relationships in organizations. Classical theory begins with a statement of the basic ingredients of any organization, and then addresses how the organization should best be structured to accomplish its objectives. There are four basic ingredients to any organization.

1. *A system of coordinated activities.* All organizations are composed of the activities and functions performed in them and the relationship among these activities and functions. A formal organization emerges when these activities are linked together.

2. *People.* While organizations are composed of activities and functions, it takes people to perform tasks and exercise authority.

3. *Cooperation toward a goal.* Cooperation must exist among the people performing their various activities to achieve a unity of purpose in pursuit of their common goals.

4. *Authority.* Authority is established through superior–subordinate relationships, and such authority is needed to ensure cooperation among people pursuing their goals.

Given that four ingredients are the basis of any organization, classical theory addressed itself to various structural properties by which the organization should best reach its goals. Four major structural principles were identified, and they are hall-marks in the history of organizational theory.

1. *Functional principle.* The functional principle is the concept behind division of labor, that organizations should be divided into units based upon performing similar functions. Thus, work is broken down to provide clear areas of specialization, which in turn improves the overall performance of the organization. Similar work activities often represent themselves as departments, which enhances coordination of activities, permits more effective supervision, and a more rational flow of work. It is the functional principle that accounts for the fact that you will typically find work functions grouped into such units as production, sales, engineering, finance, and so on, for these labels describe the primary nature of the work performed within each unit. The functional principle refers to the *horizontal* growth of the organization, that is, the formation of new functional units along the horizontal dimension.

2. *Scalar principle.* The scalar principle deals with the organization's *vertical* growth, and refers to the growth of the chain of command that results from levels added to the organization. Each level of the organization has its own degree of authority and responsibility for meeting the goals of the organization, with higher levels having greater degrees. Each subordinate should be accountable to only one superior, a tenet referred to as the *unit of command.* Classical theorists thought the best way to overcome organizational fragmentation caused by division of labor was through a well-designed chain of command. Coordination among factions would be achieved by people occupying positions of command in a hierarchy. Figure 8–1 shows a graphic representation of both the functional and scalar principles.

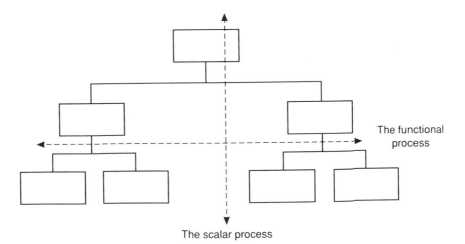

Figure 8–1 Pyramid of Organization

SOURCE: W. G. Scott, T. R. Mitchell, and P. H. Birnbaum, *Organization Theory: A Structural and Behavioral Analysis* (Homewood, Ill.: Richard D. Irwin, 1981).

3. *Line/staff principle.* A way to differentiate organizational work functions was whether they were *line* or *staff*. *Line* functions had the primary responsibility for meeting the major goals of the organization, like the production department in a manufacturing organization. *Staff* functions support the activities of the line, but are regarded as subsidiary in overall importance to line functions. Typical staff functions would be personnel and quality control. That is, while it was important to have good employees and to inspect products for their quality, the organization was not recreated to provide people with jobs or products to inspect. It was created to manufacture products (a line function), and personnel and quality control are but two staff functions designed to support the larger goal of the organization.

4. *Span-of-control principle.* The span-of-control principle refers to the number of subordinates a manager is responsible for supervising. A "small" span of control would be two subordinates, a "large" span of control might be 15. Large spans of control produce flat-shaped organizations (that is, few levels between the top and bottom of the organization); small spans of control produce tall-shaped organizations (that is, many levels). A diagram showing how the span of control affect the shape of the organization is shown in Figure 8–2.

Overview of Classical Theory. Classical theory is credited with providing the structural anatomy of organizations. It was the first major attempt to articulate the form and substance of organizations in a comprehensive fashion. The reader should clearly note there is little that is "psychological" about this view of organizations. Indeed, none of the classical organizational theorists were psychologists. The influence of psychology evidenced itself in the next school of thought on organizations, neoclassical theory. Nevertheless, while current organizational researchers regard classical theory as an antiquated view of organizations, the four principles of the theory are deeply ingrained in the way organizations are structured in real life. Problems of line/staff relationships, number of organizational levels, division of labor, coordination, and spans of control are of major concern to organizations today. It was not that classical theory was "wrong" that led to further thinking about

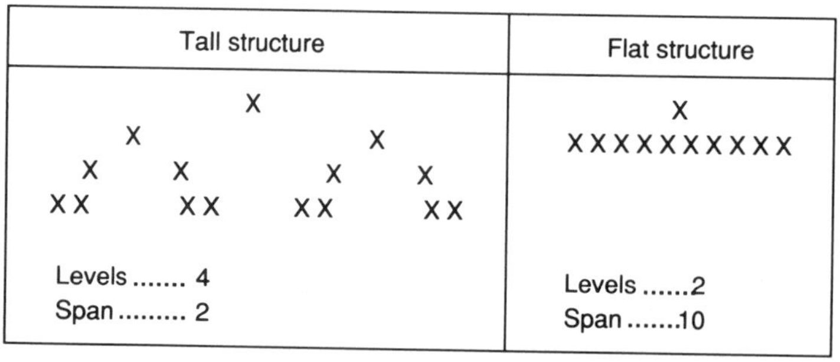

Tall structure	Flat structure
X X X X X X X X X X X X X X X	X X X X X X X X X X X
Levels .... 4 Span 2	Levels ......2 Span 10

Figure 8–2 Span of Control and Organizational Structure

SOURCE: W. G. Scott, T. R. Mitchell, and P. H. Birnbaum, *Organization Theory: A Structural and Behavioral Analysis* (Homewood, Ill.: Richard D. Irwin, 1981).

organizations but, rather, that organizations were more complex than the four classical principles would suggest. This desire to add richness and realism to organizational theory gave rise to neoclassical theory.

Neoclassical Theory

Neoclassical theory had its birth in the 1950s and early 1960s. It was identified with scholars who recognized the deficiencies in the classical school of thought. In fact, the name *neo*classical is used to connote a modernization or updating of the original (classical) theory, while still acknowledging the contributions of the latter.

It is a misnomer to call neoclassical theory a "theory" because there really is no formal theory. Rather, the theory is more a recognition of psychological/behavioral issues that serve to question the rigidity with which the classical principles were originally stated. The neoclassicists examined the four major principles of classical theory and found evidence that challenged their apparent unassailability. This evidence was based primarily upon either psychological research or an examination of "real-life" organizational problems.

The neoclassicists noted that while division of labor causes functional interdependence among work activities, it serves to depersonalize these activities so that the individual finds little meaning in them. That is, people develop a sense of alienation from highly repetitive work, which ultimately results in dissatisfaction with their work. In turn, this dissatisfaction can result in lesser efficiency caused by lowered productivity and increased absence. In short, the neoclassicists argued for less rigid division of labor and for more "humanistic" work in which people derive a sense of value and meaning from their jobs.

The scalar principle was questioned on the grounds that there are other systems that operate on people in organizations besides those imposed by formal superior-subordinate relationships. Individuals are influenced by interpersonal activities that extend well beyond those prescribed by the formal organizational structure. In short, while the scalar principle prescribes formal lines of authority, in reality there are many sources operating in an organization that influence the individual.

The line/staff principle was perhaps the easiest for the neoclassicist to challenge. The black-and-white theoretical distinction between line and staff functions is not always so clear in practice. Take, for example, the sales function. A manufacturing company's purpose is indeed to produce, but if it does not sell what it produces, the company cannot survive. What then, is the sales function—a major *line* function or an ancillary *staff* function? The neoclassicists illustrated that many staff functions are critical to the success of the organization, so the value of the distinction between line and staff is not as great as originally proposed.

Finally, what contributes to a satisfactory span of control seems far more complex than picking a number. The neoclassicists noted it depends upon such issues as the managerial ability of the superior (poor managers cannot supervise many subordinates) and the intensity of the needed supervision (you could effectively manage many more subordinates who do not require much direction than those who do require intensive direction). That is, such psychological factors as leadership style and capacity would greatly influence the determination of effective spans of control.

Overview of Neoclassical Theory.   The primary contribution of neoclassical theory was to reveal that the principles proposed by classical theory were not as universally applicable and simple as originally formulated. The neoclassicists drew heavily on behavioral research that revealed the importance of individual differences. The neoclassicists did not overtly reject classical theory. Rather than attempting to change the theory, they tried to make the theory fit the realities of human behavior in organizations. However, the neoclassicists were limited by commencing their conceptualization about organizations from the classical perspective. It became apparent by the mid-1960s that an entirely new approach to thinking about organizations was necessary. Organizations were more complex than even the neoclassicists portrayed them, which led to the formation of a radically different school of thought called modern organization theory.

Modern Organization Theory

Modern organization theory adopts a complex, dynamic view of organizations called the "systems approach." The systems approach had its origins in the biological sciences and was modified to meet the needs of organizational theory (Kast & Rosenzweig, 1972). The systems approach views an organization as existing in an interdependent relationship with its environment. The system approach asserts, "It is impossible to understand individual behavior or the activities of small groups apart from the social system in which they interact. A complex organization is a social system; the various discrete segments and functions in it do not behave as isolated elements. All parts affect all other parts. Every action has repercussions throughout the organization, because all of its elements are linked" (Scott, Mitchell, & Birnbaum, 1981, p. 44). In fact, the idea that all of the parts of the system are interdependent is the key to understanding the systems approach. All of the parts and their interrelatedness make up the "system," which is how the theory gets its name.

Modern theory asserts an organizational system is composed of five parts.

A. *Individuals.* Individuals bring their own personalities, abilities, and attitudes with them to the organization, all of which influence what they hope to attain by participating in the system.

B. *Formal organization.* The formal organization is the interrelated pattern of jobs that provide the structure of the system.

C. *Small groups.* Individuals do not work in isolation but form memberships in small groups as a way to facilitate their own adaptability within the system.

D. *Status and role.* Status and role differences exist among jobs within an organization and serve to define the behavior of individuals within the system.

E. *Physical setting.* The physical setting refers to the external physical environment and the degree of technology that characterizes the organization.

Figure 8–3 illustrates the five parts of the system and their interrelatedness. Complex interactions exist among all parts of the system. Individuals interact to form small groups, members of the groups are differentiated by status and roles, the

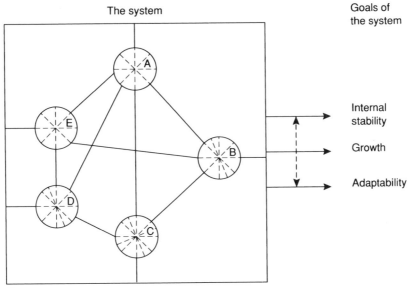

Key:
   1. Circles represent parts of the system.
   2. Broken lines represent intrapart interactions, i.e., individuals with other individuals.
   3. Solid lines represent interpart interaction.
   4. Both the solid and broken lines are the processes which tie the parts of the system together.

Figure 8–3   The Framework of System Analysis

SOURCE: W. G. Scott, T. R. Mitchell, and P. H. Birnbaum,
Organizational Theory: A Structural and Behavioral Analysis
(Homewood, Ill.: Richard D. Irwin, 1981).

physical environment affects the behavior of individuals and groups, and all exist within the framework provided by the formal organization.

    With all of these parts making up the system, it is necessary to have a means to provide coordination and linkage among them. Such functions are accomplished through communication and decision making; they permit the various parts of the system to "talk" to each other. Organizational communication occurs through a series of networks that often bear little resemblance to the formal lines of authority within the organization. Similarly, decisions often get made in ways that deviate from formal lines of authority. That is, the reality of how organizations actually conduct themselves is usually quite different from the principles established by classical organizational theory. It is also prudent to note that the Achilles' heel of most large organizations rests with failures to communicate. This makes considerable sense, given the systems perspective of organizations, in that communication is the means by which the system can be responsive to its environnment. The importance of organizational communication is the subject of Chapter 12.

    Finally, the systems approach instructs us that the parts and interactions of a system do not exist for themselves. Rather, they exist to meet the larger goals of the system, which are to attain stability, growth, and adaptability. That is, a living organism has to be stable in the sense that its parts are harmoniously integrated. Growth reflects a sense of vitality and vigor. Adaptability is critical if the organism is to be responsive to environmental changes because adaptability enables the organism to survive in times of rapid change. Thus, a healthy, successful organization is not only "effective" in meeting its business objectives but also stable, growing, and adaptable. These are the characteristics of all living organisms, be they organizations, animals, plants, or societies.

Overview of Modern Organization Theory.   Modern organization theory offers a radical departure from the classical and neoclassical schools of thought. Modern theory is premised on the systems approach, which views organizations as any other form of living organism. The purpose of an organization is to reach stability, to grow, and to adapt, as all living organisms must do to survive. You should note the abstractness of systems theory. There are no direct references to anything quite as simple as a span of control, for example. This abstractness is deliberate, for only at some degree of generality can one attempt to equate such diverse entities as organizations, plants, and animals. Modern organizational theorists believe that an understanding of something as complex as an organization requires the type of conceptualizations offered by systems theory. A systems perspective of organizations permits us to understand phenomena of organizational life that earlier theories would not permit. The balance of this chapter is devoted to gaining a deeper understanding of some of the components of an organizational or social system, and to examining some of the constructs I/O psychologists have identified that emerge from such systems.

Components of Social Systems

A *social* system is a structuring of events or happenings; it has no formal structure apart from its functioning. Physical or biological systems (cars or human beings) have structures that can be identified even when they are not functioning (electrical or skeleton structures); that is, they have both an anatomy and a physiology. There is no anatomy to a social system in this sense. When a social system stops functioning, no identifiable structure remains. It is hard for us to think of social systems as having no tangible anatomy because it is easier to understand concepts with concrete and simple components (Katz & Kahn, 1978). Social systems do indeed have components, but they are not concrete. We will examine some of them while recognizing that they are more abstract.

Roles

When an employee enters an organization, there is much for that person to learn. This includes expected performance levels, recognition of superiors, dress codes, and time demands. *Roles* ease the learning process. Roles are usually defined as the expectations of others about appropriate behavior in a specific position (Scott et al.,

1981). Each one of us plays several roles at the same time (parent, employee, club member, and so on), but we will focus on job-related roles.

Scott and associates (1981) listed five important aspects of roles. First, they are impersonal; the position itself determines the expectations, not the individual. Second, roles are related to task behavior. An organizational role is the expected behaviors for a particular job. Third, roles can be difficult to pin down. The problem is defining who determines what is expected. Since "other" people define our roles, opinions differ over what our role should be. How we see our role, how others see our role, and what we actually do may differ. Fourth, roles are learned quickly and can produce major behavior changes. Fifth, roles and jobs are not the same—a person in one job might play several roles.

We learn our role through a *role episode*, as Figure 8–4 shows. Group members have expectations about job performance. These are communicated either formally or by having the role occupant observe others in similar roles. In stage 3, the role occupant behaves as he or she believes is appropriate. If the behavior (stage 4) differs widely from the group's expectations (stage 1), the occupant gets feedback from the

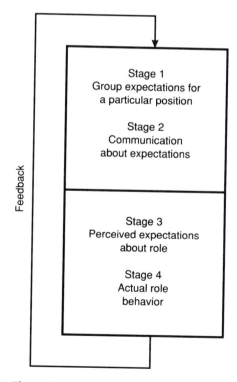

Figure 8–4   The Role Episode

SOURCE: W. G. Scott, T. R. Mitchell, and
P. H. Birnbaum, *Organization Theory:
A Structural and Behavioral Analysis*
(Homewood, Ill.: Richard D. Irwin, 1981).

group regarding the discrepancy. This is intended to alter behavior toward group expectations. The role episode is ongoing. Expectations may change over time, as might the employee's behavior.

Another aspect is *role differentiation*. This is the extent that different roles are performed by employees in the same subgroup. One person's job might be maintaining good group relations, such as a work unit coordinator. His or her role might thus require providing emotional or interpersonal support to others. Another's role might be setting schedules, agendas, and meeting deadlines; such a person is usually an administrator. When all roles in a work group fit together like the parts of a puzzle, a smoothly running, effective group results. However, all parts may not fit together. Later in the chapter, we will examine the way some organization pressures produce role problems.

Norms

Norms are shared group expectations about appropriate behavior. While roles define what is appropriate for a particular job, norms define acceptable *group* behavior. Roles differentiate positions; norms establish behavior expected of everyone in the group (Scott et al., 1981). This might concern when employees take coffee breaks, how much they produce, when they stop for the day, and what they wear. Norms are unwritten rules that govern behavior. A no-smoking sign is not a norm but a formal written rule of behavior. If employees smoke despite the sign, there is a norm that sanctions such behavior in spite of the formal rule.

Norms have several important properties. First, there is "oughtness" or "should-ness"— that is, prescriptions for behavior. Second, norms are usually more obvious for behavior judged to be important for the group. A norm might exist for *when* employees stop work before lunch. But there probably would not be a norm about *what* employees eat. Third, norms are enforced by the group. Much expected behavior is monitored and enforced through formal rules and procedures. With norms, group members regulate behavior. Sometimes formal rules and group norms clash. The no-smoking rule and group norm sanctioning smoking is an example. Unless the organization imposes sanctions on smokers (that is, rule breakers), the group norm would probably prevail. Finally, the degree that norms are shared and the degree that deviation is acceptable vary. Not all smokers might smoke in proscribed areas, and those who do not might be as accepted by the group just like those who do.

There is a three-step process for developing and communicating norms. The norm must first be defined and communicated. This can be done either explicitly ("Here is the way we do things around here") or implicitly (the desired behavior is observed). Second, the group must be able to monitor behavior and judge whether the norm is being followed. Third, the group must be able to reward conformity and punish noncomformity. Conformity enhances predictability of behavior within the group, which in turn promotes feelings of group cohesion.

Compliance with norms is enforced by positive reinforcement or punishment. Positive reinforcement can be praise or inclusion in group activities. Punishment can be a dirty look, a snide remark, or actual physical abuse. (Workers who exceeded the

"Counterclockwise, Red Eagle! Always counterclockwise!"

"The Far Side" cartoon panel by Gary Larson is reprinted by permission of Chronicle Features, San Francisco.

group norm for productivity in the Hawthorne studies were hit on the arm, which was called "binging.") Another form of punishment is exclusion from group activities. The group will often try to convince the nonconforming employee (referred to as a *deviant*) to change his or her behavior. The group will try to alter the deviant's opinion through increased communication, verbal or nonverbal. The clearer and more important the norm, the more cohesive the group, the greater the pressure will become. Eventually, the deviant will either change or be rejected. If rejected, the deviant will become an *isolate*, and pressure to conform stops. Because the group may need the isolate to perform work tasks, they will usually reach a truce; the isolate will be tolerated in work but excluded from group activities and relations. Obviously, the isolate can quit the job and try to find a better match between his or her values and the group.

Finally, norms are not always *contrary* to formal organization rules or *independent* of them. Sometimes norms greatly aid organization goals. For example, there may be a norm against leaving for home before a certain amount of work has been done. Although quitting time is 5:00 P.M., the group may expect employees to stay until 5:15 or 5:30 and finish a certain task. In this case, the deviant is one who conforms to the formal rule (that is, leaving at 5:00 P.M.) instead of the group norm. When group norms and organization goals are complementary, high degrees of effectiveness can result.

Power

In an organization, members give up some individual freedom in order to form an aggregate that can help them obtain their goals. In deference to this pursuit, individuals enter into a relationship with an organization whereby the organization and parts can control aspects of their lives. The source of the control is the *power* the organization exerts over its members. Power is a complex topic; there are many variations or bases of power. It also works in both directions: employees (individually and collectively) can exert power over the organization. We will examine power in this section and in a later chapter.

Perhaps the best analysis of power in an organization is that of French and Raven (1960). They proposed five sources or bases.

1. *Reward power.* This is the capacity of an organization (or a member in a specified role) to offer positive incentives for desirable behavior. Incentives include promotions, raises, vacations, good work assignments, and so on. Power to reward an employee is defined by formal sanctions inherent in a superior's role.

2. *Coercive power.* The organization can punish an employee for undesirable behavior. Dismissal, docking of pay, reprimands, and unpleasant work assignments are examples. This capacity to punish is also defined by formal sanctions inherent in the organization.

3. *Legitimate power.* Sometimes referred to as *authority*, this means that the employee believes the organization's power over him or her is legitimate. Norms and expectations help to define the degree of legitimate power. If a boss asked an individual to work overtime, this would likely be seen as legitimate, given the boss's authority. However, if a co-worker made the same request, it might be turned down. The co-worker has no legitimate authority to make the request, although the individual might agree out of friendship.

4. *Expert power.* The employee believes that some other individual has expertise in a given area and that he or she should defer to the "expert's" judgment. Consultants are called on for help in handling problems because they are seen as experts in certain areas. The source of expert power is the perceived experience, knowledge, or ability of a person. It is not formally sanctioned in the organization. There are also differences in the perceived boundaries of expertise. One employee may be seen as the expert on using tools and equipment; others will turn to him or her for help with technical problems. However, that expertise may not be seen as extending to other areas, like interpersonal relations.

5. *Referent power.* This is the most abstract type of power. One employee might admire another, want to be like that person, and want to be liked by him or her. The other worker is a referent, someone the employee refers to. The source of referent power is the referent's personal qualities. Cultural factors may contribute to these qualities. Younger people will often defer to an older person partly on the basis that age per se is a personal quality that engenders deference. Norms can also generate referent power. An employee may wish to identify with a particular group and will bow to the group's expectations.

Organizations differ in the extent to which they use the various bases of power. Authoritarian managers rely on reward and coercive power. Managers with a participative style rely on expert and referent power. The military relies heavily on the legitimate power inherent in military rank. Educational organizations have a high degree of expert power over their members.

Employees (individually and collectively) can also attain and use power in dealing with the organization. Power is not only a "top-down" affair. A secretary can have much power over her boss by knowing where things are filed, whom to call to get things done, and so forth. I am very aware of this when my secretary goes on vacation. I am then forced to do things on my own that she could do far more efficiently. A highly competent employee can exercise power by demanding a raise using the threat of quitting. Unless the organization is prepared to lose the employee, it might have to agree to the raise.

Unions typify a major source of employee power. They can often obtain goals (better working conditions, greater pay) more effectively than members could on their own. In forming a union, workers must forgo some individual freedom (such as paying union dues), but in return they may have greater job security. Unions also have power in that members can strike if the organization (that is, management) presents them with "unreasonable" demands. However, the converse is also true: If management feels that the union is "unreasonable," it can prevent employees from working (a lockout). Power in union/management relations is a fascinating topic and will be discussed in greater detail in Chapter 14.

Culture

One of the most recently identified components of social systems is the concept of organizational culture. The concept of culture was originally proposed by sociologists to describe societies, but we have also found it useful to describe organizations. Culture consists of the language, values, attitudes, beliefs, and customs of an organization. As can be inferred, it represents a complex pattern of variables that, when taken collectively, gives each organization its own unique "flavor." While there are many formal (and rather cumbersome) definitions of culture, one that I find most instructive is: "the way we do things around here." An organization's culture influences not only the behavior of its members but also the way they perceive and interpret behavior.

As new employees are socialized into the organization, they acquire its culture.

Individuals become socialized into the group as a result of their interactions with other members of the group. It is through common social activities that new members learn the generalized set of attitudes, values, and beliefs common to members of the social system. This socialization process makes it possible to control individual behavior and to direct it toward the larger goals of the organization. Culture does not manifest itself directly in behavior but, rather, as Schein (1985) notes, "it is the assumptions that underlie the values and determine not only behavior patterns, but also such visible artifacts as architecture, office layout, dress codes, and so on" (p. 14).

Deeply ingrained within organizational culture are communication processes, for it is through communication that culture is transmitted. It is through interactions with longtime organizational members that new recruits are enculturated. This is how new members learn the language and appropriate behavior of the group, hear its stories and legends, and observe the rites and rituals of the organization. Members must determine what is appropriate dress, how to arrange one's office, and how much latitude they have in being on time for appointments and in meeting deadlines (Barnett, 1988). Culture may also be communicated through other channels such as in-house memos, official policies, statements of corporate philosophy, and any other means of value expression.

Researchers have recently learned to differentiate the topic of *culture* from one of its predecessors, *climate*. Organizational climate refers to individual psychological perceptions of the characteristics of an organization's practices and procedures. Culture is regarded as an emergent property of group interactions, while climate refers more to people's reactions to those interactions. I/O psychologists find the concept of culture to be a richer, more accurate, and more useful way to differentiate organizations than climate. Another distinction is that culture is a more stable, enduring property of an organization; climate is subject to more rapid changes. There is still some confusion among I/O psychologists regarding whether culture and climate are truly distinct concepts, or whether the climate of an organization is but a component of its culture.

Given the newness of organizational culture among researchers, there is not a great deal of research on it. Much of the research addresses how new members learn the culture of an organization, and what means organizations use to express their culture. However, in the years ahead I anticipate researchers will find culture to be a useful way to understand some of the issues within personnel psychology. I see the concept of culture having great relevance for selection, training, and even performance appraisal. For example, the type of applicant an organization is likely to view as being acceptable is heavily tied to the values and beliefs held within the organization. Thus, new employees are selected to be compatible with the organization's culture. Training can be a direct extension of an organization's culture, initiating new members into the beliefs, values, attitudes, and behaviors of the organization. Finally, organizations differ in the standards and expectations they have for employee job performance. A "superior" employee in an organization with moderate standards for performance may be only "average" in an organization with high standards. In short,

I believe I/O psychologists will find the topic of culture to be a useful way to integrate a diverse array of research findings from many areas within our discipline (see Field Note 1).

As noted in the text, one definition of culture is "the way we do things around here." I have two clients whose cultures are extraordinarily different from each other in the way they do things.

One company is in the telephone communications business. It is only about ten years old and was created as a result of the breakup of AT&T. All the officers of the company are bright, young (only two were over 40), extremely ambitious entrepreneurs. Their (unofficial) company motto is "Ready, Fire, Aim." They make major business decisions on the basis of hunches, insight, and savvy. For example, I attended one board meeting where they decided they wanted to publish their own version of the Yellow Pages, a business telephone directory. One person was given the assignment of finding a building, another one would purchase the needed equipment, a third (the personnel director) was told to hire and train 180 new employees to staff the department. They decided to have this department operating in six weeks! A standing joke in the company is if you don't like the way things are going today, don't worry, because by next week things will be different. They refer to themselves as "cowboys," people who ride roughshod over the business terrain.

The other company is in the insurance business. The company has been in business for over 100 years. All the officers in the company are much older—no officer is under 55. They all served their time working their way up the corporate ladder. Being made an "officer" is the product of having worked at least 25 years within the company. They don't have a corporate motto, but if they did it would be "Slow But Sure." Everything they do in the company is checked and rechecked. Memos are examined and edited by people one, two, and sometimes three administrative levels above the memo writer. They start to plan their annual office Christmas party in February. There is a manual, an office procedure guide, a handbook, or written policy for every conceivable business situation or decision. The communications company committed very little to writing because conditions and people changed so rapidly any written policy would soon be obsolete.

To say these two companies have grossly different cultures would be an understatement. Each organization has its own values and behaviors, and each attracts a different type of employee. If you like rapid change and the resulting dynamic tension such change produces, you would be extremely frustrated working in the insurance company. If you like stability and predictability you would be most anxious working in the communication business. As a consultant, I had to understand their respective cultures and have my work fit in to the way they operated. Travel agents promote their business by saying you should travel to far away countries to experience different cultures. As a consultant, I have experienced different (organizational) cultures, and I haven't had to travel too far to do it.

Summary of Social System Components

Organizations have physical structures, but these alone do not define organizations. The social fabric—norms, roles, power, and culture—is a significant influence on the conduct of organization members. These components are not tangible entities, but they are as much attributes of an organization as its size. Organizations differ in norms, roles, use of power, and culture. Norms influence behavior, increasing consistency and predictability. Roles prescribe the boundaries of acceptable behavior and enhance conformity. Organizations exert many forms of power over their members to get them to behave in certain ways. These three variables all help produce uniformity and consistency in individual behavior. This is necessary in part to ensure that all organizational members are pursuing common goals. Individuals give up some freedom in joining an organization, and these constructs represent three ways freedom is limited. Organizations differ in culture just as individuals differ in personality. Similarly, just as certain personality types are better suited for some jobs, certain cultures foster certain behaviors. Together, these four constructs define an organization's social system; they are intangible but potent determinants of behavior.

Person-Environment (P-E) Congruence

Almost all I/O psychology can be viewed as the interrelationship between people and work. Not all jobs are the same, because major differences exist in tasks, responsibilities, and working conditions. I/O psychologists try to get a good match or "fit" between people and jobs, believing that all people are not equally suited for all jobs. We go about this in several ways. In personnel selection and placement, we assume the job is fixed or constant. We try to identify (that is, select and place) individuals who can best meet the demands of the job. In personnel training, we try to improve the fit by upgrading the skills of individuals to match the job requirements better.

We can also go about this process in reverse. As we will discuss later, we can assume the people are fixed. Our goal is then to restructure work to match their talents. In short, we try either to find (or shape) "pegs" (people) to fit existing "holes" (jobs) or to reshape the holes to fit existing pegs. This matching process is called *person-environment congruence* or *fit*.

There are several opinions regarding what makes a good fit between people and environments. Pervin (1968) proposes that some environments more or less match the individual's personality. A good match between them is reflected in high performance, satisfaction, and little stress. Lack of fit results in decreased performance, dissatisfaction, and stress in the system. Pervin reviewed psychological research in many areas to substantiate the importance of person-environment congruence for individual performance and satisfaction. One study found that students who were not very sociable performed better in lecture sections, while more sociable students performed better in leaderless discussion groups. The significance of person-environment congruence is very evident in the academic performance and satisfaction of college students. Rather than speaking of bright or dull students and good or bad colleges, it is more fruitful to focus on the relationship between students, curricula, and schools. The key is the interaction of the person and the environment, not one factor or the other. Research has shown that students who had authoritarian personalities had a very high dropout rate from colleges with a "liberal" attitude toward education. Those students complained about the colleges' permitting smoking in class, not requiring attendance, and expecting students to answer their own questions. The converse has also been found to be true. Students with highly flexible personalities dropped out of colleges whose policies were seen to be "repressive," that is, many required courses and required attendance in class. According to Pervin, it is the personality of the individual that determines the degree of fit with various environments.

O'Reilly (1977) conducted a laboratory study showing that certain types of people perform better in certain types of environments. He identified two types of people based on personality. One wanted a sense of achievement and personal growth in work; the other was more concerned with job security and financial reward. Two types of work tasks were created: one challenging, and the other routine. O'Reilly found that those wanting a sense of achievement and personal growth were far more satisfied with the challenging task. Those seeking job security were more satisfied in the less challenging task. Like Pervin, O'Reilly found that satisfaction with an environment (in this case, type of task) was influenced by the congruence between it and the individual's personality.

The concept of person-environment fit is a most useful framework for examining human behavior in organizations. For example, let us suppose that individuals are not fitting well with their environments. Caplan (1987) notes that we can improve PE fit by altering P (for example, by training), E (for example, by job redesign), or some combination of the two. If we assume that the environment is fixed, our efforts would be to make modifications in the type of people we hire or train. Such is the fundamental rationale of personnel psychology. Alternatively, if we assume people are fixed, we would seek to alter the environment. That is the perspective of human factors psychology. However, Schneider (1987) makes the point that the distinction between P and E is not always so clear. He asserts that human behavior occurs in organizations populated by people. It is the people who contribute heavily to organizations' being what they are, in terms of their values and attitudes (that is, culture). Therefore, according to Schneider, Ps help define Es. Accordingly, efforts to attain greater PE fit by concentrating solely on structural (nonpeople) issues will most likely not be successful. Muchinsky and Monahan (1987) also suggest that it is possible for organizations to seek people who fit "too well." That is, some organizations seek to hire people who closely mirror the values and beliefs of employees, a filtering process that results in extreme homogeneity within the organization. The danger is that new ideas and perspectives may never surface because of the intensive enculturation process that results in "everyone's being alike." We saw this issue raised in the previous chapter regarding assessment centers.

When we think of PE fit we can imagine several products that might emerge as a result of people's both fitting and not fitting with their environments. The balance of this chapter is devoted to examining several individual responses to person-environment interactions.

Individual Responses to Person-Environment Interactions

In organizations, two major forces are at work. One has to do with the individual. This includes personal factors (for example, age, sex, race), abilities, knowledges, skills, interests, and personality. These are all the things a person brings to the organization. The second major force has to do with the organization. It includes organizational factors (for example, location, size, technology), task and job demands, role expectations, norms, and culture. An individual will have to adjust to these factors if he or she accepts a job with the organization. There are a number of employee responses to this interface of individuals and organizations. We can think of them as reactions to the organization. They are not inherent in the individual or the organization but emerge from the interaction. These emergent responses have been widely studied because they influence a variety of criterion variables that are important to the organization, such as productivity, absenteeism, turnover, and satisfaction. Furthermore, we have learned that these responses can be classified into two categories: dysfunctional and functional. Dysfunctional responses are detrimental to the individual and the organization, while functional responses are beneficial.

Dysfunctional P-E Responses

Stress.   For many years, stess was studied mainly by medical researchers interested in physiological measures. Recently, however, stress has become of particular interest to I/O psychologists. We are just beginning to understand its effect on work behavior. Stress is difficult to define—it is not strictly an independent, dependent, or intervening variable. Rather, it is a collective term denoting demands that "tax" a system (physiological, social, or psychological) and its responses. Job stress involves complicated interactions between the person and the environment, particularly as they occur over time. Beehr and Newman (1978) provide the following definition: "Job stress refers to a situation wherein job-related factors interact with a worker to change (i.e., disrupt or enhance) his or her psychological and/or physiological condition such that the person (i.e., mind-body) is forced to deviate from normal functioning" (pp. 669–670).

Ivancevich and Matteson (1980) have developed a model to explain the many antecedents, outcomes, and consequences of stress. Their model is shown in Figure 8–5. The antecedents of stress (called *stressors*) come from many sources. They may originate from the physical environnment (temperature, noise), from individual-level phenomena (work overload, role conflict), from the work group (lack of cohesiveness), and from the total organization (its culture). Stressors at work can even stem from nonwork concerns, like economic problems and family relations. Feelings of stress can then be perceived by oneself. However, sometimes individuals do not know they are stressed, but their friends or associates recognize that "something is

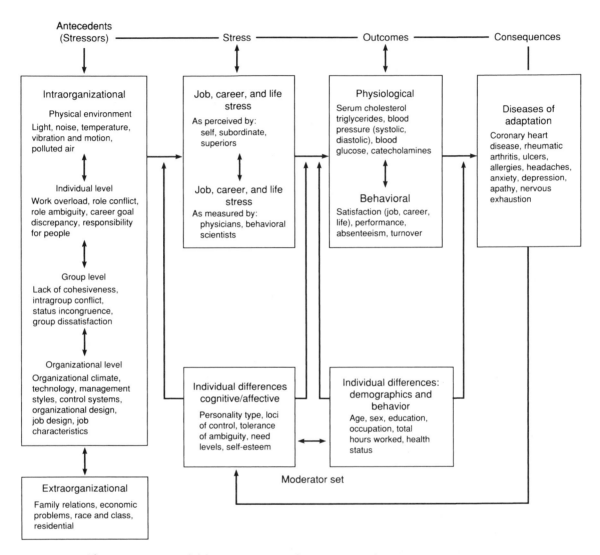

Figure 8–5 A Model for Organizational Stress Research

SOURCE: J. M. Ivancevich and M. T. Matteson, *Stress and Work: A Managerial Perspective* (Glenview, Ill.: Scott, Foresman, 1980).

wrong." The outcomes of stress are physiological changes (high blood pressure and blood sugar) and behavioral changes (less job satisfaction, greater absenteeism). The consequences of stress include heart disease, ulcers, headaches, depression, and nervous exhaustion. Stress is considered to be one of the major problems facing the contemporary worker, and occurs across all job levels, kinds of employees, and types of organizations.

Over the past few years I/O psychologists have intensively researched the area of stress. While there is much to learn, we are beginning to identify the scope of this pervasive problem. Parker and DeCotiis (1983) concluded that there are two major types of organizational stressors. The first relates to feelings of being under substantial time pressure. Individuals believe they are generally capable of doing their work but feel stressed because of the inadequate amount of time they are given to complete it. The second is chronic job-related feelings of anxiety—more of a generalized "up-tight" feeling about work in general. Eden (1982) feels that most stress is caused by "critical job events," events that are an inherent part of many jobs and cannot be eliminated by organizational redesign or better management. Major examinations would be an example of a critical job event for students. These events have been found to cause increases in anxiety, pulse rate, systolic blood pressure, and serum uric acid. Even the anticipation of upcoming critical job events can cause stress. Eden feels that preventing stress requires more than counseling people that a critical event is going to occur.

A number of studies have explored mechanisms for coping with stress. Jackson and Maslach (1982) found that police officers experiencing stress were more likely to display anger, spend time away from home, be uninvolved in family matters, and to have unsatisfactory marriages. These officers coped with the stress by smoking, drinking, and withdrawing from other people. Their wives coped with their stress by talking to friends, participating in organized groups and religious activities, and by going shopping. Indeed, Gupta and Jenkins (1984) concluded that drug and alcohol consumption are two frequently used means of coping with stress; however, they differ in their degree of social acceptance. Organizations sanction the use of alcohol, but they do not sanction drug usage (which is regarded as evidence of moral turpitude). Some companies have instituted formal stress reduction programs for their employees. These programs are offered during the normal workday, and usually attract a fairly high percentage of participants. Such programs range from time-management instructions designed to make more efficient use of the workday to progressive relaxation techniques involving special breathing exercises. Higgins (1986) reported both of these programs were successful in reducing stress among a sample of working women.

Do some people have personality traits that make them more susceptible to stress? It appears so. A distinction has been made between two types of people, called Type A and Type B. Type A people have the following characteristics: they walk, eat, and talk rapidly; are impatient; can't cope with leisure time; measure success with numbers; and are aggressive, competitive, and constantly feel under time pressure. Type B people have this profile: they are not concerned about time; don't brag; play for fun, not to win; relax without guilt; and are mildmannered and "laid-back." Type A people have a higher standing pulse rate than Type B people, and are twice as likely to develop heart disease than their Type B counterparts. It has been estimated that about 60% of the general population is Type B; 40% is Type A.

Matteson, Ivancevich, and Gamble (1987) propose that people "learn" to be Type A as a product of the values, beliefs, and fears they were exposed to in childhood. Research has addressed the fit between these types of people and their work environments. Matteson, Ivancevich, and Smith (1984) reported that Type A salespeople suffered more stress and a greater number of health complaints than Type B salespeople. Obviously, Type A employees experience considerable job stress, and seemingly gravitate toward stressful environments. Burke and Deszca (1982) related Type A behavior to preferred organizational climates. Type A individuals prefer work climates characterized by high performance standards, spontaneity, ambiguity, and toughness. The authors concluded that individuals are attracted to jobs and organizational climates that match their own behavioral and attitudinal propensities.

Stress represents a classic sample of a dysfunctional response between the individual and the environment. Job stress may be thought of as a result of trying to force "a round peg into a square hole." The peg (person) will not fit, and the hole (environment) puts pressure on the peg—a typical poor fit (see Field Note 2).

Field Note 2

In Chapter 6, I described some of my experiences working with coal miners as related to training. The story continues as the experiences related to stress.

Recall that the miners were very fatalistic about their lives. They believed when it was "their turn to go," they would be killed and there was nothing they could do about it. In short, they faced the possibility of death every day, but felt impotent in enhancing the odds of their living. However, being fatalistic does not mean blasé or indifferent. Far from it. Working in a coal mine is a highly stressful way to earn a living.

If miners escape immediate death or injury caused by a cave-in, they face the possibility of a long-term debilitating illness called "black lung disease" brought on by repeatedly inhaling coal dust. Miners get deeply stressed by continually facing these life-threatening conditions, and when they get off work, they frequently "unwind" to relieve the tension. They often "unwind" on themselves, their spouses, and their children. There is a high incident rate of drinking and drug consumption by miners. There are also serious problems of wife beating and child abuse. These problems are not endemic to the coal mining industry by any means, but are often found in occupations where employees are heavily stressed. Spouses and children are convenient outlets for the pent-up fears and anxieties experienced at work. Family members are as much the victims of job-related stress as the coal miners themselves.

Burnout.   Burnout is one of the "newer" person/environment reactions identified by I/O psychologists. Burnout is a syndrome of emotional exhaustion and cynicism that occurs among individuals who do "people-work" of some kind, such as teachers, nurses, social workers, and counselors. A major aspect of the burnout syndrome is increased feelings of emotional exhaustion. As their emotional resources are depleted, workers feel they are no longer able to give of themselves at a psychological level. Another aspect is the development of negative, cynical attitudes and feelings about one's clients. This nearly dehumanized perception of others can lead to the belief that the clients are somehow deserving of their troubles. Also, burned-out workers often feel unhappy about themselves and are dissatisfied with their accomplishments on the job (Maslach & Jackson, 1981). The research of Jackson, Schwab, and Schuler (1986) concluded there were three major components to the burnout

Certain jobs produce extreme stress—financial brokers attempting to buy treasury bonds.
Courtesy Chicago Board of Trade.

syndrome: (1) emotional exhaustion, (2) depersonalization, and (3) feelings of low personal accomplishment. This syndrome also seems to be correlated with various self-reported indexes of personal distress, including physical exhaustion, insomnia, increased use of alcohol and drugs, and marital and family problems.

Maslach and Jackson (1981) have developed a scale to measure burnout. Some of the questions from that scale are presented in Figure 8–6.

We are just beginning to understand burnout. As Meier (1983) notes, we are not yet in agreement as to the causes or definition of burnout. There is evidence that burnout is related to such diverse causes as tedium and stress, career development crises, work overload, and lack of perceived success. There is also some justification that burnout may not be limited to the "people" professions but may apply to a state of tension or energy-depletion produced by continuing frustration of personal needs on any job. We know very little about how to deter burnout. In a rare study on burnout intervention, Russell, Altmaier, and Velzen (1987) found the effects of burnout among public school teachers could be abated by receiving positive feedback concerning their skills and abilities from supportive supervisors. While our knowledge of burnout is still in the embryonic stage, it is evident burnout is yet another expense we must pay for being in jobs that exceed the limits of our human capabilities.

I feel emotionally drained from my work.

I feel used up at the end of the workday.

I feel like I'm at the end of my rope.

I worry that this job is hardening me emotionally.

I've become more callous toward people since I took this job.

Figure 8–6   Sample Questions from the Maslach-Jackson Burnout Inventory

SOURCE: C. Maslach and S. E. Jackson, "The Measurement of Experienced Burnout," *Journal of Occupational Behavior*, 2 (1981), pp. 99–113.

Role Ambiguity.   Role ambiguity refers to the difference between what people expect of us on the job and what we feel we should do. This causes uncertainty about what our role should be. There can be three reasons for this. One is that the employee doesn't understand what is expected. Second, the employee may not know how to meet expectations. (It is one thing for a salesperson to know annual sales volume should be $1 million; it is another thing to know how to bring it about.) Finally, an employee may think the job should be different.

Role ambiguity can cause significant problems on the job. It is related to stress, tension, and lower satisfaction. Medical data reveal that ambiguity may increase heart problems and lead to anxiety and depression. However, the effects of role ambiguity are not uniform, and role ambiguity seems to be more of a problem at higher organizational levels. Schuler (1975) reported that it was more strongly correlated with job satisfaction for upper-level employees than for lower-level employees. Schuler (1977a) also found that employees with high ability coped better with role ambiguity. Finally, Schuler (1977b) reported that organization structure can interact with task duties to produce role ambiguity. He found that it was less when *simple* tasks were to be performed in an organization with very formalized rules and procedures, little intergroup communication, and strict adherence to the chain of command. This was compared to *complex* tasks performed in the same type of organization. Less role ambiguity was found when complex tasks were performed in an organization with low formalization of rules, high intergroup communication, and low adherence to the chain of command. Schuler discussed the importance of congruence or fit between task complexity and organization structure in reducing role ambiguity. In this case, fit between two aspects of the organization (technological complexity and structure) benefited the employee. Based upon a review of many studies examining role ambiguity, Jackson and Schuler (1985) concluded that most of the relationships describing the potential causes and consequences of role ambiguity are likely to be influenced by other variables, like the person's age or education. That is, the causes and consequences of role ambiguity vary across different types of people.

Role Conflict.   When two or more pressures occur together so that complying with one would make doing the other more difficult, role conflict can arise (Kahn, Wolfe,

Quinn, Snoek, & Rosenthal, 1964). There are a variety of causes. It may be a function of conflicting messages (for example, "I need this report finished by tomorrow and I want it done well!"). The conflict is between the deadline and the request for high-quality work. Role conflict can also occur with promotion. A new manager may feel a conflict between new responsibilities and loyalty to former co-workers. For some women, there may be role conflict between the demands of home and job. An individual's personal values and beliefs may clash with role requirements. A used-car salesman may be torn between telling the truth about a car and trying to make a sale (see Field Note 3).

Field Note 3

Role conflict is a problem in many jobs where people feel a dual allegiance to things that are important to them. Nowhere is role conflict more evident than in the job of a foreman. Foremen represent the lowest level of management. They are responsible for the supervision of work at the level where most of it occurs. Foremen are trained to represent management, to work in a supervisory role, and to help ensure the goals of their department are met. The foreman's job is the entry point for promotions to higher-level management jobs, such as supervisor, general supervisor, department manager, and so on.

However, foremen are usually selected from the ranks of production employees. They know full well what it is like to be on the receiving end of administrative control. Foremen often end up supervising the very people who were once their co-workers. These employees expect foremen to be sym-

pathetic to their needs and positions, and to remember "what it was like" to work in the trenches.

Many times foremen find themselves in the middle. For example, upper management decides to increase production, and it is the foremen who have to implement this policy with the employees. The employees may resent having these new demands placed on them, and the foreman is a convenient outlet for their frustrations. Foremen feel pressure from both directions: the need to support management, of which they are a part, and resistance from the employees whom they supervise. Feelings of role conflict can become very intense. It is not uncommon for foremen to return to their old jobs, escaping the hassles that come from being in the middle. For those people, the pressures of role conflict simply aren't worth the rewards associated with being a foreman.

The effect of role conflict on employee attitudes and behavior has been studied. Rizzo, House, and Lirtzman (1970), and House and Rizzo (1972) studied the relationship between role conflict and job satisfaction, turnover, anxiety, and perceived threat. However, the results are not simple or clear-cut. Role conflict produced job dissatisfaction, but the strength of the relationship was affected by the employee's position. Role conflict is more strongly related to dissatisfaction for lower-level jobs, the reverse of the findings for role ambiguity (Hamner & Tosi, 1974). Keller (1975) found that role conflict was more strongly related to dissatisfaction with the boss;

role ambiguity was more strongly related to dissatisfaction with the work itself. There is also evidence that role conflict diminishes performance. Szilagyi, Sims, and Keller (1976) found that role conflict was significantly related to poor performance among professional, technical, and clerical employees in a large medical center.

Women are frequently caught in between the conflicting demands of a family and a job. Beutell and Greenhaus (1983) studied a sample of married women who had at least one child and who were attending college. Time demands for the student role created more role conflict for women whose husbands held relatively traditional sex-role attitudes. Nelson and Quick (1985) noted that the marriage/work interface is an acute source of role conflict for professional women. The authors recommend that professional women develop strong supportive mentor relationships to increase their self-confidence and self-awareness. Certainly, one way to cope with role conflict is to resign from a role. However, Chusmir (1982) found that the number of women who cope with role conflict by leaving their jobs is on the decline.

It seems that in many ways we as individuals are our own worst enemies when it comes to feelings of role conflict. As Berger-Gross and Kraut (1984) have observed, one way to view role conflict is the difference between our self-expectations and the perception of others' expectations about us. We can often lessen role conflict to some degree by lowering the expectations we have of ourselves and the standards we feel we must live up to. However, other sources of role conflict are not as subjective, and we must often seek ways to keep multiple constituencies happy. The continual searching for these ways is often a source of stress.

Functional P-E Responses

Job Involvement. Job involvement is the extent that individuals are ego involved in their work, though there appears to be more here than just ego involvement. Lodahl and Kejner (1965) define job involvement as "the degree to which a person is identified psychologically with his work, or the importance of work in his total self-image" (p. 24). They also say that involvement refers to internalizing values about the goodness or the importance of work. There is some confusion over whether job involvement is a product of person-environment interaction or is simply an individual personality variable (Rabinowitz & Hall, 1977). However, most research indicates that job involvement can be altered by the work environment, thus supporting the notion that it is a product of person-environment interface.

Job involvement has been found to be related to three sets of variables: demographic, situational, and work outcome. Saal (1978) has shown that job involvement is positively correlated with age and endorsement of the Protestant work ethic (that is, the belief that hard work is itself rewarding). Involvement is also related to job characteristics. Workers who have a greater variety of tasks and who deal with other people at work feel more job involved. Finally, involvement is consistently related to various types of job satisfaction, particularly satisfaction with work itself ($r = .52$); that is, employees who really like what they do are more job involved. Job involvement is negatively related to absenteeism. Curiously, there is no relationship between job involvement and productivity. Workers who are not job involved are no less productive than workers who are.

Lodahl and Kejner (1965) developed a 20-item questionnaire to measure job involvement. Several items from it are presented in Figure 8–7. People respond to these items by indicating their degree of agreement with each statement. The internal consistency reliability of the questionnaire has been measured with several samples of employees; an average reliability coefficient is around .80. This is adequate, but it appears some items assess aspects of job involvement that are not as clearly central to the concept as others.

While we are quite certain of the relationship between job involvement and several other variables, most of the variance in job involvement remains unexplained. People certainly do differ in their degree of involvement, but we do not really know why. More work remains to be done on the *process* that generates involvement. Is some degree of job involvement necessary or desirable in all workers? Do certain jobs inspire more involvement than others? Can people be too involved for their own good? Answers to these questions await further research. If organizations want to employ highly involved people and job involvement is strictly an individual variable, then the issue is one of personnel selection. Organizations would use a job-involvement questionnaire and hire those who score high. However, if organizations can "do" something to make employees more involved (as the job characteristics correlates of involvement suggest), then the issue also becomes one of job design. Work should be designed in such a way as to facilitate feelings of job involvement.

Organizational Commitment.   Organizational commitment is "the relative strength of an individual's identification with the involvement in a particular organization" (Steers, 1977, p. 46). It is characterized by (1) strong belief in and acceptance of the organization's goals and values; (2) willingness to exert effort for the organization; and (3) desire to maintain membership in the organization (Porter, Steers, Mowday, & Boulian, 1974). Organizational commitment has both antecedent causes and consequences (as shown in Figure 8–8). Steers (1977) proposed three sets of antecedents: personal characteristics, job characteristics, and work experiences. Personal characteristics include age and education. Job characteristics involve challenge, opportunities for social interaction, and the amount of feedback provided on the job. Finally, work experiences include such factors as attitudes toward the organization, organization dependability, and the realization of expectations within the organization.

Steers tested the *antecedents* of organizational commitment with a sample of hospital employees. He used multiple regression analysis to assess the predictive

---

I'll stay overtime to finish a job even if I'm not paid to do it.

For me, mornings at work really fly by.

Sometimes I lay awake at night thinking ahead to the next day's work.

Figure 8–7   Sample Items from the Lodahl-Kejner Job Involvement Questionnaire

SOURCE: T. M. Lodahl and M. Kejner, "The Definition and Measurement of Job Involvement," *Journal of Applied Psychology, 49* (1965), pp. 24–33.

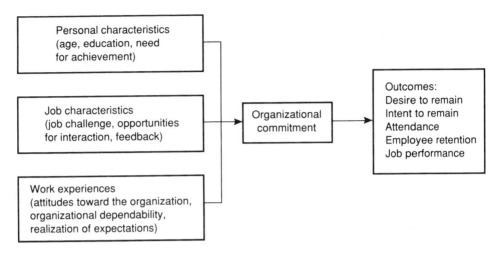

Figure 8–8   Hypothesized Antecedents and Outcomes of Organizational Commitment

SOURCE: R. M. Steers, "Antecedents and Outcomes of Organizational Commitment," *Administrative Science Quarterly*, 22 (1977), pp. 46–56. Reprinted by permission of *Administrative Science Quarterly*.

power of each variable within each of the three antecedents. He obtained multiple correlations (*R*) for personal characteristics (.55), job characteristics (.64), and work experience (.71). When the three sets were combined in a multiple regression analysis to predict organizational commitment collectively, the multiple correlation (*R*) was .81. If we square this, we get $R^2 = .65$, meaning that 65% of the variance in commitment is explained by the three types of predictor variables. This is most impressive. It indicates that we know more about organizational commitment than job involvement.

Steers tested the *consequences* by correlating commitment with a variety of outcome variables, such as attendance and performance. With the same sample of hospital employees, Steers found that commitment correlated most strongly with three variables: desire to remain with the organization ($r = .44$), intent to remain with the organization ($r = .31$), and turnover ($r = .17$). Like job involvement, organizational commitment was not related to any measures of productivity. In general, we know more about the antecedents of organizational commitment than we know about its consequences.

Mowday, Steers, and Porter (1979) developed a questionnaire measuring organizational commitment. It consisted of 15 items, with responses indicating degree of agreement. Figure 8–9 contains three items from the questionnaire.

Internal consistency reliability of the questionnaire was very high; the average figure was around .90. Mowday and associates also correlated scores on the questionnaire with selected outcome variables. The results indicated that organizational commitment correlated with intent to leave the organization at $-.45$ and with intended length of service at .51. These results, in part, suggest that the questionnaire had an acceptable degree of construct validity and that organizational commitment appears to be a useful concept for organizational research.

I am proud to tell others that I am part of this organization.

I really care about the fate of this organization.

I am willing to put a great deal of effort beyond that normally expected to help this organization succeed.

Figure 8–9 Sample Items from the Mowday et al. Organizational Commitment Questionnaire

SOURCE: R. T. Mowday, R. M. Steers, and L. W. Porter, "The Measurement of Organizational Commitment," *Journal of Vocational Behavior, 14* (1979), pp. 224–247.

Wiener (1982) has suggested that feelings of commitment to an organization are preceded by feelings of organizational identification and generalized values of loyalty and duty. Wiener feels organizational commitment can be influenced by both personal predispositions (which means companies can select people who will be more committed) and organizational interventions (which means companies can do things to make their employees more committed). Organizational research clearly indicates the value of having committed employees: they are more adaptable, have less turnover, less tardiness (Angle & Perry, 1981), and more job satisfaction (Bateman & Strasser, 1984). It has also been ascertained that American workers are no more and no less committed to their organizations than are their Japanese counterparts (Luthans, McCaul, & Dodd, 1985). Whatever differences there are in productivity between the two nationalities, they are not attributable to differences in commitment.

Self-Esteem. Korman (1970) proposed a theory of work behavior based on self-esteem. Self-esteem is the extent to which a person sees himself or herself as competent and need satisfying. People with high self-esteem feel good about themselves, feel they are competent, and anticipate success. People with low self-esteem are the opposite. Research has shown that low self-esteem is associated with coronary heart disease, while high self-esteem is associated with lack of anxiety and with life satisfaction (Tharenou, 1979). According to Korman (1970), there are three sources of self-esteem. The first, *chronic* self-esteem, is a persistent personality trait relatively consistent across situations. The second, *task-specific* self-esteem, is an individual's feeling of competence in a particular task. This is likely a function of past experience with the same or similar tasks. The third, *socially influenced* self-esteem, is a function of others' expectations. When others expect a person to perform well and communicate this, his or her feelings of competence will increase. For the purposes of our person-environment analysis, we will focus on the last two types of self-esteem.

Korman's theory presents some interesting ideas about job performance. It suggests that there are hints of self-fulfilling prophecy in job performance. People who think they will fail and believe others think the same will, according to the theory, indeed do poorly. The opposite is also true. Korman suggests that one reason some minority group employees perform poorly is that they have been socialized to fail and believe the organization expects them to. If this is valid, then the organization's influence on job performance is very important. If the organization can convey expectations of success, the pattern of "failure begets failure" may be broken.

There have been many tests of Korman's theory, particularly as it relates to employee satisfaction and performance. Many of the studies are laboratory experiments in which the subjects were led to believe that they are expected to do well or poorly on a given task. The results of such studies (for example, Greenhaus & Badin, 1974) indicate that the expectations of the environment (that is, the experimenter) do indeed affect how well people will do on the job. One of the problems with the theory, however, is that a portion of one's self-esteem—chronic self-esteem—cannot be changed; it is seen as an enduring personality trait. The organization has the capacity to influence only task-specific and social self-esteem.

A crucial issue is, which of the three types of self-esteem is most dominant or important? Research indicates that the sources of self-esteem vary in importance for different people. Organizations will be most successful in inducing effective job performance among those not dominated by chronic self-esteem. The most successful people should, in theory, be those with high chronic self-esteem who are made to feel high task-specific esteem and social self-esteem by the organization. The implications of Korman's theory are that an organization can, through carefully developed personnel selection and training programs, be staffed with employees who are high in self-esteem and thus will be effective on the job.

Dipboye (1977) has criticized Korman's theory because there are other explanations for why those low in self-esteem behave as they do. Specifically, Dipboye believes that people with low self-esteem are used to failure and will not put out much effort, making expected future failures easier to accept. A person who fails because of a lack of effort can rationalize the failure more readily than a person who tries very hard and still fails. While Korman (1977) does not agree with Dipboye's criticisms regarding why low self-esteem produces the behavior it does, it is evident that self-esteem does play a role in a person's job performance. To the extent that an organization can influence an individual's expectations of performance, and that expectations do affect performance, self-esteem is another aspect of person-environment interface that warrants our attention.

Overview of Individual Responses to Person-Environment Interactions

In this section, seven individual responses to person-environment interactions were presented: stress; burnout; role conflict; role ambiguity; job involvement; organizational commitment; and self-esteem. The first four are clearly "bad" for the individual. No benefits have yet been identified with them. We can view these four responses as the painful price that some people have to pay for certain person-environment interactions.

The remaining three concepts are beneficial. High job involvement, organizational commitment, and self-esteem appear to be desirable. Low levels seem harmful. It is also interesting that each of the last three responses is related to a different unit of analysis. Self-esteem, while influenced by environmental factors, is most directly tied to a person's own personality. Job involvement involves a person's feelings for his or her job. Finally, organizational commitment is a person's sense of identity with an entire organization.

MAJOR CHAPTER OBJECTIVES IN REVIEW

After having read this chapter, you should know:

1. Three schools of thought on the structure and development of organizations.
2. Components of social systems.
3. Concept of person-environment congruence.
4. Dysfunctional responses to person-environment congruence.
5. Functional responses to person-environment congruence.

CASE STUDY—Should Sex Make a Difference?

Paula Scott was examining the notes she had taken on three applicants for a management position. Scott was a manager herself and had worked her way up from a clerical job. She was the only female manager on a staff of seven and was acutely aware of her sex in her corporate position. Scott was highly respected by her peers, and her boss often praised the quality of her work. She took pride in her work, and she had the satisfaction of knowing she had made it on the basis of competence. Yet, she felt that being a woman had been a handicap for her over the years. She really thought she would have been promoted to her current position sooner if she had been a man. It was tough to break into an all-male management staff, and she questioned whether some of her male colleagues would have endured the same frustrations she had accepted. Scott demanded and got high performance from her staff. Her subordinates regarded her as a no-nonsense type of manager, someone who set high standards for them as well as herself. They admired her tenacity and perseverance in the company. Many felt she was the most talented manager on the staff.

Scott perused her notes. The management staff had interviewed each applicant, and at three o'clock they would meet to make their selection. The person chosen would become the eighth manager on the staff. Two of the candidates were male, the third female. The applicant selected must step in and assume a great deal of responsibility quickly. Scott knew if a bad choice were made, it would only mean more work for her and the other managers. A lot was riding on the decision, and nobody wanted to blow it.

On the basis of the interview and past work experience, Roger Morgan appeared to be the most qualified. Scott was sure the other managers would support him. A close but definite second was Claire Hart. Hart came across very well in the interview, but her academic training wasn't in business even though she had several years of business experience. Finally, Kevin Joyce seemed a distant third. His background, training, and experience weren't as strong, and his interview performance didn't help his case either.

Scott was torn between Morgan and Hart. Morgan appeared to be the stronger candidate, but his career had been handed to him. He was a business major from an excellent university and had six years of experience in his uncle's company. Hart got her degree in sociology, but she worked her way up to a responsible position after five years with the same company. Scott figured Hart got few breaks along the way, and whatever she got, she undoubtedly earned. Scott saw some of herself in Hart. She would like to have another female manager on the staff since she was tired of being the company token. If the company were going to be more responsive to the talents of women, the candidacy of Hart would be a good test case. Scott believed she and Hart could be two role models for other women in the company.

Yet, Morgan was also truly qualified. It shouldn't be held against him that he went to work for a relative. He came very highly recommended, and nothing about his credentials or personal conduct was objectionable. If Scott plugged Hart too strongly, she feared she would lose some of her reputation for being objective and performance-oriented. She could ill afford to lose her credibility by backing Hart primarily because she was a woman. If Hart had been a man, Scott's choice of Morgan would be fairly clear-cut. Yet if she didn't take a stand on Hart, she saw little chance for change.

Scott thought maybe she should support Morgan and secretly hope he wouldn't take the position. Surely, they would then offer it to Hart. No, she concluded, that's too much of a gamble. If she wanted Hart to join the company, and she knew she did, she would just have to support her outright from the start.

Questions

1. What is the source of role conflict in this case?

2. Do you think Paula Scott is justified in considering Claire Hart partly on the basis of gender?

3. Do you think Scott would have given as much thought to Hart's candidacy if Scott weren't the only woman on the management staff?

4. Do you think there is a way for Scott to reduce her role conflict without jeopardizing her personal values and professional integrity?

5. On the basis of the information presented, which candidate would you support for the position?

9

Job Satisfaction

Job satisfaction is one of the most researched areas in I/O psychology. Locke (1976) estimated that over 3,000 articles have been written on the topic, and that figure is probably low. Why has the subject aroused so much interest? There are three reasons, which, at the risk of oversimplifying, I shall call *cultural*, *functional*, and *historical*. They are implicit rather than explicit because few researchers ever formally state their reasons. However, these reasons can be distilled from the research.

The first reason is *cultural* in the sense that as a nation we value individual freedom, personal growth, and "opportunity." Such values stem from formal documents like the Bill of Rights, a doctrine that has guided the political and social evolution of this country for over 200 years. They also stem from the belief that the United States is the "land of opportunity," as attested by the millions who emigrated from their native countries for a chance at a new life. A work ethic was also developed as part of the fabric of American life, one that is formulated on the "pursuit of happiness," to which work contributes. Thus, concern over whether people like their jobs, their freedom to express feelings, and their ability to alter their destiny through work are hallmarks of American tradition. We believe implicitly that everyone has a right to a rewarding, satisfying job. I know of only *one* Soviet study on job satisfaction (Phillips & Benson, 1983). In the Soviet culture, feelings about work are not important. In fact, according to Phillips and Benson, only recently have the Soviets turned to the field of psychology for answers to their industrial problems. In certain European countries, like Germany, Sweden, and Holland, there has been a long-standing concern for industrial democracy, in which the feelings of workers are of major importance. However, in some other European countries (De Wolff & Shimmin, 1976) and in other parts of the world, interest in the quality of work life is just emerging.

The second reason for interest in job satisfaction is *functional*. The concept of job satisfaction has intrinsic value. But research has shown that satisfaction is also related to other important variables like absenteeism, turnover, and performance. (We will examine these relationships in more detail later.) Though we do not know if job satisfaction has a *causal* relationship with these variables (for example, high job satisfaction will cause a worker to be absent less often), we do know that feelings of high job satisfaction are *associated* with certain levels of them. Because we want less absenteeism, less turnover, and better performance, increasing job satisfaction might help in meeting these objectives.

Indeed, Mirvis and Lawler (1977) applied cost-accounting procedures to the consequences of employee attitudes. The authors measured the attitudes of bank tellers and their absenteeism, turnover, and performance as indexed by cash shortages. They remeasured these variables later, after the banks had instituted programs to make the tellers' work more satisfying. Results showed that as teller attitudes improved, there were changes in job behavior. The authors calculated how much these changes were worth to the bank in dollars and cents. The results were impressive. If all bank tellers' scores on the job satisfaction questionnaire could be elevated by one-half of a standard deviation over a one-year period (through the efforts of the bank to make their work more satisfying), the estimated improvements in performance on the job led to a *direct* saving of $17,664. The potential *total* cost savings (including savings from not having to recruit, hire, and train new employees) came to over $125,000! The results showed a definite functional relationship between increased job satisfaction and improvement in organization effectiveness.

Finally, there is a *historical* basis to job-satisfaction research. The Hawthorne studies began in the 1920s as research on the effects of work breaks and illumination on productivity, but the emphasis soon shifted to *attitudes*. Research revealed that employees had strong feelings about work. The Hawthorne studies dramatically shifted the work variables studied by psychologists. Economic and structural variables became less important, and interpersonal and attitude factors began to be emphasized. A few years after the first report of the Hawthorne studies was published, the first intensive study of job satisfaction appeared. Hoppock (1935) examined the factors affecting satisfaction on the job (fatigue, working conditions, supervision, and achievement). During World War II, interest in leadership was aroused; the results of many studies emphasized the importance of satisfaction with a leader. In the late 1950s and early 1960s, attention was given to designing jobs that were more satisfying. This early research was the nucleus for current work on changing the environment (designing jobs) to improve work life.

The cultural, functional, and historical bases of interest in job satisfaction resulted in a vast amount of research. In this chapter, we will examine job satisfaction from many perspectives. These include theories about what makes people satisfied, how to measure job satisfaction, and how it relates to other concepts. It is useful to think of job satisfaction as another example of person-environment congruence (Seybolt, 1976). As we will see, there are differences in people and in jobs (environments) that result in varying degrees of job satisfaction.

The Concept of Job Satisfaction

Like any feelings of satisfaction, job satisfaction is an emotional, affective response. *Affect* refers to feelings of like or dislike. Therefore, job satisfaction is the extent to which a person derives pleasure from a job. Locke (1976) defines it as "a pleasurable or positive emotional state resulting from the appraisal of one's job or job experiences." Unlike morale, which is a group response, job satisfaction is strictly an *individual* response. The morale of a group could be high, but a person in the group could be dissatisfied. The converse could also be true. Similarly, satisfaction is distinct from job involvement. People who are highly involved in their jobs take their work seriously, and their feelings are strongly affected by job experiences. Involved individuals will probably feel very satisfied or dissatisfied with their jobs, depending on their degree of success in them. Individuals who are not involved will probably experience less extreme responses.

It was initially thought that people could have an overall feeling of liking for a job, ranging from very low to very high. This was known as *global* job satisfaction. We later learned that many factors contribute to how a person feels about a job. People can have different feelings about their co-workers and their pay, and both contribute to overall feelings about their jobs. Thus, two people could feel the same level of global job satisfaction but for different reasons. One might be very pleased with her co-workers but unhappy with her pay. This would result in "moderate" global job satisfaction. A second person might be moderately pleased with both his co-workers and his pay and thus also have a moderate level of satisfaction.

Psychologists realized that people can feel differently about various aspects of a job. Because these feelings could be masked by assessing only global satisfaction, psychologists began examining *job-facet* satisfaction. This involves measuring how people feel about various parts of a job. As Locke (1976) said, "A job is not an entity but a complex interrelationship of tasks, roles, responsibilities, interactions, incentives, and rewards. Thus a thorough understanding of job attitudes requires that the job be analyzed in terms of its constituent elements" (p. 1301).

What are the facets of a job, and how many are there? There is no one number that holds for all jobs. Jobs differ, and certain facets are more prevalent in some jobs than others. Identifying facets has proceeded along two lines: statistical and conceptual. The *statistical* approach involves analyzing employee responses to job attitude questions (for example, "How much do you like your boss?" "How satisfied are you with your pay?"). Responses are intercorrelated, and clusters or factors are created based on similarity of response. These factors thus become the facets of a job as perceived by the employees.

The *conceptual* approach involves specifying the facets to be examined in light of

FRANK AND ERNEST   by Bob Thaves

the research goals. The facets are identified from the researcher's intuition, perhaps from a theoretical perspective. No matter which method is used, results usually reveal from five to twenty facets that contribute to satisfaction. Some facets are common to all jobs; others are job specific.

Locke (1976) summarized the facets contributing to employee satisfaction as shown in Table 9–1. The facets shown are fairly common to all jobs. Most employees quickly form impressions about the nature of their work, pay, promotion opportunities, and so on. Locke distinguishes events (conditions at work) from agents (people). Events are ultimately caused by someone or something, and agents are liked or disliked because they are seen as doing (or not doing) something. Employees can be satisfied with certain events (pay) but dissatisfied with certain agents (supervisors). Similarly, they can be dissatisfied with work (the event) because their abilities are not being fully used (they are the agents). Locke classified the facets into logical groupings, providing an understanding of how and why some facets are liked or disliked. Research by Ben-Porat (1981) has verified that the agent/event framework is a useful one for examining job satisfaction.

TABLE 9–1 *Effects of Various Events, Conditions, and Agents on Job Satisfaction*

Source	Effect
Events or conditions:	
Work itself: challenge	Mentally challenging work that the individual can successfully accomplish is satisfying.
Work itself: physical demand	Tiring work is dissatisfying.
Work itself: personal interest	Personally interesting work is satisfying.
Reward Structure	Just and informative rewards for performance are satisfying.
Working conditions; physical	Satisfaction depends on the match between working conditions and physical needs.
Working conditions: goal attainment	Working conditions that facilitate goal attainment are satisfying.
Agents:	
Self	High self-esteem is conducive to job satisfaction.
Supervisors, co-workers, subordinates	Individuals will be satisfied with colleagues who help them attain rewards.
	Individuals will be satisfied with colleagues who see things the same way they do.
Company and management	Individuals will be satisfied with companies that have policies and procedures designed to help them attain rewards.
	Individuals will be dissatisfied with conflicting and/or ambiguous roles imposed by company and/or management.
Fringe benefits	Benefits do not have a strong influence on job satisfaction for most workers.

SOURCE: Adapted from E. A. Locke, "The Nature and Causes of Job Satisfaction," *Handbook of Industrial and Organizational Psychology*, M. D. Dunnette (ed.). In F. J. Landy and D. A. Trumbo, *Psychology of Work Behavior*, rev. ed. (Pacific Grove, Calif.: Brooks/Cole, 1980).

Since there are many facets to job satisfaction, it seems logical that some are more important to an individual than others. For some people, pay may be more important than working conditions. Indeed, Kraut and Ronen (1975) showed systematic differences in the importance of 14 facets among samples of salesmen and repairmen in five countries. Their degree of importance was quite constant among employees across the five countries.

When psychologists attempt to *weight* facets by degree of importance, the results generally have *not* improved understanding of satisfaction. Several studies (for example, Ewen, 1967; Mikes & Hulin, 1968) showed that weighting facets by importance to the individual does not improve prediction of certain criterion variables (like turnover) beyond what is attained by weighting all facets equally. The best explanation is that when people rate satisfaction with a single facet, they also indirectly judge its importance (Dachler & Hulin, 1969). Having strong feelings of satisfaction or dissatisfaction indicates that the facet is important enough to feel strongly about. Conversely, neutral feelings of satisfaction typically mean that the facet really does not matter much. In sum, weighting satisfaction ratings does not add any unique information and thus does not improve predictive ability.

Theories of Job Satisfaction

Several theories have been proposed to explain why people are satisfied with their jobs. None of them have garnered a great deal of empirical confirmation, which suggests that job satisfaction is a complex phenomenon with many causal bases and that no one theory to date has been successful in incorporating all of them. As is usually true with multiple theories about a single phenomenon, each theory seems to explain a piece of the puzzle, but a complete understanding is beyond its scope. We will examine four very different approaches to studying job satisfaction. This will be by no means a comprehensive review of all theories, but it will give some insight into the ways in which job satisfaction has been examined. The interested reader can refer to Locke (1976) for a more exhaustive review.

Intrapersonal-Comparison Processes

According to McCormick and Ilgen (1980), "the most widely accepted view of job satisfaction assumes that the degree of affect experienced [by a person] results from some comparison between the individual's standard and that individual's perception of the extent to which the standard is met" (p. 306). Degree of satisfaction is the difference between the standard and what is actually received from the job. *Intrapersonal-comparison* theories compare what a person wants (the standard) with what he or she receives. The smaller the difference, the greater the feeling of satisfaction. These theories are called *intrapersonal* because the comparisons occur within each individual.

The standard and its derivation must be defined. Some researchers believe the standard consists of human *needs*. Needs are inborn and, it is believed, basic to everyone. Needs are generally classified into two categories: *physical* needs required for bodily functioning (air, water, food), and *psychological* needs required for mental functioning (stimulation, self-esteem, pleasure). A satisfying job would fulfill the basic psychological needs (for example, adequate income) and provide self-esteem and personal recognition. The research of Schaffer (1953) and Porter (1962) exemplifies the view of job satisfaction as a function of need fulfillment.

Other researchers believe the standard is derived from human *values* rather than needs. Values are what a person desires or seeks to attain and are acquired over time. All people have the same basic needs, but they differ in what they value. Values determine the choices people make as well as their emotional responses to those choices. A satisfying job would then provide an opportunity to attain valued outcomes. The research of Locke (1969) and Mobley and Locke (1970) supports this view.

It seems that value-based theories are more flexible than need-based theories. All people have the same needs. It could thus be argued that affective reactions to jobs would be uniform, based on how the jobs meet constant human needs. However, this clearly is not the case. There are great differences in individual satisfaction with the same job. In defense of need theories, it can be argued that people may have the same needs, but they differ in the *strength* of those needs. Thus, a person with a strong need for self-esteem might be dissatisfied with a certain job. Another, with a weaker self-esteem need, might be quite satisfied with the same job. On the other hand, people certainly have different values, which explains differences in job satisfaction. Someone who valued monetary rewards and personal challenge would probably not be satisfied with a low-paying, routine job. However, someone who valued earning just enough to make ends meet without being mentally taxed might be quite satisfied with such a job.

Intrapersonal-comparison-process theories are based on the extent to which a job is perceived to meet a person's needs or values. If there is a wide discrepancy between what is needed or desired and what is obtained, job dissatisfaction will result. A job could become dissatisfying if the strength of a person's needs were to change or if new values were acquired. To carry the theory to an extreme, if a person worked in a social vacuum (no other people) but needs or values were met, satisfaction would result. This *intrapersonal*-comparison process is distinctly different from the next theory of job satisfaction, which involves *interpersonal* comparisons.

Interpersonal-Comparison Processes

The basis of the interpersonal-comparison theory is the belief that people compare themselves to others in assessing their own feelings of job satisfaction. Rather than being intrapersonal (based on needs or values), comparisons are made within a social system, that is, *interpersonally*. An individual observes others in similar jobs and infers how satisfied they are. The person compares himself or herself to these other people and then derives feelings of satisfaction based on how they feel about their jobs (Salancik & Pfeffer, 1977).

Weiss and Shaw (1979) conducted a study illustrating the influence of the individuals perceptions of others' satisfaction. They developed a training film showing people working on an electrical assembly line. Two types of tasks were shown, one routine and boring, and the other interesting. Throughout the film, the actors made comments reflecting negative or positive feelings. Each participant in the study then worked on one of the two tasks and rated his or her satisfaction with it. Results indicated that their feelings were influenced by the reactions of the people performing the same task in the film. Weiss and Shaw thus suggested that a sense of satisfaction is derived by observing others.

What the interpersonal-comparison theories have in common with the need- or value-based comparison process theories of job satisfaction is the belief that affective feelings about work are comparative. The two sets of theories differ on the basis on which comparisons are made. If a hypothetical individual worked in a social vacuum, interpersonal comparison theories would say that he or she could not assess job satisfaction.

The idea that social factors influence feelings of satisfaction is intuitively appealing. Certainly a lot of research in social psychology indicates that we assess ourselves by our perceptions of others. It therefore is reasonable to assume that social comparisons operate in job satisfaction.

Opponent-Process Theory

Landy (1978) proposed a radically different job-satisfaction theory. He said that the causal basis of satisfaction is physiological, involving the central nervous system. An individual's satisfaction will change over time even if the job remains constant. As an example, a job tends to be more interesting during the first few weeks than it is after several years. This reaction had been previously dismissed as simply "boredom," with no explanation provided. Landy, however, suggested that there are mechanisms within individuals that help them maintain emotional equilibrium. Since satisfaction and dissatisfaction are in part emotional responses, these mechanisms are thought to play a role in job satisfaction.

Opponent process refers to opposing processes for dealing with emotion. For example, if a person is very happy, there is a physiological response that opposes this emotional state and attempts to bring the person back to a neutral level. Extreme emotion (positive or negative) is seen as damaging to individuals. Physiological mechanisms are designed to protect a person from these extreme states. Landy suggests that the reason people differ in job satisfaction is that they differ in terms of the stage of their protective physiological functions.

When a stimulus (a job) is introduced, it produces either a positive or negative reaction. Once the emotion exceeds a certain level, an opponent process automatically brings it under control. When the stimulus disappears (a person stops work for the day), the emotion stops and the opponent process recedes. In theory, each time the protective mechanism is activated, it becomes stronger. Thus, it is more intense in reducing extreme emotion over time; that is, a person becomes more neutral about a job the longer he or she is in it. If Landy's theory is right, we have an explanation for boredom on the job. Many people assume that a job loses its stimulating effect over time, resulting in boredom. Opponent-process theory suggests that the degree of stimulation remains unchanged, but the opponent process becomes stronger. Therefore, it is not jobs per se that are boring but people's repeated exposure to the same jobs that results in a very strong physiological response that prohibits elation or pleasure.

Virtually no data exist on the validity of Landy's theory. The theory offers an explanation for boredom but does not explain why people become *more* satisfied or dissatisfied (rather than bored) with their jobs over time. Also, we know that some people who have been on the same job for a long time are either very pleased or displeased. It is too early to judge the theory's value in explaining job satisfaction. It seems useful for explaining some aspects and deficient for explaining others, but this criticism can be leveled at *any* theory of job satisfaction. Landy's is a fresh approach. It illustrates how I/O psychologists might draw on other sciences to explain phenomena of interest.

Two-Factor Theory

No theory has generated as much research and controversy as Herzberg's *two-factor theory*. Herzberg, Mausner, and Snyderman (1959) originally dealt with job satisfaction among engineers and accountants. They conducted individual interviews, asking subjects to describe when they felt very good or bad about their jobs. The workers described incidents that had led to feelings of satisfaction and dissatisfaction. The interviews were *content analyzed* for common themes or ideas in the responses. This was done to determine (1) what kinds of things were mentioned when people described the times they were very satisfied, (2) what kinds of things were mentioned when people described the times they were very dissatisfied, and (3) whether there was any difference in what was described in each circumstance.

Results showed that certain factors were associated with high satisfaction and others with dissatisfaction. The authors found that descriptions of good times included such things as achievement, recognition, advancement, and responsiblity. Since all related to the jobs' content, they were called *content* factors. Descriptions of bad times were characterized by factors such as company policy, supervision, salary, and working conditions. These factors all related to the jobs' context and were therefore labeled *context* factors.

Herzberg proposed two general classes of work variables: (1) *satisfiers*, content factors that result in satisfaction, and (2) *dissatisfiers*, context factors producing dissatisfaction. Because of this organization, the theory has come to be known as the two-factor theory. Herzberg then went on to propose what is perhaps the most controversial aspect of his theory. He said that when a job provides a lot of content factors—that is, a sense of recognition, achievement, and so on—the employee will feel satisfied at work. When these factors are absent from a job—there is no sense of recognition, advancement, and so forth—the employee will *not* be dissatisfied but will feel neutral or indifferent. Alternatively, when a job provides a lot of context factors—such as good salary or pleasant working conditions—an employee will *not* feel satisfied but will feel neutral or indifferent toward the job. When these factors are absent from a job—poor salary or unpleasant working conditions—the employee will feel dissatisfied. Thus, with *satisfiers*, a high degree of reward will result in satisfaction and a low degree of reward will result in indifference. Conversely, with *dissatisfiers*, a high degree of reward will result in indifference and a low degree of reward in dissatisfaction. This relationship, which is the most controversial part of Herzberg's theory, is shown graphically in Figure 9–1. Thus, according to Herzberg, jobs should be designed so there will be a high degree of reward provided by both *context* factors (to avoid dissatisfaction) and *content* factors (to ensure satisfaction).

Herzberg's theory has been criticized on two points. The first is the method of data collection. Herzberg assumed that those interviewed could and would accurately report the conditions that made them satisfied or dissatisfied with their jobs. Unfortunately, when a person describes something favorable, there is a tendency to attribute it to the person's own accomplishments (content items). Conversely, in describing an unpleasant experience, a person is more apt to blame others (context items) rather than accept the blame personally. Many critics attribute the

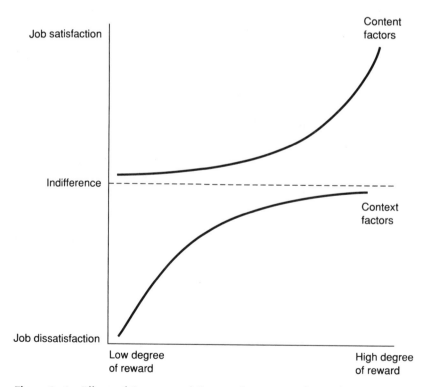

Figure 9–1 Effects of Content and Context Factors on Job Satisfaction

"two factors" to this tendency. It means the results are really only artifacts of the method used.

The second major criticism is that many studies have failed to replicate Herzberg's findings (for example, Ewen, 1964; Hinrichs & Mischkind, 1967). Such studies have shown that both content and context factors contribute to satisfaction and dissatisfaction. If people feel no sense of achievement or recognition, their response is likely dissatisfaction rather than indifference. Similarly, people can get pleasure from salary and working conditions. At best, these factors do not have to result in indifference. Thus, the validity of Herzberg's classification is suspect. In summarizing tests of Herzberg's theory, King (1970) found little evidence to support it.

The reaction of I/O psychologists to Herzberg's theory is mixed, but most evaluations are negative. McCormick and Ilgen (1980) strongly reject it: "The two-factor theory no longer deserves consideration" (p. 308). Landy and Trumbo (1980) are more positive: "On the whole, Herzberg has had a positive effect on the research on job satisfaction" (p. 407). The theory is popular among practitioners because it is certainly "elegant" and straightforward. There are no references to intangible values or needs, no comparative others are needed to explain satisfaction, and certainly there are no references to mysterious functions of the nervous system. According to Herzberg, satisfaction derives from conditions of work. I'm sure that much of the theory's appeal lies in its simplicity. Unfortunately, however, the theory has received little empirical support.

Review of the Four Satisfaction Theories

After reading about the four satisfaction theories, you should have some understanding and appreciation of the approaches to job satisfaction (see Field Note 1). According to the need- and value-based theories, satisfaction is the extent to which a job meets needs or fulfills values. It is an individual process. Social-comparison theories postulate that satisfaction is derived from a comparison with others in similar jobs. This is a social process. The opponent-process theory indicates that satisfaction is physiological. The central nervous system is responsible for satisfaction, particularly with regard to protecting a person from extreme emotions. Finally, the two-factor theory postulates work conditions as the sources of satisfaction. Content and context factors determine how satisfied a person will be. The four theories are summarized and evaluated by the criteria of empirical support and industrial applicability in Table 9–2.

The most popular theory of job satisfaction (in terms of the amount of research generated) has been the two-factor theory, though the comparative-process theories are currently seen as the most defensible. Each theory has, in it own way, contributed to our understanding of job satisfaction. It seems unlikely that researchers will develop *the* theory of job satisfaction. Such a theory would be an integration of the existing theories, each of which explains a component of job satisfaction.

TABLE 9–2   *Summary and Evaluation of the Four Job-Satisfaction Theories*

Theory	Source of Satisfaction	Empirical Support	Industrial Applicability
Intrapersonal-comparison theory	Comparison of personal needs or values with outcomes and rewards provided by a job.	*Mixed* More positive than negative, but difficult to pin down source of people's values and needs.	*Moderate* Applicable to the extent to which people have common needs or values that jobs can satisfy.
Interpersonal-comparison theory	Comparison of self to others in social network to infer feelings of satisfaction.	*Mixed* Some support that how people feel about themselves is a product of how they view others around them.	*Limited* Companies would have to employ happy people who also make others feel good in comparison.
Opponent-process theory	Feelings of satisfaction and dissatisfaction are products of the physiology of the body's central nervous system.	*Untested* Theory has been proposed but not tested. In fact, the theory may not be testable.	*Limited* Companies can do little (if anything) to alter the physiological makeup of their employees, and ethically may be precluded from attempting to do so.
Two-factor theory	Feelings of satisfaction are caused by job-content factors; feelings of dissatisfaction are caused by job-context factors.	*Weak* Many studies find both content and context factors lead to feelings of both satisfaction and dissatisfaction.	*High* Much of the theory's appeal rests with the prospects of maximizing factors leading to satisfaction and minimizing factors leading to dissatisfaction.

Field Note 1

What if you could go back in time 100 years? Pretend it's the late 1800s and you are on a mission to assess the job satisfaction of American workers. What do you think you would find? Certainly employment conditions then were grossly different from what they are today. Back then people earned a fraction of what they now earn, but everything cost a fraction of what it costs today as well. There were no employer-paid medical plans, paid holidays, air-conditioned offices, retirement benefits, or employee cafeterias. People often worked twelve-hour days, had no modern tools or equipment, worked under dehumanizing and unsafe conditions, and received no unemployment compensation or welfare if they were out of work. How do you think these people would describe their work lives?

You might think they would be most unhappy with their jobs because they were lacking many of the comforts we take for granted. Yet, they would not know what it was they were missing because you, not they, would have the benefit of hindsight. The interpersonal-comparison theory of job satisfaction says that people assess their feelings in comparison to those around them. Perhaps workers 100 years ago would have no basis on which to realize how rough they had it. Yet, those workers certainly had better employment conditions than *their* predecessors did 100 years before them.

How would you explain the job satisfaction of today's workers? Shouldn't we be delighted with our jobs, given what our ancestors had to endure? Or are we always caught up in the tide of rising expectations: the more we get, the more we want and the more easily we are disappointed or unhappy when we do not get it? Over the past 100 years, our national level of education has been greatly elevated. Has this "progress" somewhat backfired on us in that we now want more challenge from jobs than they can reasonably provide? Think about the American work life today versus that of 100 years ago. How would you explain the levels of job satisfaction you think you would find in both samples?

Measurement of Job Satisfaction

Surveys have been developed for measuring job satisfaction just as they have been developed for other attitudes. Some have been used extensively. Others were developed for a single study. There is nothing "wrong" with each researcher's developing a measure, but the measurements must be reliable and valid. However, comparing studies that use different measures may be a problem. Some surveys measure global satisfaction and others facet satisfaction (and not always the same facets). Thus, the literature on job satisfaction is confusing. In recent years, more researchers are using standardized surveys. This permits across-study comparison, which is of value for arriving at generalizations about job satisfaction. Three surveys are particularly popular and have been the objects of intensive research. We will examine each of them in some detail.

Job Descriptive Index

The Job Descriptive Index (JDI), developed by Smith, Kendall, and Hulin (1969), is the most often used and researched measure of job satisfaction. The questionnaire measures five facets: satisfaction with work itself, supervision, pay, promotions, and co-workers. Each facet consists of nine or eighteen items. These are either words ("routine") or short phrases ("gives sense of accomplishment"). The employee indicates whether or not the item describes the job. He or she can also give a response of "uncertain." Each item has a scale value indicating how descriptive it is of a satisfying job. Sample items are given in Figure 9–2. Five scale scores reflecting satisfaction for each of the facets are tabulated. The total score on the JDI has also been used to reflect overall job satisfaction; however, we now believe that overall job satisfaction is more than the sum of facet satisfactions (Scarpello & Campbell, 1983).

Research showed the questionnaire to be useful. Smith, Smith, and Rollo (1974) found the JDI measured satisfaction equally well for Blacks and Whites. The authors also confirmed that it successfully measured different facets of satisfaction. Schneider

Think of your present job. In the blank beside each word or phrase, write
Y for "yes" if it describes your job
N for "no" if it does *not* describe your job
? if you cannot decide

Work	Pay	Promotions	Co-workers	Supervision
—— Routine	—— Bad	—— Dead-end job	—— Talk too much	—— Up-to-date
—— Satisfying	—— Highly paid	—— Promotion on ability	—— Ambitious	—— Hard to please
—— Good	—— Less than I deserve	—— Infrequent promotions	—— Lazy	—— Asks my advice
—— On your feet	—— Income provides luxuries	—— Good chance for promotion	—— Loyal	—— Around when needed

Figure 9–2 Sample Items from the Job Descriptive Index

SOURCE: P. C. Smith, L. M. Kendall, and C. L. Hulin, *The Measurement of Satisfaction in Work and Retirement* (Skokie, Ill.: Rand McNally, 1969). Copyright © 1975, Bowling Green State University, Department of Psychology, Bowling Green, Ohio 43403.

and Dachler (1978) reported that test/retest reliability of the JDI over a 16-month interval was .57. They felt this was high enough to justify the JDI in longitudinal studies because satisfaction can change over time. McCabe, Dalessio, Briga, and Sasaki (1980) found a Spanish version of the JDI that was of comparable quality to the English version. However, Yeager (1981) suggested that the JDI may measure more than five facets. Some of the original scales seem to consist of multiple dimensions. For example, the supervision scale could be broken down into satisfaction with the supervisor's ability or performance and interpersonal skills. Nevertheless, the JDI seems to deserve its reputation as the best measure of satisfaction currently available.

Minnesota Satisfaction Questionnaire

The Minnesota Satisfaction Questionnaire (MSQ) was developed by Weiss, Dawis, England, and Lofquist (1967). It is the second-most-popular measure of satisfaction. Like the JDI, the MSQ also measures satisfaction with facets of a job. Twenty are included, such as creativity, independence, supervision-human relations, supervision-technical, and working conditions. Each facet is composed of five items. The individual responds on a five-point scale ranging from "very satisfied" (5) to "very dissatisfied" (1). Sample items are presented in Figure 9–3.

With 20 scales of five items each, the MSQ takes more time to complete than the JDI. However, research has shown that four of the scales (satisfaction with advancement, compensation, co-workers, and supervision-human relations) correspond roughly to four of the five scales in the JDI (satisfaction with promotions, pay, co-workers, and supervision, respectively). Gillet and Schwab (1975) administered the MSQ and the JDI to a sample of production workers and intercorrelated the responses. These four pairs of scales seem to measure the same facets. Thus, responses were expected to be similar. Validity coefficients converged in a range of from .49 to .70. These coefficients are not very high. They suggest, for example, that satisfaction with co-workers as measured by the JDI is not equivalent to the same facet as measured by the MSQ. So, questionnaires that seem to measure the same dimensions of a job may in fact not have a great deal in common. The study underscores the difficulty of making comparisons based on different measures.

How many facets of job satisfaction a questionnaire should measure is debatable. The JDI measures five, the MSQ 20. Data clearly indicate that these facets are not independent. As discussed, the number and kind of dimensions should be determined by the issues of interest to the researcher. In both the MSQ and the JDI, two dimensions of satisfaction with supervision are measured. In the MSQ, the two dimensions (satisfaction with supervisor's human relations and technical abilities) are listed as two separate scales. These were established by the researchers *before* data were collected. The JDI contains only one satisfaction-with-supervision scale. However, research (for example, Yeager, 1981) indicates that this one scale involves two dimensions of leadership. Thus, these dimensions were identified *after* the data were collected and analyzed. Similar conclusions can be drawn about an issue (in this case, satisfaction with supervision) via two different routes. This reflects the differences between the inductive and deductive modes discussed in Chapter 2.

	Very Dissatisfied	Dissatisfied	Neutral	Satisfied	Very Satisfied
On my present job, this is how I feel about:					
1. Being able to keep busy all the time	___	___	___	___	___
2. The chance to work alone on the job	___	___	___	___	___
3. The chance to do different things from time to time	___	___	___	___	___
4. The chance to be somebody in the community	___	___	___	___	___
5. The way my boss handles his men	___	___	___	___	___
6. The competence of my supervisor in making decisions	___	___	___	___	___
7. The way my job provides for steady employment	___	___	___	___	___
8. My pay and the amount of work I do	___	___	___	___	___
9. The chances for advancement on this job	___	___	___	___	___
10. The working conditions	___	___	___	___	___
11. The way my co-workers get along with each other	___	___	___	___	___
12. The feeling of accomplishment I get from the job	___	___	___	___	___

Figure 9-3 Sample Items from the Minnesota Satisfaction Questionnaire

SOURCE: D. J. Weiss, R. V. Dawis, G. W. England, and L. H. Lofquist, *Manual for the Minnesota Satisfaction Questionnaire,* Minnesota Studies on Vocational Rehabilitation 22 (Minneapolis: University of Minnesota, Industrial Relations Center, Work Adjustment Project, 1967). From *Contemporary Approaches to Interest Measurement,* ed. Donald G. Zytowski (Minneapolis: University of Minnesota Press). Copyright © 1973 by the University of Minnesota.

Faces Scale

The third-most-common satisfaction measure is the Faces Scale developed by Kunin (1955). This single-item scale is very different from the others. It measures global satisfaction and, as opposed to words or phrases, the scale points are drawings of a human face, as shown in Figure 9–4. In looking at this figure, one would think that Kunin simply took a few minutes to sketch some faces. Actually, a series of scale-construction procedures were used to create equal scale intervals. The Faces Scale is a good measure of overall satisfaction and is widely applicable. Since words are not used, there is less ambiguity about the meaning of the scale points. The person simply checks the face that reflects how he or she feels about the job in general. Kunin's Faces Scale is applicable for both males and females, though Dunham and Herman (1975) developed a version showing female faces.

Many researchers have used one of the above three scales to assess job satisfaction. However, as Wanous and Lawler (1972) state, there is no one best measure of job satisfaction. Certain measures related more strongly to certain variables than others. Indeed, the research we will review indicates that various facets have different correlations with various criterion variables. The selection of a satisfaction questionnaire should therefore be guided by two things: first, it should provide reliable and valid assessments; second, it should measure the facets of satisfaction that are of greatest interest to the researcher.

Relationship Between Job Satisfaction and Personal Variables

Several studies dealt with the relationship between job satisfaction and such personal variables as age, race, and sex. The results are only moderately consistent; that is, we cannot say that males are always found to be more satisfied than females or Whites more so than Blacks. In one study a given group will be found to be more satisfied

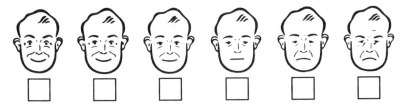

Put a check under the face that expresses how you feel about your job in general, including the work, the pay, the supervision, the opportunities for promotion, and the people you work with.

Figure 9–4   The Faces Scale of Job Satisfaction

SOURCE: T. Kunin, "The Construction of a New Type of Attitude Measure," *Personnel Psychology, 8* (1955), pp. 65–67.

than another, yet another study may reverse these findings. However, we will examine some findings in detail and try to explain the results.

Age

The results from some studies (for example, Hulin & Smith, 1965; Gibson & Klein, 1979) suggest that *global* job satisfaction increases with age, especially for males. Thus, the most dissatisfied workers are the youngest and the most satisfied are those nearing retirement.

The relationship between job-*facet* satisfaction and age is not so uniform. Hunt and Saul (1975) reported that satisfation with work, supervision, working conditions, and co-workers increased with age in a sample of males, but the only significant positive relationship for females was for satisfaction with work. Satisfaction with promotion opportunities was negatively related to age for both sexes. There was no relationship between age and satisfaction with pay for males; a negative relationship was found for females.

Later studies report different findings. In a review of many studies conducted on age and job satisfaction, Rhodes (1983) reports that the only facet showing a consistent positive relationship with age is satisfaction with work itself; that is, older workers like what they do more than younger workers. The relationship between age and the other facets seems to be much more variable across studies.

There are several explanations for the relationship between age and job satisfaction. One is that younger, dissatisfied workers eventually quit to find jobs that will satisfy them and employees who like their jobs remain; hence the relationship between age and job satisfaction. A second explanation is that growing older promotes satisfaction. Over time, individuals become more realistic about what they can expect from a job, and this maturation results in greater satisfaction. A third explanation is based on the notion of cohorts. Here, *cohorts* are groups of employees who enter the labor force at the same time. Each succeeding generation of cohorts may be less inclined to enjoy its jobs, perhaps due to a decline in the work ethic or some other change in formative influences. If this is true, there will be a positive relationship between age and satisfaction. Employees do not become more satisfied over time but, rather, there are group differences in satisfaction. Employees in the 50-to-55-year old cohort, for example, are more satisfied than employees in the 20-to-25-year-old cohort.

Longitudinal (as opposed to cross-sectional) analyses would determine which theory is correct. In the cohort explanation, patterns of satisfaction would be stable over time. In the aging explanation, satisfaction should increase. However, aging and cohort effects might also interact to produce feelings of increased satisfaction with age. Janson and Martin (1982) conducted a lengthy investigation into *why* overall job satisfaction increases with age. They were unable to provide evidence in support of any of the theoretical positions. In short, job satisfaction does increase with age, but we do not know why. Whatever the explanation, the empirical results are far more consistent for global than for facet satisfaction.

Race

Studies comparing racial-group satisfaction have been limited to mainly Black-White differences. The results are fairly consistent, but Black-White differences in satisfaction are not very great.

Some of the early studies compared Blacks and Whites in terms of whose needs were more satisfied on the job. For example, Slocum and Strawser (1972) reported that Black certified public accountants were less satisfied than their White counterparts along a number of dimensions, including needs for esteem, autonomy, self-actualization, and compensation.

Weaver (1977) found that Whites were more satisfied with their jobs overall. Results were based on a national opinion poll of full-time employees. However, the difference, while statistically significant, was not very large. Weaver (1978a) extended his research to correlates of job satisfaction and found little difference between Blacks and Whites in satisfaction with various job aspects. For example, the correlation between satisfaction and autonomy was .12 for Whites and .13 for Blacks. While some differences between races were found, it appears that Blacks and Whites are more similar in their feelings about work than they are different. This suggests that though Blacks may be somewhat less satisfied in *level* of job satisfaction, the *degree of association* between satisfaction and other variables is comparable for the two races.

Jones, James, Bruni, and Sells (1977) suggested that Black-White differences in satisfaction are not as important as understanding why they occur. Only one study (Moch, 1980) systematically dealt with explanations. Moch investigated two potential determinants of satisfaction: structural and cultural. Structural explanations state that systematic differences in the way employees are treated account for racial differences in satisfaction. An example would be Black employees' having fewer promotion opportunities. Cultural explanations attribute satisfaction differences to beliefs, values, or psychological states. Moch tried to assess the effects of these two types of variables on the global satisfaction of Blacks, Whites, and Mexican-Americans. He measured structural variables, such as work-group assignments and position in the organization, as well as cultural factors like the importance of interpersonal relations and intrinsic/extrinsic rewards. Moch then determined to what extent satisfaction was related to these factors. The results indicated that structural and cultural factors play a small but significant role.

Moch's findings were also somewhat discouraging about what organizations can do to improve feelings of satisfaction. Certainly, promotion opportunities and work assignments that modestly influence satisfaction can be improved; however, cultural factors cannot be altered. As Moch states, "It may be that the differential satisfaction by race . . . can only be erased through broad racial and cultural change rather than through conscious management policy. If so, it may be a long time before people of different races report relatively equal degrees of satisfaction" (p. 305).

More research should be done on why such differences do or do not occur. If structural factors are a cause of differential satisfaction, an organization should have the power to alter these inequities. However, if cultural factors are a major cause of satisfaction differences, we have few options with which to improve the situation. The effects of years of discrimination cannot be erased quickly. As Moch stated, it may take a long time to reach equity in satisfaction among different races. At the very least, research on the causes of racial effects helps in identifying what can be done to improve satisfaction as well as those factors that cannot be controlled.

Sex

Research on the relationship between job satisfaction and sex is inconsistent. Some studies report that males are more satisfied than females; others report the opposite; and still others report no differences. Hulin and Smith (1964) think sex differences are due to differences in education, pay, and tenure, and that males and females are equally satisfied with their jobs when these factors are controlled for. Sauser and York (1978) found this to be correct in their study of government employees. Males were more satisfied in global terms and also with regard to such facets as promotions, supervision, and work. When work differences between the sexes in education, pay, and tenure were considered, there were no important differences between males and females. The only significant finding was that women were more satisfied with pay than men. It appears that male/female differences per se do not account for much variance in job satisfaction. Rather, it is other variables (such as education) that are correlated with sex that best explain these differences.

Several studies have tried to find the sources of job satisfaction for men and women. Andrisani and Shapiro (1978) reported that females derived satisfaction from both content and context factors. Results were similar to studies that tested the validity of Herzberg's theory with men. Women derive satisfaction from both intrinsic and extrinsic factors. Weaver (1978c) directly compared sources of satisfaction for samples of men and women. He found that both sexes derived satisfaction from the same factors, that is, prestige, income, autonomy, and education. Weaver concluded,

> It should be unnecessary, therefore, for researchers to distinguish between the sexes when investigating the functional relationships between job satisfaction and the determinants included in this study; nor should management expect male and female workers to differ in the way their morale is affected by changes in the conditions of work which are related to these determinants [p. 271].

It would be a mistake, however, to conclude that women and men have the same feelings about work. Traditionally, married males have been the principal wage earners in a family, and females have had the main responsibility for child rearing. As more married women return to work, they experience role conflict that influences their feelings about their jobs. Andrisani and Shapiro (1978) state,

> [The] conflicting responsibilities at work and at home among these [females] with dual careers may prevent such working women from utilizing their productive talents to the best advantage. As a consequence, many may be compelled to accept unfulfilling jobs in order to keep market work from too seriously interfering with family responsibilities [p. 30].

To reduce role conflict, some women and have to take jobs that do not fully use their skills and abilities. They may also be forced to put less importance on work than do males, given the demands of their personal lives. Therefore, for at least some parts of the female labor force, feelings of satisfaction and the importance of work must be weighed against responsibilities in other aspects of their lives. Most males, on the other hand, do not experience such conflicting role pressures.

Review of Personal Correlates of Job Satisfaction

In considering the relationship between personal variables (age, race, sex) and job satisfaction, one must keep several points in mind. While there are age, race, and sex differences, they are not large. The variance in satisfaction caused by these variables was estimated at between 2% and 5% (Landy & Trumbo, 1980). Furthermore, when other variables (status, education, and pay) are held constant or controlled for, their effect is even less.

It is very difficult to find two groups of people who differ only with regard to age, race, or sex. Statistical methods can be used to control for variables known to affect satisfaction (like pay), but we assume that variables not controlled for do not influence satisfaction, and this may be incorrect. For example, if systematic differences (like cultural factors) exist between two groups, they, and not race per se, determine differences in satisfaction. Moch's study (1980) showed that cultural differences did affect satisfaction, so perhaps racial differences should be seen as cultural differences.

Landy and Trumbo (1980) make the point that lower satisfaction of females and blacks may simply be a case of the have-nots versus the haves. White males have usually held better jobs, and females and Blacks have held lower-paying, lower-status ones. Thus, it is not surprising that people in "good" jobs (White males) like what they do more than those in "bad" jobs (Blacks and females). Saying that all White males have good jobs and all Blacks and females have bad jobs is an oversimplification, but job satisfaction data make more sense if we talk about differences in types of jobs rather than types of people. Under ideal conditions, we would match people on all relevant variables except for age, race, and sex. We could then see what percentage of the variance in satisfaction these variables explain. Some researchers think the effect would vanish under such conditions. Since we can never have such an experiment, we must be aware of possible contamination by other uncontrolled variables (see Field Note 2).

Field Note 2

One of the fascinating things about people is their diversity, particularly as it relates to their likes and dislikes about work. While there are a few "common denominators" that cut across all jobs from which people seem to derive pleasure or displeasure, for the most part we have different tastes and preferences for work. For that we all should be most grateful, for if we all sought the same jobs, society would suffer. There would be intense competition for a few select jobs, and the rest would go unfilled. What seems evident is that people can satisfy their needs through work in a multitude of ways.

Several years ago, Studs Terkel wrote a book entitled *Working*. It is the chronicle of a seven-year project of interviewing hundreds of people about their jobs. The following are selected quotations from Terkel's book. Notice the diversity of ways in which people's needs are fulfilled (or unfulfilled) through their jobs.

Hots Michaels, player at piano bar in New York Hotel:

Because I enjoy the action, I enjoy people. If I were suddenly to inherit four million dollars, I guarantee you I'd be playin' piano, either here or at some other place. I can't explain why. I would miss the flow of people in and out.

Cathleen Moran, a nurse's aide:

I really don't know if I mind the work as much as you always have to work with people, and that drives me nuts. I don't mind emptying the bed pan, what's in it, blood, none of that bothers me at all. Dealing with people is what I don't like. It just makes everthing else blah.

Nora Watson, editor:

Jobs are not big enough for people. It's not just the assembly line worker whose job is too small for his spirit, you know? A job like mine, if you really put your spirit into it, you would sabotage immediately. You don't dare. So you absent your spirit from it. My mind has been divorced from my job, except as a source of income, it's really absurd.

Elmer Ruiz, gravedigger:

Not anybody can be a gravedigger. You can dig a hole any way they come. A gravedigger, you have to make a neat job. I had a fella once, he wanted to see a grave. He was a fella that digged sewers. He was impressed when he seen me diggin' this grave—how square and how perfect it was. A human body is goin' into this grave. That's why you need skill when you're gonna dig a grave . . . I start early, about seven o'clock in the morning, and I have the part cleaned before the funeral. We have two funerals for tomorrow, eleven and one o'clock. That's my life . . . I enjoy it very much, especially in summer. I don't think any job inside a factory or an office is so nice. You have the air all day and it's just beautiful. The smell of the grass when its cut, it's just fantastic. Winter goes so fast sometimes you just don't feel it.

Relationship Between Job Satisfaction and Employment Conditions

Many researchers have been interested in the relationship between people's feelings about their jobs and employment conditions. The set of variables that constitute "employment conditions" is very large. An exhaustive review of their relationships to job satisfaction is beyond the scope of this book. Instead, we will look at four sets of work-related variables: status, unions, pay, and employee ownership.

Status

Weaver and Holmes (1975) examined the work satisfaction of both women employed full time and full-time homemakers. They analyzed data from a national survey of 629 females; 331 with full-time jobs and 298 who reported their full-time activity as keeping house. The women responded to the question "On the whole, how satisfied are you with the work you do—would you say that you are very satisfied, moderately satisfied, or a little dissatisfied?"

Weaver and Holmes also collected information on demographic variables like age, marital status, education, and family income. Fifty-two percent of the respondents with full-time jobs and 53% of the homemakers reported being very satisfied with their work. The difference between the two groups (1%) was not significant. The responses were reanalyzed in terms of the demographic characteristics of the respondents. The only significant difference occurred in families with an annual income they perceived as below the national average; in this case, women who were homemakers were more satisfied than women who held full-time jobs. Apparently the latter were dissatisfied because they were still below the national average in spite of their financial contribution. Weaver and Holmes felt their findings cast doubt on the hypothesis offered by some authors that satisfaction of women with full-time jobs would be less than that of full-time homemakers.

Ronen (1977) examined the job-facet satisfaction of paid and unpaid industrial workers. In the United States, it is difficult to think of industrial workers who are not paid. But in Israel, such a condition can exist among members of a *kibbutz*. Ronen offers this description:

> A kibbutz is a voluntary collective settlement operating as a single economic unit and governed by a general assembly composed of all [its] members. Kibbutz members' needs are provided on a egalitarian basis and include food, clothing, housing, medical care, recreation, and equal pocket money, all of which are based on need and not on the level or style of their work or participation [p. 585].

Ronen administered the JDI (translated into Hebrew) to a sample of 135 unpaid kibbutz workers and 187 paid city workers. The pay scale of the JDI was not given to the kibbutz workers.

Ronen wanted to see whether the general pattern of job-facet satisfaction scores was comparable for the two groups. He correlated the JDI scores with overall measures of job satisfaction. Levels of importance for the facets of job satisfaction were identical for the JDI scores. The most important facet (strongest correlate with overall job satisfaction) was satisfaction with supervision, followed by work, promotions, and co-workers. Ronen concluded that the nonmonetary aspects of satisfaction could be distinguished as clearly for unpaid as for paid workers and that the former could be studied independently of attitude toward pay. It would be interesting to know whether the *level* of satisfaction with each facet was also comparable for the groups. Perhaps workers who are unpaid derive more (or less) satisfaction from the work itself. Unfortunately, Ronen did not deal with this.

Miller and Terborg (1979) measured facet satisfaction of 665 part-time and 399 full-time employees of a general retail store. The results revealed that the full-time employees were significantly more satisfied overall, and with their work and benefits, than were the part-time employees. The two groups did not differ on satisfaction with supervision, pay, or advancement. The part-time employees were no more satisfied with any facet of their jobs than were the full-time employees. Miller and Terborg explained the results on the basis of the partial inclusion of part-time employees in the work force. Part-time employees may tolerate organization demands differently. They may choose part-time work because of the time demands of other commitments. Part-time employees may be less satisfied because they are less included in the organization. They may be dissatisfied with benefits (insurance, vacation) because they receive fewer of them due to their status.

Unions

Schriesheim (1978) studied the relationship between satisfaction and voting in a union election. The sample consisted of 59 production workers who had recently voted in a union election in which union representation was defeated by two votes. Schriesheim wanted to see whether attitudes could be used to predict how employees voted. Using the MSQ, he collected data on four noneconomic facets of satisfaction (independence, variety, creativity, and achievement) and four economic facets (security, company policy, pay, and working conditions). He also collected data on employee attitudes toward both the local union and unions in general. The findings from the study are reported in Table 9–3.

The more positive the attitude toward the local union ($r = .57$) and unions in

TABLE 9–3 *Variable Correlations with Prounion Voting*

Variable	r
Attitude toward the local union	.57
Attitude toward unions in general	.51
Total noneconomic satisfaction	−.38
Independence satisfaction	−.36
Variety satisfaction	−.04
Creativity satisfaction	−.17
Achievement satisfaction	−.36
Total economic satisfaction	−.74
Security satisfaction	−.41
Company policy satisfaction	−.55
Pay satisfaction	−.60
Working conditions satisfaction	−.76
Total noneconomic and economic satisfaction	−.64

SOURCE: C. A. Schriesheim, "Job Satisfaction, Attitudes toward Unions, and Voting in a Union Representation Election," *Journal of Applied Psychology, 63* (1978), pp. 548–552.

general ($r = .51$), the more likely the employee was to cast a vote in favor of the union. However, a more potent predictor of the union vote was satisfaction with economic facets. The correlation for individual economic facets ranged from $-.41$ (for security) to $-.76$ (for working conditions). As a group, all four economic facets correlated $-.74$ with the prounion vote. Satisfaction with noneconomic facets was not as strong a predictor. The correlation for these facets was $-.38$ with the prounion vote. Schriesheim was able to show that a tendency toward unionization was mainly a function of dissatisfaction with economic facets. So, to avoid unionization, an organization would be wise to improve economic factors (job security, pay benefits). Schriesheim's study provided support for the adage that workers "vote their pocketbooks."

A second study on work attitudes as predictors of union activity was done by Hamner and Smith (1978). The authors sampled over 80,000 employees in 250 units of a large organization. In 125 of these units, some union activity had occurred shortly after the survey was taken; in the other 125 units, there was no union activity. The study was meant to determine whether satisfaction could predict the degree of union activity (ranging from no activity at all to holding an election that the union won). A 42-item satisfaction questionnaire was used, and responses were correlated with degree of union activity.

Thirteen of the items correlated significantly with the criterion. These involved supervision, co-workers, company identification, amount of work, physical surroundings, and kind of work. When the 13 items were combined in a multiple regression equation, the resulting squared multiple correlation was .30. In other words, approximately 30% of the variance in union activity could be explained by the responses to these 13 items. The results showed that attitudes can predict behavior. They also indicated that satisfaction surveys can be used by management to make changes that will reduce dissatisfaction with work. Without such changes the likelihood of unionization probably increases.

The purpose of the study of unions and job satisfaction by Odewahn and Petty (1980) was different. The authors compared satisfaction of 102 unionized and 76 nonunionized employees of a residential mental health care facility. All were given the JDI. Responses were statistically adjusted for differences between the two groups in education and tenure variables relating to job satisfaction. Nonunionized employees were significantly more satisfied with work and pay. Differences in satisfaction with promotion, co-workers, and supervision were not significant. Odewahn and Petty believe their results should be of particular interest to union leaders. They feel that employee attitudes toward the company and the union may predict the outcome of union elections. Certainly the results of the previous two studies support their position.

Pay

Two noteworthy studies investigated satisfaction with one particular job facet: pay. Why people are dissatisfied with pay has long interested I/O psychologists. Such dissatisfaction may promote poor performance, work stoppages, absenteeism, turnover, and overall satisfaction (Lawler, 1971). Dyer and Theriault (1976) studied pay satisfaction in three samples of U.S. and Canadian managers with the JDI pay scale. The managers also provided information on their current pay level, the personal inputs they brought to the job (such as training, experience, seniority, effort, and performance), and the priority they felt should be given to several factors in making salary decisions. Each of these variables was correlated with the JDI pay scale. The best single predictor was level of pay; the more people are paid, the more satisfied they are with their pay. Also, managers who felt that not enough importance was placed on the cost of living in making salary decisions were dissatisfied with their pay. All the variables accounted for between 34% and 45% of the variance in pay satisfaction for the three samples. The authors concluded that their study adds to our understanding of why people are satisfied with pay. However, we still have more to learn; over half the total variance in pay satisfaction remains to be explained.

A second study in this area was conducted by Weiner (1980). It assessed pay satisfaction in a sample of public-service employees by using the pay scale of the MSQ. It also collected information on attitudes toward unionization, turnover, and absenteeism. All variables were intercorrelated. Results showed that the more satisfied people are with pay, the less favorable is their attitude toward unionization. Weiner also showed that the more dissatisfied employees are with pay, the more likely they are to be absent and to quit. As with the previous study, a great deal of variance in pay satisfaction remains unexplained, but attitudes toward pay relate to important job behaviors as well as other attitudes.

Employee-Owned Companies

In many cases employees are dissatisfied with their jobs and attribute many of their employment woes to the companies' owners and bosses. What happens when the employees themselves own the company? This can happen in some special cases. For example, workers facing unemployment due to impending business closures have managed to purchase the financially threatened business. Another way for employees to become owners of their own companies is by being awarded shares of stock in the company as a form of compensation. However it happens, the employees themselves are in effect the owners (and ultimate bosses) of their own companies. What is the job satisfaction of workers in this employment context? Strangely enough, what information we do have reveals the results are not all that different from the case of more conventional companies.

Hammer and Stern (1980) found that despite being the actual owners of their companies, workers still tended to view top management as the owners. Also, rather than having an equal voice in making decisions, the workers preferred letting management make many of them. In another study, Hammer, Landau, and Stern (1981) discovered that after a company transferred to being employee owned, the amount of voluntary absenteeism (that is, absenteeism for which the employees did not have a legitimate excuse) decreased, but the amount of involuntary absenteeism (that is, being out sick) increased. In general the total amount of employee absence did not change, but there was a proportionate change in the two types of absence. In a study of job satisfaction, Long (1982) found that after changeover to employee ownership, attitudes of employees remained where they had been two years previously. Then there was a sharp decline in employee satisfaction, which occurred despite there being a steady increase in the value of the company's stock. After reviewing many companies that have employee stock-ownership plans (Klein, 1987) concluded that employee turnover is low and job satisfaction is high when management is strongly committed to employee ownership and there is extensive communication about the stock program.

While we do not know a lot about the attitudes of workers in employee-owned companies, it seems that employee ownership is not a panacea for employee discontent. Employee owners seem to face the same ailments and problems as do workers in conventional companies. In fact, it might be argued that job satisfaction among employee-owners might even be lower because they now have the burden of making difficult decisions and resolving complex problems.

Review of Employment-Condition Correlates of Job Satisfaction

As shown, employment factors do influence feelings of satisfaction. Feelings of satisfaction are, in turn, related to subsequent behavior. The Miller and Terborg (1979) study showed that part-time employees were more dissatisfied. Therefore, we might expect less productivity, more absenteeism, or more turnover in this group. The studies relating job satisfaction to unions reported significant results. In the Schriesheim (1978) and Hamner and Smith (1978) studies, employee attitudes about their jobs were good predictors of their vote in union elections. The appeal of unions seems to be based on the belief that they can change the causes of dissatisfaction. If employees are satisfied with their jobs, the union has much less of a chance of representing them since fewer benefits are attributable to the unions. Indeed, Berger, Olson, and Boudreau (1983) concluded that unions affect worker job satisfaction only indirectly. Unions serve to fulfill certain employee needs (for example, job security established by means of seniority systems), and it is the fulfillment of these needs that contributes to workers' satisfaction with their jobs. The Dyer and Theriault (1976) study showed that pay satisfaction is a function of many variables; the Weiner (1980) study illustrated that dissatisfaction with pay can lead to a number of undesirable behaviors. The research on employee-owned companies indicates that worker job satisfaction is in general certainly no greater than found in conventional companies, and perhaps may even be lower. Generally, it seems that there are some fairly strong relationships between work conditions and employee's attitudes toward their jobs.

Relationships Between Job Satisfaction and Job Behavior

Job satisfaction has long been seen as a major criterion variable in I/O research. Other important variables are absenteeism, turnover, and performance. This section reviews the relationships among these variables, recognizing that the satisfaction-performance relationship is one of the most intriguing and often-studied topics in I/O psychology.

Absenteeism

It makes sense that employees who do not like their jobs are absent more often. However, research (for example, Muchinsky, 1977; Porter & Steers, 1973) has shown that rarely does the correlation between satisfaction and absenteeism exceed $-.35$. There is also some evidence that the various facets of job satisfaction are differentially related to absence, with satisfaction with work being a consistent predictor (Terborg, Lee, Smith, Davis, & Turbin, 1982). We will examine three studies that offer insight into this relationship.

Smith (1977) took advantage of a natural occurrence to study how predictive job attitudes are of absenteeism. Smith examined attendance in one Chicago company on the day after a major snowstorm, when it took special effort to get to work. He had previously collected data on a number of satisfaction facets, including supervision, work, future with the company, and pay. Smith then correlated these scores with attendance. He also conducted the same analysis with a sample of New York employees unaffected by the snowstorm. Average attendance on that day in Chicago was much less (70%) than in New York (96%). The results are shown in Table 9–4.

Every measure of job satisfaction predicted attendance in Chicago, but none predicted attendance in New York. The best predictor was the career-future scale, suggesting that those who were most satisfied with their prospects put out the special effort needed to get to work that day. Smith concluded that satisfaction measures can predict job behavior (in this case attendance) when that behavior is under the employee's control. The results reported by Smith for the Chicago sample are certainly above the averages reported for the satisfaction-absenteeism relationship. Without mitigating circumstances (as in the New York sample), the relationship between satisfaction and absenteeism is quite modest.

Ilgen and Hollenback (1977) investigated the relationship between satisfaction and absenteeism over a 20-month period with a sample of secretaries. They measured absence with the MSQ. The resulting correlation was only $-.09$. The authors proposed two reasons. One was that if the company allows frequent absences (for

TABLE 9–4   *Correlations between Job Satisfaction and Attendance Levels on Individual Days for Chicago and New York Groups*

Scale	Chicago*	New York†
Supervision	.54	.12
Amount of work	.36	.01
Kind of work	.37	.06
Financial rewards	.46	.11
Career future	.60	.14
Company identification	.42	.02

* Group following storm.
† Group following no storm.
SOURCE: F. J. Smith, "Work Attitudes as Predictors of Attendance on a Specific Day," *Journal of Applied Psychology, 62* (1977), p. 18.

example, sick days, excused absences), employees will take advantage of them regardless of satisfaction. In fact, Ilgen and Hollenback argue, company policies that permitted absence should *increase* satisfaction. The second explanation was that if few rewards or sanctions were tied to absenteeism, probably no relationship would exist between satisfaction and absence; that is, if employees were neither rewarded nor punished for absence, their feelings about their jobs would be independent of attendance. A correlation of $-.09$ indicated that the two constructs were nearly independent statistically, if not conceptually. The authors believed that significant satisfaction-absenteeism relationships would occur only if rewards (promotions, raises) were based on attendance.

Finally, Steers and Rhodes (1978) proposed a model of attendance in which satisfaction plays a major role. The model is shown in Figure 9–5. Note that several

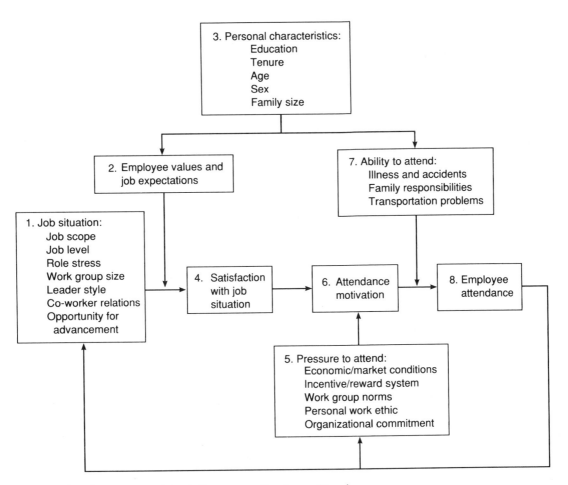

Figure 9–5   Major Influences on Employee Attendance

SOURCE: R. M. Steers and S. R. Rhodes, "Major Influences on Employee Attendance: A Process Model," *Journal of Applied Psychology, 63* (1978), pp. 391–407.

factors intervene between satisfaction (box 4) and attendance (box 8). Such factors as pressure to attend (economic factors, work group norms, and incentive or reward systems), motivation to attend, and ability to attend (taking into account family responsibilities and transportation problems) intervene. Given the many variables between satisfaction and attendance, it is not surprising that both strong and weak relationships between the two were reported. A person who liked his or her job but had no pressure, low motivation, and limited ability to attend would probably have more absences despite higher satisfaction. Steers and Rhodes did an excellent job of outlining the factors affecting attendance. They show that the link between satisfaction and attendance is neither simple nor direct.

Turnover

Muchinsky and Tuttle (1979) summarized 39 studies of the relationship between satisfaction and turnover. In all but four the relationship was negative. It appears, then, that the more people dislike their jobs, the more likely they are to quit. The magnitude of the satisfaction-turnover relationship, on average, is about −.40.

As an example of such work, Hulin (1966) matched clerical employees who quit with those who did not via several demographic variables. Hulin obtained satisfaction measures for all employees before any quit. He found that the mean satisfaction score for those who eventually did quit was significantly lower than for those who stayed with the company. Thus, it appeared that turnover could be predicted on a group basis, though the data did not permit individual prediction. Two years later, Hulin (1968) repeated the study in the same company and got the same results. Changes in company practices meant to reduce turnover by improving satisfaction were also successful.

Mobley (1977) proposed a model of employee turnover based on several hypothesized links between satisfaction and quitting. Such links included thinking about quitting, looking for another job, intending to quit (or stay), and actually deciding to quit (or stay). Mobley contended that feelings of dissatisfaction provoke thoughts of quitting, which in turn prompt the search for another job. If the costs of quitting are too high, the person may reevaluate the job (producing a change in satisfaction), think less about quitting, and/or use other responses like absence or passive behavior. If the costs are not too high and the other job looks good, this will stimulate the intention to quit, followed by actual quitting. If the alternative job is not good, the situation may stimulate the intention to stay. Mobley's model was a major step forward in thinking of the process from job dissatisfaction to turnover instead of repeatedly assessing the direct relationship between satisfaction and turnover.

Mobley, Horner, and Hollingsworth (1978) tested the model, as presented in Figure 9–6. They measured the satisfaction of some hospital employees. The authors also obtained measures of the other variables in the model. Turnover data were collected for 47 weeks after collection of the satisfaction data. Using correlation and multiple regression analysis, Mobley and associates tried to predict turnover from the variables in the model. Overall job satisfaction was found to correlate −.54 with thinking of quitting, −.54 with intention to search, −.49 with intention to quit or to

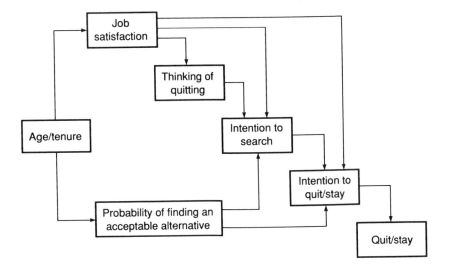

Figure 9–6   A Representation of the Intermediate Linkages in the Employee Turnover Process

SOURCE: W. H. Mobley, S. O. Horner, and A. T. Hollingsworth, "An Evaluation of Precursors of Hospital Employee Turnover," *Journal of Applied Psychology, 63* (1978), pp. 408–414.

stay, and −.21 with actual turnover. When all the variables shown in Figure 9–6 were combined to form a multiple regression equation, the multiple correlation for intention to quit was .75, while that for actual quitting was .51. Mobley and associates were able to demonstrate that cognitive and behavioral phenomena intervene between feelings of job satisfaction and actual quitting. Clearly, employee turnover is predicated on more than feelings of unhappiness about a job.

Satisfaction is a determinant of turnover, but the economic context must also be considered. Muchinsky and Morrow (1980) believe that satisfaction will be a better predictor of turnover in good economic times. They postulate that under conditions of high unemployment, employees would rather endure feelings of dissatisfaction than be out of work. Under good economic conditions with plentiful jobs, dissatisfaction could readily result in turnover if other jobs are available. Carsten and Spector (1987) tested the model proposed by Muchinsky and Morrow by comparing the relationship between job satisfaction and employee turnover over a 36-year period that was marked by diverse economic conditions. They found the correlations between satisfaction and turnover ranged from −.18 to −.52, providing support for the hypothesis that economic conditions moderate the relationship between the two concepts.

Performance

Probably no other topic has generated as much interest as the relationship between satisfaction and performance. The reason is obvious: we would like employees to be *both* happy and productive. Early research determined whether there was a relationship between the two. Two major studies (Brayfield & Crockett, 1955; Vroom, 1964) reached the general conclusion that they were related either not at all or only slightly. Vroom reported a median correlation of .14 across 23 studies of the satisfaction-performance relationship. Subsequent research revealed that certain types of performance were more related to satisfaction than others. A controversy then arose over whether satisfaction causes performance or performance causes satisfaction. The first view led to the belief that the way to have productive workers is to first make them happy. Today, however, the opposite view is held: People get pleasure from their work after finding they are good at it—performance leads to satisfaction. It is difficult to establish causality between any two variables, but some careful laboratory research (for example, Wanous, 1974) has indicated that the latter view seems more defensible.

The case has not been cleared completely. Organ (1977) has described some conditions supporting the former position. As Lorenzi (1978) commented, the implications of which view is correct are significant. If the performance-causes-satisfaction view is correct, managers should base rewards on past performance in the belief that this will reinforce desired performance. If the satisfaction-causes-performance view is correct, managers should reward regardless of performance so that employees will show their gratitude by performing better in the future. Most evidence favors the performance-causes-satisfaction view. But the controversy continues (for example, Sheridan & Slocum, 1975) and, given its implications, will probably never be totally resolved.

Some efforts have been made to study the satisfaction-performance relationship in certain types of jobs. One approach has been to create boring and stimulating jobs in a laboratory paradigm or to find such jobs in a field model. One reason for making jobs more stimulating is to enable jobholders to experience satisfaction when they perform well. Thus, it appears that the satisfaction-performance relationship will be stronger in a stimulating job than in a boring one. The research results on this issue have produced conflicting conclusions. Baird (1976) obtained just the opposite result—namely, that satisfaction with work is correlated with performance only in the boring job. Opposite and mixed results for the same type of study have been reported by Ivancevich (1978, 1979).

Other studies have investigated the conditions under which satisfaction and performance are related. Jacobs and Solomon (1977) found that the relationship is stronger when rewards are based on performance. Thus, people whose pay is based on performance (like salespeople on commission) should be more satisfied with their performance than others paid on an hourly rate (Cherrington, Reitz, & Scott, 1971).

In general, however, the satisfaction-performance relationship is not very large and certainly not consistent across different samples of jobs. A review of many satisfaction-performance studies by Iaffaldano and Muchinsky (1985) revealed that the best estimate of the true correlation between the two concepts, controlling for a variety of statistical errors, is .17. This correlation is not nearly as great in magnitude as some theoreticians and practitioners would intuitively believe. Its implication is that organizational attempts to enhance both worker satisfaction and performance simultaneously will likely be unsuccessful. The reason is that the two concepts are, for the most part, unrelated to each other. In fact, some organizational attempts to increase productivity (for example, cracking down on employees through tough supervisory practices) may well serve to decrease job satisfaction.

Fisher (1980) pointed out that low satisfaction-performance correlations often emerge because researchers try to relate a *general* attitude (overall satisfaction) with a *specific* behavior (performance of some task). Fisher contends that researchers should use attitude measures that are as specific as the performance measures. Without such a "fit," the two variables will probably never correlate highly. The effect of Fisher's contention remains to be seen. What is clear is that performance and satisfaction are popular and important criterion variables in I/O psychology. Thus, research on the conditions under which they are related or dissimilar will continue (see Field Note 3).

Field Note 3

The relationship between how well you do your job and how happy you are in doing it has intrigued people for decades. On an intuitive level many people think these two concepts should go together. After all, most people like what they are good at and dislike things they cannot do well. Yet many research studies have revealed there is little in common between performance and satisfaction. Why? It seems both variables have many complicated causes, and the link between them is not as simple or direct as it might initially appear. How productive you are depends on your motivation, your ability, and having a work environment that permits you to be productive (for example, having good tools). How happy you are in your work depends upon several factors: how happy you are in life and general disposition, your expectations for your job, and the reference group with whom you compare yourself. Added to these multidetermined con-

cepts are the problems of measurement; there is always a certain amount of error in assessing how productive or happy we really are. When you add it all up, it probably is *not* all that surprising that we do not find consistently strong relationships between the two.

However, some people persevere in searching for a definitive satisfaction-performance relationship as if it were the Holy Grail. They *expect* the two concepts to be related, so they repeatedly look for the connection. Psychologists have a fancy name for this phenomenon: "persistence in the illusion of validity." Probably no other relationship in all of I/O psychology has been studied so often with such negative results as the satisfaction-performance relationship. Most topics that repeatedly produce negative findings usually fall out of favor among researchers. However, this topic will probably continue to taunt researchers as a seductive mystery waiting to be unraveled.

Review of Job Satisfaction–Job Behavior Relationships

Job satisfaction is slightly correlated with absenteeism; low negative correlations are most often reported. Though the magnitude of the relationship is not great, the results of many studies have been quite consistent. Nicholson, Brown, and Chadwick-Jones (1976) concluded that many other factors intervene in the satisfaction-absenteeism relationship. The Steers and Rhodes (1978) model indicates some of these mediating factors, particularly the importance of pressure and ability to attend.

The relationship between dissatisfaction and turnover is fairly substantial; correlations in the .40s have been common. However, as with absenteeism, the relationship is not direct. People do not quit their jobs simply because they are dissatisfied. Mobley (1977) and Mobley and associates (1978) described some factors that intervene between satisfaction and turnover, such as the attractiveness and relative cost of other employment. The relationship between satisfaction and turnover is also limited by economic conditions. Mild dissatisfaction may lead to turnover when jobs are plentiful; feelings of strong dissatisfaction may be endured if the only other option is unemployment.

The relationship between satisfaction and performance is of great interest to I/O psychologists. Most research indicates the two are only slightly related. Research favors the argument that performance causes satisfaction rather than vice versa. Some studies have tried to identify the conditions that strengthen the relationship. Employees who are paid based on performance experience stronger satisfaction-performance relationships. Given the salience of satisfaction and performance as criterion variables, research on their interrelationship will probably continue.

Relationship Between Job Satisfaction and Life Satisfaction

Our final set of studies examines the relationsip between job satisfaction and satisfaction with life in gereral. To what extent are work and nonwork attitudes related? Is work more important to some people than to others? These types of questions guided the research in this area. On theoretical grounds, Kabanoff (1980) discussed three explanations for the relationship between work and nonwork satisfaction. The first is *compensation*. High satisfaction in one domain (work) may *compensate* for less satisfaction in the other (nonwork). The second explanation is *spillover*. High satisfaction (or dissatisfaction) in one area will *spill over* into the other area. Thus, one would expect roughly equal satisfaction in both areas as the feelings generalize. The third explanation is *segmentation*. Segmentation theory postulates that social experiences in life are *segmented* or kept separate by individuals; that is, the worlds of work and leisure are essentially psychologically separate. Thus, the amount of satisfaction a person feels with these two areas need not be related at all.

There is no definite empirical support for any of the explanations. Kabanoff attributes this to methodology problems, particularly in measuring nonwork satisfaction. However, each theory has received some empirical support. We will now examine some studies testing the relationship between work and nonwork satisfaction.

Dubin (1956) proposed the concept of *central life interest*. He defined this as an expressed preference for behaving in a given locale. Some people see work as a central life interest. These individuals, whom Dubin calls *job-oriented*, should have a high

In some jobs, feelings of satisfaction are very intense. Larry Morris/NYT Pictures

evaluation of work and would score relatively high on satisfaction measures. Other individuals, whom Dubin calls *non-job-oriented*, have central life interests other than work (church, family, or community). A smaller portion of this group should have strong feelings of job satisfaction. A third group may express no clear preference. They have a *flexible-focus* central life interest. For this group, we would expect a small relationship between central life interests and job satisfaction.

Dubin and Champoux (1977) tested these hypotheses with samples of male blue-collar and female clerical workers. Each person in the study completed a measure of central life interest assessing their environment preference (job, nonjob, no preference). They also completed the JDI measure of job satisfaction. When satisfaction scores were computed for each group, the general level of job satisfaction was found to be highest among those with a job-oriented central life interest. Satisfaction was lowest among workers with a non-job-oriented central life interest. Those with a flexible focus had intermediate scores. The results supported the hypothesis for job-oriented people. But the results for people with flexible focus were not as originally proposed. The authors concluded that this was reasonable. Because some of the environmental preferences for this group included the world of work, their job satisfaction scores *should* have fallen between those of the other groups.

Orpen (1978) correlated measures of job and life satisfaction in a sample of first-line managers. He administered two questionnaires at two different times. The correlations between the two variables were .31 and .24. The design of Orpen's study suggested some causal relationship between job and life satisfaction. He concluded that differences in job satisfaction cause differences in fulfillment of life satisfaction outside the job. He also concluded that satisfaction in one area spills over into the other. Current thinking on the job satisfaction-life satisfaction relationship suggests that the two concepts have a reciprocal causal relationship, meaning each influence the other (Schmitt & Bedeian, 1982).

We are now beginning to understand that the segmentation theory is probably incorrect—that is, it seems unlikely that people can completely divorce feelings about their job from feelings about life in general. Jamal and Mitchell (1980) concluded that individuals who cannot appreciably satisfy their psychological needs in their work environment have either a low or, at best, moderate level of mental health. Individuals whose needs are relatively much more satisfied in the work environment show either a high or moderately high level of overall mental health. Thus there appears to be a bond between feelings of satisfaction in the work and nonwork domains. Weaver(1978b) summarizes it as follows:

> Thus, happiness seems to be a generalized phenomenon, according to which employees are either generally satisfied or generally dissatisfied across a broad totality of life, with relatively few employees experiencing a significant satisfaction-happiness relationship in only one of a few aspects of life. . . . The happiness of most employees would rarely come entirely from a satisfying job, with little or no support from satisfaction in other domains of life [p. 839].

An emerging trend among I/O psychologists is to consider the concept of job satisfaction in a more holistic fashion. That is, how satisfaction with one's job relates to one's physical health, leisure activities, family life, and eventually to retirement from the work force. Increasingly, more companies are building gymnasium-type facilities for recreational activities. Designed for employee use during the workday, these facilities often include weight-lifting apparatus, aerobic exercises, jogging courses, and calisthenics programs. They are designed in the belief that physical well-being contributes to healthy job attitudes. Such facilities also enhance the attractiveness of these companies as employers. Progressive companies are also providing leisure counseling to their employees. Leisure counseling attempts to match an individual's attitudes (for example, personality) with leisure activities that the person should presumably enjoy. The leisure activities usually involve other people, so they provide a means of developing a social-support network for the person. The linkage between family and work life has long been ignored by researchers, and we are now witnessing research on the importance of this bond ranging from company-sponsored child day-care centers to the problems of dual-career couples. Finally, I/O psychologists are beginning to make inroads in an area long the province of gerontologists (researchers who study aging), that of the retirement process. The research by Beehr (1986) on retirement, Lounsbury and Hoopes (1986) on leisure activities, and Zedeck (1987) on family issues illustrate the more integrative manner in which I/O psychologists are coming to view job satisfaction.

Review of Job Satisfaction–Life Satisfaction Relationship

Job satisfaction is but one aspect of feelings of satisfaction with life in general. Among those for whom work is a central life interest, such feelings are more pronounced. Feelings of job satisfaction also contribute to general mental health. The relationship between job satisfaction and life satisfaction varies for different groups. The results of Weaver's (1978b) study suggest that degree of happiness is fairly pervasive: People are either generally satisfied or dissatisfied with the many factors that contribute to overall happiness. For most people, it is unlikely that a satisfying job can compensate for dissatisfaction in other areas of life. I/O psychologists are beginning to study factors relating to job satisfaction that extend far beyond the workplace.

Concluding Comments

A question often raised in the popular press is whether job satisfaction is increasing or decreasing. The answer is complex, given the many facets of job satisfaction and the difficulties in drawing accurate inferences from longitudinal studies. Two studies have tried to address the issue with somewhat conflicting results. Weaver (1980) assessed the job satisfaction of over 4,000 workers examined from 1972 to 1978. He reported no significant changes in global satisfaction among full-time employees (see Table 9–5). The responses were highly consistent over the seven-year period. Furthermore, over 85% of the respondents in each year were satisfied with their jobs. Weaver thus concluded that the global measure of job satisfaction is very stable, and as a measuring device, it may be unresponsive to changes in society.

A very large study by the Opinion Research Corporation (1981) reached a somewhat different conclusion. The attitudes of more than 25,000 workers from 400 companies were sampled over a 28-year period. This study differed from Weaver's (1980) in that it collected data about many facets of work. Feelings of job security among managers were found to be lower now than they have ever been. However, clerical and hourly employees were reported to feel more secure than at any time in the past 20 years. Most employees were found to be feeling more dissatisfaction with

TABLE 9–5 *Reported Job Satisfaction Among Full-Time Workers in the United States, 1972–1978*

Attitudes	Year of Survey							
	1972	**1973**	**1974**	**1975**	**1976**	**1977**	**1978**	$\bar{X}$
Very satisfied	48.8%	50.0%	51.2%	56.8%	55.8%	49.5%	52.0%	51.8%
Somewhat satisfied	36.6	37.4	36.7	31.8	32.6	39.2	37.2	36.1
A little dissatisfied	11.2	9.0	8.5	8.1	8.5	9.6	7.9	9.0
Very dissatisfied	3.4	3.6	3.6	3.3	3.1	1.7	2.9	3.1
Total satisfied*	85.4	87.4	87.9	88.6	88.4	88.7	89.2	87.9

* The combined percentage who responded "very satisfied" or "somewhat satisfied."
SOURCE: C. N. Weaver, "Job Satisfaction in the United States in the 1970's," *Journal of Applied Psychology, 65* (1980), pp. 364–367.

intracompany communication. The results were quite complex. In general, it seems that job satisfaction is falling for some groups of employees but rising for others. Perhaps the differences between the two studies stemmed from the more varied sample, longer time period, and use of facet (as opposed to global) satisfaction in the latter. A complex question warrants a complex answer. The question of rising feelings of job dissatisfaction is difficult to answer in a simple manner. Though workers may complain more now, maybe it is just that they are more willing to *voice* their complaints than ever before.

Nord (1977) made the point that I/O psychologists can improve our understanding of job satisfaction if they direct their research efforts toward helping improve employee satisfaction. He feels that too often scientists address esoteric issues and lose sight of the groups who could benefit from their research. Job satisfaction is certainly a valid area of inquiry since it affects the daily lives of millions of workers. Nord contends that by making research more relevant for practitioners, we will develop a healthier and more balanced perspective. Wiggins and Steade (1976) have expressed a similar idea. They feel that job satisfaction is a social concern that we must consider as we try to improve the quality of life. Job satisfaction, therefore, has important practical implications for workers as well as for scientific investigation. We should never lose sight of our mission as scientists. But we should also not fail to grasp the importance of satisfaction for workers.

MAJOR CHAPTER OBJECTIVES IN REVIEW

After having read this chapter, you should know:

1. Four major theories of job satisfaction and the basis of their explanation as to why people like their jobs.

2. Major methods of measuring job satisfaction.

3. Relationships between job satisfaction and employment conditions.

4. Relationships between job satisfaction and job behavior.

5. Relationships between job satisfaction and life satisfaction.

CASE STUDY—*Do You Like Your Job?*

Gil McKee contemplated his drink. After a hectic day, he was trying to unwind in a bar frequented by business people. He looked up to notice an old college friend coming through the door. It had been almost two years since he had seen Barry De Nisi when they were in the same marketing class.

"Barry," McKee yelled out over the din in the bar. "Have a seat. I haven't seen you in ages. I didn't know you were in town."

"I've been at Allied Insurance as a management trainee for the past eighteen months," replied De Nisi. "How about you?"

"I'm with Stoner and Young, an advertising agency. I've been with them for almost a year," said McKee.

"What's it like?" asked De Nisi. "I hear they're a pretty high-pressure outfit."

"I don't know where you get your information," McKee responded, "but you're right. The pay is really good, but they get their pound of flesh from us every day. The people I work with are very sharp, but they're real competitive. I think Stoner and Young has an unwritten policy. They like to pit all the new people against each other, and the 'winner' gets promoted. People who don't get promoted don't seem to last very long. They either look elsewhere or get asked to look elsewhere, if you know what I mean."

A sympathetic look crossed De Nisi's face. "I have my own hassles at Allied, but they're different. My salary is pretty low, but I think I'm close to a promotion. I'd better be. When I started, they said we'd be moving up after nine months of training. Those nine months became twelve, then fifteen. I've been there eighteen months now, and nobody in my group has moved up yet. We've had two resignations in the positions above mine, so they'll be moving two of us up soon. I hope I'm one of them. Their policy is to bring you along slowly. There's a lot of legal stuff to learn. I've picked up a lot, but I'm getting anxious to use it. My boss is terrific. Right when I feel really frustrated, he takes me aside and says I'm doing great. He shows me the corporate staffing projections and says he'll recommend me highly for an opening. I guess I'm just too impatient."

McKee stared back at his drink. "My boss is a dunce, but he's a slick dunce. He surrounds himself with people that make him look good. They do all the work; he gets all the credit. I've learned more from my peers than I have from him. I don't understand how someone like that survives in Stoner and Young. You'd think by now they'd be onto him. He must be a better actor than I give him credit for."

"You like what you do?" asked De Nisi.

"Yeah, it's interesting stuff," answered McKee. "A lot more complicated than what we learned in college. Some of our professors ought to go out in business for a while as a refresher course. They didn't teach us about company politics. I never had a course in making my boss look good, but that's what I do."

They both fell silent for a while. Finally De Nisi said, "Say, the Yankees are in town on Friday night. You want to catch the game with me?"

"I'd like to, Barry," said McKee, "but Rita has really been on my back lately about bringing a lot of work home. I promised her we'd go dancing Friday night. Maybe later, okay?"

"Sure," De Nisi replied, "right after we both get promoted."

They both laughed, and De Nisi reached for his coat.

Questions

1. How would you assess the job-*facet* satisfaction of both De Nisi and McKee?

2. Which person feels the more *overall* satisfaction with his job, and why?

3. Do the two men attach different degrees of importance to the various facets of their jobs? If so, which facets seem most important for whom?

4. Does any one theory of job satisfaction seem particularly useful in explaining McKee's feelings about his job?

5. Is there any information in the case that would lead you to speculate on the relationship between job and life satisfaction?

10

Work Motivation

Motivation was one of the first topics researched in psychology. Some of the most grand (if not grandiose) theories have been theories of motivation. Such psychologists as Hull, Skinner, and Tolman proposed explanations of why people behave as they do. However, these theories were broad and limited in explaining the motivation of industrial workers. Consequently, I/O psychologists developed a second set of theories to explain the behavior of employees in a work setting. These are more concentrated in scope. They deal with human motivation in a refined context of which work motivation is but a subset. However, theoretical constructs may be modified to explain behavior in the two domains.

Within the work world, there is no shortage of pat explanations for behavior. Various levels of performance are "explained" by such comments as "She's just lazy," "He's a real hustler," or "People will do anything if you pay them enough." Unfortunately, human behavior is not so simple. Motivation is one of the most complex phenomena. People are motivated by many factors. Furthermore, the same people can be motivated by different factors in different situations. In this chapter, we will look at several theories of motivation. As will be seen, they offer fairly complex explanations for work behavior.

Ability, Performance, Situational Constraints, and Motivation

Consider this conversation:

Supervisor: George just isn't motivated any more!

Foreman: How can you tell?

Supervisor: His productivity has fallen off by more than 50%.

This conversation reflects a stereotypical misconception about motivation. Motivation is a hypothetical construct: Its existence has to be inferred from observation. In this case, the supervisor infers the worker's level of motivation based on the latter's behavior (productivity).

However, motivation and performance are not the same. A highly motivated person may not perform very well. The reason is that *performance*, in theory, is the product of motivation and ability moderated by situational constraints. *Ability* is the individual's capability for performing certain tasks. It is a necessary but insufficient precursor of performance. *Motivation* is the individual's *desire* to demonstrate the behavior and reflects willingness to expend effort. *Situational constraints* refer to factors in the work environment that hinder performance. For example, a carpenter who has lost all his tools cannot be productive no matter how great his talent or motivation. When someone has (1) no ability, (2) no motivation, or (3) pressing situational constraints, performance will be poor. If a person has no musical ability, all the motivation in the world will not make him or her a good musician. People perform best when they have the needed resources, abilities, *and* the desire to perform a task well. Motivation, therefore, is but one factor determining performance.

Work Motivation

Steers and Porter (1975) identified three major components of motivation. The first is *energizing*—a force within people that arouses behavior. The second involves *direction*: people may direct their efforts to certain situations and not others. A good motivation theory should explain why these choices are made. Finally, motivation involves *maintenance*. People will persevere in some tasks and end others quite quickly. Theories of work motivation concern the behavior of workers over an extended time (for example, a career). Thus, maintenance is a particularly important component. Steers and Porter define work motivation as "*conditions which influence the arousal, direction, and maintenance of behaviors relevant in work settings*" (italics added).

Two Perspectives on Motivation

Motivation has traditionally been viewed from one of two perspectives: trait theory and environmental theory.

Trait Theory.   According to the *trait theory*, motivation is an enduring characteristic; some people have it and some do not. People are presumed to be born with a certain level, which remains stable over their lives. Accordingly, highly motivated people never "lose" it and poorly motivated people never acquire it. If you were a manager who wanted highly motivated workers, your strategy would be to hire people who were judged as possessing this trait. Thus, you would assess a person's motivation just as you would such attributes as typing ability, physical strength, or mechanical aptitude. Because many practitioners subscribe to this theory, you might think that there are many tests to assess "how much" motivation a person has, just as there are for intelligence and ability. Such is not the case; only a few tests of this kind have been developed. One was designed by Wherry and South (1977). The test contained seventy items. Responses were on a scale from 1 ("I almost never feel that way") to 5 ("I almost always feel that way"). Examples of items are shown in Figure 10–1. Wherry and South administered the test to 240 workers in 35 organizations and correlated the scores with criterion measures, such as job satisfaction, salary, and job level. High scores on the motivation test were related to greater satisfaction, higher salary, and higher job level.

This test provided evidence that individual differences in motivation can be assessed. We can differentiate poorly from highly motivated people to some degree. However, these types of tests are not as popular as intelligence and aptitude tests, presumably because responses can be faked. With an aptitude test, there is one correct answer per question (for example, "What is the square root of 64?"). In contrast, we do not know whether a person is truthful when he or she says, "I like to expend a lot of energy." Furthermore, we do not know a person's frame of reference. If a motivational test is given for personnel selection, applicants can respond in ways they think would make them look highly motivated. This is especially true when the most desirable response is obvious. Though some tests (like the MMPI) have a built-in scale with which to detect faking, most do not. It would be nice if we could develop "fake-proof" questions for accurately assessing motivation. To date, we have not been very successful.

Environmental Theory. According to the *environmental theory*, situational or environmental factors determine motivation; given the right set of circumstances, people can be "made" to be motivated. Rather than proposing that some people are highly motivated and some are not, this view assumes that all people can become highly motivated if the necessary factors are present in the environment. Consequently, it focuses on understanding what these "motivation-inducing" factors are and how they affect human behavior. Research from this perspective has sought to determine to what degree motivation is enhanced by attributes of the work performed, the individual's relationship with co-workers, and rewards made contingent upon performance.

Both perspectives have some merit. As the trait theory suggests, some people are

---

Desire promotion based on ability rather than seniority.

Spend much of my free time in self-improvement.

Like to keep my output at a high level.

Would rather work than loaf.

Like to expend a lot of energy.

Come to work early and stay late as a rule.

Believe in setting goals and achieving them.

Want to work my way to the top eventually.

Figure 10–1 Sample Items from Wherry and South's Work Motivation Scale

SOURCE: R. J. Wherry and J. C. South, "A Worker Motivation Scale," *Personnel Psychology, 30* (1977): pp. 613–36.

FRANK AND ERNEST   by Bob Thaves

I THINK OF MYSELF AS BEING IN MOTIVATION RESEARCH -- EVERY MORNING I WONDER WHY I GO TO WORK.

THAVES 2-11

©1975 Newspaper Enterprise Association, Inc.

indeed more motivated than others. However, the world is not divided into sloths and dynamos. Rather than "some have it and some don't," the idea that "some have more of it than others" is more realistic. The environmental theory is quite exciting for those interested in designing effective organizations. If motivation can be improved, organizations need not be passive, only hoping to "find" motivated workers. Research has found factors that induce motivation. Therefore, a *balanced* perspective of motivation is most reasonable. There are differences in both people and environments that account for variations in motivation (see Field Note 1).

Field Note 1

The distinction between the trait and environmental approaches to motivation is a fascinating one and has far-reaching implications for the world of work. The trait approach is premised on the assumption that motivation is a trait like any other, such as sociability. Thus, people vary in terms of how much of this trait they have, ranging from little, if any (these people are called "lazy"), to a lot (these people are called "ambitious"). Many job announcements seem to endorse this perspective as they clamor for "eager, hard-driving, high-energy go-getter" candidates who will bring to the jobs the levels of motivation needed for success. This trait is often deemed highly critical for managerial jobs.

The alternative approach is based on the idea that there are forces in the environment that will motivate people. These forces can range from inspiring talks and speeches (the athletic-coaching profession is a classic example) to the characteristics of certain tasks that motivate people to do a good job (these will be reviewed in Chapter 13). The assumption underlying this approach is that just about anyone can be transformed into a charged-up performer if exposed to the proper stimulation. Thus, people can attend "motivation clinics" designed to unleash the driving potential that supposedly resides within everyone. This "unlocking mechanism" has been the object of intensive search for decades.

Imagine yourself as a company president. Would you look to *hire* people who were already motivated to succeed prior to joining your company? Lee Iacocca, a respected and popular corporate executive, refers to these people as those in whom "a fire burns in their belly." Alternatively, would you turn your attention to the workplace itself and seek to staff the organization with inspiring managers who will "turn on" the work force? Perhaps you would try to design work in such a way as to motivate the people who perform it. The answers to these questions have intrigued I/O psychologists since the inception of our profession and have profound economic and social consequences.

Motivation Theories

Most of this chapter is devoted to seven theories of work motivation. The concluding section attempts to integrate and synthesize the research on motivation, underscoring areas of convergence as well as divergence. The reader will undoubtedly be struck by the multitude of ways in which work motivation has been conceptualized. Perhaps no other area of I/O psychology has produced such a differing array of perspectives on the same topic.

One might also view the number of different theoretical perspectives as implicit testimony to the complexity (and our limited understanding) of work motivation as a construct. As McCormick and Ilgen (1980) say, the many orientations are "a blessing and a curse." They are a blessing in that they expand our understanding, yet a curse because they also make the likelihood of a simple, unified theory quite remote. It would be futile to determine which theory is "right"; they all have strengths and weaknesses. Understanding the theories and their empirical support can help in designing personnel policies and work that will encourage desirable behavior.

Each of these theories will be presented in three sections: a *statement* of the theory, *empirical tests*, and an *evaluation*.

Need-Hierarchy Theory

Statement of the Theory.   One of the major theories of motivation was developed by psychologist Abraham Maslow. It is called the *need-hierarchy theory*. Most of Maslow's writing was *not* concerned with work motivation. Only later in his career did Maslow become interested in applications of his theory. Most of its uses were derived from other researchers' examinations of its relevance for industrial organizations.

According to Maslow (1954, 1970), the source of motivation is certain needs. Needs are biological or instinctive; they characterize humans in general and have a genetic base. They often influence behavior unconsciously. What causes people to behave as they do is the process of satisfying these needs. Once a need is satisfied, it no longer dominates behavior, and another need rises to take its place. Need fulfillment is never ending. Life is thus a quest to satisfy needs.

Much of Maslow's theory identifies needs, but the second component explains how the needs relate to one another. Maslow proposes five types of needs: physiological, safety, social, self-esteem, and self-actualization. *Physiological* needs are the most basic; their fulfillment is necessary for survival. They include the need for air, water, and food. *Safety* needs include freedom from threat, danger, or deprivation. They involve self-preservation. Today, most of our safety needs are met, but people experiencing disasters like hurricanes or riots have had their safety needs threatened. *Social* needs include the desire for association, belonging, companionship, and friendship.[1] These involve an individual's ability to exist in harmony with others. *Self-esteem* needs include self-confidence, recognition, appreciation, and the respect of one's peers. Satisfaction of these needs results in a sense of adequacy; their thwarting produces feelings of inferiority and helplessness. The last type of need is *self-actualization*; it is the best known and least understood in Maslow's scheme. Self-actualization is realization of one's full potential—in Maslow's words, "to become more and more what one is, to become everything that one is capable of becoming."

As mentioned, the second part of the theory concerns how these needs are related. According to Maslow, they exist in a *hierarchy*. At the base are the physiological needs, which must be met first and continuously. The remaining needs are placed in order, culminating with the highest need, self-actualization. Physiological and safety needs are referred to as *basic*; social, self-esteem, and self-actualization needs are *higher-order* needs. The need hierarchy theory is illustrated in Figure 10-2.

Maslow proposed several points regarding the need hierarchy:

1. Behavior is dominated and determined by the needs that are unfulfilled.

2. An individual will systematically satisfy his or her needs by starting with the most basic and working up the hierarchy.

3. Basic needs take precedence over all those higher in the hierarchy.

The first proposition is fundamental: once a need is fulfilled, it will no longer motivate behavior. A hungry person will seek food. Once the hunger is satisfied, it will not dominate behavior. The second proposition involves *fulfillment progression*. This means that a person will progress through the needs in order, moving on to the next one only after the preceding one has been fulfilled. We all spend our lives trying to fulfill these needs because, according to Maslow, only a small percentage of people have fulfilled the self-actualization need. Maslow also says this need can never be fully satisfied. The third proposition stresses that the needs basic to survival always have a higher priority.

The theory has several implications for work behavior. When pay and security are poor, employees will focus on those aspects of work necessary to fulfilling their basic needs. As conditions improve, the behavior of supervisors and their relationship with the individual take on increased importance. Finally, with a much improved environment, the role of the supervisor diminishes and the nature of the work reemerges. However, work is now important in self-actualization and not in fulfilling basic needs.

---

[1] Some authors also refer to social needs as love or belongingness needs.

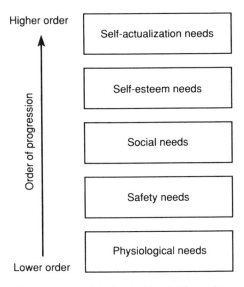

Higher order

Self-actualization needs

Self-esteem needs

Order of progression

Social needs

Safety needs

Physiological needs

Lower order

Figure 10–2 Maslow's Need Hierarchy

SOURCE: A. H. Maslow, *Motivation and Personality,*
2nd ed. (New York: Harper & Row, 1970).

The theory also predicts that as people move up in the management hierarchy, they will be motivated by increasingly higher-level needs; thus, managers at various levels should be treated differently. Additionally, employees can be expected always to want more. The organization can never give enough in terms of individual growth and development. It is the nature of the self-actualization need that once activated and satisfied, it stimulates an even greater desire for satisfaction. Thus, it is a continuing source of motivation (Miner, 1980).

Empirical Tests of the Theory. The ultimate test of any theory is empirical support, but a problem with Maslow's theory involves measuring the variables. Because he did not provide operational definitions of his variables, measuring them and testing the theory have fallen to other researchers.

Research has focused mainly on the existence of the five needs and their hierarchical arrangement. Porter (1961) developed a need-satisfaction questionnaire for assessing the degree of fulfillment and importance of the five needs. Using a 7-point scale, Porter asked people to indicate (1) how much of a given need is present in their lives now, (2) how much there should be of this need, and (3) how important the need is. By subtracting the second variable from the first, Porter obtained a measure of *relative deficiency*—the difference between what people have and what they want. Using this method, Lawler and Suttle (1972) sampled a group of lower-level managers at two points in time separated by six months. The median stability (test/retest reliability) of the need measures over this six-month period was found to be only .38. This is evidence that either the managers' needs changed over the six months or the measurement was somewhat unreliable. Lawler and Suttle also found that needs exist in a two-level hierarchy (as opposed to the five Maslow proposed). The basic biological needs are on the bottom and all other needs on the top.

Mitchell and Mougdill (1976) assessed the needs of several samples of accountants and engineers in Canada using a questionnaire similar to Porter's (1961). Again the results did not support a five-level hierarchy. Their data suggested that security needs are distinct from the others and the remaining needs clustered as a group. Although the authors did not totally reject the five-level hierarchy, their data clearly did not support it.

Betz (1984) found mixed support for the theory. On the negative side, she found that need importance was not related to need deficiency. Yet, as the theory predicts, Betz found a positive correlation between need fulfillment and life satisfaction.

Finally, Wahba and Bridwell (1976) reviewed all earlier research on Maslow's theory. They concluded that the theory has received little clear or consistent support. Some of Maslow's propositions were totally rejected; others received mixed or questionable support. Most support was for the importance of the basic needs; the least evidence was for the higher-level needs. The number of needs appeared questionable, as did the idea of fulfillment progression.

Evaluation of the Theory.   It is tempting to dismiss most of Maslow's theory, given the lack of support, but there are a few points that suggest a more positive verdict. First, it is not a "theory" in the usual sense. Maslow did not propose testable hypotheses. As Wahba and Bridwell (1976) said, "Maslow's need hierarchy theory is almost a nontestable theory" (p. 234). It was based on logical and clinical insights into human nature rather than on research findings. Furthermore, Maslow did not discuss any guidelines for empirical tests of his theory. Many questions remain, and the way the theory is tested is open to interpretation. For example, what is the time span for the unfolding of the hierarchy? Is there a relationship between age and the need we are trying to satisfy? How does the shift from one need to another take place? Do people also seek to fulfill needs by going *down* the hierarchy? These questions are very important; they affect how we would use the theory in the work environment.

The vagueness of the theory also leaves some nagging issues unanswered. According to Maslow, we systematically progress from one need in the hierarchy to the next. Yet, we all need to eat, drink, and breathe every day. We never really have our physiological needs satisfied. We try to fulfill our self-esteem needs even if our social needs are not fully satisfied. Rather than going through the hierarchy in stages, perhaps we attempt to satisfy all needs concurrently. Maslow did not deal with this speculation.

Maslow's theory, a highly abstract statement about humankind, is far more philosophical than empirical. But his notion of self-actualization is well ingrained in the way we think about our mission in life. His writing has generated a great deal of thought about the nature of humankind in general. While Maslow's theory is deficient in explaining day-to-day behavior at work, his contributions to the field of psychology as whole should not be ignored.

ERG Theory

Statement of the Theory. A second major theory based on needs was proposed by Alderfer (1969, 1972). Its name is *ERG theory*, which stands for three types of needs: existence, relatedness, and growth. Alderfer defined them as follows:

1. *Existence needs.* These are material and are satisfied by environmental factors, such as food, water, pay, fringe benefits, and working conditions.

2. *Relatedness needs.* These involve relationships with "significant others," such as co-workers, superiors, subordinates, family, and friends.

3. *Growth needs.* These involve the desire for unique personal development. They are met by developing whatever abilities and capabilities are important to the individual.

Alderfer proposed ERG in response to the shortcomings of Maslow's theory. His theoretical variables also involve specific measures. Alderfer's theory differs from Maslow's on three important dimensions.

1. He proposed three need categories in contrast to Maslow's five. The correspondence between them is shown in Figure 10–3.

2. Alderfer arranged his needs along a continuum as opposed to a hierarchy. The continuum, as shown in Figure 10–4, is concreteness. Existence needs are the most concrete and growth needs the most abstract.

3. According to Maslow, a person only moves *up* the need hierarchy (fulfillment progression). Alderfer, on the other hand, allowed for "movement" *back and forth* on the continuum. Moving toward fulfillment of the growth and relatedness needs was also called fulfillment progression by Alderfer. Moving back toward the fulfillment of more concrete needs, however, was referred to as *frustration regression*. Alderfer meant that if a person became frustrated in satisfying higher needs, he or she would regress toward fulfilling lower needs.

The two theories also differ on need fulfillment, particularly with respect to

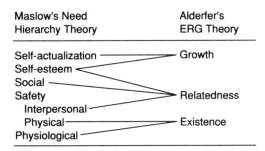

Maslow's Need Hierarchy Theory

Alderfer's ERG Theory

Self-actualization —————— Growth
Self-esteem
Social
Safety ——————— Relatedness
  Interpersonal
  Physical ——————— Existence
Physiological

Figure 10–3 Comparison of Maslow's Needs to Alderfer's Needs

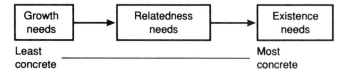

Figure 10–4 Alderfer's Continuum of ERG Needs

motivating properties of unfulfilled needs. According to Maslow, the less social needs, for example, are satisfied, the more they will be desired. To Alderfer, the less relatedness needs are satisfied, the more existence needs will be desired. The same relationship holds for growth needs: if not satisfied, they will be supplanted by relatedness needs. Here again is the concept of frustration regression, which permits a person to seek fulfillment of more concrete needs if the more abstract needs are not satisfied.

Empirical Tests of the Theory. There are relatively few tests of ERG theory. One study testing Maslow's theory (Hall & Nougaim, 1968) reported results that became a partial basis for Alderfer's theory. Hall and Nougaim found that the more a need is satisfied, the more important it becomes. Maslow's theory would predict that satisfaction at one level would correlate positively with importance at the next level.

Another study (Wanous & Zwany, 1977) provided strong support for ERG theory, especially the existence of the three needs. The authors also found that the three were relatively independent of one another and could be measured reliably. They found support for the notion that people progress through the three needs as Alderfer proposed. Wanous and Zwany concluded that there was some hope for using Alderfer's theory in management. According to Maslow, a satisfied need is not a motivator; therefore, "today's successful motivator becomes obsolete tomorrow" (p. 96). However, Wanous and Zwany found the opposite: Both relatedness and growth needs can become *more*, not less, important when highly satisfied. This is obviously encouraging for organizations seeking to motivate employees.

Evaluation of the Theory. Alderfer's ERG theory has received more support than Maslow's need-hierarchy theory. But many of the same problems plague both. Exactly what constitutes a need is still unclear, especially its psychological and/or physiological basis. Also, people engage in behavior that is seemingly unrelated to need fulfillment. Campbell and Pritchard (1976) stated that Alderfer's definition of needs is "as slippery as ever and . . . represents no major conceptual breakthrough" (p. 77). In addition, needs are quite amorphous. Can managers "instill" certain needs to motivate employees? Are employees who are trying to satisfy existence needs less productive than those striving to fulfill growth needs? Needs are nebulous for counseling an employee on improving performance. We have little advice to offer, say, regarding changing from existence to relatedness needs as a basis for behavior.

Alderfer's theory, while less general than Maslow's, is also quite removed from reality. Wanous and Zwany (1977) concluded that need theories may be of little value in day-to-day management. This might explain why relatively little research has been done on ERG theory.

Equity Theory

Statement of the Theory. Adams (1965) proposed a theory of worker motivation drawn from the principle of social comparison. How hard a person is willing to work is a function of comparisons of the effort of others. The theory has perceptual and social bases, since motivation is a function of how a person sees himself or herself in comparison to other people. Adams has suggested that motivation has a social rather than biological origin.

Equity theory has four major parts:

1. Because it is a perceptually based theory, the individual perceives himself or herself in comparison to others. The person who does the perceiving is called *Person*.

2. It is postulated that Person compares himself or herself to another individual. This other person is called *Other*.

3. All of the assets Person brings to the job constitute the third component; collectively they are referred to as *Inputs*. Inputs can include Person's education, intelligence, experience, skill, seniority, effort level, health, and so on. They are anything of perceived value or importance that Person brings to the job.

4. All benefits Person derives from the job are the fourth component; collectively referred to as *Outcomes*. Outcomes can include pay, benefits, working conditions, status symbols, seniority benefits, and so forth. They are those factors Person perceives as being derived from employment.

The theory states that Person forms a ratio of his or her inputs to outcomes and compares it to perceptions of Other's inputs:outcomes ratio. Adams assumes that people can quantify both their inputs and outcomes into common scale units. For example, Person will consider all the inputs she brings to the job; let us say they total 50. Person will assess her outcomes in the same manner; again let us assume they total 50 units. Person's ratio is therefore 50:50. Person then compares her ratio to what she perceives Other is putting into his job and deriving in outcomes from it. Let us assume Person assesses Other's inputs and outcomes to be 50 units each. We now have two ratios as assessed by Person:

Person, 50:50 and *Other,* 50:50

The equality of the ratios as perceived by Person represents *equity* (literally, "fair"). If Person perceives Other as deriving 100 units of outcomes from his job (due to more pay, higher status) but also contributing 100 units of inputs (due to greater education, more experience), this would also represent equity to her. Other is getting more out of the job than Person but is also putting more in; that is, 50:50 equals 100:100.

What happens if Person's ratio is different from Other's—that is, 50:50 versus

50:75? Both Person and Other are perceived as contributing the same amount of inputs (50 units), but Other is deriving more outcomes (75 units). According to Adams, this situation would represent *inequity*, or "unfairness," in the sense that Person perceives Other to be getting more out of the job although both are contributing the same number of inputs.

According to Adams, feelings of inequity cause tension, which Person will become motivated to reduce. The greater the inequity between Person and Other, the greater the tension and the greater the motivation to reduce it. Thus, for Adams, the source of motivation is feelings of tension caused by perceived inequity. Feelings of inequity are necessary for motivation to occur, for if Person perceives herself as being in an equitable relationship with Other, she will not be motivated.

Adams proposed two types of inequity. *Underpayment* refers to Person's perception of herself as deriving *fewer* outcomes from a job than Other when both are contributing comparable inputs. An example of underpayment inequity would be

Person, 50:50 and *Other*, 50:75

Overpayment refers to Person's perception of herself as deriving *more* outcomes from a job than Other when both are contributing comparable inputs. An example of overpayment inequity would be

Person, 50:75 and *Other*, 50:50

Adams felt that people could alter their motivation levels in an attempt to bring feelings of inequity back into line. The drive to reduce the tension caused by inequity would manifest itself in more or less effort being put into the job, which is a form of input. Adams said that how inequity was reduced would be a function of the method of payment: hourly (wages determined per unit of time, such as $3 per hour) and piece rate (wages determined per unit of production, such as 25 cents per object).

Most of the research done on equity theory was conducted in laboratory or field experiment paradigms. In order to test the theory, feelings of overpayment and underpayment had to be induced in the subjects. Such inducements were created by the following types of manipulations. The experimenter, posing as a manager or supervisor of some fictitious company, would place an ad in a local newspaper announcing part-time job openings. At the employment interview, subjects (who did not know this was a psychology experiment) would be told the job paid a certain hourly rate (such as $3 per hour) or piece rate (such as 25 cents per object produced). They would then start work at this rate. After a few days, the experimenter would say, "We just received a large contract from the government, and we now can pay you more money. Starting tomorrow, you will make $5 per hour (or 40 cents per object)." This manipulation was meant to induce feelings of overpayment. Subjects would be paid more for doing the same job. To induce feelings of underpayment, the experimenter would say, "We have just experienced a major cutback in financial support due to the loss of a contract. Starting tomorrow, we can pay you only $2 per hour (or 15 cents per object)." These experimental instructions would be given to some subjects and not others. Thus, some people would work at the "new" rate and others would continue to work under the original rate. The first few days of employment were designed to set base rate expectations about the job. After this period the amount of compensation for the same work would either go up (in the overpayment condition) or down (in the underpayment condition). The question to be answered was, what would these people do as a result of feelings of inequity? Given two types of inequity (underpayment and overpayment) and two compensation systems (hourly and piece rate), four sets of hypotheses were proposed as to how Person would reduce feelings of inequity:

Overpayment—hourly. In this condition, it is predicted that subjects would try to reduce the inequity caused by overpayment by working harder or expending more effort. By increasing their inputs (effort level), they would reduce feelings of inequity. The increased effort was predicted to manifest itself in increased quantity or quality of production.

Overpayment—piece rate. In this condition, subjects were being paid more for every object produced. Therefore, it was predicted that to reduce feelings of inequity, they would work harder as a means of increasing their inputs. However, if their increased effort resulted in a greater *quantity* of output, the feelings of inequity would be magnified even more. Thus, it was predicted that the subjects in this condition would produce fewer but higher-quality objects than before.

Underpayment—hourly. In this condition, subjects were now being paid less than they were before. It was predicted that as a means of reducing inequity, subjects would lower their effort to accommodate their decrease in outcomes. Decrements in product quantity and quality were predicted.

Underpayment—piece rate. In this condition, subjects are now being paid less than before for every object produced. It was predicted that in order to compensate for this loss in pay, subjects would produce more but appreciably lower-quality objects.

Empirical Tests of the Theory. A fairly large number of studies have tested some or all of the predictions made by equity theory. In an early study, Adams and Rosenbaum (1962) used both payment systems in studying the effects of inequity on performance in the job of interviewer. Certain groups of subjects were made to feel over- or underpaid; others were made to feel they were paid equitably. For the most part, the data supported the theory. Overpaid subjects conducted significantly more interviews only when paid by the hour. The quality of the interviews (measured by completeness and detail) was higher for those overpaid when a piece-rate system was used. A study by Pritchard, Dunnette, and Jorgenson (1972) also supported the theory in that overpaid subjects tended to process more catalogue orders than equitably paid subjects.

Most studies found that equity predictions held up best in the underpayment conditions. Also, the results of studies using hourly payment were stronger than those with piece-rate payment. These findings have important implications, which we will discuss shortly.

The original theory proposed that people expend more or less effort to reduce inequity. These are called *behavioral* ways of reducing inequity. As mentioned, one way to reduce inequity would be to adjust the level of effort expended—changing one's inputs, as the theory postulates. A second behavior mode of reducing inequity would be to alter one's outcomes, such as by asking for a raise if one felt underpaid. A third technique would be to get Other to change his or her inputs or outcomes by using peer pressure to get Other to work faster or slower. Finally, if all else failed, Person could always quit a job if it were perceived as being too inequitable.

Research has shown, however, that there are also *cognitive* ways to reduce inequity. By *cognitive*, we mean that a person does not have to "do" anything; rather, he or she reduces inequity through mental processes. One way is for Person to distort views of his or her inputs or outcomes. For example, Person could think, "I'm not really working that hard. After all, I spend a fair part of my day just talking to my friends." Outcomes could also be distorted in a similar way. A second technique is for Person to distort Other's inputs or outcomes; for example, "She really has to put up with a lot from her supervisor that I don't have to take." Finally, if a particular Other made Person feel inequitable, Person could always find a new Other for comparison. Equity theory does not state who Other has to be. The methods of reducing inequity (both behavioral and cognitive) are listed in Table 10–1.

Most experiments on equity theory have supported the predictions made. Problems occur not because the theory is "wrong" but because hypotheses and predictions are not very precise. There are several ways of reducing inequity, and the theory does not specify which will be chosen. A second problem involves time. Many of the experiments studied behavior for short periods, from ten minutes to 30 days. As with any motivation theory, we are interested in the long-term effects on behavior. Some of the implications of this will be addressed in the next section.

Evaluation of the Theory. A number of authors (Pritchard, 1969; Goodman & Friedman, 1971) have expressed concern over both the substance and implications of the theory. To date, the research on equity theory has addressed itself to the outcome of financial compensation. Yet, financial compensation is but one of many outcomes derived from a job. We know very little about the effects on motivation of manipulating other outcomes. The results of most of the studies have found fairly strong support for the underpayment predictions but less support for the overpayment ones. One of the consequences of inequity caused by underpayment is an increase in job

TABLE 10–1 *Modes of Reducing Inequity*

Behavioral modes of inequity reduction:
1. Change inputs.
2. Change outcomes.
3. Get Other to change inputs or outcomes.
4. Quit job for more equitable one.

Cognitive modes of inequity reduction:
1. Distort own inputs or outcomes.
2. Distort Other's inputs or outcomes.
3. Change comparison Other.

dissatisfaction. We know that this is associated with increased absenteeism and turnover. We will have accomplished very little in the work force if, in the name of increased motivation, we make people feel underpaid and thus have them turn around and be absent from work and/or quit.

In theory, feelings of overpayment will cause a person to work harder to produce more or higher-quality products. However, research has shown that such feelings do not last very long (Carrell & Dittrich, 1978). People seem to have a very high threshhold for overpayment (that is, it takes a large increment for people to feel overpaid) but a low threshhold for underpayment (that is, it takes only a small decrement for people to feel underpaid). Given that feelings of overpayment are short-lived, an organization that doubled the wages of its employees every two months to make them feel consistently overpaid would soon be bankrupt. Huseman, Hatfield, and Miles (1987) suggest that individuals differ in their sensitivity to feeling over- or underrewarded. They believe that "benevolents" are employees who more likely feel a sense of being overrewarded than do "entitleds."

Finally, the whole issue of organizations deliberately manipulating their employees to induce feelings of inequity raises serious moral and ethical questions. Few employees would like working for an organization that willingly made them experience inequity.

On the positive side, the notion of equity is important. As a motivation theory, however, it has some practical limitations. Notions of equity are of great concern in compensation issues. Organizations strive to maintain *external* equity (salaries and wages comparable to those in other companies in the area and industry) and *internal* equity (salaries and wages comparable within the company). A major problem in industry today is that many recent college graduates command starting salaries above those offered by companies. Organizations have to remain financially competitive if they are to hire new employees yet also be fair to existing employees. An interesting paradox is that in compensation administration, *equity* in salaries and wages must be maintained; in equity theory, it is necessary to maintain *inequity* for the purposes of motivation (see Field Note 2).

Despite the problems, it is established that people expend effort in relation to the effort of others in the work force (Middlemist & Peterson, 1976). Social comparison is valid; what we do is in part a product of what others around us do. The theoretical origins of equity are both justified and accurate, in that there is a social component to motivation. Equity theory should be lauded for its attempt to consider this phenomenon as a basis for work motivation. Unfortunately, the path from the scientific statement of equity theory to the practice of motivation in the day-to-day work world is strewn with large boulders instead of small pebbles.

Field Note 2

Most formal studies of equity theory have occurred in field experiment or laboratory conditions. However, some researchers have used the tenets of equity theory to explain naturally occurring phenomena. Lord and Hohenfeld (1979) applied equity theory to explain the on-the-field performance of some major league baseball players.

A player who plays for a team signs a contract for certain duration (say, three years) at a specified salary. At the end of the contract term, both the player and the team must negotiate a new contract. Sometimes the player and team cannot agree on a new contract because the player feels he is worth more money than the team offers him. In short, the player feels underpaid in comparison to what other players are receiving. In this case the player may engage in a process known as "playing out his option." What this means is that he will continue to play for the same team for one more year without a contract. This year is called the "option year." At the end of the option year, the player is free to sign with any other baseball team in the major leagues. However, during the option year the player receives a lower salary than he did when he was under contract. Therefore, his feelings of underpayment are intensified for two reasons. One is that he feels he is worth more than he *was* being paid under the old contract. Two, in the option year, he is paid even less than before.

According to equity theory, perceptions of underpayment should produce lower performance. Lord and Hohenfeld studied a sample of twenty-three baseball players who were unable to reach an agreement with their teams for a new contract and thus played out their option year. The authors selected four criteria of job performance for the players: batting average, home runs, runs batted in, and runs scored. They compared the player's performance on these criteria prior to the option year with their performance during it. Equity theory would postulate that because the players felt underpaid, their performance on these four factors would be lower during the option year. The results supported the hypothesis for the first three performance indexes but not for runs scored. The findings were consistent across the players, over time, and over the performance indexes. They indicated that, at least in this sample, feelings of underpayment did produce lower job performance, as equity theory would have predicted.

Expectancy Theory

Statement of the Theory. *Expectancy theory* originated in the 1930s, but at that time it was not related to work motivation. Georgopoulos, Mahoney, and Jones (1957) were the first to apply the theory in a work environment. However, it was a book by Vroom (1964) that catapulted expectancy theory into the arena of motivation research. In the past 25 years, expectancy theory has been the most popular and prominent motivation theory in I/O psychology. Since Vroom's formulation, several other researchers have proposed modifications (Graen, 1969; Porter & Lawler, 1968). We will not examine all of the variations but will focus on key elements.

This is very much a cognitive theory. Each person is assumed to be a rational decision maker who will expend effort on activities that lead to desired rewards. Individuals are thought to know what they want from work and understand that their performance will determine whether they get the rewards they desire. A relationship between effort expended and performance on the job is also assumed.

The theory has five major parts: job outcomes, valence, instrumentality, expectancy, and force.

Job Outcomes.   Job outcomes are things an organization can provide for its employees, such as pay, promotions, and vacation time. There is no theoretical limit to the number of outcomes. They are usually thought of as rewards or positive experiences, but they need not be. Getting fired could be an outcome, as could being transferred to a new location. Outcomes can also refer to intangibles like feelings of recognition or accomplishment.

Valence.   Valences are the employee's feelings about the outcomes provided. They are usually defined in terms of attractiveness or anticipated satisfaction to the individual. Valences are generated by the employee; that is, he or she would rate the anticipated satisfaction from (that is, ascribe a valence to) each outcome considered. Rating is usually done on a −10 to +10 scale. The individual can indicate whether an outcome has positive or negative valence. If the employee anticipates that all outcomes will lead to satisfaction, varying degrees of positive valence will be given. If the employee anticipates that all outcomes will lead to dissatisfaction, varying degrees of negative valence will be assigned. Last, if the employee feels indifferent about the outcomes, a valence of zero will be given. The employee will generate as many valences as there are outcomes.

Instrumentality.   Instrumentality is defined as the perceived degree of relationship between performance and outcome attainment. This perception exists in the mind of the individual. Instrumentality is synonymous with the word *conditional* and literally means the degree to which the attainment of a certain outcome is conditional upon the individual's performance on the job. For example, if a person thought that increases in pay were totally conditional on performance, the instrumentality associated with that outcome (a pay raise) would be very high. If a person thought that being transferred was totally unrelated to job performance, the instrumentality associated with that outcome (a transfer) would be very low. Like valences, instrumentalities are generated by the individual. He or she evaluates the degree of relationship between performance and outcome attainment on the job. Instrumentalities are usually thought of as probabilities (which therefore range between 0 and 1.0). An instrumentality of 0 means the attainment of that outcome is totally unrelated to job performance; an instrumentality of 1 means the attainment of that outcome is totally conditional upon job performance. Just as there are as many valences as there are outcomes, there are as many instrumentalities as there are outcomes.

Expectancy.   Expectancy is the perceived relationship between effort and performance. In some jobs, there may not seem to be any relationship between how hard you try and how well you do. In others, there may be a very clear relationship: the harder you try, the better you do. Expectancy, like instrumentality, is scaled as a probability. An expectancy of 0 means that there is no probability that an increase in effort will result in an increase in performance. An expectancy of 1 means it is certain that an increase in effort will be followed by a corresponding increase in performance. As with the valence and instrumentality components, the individual generates the expectancy for his or her job. After thinking about the relationship between effort and job performance, the individual makes an assessment of it (ascribes an expectancy). Unlike the previous components, there is usually only *one* expectancy value generated by the person to reflect the effort-performance relationship. The best way to establish expectancy is through feedback from a job (Janz, 1982).

Force.   The last component is force. Force is the amount of effort or pressure within the person to be motivated. The larger the force, the greater the hypothesized motivation. Mathematically, force is the product of valence, instrumentality, and expectancy, as expressed by the following formula:

Formula 10–1

$$\text{Force} = E\left(\sum_{i=1}^{n} V_i I_i\right)$$

This formula can better be explained with the aid of the information in Figure 10–5. It shows the components that constitute expectancy theory. Job outcomes (*0*), rated valences, instrumentalities, and expectancy are presented for a hypothetical employee. To compute this individual's force, we multiply the valence for an outcome by its corresponding instrumentality and then sum these numbers. Therefore,

Formula 10–2

$$(7 \times .5) + (6 \times .3) + (2 \times .2) + (9 \times .8) = \sum_{i=1}^{4} V_i I_i = 12.9$$

We then multiply 12.9 by the listed expectancy of .75, which yields a force score of

Formula 10–3

$$E\left(\sum_{i=1}^{4} V_i I_i\right) = .75(12.9) = 9.7$$

This product (9.7) represents the amount of force within the person to be motivated. It is the end product of the information on valence, instrumentality, and expectancy. Now that we have this force score, what do we do with it? You can think of it

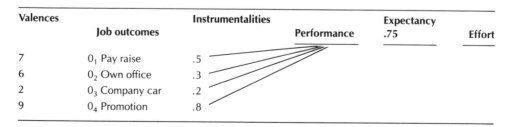

Valences	Job outcomes	Instrumentalities	Performance	Expectancy .75	Effort
7	0_1 Pay raise	.5			
6	0_2 Own office	.3			
2	0_3 Company car	.2			
9	0_4 Promotion	.8			

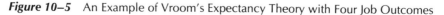

Figure 10–5   An Example of Vroom's Expectancy Theory with Four Job Outcomes

as a predictor of how motivated a person is. As with any predictor, the next step is to correlate it with some criterion. Because the force score predicts effort, the criterion must also measure effort. The most common measure of effort is a subjective assessment, usually a rating: the individual renders a self-assessment of his or her effort, the individual's supervisor makes the judgment, or peer assessments are used. The number of hours spent studying each week has been used in trying to predict the motivation of students. In one type of validation paradigm of expectancy theory, force scores are calculated for a group of people as well as criterion measures of effort. If the theory is valid, the greater the person's force score, the greater should be the effort. The validity of the theory is typically assessed by correlating the force scores with the criterion of effort. High correlations between the two variables would substantiate the theory; low correlations would disconfirm it. We will examine the validation process more closely in the next section.

Expectancy theory provides a rich rational basis for understanding motivation in a given job. Each component is a framework for analyzing the motivation process. First, we should consider the outcomes provided and their rated valence. If a person feels indifferent about the outcomes (they have a low valence), there is no reason to work hard for their attainment. According to expectancy theory, therefore, the first ingredient for motivation is desired outcomes. Second, the person must believe that there is some relationship between job performance and outcome attainment (instrumentalities must be high). If a person wants the outcomes but does not see performance as a means of getting them, there is no link between what is done and what is wanted. Reward practices and the role of the supervisor are crucial in establishing high instrumentalities. If a supervisor says, "Your performance has been very good lately; therefore, I will reward you with a raise [or promotion]," the individual will see that the attainment of a pay raise or a promotion is conditional on (instrumental to) good performance. Conversely, if a supervisor says, "We don't give pay raises or promotions on the basis of performance; we grant them only on the basis of seniority," the individual will not be motivated to perform well to attain these outcomes. Perhaps the only motivation will be to work hard enough not to be fired, so that these outcomes would eventually be attained through increased service with the organization. When outcomes are made contingent on performance and the individual understands this relationship, expectancy theory predicts that job performance will be enhanced.

Finally, the notion of expectancy is crucial. People must see a relationship (an expectancy) between how hard they try and how well they perform. If expectancy is low, it will make no difference to them whether or not they work hard because effort and performance seem unrelated. When I first started college, I was a chemistry major. I desired certain outcomes (for example, good grades, a sense of accomplishment). I also realized that attaining these outcomes was conditional on my performance in classes. I had high valences for both the outcomes and the perceived high instrumentalities. However, after three agonizing semesters, my expectancy was near zero. It did not seem to matter how hard I tried; I just could not alter my (low) performance in chemistry classes. My overall motivation fell dramatically along with my performance, and I eventually chose a new major. In retrospect, I realize I lacked the abilities to perform well as a chemist. All the motivation I could muster would not lead to good performance.

The idea of expectancy also explains why some jobs seem to create high or low motivation. On assembly lines, group performance level is determined by the speed of the line. No matter how hard a person works, he or she cannot produce any more until the next object moves down the line. The employee soon learns that he or she need only keep pace with the line. There is thus no relationship between individual effort and performance of the line. Alternatively, sales jobs are characterized by high expectancy. Salespeople who are paid on commission realize that the harder they try (the more sales calls they make), the better their performance (sales volume). Expectancy theory would predict that motivation is greatest in jobs with high expectancies.

In summary, expectancy theory is very good at diagnosing the components of motivation. It provides a rational basis on which to assess people's effort expenditure.

Empirical Tests of the Theory. Implicit in expectancy theory is a measurement issue. The theory revolves around the relationship among valences, instrumentalities, and expectancy. Thus, measuring them with a high degree of reliability is important. A second issue is what to do with these concepts after we have measured them. Various studies have dealt with both issues.

Research on reliability of the valence, instrumentality, and expectancy measures is quite positive (Mitchell, 1974). Reliability estimates in the .70s and .80s are not uncommon for valence and instrumentality. This is taken to mean that preferences for outcomes (valences) and perceptions of outcome-performance relationships (instrumentalities) are fairly stable. Reliability of expectancy is somewhat lower; these coefficients cluster in the .50-to-.60 range. This suggests some variability in perception of the extent to which increasing effort leads to increasing performance. Perhaps situational factors (like feedback from supervisors) induce variation in perceptions of this concept. While some studies (for example, Dachler & Mobley,1973; De Leo & Pritchard, 1974) have reported lower reliabilities for these components, on par it seems that the stability of the measurements is not a major problem.

Expectancy theory further states that the components should be multiplied to yield a force score. Before numbers can be multiplied, they must have ratio-scale properties. The three components of the theory have only interval-scale properties at best, and in some research designs they are measured in a way that they have only ordinal-scale properties. Schmidt (1973) stated that the multiplication of these components not only violates the principles of measurement but may also yield spurious results. Schmidt feels that until we can measure these components with more precision, we should not be multiplying them together. However, Arnold and Evans (1979) countered Schmidt's argument by developing a statistical procedure that permits the multiplication of these terms even though they are not measured on a ratio scale.

The measurement issue is significant because we multiply these components together to enhance prediction of the criterion. By violating measurement asssumptions, we may delude ourselves about the predictive power of the theory. Some research (for example, Mitchell & Knudsen, 1973; Muchinsky & Taylor, 1976) has shown that equally good predictions can be made by eliminating a component (for example, valence) from the theory or by simply *adding* rather than multiplying the components. Thus, on theoretical grounds, we should measure all the components and multiply them, but on empirical grounds, we can make equally good predictions with alternative procedures. Research on this aspect of the theory suggests that the three components do not add unique information (similar to the finding on weighting the facets of job satisfaction by their importance), so reduced theoretical formulations have comparable predictive power. Limitations in our ability to measure the components may cause empirical findings to deviate from the postulations made by the theory.

Research has also been done on the specific predictions the theory tries to make. It has taken two approaches. One assumes the theory tries to distinguish the "most-motivated" from the "least-motivated" people in a group. With one force score derived for each person, supposedly the person with the highest score is the most motivated and the person with the lowest score the least. This type of approach is called an *across-subjects* design, because predictions are made across people.

The second approach tests the theory differently. Here the theory assumes that each person is confronted with many tasks, and then predicts on which tasks each will work the hardest and on which he or she will expend the least effort. The theory is expanded to derive a force score for each task under consideration, and a criterion of effort is obtained for each. For *each* person, a correlation is computed between predictions of effort made by the theory and actual amounts of effort expended on the tasks. This type of approach is called a *within-subjects* design; predictions are made for each individual separately.

Validation studies generally find better predictions for the within-subjects design than the across-subjects design. Average validity coefficients for the across-subjects design are usually in the .30s to .40s (for example, Lawler & Porter, 1967; Pritchard & Sanders, 1973). Average validity coefficients for within-subjects designs are usually in the .50s to .60s (Matsui, Kagawa, Nagamatsu, & Ohtsuka, 1977; Muchinsky, 1977). The theory seems better at predicting various levels of effort an individual will expend on different tasks than at predicting gradations of motivation across different people (Kennedy, Fossum, & White, 1983). These validity coefficients are quite impressive; they are generally higher than those reported for other motivation theories.

In a major study on incentive motivation techniques, Pritchard, De Leo, and Von Bergen (1976) reported that a properly designed, successful program for motivating employees will have many of the attributes proposed by expectancy theory. Among the conditions they recommend for a program to be successful are the following:

1. Incentives (outcomes) must be carefully sought out and identified as highly attractive.

2. The rules (behaviors) for attaining the incentives must be clear to both those administering the system and to those actually in it.

3. People in the system must perceive that variations in controllable aspects of their behavior will result in variations in their level of performance and, ultimately, their rewards.

In somewhat different words, these three conditions for an effective incentive motivation program reflect the concepts of valence, instrumentality, and expectancy, respectively. The importance of having desired incentives is another way of stating that the outcomes should have high valence. The clarity of the behaviors needed to attain the incentives reflects the strength or magnitude of the instrumentalities. The ability to control levels of performance through differential effort expenditure is indicative of the concept of expectancy. In short, expectancy theory contains the key elements of a successful incentive system as derived through empirical research. While not all research on expectancy theory is totally supportive, the results generally have tended to confirm its predictions (Schwab, Olian-Gottlieb, & Heneman, 1979).

Evaluation of the Theory. Expectancy theory is a highly rational and conscious explanation of human motivation. People are assumed to behave in a way that will maximize expected gains (attainment of outcomes) from exhibiting certain job behaviors and expending certain levels of effort. To the extent that behavior is not directed toward maximizing gains in a rational, systematic way, the theory will not be upheld. Whenever unconscious motives deflect behavior from what a knowledge of conscious processes would predict, expectancy theory will not be predictive (Miner, 1980). Research suggests that people differ in the extent to which their behavior is motivated by rational processes. This was quite apparent in one of my own studies (Muchinsky, 1977). I examined the extent to which expectancy theory predicted the amount of effort college students put into each of their courses. With a within-subjects design, the average validity of the theory for all students was .52; however, for individual students it ranged from −.08 to .92. Thus, the theory very accurately predicted the effort expenditure of some students but was unable to predict it for others. This supports the idea that some people have a very rational basis for their behavior, and thus the theory works well for them; others appear to be motivated more by unconscious factors, and for them the theory does not work well (Stahl & Harrell, 1981).

Additional research (Broedling, 1975; Lied & Pritchard, 1976) has shown that there are some personality correlates of expectancy theory. Individuals for whom the theory is most predictive have an internal, as opposed to external, locus of control. Such people believe that events in their lives are largely subject to their own influence. Individuals with an external locus of control see themselves as being largely at the mercy of fate. Given the rational emphasis of expectancy theory, it is not surprising that individuals with an internal locus emerge as more strongly motivated.

While problems still exist with measurement of the components (Ilgen, Nebeker, & Pritchard, 1981), in general empirical support for the theory is quite strong. Expectancy theory also has limitations in terms of applicability to different types of people. Despite these problems, the prevailing consensus is that it is one of the dominant motivation theories in I/O psychology today. While other motivational theories also show promise for explaining selected aspects of behavior, probably none has received the consistent support or has the generalizability of expectancy theory.

Reinforcement Theory

Statement of the Theory. *Reinforcement theory* is one of the older approaches to motivation; what is novel is its application to industrial workers. It is also referred to as *operant conditioning* and *behaviorism*. Its origins are in B. F. Skinner's work on the conditioning of animals. It was not until the 1970s that I/O psychologists began to see some potential application of reinforcement theory to the motivational problems of employees.

The theory has three key variables: stimulus, response, and reward. A *stimulus* is any variable or condition that elicits a behavioral response. In an industrial setting, a *response* would be some measure of job performance, like productivity, absenteeism, or accidents. A *reward* is something of value given to the employee on the basis of the elicited behavioral response; it is meant to reinforce the occurrence of the desired response. Most attention has been paid to the response-reward connection. Based on research with animals, four types of response-reward connections or contingencies have been found to influence the frequency of the response:

Fixed interval. The subject is rewarded at a fixed time interval, such as every hour. Those paid on an hourly basis can be thought of as being rewarded on a fixed-interval basis.

Fixed ratio. The subject is rewarded as a function of a fixed number of responses. For example, a real estate salesperson who gets a commission after each sale is rewarded on a fixed-ratio schedule. In this case, the reward schedule is said to be *continuous*.

Variable interval. The subject is rewarded at some time interval, which varies.

Variable ratio. Reward is based on behavior, but the ratio of reward to response is variable. For example, the above salesperson might sometimes be paid after each sale and at other times after two or three sales. The person would be paid on the basis of the response (that is, making a sale), but the schedule of payment would not be constant.

Advocates of reinforcement theory believe that the magnitude of the subject's motivation to respond can be shaped by manipulating these reinforcement schedules.

A number of authors (for example, Jablonsky & De Vries, 1972; Nord, 1969) have discussed the potential benefits and liabilities of using reinforcement theory as a basis for motivating employees. Nord said that this entails placing the control of employee motivation in the hands of the organization since organizations can "regulate" the energy output of employees by manipulating reinforcement schedules. Nord thinks most people would like to feel in control of their own lives rather than being manipulated into certain behavior patterns by the organization. The issue of responsibility for controlling behavior is very sensitive, because it entails ethical considerations for employee welfare. If employees work themselves to exhaustion through mismanagement of their own efforts, they are responsible for their own actions. However, those who are manipulated into expending excessive effort have been victimized by a force beyond their control, and the organization should be held responsible for their condition. Issues of ethical responsibility for behavior are not central to the theory, but they are important when the theory is applied in daily life. Whenever anything is "done" to someone by an outside agent, the question of *whose* values (the individual's or the agent's) are being optimized arises.

Empirical Tests of the Theory. Empirical tests of reinforcement theory have involved determining which schedule of reinforcement has the greatest effect on increasing the occurrence of the desired behavioral response. In a series of studies involving tree planters, Yukl and Latham (1975) and Yukl, Latham, and Pursell (1976) compared the effectiveness of various schedules of reinforcement. Some planters were paid on a fixed-interval schedule (hourly pay); others were paid based on the number of trees they planted. Employees paid on a ratio schedule were significantly more productive (planted more trees). Pritchard, Leonard, Von Bergen, and Kirk (1976) examined the effect of different payment schedules on employees' ability to pass self-paced learning tests of electrical knowledge. Some employees were paid a flat hourly wage and others according to the number of tests they passed. Two types of ratio-payment schedules were used: fixed (the employee was paid after passing every third test), and variable (the employee was paid after passing a variable number). The results of the study are shown in Figure 10-6. Employees paid contingently (that is, based on their performance) passed 60% of the tests; those paid by the hour passed about 40%. Results also showed no difference in test performance between fixed- and variable-ratio reinforcement schedules. A later study by Pritchard, Hollenback, and De Leo (1980) confirmed that ratio schedules were more effective than interval schedules. However, there is no apparent difference among the various types of ratio schedule. Saari and Latham (1982) found that ratio schedules of reward were associated with higher perceived levels of task accomplishment and feedback than continuous-reward schedules.

Research on reinforcement theory is not limited to measures of productivity. Pedalino and Gamboa (1974) described how the theory could be used to decrease absenteeism. The authors devised a plan whereby every employee who came to work on time was dealt one card from a poker deck. Each day, the attending employees were dealt a new card. At the end of the week, the employee with the best poker hand won $20. In this case, the desired response (attendance) was reinforced through monetary reward. Attendance under this plan was greater than before the program was introduced.

Evaluation of the Theory. Research clearly indicates that the principles of reinforcement theory do "work." However, the theory suffers from some limitations in industrial settings. As Mawhinney (1975) noted, current applications of reinforcement theory tend to ignore individual differences in what are valued as rewards. In the Pedalino and Gamboa study, for example, it was assumed that all the employees were interested in playing poker and would respond positively to a gambling or lottery situation. Vast individual differences in preferences would have precluded the

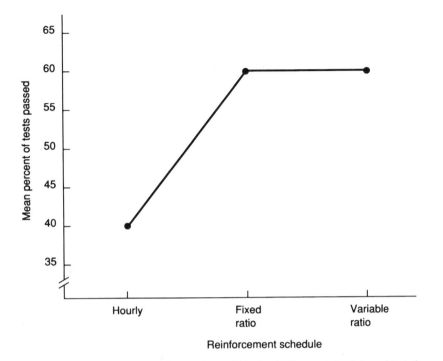

Figure 10–6   Percentage of Tests Passed Under Different Schedules of Reinforcement

SOURCE: R. D. Pritchard, D. W. Leonard, C. W. Von Bergen, and R. J. Kirk, "The Effect of Varying Schedules of Reinforcement on Human Task Performance," *Organizational Behavior and Human Performance, 16* (1976), pp. 205–230.

success of any such program. Second, reinforcement has been primarily limited to studies of quantity of production. We don't know very much about how *quality* of performance is affected, the long-term effects of various reinforcement schedules, or people's attitudes toward such incentive methods.

The use of reinforcement theory in industry has its share of supporters (Hamner & Hamner, 1976) and detractors (Locke, 1977). Advocates of the theory cite its wide applicability for solving problems. Hamner and Hamner reviewed the uses of reinforcement theory in industry and reported such applications as absence and turnover reduction, productivity enhancement, and improving supervisory training. The experiences of Emery Air Freight constitute one of the biggest success stories on reinforcement theory. Emery reported $3 million in cost saving after having adopted a system of positive reinforcement. Other companies have also reported successful applications of the theory. What does seem to be of concern regarding the theory are possible ethical matters associated with the reinforcement of behavior. How ethical is it for an organization to use a payment system that increases productivity but may cause adverse side effects? Sweden has condemned piece-rate payment schedules because they cause tension and ultimately damage the mental and physical well-being of workers. There is also evidence that workers in short-cycle, monotonous jobs prefer hourly rates to piece rates. They complain that piece-rate systems "control" them (or at least their behavior), which is the precise intent of the system. Despite these legitimate ethical concerns, reinforcement theory has a history of producing desired changes in work behavior. Unlike other motivational theories, its focus is not on the individual but on environmental factors that shape or modify behavior. While problems exist regarding implementation of the theory, they address only its applicability rather than its validity (see Field Note 3).

Field Note 3

Reinforcement theory is premised on rewarding desired behavior. The stronger the link between the behavior and the reward, the greater becomes the probability of the behavior. However, in an organizational context it is sometimes difficult to tie rewards to a particular behavior because many behaviors are typically elicited concurrently. It is thus possible to obscure the connection between reward and the desired behavior, which therefore decreases the probability of the behavior's occurring. In an extreme case, everything gets turned around: the behaviors that organizations have tried to encourage get punished, and those that they have tried to discourage actually get rewarded. Kerr (1975) described how this can happen.

Orphanages are organizations created as residences for children prior to their being placed in private homes. The orphanage therefore is theoretically interested in placing as many children as possible in good homes. Orphanages receive state funds to assist them in their operations. Since the primary goal is to place children in good homes, the means by which the orphanage is run should be directed toward this objective. However, such is not the case—the reward system created by the orphanage's management often drives the process in reverse for the following reasons:

1. The number of children enrolled in the orphanage often is the most important determinant of the size of its allocated budget.

2. The number of children under the director's care will affect the size of the support staff, which also is a determinant of the budget.

3. The total organizational size will largely determine the director's prestige at annual conventions, in the community, and so on.

Therefore, to the extent that staff size, total budget, and personal prestige are valued by the orphanage's executive personnel, it becomes rational for them to make it *difficult* for children to be adopted. Thus, the reward system reinforces the exact opposite of the behavior for which the orphanage was created, that is, the placement of children.

Vast amounts of research indicate that schedules of reinforcement can indeed motivate behavior to occur in certain patterns. However, the *direction* of that behavior is not always consistent with organizational goals.

Goal-Setting Theory

Statement of the Theory. *Goal setting* is a motivation theory based on the assumption that people behave rationally and consciously. The crux of the theory rests on the relationship among conscious goals, intentions, and task performance. Its basic premise is that conscious ideas regulate a person's actions. Goals are what the individual is consciously trying to attain, particularly as related to future objectives.

According to Locke (1968), goals have two major functions. They are a basis for motivation and they direct behavior. A goal provides guidelines for deciding how much effort to put into work. Goals are intended behaviors; in turn, they influence task performance. However, two conditions must be met before goals can positively influence performance. First, the individual must be aware of the goal and know what must be accomplished. Second, the individual must *accept* the goal as something he or she is willing to work for. Goals can be rejected because they are seen as too difficult or too easy or because the person does not know what behaviors are needed for goal attainment. Acceptance of the goal implies the individual intends to engage in the behavior needed for goal attainment.

Locke's theory of goal setting states that more difficult goals lead to higher levels of job performance. Locke believed that commitment to a goal is proportional to its difficulty. Thus, more difficult goals engender more commitment to their attainment (Steers & Porter, 1974). Goals can also vary in specificity. Some goals are general (for example, to be a good biology student), and others are more specific (to get an "A" on the next biology test). The more specific the goal, the more concentrated the individual's effort in its pursuit, and the more directed the behavior (Terborg, 1977). It is also important for the person to receive feedback about task performance; this serves as a guide as to whether he or she should work harder or continue at the same pace.

Therefore, according to goal-setting theory, the following factors and conditions would induce high motivation and task performance. Goals are behavioral intentions that channel our energies in certain directions. The more difficult and more specific the goal, the greater will be our motivation to attain it. Feedback on our performance in pursuit of the goal tells us whether our efforts are "on target." The source of motivation, according to goal setting, is the desire and intention to attain the goal; this must be coupled with the individual's acceptance of the goal. Rather than dealing with motivation as a product of innate needs, feelings of inequity, or schedules of reinforcement, goal setting assumes people set acceptable target objectives and then channel their efforts in pursuit of them.

Empirical Tests of the Theory. For the most part, empirical tests of the theory are quite supportive. Latham and Yukl (1975a) reviewed over 25 field studies of goal setting, and nearly all substantiated the theory. As an example, Latham and Baldes (1975) studied truck drivers hauling logs to lumber mills. Performance was studied under two conditions. First, drivers were told only to "do their best" in loading the trucks. After a time, they were told to set a specific and rather hard goal of loading their trucks up to 94% of the legal weight limit. (The closer to the legal limit, the fewer trips were needed.) Each truck driver got feedback by means of a loading scale indicating tonnage. Figure 10–7 shows the drivers' performance over a 48-week period. At the onset of goal setting, performance improved greatly; however, the cause is not clear-cut. One explanation may be due to the effects of goal setting. Another could be a sense of competition among the drivers as to who could load the truck closest to the legal limit. (The decline in performance between the fourth and fifth blocks was due to the truck drivers' "testing" of management to gauge its reaction.) In any case, the study clearly showed that performance under goal setting was superior to the "do-your-best" condition.

In another study, Latham and Yukl (1975b) compared the effectiveness of three types of goal setting on the performance of logging crews. One method of goal setting was simply to tell the crew members to "do their best." The second was to designate or assign goals to the crew members. The third was to have the loggers participate in setting their own goals. The results showed that participation produced better performance and more frequent goal attainment. The average goal level set by the loggers was greater than that set for the assigned group, which suggests that the performance difference was due in part to greater goal difficulty in the participative condition.

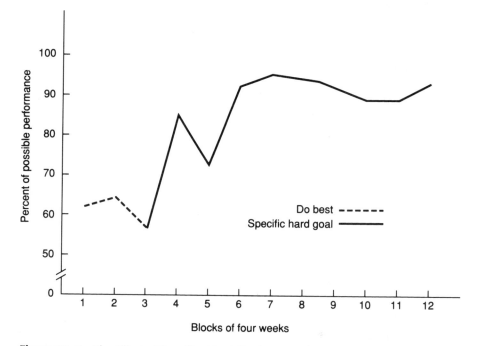

Figure 10–7 The Effect of Specific, Hard Goals on Productivity

SOURCE: G. P. Latham and J. J. Baldes, "The Practical Significance of Locke's Theory of Goal Setting," *Journal of Applied Psychology, 60* (1975), pp. 122–124.

Also, goal attainment was highest with participation despite more difficult goals. This suggests that goal acceptance is increased by participation.

While goal setting has been found to be effective in reaching certain levels of task performance, some research shows that groups differ in their acceptance of goals and in the behavior they see as being related to goal attainment. Ivancevich and McMahon (1977) compared Black and White technicians in a goal-setting program. Blacks were found to want more feedback and participation in the goal-setting process; Whites wanted more difficult goals. Thus, there appear to be race-linked differences in acceptance of goal setting, and additional moderating differences may be found in future research. While variation does exist in terms of task behaviors and acceptance of goal setting, research indicates that goal setting produces better performance than the absence of goals or very general goals. As Latham and Marshall (1982) have stated, the key issue appears to be not *how* a goal is set but *whether* the goal is set.

Evaluation of the Theory. You should be struck by the elegance and simplicity of goal-setting theory. There are no references to innate needs, perceived instrumentalities, or comparison others; the theory is not based on abstract concepts or hypothetical constructs. The theory states that the most effective task performance is obtained by intentionally channeling one's efforts in pursuit of a desired objective or goal. Difficulty and specificity of the goal influence performance, as do the amount and nature of feedback. There are some differences in performance between goals that are assigned and those that are self-selected. Different types of people also prefer different types of goals. But it is clear that goal setting elicits better performance.

Goal setting seems to be generalizable as a theory of motivation. It is not limited in applicability to highly rational people, though it does assume that people consciously follow through with their intentions. The theory has a cognitive basis: employees must think about the goals they want to pursue; they must decide whether the goals are acceptable; they must understand what behaviors they have to exhibit to attain the goal; and they must know how to evaluate feedback on their progress. Research on feedback (for example, Erez, 1977; Kim & Hamner, 1976) has shown that feedback is critical for optimal performance, but that people differ in their ability to use the information provided. There is also evidence that goal setting is effective for groups as well as individuals. Thus, a work group can set a goal to decrease scrap rate, for example, or to increase productive output. Group goals can be more difficult to attain, however, because in many cases the success of the overall group depends on more than just the success of individual members. A basketball team may set a goal of winning so many games a season, but its success will be determined by more than just the number of points scored by each player. Member coordination and integration must also be considered. One player might help the team by passing, another by rebounding, and the others by shooting.

Certain situational factors must also be present. A production worker, for instance, cannot increase the speed of an assembly line. In some cases, effort or desire alone may not be enough for goal attainment. Reasonable opportunity must be provided. Perceptions of this opportunity may be a deciding factor in whether a person accepts a goal.

Locke, Shaw, Saari, and Latham (1981) reviewed 12 years of goal-setting research studies and came to the following conclusion: 90% of the studies show that specific and challenging goals lead to higher performance than easy goals, "do-your-best" goals, or no goals. Goal setting was found to improve task performance when (1) subjects have sufficient ability; (2) feedback is provided on progress in relation to goals; (3) rewards are given for goal attainment; (4) management is supportive; and (5) individuals accept assigned goals. Tubbs (1986) concluded that the concepts of goal difficulty, goal specificity, and participation in the goal-setting process were all supported by empirical research studies. However, the principles of goal setting were empirically supported more often in laboratory than field studies. Tubbs also discovered that individuals are more willing to accept and work for an extremely difficult goal when they know that they will not have to do so for any extended period. In summary, the overall verdict on the value of goal setting as a theory of motivation is overwhelmingly positive. Quite clearly, setting goals does enhance performance. More recently, attention is being turned to *why* goals enhance performance (Mento, Steel, & Karren, 1987), and *how* people become committed to reaching a goal (Hollenbeck & Klein, 1987).

The concept of goal setting underlies management by objectives (MBO), a management technique meant to increase performance through goal setting (McConkie, 1979). There are many variations of MBO. In principle, a worker and his or her supervisor set objectives for the worker's future performance. It is thought that by thus allowing the worker to take part in the goal-setting process, his or her commitment to the goal will be greater. Though it is beyond our scope to fully discuss MBO, it is important to know that it is an actual management tool derived from empirical research on goal setting. Industry's adoption of a procedure developed through scientific investigation is a fair indication that the procedure does indeed "work" outside the laboratory. Research on MBO, and on goal setting in general, is quite supportive. We are not totally clear on causal relationships and need more research on issues relating to goal setting. But I/O psychologists are convinced that goal setting is a way of increasing task performance. Landy and Trumbo (1980) feel that the diverse goal-setting findings should be placed in a coherent framework general enough to embrace many work behaviors. Then goal setting may become the most reasonable approach to work motivation.

Intrinsic Motivation

Statement of the Theory. Deci (1975) proposed that people expend effort due to *intrinsic* as well as extrinsic motivation. If extrinsically motivated, people perform tasks because of the external rewards (for example, money) such behavior will provide. If intrinsically motivated, they perform tasks for the inherent pleasure derived from engaging in those behaviors. Deci believed that people like to be responsible for their own actions, as opposed to believing something (external) is done to them. When people are made to behave in certain ways through punishment or rewards, they lose control over their actions. Deci believes jobs should be created

When people have equivalent ability and opportunity, their level of performance is determined by their motivation. Duomo Photography, Inc.,/Steven E. Sutton

so as to give people feelings of competence and pleasure and at the same time make them feel they are in control of their actions. These conditions would induce intrinsic motivation. In theory, an intrinsically motivated person will be more satisfied and committed to a task than a person who is extrinsically motivated.

Most researchers believe that motivation is additive. People will make an effort because a task is enjoyable (intrinsically motivating) and because it offers external reward (extrinsically motivating). Deci, however, does not share this belief. He feels that when external rewards are tied directly to performance, intrinsic motivation declines. Thus, Deci suggests that paying people for doing a task that they also like will decrease their intrinsic motivation. The issue becomes one of a changing locus of causation. If people are paid for performing a task, their behavior is caused by the external reward. As the locus of control for their actions shifts to something in the environment, they lose intrinsic motivation because they are no longer performing the task for the feelings of competence and self-control. Deci argues that externally rewarding people for doing tasks they enjoy will, in the long run, decrease motivation.

Empirical Tests of the Theory. Deci derived most of the support for his theory in laboratory studies involving puzzles and games. For example, Deci (1972) conducted a study in which some subjects were paid hourly and others contingently for working on puzzles they found enjoyable. Contingently paid subjects were rewarded for every puzzle they correctly solved. After the session, the subjects were given a chance to keep working on the puzzles for no pay. Deci discovered that subjects who were paid contingently spent less time working on the puzzles in the nonpay period than those subjects who were paid hourly. He concluded that when external rewards (money) are tied directly to performance (contingent payment), intrinsic motivation (desire to work on an enjoyable task) decreased.

Deci conducted other, similar studies. The paradigm was consistent. People were paid to perform a pleasurable task either contingently or not. Contingently rewarded subjects spent less time performing the same task in a "free period." Several others investigated the extent to which external rewards decreased intrinsic motivation. The majority of these studies (for example, Hamner & Foster, 1975; Phillips & Lord, 1980) did not clearly support Deci's contention that contingent payment decreases intrinsic motivation. People may not believe that contingent reward means their actions are being controlled by external forces. Alternatively, the effect of contingent payment may not be strong enough to diminish intrinsic motivation. These studies did not replicate Deci's findings, but they challenged the assumption that intrinsic and extrinsic motivation are additive. These studies did show that Deci was correct in stating that motivation is not simply additive (Pritchard, Campbell, & Campbell, 1977). If people perform a task for sheer pleasure, paying them will not necessarily add to their motivation to perform it. This research shows that external rewards can enhance motivation for certain, but not all, tasks.

Evaluation of the Theory. Theories of intrinsic motivation suffer from many theoretical, methodological, and practical problems. On the theoretical side, there is confusion about what is meant by "intrinsic"—that is, whether it applies to the individual or the task (Scott, 1976). If one person finds a task boring but another finds it interesting, what is "intrinsic" seems to be within the individual. If many people find one task (a puzzle) fun but another (sorting cards) dull, what is "intrinsic" seems to be within the task. Whether theories of intrinsic motivation relate to differences in people or in jobs is unclear. What is intrinsic and what is extrinsic are also unclear (Dyer & Parker, 1975). What one person sees as extrinsic (the pay increase associated with a promotion) another might see as intrinsic (the gratification of accomplishment). The failure to differentiate clearly intrinsic from extrinsic rewards greatly undermines the basis of Deci's contentions.

Intrinsic motivation is dominated by laboratory research. Mawhinney (1979) and others feel the theory should be tested under field conditions as well. Problems with methodology underscore problems with the theory itself. Usually researchers have to sort through an array of potential tasks carefully to find one that subjects uniformly believe is interesting. If such "intrinsically motivating" tasks are so hard to come by, one can question the applicability of the theory. Also the time subjects spend working on the task in the free period (the typical dependent variable in such studies) is usually measured in *seconds* or *minutes*. If a person spends five extra minutes putting a puzzle together, broad conclusions are drawn on the generalizability of the findings. Obviously, for industrial applications, such generalizations are absurd. We are interested in the persistence of behavior over months and years, not minutes. As with equity theory, the limitations of laboratory studies testing intrinsic motivation are particularly acute.

Finally, we can ask about the practical implications of intrinsic motivation. We seem to have no firm guidelines as to what an organization can do to pay people for jobs they find intrinsically motivating. Deci would recommend they be paid noncontingently; other researchers are not so certain. How long an intrinsically motivating task will remain so is also debatable. A puzzle may lose its appeal if a person has to work on it eight hours a day, five days a week. We can conclude that some people find some tasks enjoyable (at least for short periods); when they are paid to perform these tasks contingently, such tasks lose some of their appeal (at least the person's desire to perform the task decreases). There are anecdotes about people who like their jobs so much they would do them for little or nothing, but the average worker is not in that position. It seems that theories of intrinsic motivation have not been of much help in explaining work motivation. The research indicates that perhaps recreational pursuits (doing puzzles) must be intrinsically appealing if they are to sustain interest—but if it were not for jobs that paid external rewards, people would not have the time or money to pursue such activities.

Overview and Synthesis of Work Motivation Theories

Integrating theories of work motivation is an awesome task. At this stage of development, it is probably impossible. We can step back and view these theories from a broad perspective, highlighting major points of divergence and convergence. Landy and Trumbo (1980) made the astute observation that theories of work motivation are often more complex than the behavior they try to explain. The preceding sections dealt with each of these complex theories in detail; we will now attempt to simplify the perspectives.

The seven theories discussed roughly reflect three different views of motivation. Need theories and the theory of intrinsic motivation presume that people are motivated by internal factors. These are either innate needs causing us to seek fulfillment or feelings of pleasure and self-control from performing tasks we find enjoyable. Expectancy theory and goal-setting theory presume that people are rational. After carefully considering our wants and the relationship between behavior and attaining desired outcomes or goals, we make an effort to maximize the chances of obtaining what we want. Equity theory and reinforcement theory presume we are motivated by external factors. According to equity theory, our perceptions of what others are giving and getting are involved. With reinforcement theory, motivation is a product of a schedule of rewards. We are left with diverse theoretical perspectives: motivation springs from within us due to unconscious forces; it is a product of rationally calculating what we must do to get what we want; or it is a result of things that are "done" to us.

Which perspective is most defensible? There is some research support for all of them, but some theories have received more confirmation than others. This is, in part, what makes motivation so intriguing. No theories are absolutely "wrong." But no theory to date has received so much support that it can be declared *the* theory of motivation. Even those receiving most of the research support make different predictions. Probably the two best theories of work motivation are expectancy theory and goal-setting theory. Expectancy theory advocates setting easy goals to maximize motivation—the probability of effort's resulting in attainment is very high. Goal setting advocates the opposite: setting difficult goals. Perhaps the theories differ on this point only with regard to time. Easier goals should first be set so people can build up confidence (expectancy) that effort will result in performance, which will lead to outcome attainment. As expectancy grows, progressively harder goals could be set, leading to even greater attainment. Goal-setting theory stresses the difficulty of the goal; expectancy theory stresses the perceived relationship among effort, performance, and outcome attainment. Thus, predictions made by each theory need not be contradictory.

If we could distill the best of each of the seven theories, we would arrive at the following conclusions. Need theory reminds us that individual differences are important and that our efforts will always be channeled toward survival before social fulfillment. Different people have different needs and desires; any good theory of motivation must allow for this. Equity theory emphasizes that what we do is in part a product of what people around us do. We are social creatures; we do not exist in a vacuum. What we eat, how we dress, and how hard we work are all determined to some degree by other people in our environment. Expectancy theory raises motivation to a level of conscious choice. We deliberately choose how hard to work based on the gains we expect to receive from our efforts. If we do not see any benefit to be gained from our efforts, we will not be motivated. Goal-setting theory stresses that motivation is maximized by setting specific target objectives; such goals can prevent an ineffective diffusion of effort. Reinforcement theory states that when people are rewarded on units of performance as opposed to units of time, their motivation is greater. Finally, intrinsic-motivation theory suggests that people prefer to expend effort on tasks that enhance feelings of personal control and competence. A composite theory of motivation, drawing on the strengths of existing theories, would ideally include these findings as established by research. A general summary of all the motivation theories is presented in Table 10–2.

Mitchell (1982) feels that we must strive to integrate our existing theories of motivation. We don't need more theories of motivation; rather, we need to consolidate those that we already have. Some researchers have attempted to do just that. For example, Garland (1984) combined elements from both expectancy theory and goal-setting theory. He found that both goal levels and expectancy made independent contributions to variance in performance. Furthermore, Perry and Porter (1982) observed that most of what we know about motivation comes from private-sector

TABLE 10–2 *Summary and Evaluation of Work-Motivation Theories*

Theory	Source of Motivation	Empirical Support	Industrial Applicability
Need theory	Unconscious, innate needs	*Weak:* Little support for proposed relationships among needs.	*Very limited:* Theory lacks sufficient specificity to guide behavior.
Equity theory	Drive to reduce feelings of tension caused by perceived inequity	*Mixed:* Good support for underpayment inequity, weak support for overpayment inequity.	*Limited:* Social comparisons are made, but feelings of inequity can be reduced through means other than increased motivation.
Expectancy theory	Relationship among desired outcomes, performance-reward, and effort-performance variables	*Moderate-strong:* More strongly supported in within-subject than across-subject experiments.	*Strong:* Theory provides a rational basis for why people expend effort, although not all behavior is as consciously determined as postulated.
Reinforcement theory	Schedule of reinforcement used to reward people for their performance	*Moderate:* Ratio reinforcement schedules evoke superior performance compared to interval schedules, but little difference exists among various ratio schedules.	*Moderate:* Contingent payment for performance is possible in some jobs, although ethical problems can be present in an organization's attempt to shape employee behavior.
Goal-setting theory	Intention to direct behavior in pursuit of acceptable goals	*Moderate-strong:* Performance under goal-setting conditions usually superior to conditions under which no goals are set.	*Strong:* Ability to set goals is not restricted to certain types of people or jobs.
Intrinsic motivation theory	Feelings of competence and self-control that come form performing enjoyable tasks	*Mixed:* Extrinsic and intrinsic rewards do not seem to be purely additive, but extrinsic rewards do not always decrease intrinsic motivation.	*Very limited:* Little evidence that intrinsically motivating tasks remain intrinsically motivating for long periods of time.

(business and industry) employees, and we need to expand our theories to include public organizations.

To what extent have these theories improved understanding of motivation in the work force? Any manager who adopted one theory to the exclusion of the others would probably not be very successful. Motivation is very complicated, and no one theory always "works." Pinder (1977) makes the point that when the practitioner asks, "How do I motivate my employees?" the researcher's answer should indeed be tentative. There are no automatic solutions to problems of worker motivation—if there were, you wouldn't have read about seven different theories. As Pinder states, given the degree of empirical support, total application of a theory in industry is simply premature. We do not know enough to offer pat solutions; simple answers rarely serve complex problems. What you should have learned from this chapter is that many approaches exist and understanding all of them is necessary in order to appreciate the intricacies and dynamics of motivation in the work force.

MAJOR CHAPTER OBJECTIVES IN REVIEW

After having read this chapter, you should know:

1. Two fundamental perspectives of motivation.

2. Conceptual basis and degree of empirical support for the following motivational theories:
   a. Need
   b. Equity
   c. Expectancy
   d. Reinforcement
   e. Goal setting
   f. Intrinsic

3. Sense of perspective on how each theory contributes to our understanding of motivation.

CASE STUDY—What to Do with Harry?

Joe Collins, production manager of York Tool and Die Company, tapped Harry Simpson on the shoulder. "Harry," Collins said, "I'd like to talk to you in my office."

"Right now?" asked Simpson.

"Right now," Collins replied.

Simpson took off his safety goggles and put them on the rack.

He was a line foreman, and it was unusual to be called away from his line. He figured it had to be something big; otherwise Collins would have waited until break.

"Hey, Willie," Simpson yelled at his lead man, "cover for me, will you? I've got to talk to Joe."

Simpson walked into Collins's office and sat down. The look on Collins's face told him it wasn't going to be good news.

"Harry, I've known you for eight years," Collins began. "You've always kept your nose to the grindstone. You've been conscientious and diligent. I've had fewer problems with you than with most of the other foremen. But lately things have been different. You've come to work late five times in the past month. You've been late turning in your weekly production sheets. The scrap rate of your line has been going up, too. I was also told that Willie had to spend a lot of time breaking in the two new guys. That's your job. What's going on, Harry?"

Simpson shuffled his feet and cleared his throat. "I didn't realize these things were happening."

"You didn't know you were late?" Collins was incredulous. "You've been coming to work at 7:30 for eight years. When you punch in at 7:45, you're late, and you know it."

"I don't know, Joe, I just haven't felt 'with it' lately." Simpson explained. "Doris says I've been moping around the house a lot lately, too."

"I'm not here to chew you out, Harry," Collins replied. "You're a valuable man. I want to find a way to get you back in gear. Anything been bugging you lately?"

"Well, I've finally figured out I'm not going to make it to supervisor. At least not in the near future. That's what I've been working for all along. Maybe I've hit my peak. When Coleman made it to supervisor, I figured I'd be the next one up. But it never happened. I'm not sore—Coleman is a good man, and he deserved it. I just feel kind of deflated."

"You're well respected by management, Harry, and your line thinks you're great too. You've set a tough example to live up to. I want you to keep it up—we need people like you."

"I know I have an important job," said Simpson, "but I figure I can't get ahead anymore, at least not on how well I do my job. I guess it boils down to luck or something."

"What if I give you a new line to run?" Collins asked. "Would that give you a new challenge?"

"No, I wouldn't want that, Joe," replied Simpson. "I like my line, and I don't want to leave them."

"All right Harry, but here's the deal," Collins stated. "I want you to cut back on the lateness, pronto. Get your production reports in on time, and watch the scrap. With the price of copper going up, we've got to play it tight. Oh, and give Willie a break. He's got enough to do. Does this sound okay to you?"

"Yeah," Simpson said. "You're only telling me to do what I'm supposed to be doing."

"Keep at it, Harry," Collins said with a smile. "In two more years, you'll get a ten-year-pin."

Simpson got up to leave. "It won't pay the rent, but I'd like to have it."

Simpson walked back to the line. Willie looked up and saw him coming.

"What'd Joe want?" Willie asked.

"Oh, nothing much," Simpson replied.

Willie knew Simpson was hiding something, and Simpson figured Willie knew what it was.

Questions

1. Which theory of motivation do you feel best explains Simpson's recent behavior?

2. What would equity theory have predicted about Simpson's behavior following the promotion of Coleman?

3. In terms of expectancy theory, how would you describe Simpson's valence for a promotion and its instrumentality?

4. What psychological needs did Collins appeal to in talking to Simpson?

5. How might you use reinforcement theory to shape the behavior of Simpson in the areas needing attention?

11

Leadership

When you think of leadership, many ideas come to mind. Your thoughts might relate to power, authority, and influence. Maybe you think of actual people—Washington, Lincoln, Churchill, Napoleon—or what effective leaders do. In short, the concept of leadership evokes a multitude of thoughts, all of which in some way address causes, symptoms, or effects of leadership.

In this chapter we will examine how I/O psychologists have tried to grapple with the multifaceted concept of leadership, particularly as it relates to behavior in the world of work. Research on leadership has been diverse because various investigators have approached the concept from different perspectives. Some research has examined what strong leaders are like as people by looking at demographic variables, personality traits, types of skills, and so on. Without *followers* there can be no leaders; accordingly, some research has examined leader-follower relations. Presumably "strong" leaders accomplish things that "weak" leaders do not; thus another area of research is on the *effects* of leadership. An interesting question addresses contextual effects in leadership—for example, is leadership of a prison more demanding than that of a business organization? Thus, the *situation* in which leadership occurs has attracted much attention. Other areas of interest within the domain of leadership research have also been investigated.

In this chapter, we will examine the research on many of these leadership perspectives. Unlike the area of worker motivation, whose multiple theories are all aimed at explaining why and how people expend effort, the area of leadership is characterized by varying topics of investigation. While such diversity of interest expands our basis of understanding, it also creates ambiguity as to exactly what leadership is all about (Pfeffer, 1977).

Interest in leadership concerns the I/O practitioner as well as the scientist. In fact, leadership is one of the richer areas of interplay between the two—it has had a healthy influx of ideas from both camps. Identifying and developing leaders is a major concern of industry today. Companies often train their higher-level personnel in skill areas (interpersonal relations, decision making, planning) that directly affect their performance as leaders. In Greensboro, North Carolina, there is an organization called the Center for Creative Leadership whose purpose is to enhance, through training, the leadership abilities of key industrial and business personnel. Not surprisingly, the military is also greatly concerned with leadership. It sponsors a wide variety of research projects that have the potential for enhancing our understanding of this subject. In summary, the balance between the theory and practice of leadership is fairly even as a result of this dual infusion of interest.

Major Substantive Topics of Interest in Leadership Research

Because of the many facets of leadership, researchers have focused on selected areas (Barrow, 1977). We can group these studies into six major categories.

Positional Power

Some investigators view leadership as exercise of *positional power*: the higher the position in the organizational hierarchy, the more power the position has. As discussed in Chapter 8, there are several kinds of power. In the leadership context, we are most concerned with legitimate power: the formal power given to a position. The positional power of a company president exceeds that of a manager; in turn, the manager has more power than a secretary. Viewing leadership in terms of positional power separates the person from the role. Little attention is given to individual's attributes; most is aimed at the use of positional power. Organizational theorists speak of such terms as *the power of the presidency* and *administrative clout*, issues not really related to the people in such positions. Sometimes history judges leaders on their inability to use all the power their positions give them. Other leaders try to exceed the power granted their positions. In some countries, leaders emerge by seizing power through military or political coups. Leadership, according to this perspective, is inherent in an organizational position based on the concept of power.

Some researchers have studied the tactics organizations use to influence other organizations and people. Kipnis and Cosentino (1969) found that military supervisors rely more on direct attempts to change subordinate behaviors through corrective power (for example, punishments), while industrial supervisors rely more on persuasive power (for example, diagnostic talks). In a study of interorganizational relations, Wilkinson and Kipnis (1978) found that leaders use both strong and weak influence tactics depending on the perceived power of the organization they are trying to influence. When the target organization is seen as more powerful than the initiating one, the latter will use gentle tactics like persuasion and ingratiation to exert influence. When the target is seen as less powerful, leaders will resort to stronger tactics (such as threats of ending relationships and legal action).

In the total spectrum of leadership research, a relatively small number of studies have been done on positional power. Many I/O researchers find it hard to separate leadership itself from the characteristics of people in leadership positions. But research on positional power has shown that some leadership issues transcend individual differences.

The Leader

Characteristics of individual leaders have been one of the most researched areas of leadership. Most leadership theories are based on understanding the differences among personal traits and behaviors. This is almost the opposite of emphasis on positional power, which minimizes individual differences. Many early studies leaned toward demographic and personality variables. Others studied what behaviors individual leaders exhibit that influence the judgment of whether they are strong or weak leaders. Statements like "Strong leaders radiate confidence" or "Weak leaders are indecisive" reflect the school of thought that stresses the importance of the leader in examining the leadership process. Research has been done on the *selection* of people into leadership positions; other research has been devoted to *training* people to enhance their leadership skills. Both leaders' sex (for example, Bartol & Wortman, 1975) and leaders' race (for example, Bartol, Evans, & Stith, 1978) have been examined as variables. Research has also been done on how the behavior of individual leaders affects subordinate motivation (for example, Klimoski & Hayes, 1980). The significance here is the focus on leader characteristics or behavior and their influence on others. This is a classic I/O psychology perspective, and it is the most popular in leadership research literature.

The Led

An area that is of growing interest is that of the characteristics of the followers, or the led. This is quite a shift in emphasis from the preceding area, in that leadership is construed more in terms of who is led than who does the leading. Casual observation suggests that some people are easier for leaders to work with than others. Military leaders have long known that some groups of recruits are more responsive, cohesive, or productive. Teachers have noted variations among student classes. Industrial-training directors have found this among various trainee groups. We thus have evidence that a leader's performance is not the same across different groups of followers. Studies by Lowin and Craig (1968) and Greene (1975) showed that certain characteristics of subordinates (most notably performance) can cause changes in leader behavior. We might label this class of studies "followership" research.

As an example, consider the case of a high school science teacher. The material may remain fairly constant over time, but the teacher's behavior may vary depending on the students. One year the teacher may have a class of bright, motivated students who quickly grasp the material. The teacher may respond by offering the class more advanced topics, laboratory experiments, or field trips. In another year, the teacher could have students who have difficulty learning the material. The teacher may have to instruct at a slower pace, use more examples, and hold help sessions. Other variables include class size, disciplinary problems, and student backgrounds. Thus, attributes of the led (the students) as indexed by their intelligence, motivation, number, interpersonal harmony, and background would be examined as factors affecting the behavior of the leader (the teacher).

We do not know as much about followers as we do about leaders. Studying followers usually involves studying groups as opposed to individuals, and groups are far more variable and difficult to study. Viewing the leadership process from the perspective of those who are led is fairly new in I/O psychology, but we are learning that followers can influence leaders just as we have long known the converse to be true.

Influence Process

Rather than focusing on either the leaders or the led, some researchers have found it instructive to examine the relationship or link between the two parties, particularly as they influence each other. Here researchers give their attention to the dynamics of this relationship, although they may also consider characteristics of both the leaders and the followers. In a general sense, what leaders "do" to a group is to influence its numbers in pursuit of some goal. Research on the influence process examines how this process is enacted.

The concept of influence entails how one person's actions affect those of another. As Cartwright (1965) notes, there are several methods of influence, including (1) coercion, (2) manipulation, (3) authority, and (4) persuasion. *Coercion* involves modifying behavior by force. *Manipulation* is a controlled distortion of reality as seen by those affected. People are allowed to see only those things that will evoke the kind of reaction desired. In the case of *authority*, agents appeal to a mutual decision giving them the right to influence. *Persuasion* means displaying judgment in such a way that those exposed to it accept its value. Researchers study how these methods are used in leader-follower relations. As an example, Greene and Schriesheim (1980) studied two types of leader behavior: instrumental and supportive. In instrumental leadership, a leader clarifies the group's goals. A supportive leader is friendly and considerate of others' needs. Greene and Schriesheim classified various work groups by size. The results showed that relatively small groups were most influenced by a supportive leader, and that instrumental leadership worked better in larger groups (perhaps because it brings order and structure to the group).

Like the above study, research on influence process tends to be fairly complex. It usually involves analysis of several variables. Perhaps more than in any other leadership area, this research has shown the intricacies and many facets of leader-group relations.

The Situation

Leadership research has also been directed at the situation or context in which leader-group relations occur. These factors can greatly affect the types of behaviors a leader has to exhibit to be effective. Imagine the leader of a Boy Scout troop, the supervisor of a production crew, and the warden of a prison. Each faces a different situation. Research on situational factors has tried to identify how various contexts differ and what effect they have on leader behavior.

Fiedler (1964) was one of the first researchers to acknowledge the importance of the context in which leadership occurs. One factor he considered important was how leaders and groups get along. Some leader-group relationships are friendly and positive, others are indifferent, and still others may be hostile. Fiedler says it is easier to be a leader where there are friendly relations, and difficult in a hostile atmosphere. He also proposed some other factors that differentiate leadership situations, which will be discussed later.

Depending on the context in which leadership occurs, different types of leader behavior will be called for. As an example, Green and Nebeker (1977) studied two types of leadership situations, one favorable and one unfavorable. In the favorable situation, leaders emphasized interpersonal relations and were supportive of the group members. However, in the unfavorable situation, the leaders became more task oriented and more concerned with goal accomplishment than with interpersonal relations. Green and Nebeker were able to show that different situations evoke different styles of leadership behavior.

Leader Emergence Versus Leader Effectiveness

The final category we will consider is the effectiveness versus emergence of leaders. Some leadership researchers are interested in the dynamics of what causes leaders to emerge within a group. This emergence process can either be formal (that is, a person is designated to be the leader) or informal (that is, a person evolves as the leader of a group without having been so designated). Researchers would examine such possible characteristics as the age, sex, and physical appearance of the leader, or would consider verbal and nonverbal behaviors associated with the subsequent emergence. Also of possible interest might be the characteristics of the group from which the leader emerged. In short, leader emergence is concerned with the process that results in someone's being regarded as the leader of a group.

Research on leader effectiveness is concerned with the performance of the leader. What are of concern in this line of research are the characteristics of the leader (or the group) that are associated with evaluation of leader quality, and in establishing the criteria for effective leaders. In the former case, effective leaders might be identified as people who possess certain characteristics, such as verbal fluency, sensitivity, decisiveness, and so on. In the latter case, effective leadership might be regarded as success in task completion (that is, an effective leader gets the job done), or in terms of the acceptance of the leader by the group (that is, an effective leader has group support). Issues associated with both leader emergence and leader acceptance have long been of interest to I/O psychologists.

Overview

Leadership researchers do not limit their studies or theories to just one of these six areas. A researcher interested in influence processes might consider in which situations influence attempts will be successful. Interest in leader traits may also include consideration of follower traits. My purpose in describing these areas is to highlight major categories of leadership research and acknowledge their different units of analysis while realizing the areas are not mutually exclusive. Table 11–1 summarizes the six major research areas and lists the types of topics and questions each area tends to address.

Established Theories of Leadership

Over time, researchers have proposed various leadership theories as they did with motivation theories. Motivation theories were distinct from one another; the newer theories rarely included concepts from the older ones. However, leadership theories have a cumulative effect. Some of the newer ones include concepts or principles first developed in previous theories. This is a healthy development in theory evolution since theorists do not have to begin at square one each time.

A second feature of leadership theories is their growing complexity. The early theories were quite simplistic—they tried to explain leadership on the basis of a few variables. The newer theories are far more complex in that they include a variety of elements. The profusion of empirical studies on diverse areas of leadership parallels

TABLE 11–1 *Topics and Associated Issues in Leadership Research*

Topic	Unit of Analysis	Variables of Interest	Research Questions
Position power	Organizational roles and positions	Influence tactics; use of power	Under what conditions will organizations resort to strong influence attempts?
The leader	Individual leaders	Personality characteristics; leader behaviors	What traits and/or behaviors differentiate effective versus ineffective leaders?
The led	Work groups and subordinates	Group size; experience of subordinates	What types of subordinates desire close supervision?
Influence process	Superior-subordinate interface	Receptivity to influence; nature of influence attempts	Under what conditions are leaders most susceptible to subordinate influence attempts?
The situation	Environment or context in which leadership occurs	Situational effects on leader behavior; factors defining favorable situations	How do various situations modify leader behavior?
Leader emergence versus effectiveness	Individuals and/or groups	Group dynamics and individual characteristics	How do individuals become recognized as leaders?

the extent to which theory developers have tried to incorporate their findings. Some of the newer leadership theories are among the most complex in all of I/O psychology.

We will look at six established leadership theories in this chapter. I call them "established" theories because they have been in existence a fairly long time and have been the subject of extensive research. Five are classified primarily as *descriptive*. The first four of these focus on the leader but also address the followers and the situation. The fifth theory takes a different tack; it examines leadership mainly from the perspective of influence. The final theory is classified as *normative*; it tries to prescribe (as opposed to describe) the leader's behavior. We will explore each theory and its supporting research.

Trait Theory

Though not a full-fledged "theory" in terms of stated hypotheses and postulates, *trait theory* is the oldest approach to leadership. It views leadership solely from the perspective of the leader. In particular, it identifies personal traits associated with leader effectiveness, such as physical features and personality characteristics.

A three-step process is used to identify the traits associated with leader effectiveness:

1. Identify effective and ineffective leaders through some external criterion, such as subjective judgment of their effectiveness.

2. Measure both types of leaders on demographic and personality variables. Demographic variables could be age, height, weight, sex, and race. Personality variables could be ambition, authoritarianism, dominance, judgment, and self-confidence.

3. Determine if effective leaders could be differentiated from the ineffective on the basis of one or more of these traits. Such a trait, if found, would be called "a critical leadership trait."

Stogdill (1948) and Hollander and Julian (1969) reviewed trait literature and found little or no connection between personal traits and leader effectiveness. Even if a connection were consistently found, other problems would ensue. There are too many variables and there is no rational guide to selecting them. It is "shotgun empiricism" in its worst form. Also, many personality scales used to assess the personality traits have very low reliability. Last, trait theory gives no basis for explaining *why* the critical leadership traits operate as they do. What if effective leaders were found to be tall, heavy, and dominant? How would those variables account for variation in effectiveness?

Brown (1954) observed: "The longer and more comprehensive the list of qualities, the more obvious it must be that their possession would be of no use as a junior leader in industry, for he would inevitably be in demand elsewhere as a Prime Minister, or maybe as a Archangel" (p. 219). But the myth of the trait approach to leader identification prevails. Famous World War II leader General Douglas

MacArthur was described as "someone who just looks like a leader." His associate General Omar Bradley had physical features and a general demeanor that prompted some people to question his face validity as a leader. Yet, despite their different physical structures and personalities, both men were among the most effective military leaders in our nation's history.

Dissatisfaction with trait theory gave birth to the second major theory in leadership research: behavior theory.

Behavior Theory

Behavior theory, like trait theory, studies leadership by looking at the leader. But unlike trait theory, it sees leadership in terms of what leaders do, not what traits they have. According to behavior theory, effective leaders can be differentiated from ineffective leaders on the basis of their performing different behaviors. The research strategy behind the behavioral approach is as follows. First, people in leadership positions are studied by direct observation and survey questionnaires. This determines the types of work behaviors they show. One example might be a supervisor's publicly reprimanding an employee for poor job performance. Another could be a surpervisor who shows a new employee how to use certain equipment. Next, these behaviors are placed into categories on the basis of similarity. These categories are then put into a checklist or other type of classifying scheme. The checklist is used to evaluate behavior through techniques such as "yes-or-no" questions ("Does the leader follow this behavior on the job?") or frequency scales ("How often does this behavior occur?"). Last, leader effectiveness is judged, usually in terms of work-group productivity, absences, turnover, or morale. If certain leader behaviors systematically relate to these effectiveness indexes, we then have a solid empirical basis on which to judge leadership. The behavioral approach is far more fruitful than the trait approach in explaining leadership.

The most famous of all the behavioral studies of leadership were conducted at Ohio State University. They started in the early 1950s and continued for many years. They had such a dominant impact on leadership research that they have come to be known collectively as the Ohio State studies. They are probably best known for two major contributions to the leadership literature: first, they provided a number of questionnaires to measure leadership; second, they identified two dimensions of leadership later found to be highly reliable and valid.

The researchers began by developing many questionnaire items on what supervisors do in their leadership roles. Such items as "He knows about it when something goes wrong" and "She calls the group together to talk things over" are examples. The items were placed into such general categories as domination, evaluation, and communication. Then the questionnaires were given to a wide variety of people in leader-group relations, such as in military, business, industrial, and academic organizations. The subordinates described the leaders' behaviors on each of the categories. The results showed overlap in these descriptions across the categories. Using a procedure called *factor analysis*, which reduces a large number of questionnaire items to a smaller number of factors based on similarity of content, two factors were found to underlie leader behavior: *consideration* and *initiating structure*.

Fleishman and Harris (1962) define these factors as follows:

> *Consideration.* Includes behavior indicating mutual trust, respect, and certain warmth and rapport between the supervisor and his group. This does not mean that this dimension reflects a superficial "pat-on-the-back, first-name calling" kind of human relations behavior. This dimension seems to emphasize a deeper concern for group members' needs, and includes such behavior as allowing subordinates more participation in decision making and encouraging more two-way communication.
>
> *Structure.* Includes behavior in which the supervisor organizes and defines group activities and his relation to the group. Thus, he defines the role he expects each member to assume, assigns tasks, plans ahead, establishes ways of getting things done, and pushes for production. This dimension seems to emphasize overt attempts to achieve organizational goals [pp. 43-44].

Several questionnaires were developed to assess the content of leader behavior as reflected by these two factors. The first, the Leader Behavior Description Questionnaire (LBDQ), is completed by a *subordinate* who describes how the leader behaves in various situations. A second questionnaire, the Leader Opinion Questionnaire (LOQ), is completed by a *supervisor* and deals with questions on ideal methods of supervision. Sample items from the LBDQ and the LOQ are presented in Figures 11–1 and 11–2.

Over time, many studies were made of the psychometric properties of these questionnaires. Schriesheim and Kerr (1974) and Schriesheim and Stogdill (1975)

Structure	Consideration
1. He schedules work to be done.	1. He is friendly and approachable.
2. He emphasizes the meeting of deadlines.	2. He makes group members feel at ease when talking to them.
3. He lets group members know what is expected of them.	3. He does little things to make it pleasant to be a member of the group.

Figure 11–1   Sample Items from the Leader Behavior Description Questionnaire

Structure	Consideration
1. Put the welfare of your unit above the welfare of any person.	1. Give in to your subordinates in your discussions with them.
2. Encourage after-duty work by persons of your unit.	2. Back up what persons under you do.
3. Try out new ideas in the unit.	3. Get approval of persons under you on important matters before going ahead.

Figure 11–2   Sample Items from the Leader Opinion Questionnaire

found clear support for the value of LBDQ in studying leadership, but LOQ appears to have lesser value. About 80% of leader behavior variance could be explained by the consideration and initiating structure factors (Hemphill, 1950; Stogdill & Coons, 1957). Cross-cultural studies (for example, Tscheulin, 1973) also supported the existence of these factors.

The Fleishman and Harris study (1962) revealed that even the two leadership factors can interact in their effect on subordinate behavior. The authors examined to what degree the leader's consideration and initiating structure influenced the subordinate's grievance rate. The results of this study are shown in Figure 11–3. Leaders low in consideration incurred the highest grievance rates; those high in consideration

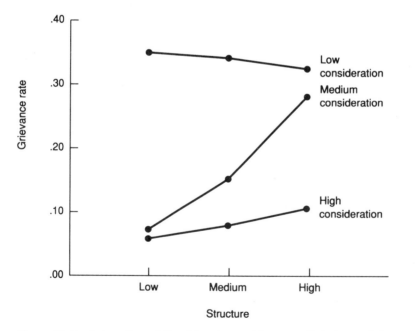

Figure 11–3   Interaction of Consideration and Structure Relating to Grievance Rate

SOURCE: E. A. Fleishman and E. F. Harris, "Patterns of Leadership Behavior Related to Employee Grievances and Turnover," *Personnel Psychology, 15* (1962), pp. 43–56.

incurred the lowest. For leaders with medium degrees of consideration, degree of structure determined the grievance rate. Leaders low in structure incurred few grievances, but those high in structure incurred many. In short, the grievances of subordinates were determined by the combination or the interaction of the leader's consideration and initiating structure. The results from these types of studies showed that the leader's behavior does indeed influence the work group on a number of factors. But the relationship between the two is not simplistic.

In viewing a leader's behavior as measured by consideration and initiating structure, it becomes apparent on the basis of the validation studies that certain behaviors result in more desirable outcomes than others. The Fleishman and Harris study (1962), for example, showed that highly considerate leaders incur low grievance rates, and other research has shown leaders demonstrating high structure have highly productive work groups (for example, Schriesheim, House, & Kerr, 1976). The relationship *between* consideration and initiating structure is important because both factors have been found to influence other variables. If the relation between them is negative, a high score on one factor would be paired with a low score on the other. If the correlation is positive, scores on both factors would co-vary positively. If the correlation is zero, a wide range of combinations of consideration and initiating structure would be possible.

It was originally proposed that the two factors were independent or unrelated to each other. However, later empirical work has shown that the two factors are rarely independent (Weissenberg & Kavanagh, 1972). Some studies (for example, Larson, Hunt, & Osborn, 1976) report correlations in excess of .70. These findings suggest that subordinates who describe their leader's behavior see these two factors as being related. Thus, leaders who are described as exhibiting low feelings of consideration for their subordinates are also frequently seen as providing little guidance for goal attainment. However, not all desirable organizational outcomes (for example, low turnover, high satisfaction) are associated with high scores on these variables. Sometimes low scores are desirable, and in many cases, the relationships are moderated by other variables. It would be best for the organization if these two leadership dimensions were unrelated to each other. That would allow for the greatest flexibility in leader behavior. However, research indicates that subordinates see these aspects of leader behavior as positively related to each other, thus diminishing the likelihood of the desired flexibility in leader style.

Overview of Behavior Theory. The behavioral approach to leadership was a big advance over the trait approach. Effective leadership became transformed into what leaders *do* as opposed to who they *are*. Emphasizing behaviors focused attention on *training* leaders to be more effective. Behaviors are far less ambiguous than traits. It is far more useful to describe a leader as one who "never gives subordinates a chance to voice their feelings" than to say the leader is "highly dominant."

The Ohio State studies exemplified the behavioral approach to leadership. They provided reliable means to measure leader behavior. The identification of consideration and initiating structure, factors that account for the majority of variance in leader behavior, was a major advance in understanding leadership. While later approaches to

Four presidents of the United States: What leader behaviors and characteristics would describe these individuals? Wide World Photos

leadership have added to our knowledge, probably no other theoretical perspective advanced the discipline as much as the behavioral approach.

Fiedler's Contingency Theory

The next phase in the evolution of leadership theory was Fiedler's *contingency theory*. His major contribution was his recognition that the effectiveness of leaders depends on the situations in which they operate. The origins of Fiedler's thesis stemmed from some research he did on clinical therapists. Fiedler (1951) discovered that effective therapists viewed their patients as being similar to themselves; ineffective ones viewed them as being dissimilar. Thus, the therapists' effectiveness was not independent of the situations in which they worked. Fiedler extended his findings and developed a theory of leader effectiveness applicable to a broad range of leader-group situations.

There are three major parts to Fiedler's theory.

Least-Preferred Co-Worker Scale. The first part of Fiedler's theory addresses individual differences among leaders. Leaders can differ from one another on many dimensions (intelligence, personality, experience, and so on). Fiedler did not find these factors to be particularly useful, so he developed a new method to identify types of leaders: a paper-and-pencil measure called the least-preferred co-worker (LPC) scale. The scale uses a series of bipolar adjectives to describe someone's personality (pleasant-unpleasant, friendly-unfriendly, and so on). There are eight scale points between the adjectives. The leader is instructed to think of the one person he or she would least like to work with due to incompetence; that person is the least-preferred co-worker. The leader then rates or describes this person on the LPC scale. The positive ends of the scale (pleasant, friendly) have high numerical values; the low ends (unfriendly, unpleasant), low values. The total score is called the LPC score. A high LPC score indicates that the leader can differentiate the person's competence from his or her personality. It is an accepting description of the least-preferred co-worker's personality (for example, "You're incompetent as a co-worker, but you are a pleasant person"). A low LPC score is a rejecting description ("You're incompetent as a coworker, and you also have an unpleasant personality").

In a later study, Fiedler (1967) said that a leader's LPC score reflects his or her style of leadership. Low-LPC leaders are more task oriented, are more controlling in their leadership role, and tend to score higher on initiating structure variables from the Ohio State leadership scales. High-LPC leaders are more relationship oriented, are more permissive in their leadership role, and tend to score higher on consideration variables from these scales. LPC scores are also related to cognitive complexity. Low-LPC leaders tend to be cognitively simple; they do not differentiate judgments of personality from those of competence. High-LPC leaders tend to be cognitively complex; they can differentiate personality judgments from competence ones. We will examine the empirical research on LPC scores a bit later. Suffice it to say for the moment that they are the means by which Fiedler identifies different types of leaders.

Situational Favorability.   The second part of Fiedler's theory involves how he measures differences in situations where leadership occurs. Fiedler thinks it is easier to be a leader in some situations than others. He proposed three variables to account for this. Each factor has two levels. The first factor, *leader-group relations*, deals with how well the leader and the group get along. When leader-group relations are good, the leader is accepted, the group members are loyal, and the leadership job is much easier. When leader-group relations are poor, the leader is rejected, and there is hostility between the leader and the group.

The second factor, *task structure*, is the clarity of the steps needed to complete a task. Some tasks have high structure; they are straightforward, steps involved are clear-cut, and everyone knows how to get the job done. Other tasks have low structure; what has to be done is not as clear and roles are ambiguous.

The third factor, *leader position power*, is the amount of legitimate authority and number of sanctions available to the leader. Some leadership positions have high power (a company president); others have low power (the social chairperson of a club).

After defining these three factors, Fiedler combined the two levels of each factor to yield eight (2 × 2 × 2) types of situations—what he calls *octants*. These are illustrated in Figure 11–4. Note that the octants differ in their favorability. Octant 1 is the most favorable: good leader-group relations prevail, there is high task structure, and the leader has a lot of power. Octant 8 is the least favorable: poor leader-group relations prevail, there is low task structure, and the leader has little power.

Factors Determining
Situational Favorability

Leader-group relations	Good	Good	Good	Good	Poor	Poor	Poor	Poor
Task structure	High	High	Low	Low	High	High	Low	Low
Position power	High	Low	High	Low	High	Low	High	Low

Octant	1	2	3	4	5	6	7	8

(High)   (Low)

Situational favorability

Figure 11–4   Factors Defining Situational Favorability According to Fiedler's Contingency Theory

The most influential factor determining situational favorableness is leader-group relations. The four most favorable situations have high leader-group relations. Thus, this second part of Fiedler's theory is independent of the characteristics of the leader since it relates only to differences in situations.

Matching Leaders and Situations.   In the final part of the theory, Fiedler integrates the first two parts and makes specific predictions about leader effectiveness. There are differences in leaders (as indexed by LPC scores) and in situations (as indexed by situational favorableness), and certain types of leaders are predicted to be more effective in certain types of situations. Fiedler proposed that low-LPC leaders are more effective in both highly favorable and highly unfavorable situations. High-LPC leaders are more effective in moderately favorable situations. The basis for these hypotheses is as follows. Moderately favorable situations are characterized by considerable differentiation among the various factors; some are positive and some are negative insofar as leader control and influence are concerned. Because a high-LPC leader is cognitively complex, he or she can differentiate factors in the environment. Thus, a cognitively complex person and a highly differentiated environment are a good match. A low-LPC leader does not differentiate among factors in the environment. He or she is better off in either a highly favorable and highly unfavorable situation; that is, all the factors are either high or low. Therefore, a good match would be that of undifferentiated types of people and undifferentiated types of situations. Figure 11–5 illustrates Fiedler's best match between leaders and situations.

Evaluation of Fiedler's Theory.   The ultimate test of any theory's validity is the extent to which it predicts the criterion of interest. With Fiedler's theory, the criterion is leader effectiveness, defined in terms of performance by the group in its major assigned task. The measure most often used is a rating of group performance.

On par, tests of Fiedler's theory have had mixed results. Most studies give some support (that is, performance in some octants is more predictable than in others);

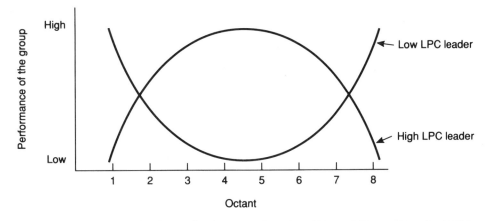

Figure 11–5 Proposed Relationship between Situational Favorability and Leader LPC Score as They Affect Group Performance

only a few give no support. Negative findings have been reported by Graen, Alvares, Orris, and Martella (1970) and Vecchio (1977). In defense of his theory Fiedler (1971) argued that the results, while not as strong as he would like, exceed the levels dictated by pure chance. To his credit, Fiedler has responded to criticism (Ashour, 1973) and tried to modify the theory.

Most of the problems with Fiedler's theory have been with the LPC measure. It is not clear what construct this scale really measures. Evans and Dermer (1974) said the scale more readily measures dogmatism than cognitive complexity. Stinson and Tracy (1974) and Rice (1978) reported problems with the scale's reliabilty and construct validity. Shiftlett (1981) questioned the adequacy of the cutting score, which supposedly separates high from low LPC scores. That is, when you dichotomize a continuous variable (LPC scores) into two groups (high and low), you must have a highly accurate scale that permits such a split to occur. Although Fiedler's theory addresses only high and low LPC scores, some researchers have *trichotomized* LPC scores into high, middle, and low. What are *middle* LPC people like? Kennedy (1982) found that middle-LPC leaders were generally superior to both high- and low-LPC leaders in situations described by the model. He also found middle-LPC leader performance to be largely independent of the situational factors that affect the performance of high- and low-LPC leaders. In short, the LPC component of Fiedler's theory has been the target of considerable criticism.

Subsequently, Fiedler has taken a further tack. He advocates social engineering (Fiedler, 1965)—restructuring the job (to make it more or less favorable) to fit the leader. Alternatively, the leader could be selected (high or low LPC) to fit the job (its degree of favorableness). Fiedler and his associate (Fiedler & Mahar, 1979a, 1979b) developed a self-paced learning program to train people to become more effective leaders. The training, called Leader Match, teaches leaders what they can do to change the favorableness of the situation to best match their LPC scores, for example, by making more routine-work assignments. Csoka and Bons (1978) compared two groups of student military leaders, one of which received the leadership training. The leaders' performances were rated by peers and superiors. According to the authors, leaders who received Leader Match training performed better than the control leaders. In another test of Leader Match, Leister, Borden, and Fiedler (1977) studied two groups of naval officers; one received the training and one did not. Superiors rated the performances of members of both groups before the training and again six months later; the officers trained with Leader Match received superior performance ratings. However, Kabanoff (1981) is critical of Leader Match, and feels that Fiedler has overstated the importance of congruence between a leader's style and the situation in determining group performance. Kabanoff believes that other factors besides congruence determine how successful a leader will be. Also, Jago and Ragan (1986) concluded the training principles of Leader Match do not follow from the tenets of contingency theory, the supposed basis of the program.

In addition to stressing the importance of the situation, Fiedler also devised a way to change the situation to fit the leader's style. This is the classic human-factors approach to performance: Assume the people are "fixed" and vary the environment. The Ohio State studies took the opposite approach: select or train leaders to fit the job.

Overview of Fiedler's Theory.   Some authors (for example, Kerr et al., 1974) acknowledge that though Fiedler did not invent the contingent approach to leadership, he did elevate the importance of situational factors to the same level as leader characteristics. Fiedler changed the emphasis of leadership research from looking at just leaders' traits and behaviors to looking at both the leader and the context in which leadership occurs. It is also instructive to recognize the confluence of sources from which Fiedler developed his theory. His measure of leader position power reflects the importance that some researchers place on position power (as discussed earlier) in the role of leadership. His measure of the least-preferred co-worker draws on the importance of studying the leader in the leadership process. While what the LPC scale actually measures is a matter of debate, it seems to be associated to some degree with the perspective of examining personality factors and traits in leadership. Fiedler's measure of situational favorableness is the prototype for leadership research that stresses the situation. He is less concerned with explicit leader behaviors, though research has shown that high- and low-LPC leaders do behave differently in their leadership roles.

On par, Fiedler's theory has been supported empirically more than it has been refuted. Strube and Garcia (1981) found the theory to be very robust in predicting group performance, and thus acclaimed the theory's veracity. Peters, Harthe, and Pohlmann (1985) found somewhat differential support for the theory as a function of the method used to test it. They found empirical support for seven of the octants in laboratory studies, but support for only four octants in field studies. In particular, octant 2 (where leader-group relations are good, the task is clear-cut, but the leader has relatively little power) seems to be a more favorable situation in which to be a leader than octant 1, in theory the most favorable situation. Perhaps octant 2 is indeed the most favorable situation, because when the leader and the group get along, and the task is straightforward, the leader may not *need* a lot of power. The most commonly used criterion in validation studies of Fiedler's theory is group performance. However, a second criterion may be considered as an index of the leader's success: subordinate satisfaction. Rice (1981) found support for the contingency model when subordinate satisfaction was used as the criterion.

Fiedler's theory has contributed a great deal to the field of leadership research. It has pointed research in new directions. Some researchers have proposed additional factors that contribute to situational favorability. Others modified the LPC scale. Yet other studies proposed new approaches to classifying situations. In short, the theory has been a catalyst for leadership researchers. As a result of it, when we are asked what makes for an effective leader, the answer is "It depends" (that is, leader effectiveness is a contingent phenomenon).

The course of leadership research changed after Fiedler's theory, and the contingency theme was magnified even more in the next major theory of leadership: path-goal theory.

Path-Goal Theory

In the previous chapters, we discussed job satisfaction, motivation, and leadership. Each of these theories addresses a limited aspect of human behavior. But in real life, how we feel about our boss, how motivated we are, and how satisfied we feel are not independent of one another. *Path-goal theory* integrates job satisfaction, motivation, and leadership. Though mainly a theory of leadership, it also explains subordinate motivation and job satisfaction.

Path-goal theory is a type of contingency theory. However, it is more complex than Fiedler's theory because it includes a broader range of variables. Path-goal theory is relatively new, so it is still evolving and being tested (Keller, 1989). Proposed by House (1971) and House and Mitchell (1974), the theory stresses mainly the behaviors a leader must exhibit in order for the subordinates to attain their goals. As a process theory, path-goal is loaded with links among variables.

We will begin by examining the theory's two major postulates:

1. Leader behavior will be acceptable and satisfying to subordinates when they see it as an immediate source of satisfaction or being instrumental in obtaining future satisfaction.

2. Leader behavior will increase subordinate effort expended when subordinates see effective performance as a means of satisfying important needs and the leader as an aid in attaining effective performance.

These postulates are not simple. They involve subordinate perceptions of the leader's behavior, determining how the leader's behavior affects subordinate motivation, and assessing the degree to which the leader's behavior facilitates subordinate goal attainment. Path-goal theory has its roots in the expectancy theory of motivation. "Goals" are the outcomes that subordinates desire, and "paths" are the behaviors that have to be exhibited to attain these goals. In a nutshell, path-goal theory explains how the leader facilitates subordinate goal attainment. Note that path-goal theory shifts the focus from the leader's characteristics to his or her effect on subordinate motivation.

The theory states that a leader must be able to manifest four different styles of behavior derived from previous research on work behavior:

1. *Directive leadership.* The leader provides specific guidelines to subordinates on how they perform their tasks. The leader should set standards of performance and provide explicit expectations of performance. This style reflects initiating structure from the Ohio State studies.

2. *Supportive leadership.* The leader must demonstrate concern for the well-being of the subordinates and must be supportive of them as individuals. This style reflects the consideration factor from the Ohio State studies.

3. *Participative leadership.* The leader must solicit ideas and suggestions from subordinates and invite their participation in decisions that directly affect them. The origins of this style of leadership stem from research on the value and importance of participative decision making (Likert, 1961).

4. *Achievement-oriented leadership.* A leader must set challenging goals, emphasize improvements in work performance, and encourage high levels of goal attainment. This style of leadership is directly related to the findings from the goal-setting theory of motivation and other approaches that emphasize achievement motivation.

Effective leaders need all four of these styles since each one produces different results. But when should a leader use which style? It depends on a number of situational factors (note the contingency basis here). To date, two types of contingency factors have been identified.

Some of the situational factors relate to characteristics of the subordinates, others to environmental factors. Two subordinate characteristics are perceived ability and locus of control. Subordinates who believe they have a lot of ability are less accepting of the directive leadership style. They think they need little guidance and direction from their leader. Subordinates with an internal locus of control are more satisfied with the participative leadership style; those with an external locus of control favor the directive style. In short, internals like to be asked; externals like to be told. One environmental factor is the nature of the task being performed. The more dissatisfying and unpleasant the task, the more subordinates resent the directive leadership style. Leader behavior is motivating to the extent that it helps subordinates cope with environmental uncertainties, threats, or frustration.

What effect do these leader behaviors have? According to path-goal theory, the leader can influence subordinates' perceptions of their jobs by (1) removing obstacles from the paths to desired goals, (2) rewarding subordinates for attaining their goals, and (3) helping subordinates clarify paths to valued goals. Thus, the leader is one who helps subordinates do the things that must be done to obtain the desired rewards.

Finally, if the leader is successful, what will happen? First, subordinate job satisfaction will result since the job is seen as a vehicle for providing desired rewards.

Second, the leader will be accepted by the subordinates and be seen as instrumental in helping the subordinates attain their desired rewards. Finally, subordinate motivation will be high since, according to the postulates of expectancy theory, the leader provides feedback to show that effort leads to performance (expectancy) and that performance results in reward attainment (instrumentality). The entire path-goal theory is presented graphically in Table 11–2.

Path-goal theory is an "organizational care package"—many good things are supposed to happen if the theory works. Indeed, the theory is quite imposing, considering all that it purports to accomplish. Recently, a number of tests have been made, but given the theory's complexity, only parts of it have been tested. Many tests looked at two of the four leadership styles (usually directive and supportive); others studied the results (for example, satisfaction, role clarity) of using certain leadership roles. Test results are indecisive. The theory can be judged on two dimensions: internal logic and empirical verifiability. The theory's logic seems sound: an effective leader should facilitate subordinate job satisfaction and motivation. But it is difficult to verify the theory's predictions. Like Maslow's theory, one major problem has to do with measurement. Concepts like path, goal, supportive leadership, directive leadership, and so on, can be interpreted differently when put into operation.

A number of other issues have been raised. Greene (1979) conducted a study of path-goal theory that largely *supported* the predictions made, yet he raised questions about causation among the variables. The theory states that leader behavior style causes certain subordinate attitudes and behavior. Greene feels that the attitudes and behavior of the subordinates can cause changes in the style used by the leader. This reflects the school of thought that subordinates influence leaders just as leaders influence subordinates. Mawhinney and Ford (1977) have stated that because path-

TABLE 11–2 *Path-Goal Theory of Leadership*

Leader Behavior	Contingency Factors	Subordinate Attitudes and Behavior
1. Directive	1. Subordinate characteristics	1. Job satisfaction; job → rewards
2. Supportive	a. Locus of control	
3. Participative	b. Perceived ability	2. Acceptance of leader; leader → rewards
4. Achievement-oriented	c. Authoritarianism	
	.	3. Motivational behavior; effort → performance performance → rewards
	.	
	.	
	.	
	2. Environmental characteristics	
	a. Nature of the task	
	b. Formal authority system	
	c. Primary work group	
	.	
	.	
	.	

goal theory is based on expectancy theory, there is a tendency to view the theory from a cognitive, rational perspective. They argue that an operant interpretation of path-goal theory results is also plausible, that the behavior of subordinates can be explained by the reinforcing behaviors of the leader. They support the logic of the theory but feel the operant perspective can explain the results as well as the cognitive perspective. Which perspective is more defensible depends on finding a condition where the two theories make opposite predictions. But such a test awaits further research. Fulk and Wendler (1982) noted that while three major outcomes are supposed to follow from use of the theory (employee job satisfaction, acceptance of the leader, and employee motivation), the most commonly observed (and measured) outcome is that of job satisfaction.

Overview of Path-Goal Theory. Path-goal theory is a confluence of many other theories. The four types of leader behavior styles were distilled mostly from the Ohio State studies. The perspective that leadership is a contingent phenomenon draws heavily on Fiedler's work. The hypothesis that a job provides desired rewards comes from existing theories of job satisfaction. The notion of a leader's being instrumental for subordinate goal attainment has its roots in expectancy theory. Path-goal theory is perhaps the most complex of all the theories in I/O psychology. It is also the most comprehensive. We should not let the lack of supporting data sour us on its value. As a research strategy, it would be advisable to get better measures of the variables and continue to look for additional contingency factors. In fact, as shown in Table 11–2, the search for contingency factors is still being conducted. Although the theory needs a lot of further work (see Field Note 1), it provides us with a rational basis for synthesizing our knowledge about work behavior, which heretofore we have addressed in piecemeal fashion. While at this time the goals of the theory may be held in higher esteem than the theory itself, path-goal theory provides a strong basis for increasing our understanding of work behavior beyond just the topic of leadership.

Field Note 1

The path-goal theory of leadership is a complex explanation of how leaders should behave. As with anything that is complex, there is a lot that can go wrong. One of the contingency factors is subordinate characteristics; that is, the leader should, based on what the subordinates are like, invoke different leader styles. There is a fine line between exhibiting different leader styles to different people on a consistent basis, and being perceived as "wishy-washy" or "playing favorites." For example, research has shown that individuals who have an internal locus of control prefer the participative leader style, and that those with an external locus prefer the directive leader style. Simply put, you ask internals and you tell externals.

If you followed path-goal theory to the letter, you would ascertain the locus of control of all your subordinates, and would then treat them differently (that is, use a different leadership style) depending upon the results. However, unless the subordinates are made aware of the "contingent logic" in your treatment of them, using different styles might be perceived as favoritism, bias, or inconsistency. It may appear that you *ask* your favorites what they want to do, but *tell* everyone else what to do. Unless all subordinates understood the contingent basis of your leadership style, you could be accused of inflicting differential treatment. This is often perceived as being unfair and can be the kiss of death for some leaders.

There are also some internal contradictions in the theory. Research has shown that leaders should *not* use the directive style with subordinates who perform unpleasant tasks.

What style should they use with a subordinate who has an external locus of control (who would respond to the directive style) *and* who performs an unpleasant job (in which case the directive style should *not* be used)? This is the problem with multiple contingency factors—they can serve to push the leader in opposing directions. Path-goal theory is almost too complex for its own good. Each new contingency factor added to the theory further adds to the probability of the theory's being difficult to enact in a practical setting.

Mutual-Influence Theory

As a departure from the progression of the last four leadership theories, some theories limit their view of leadership to the exchange of mutual influence between the leader and followers. As opposed to thinking in terms of leader characteristics or situational factors that moderate leader effectiveness, *mutual-influence theories* focus on the dynamics of the leader-follower relationship, stressing the link between the two rather than either role individually.

Herold (1977) conceptualized leadership as a dyad and focused on the relationship between the two partners. He discovered that through his or her own behavior, each partner in a dyad, whether leader or subordinate, will affect the other's behavior and/or attitudes. So leadership is just a special case of this two-way influence process. However, in a typical situation, the leader has more power. Herold showed that while the influence process is reciprocal, powerful leaders affect subordinate behavior more than powerful subordinates affect leader behavior. Herold felt conceptualizing leadership as a *vertical dyad* (a superior and subordinate) would be the best unit of analysis.

Another researcher who used the mutual-influence process in a dyad is Graen. Graen and his associates (for example, Dansereau, Graen, & Haga, 1975) proposed what they call the *vertical dyad linkage model* of leadership or what is sometimes referenced as "leader-member exchange theory." According to the theory, leaders differentiate their subordinates in terms of (1) competence and skill, (2) extent to which they can be trusted (especially when not being watched by the leader), and (3) their motivation to assume greater responsibility within the unit. Subordinates identified by the leader with these attributes become members of what Graen calls the *in-group*. In-group members go beyond their formal job duties and take responsibility for completing tasks that are most critical to the success of the work group. In return, they receive more attention, support, and sensitivity from their leaders. Subordinates who do not have these attributes are called the *out-group*; they do the more routine, mundane tasks of the work group and have a more formal relationship with the leader. Leaders influence out-group members by using formal authority, though this is not necessary with in-group members. Thus, leaders and subordinates use different types and degrees of influence depending on whether the subordinate is in the in- or out-group.

In addition to providing a new way of conceptualizing the leadership process, the vertical dyad linkage model underscores a major methodological issue in leadership research. Traditionally, perceptions of the leader (as in the LBDQ) are averaged across respondents to get a "typical" measure of him or her on some dimension. However, this model suggests that the leader-member exchange between a supervisor and each subordinate should be approached as unique. If a leader is very considerate of in-group members and very inconsiderate of out-group members, a statistical average will give a false picture. As opposed to thinking of ten subordinates in a work group as one unit, the theory recommends that the leadership of this group be construed as ten leader-subordinate dyads. This perspective was supported in a study by Graen, Liden, and Hoel (1982) that addressed the effect of leadership on turnover. When conceptualized in terms of overall leadership style, leadership was not helpful in predicting turnover. However, when the problem was conceptualized as a series of leader-subordinate dyadic interactions, leadership *was* an effective predictor of turnover. Vecchio (1982) found the dyadic approach useful in explaining the attitudes of employees toward their supervisors, and Vecchio and Gobdel (1984) found the model predictive of employee performance and propensity to quit. In a review of the theory, Dienesch and Liden (1986) concluded there are three psychological bases for the "exchange" between the superior and subordinate. *Personal contribution* refers to the perception of the amount, direction, and quality of work-oriented activity each member puts forth toward the mutual goals of the dyad. *Loyalty* is the expression of public support for the goals and personal character of the other member. *Affect* is the degree of liking the members of the dyad have for each other. The authors refer to these three dimensions as the "currencies of exchange" within the dyad.

In summary, the mutual-influence theories focus on the linkage between supervisors and subordinates and how both parties influence each other. Leadership is a special type of influence process, and what is special is the unequal nature of the power roles in the dyad. This view also transforms leadership from a purely independent variable to one that is also dependent. Thus, leadership affects and is affected by other variables.

Vroom-Yetton Contingency Theory

The final theory of leadership is quite different. First, the *Vroom-Yetton theory* is normative: it tells leaders how they should behave. While Fiedler's contingency theory and path-goal theory also have some normative components (that is, the behaviors a leader should exhibit are contingent on other factors), they are not nearly as prescriptive. Second, the Vroom-Yetton theory deals with only one aspect of leadership: decision making.

The essence of the Vroom-Yetton model is the degree to which a leader allows subordinates to participate in the decision-making process. Depending on what the leader is trying to accomplish, certain leader behaviors (for example, the degree of subordinate participation in decision making) produce certain outcomes. In particular, the model proposes three types of decision-making styles the leader should utilize, depending upon the outcomes desired. *Autocratic* (A) decisions are made primarily by the leader; *consultative* (C) decisions are made by the leader and the group in concert; and *group* (G) decisions are made exclusively by the group. Vroom and Yetton (1973) developed a model of decision-making strategies for the leader to follow, depending on certain aspects of the decision problem.

Vroom and Yetton outlined five types of leader decision making behaviors:

1. The manager personally solves the problem or makes the decision using information available at the time (A1).

2. The manager gets the necessary information from subordinates and then decides on a solution (A2).

3. The manager shares the problem with relevant subordinates individually, getting their ideas and suggestions without bringing them together as a group, and then makes the decision personally (C1).

4. The manager shares the problem with subordinates as a group, gets their collective ideas and suggestions, and then makes the decision personally (C2).

5. The manager shares the problem with subordinates as a group and is willing to accept any solution that has group support (G2).

To help the manager select a certain decision-making strategy, Vroom and Yetton proposed a number of decision rules or criteria. These are (1) the *quality* of the decision, (2) the *acceptance* of the decision by the subordinates, and (3) the *time* needed to make the decision. These are the contingency factors in the Vroom-Yetton theory that determine which decision-making style the leader chooses. In reviewing the five types of leader behavior, you can see that some behaviors will need less time and others are more likely to produce greater subordinate acceptance of the decision.

Next, the authors use a *decision tree*, a graphic way to display various decision options. The "path" of the tree is determined by yes or no answers to seven questions (see Figure 11–6). Depending on the answers, fourteen problem types can emerge.

With certain leader behaviors, less time is spent making the decision. However, time is not the only criterion in selecting a decision strategy. Group acceptance of the decision and the process of group development are also important. Table 11–3 shows three columns of variables. Column 1 shows the fourteen problem types identified in Figure 11–6. The variables in column 2 indicate which of the five leader behaviors will result in the least amount of time being spent on the problems. The third column shows how the ordering of the other leader behaviors would facilitate group development. A manager who uses one of these strategies might spend more time on the problem than necessary but have the advantage of an increasing amount of group development. Moving to the right across the third column, time minimization is

Questions

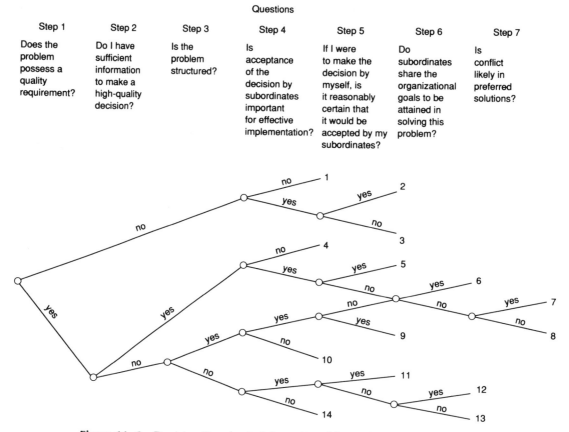

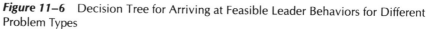

Figure 11–6 Decision Tree for Arriving at Feasible Leader Behaviors for Different Problem Types

SOURCE: Adapted from V. H. Vroom and P. W. Yetton, *Leadership and Decision-making* (Pittsburgh: University of Pittsburgh Press, 1973). Reprinted by permission of the University of Pittsburgh Press.

increasingly traded off against subordinate group development. The final behavior in column 3 is G2, letting the subordinates make the decision.

Most of the tests of the Vroom-Yetton theory have been comparisons of what the theory says managers should do versus what they actually do. We have less information on whether managers perform better when they follow the theory. Many of the subjects in these tests have been actual managers who report how they deal with a particular problem. Research shows that managers share decision-making responsibilities when they feel their subordinates can be trusted. When Jago and Vroom (1977) studied managers at four organizational levels, they found greater use of participative methods at higher levels. Hill and Schmitt (1977) found that leaders apparently do make decisions based on the problem attributes (that is, quality, time, acceptance). These decisions are fairly consistent with the theory's predictions, espe-

TABLE 11–3 *Feasible Leader Behaviors for Each of Fourteen Problem Types*

Problem Type	Behavior Resulting in Least Time Spent on Problem	Behavior Providing for Increasing Amounts of Group Development			
1	A1	A2	C1	C2	G2
2	A1	A2	C1	C2	G2
3	G2				
4	A1	A2	C1	C2	G2
5	A1	A2	C1	C2	G2
6	G2				
7	C2				
8	C1	C2			
9	A2	C1	C2	G2	
10	A2	C1	C2	G2	
11	C2	G2			
12	G2				
13	C2				
14	C2	G2			

SOURCE: V. H. Vroom and P. W. Yetton, *Leadership and Decision-making* (Pittsburgh: University of Pittsburgh Press, 1973). Reprinted by permission of the University of Pittsburgh Press.

cially with regard to the time criterion. The authors also confirmed that some leaders are more concerned with decision quality and others with decision acceptance. Vroom and Jago (1978) reported that use of the theory enhanced decision acceptance; lesser gains were made in decision quality.

Nevertheless, Field (1979) has criticized these tests on the grounds that almost all the variables are assessed through self-reports of managers. He proposed that some external measures of these variables would result in a stronger test. Field (1982) tested the model in a way that utilized the results of solving actual decision problems as the criterion and found considerable support for it. When leaders followed the prescriptions of the model, 49% of the decisions were effective. However, when decision styles that did not follow the model's prescriptions were utilized, only 36% of the decisions were effective. Jago and Vroom (1982) discovered some sex differences in the use of the leader behaviors. Females who used the autocratic decision-making style were perceived negatively by their subordinates (even when the model prescribed use of the autocratic style), while males who used the autocratic style received modest but positive evaluations. Heilman, Hornstein, Cage, and Herschlag (1984) discovered that autocratic leader behavior was never rated as more effective than consultative or group leader behavior, even when the situation was one in which autocratic behavior was prescribed by the Vroom-Yetton model. It seems subordinates like to have their opinions solicited in problem solving even when their input may not be desired for problem resolution (see Field Note 2).

There seems to be fair empirical support for the Vroom-Yetton theory. Leaders can manipulate decision time, quality, and acceptance by using various decision-making styles or behaviors, but there is always a trade-off: the most expedient behaviors do not always result in acceptable or high-quality decisions. Conversely, decision strategies aimed at producing high group acceptance can take a long time. However, as a theory of leadership, the Vroom-Yetton model is narrow in scope. While decision making is an important aspect of leadership, it is by no means the *only* aspect. The Vroom-Yetton model is not on the same level as Fiedler's theory or path-goal theory in terms of inclusiveness of leadership issues. Though empirically supported, the theory will have to be expanded to be comprehensive. But as limited as the theory is, it is imbued with the contingency flavor that has so dominated leadership research in the past twenty years.

Field Note 2

One of the leader styles proposed by both path-goal theory and the Vroom-Yetton model is participative leadership, which refers to allowing subordinates to participate in the decision-making process. I/O psychologists have experienced considerable difficulty in figuring out the conditions under which this style is effective. Many factors seem to contribute to its success. We can start with the leader. Some individuals like to retain the decision-making authority inherent in their leadership roles, and do not like to relinquish it to their subordinates. One basis for their feelings is that leaders have more expertise than their subordinates, so why dilute the quality of the decision by delegating it to others? Some leaders solve this problem by giving subordinates the authority to make trivial decisions, or what is sometimes called "throwing them a bone."

Another problem is the subordinates. Most of us like to have our feelings solicited in matters that pertain to us, but there are wide individual differences. Some subordinates like to get involved in fine-grained,

nitty details of decisions, and others do not. Some subordinates resent having to make all sorts of decisions. If they are going to be burdened with the responsibility for making administrative decisions, then they want the salary and title that traditionally come with it. When invited by the boss to participate in certain decisions, they are inclined to feel "That's your job, not mine." Willingness to participate is also moderated by the nature of the decision problem. Some problems are fair game for employee involvement, and others are not.

Finally, there are cross-cultural differences in the acceptance of participative leadership. A leading U.S. company once opened a production plant in Latin America. Using the latest leadership ideas that had been learned in the United States, company officials invited the native employees to participate in a wide range of work-related decisions. Within a short period of time after the plant opened, turnover was running exceedingly high. When the company investigated the cause of the turnover, it was shocked to learn its own management practices were primarily responsible. The employees attributed management's participative style as evidence of its ignorance as to how to run the plant. The employees were saying, in effect, "We're the workers, not management. If you don't know how to run your own plant, how do you expect us to know?" Effective use of the participative leadership style is more complex than you might think.

New Theories of Leadership

Leadership is one of the most exciting areas of I/O psychology because of the continuous stream of approaches being formulated. We will examine four of these newer theories, all of which lack the extensive research base of the established theories. What is, in my opinion, intriguing about these theories is not that they attempt to explain the *content* of leadership. Rather, they offer explanations of leadership as a fluid *process*. That is, leadership is viewed more as a means to an end rather than an entity unto itself. While these theories lack extensive research support, they represent some fascinating new ways to think about an old problem.

Cognitive-Resource Utilization Theory

Fiedler proposed a new theory of leadership that draws upon his earlier contingency theory: cognitive-resource utilization theory. Cognitive resources refer to the intelligence, technical competence, or job-relevant knowledge possessed by the leader. The theory addresses how and under what conditions leaders should utilize their cognitive resources to lead their groups. Fiedler and Garcia (1987) propose that when leaders employ directive leader behavior, are not under stress, and enjoy the support of their followers, they will make the most effective use of whatever cognitive resources they possess.

The major focus of cognitive-resource utilization theory is to unravel the conditions for optimum use of leader abilities. The theory asserts that leaders possess two general types of resources to help resolve problems: their prior experience and their intelligence. When a group is under stress because of the tense relationships leaders have with the subordinates, leaders rely on prior experience in leading the group and do not make effective use of their intelligence. Fiedler believes that stress is a variable that can be managed effectively. Thus, through the management of stress it is possible to increase the application of intelligence by leaders—that is, to make fuller utilization of cognitive resources. The theory postulates under which conditions leaders should draw more heavily upon either their prior experience or their intelligence to resolve leadership problems. Similar to contingency theory, Fiedler incorporates both situational and personal variables into his theory of leadership. You can think of cognitive-resource utilization theory as a specification of the process leaders should utilize in dealing with various types of situations to effectuate the success of the group.

Implicit Leadership Theory

All of the previous theories of leadership discussed in this chapter presume that leadership is something that is "out there" for real, and the various theories are merely different ways to explain what it is. A radically different view is that leadership exists only in the mind of the beholder, usually the follower. It may be that "leadership" is nothing more than a label we attach to a set of outcomes. That is, we observe a set of conditions and events and make the attribution that leadership has occurred or exists. Implicit leadership theory regards leadership as a subjectively perceived construct rather than an objective construct. Implicit leadership theory is also referred to by other names, including attribution theory of leadership and social information processing theory.

Lord and his associates have made the greatest contribution to this view of leadership. For example, Lord, Foti, and Phillips (1982) concluded that individuals hold conceptions of prototypic leaders (that is, what they think leaders are like) and then evaluate actual leaders according to their conceptions. People judged as "good" leaders are likely to be those whose actions and demeanors conform to the conception we hold. Thus, "effectiveness" in leadership is not determined objectively but through the confirmation of expectations. Phillips and Lord (1981) discovered that individuals develop global impressions of leader effectiveness and then use those global impressions to describe specific dimensions of leader behavior. Thus, individuals make confident judgments of behavior they had no opportunity to observe, much in the same way halo error operates in performance appraisal. Implicit leadership theory poses a vexing dilemma for the assessment of leaders through questionnaires, as the LBDQ. We don't know if what these questionnaires measure is the actual behavior of the leader or the cognitive set of the rater. While Lord (1985) and Foti and Lord (1987) have proposed strategies to aid in the measurement of leaders, the issues raised by implicit leadership theory challenge the very foundation upon which most of our knowledge of leadership is based.

Charismatic Leadership Theory

Perhaps the most noteworthy characteristic of charismatic leadership theory is the choice of its dependent variables. Rather than examining the more traditional variables of group performance and member satisfaction, charismatic leadership theory examines such variables as the followers' self-esteem, trust, and confidence in their leader, and followers' motivation to perform above and beyond the call of duty. House and Singh (1987) describe the thrust of charismatic leadership as follows:

> . . . in contrast to traditional leadership theories which describe leaders in terms of task- and person-oriented leader behavior, [charismatic leadership theory] describes leaders in terms of articulating and focusing a vision and mission, creating and maintaining a positive image in the minds of followers, setting challenging expectations for followers, sharing confidence in and respect for followers, and behaving in a manner that reinforces the vision and the mission [p. 684].

Charismatic leaders are regarded as individuals who provide for their followers a vision of the future that promises a better and more meaningful life.

It should be apparent that a strong historical antecedent of charismatic leadership theory is trait theory. Rather than providing a lengthy list of leadership traits, charismatic leadership theory focuses upon one trait: charisma. Charisma is defined as "the special quality that gives an individual influence or authority over large members of people" (*Random House Dictionary*, 1984). Charismatic leadership theory has little to offer the area of leadership training because either you are blessed with having charisma or you are not. The theory seeks to explicate the power and influence of those leaders who are judged to be "charismatic," but first assumes that such people exist and can be so identified. Charismatic leadership theory takes a tack rarely witnessed in leadership research; it identifies real-life historical figures (for example, President John F. Kennedy) and seeks to explain why they were successful leaders (House, 1985). I regard charismatic leadership theory as dealing with a relatively small but important piece of the leadership puzzle: a study of selected individuals who united diverse followers and wrought great change through the sheer dint of their personality.

Substitutes for Leadership

We conclude this section on new theories of leadership with an area of research that is not so much formal theory as it is a body of findings that reveal that leadership is a process, a process that can be substituted for.

Kerr and Jermier (1978) have asked what it is that organization members need to maximize in seeking organizational and personal outcomes. They conclude that employees seek both guidance and good feelings from their work settings. Guidance usually comes from role or task structuring; good feelings may stem from any type of recognition. The authors feel that although these factors must be present, they do not necessarily have to come from a superior. While a leader may provide guidance and recognition, so may other sources. In those cases where guidance and recognition are strongly provided by other sources, the need for formal leadership is diminished. The authors reference *substitutes* for leadership and highlight the point that a leader is merely a vehicle for providing these services. Indeed, recently some organizations have experimented with abandoning foremen and supervisor positions, leaving such traditional leadership positions in the hands of the employees organized into special work teams. Such operating procedures are implicit testimony to the practical feasibility of having substitutes for formal leaders.

While not all leadership positions have been abandoned in these organizations, there is evidence that the concept of leadership does not have to be vested in a formal position. Howell and Dorfman (1981) tested the validity of whether leader substitution can replace or "act in the place of" a specific leader. They examined whether such leader substitutes as having a closely knit cohesive work group and tasks that provide feedback concerning performance served to take the place of a formal leader. The authors found partial support for the substitution of leadership, giving some credence to the idea that leadership need not always reside in a person. Further support for leader substitutes was provided by Pierce, Dunham, and Cummings (1984). They examined four environmental sources from which employees get structure and direction in how to perform their work: the job itself; technology; the work unit; and the leader. The authors found that only when the first three sources of structure were weak did the influence of the leader strongly affect employees. It seems that employees can derive typical leader qualities (that is, structure and direction) from inanimate sources in their environments, and that leadership functions need not be associated with someone in authority. It is thus possible to envision a successfully operating leaderless group in which the job itself provides direction in what to do (initiating structure) and the work group members support and tend to one another (consideration) (see Field Note 3).

There is also evidence that some individuals are capable of directing themselves, a concept called "self-leadership." Manz (1986) found some employees could lead themselves if their values and beliefs were congruent with those of the organization. The concept of self-leadership helps to explain why some individuals who are capable of monitoring their own behavior resist the directive leadership style, a finding reported from path-goal theory. In summary, the research on substitutes for leadership suggests that leadership can be thought of as a series of processes or functions for facilitating organizational and personal effectiveness. These processes or functions need not necessarily emanate from a person in a formal leadership role but may be derived from characteristics of the work being performed by the group members.

Field Note 3

I once had an unintended firsthand exposure to what I/O psychologists refer to as "substitutes for leadership." I was on vacation and had the opportunity to tour a small company that made handcrafted shoes. The production area of the company looked like something out of a fairy tale. The company employed about twenty cobblers. Cobblers make shoes on what is called a last. For example, lace shoes would be made on one last, loafers on another, boots on another, and so on. Each cobbler was hunched over his last, fashioning a pair of shoes from leather stock. The room was saturated with the rich aroma of leather. The youngest cobbler had been working there for 16 years, the oldest over 40 years. Their fingers were callused and stained from continuously working with leather. They worked slowly but methodically, developing shoes from a pattern (customers would trace their feet on a piece of paper, which served as the pattern). There was no automated equipment, only hand tools. Every cobbler was an expert in making a certain style of shoe, and generally stayed with making one style. There were some seasonal variations in orders; more boots were made in the winter and more casual shoes were made in the summer. Every cobbler was a craftsman in the truest sense of the word. The year was 1986, but it might as well have been 1886.

While I visited the company as a tourist, the I/O psychologist in me began to creep out. I asked the person who showed me around, "To whom do these cobblers report?" I was told, "No one. We all used to report to the president and founder of the company, but he died eight years ago." I said,

"Who tells these cobblers what to do?" He said, "No one. They know what to do. That's why they work here." I said, "Who runs staff meetings?" He said, "No one. We don't have meetings. Hilda answers the phone and sends out the bills. I order the leather from our suppliers and keep the books. Everyone else makes shoes." I said, "How do you evaluate the work of these cobblers?" He said the finished pair of shoes provided an assessment of the cobbler's work. If the shoes didn't look right, they would be remade. He couldn't remember the last pair of shoes that were defective. If a customer says the shoes didn't fit properly, the cobbler who made them reworks them until they do fit. I concluded my visit by asking two cobblers what they liked most about their jobs. What I had envisioned as an endless series of shoes, they saw differently. They said it felt gratifying to make something useful with their hands.

Each pair they made was a measure of their work, and they took great pride in their work. They also said no two pair of shoes were ever the same. Since they were custom-made shoes, people differed in the size of their feet and their preference for color.

My experience at the shoe company reaffirmed that in some circumstances formal leadership is not necessary. That is, the function that leadership provides, as a sense of direction for one's work and providing support for doing it, can be derived from other sources. The cobblers didn't need direction in how to do their work, and the nature of the work they did provided feedback and support. Thus, as the research suggests, there can indeed be substitutes for leadership. The fact that some work groups can prosper without leaders gives us a clue as to the conditions under which it is needed.

The bulk of this chapter has been devoted to a explication of ten leadership theories. As noted earlier in the chapter, the theories differ not only in their orientation toward leadership but also in terms of the variables they examine and the research questions that guide their development. As a way to aid the reader in classifying and organizing these theories, Table 11–4 presents the ten theories and describes their major focus or perspective of leadership.

Women in Leadership Roles

We conclude this chapter with a departure from theories of leadership to an issue that has considerable practical relevance in the business world of today. It concerns women serving in leadership roles, and the issues and problems they face. As increasingly more women have entered into business and professional careers, I/O psychologists have been able to establish a fairly substantial research base on the topic. Most of what we know is based upon women in *managerial* roles.

While women have been a dominant force in the labor market for many years, only recently have greater strides been made to place them into management positions. Males who want to be managers must be trained to develop administrative skills, but females have an even greater array of skills to master. Many of the problems facing women in management are attitudinal—attitudes women hold about themselves and attitudes about women held by others. These problems relate to role stereotypes, feelings of low self-esteem, and negative assessments of women's compe-

TABLE 11–4 *Ten Leadership Theories and Their Associated Focus or Perspective of Leadership*

Theory	Focus or Perspective
1. Trait	Personal characteristics of individuals that contribute to performance as leaders
2. Behavior	Behaviors exhibited by individuals that contribute to performance as leaders
3. Contingency	The interaction of situational and individual characteristics that results in group performance and member satisfaction
4. Path-Goal	How the use of various leadership styles contingent upon subordinate and environmental factors results in goal attainment
5. Mutual Influence	How superiors and subordinates influence one another in a leader-member relationship
6. Vroom-Yetton	Characteristics of decision-making tasks that determine the behavioral style of leader
7. Cognitive-Resource Utilization	The conditions under which individuals utilize various intellectual resources at their disposal in leadership roles
8. Implicit	The phenomenon of leadership resides in the minds of observers, who attribute its occurrence to perceived events and outcomes
9. Charismatic	How individuals perceived as possessing the personality trait of charisma conduct themselves in leadership roles
10. Substitutes	The conditions under which formal leaders may be substituted for by characteristics of subordinates and the tasks they perform

tence. O'Leary (1974) discussed how these factors are barriers for women. Among the objective problems women face in management are factors relating to role conflict and educational background. Role conflict is the product of tension caused when two or more roles must be filled at the same time but they do not blend well. Traditionally, females have had the main responsibility for homemaking and raising children. But a manager's job requires a major commitment of time and energy, and many women are caught in a bind. They feel they cannot be both a competent manager and a competent homemaker. Also, many managers have either a business or technical education background. These majors have typically been male dominated, though more females are now entering them. Women who do not have this training find it hard to compete for managerial jobs with men who do.

Becoming a successful business manager is an arduous task for anyone. Some recent research has investigated other ways by which this training process can occur. Hunt and Michael (1983) explored the concept of new managers having a mentor. *Mentors* are older, more experienced individuals who advise and shepherd new people in the formative years of their careers. They are professionally paternalistic and serve in a "godparent" role. Hunt and Michael discovered four stages to the mentor relationship. The first is the initiation phase, where the more powerful and professionally recognized mentor recognizes the apprentice as a protégé. The second is the protégé phase, where the apprentice's work is recognized not for its own merit but as the by-product of the mentor's instruction, support, or advice. The third is the breakup stage, where the protégé goes off on his or her own. If the mentor/protégé relationship has not been successful to this point, this will be the final stage. However, if it has been successful, both parties continue on to the lasting-friendship stage. Here the mentor and the protégé have more of a peer-like relationship. The protégé may become a mentor but does not sever ties with the former mentor.

Mentoring is a time-honored way for young professionals to break into the ranks. While this process has historically been very successful for males, it is less effective for females. Why? Most mentors are male and represent the most-senior people in the field of management. Women who adopt male mentors must tread a fine line between getting too close to them and not being too distant. Females with male mentors may be confronted with allegations of a sexual relationship between them, which will weaken the former's professional credibility. Male mentors (particularly if they are married) do not want such allegations aimed at them either because the allegations will also threaten their professional integrity. Sometimes a mentor must be overtly critical of a protégé's work. In such a case, a female protégé may question whether she is being criticized in part for being a woman ("Would he have said the same thing to a male protégé?"), and male mentors become fearful of being charged with sexual harassment.

Sexual harassment (Faley, 1982) covers activities ranging from abusive language to solicitations for sexual favors, but their common basis is that they are directed by members of one sex (typically male) to the other (typically female). Konrad and Gutek (1986) discovered there is a basic difference between men and women in personal orientation toward sexual harassment and how they define it. Women perceive a broader span of behaviors as being harassing than men. The "solution" to all these problems, real and potential, is that many (male) mentors will simply refuse to work with (female) protégés. Rather than risking allegations of sexual misconduct and possible charges of sexual harassment, the mentors solve the problem by avoiding it. Females, too, become leery of entering a professional relationship with male mentors when there is such a power differential. Female protégés can be taken advantage of by male mentors who withhold their support and advice unless the women capitulate to their advances. The culmination of all these divisive forces is the exclusion of more women than men from this mentoring relationship. Given that mentoring is an established method for career development, you can see that some women are at a built-in disadvantage over their male counterparts. Noe (1988) feels the relative exclusion of women from mentoring produces a lack of female role models.

What internal support systems are available for women in their managerial career development? One method is peer relationships: women help one another. Kram and Isabella (1985) described how peer relationships are important in career development. They found there are three types of peers. One is the *information* peer, a person with whom you can exchange information about work in the organization. You share a low level of disclosure and trust, and there is little mutual emotional support. The second type is the *collegial* peer, with whom you have a moderate level of trust and engage in some self-disclosure. Collegial peers provide increased emotional support and feedback and engage in more intimate discussions. The third type is the *special* peer, with whom there are no pretenses and formal roles. You reveal ambivalence and personal dilemmas as you would to few other people in your life. You need not limit peer relationships to members of the same sex, but special peers will most likely be of your sex. Furthermore, the value of peer relationships to career development is not limited to females. However, because of the problems females have in mentoring relationships, the importance of the peer relationship in career development is accentuated for women.

The reader should note there is relatively little formal recognition of gender differences in the established theories of leadership. In terms of theory development, researchers have generally considered leadership issues to be independent of gender. Perhaps continued research along the lines advocated by the newer theories of leadership will incorporate the research findings on mentor and peer relationships. I believe the charismatic and implicit theories of leadership would be sensitive to the types of gender differences in leadership issues identified by past research.

Overview of Leadership Research

Unlike some areas of personnel psychology that are markedly devoid of theory, there is certainly no shortage of theories of leadership. Motivation and leadership are among the two most heavily theoretical areas of I/O psychology. In my opinion there is little debate among I/O psychologists as to what motivation is; accordingly the various theories of motivation simply reflect different ways to conceptualize it. However, I don't feel the same holds in the area of leadership. Some of the (older) leadership theories seek to define "what" leadership is; other theories seek to explain how leadership skills should be used to produce certain desirable outcomes; and yet other theoretical orientations question whether leadership objectively exists at all. The newer theories have transformed leadership into something far more abstract than did their precursors. Scientists often conclude after a lengthy study that the research issues they addressed were far more complex than what they initially thought. I believe the same can be said about I/O psychology and the study of leadership.

Meindl and Ehrlich (1987) discussed what they called "the romance of leadership" as it relates to assessments of organizational performance. In their study subjects give better evaluations to performance outcomes attributed to leadership factors than they gave to the exact same outcomes when they were attributed to nonleadership factors. The authors concluded that leadership has assumed a heroic, larger-than-life quality in the minds of people. Meindl and Ehrlich believe leadership may serve more of a symbolic role, causing people to feel assured and confident that the fate and fortune of an organization are in good hands. Thus leadership may not account for as much of an organization's success as we believe, but 'leadership' has a symbolic value in producing subordinate support, which may then paradoxically produce organizational effectiveness. Although these authors' view of leadership is from the implicit school of thought, I suspect this perspective may be a dominant influence in how I/O psychologists in general come to view the topic of leadership in the years ahead.

MAJOR CHAPTER OBJECTIVES IN REVIEW

After having read this chapter you should know:

1. Major topics of interest among leadership researchers.

2. Major theories of leadership and associated empirical support for:
    a. Trait theory
    b. Behavior theory
    c. Contingency theory
    d. Path-goal theory
    e. Mutual-influence theory
    f. Vroom-Yetton theory

3. New and evolving theories of leadership:
    a. Cognitive-resource utilization theory
    b. Implicit leadership theory
    c. Charismatic leadership theory
    d. Substitutes for leadership

4. Major issues associated with women in leadership positions.

CASE STUDY—What Type of Leader Do I Want?

Ruth McFadden faced a decision she couldn't put off any longer. As vice-president of the Reliance Insurance Company, she had five departments reporting to her. Four departments were running smoothly but the fifth had been troublesome for a long time. It was the Claims Department. The department was responsible for verifying insurance claims filed by policyholders, and authorizing payments to health care providers. The manager of the department had just resigned, to no one's surprise. The department was a real pressure cooker. The volume of medical claims had increased by 28% over the past year, but the department was able to add only two new people. Everyone was feeling overworked. With the ever-changing complexities of the insurance business, an increasing percentage of claims required greater verification. Not all the services provided by health care providers were covered under the various insurance policies offered by the company. The company had recently switched to larger computers to help accommodate the processing of claims, but there were still many bugs in the system. Consequently, the work flow would often get backed up. Turnover was a concern in the department, and employees would seek to transfer to more tranquil departments, or would simply quit the company. Everyone at Reliance knew the Claims Department was the fast track to high blood pressure.

McFadden was faced with picking a new manager for the department. Both final candidates were current employees of the department, and both had great strengths but in different areas. McFadden knew her choice would be critical to the welfare of the department. One candidate was Esther La Quinta. She was extremely knowledgeable about the job from a technical standpoint. McFadden felt La Quinta could lead by example. She was one of the most proficient claims processors in the department. She knew all the operating policies governing payments, and helped debug the new computer system when it was installed. She was often utilized within the department as a resource—someone to turn to for advice on how to get something done. If anyone in the department was an expert on claims payments, it was La Qunita. However, she had some trouble getting along with people. She had a quick temper, and was not very patient in dealing with people who weren't as skilled as she was, which was just about everyone. If the work situation in the department was already stressful, putting her in charge might be like pouring gasoline on a fire. Yet, McFadden thought, she might bring more order to the department by her vast technical ability.

The other candidate was Arlene Davidson. Davidson had great interpersonal skills and was truly liked by all her co-workers. She was a calming influence within the department, helping people through difficult times by being supportive of their efforts. She just seemed to have a way with people that inspired trust and mutual concern. However, Davidson, unlike La Quinta, was not a particularly proficient claims processor. Her work was satisfactory, but nothing more. She seemed intimidated by the new computer system, and frankly admitted she preferred the old system. Putting Davidson in charge of the department would definitely help matters in some regards, but her lack of technical expertise was a real liability. McFadden wondered just who would get the work out if even the manager didn't know what to do.

McFadden was faced with a dilemma. Each candidate had major strengths that were sorely needed in the department. Yet each was lacking in something that was also needed. Each woman could provide leadership ability in her own area, yet their respective shortcomings could well be their undoing. McFadden did not envision any foreseeable changes in the makeup of the department. The volume of work was likely to keep increasing, and would not get any easier to process. With the recent turnover of the manager, there was an added sense of turmoil in the department. McFadden wondered if she should start dispensing tranquilizers to the employees. She felt in a real bind. The Claims Department was critical to the success of the company, and the manager of the department was critical to the success of the department. If she picked the wrong person to lead the department, McFadden knew she might have to go through this all over again. Once, she thought, was enough.

Questions

1. Are there characteristics of the work situation that suggest whom to select for this managerial position? Which ones and why?

2. Do you think it would be easier to train La Quinta in interpersonal skills, or Davidson in technical skills? Why?

3. Do you feel it is more important for a leader to provide technical expertise to subordinates or to facilitate harmony among them?

4. Does McFadden have any other options besides picking La Quinta or Davidson? What might they be, and what are the costs and benefits of doing so?

5. Which theories of leadership do you find to be useful in helping decide what to do in this case?

12

Organizational Communication

Organizational communication is somewhat of an enigma. It is not nearly as heavily researched as job satisfaction, motivation, or leadership; in fact, I/O psychologists have only begun systematic studies in the past 15 to 20 years. One explanation for this historic lack of research is that communication is more an organizational than an industrial topic. In the gradual movement to study more organizational topics, communication has acquired a new recognition and importance in the discipline. Organizational communication is a vitally important topic because communication is central to the concept of an organization. The following quotations illustrate the esteem in which communication is held by organizational scholars:

"The first executive function is to develop and maintain a system of communication" (Barnard, 1938).

"When communication stops, organized activity ceases to exist. Individual uncoordinated activity returns" (Hicks, 1967).

"The communication system serves as the vehicle by which organizations are embedded in their environments" (Guetzkow, 1965).

As Rogers and Agarwala-Rogers (1976) have noted, a major reason for studying organizational communication is that it occurs in a highly structured context. An organization's structure can greatly affect the communication process—communication from a subordinate to a superior is quite different from communication between peers.

Communication is the lifeblood of an organization. It pervades the organization's activities. It is the key means through which individuals understand their organizational roles, and it integrates organizational subunits. Watson (1982) demonstrated that people's roles within an organization could be accurately inferred from the communication patterns among them. Watson found that individuals in leadership roles showed resistance to others' attempts to control a conversation, while subordinates showed compliance. Communication is a means for making decisions, obtaining feedback, and pursuing organizational goals. It is the thread that holds the various interdependent parts of an organization together. If we can learn about communication within an organization, we will have learned a lot about that organization.

Definition of Communication

Probably no other concept has as many definitions as "communication." Dance (1970) identified over 95 definitions of communication that researchers have used. For our purposes we can define *communication* as "the exchange of information between a sender and receiver and the inference of meaning between participants" (O'Reilly & Pondy, 1979). While not all communication occurs in an organizational context, such a context does produce a more restrictive consideration of communication. These restrictions may result from organizational roles (superior versus subordinate), norms (what can and can't be discussed), and structure (lines of authority). Given a typical organizational structure, communication can occur on at least three major levels:

1. *Interpersonal* communication between a sender and a receiver, such as a superior and a subordinate.

2. *Intraorganizational* communication between groups or subunits of the organization, such as between the production and the sales departments.

3. *Interorganizational* communication between organizations, such as between a chemical company and a federal regulatory agency.

Roberts, O'Reilly, Bretton, and Porter (1974) noted that organizational communication may be viewed from any or all of these levels. In a more general sense, Farace and MacDonald (1974) defined organizational communication as the process by which organizationally relevant information is transmitted and received. Organizational communication is a subset of communication in general, a process that is affected by, and in turn affects, all the defining properties of an organization.

Purposes of Communication

Organizational communication has many purposes. It is involved in such processes as leadership, influence, control, planning, and decision making. Behind each of these are functions that communication serves to enhance. Scott and Mitchell (1976) have proposed four such functions of communication:

1. Control—to clarify duties and establish authority and responsibility.

2. Information—to provide the basis for decision making.

3. Motivation—to elicit cooperation and commitment to organizational objectives.

4. Emotive—to express feelings.

A performance-appraisal interview between a superior and a subordinate may manifest all four of these functions. The superior may review a subordinate's goals and objectives as a basis for establishing an evaluative framework—clearly a control function. The subordinate may discuss problems on the job, which can serve as a basis for deciding how the job might best be restructured. If the superior and subordinate reach agreement on goals for the future, the motivational properties of such communication can elicit greater commitment to goal attainment. Finally, the subordinate may air feelings of pleasure and displeasure about various aspects of the job. Other organizational practices also reflect these functions, though some may have a more narrowly defined purpose. Shortly, we will examine several organizational practices and constructs and see how communication is centrally related to each.

A Model of Communication

There are four major components in the communication process: source, message, channel, and receiver. This is referred to as the S-M-C-R model of communication (Berlo, 1960). Though somewhat oversimplified, it is a useful framework for analyzing the communication process. The model in Figure 12–1 shows the four major components plus two others: effects and feedback.

1. Source. The source is the originator of the message. It may be an individual or an institution.

2. Message. The message is the stimulus—the idea—that the source transmits to the receiver. It is what the process of communication is primarily about. Messages may be language symbols (words), nonverbal symbols (facial or bodily gestures), or pictures. *Meanings* are references, such as ideas, images, and thoughts, that the source and the receiver have in common. Without shared meanings, communication cannot occur. Many communication failures are due to mistaken assumptions by the

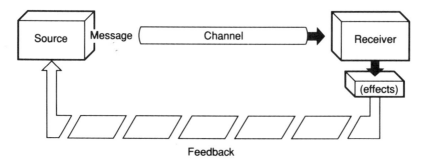

Figure 12–1   The S-M-C-R Model of Communication

SOURCE: David K. Berlo, *The Process of Communication: An Introduction to Theory and Practice.* Copyright © 1960 by Holt, Rinehart and Winston, Inc. Reprinted by permission of Holt, Rinehart and Winston, CBS College Publishing.

source or the receiver about the meaning of a symbol they have exchanged. Berlo stated, "Meanings are in people, not in the message." He meant that words have no meanings in themselves; their meanings are assigned by the source and the receiver.

3. **Channel.** The channel is the means by which a message travels from a source to a receiver. It is the path through which the message is physically transmitted. Channels can be classified into mass media or interpersonal channels. Mass media channels (newspapers, books, radio, and television) enable a source to reach many receivers. Interpersonal channels usually involve a face-to-face exchange between a source and a receiver.

4. **Receiver.** The receiver is the recipient of the message. Receivers are often ignored by the source, which results in a failure to communicate. Some sources are source oriented—for example, textbook authors sometimes write for their colleagues and go over the heads of their student readers. Other sources are message oriented; that is, they know a great deal about the topic but cannot express it meaningfully to their receivers. Still other sources are channel oriented, preoccupied with one channel of communication (writing memos instead of calling a staff meeting). Effective communicators must be receiver oriented because the receivers are the object of the communication.

5. **Effects.** Communication effects are the changes in receiver behavior that occur as a result of transmitting the message. Effective communication is communication that results in changes in receiver behavior that were intended by the source. There are three major types of communication effects: changes in receiver *knowledge*, *attitude*, and *overt behavior*. Normally, but not always, these effects occur in sequence: a change in knowledge (for example, a new company policy) precedes a change in attitude (attitude toward tardiness), which precedes a change in overt behavior (coming to work on time).

6. **Feedback.** Feedback is a response by the receiver to the source's message. The source may take account of feedback in modifying subsequent messages. *Positive feedback* informs the source that the intended effect of a message was achieved; *negative feedback* informs the source that the intended effect of a message was *not* achieved.

To illustrate, I am the source of this communication. The message is the content of I/O psychology. The channel is the printed medium, in this case a book. College students are the primary receivers of the message. The effects of the message are, I hope, a change in receiver knowledge and possibly a change in attitude (about I/O psychology) and overt behavior (perhaps seeking employment in the field of psychology). Feedback—both positive and negative—will be the basis for my revisions in the next edition.

The S-M-C-R model is a useful way to understand the process of communication. Failures to communicate can be caused by "breaks" in any or all of the model's components. Research on organizational communication has also shown some interesting correlates of each component. We will examine these findings later in the chapter.

Communication in Work Behavior

Communication is basic to an organization's functioning since it pervades many aspects of work behavior. We will discuss five topics—selection, job performance, performance appraisal, training, and organizational climate— in terms of their relevance to communication. But keep in mind that communication affects, directly or indirectly, probably every substantive area in I/O psychology.

Selection

The applicant's ability to communicate a desirable impression is of fundamental importance in personnel selection. Applicants have been known to be denied employment because of poor written communication skills revealed on the selection instrument being used. Levine and Flory (1975) have noted that some applicants hurt their chances by not listing full details on an application blank. Some application blanks

Sometimes the meaning of the message is lost between sender and receiver. H. Armstrong Roberts

require applicants to explain why they would like to have the job. The answers are sometimes so disjointed and illogical that they cause the applicants to be turned down.

Letters of recommendation are another type of selection device heavily influenced by written communication. Referees are sometimes unable to adequately describe the applicant for the prospective employer. I have received hundreds of letters of recommendation written for applicants to graduate school. One of the more memorable ones contained this sentence: "If you knew Ralph as I know Ralph, you would think of Ralph as I think of Ralph." Was this an endorsement or a condemnation of Ralph? Obviously the message was distorted between the source (the referee) and the receiver (me).

Effective oral communication skills are critical when the selection instrument is an interview. This holds for both the interviewer and the applicant. The interviewer attempts to foster a positive image of the company as an attractive employer. The applicant tries to impress the interviewer with his or her credentials. The nature of the oral expression and nonverbal behavior of both parties can have a great bearing on the outcome of the selection interview (Schmitt, 1976). Inarticulateness, reticence, verbosity, and redundancy all contribute to lower evaluations. People who cannot express themselves orally suffer negative judgments of their capabilities, particularly in jobs that require a great deal of oral communication. Many seemingly qualified applicants never get a foot in the door because they cannot communicate their skills and abilities effectively.

Job Performance

For some jobs, neither written nor oral communication ability is crucial to job success (such as in some kinds of manual labor). However, the ability to communicate is an important dimension of success for many jobs—for some, in fact, it may be the dominant dimension. Jobs that require interpersonal skills need to be filled by people with communication ability. A survey of major corporations revealed that ability to communicate was the prime requisite of a promotable executive (Randle, 1956).

Given the highly technical nature of many businesses today, clarity in written communication is particularly important. Fielden (1964) noted that many managers cannot write. He suggests using a written performance inventory to evaluate managers' writing skills on four factors: readability, correctness, appropriateness, and thought. Fielden also contends that managers can be trained to write more effectively once their deficiencies have been identified. In a later study, Fielden (1982) suggests that the tone of a written message can be as influential as the content. He advocates the use of a different tone, depending on whether the sender is in a more or less powerful position than the reader.

Oral communication skills are also related to job performance. Wilcox (1959) said that if a person does not understand a *written* report, he or she may reread it, refer back or ahead, or even consult other sources. *Oral* communication disappears into thin air. Therefore, to aid in understanding, voice and language skills must be developed. In an empirical study, Pace (1962) demonstrated that differences between effective and ineffective sales representatives were due to differences in oral communication skills. Less effective representatives were deficient in their use of special types of persuasive communication.

Though most educational and training programs stress knowledge, they rarely teach how to communicate that knowledge to others, even when it is a vital part of the job. Many business and educational leaders make comments like: "It's really too bad about Mr. (or Professor) Jones—he knows his material, but he just can't communicate it to his subordinates (or students)." Effective communication skills are trainable. (We will discuss communication training shortly.)

Performance Appraisal

In Chapter 7, we discussed the importance of the performance-appraisal interview. Superiors should communicate to the subordinate which performance objectives are being reviewed and how well the subordinate is performing on them. A number of studies have revealed several communication correlates of employee satisfaction with the appraisal interview. Nemeroff and Wexley (1977) found that the proportion of time the subordinate spoke in the interview was positively correlated with subordinate satisfaction. Burke, Weitzel, and Weir (1978) reported that subordinates who were allowed to communicate their ideas about planning improvements in their performance subsequently performed better on the job. While the performance-appraisal interview is but one avenue of superior/subordinate communication (Jablin, 1979), the content and process of this communication are related to both subordinate satisfaction and performance.

Other research has studied how employees learn about how well they are performing their jobs. Ashford and Cummings (1983) believe that individuals are motivated to seek feedback from the organization with regard to how well they are doing and how certain behaviors are being perceived and/or evaluated by others. Greller and Herold (1975) identified five sources from which employees receive information about their job performance: the formal organization, superiors, co-workers, the task itself, and personal thoughts and feelings. The authors proposed that the value of these sources for providing appraisal information increases as one moves from psychologically distant sources (the formal organization) to psychologically nearer sources (personal thoughts and feelings). A later study by Hanser and Muchinsky (1978) confirmed the validity of these sources of information. They found that the nearer sources (the task and personal thoughts and feelings) communicated more information to employees than the more distant sources. Finally, Hanser and Muchinsky (1980) showed that the amount of trust employees have in their superiors is related to how accurate and reliable they perceive appraisal information to be.

Thus, appraisal information is communicated to employees from several sources. How believable the information is (especially from superiors) is related to interpersonal trust and affect. The value of performance appraisal information depends on its source.

Training

Communication is important in developing and implementing a training program. The goals of the program should be clearly explained along with the actual content of the training material. If the employees do not understand the message, they will have a very limited opportunity to acquire skills. Because many training programs are in highly technical areas (for example, use of computers), there is a tendency for trainers to lapse into jargon that they understand but that may be foreign to the trainees. As an occasional trainer myself, I have been guilty of this oversight. A company would hire me to train supervisors on how to appraise their employees' performance. At first, I would use expressions like "criterion-related validity," "freedom from contamination," "a minimum of halo error," and so on. Blank stares from the supervisors communicated (nonverbally) to me that I was not communicating (verbally) with them. I knew what I was saying, but I was not getting my message to them, given their level of education and experience. I learned to translate "criterion-related validity" into "the ratings of performance have to be related to how well people are doing their job."

Companies also train their employees directly in how to communicate. Rogers and Farson (1969) described a procedure designed to help people listen, the first step in helping them to understand. Listening is a skill and, like most other skills, can be acquired with practice. The trainee is given a message and is asked to paraphrase it. The differences in what people hear (and see) are amazing—a phenomenon that exasperates police trying to obtain eyewitness testimony about a crime (Woocher, 1977). Oral communication skills can be enhanced by using videotape and other transcription methods. Company executives may go through such communication training, particularly when they are under public scrutiny (Powell, Heimlich, & Goodin, 1980). Written communication skills can be enhanced through workshops and other training methods (for example, Fielden, 1964). Recently, certain types of businesses (such as insurance) have come under fire for issuing documents (for example, policies) that the average person cannot understand. The ability to communicate is becoming an increasingly common area of training.

Organizational Climate

Organizational climate is the combined perceptions of individuals that are useful in differentiating organizations according to their procedures and practices. One climate factor relates to organizational communication—that is, organizations can be differentiated in part on the basis of their communication practices. Sims and La Follette (1975) identified a climate factor they called *openness of communication*; it involved communication between employees and management. Specific items covered managers' willingness to accept and act on subordinates' ideas and management's career counseling of subordinates. Some organizations have receptive climates for communication: open-door policies that encourage employee contact with superiors. Other organizations have more formal communication structures: employees communicate only through channels of authority. Organizations can greatly shape communication behavior by supporting or suppressing open communication.

Some communication climates are better than others for pursuing certain organizational goals. Muchinsky (1977b) correlated several communication variables with measures of both climate and job satisfaction. The perceived accuracy of communication and employee satisfaction with communication were related to the interpersonal atmosphere in the organization, perceptions of management, and judgments about organizational practices. Employees who were dissatisfied with communication and who felt that most communication was inaccurate did not like the interpersonal atmosphere, felt negative toward management, and were critical of the way the organization conducted itself. In addition, employees who felt communication was accurate and were satisfied with it were generally satisfied with their work, their supervision, and their co-workers. Perceptions of organizational communication are vital if a company wants to foster positive feelings in their employees.

Nonverbal Communication

Nonverbal communication refers to the messages we communicate without words. They are powerful and often unintended indicators of how we feel. It has been suggested that while we all can use words to deceive, our nonverbal communications reveal the truth about ourselves. Knapp (1972) presented three major categories of nonverbal communication: *kinesics* (body movements such as eye contact, head nodding, posture, and gestures); *paralanguages* (such as saying "mm-hmm" or "uh-huh"); and *proxemics* (the physical distance between people). We are just beginning to understand what role nonverbal behaviors play in organizational life.

Much of our knowledge is based on studying the employment interview. For example, Imada and Hakel (1977) showed subjects films of simulated employment interviews under two conditions. Under one condition there was a high degree of eye contact by the interviewee, a lot of smiling, an attentive posture, and many hand gestures, and the interviewee sat near the interviewer. Under the other condition the opposite nonverbal behaviors were evidenced. The actual words spoken in both interviews were identical.

What effect did these nonverbal behaviors have on the subjects' evaluation of the candidate? Results showed 86% of the subjects recommended for hire the candidate who exhibited the strong nonverbal behavior; only 19% of the subjects recommended the other candidate. The authors concluded that the judicious use of nonverbal behavior creates a highly favorable first impression in the employment interview.

There has also been research on the effects of nonverbal communication in other areas. Steckler and Rosenthal (1985) had subjects evaluate the competence of both males and females when they were communicating orally to their bosses and to peers. Females were rated as more competent both verbally and nonverbally when they were addressing their bosses. Males, on the other hand, were rated as more competent when they were addressing their peers. The authors concluded that females make an effort to sound more competent to the people who would be most likely to doubt their abilities. Males sound more competent when addressing their peers because of their competitiveness with them, letting co-workers know they are confident and successful. Their lower competence rating when communicating to their bosses may reflect an attempt to reassure them that they are not in direct competition for their jobs. From Chapter 7 on performance appraisal, there is evidence that the physical attractiveness of females is a factor in their evaluations. Gifford, Ng, and Wilkinson (1985) reported that employment interviewers rated job applicants as having greater motivation and social skills when the applicants smiled more, used hand gestures, dressed stylishly, and were talkative. De Meuse (1986) concluded that the frequency of smiling and head nodding is related to overall performance evaluation. Smiling, approving, accepting people seem to receive higher evaluations than their more reserved counterparts. Research on proxemics indicates that distances of 4 to 5 feet seem most comfortable for many North Americans; greater distance is perceived as aloofness.

Nonverbal communication modes cannot be completely understood apart from verbal communication modes. Sometimes the two modes complement each other (an applicant keeps close eye contact and professes interest in the job). Other times, the two modes yield conflicting messages (an applicant yawns while saying the job sounds interesting). We clearly have more to learn about nonverbal communication. Most nonverbal communication is very subtle; while we concentrate on the words being spoken, we unwittingly are influenced by nonverbal behaviors (see Field Note 1). Rehearsing nonverbal behaviors may be more instrumental in getting a job than rehearsing a series of answers to anticipated questions.

Field Note 1

Nonverbal communication has strong cultural ties; that is, what is regarded as acceptable or unacceptable nonverbal social behavior varies across cultures. Several years ago I attended a talk in which the speaker addressed some of the problems associated with the culture clash among diplomats at the United Nations in New York. One particular problem related to proxemics, the issue of how physically close you get to people when conversing with them. One member nation had scheduled a party and invited diplomats from many countries to attend. Two nations each sent one of their diplomats with instructions to discuss some issue, for it is at these types of social affairs that business is often conducted. After going through the recep-

tion line, the two men paired off in a large ballroom.

One diplomat was from a northern European country; the other was from a country in the Middle East. Apparently people from northern Europe prefer greater physical distance between discussants than do people from the Middle East. The diplomat from the Middle East would stand close to the northern European when engaging him in conversation. While listening and talking, the latter would discreetly move first one foot backward and then the second to increase the distance between them. Whereupon the diplomat from the Middle East would move ahead to regain his loss. Over the course of an hour, the diplomat from northern Europe had backpedaled almost completely around the ballroom, and the diplomat from the Middle East had inched his way forward the same distance as he tried to stay near.

When they got back to their respective embassies, both were asked whether the meeting at the party had been successful.

Both diplomats independently agreed that it had not gone well. The northern European diplomat described his associate as "incessantly pushy," while the diplomat from the Middle East described his counterpart as "cold and standoffish."

Techniques of Communicating in Organizations

There are many ways that parts of an organization can communicate with one another and a lesser number of ways that an organization can communicate with other organizations. We will examine some of the more widely used techniques and comment on their particular purposes. We will classify the techniques on the basis of whether they are used mostly for downward communication (that is, from sources high in the structure to receivers in lower-level positions) or for upward communication (that is, from sources in lower-level positions to receivers high in the structure).

Downward Communication

Letters, Meetings, and the Telephone. Before sending any message downward, senders must know what audience they want to reach and how to reach it most effectively. Three of the most common techniques of organizational communication are group meetings, telephone, and letters or memos. Oral media (meetings and telephone) provide personal interchange, are highly adaptable to a wide variety of situations, and can be used when time is crucial. Written communication, on the other hand, is required when the action called for is complex and must be done in a precise way. The written word is not distortion proof, but it has less distortion than its oral counterpart. Written communication provides a permanent form of record keeping, which is often desirable. It's also easier to reach 100 people with a single letter than to make 100 phone calls or schedule a time for 100 people to meet. However, each of these techniques can lose effectiveness if overused. A distinguished visitor from Europe once said that Americans spend too much time in meetings and on the phone. There is certainly no shortage of paperwork that crosses my desk on matters ranging from the crucial to the irrelevant. The sheer volume of junk mail I receive each week makes the truly valuable correspondence especially significant. Between lecturing to my classes, talking with students, reading correspondence, attending staff meetings, and answering the phone, there are days when all I seem to do is engage in varieties of organizational communication.

Recent research on managerial communication reveals the importance of several factors that affect credibility. Morrow, Lowenberg, Larson, Redfearn, and Schoone (1983) had members of a professional personnel organization evaluate the quality of business memos as a function of the author's sex and organizational position. The same memo was rated of higher quality when it was attributed to a female executive than when it was attributed to a female subordinate. There was no corresponding effect for memos supposedly written by male authors (see Field Note 2).

Whitely (1984) identified several dimensions of verbal communication that influence the behavior of managers making oral presentations. Among them were duration of message, size of group being addressed, content of message, and message initiator (oneself or others). D'Aprix (1982) noted that many business managers view the time spent engaging in face-to-face communication as a burden, an activity that interrupts their real work. However, as the author notes, management *is* communication, and the face-to-face mode is often regarded as the most effective means of communication. One source of job-related stress (for example, Gupta & Beehr, 1979) involves the anxiety produced by excessive communication at work. A second but less severe consequence is communication *overload*, which occurs when people receive more information than they can process. We will examine communication overload in greater detail later in the chapter.

Field Note 2

Have you ever written something that was criticized for being "too vague?" I continually advise my students to communicate clearly and directly. Believe it or not, there are times when being vague is the proper and appropriate thing to do. According to Fielden (1982), this occurs under certain circumstances when a person of lesser stature (a subordinate) addresses someone of greater stature (a superior). For example, in writing a memo to your boss, you clearly and concisely lay out the facts and conditions of some case. Then you come to that part of the memo where you would like to recommend your boss take certain action, given the situation. It is here where Fielden advises you to be vague. You should not come out and say what is on your mind, because that would be tantamount to telling your boss what to do. Your boss would "lose face" if it appeared he

or she was incapable of making the correct decision and had to rely on you for direction. Also your boss might interpret your assertiveness as evidence that you want his or her job, since you appear good at telling people what to do.

The solution to this problem is to be vague and indirect in your memo regarding the appropriate course of action your boss should take. Give your boss some leeway to make up his or her own mind, and then hope for the best. If you are clever and somewhat manipulative, you can present the facts in such a way that the desired action is self-evident. However, it has been my experience that some people can be exceedingly obtuse and will not make the "right" decision unless you lay it out for them. My general advice to the contrary: vagueness does have its place in communication—just don't overdo it.

Manuals.   Company manuals are another technique of downward communication. A manual is an integrated system of long-term instructions, brought together between covers, classified, coded, indexed, and otherwise prepared so as to maximize its reference value (Redfield, 1953). Manuals have a high degree of authority and are very formal. They are prepared by the company and intended for a limited audience. Manuals deal mostly with policy, procedure, or organization. A typical supervisors' manual focuses on institutional policy and procedure, personnel administration, and organization structure and interdepartmental relationships. Manuals are usually in the form of loose-leaf notebooks so they can be easily revised. Because manuals are technical and complex, employees should be *trained* in how to use them. A 300-to-500-page technical manual can be quite imposing to a new employee. It will probably collect dust if the employee is simply told, "Here it is in case you ever need it."

Handbooks. Handbooks are usually less authoritative, less formal, less rigidly controlled, and generally applicable at lower organizational levels. Handbooks are also smaller than manuals. The employee handbook is the most popular type; it outlines the duties and privileges of the individual worker. Handbooks have a low-key, friendly, and personal approach; in fact, many of the most stringent company rules may be shown in cartoons. A handbook can simplify material from the manual so that it is more appropriate for a new audience. In one organization, the handbooks were so much more practical that even higher-level supervisors used them instead of their manuals. This was unfortunate since the manuals were much more authoritative and comprehensive. Handbooks are revised less often than manuals, because they are written at a more general level and thus become outdated less quickly.

Newsletters. Company newsletters are usually issued biweekly or monthly. Informal and rarely technical, they are a means of disseminating information to a large number of employees. Newsletters might contain stories about employees cited for perfect attendance or superior job performance, announcements of company social functions, questions and answers about employment issues, and so on. Newsletters are morale boosters; they help make employees in diverse jobs feel that they are part of the whole. Unlike a manual, which communicates specific, job-related information, a newsletter has a mix of personal, social, and work-related information.

Upward Communication

Three techniques are used particularly in upward communication.

Suggestion Systems. A suggestion system is a procedure whereby employees can submit ideas or suggestions for improving company effectiveness. The suggestions are then evaluated by a panel of managers, and the valuable ones are acted on. The initiator of an idea usually gets a cash award (the amount depends on how useful the suggestion is to the company). Large organizations today often award employees over $1 million a year for their suggestions. Some companies use letters of commendation, certificates of merit, and insignia in place of cash, though financial awards are still the most prevalent. Actual suggestion boxes may serve as receptacles for the ideas, or the suggestions may be forwarded through administrative channels.

The rationale behind suggestion systems is that employees are in the best position to contribute ideas for making their jobs more effective. The suggestion system is thus a way to communicate such ideas to the organization. Though some have alleged that there is inequity between the suggestion's value to the company and the size of the cash award, the system is a long-standing practice of upward communication.

Grievances.   As discussed in Chapter 3, grievances are formal written complaints submitted by employees regarding alleged unfair treatment on the job. Grievances can cover almost any topic: working conditions, promotions, pay, disciplinary action, supervision, and work assignments. There are usually several steps in the grievance process. First, the grievance is reviewed by the employee's immediate supervisor. If the grievance cannot be resolved, the next step might be to appeal the grievance to a work unit superintendent. Further steps might involve the company's industrial relations office or use of an outside mediator. The grievance process is more formal in a unionized company, an issue we will discuss in greater detail in Chapter 14.

The grievance process is an established system for allowing employees to air their complaints. The receivers of these messages are usually responsible people who have the power to make justifiable corrections. Without such a system, an employee could channel dissatisfaction in counterproductive ways, such as lowered productivity, increased absenteeism, drug dependence, sabotage, or turnover. Employees do sometimes resort to these when company officials repeatedly ignore grievances or refuse to act on them. Grievances are more than just blowing off steam; they are a way for employees to communicate feelings of injustice in the workplace. Organizations should always have a formal grievance process since grievances are as important as suggestions in upward communication.

Attitude Surveys.   Attitude surveys are probably *the* classic form of upward communication. They are often conducted annually or biannually. The organization uses the survey to learn about employees' feelings and attitudes on many employment issues. The surveys are usually administered by an outside consultant. Responses are anonymous, so employees can speak their minds without fear of identification or reprisal. The employees either complete the surveys at their work stations or in groups in the company cafeteria or meeting rooms. Figure 12–2 shows sample questions from an attitude survey.

Some surveys deal strictly with opinions or attitudes; others add some factual questions to assess employees' knowledge, such as about company benefits. The results are tabulated, and a report is prepared. The company then acts on the information provided. If the employees lack knowledge about the company retirement plan, for example, the company might explain it in more detail. If many employees are dissatisfied with a certain area, such as working conditions, the company should either make improvements or explain why it cannot. The company must respond to the results of the survey, or no one will take the survey seriously. Furthermore, employees will resent being surveyed if the company does not act on their feelings.

1. Do you feel free to discuss problems or complaints with your supervisor?
   a. Always
   b. Usually
   c. Sometimes
   d. Seldom
   e. Never
2. Are your suggestions for changes in the methods of doing your work, which will allow you to work more effectively, carefully considered?
   a. Always
   b. Usually
   c. Sometimes
   d. Never
   e. Have not made any suggestions
3. How useful are the bulletin boards as a means of communication?
   a. Very useful
   b. Useful
   c. Of some use
   d. Of no use
   e. I don't read the bulletin boards
4. Compared to other companies in the area, how do you rate the company's dental insurance program?
   a. Better than other companies'
   b. About the same
   c. Not as good
5. State in your own words what you like best about working for the company.

Figure 12–2   Sample Questions from an Employee Attitude Survey

Attitude surveys can give potent and sometimes surprising information. Employees may admit to doing things differently than the company handbook suggests. Management may find such "discrepancies" annoying or embarrassing, but it would be foolish to ignore them. Attitude surveys can be of tremendous value if employees answer them honestly and management acts on the information they provide.

Methods of Studying Organizational Communication

Organizational communication has been studied with field and laboratory methods. Questionnaires, interviews, observation, and experimental paradigms have all been used (Greenbaum, 1974); in fact, Porter and Roberts (1976) commend the diversity of research methods used in this area. However, a number of research methods are used exclusively or primarily in the study of organizational communication. We will examine four of these methods in some detail.

Activity Sampling

Activity sampling is a field technique in which the investigator records and analyzes communication in process at many points in time and then makes generalizations from these samples. For example, a group of interviewers might ring a bell and then immediately ask each person how he or she was communicating when the bell rang (face-to-face and phone conversations, letters being written or read, purpose of the communication, and so on). Multiple samples can be taken on several consecutive days to get a communication baseline. While the method has been used in a number of studies, it requires a lot of cooperation between the researchers and the subjects. Since studying communication can disrupt work, the techniques used must be unobtrusive.

Sociogram

The sociogram was first developed by sociologists to study group formations. In communication, a sociogram is a graphic portrayal of who communicates with whom in a group. During a set period of time (such as one day), an investigator records interpersonal communication patterns within a work group using a tally sheet or some other coding device.

The sociogram in Figure 12–3 shows a seven-person work group. Person 1 communicates with everyone in the group except person 7 and is probably (but not necessarily) the group leader. He or she is called a "star," a person who communicates with almost everyone else in the group. Persons 2, 3, and 4 form a triad; they communicate with one another as well as with person 1. Persons 5 and 6 form a dyad; they communicate only between themselves and with person 1. No one communicates with person 7, the "isolate." The sociogram is often combined with other methods to get a global perspective of communication patterns. A sociogram does not show the nature of the communication; this has to be collected by another method.

Ecco Analysis

Ecco analysis is a questionnaire-based method developed by Davis (1953). *Ecco* is derived from the words "Episodic Communication Channels in Organization." The basic purpose of the method is to find out when each person first received a certain piece of information. Employees answer the same questionnaire at the same time. The results show the pattern by which information spreads through the organization. For example, Mike and Lorraine said they first got the information from Nick, who said he got it from Ben. The pattern is therefore Ben to Nick to Mike and Lorraine.

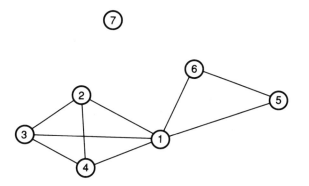

Figure 12–3   A Sociogram Showing Communication Patterns in a Seven-Person Work Group

In practice, the researcher selects an event or piece of information as the subject of the investigation—for example, a major company official is going to quit to take another job. The questionnaire might consist of the sentence, "Jim Link is leaving Fleischman's soon to enter the banking business in Norwalk." Each employee will receive this questionnaire, which might be distributed at the start of the workday. The accompanying instructions ask, "By noon yesterday did you know the information below or any part of it?" The employees then respond by indicating which part of the information they knew, who first told them the information, and the medium by which the information was communicated.

Davis (1953) says ecco analysis has a dynamic quality because it portrays a sequence of communications about an event. It shows the spread of a piece of information from its origin to all persons in the organization who knew it at the cutoff hour (for example, noon). In an empirical test, Davis showed that information was communicated to others who worked at the same job level in the same function. Relatively few people spread the information; most were only passive receivers. In general, ecco analysis has adequate reliability and validity and is most useful for studying the flow of information in an organization.

Flesch Index

Flesch (1948) developed a method to study written communication that has been used for over 40 years. His quantifiable method for calculating the reading ease of written material is based on two factors: (1) the number of syllables per 100 words, and (2) the average length of a sentence in words. Using regression analysis he derived the following equation:

Reading ease = 207 − .846 (word length) − 1.015 (sentence length).

The derived reading-ease score puts a piece of writing on a scale between 0 (practically unreadable) and 100 (easy for any literate person). We can find the reading ease of this book by subjecting a sample of my writing—first paragraph of Chapter 1—to Flesch's formula. First, count out a 100-word sample of writing. Our sample concludes with the word *image* in the sixth sentence of the first paragraph. Next, count the number of syllables in this 100-word passage; the total comes to 177. Then, compute the average number of words in the sentences used in the 100-word sample. That figure (including the complete sixth sentence) is 17.5 words, based on 105 words in six full sentences. Therefore, the reading-ease score of this book, based upon the first paragraph of Chapter 1, is:

Reading ease = 207 − .846(177) − 1.015(17.5) = 39.5.

Flesch's normative standards for gauging reading ease are shown in Table 12–1. As can be seen, the writing style associated with a reading-ease score of 39.5 is "difficult." The classification of "high school or some college" does indeed describe the level of this book.

Flesch's formula is relevant for many areas of organizational communication. It is a way to gauge if the written message is suitable for the intended audience; for

TABLE 12–1   *Pattern of Reading Ease Scores*

Description of Style	Average Sentence Length	Average Number of Syllables per 100 Words	Reading Ease Score	Estimated School Grades Completed	Estimated Percent of U.S. Adults
Very easy	8 or less	123 or less	90 to 100	4th grade	93
Easy	11	131	80 to 90	5th grade	91
Fairly easy	14	139	70 to 80	6th grade	88
Standard	17	147	60 to 70	7th or 8th grade	83
Fairly difficult	21	155	50 to 60	Some high school	54
Difficult	25	167	30 to 50	High school or some college	33
Very Difficult	29 or more	192 or more	0 to 30	College	4-5

SOURCE: R Flesch, *The Art of Readable Writing* (New York: Harper & Row, 1974).

example, manuals, handbooks, memoranda, and so on can inadvertently be written over the heads of their readers. Reading-ease scores can also be associated with levels of education. Some paper-and-pencil selection tests have been "written" for the college-graduate level, yet the job requires only a high school education. In such a case, the test must be rewritten to coincide with the job's educational requirements. Because Flesch's method is a quantitative way to assess readability, it is a useful diagnostic device.

The Effects of Organizational Structure on Communication

The structure of an organization is its anatomy and the ways in which all the parts interrelate in pursuit of its goals. Structure can influence communication in the organization by limiting and guiding its flow. In fact, some authors (for example, Roberts & O'Reilly, 1978) think of differences among organizations in terms of differences in communication structure. A main purpose of communication within an organization is to help maintain *coordination* among the parts. Depending on the organization's structure, communication can enhance coordination among the parts in different ways. We will examine how three dimensions of organizational structure influence communication.

Size

Perhaps the most obvious structural factor is the organization's size. In a small organization, formal communication rarely exceeds face-to-face interactions. Four or five employees of a gas station can communicate with one another and with customers without letters, memoranda, staff meetings, or phone conversations.

However, what are the communication needs of the large oil company that controls the local gas station (and many others)? The company may have hundreds or even thousands of retail dealerships. It might also be involved in oil exploration, refining, and transportation, as well as other petroleum-related products, such as chemicals. An organization of this size could not survive on just face-to-face communication; it needs the full gamut, particularly written communication. Speed of communication is obviously much slower than in the local gas station. Though all the station's employees need to be equally informed about job-related matters, this is not true of the parent company's employees. For instance, employees in the credit card department do not need to know about problems in the refinery. Thus, communication in a large organization is far more selective and limited (otherwise, the employees would suffer from overload), but the *need* for communication in the parent company is much more acute. There are more parts to coordinate and thus more chances for information to be omitted or distorted. The organization's structure limits possible interactions among group members (O'Reilly & Roberts, 1977a). Its size is a major structural determinant of group interactions and thus a major determinant of the nature and frequency of communication.

Centralized/Decentralized Shape

In a highly centralized organization, vertical (upward and downward) communication is stressed, and there is a lot of "distance" between the top and bottom levels. Communication flows between levels along established lines of authority. How much the organization is mechanized can also influence the amount of vertical communication. Simpson (1959) found that with low mechanization, vertical communication (as indexed by the need for close supervision) was high because supervisors continually had to monitor the work of subordinates. Under conditions of medium mechanization (a typical assembly line), the need for vertical communication was far smaller since the line set the pace of work. Under conditions of high mechanization (highly automated plants), the need for vertical communication was again high because of the necessity of dealing with frequent and serious machine breakdowns.

In a decentralized organization, there are fewer levels of authority. The work units are distributed more horizontally (along similar functional lines). There is a greater emphasis on horizontal communication (among similar work units). Horizontal communication is aimed more at resolving problems and coordinating the work flow; vertical communication is aimed more at issues of control. In a centralized organization, there is a greater desire to maintain control through formal lines of authority. In a decentralized one, there is more need for integration among interdependent parts. Vertical communication is based on power relationships (for example, superior/subordinate); horizontal stresses cooperation among parties at equal levels of power. Employees in highly centralized organizations often say that "everything is done by the book" (heavy emphasis on policies and procedures). Employees in highly decentralized organizations say that communication is informal and that they must "get along with each other" to accomplish their objectives.

Centralized/decentralized shape is not an either/or phenomenon—most companies have some attributes of each. But the shape of the organization influences the use of certain types of communication, which in turn are based on power relationships; that is, the link between shape and communication is strong but indirect. Managers transferred from corporate headquarters to a regional office notice the difference in the way things get done. Power-based, vertical communication is often the norm at headquarters but may not suffice in a regional office. People notice the same thing when they leave the military for civilian jobs. Shape, like size, limits the types of communication an organization uses.

Degree of Uncertainty

Some organizations must deal with changes in technology, labor markets, and the availability of raw materials. In this complex environment, uncertainty threatens the organization's ability to survive and attain its goals. Galbraith (1973) has stated the basic effect of uncertainty is to limit the organization's ability to preplan or to make decisions about activities in advance of their execution. O'Reilly and Pondy (1979) think that uncertainty increases the need for communication among members if the organization is to be effective. In support of this position, Tushman (1978) reported that the more complex the task in a research lab, the greater the amount of technical communication required. Bacharach and Aiken (1977) found that the more routine the task in a work group, the less the employees communicate. Other studies have supported the relationship between uncertainty and communication.

The more uncertainty an organization faces, the greater its need to communicate. The investment industry is a prime example. In this highly uncertain environment, no person or organization has yet found the key to predicting the stock market. Investment companies, therefore, continually need to communicate about financial matters.

The ability to reduce uncertainty through communication is directly related to the effectiveness of the organization. For some companies, it is the difference between adequate and superior performance; for others, between survival and demise. A company that tried to buy and sell stocks at last week's prices would soon be out of business.

Communication Structure Variables

When we think of structural variables, we tend to think of *organizational* structure. But there are a number of variables that pertain to *communication* structure that, alone or in concert with organizational structure variables, influence and control the flow of information. We will examine three communication structure variables.

Communication Networks

A communication network refers to the accessibility of channels of communication among people. Some networks are restrictive: one person communicates with one other person. Other, far more flexible networks allow communication among large numbers of people. Most of the research on communication networks has used laboratory methods and typically examined a network of a certain size, such as five people. By using an intercom or allowing subjects to pass messages through partitions, an experimenter could control who communicated with whom. Several possible five-person networks are shown in Figure 12–4.

A typical study involved giving the subjects a problem to solve collectively, requiring them to share information. (For example, each subject was given a card with five symbols on it, and the group had to find out which symbol was common to all cards.) Measures of performance included the accuracy (correctness) of the group's decision and how much time it took to reach it. The subjects also had to assess group morale in the network.

In terms of problem-solving efficiency, when the task was simple (symbol identification), the centralized wheel, chain, and Y networks (see Figure 12–4) were superior to the circle and all-channel networks (Leavitt, 1951). For more complex problems (as in human relations), the decentralized all-channel and circle networks were faster, made fewer errors, and exchanged more ideas. Similar findings occurred for group morale: the decentralized networks had higher morale than the centralized ones (Shaw, 1964).

What do the findings mean? Though generalizing from the laboratory to the organization should be viewed with caution (Burgess, 1968), there are some meaningful implications. First, for a relatively simple task (as in automated production), the company does not need a system to enable all employees to communicate with one another; such a decentralized communication structure might only confuse matters. However, if an organization is faced with complex problems (as many are), a more decentralized communication structure is desirable. A more rapid exchange of ideas is possible with an all-channel network. An organization can hurt its own cause by forcing members to communicate only through centralized channels of authority; a more open and interconnected system is better. Likewise, forcing people to communicate with one another through strict parliamentary procedure (that is, requiring all communication to flow through a central person) may foster low morale. In general, research indicates that, except as noted, a decentralized communication network is preferable. The supervisor or manager who has an open-door policy in effect produces an all-channel network. The findings from these studies suggest that the most efficient communication structure may not match the company's organizational structure.

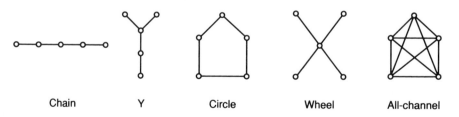

Chain   Y   Circle   Wheel   All-channel

Figure 12–4   Various Five-Person Communication Networks

Communication Roles

The research on communication networks revealed the importance of *communication roles*, the communication functions that people serve within the network. People in central positions within the network are normally more active in communicating and subsequently more satisfied. They have more potential power, both to pass on or withhold information and to introduce new information into the network. We will examine two communication roles: (1) people in positions to control information (*gatekeepers*), and (2) people in positions to bring new information into a group (*liaison*).

Gatekeepers.   To some extent, anyone who can decide what information to pass on to others is a gatekeeper. However, some jobs have more opportunity for gatekeeping than others. Secretaries and administrative assistants are gatekeepers when they decide which matters get to their bosses' attention (O'Reilly & Pondy, 1979). The role of gatekeeper has considerable power.

Research on gatekeeping shows that the power to control information flow is indeed a good way to affect certain outcomes. For example, Pettigrew (1972) described a study in which a company was contemplating buying an expensive computer system. One person within the company was able to control the timing and substance of information sent to the decision-making group. This control allowed the individual to orchestrate the purchase decision. Many administrators tell subordinates "only the information they need to know," but opinions differ over what subordinates need to know. Most employees complain that their superiors withhold too much information rather than not enough.

Gatekeeping occurs in both upward and downward communication. Subordinates sometimes screen out information they think is not important enough for their superiors' attention (upward). Superiors sometimes limit the flow of information to their subordinates (downward). Gatekeeping is a double-edged sword. Failure to gatekeep at all results in information overload; receivers get more information than they can process. Too much gatekeeping results in lack of communication; employees are kept in the dark on matters they feel they should know.

Liaisons.   In many organizations liaisons keep groups informed of one another's activities. Usually, the groups involved do not interact often, so the liaison transmits and receives information among them. The need for liaisons is greater in organizations with highly differentiated work groups or departments. While these groups normally work independently, occasionally they must communicate with one another. This is where the liaison's role is important. Figure 12–5 shows a liaison's role in work groups.

In a study of the plastics industry, Lawrence and Lorsch (1967) found that companies that used liaisons to link highly differentiated departments were more successful than firms that did not. Who serves as a liaison? Schwartz and Jacobson (1977) studied communication in a university and found that liaisons had a legitimate responsibility to involve themselves in the operations of various work groups. Such

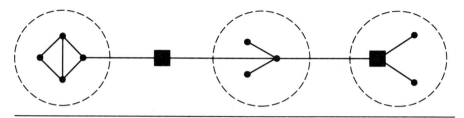

NOTE: The dashed lines represent extant work groups, squares represent liaison role persons, solid circles are nonliaison role persons, and the solid lines represent frequent interpersonal contacts. The liaison role person at the left is not a member of any existing work group, while the liaison role person at the right is a member of a work group.

Figure 12–5 Communication Structure Among Three Work Groups

people were usually administrators who served on various academic committees. Liaisons are welcome in complex organizations because they "let the right hand know what the left hand is doing." Liaisons facilitate coordination among groups, an ability that may be vital to the organization's effectiveness.

Communication Modalities

Communication modalities are the means by which information is communicated between individuals. Face-to-face communication is the most general means of communication throughout an organization. Oral communication is the most effective for exchanging ideas, concepts, or information that needs clarification or elaboration that would not be possible with written communication. People prefer face-to-face interactions in communicating. Muchinsky (1977b) found that frequency of face-to-face communication was positively correlated with work satisfaction and frequency of written communication negatively correlated.

But there are many occasions where face-to-face communication is not enough to meet the organization's needs. The more formal the communication, the greater the need to put it in writing. Technical material is best communciated in writing so that it can be studied and used later as a reference. It is also more efficient to communicate standard information (for example, an orientation program for new employees) in a handbook rather than repeating it orally to each employee. In many cases, a combination of oral and written modes is used; for example, ideas can be exchanged at a meeting and later transcribed into minutes. With the growing trend to hold corporations accountable for their actions, many companies have had to document their communications for future reference. Due to increased litigation, companies have resorted to "paper trails" of documents so they can defend their actions in court.

Communication modes are also misused. I get stacks of letters and memos on matters that could more effectively be handled by a meeting or a phone call; conversely, I attend meetings on matters that could more effectively be handled in writing. Some communicators are "channel-bound"—they use one channel to solve all their communication needs. But while certain modes are more effective in particular cases, the final choice can be partly determined by cost.

Communication Process Variables

In this section, we will discuss the variables that directly affect communication among individuals: *communication process variables*.

Accuracy

"Accuracy" refers to the correctness of the message transmitted from the source to the receiver. Most of the research on accuracy deals with *perceived* accuracy: the extent to which the receiver perceives the information as correct. In a sense, the accuracy of information can be thought of as its validity. But again, do not confuse validity with reliability. Some sources are reliable (giving consistent and predictable messages), yet the messages are inaccurate. The Soviet newspaper *Pravda* consistently reports news favorable to the Communist party, but Western countries question its accuracy.

What factors contribute to perceived accuracy of information? O'Reilly and Roberts (1976) studied the relationship between perceived accuracy and credibility (believability) of the information source. General trustworthiness and expertise of the source were positively correlated with perceived accuracy of the information. People who are trusted for their honesty and others for their expertise are perceived to supply accurate information.

Two other correlates of perceived accuracy have been identified. Roberts and O'Reilly (1974) found that superiors with a great deal of influence in the organization were seen as providing accurate information. One reason that influential superiors have clout is due to their referent power, which has a basis in knowledge and information. Hanser and Muchinsky (1980) reported that trust in the superior also contributed to perceptions of accurate information. Superiors who were trusted by their subordinates were perceived as supplying more accurate performance-appraisal information. In short, perceptions of accurate information are related to three factors: the credibility of the source, the influence of the source, and the amount of trust in the source.

FRANK AND ERNEST by Bob Thaves

WHEN YOU VOTE AGAINST A MOTION TO TABLE A RESOLUTION OPPOSING RECONSIDERATION OF THE VETO OF A BILL, WHAT ARE YOU DOING REALLY?

THAVES

© 1983 Newspaper Enterprise Association, Inc.

Openness

Open communication means a free flow of information and feelings between two or more people. Some people are very guarded; they choose their words carefully. Diplomats are well known for this (and what they say often has to be "translated" into more comprehensible language).

Research on communication openness is limited, but we do know a few of its correlates. O'Reilly and Roberts (1976) reported that a source's credibility is associated with how uninhibited the communication is perceived to be. Research shows that people have more contacts (both job related and social) in a group in which communication is seen to be open. The results suggest that individuals tend to minimize contact with information sources that provide guarded and stilted communication. Guarded communication is a way of maintaining role distance; a lack of candor in communication serves to prevent the parties from becoming psychologically "close." Guarded communication occurs more often in situations where different role status exists. Someone in a higher-status role may refuse to communicate with someone in a lower-status role as a means of maintaining the status differential. The willingness of the higher-status person to be candid varies directly with the magnitude of the discrepancy in role status.

Distortion

Information distortion is the incorrect reproduction of objectively correct information. Gaines (1980) suggests there are three types of distortion. *Puffing* is accenting or exaggerating either favorable or unfavorable aspects of a situation. *Sieving* is the selective filtering of positive or negative details. *Withholding* is the complete omitting or suppressing of positive or negative situational details. Distortion can be caused by either unconscious or deliberate alteration. All too often in an organization, the same message is not received by all parties. After people "exchange notes" on a particular message, there often remain subtle differences in content (for example, "Well, the way I heard it was . . . "). Somewhere along the communication network distortion has occurred.

What causes distortion? A study by O'Reilly (1978) showed several correlates of information distortion. Senders suppress important unfavorable information sent to superiors and accent favorable information about themselves. Subordinates often screen information before sending it upward to avoid upper-echelon overload, but deliberate distortion can have a negative affect (Athanassiades, 1973). This is especially true when important but unfavorable information is suppressed while irrelevant but favorable information is sent. Superiors may lose the ability to discriminate between the relevant and irrelevant with a consequent loss in decision-making performance. O'Reilly also found that low trust in the receiver results in much more suppression by senders, especially when the information reflects unfavorably on the sender. While distortion also occurs in the downward direction (for example, O'Reilly & Roberts, 1974), it appears that downward communication is less susceptible to the suppression of unfavorable information and the magnification of favorable information. Downward communication is seemingly marked more by gatekeeping (the withholding of certain information) than by the alteration or distortion of information; that is, senders passing information downward screen out information not perceived to be relevant for subordinates' tasks.

Overload

Information overload occurs where there is more information than can effectively be processed. The converse of overload is underload: an inadequate amount of information present. Overload is more prevalent than underload. Most of the research on overload deals with its consequences, though an interesting line of research would address what conditions cause it. Meier (1963) studied overload in a library. As requests for library service increased beyond the system's capacity, employee stress and confusion increased and service broke down.

Overload and *underload* are difficult to define precisely. The terms deal with both the amount of information and a person's ability to process it. The same amount of information may be an overload for one person and an underload for another. Therefore, these terms deal more with subjective appraisals than objective measures. In a study on the effects of overload, O'Reilly (1980) found that the volume of information in an environment affects individual satisfaction and performance differently. Overloaded people were more satisfied with communication than those who were underloaded, but overloaded people performed worse on the job. Individuals seem to want more information than they can use, and when they have it they feel more confident about their decisions even though these may actually be of lower quality. Rather than getting more information, they might make better use of existing information. The research on overload rebuts the contention that "more is better."

Miller (1960) reports several individual responses to overload, most of them negative. These responses include (1) omission—failing to process some of the information; (2) error—processing information incorrectly; (3) filtering—separating out less significant and less relevant information; (4) approximation—categorizing input and using a blanket response; and (5) escaping—avoiding the information. Some of these methods are more effective than others. The appropriateness of a response is determined by the task involved and the feedback received after using it.

Chronic and excessive overload can cause psychological stress and tension. Using Miller's terms, I combine of filtering and approximation responses to deal with information overload. I sort my mail into first- and third-class letters (filtering), and throw away all third class unopened (approximation). My rationale is that if the letter was not worth being sent first-class, it was not worth reading. To date, I have not (knowingly) lost any golden opportunities (see Field Note 3).

Field Note 3

When an organization produces a quantity of written documents sufficiently large to cause overload, it must identify each document ac-cording to its salience or criticality. Without such a classifying system, the truly important documents would get lost amidst all the trivial ones. The United States government, including all its departments, agencies, and bureaus, produces hundreds of thousands of documents every year. How does it keep them all straight? With a classification scheme based on the sensitivity of the document. Documents that are considered highly sensitive and are intended for limited audiences are called "classified." Within all classified documents there is a special coding system based on the delicacy of the subject matter being discusssed. The most sensitive documents are classified as "Top Secret," which is one way of insuring that they will be regarded as important and thus will not get lost in the shuffle.

Given the sheer volume of documents produced by the government, many of those that were *not* marked "Top Secret" got overlooked. Government employees began to realize that often only documents marked "Top Secret" got read and got acted upon. Consequently, increasingly more documents were marked "Top Secret" to strengthen the likelihood that they would be regarded as important. As a result, the government became flooded with "Top Secret" documents and that once-special rating lost much of its original value. Were all these "Top Secret" documents truly so sensitive? Not really, but the absence of the "Top Secret" rating could relegate many documents to obscurity. The government became victimized by its own classification scheme, caused entirely by communication overload.

The Outcomes of Communication

If communication in organizations is truly important, it should relate directly to important outcomes, such as performance and satisfaction (O'Reilly & Pondy, 1979). These relationships do indeed exist.

Performance

We can view performance on a number of levels, including individual task performance, group productivity, and the effectiveness of entire organizations. Research shows that communication does influence performance. We have long known (for example, Arps, 1920) that knowledge of results and feedback facilitate performance. Whether the feedback comes from the organization, a supervisor, co-workers, or the task itself (Greller & Herold, 1975), it has both informational and motivational components. Feedback focuses attention on relevant aspects of the task and gives direction as to which behaviors are most desirable or appropriate. Feedback improves job performance in many tasks, ranging from visual search (Mudd & McCormick, 1960) to complex decision making (Schmitt, Coyle, & Saari, 1977). While excessive feedback can cause information overload and decreased performance (Ilgen, Fisher, & Taylor, 1979), with no feedback, behavior is directionless and random.

At the group level, communication is associated with effectiveness. Zand (1962) found in a laboratory study that groups with higher levels of trust and more open communication were better able to solve problems and deal with conflict. O'Reilly and Roberts (1977b) studied 43 U.S. Navy work teams and found that more effective work teams had more open and accurate communication. Special police units (SWAT teams) trained in assault tactics feel that intragroup communication is basic to the efficiency of their units.

While we know less about the relationship between communication and performance at the organizational level, evidence shows that more effective organizations have more information flow across subunits (Lawrence & Lorsch, 1967). Snyder and Morris (1984) examined the impact of communication on total organizational performance. They used several objective measures of overall organizational performance as correlates of communication variables among twelve district organizations within a social service system. The authors found the quality of supervisory communication and the degree of information exchange within the peer work group were related to financial and workload measures of overall organizational performance. Research has also shown that well-developed employee orientation programs can quickly socialize a new employee with a minimum of disruption in the company's work procedures (Marion & Trieb, 1969). Since clear and informative manuals enhance efficiency, many companies hire professionals to write them.

Because there are so many facets to communication, researchers must specify which dimensions of communication they feel will enhance performance. Some indexes of communication may be more related to performance than others. For example, Muchinsky (1977a) suggested there may be no correlation at all between *frequency* of communication and subordinate performance. Two employees may engage in upward communication to an equal degree but for different reasons. One employee may be giving advice and service to a supervisor; the other may need constant guidance and direction. Obviously, the communication differs in content and purpose. Thus, the *nature* of upward communication may correlate with individual performance, and its frequency may not.

In summary, variations in individual, group, and organizational performance can be identified on the basis of variations in communication. Increasing amounts and types of communication enhance performance up to the point of overload.

Satisfaction

Much evidence links communication with satisfaction. O'Reilly (1978) reported that people who felt they were the victims of distorted communication had feelings of low satisfaction. O'Reilly (1980) found that people who experienced information overload were satisfied with their jobs even though the extra information hindered their performance. Individuals who experienced underload were all dissatisfied. Dissatisfaction is also associated with deliberate omission or distortion.

Muchinsky (1977b) identified several communication correlates of job satisfaction. Perceived accuracy of information correlated positively with both facet and overall job satisfaction. Gatekeeping correlated negatively with satisfaction (employees do not like to have information withheld from them). As in other studies, Muchinsky found high job satisfaction is associated with the opportunity to initiate face-to-face interactions. Finally, satisfaction with communication was positively correlated with all aspects of job satisfaction. These relationships are shown in Figure 12–6. Taking a similar view, Hatfield and Huseman (1982) reported the more supervisors and subordinates agreed on the nature and quality of the communication be-

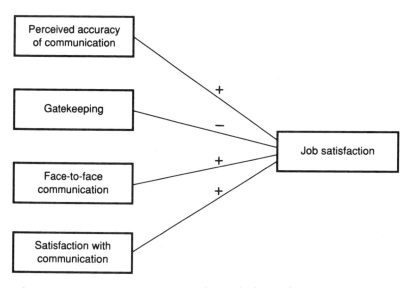

Figure 12–6   Communication Correlates of Job Satisfaction

SOURCE: P. M. Muchinsky, "Organizational Communication: Relationships to Organizational Climate and Job Satisfaction," *Academy of Management Journal, 20* (1977), pp. 592–607.

tween them, the more satisfied were the subordinates with their work, supervision, and the jobs themselves.

People like to be informed and knowledgeable about work-related information. They don't like to be excluded or to have messages altered en route. People want more information than they can effectively process, probably because lack of information breeds insecurity and while overabundance allows them to choose which information to process. Information and the ability to communicate it are forms of power. Power can aid in goal attainment, or it can be misused; failure to communicate is a failure to exercise power adequately.

Summary

The inability to communicate can be due to problems with the source, receiver, message, or channel. Many factors have to work in harmony for communication to occur. In the course of this chapter, we discussed these factors and how they are influenced by a number of extraneous variables.

Communication is a pervasive characteristic of organizations—indeed, without some form of communication, organizations would cease to exist. Communication is the "glue" that holds the parts together. The ability to communicate effectively is extremely important. People with well-developed oral and written communication skills are highly valued by organizations. Communication process variables such as gatekeeping, openness, distortion, and overload influence individual satisfaction and job performance. An organization's structure (size, shape) affects its communication patterns, which in turn are related to individual behavior and attitudes.

MAJOR CHAPTER OBJECTIVES IN REVIEW

After having read this chapter you should know:

1. S-M-C-R model of communication.

2. Basis upon which communication pervades many topics of interest in I/O psychology.

3. Nonverbal communication and its manifestations.

4. Upward versus downward communication within organizations.

5. Communication structure variables, including networks, roles, and modalities.

6. Communication process variables, including accuracy, openness, distortion, and overload.

7. How communication influences both performance and satisfaction.

CASE STUDY—What Do You Want to Know?

The soft drink machine in the lunchroom of the Conover Radiator Company flashed the message "Exact Change Only." Wanda Gilman turned to the woman next to her and asked if she had change for a quarter. Patty Sniezek handed her two dimes and a nickel, and Gilman deposited 60 cents in the machine.

"You new here?" Gilman asked of Sniezek.

"Yes," Sniezek replied, "I just started work last Monday. I'm over in the Molding Department. The only thing I've figured out so far is how to find the bathroom, lunchroom, and time clock."

"You'll get used to it," Gilman said as she headed for a table. "Sit down, and I'll fill you in."

Both women opened their lunches. "The first thing you got to know," Gilman began, "is who to talk to and who to avoid. If you're in Molding, get to know Connie Rosini. Whatever is happening, Connie knows about it first, and it's usually straight. By the time it gets passed around the floor, people get it all twisted around. I used to be in Molding, and Connie would give me the lowdown."

"How about Phil Tesatore?" Sniezek asked. "He's my foreman, and he was the one who explained my job to me."

"Tesatore? Are you kidding?" Gilman mockingly asked. "He's bucking for a management job. He'll tell you the party line but only what he wants you to hear. Half of what he tells you is wrong, and the other half is old. I bet you won't see much of him any more. After he does his bit breaking in the new people, he takes off. They call him the 'phantom.' He's probably greasing up somebody for a promotion right now."

"They told me in Personnel that he would answer any questions I might have," Sniezek stated.

Gilman shook her head in disbelief. "Look," she said, "about six months ago they changed the parking assignments in the lot. Tesatore whipped up a memo to explain it to everyone in the department. By the time he made his big announcement, everybody already knew about it. Connie got the word and spread it around first. Tesatore gave some line about 'less congestion' in the lot when we leave work, but we figured the real reason was so the foremen and supervisors could park closer to the door."

"And another thing," Gilman cautioned, "if your machine jams, go ask Red Martin what to do. If he can't fix it himself, he'll know who to contact. If you go through channels, it could be hours—and then they'll hold you responsible for catching up on what you missed."

"They did give me a manual to read on my machine," Sniezek explained. "They said it wasn't tough to figure out, but I really don't understand it."

"Don't worry about it," Gilman said. "Nobody reads those damn things anyway. They must have been written a hundred years ago."

"There is one thing maybe you could help me with," Sniezek said. "Do you know where I can get a good babysitter? They told me to check the bulletin board and the newsletter for announcements, but I can't find any."

"The bulletin board and newsletter usually tell you things like who got the highest score in bowling last month. Big deal! See Betty Felice over in the Crating Department. I hear her sister takes in a lot of kids. Maybe she can help you."

"Speaking of bowling," Gilman added, "do you bowl?"

"A little," Sniezek answered.

"Do you want to get on the team for the summer league?" asked Gilman.

"I'd like to," Sniezek said. "They told me the sign-up announcement would come out in a few weeks."

"By the time the sign-up sheets come out, the team will already be filled. If you want in, I'll get you on today," Gilman instructed.

Sniezek nodded her head. Gilman tapped another woman on the shoulder, said something inaudible, and motioned her head toward Sniezek.

The woman looked up at Sniezek and said, "What's your name?"

Questions

1. How does Gilman assess the credibility of the formal channels of communication?

2. How would Gilman evaluate Rosini and Tesatore in terms of such factors as openness and distortion of communication?

3. Will Sniezek's job satisfaction and performance be affected by her exposure to Gilman? If so, in what ways?

4. In Chapter 8, we discussed the topic of roles. What roles do Rosini and Gilman fill in the organization?

5. Do you feel the discrepancies between what is communicated formally versus informally are inevitable in a large organization? What factors might contribute to the size of a discrepancy?

4

The Work Environment

13

Job Design and Organization Development

Organizations constantly try to maximize the "fit" between worker and workplace. The better the fit, the more likely the organization will be effective and smooth running. Thus far, our discussion of increasing the fit (what we called "person-environment congruence" in Chapter 8) centered on the worker. Using the peg-and-hole analogy, we discussed finding new pegs that fit existing holes (personnel selection) or reshaping existing pegs for better fit (personnel training). However, the problem of fit can be approached by trying to change the shape of the hole. It is possible to change the workplace instead of, or in addition to, changing the worker. The overall purpose is to increase organization effectiveness. This may show itself in greater productivity, lower cost, increased satisfaction, less turnover, and so on.

In this chapter, we will examine two approaches to changing the workplace. One focuses on changing a *job* and is called *job design*. The other has a larger scope and involves more than just a job. It is called *organization development*. The two approaches are not unrelated; some authors consider job design a part of organization development. However, organization development usually involves reorganizing many components of the workplace; job design has a more narrow scope.

To Alter the Worker or the Workplace?

The choice of whether to change worker or workplace is not easy. It is also not strictly an either/or choice; efforts to change the work environment may be made at the same time that workers are being changed. Usually, though, there is more emphasis on changing one or the other. There is no magic formula telling the I/O psychologist which side deserves more attention. This is a matter of professional judgment, best guided by the psychologist's experience with the organization.

The history of the organization's problems is usually the best place to begin. If a company has been successfully manufacturing a product or providing a service, it would be better to replace a few workers who do not perform well than revamp the entire organization. If large parts of the work force have difficulty adjusting to work demands, personnel training may be the best method of raising skill levels to match organization needs. However, when problems seemingly reappear independent of *who* performs the work, thought must be given to altering the workplace. As a rule, it is more difficult to alter the workplace than the workers. Changing one part of an organization usually will have intended or unintended effects on the rest of the organization.

Because organizations are designed to have interchangeable human parts, their life spans can exceed the working life spans of its employees. The complexities of personnel selection, placement, and training notwithstanding, the workplace is less alterable than the work force. Successful organizations learn to alter both as conditions demand. In this chapter, we will look at ways of changing the workplace, recognizing that the constant search for good "fit" warrants giving attention to both sides of the relationship.

Job Design

Historical Overview

Job design originated in the early years of this century. Frederick Taylor, a founder of industrial psychology, believed that efficiency could be improved by carefully designing work to increase productivity. Taylor advocated structuring jobs for simplification and standardization. Simplification meant breaking jobs into small tasks and then having each worker perform a small part of a total operation. A worker does this task repeatedly; the result is extreme specialization. For example, a job might be to connect two pieces of metal with a bolt. This is one part of an entire operation, and it might be repeated over 100 times every hour. Other workers perform similar specialized tasks until the entire product is finally produced through the total efforts of all workers. The work process is also standardized, that is, the sequence of activities performed is the same.

Taylor's approach did improve productivity. Workers were able to produce more goods. Also, the skill levels needed for these specialized tasks were lower, as was the time needed to train workers. In the short run, this approach resulted in economic efficiency. In Taylor's time, economic conditions were not good, jobs were relatively scarce, and people were grateful for whatever work they could get. However, this approach also produced problems. Workers rebelled at highly specialized, routine jobs. Monotony produced boredom, which, when coupled with lack of challenge and a sense of depersonalization, led to dissatisfaction (Dunham, 1979). The behavioral consequences of work simplification and standardization are presented in Figure 13–1.

The dissatisfaction resulting from Taylor's approach showed itself in ways that

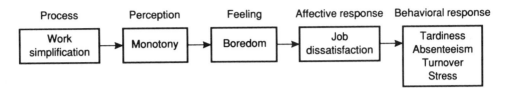

Figure 13–1   Behavioral Consequences of Work Simplification

detract from efficiency: lateness, absenteeism, turnover, stress, drug use, and sabotage. Over time, the problems were exacerbated by changing worker populations. At the turn of the century, workers were relatively uneducated and jobs were scarce: workers were not very critical of the jobs. As the educational attainment of workers increased and more jobs became available, workers were no longer content with jobs that provided little other than income. The economic gains of increased efficiency were offset by reactions to the simplified jobs. The pendulum swung back. Companies realized that efficiency could be enhanced by designing jobs that were gratifying. This has been called the *humanization* of work. Research on job design describes attempts to make jobs "better" by making them more meaningful and rewarding.

Job Enlargement and Job Enrichment

In the 1940s and 1950s, organizations began to realize the structure of jobs must be changed from specialization of work to greater satisfaction of employee needs. During this time, two "job-change" strategies became popular: job enlargement and job enrichment. In theory, the two are different. In practice, they have a lot in common. *Job enlargement* means increasing the number and variety of tasks a worker performs. *Job enrichment* means increasing a worker's control over the planning and performance of a job and participation in setting organization policy (Lawler, 1969). Job enlargement involves expanding the scope of a worker's job duties. An example might be a production worker's responsibility for assembling several parts, as opposed to one, of a piece of equipment. Job enrichment involves giving the worker more autonomy and decision-making power over when and how work operations are performed. At the core of both programs was the belief that motivation would be better if workers had more sense of achievement in their work.

Many early studies examined the effects of job enlargement and/or enrichment on worker behavior and attitudes. One can think of these as field studies—they compared on-site performance before and after job change. Several studies reported increases in either attitude or performance as a result of job-design changes. However, the research was not of the best quality since it rarely used control groups. A company would often introduce new technology along with changes in work operations. It was thus impossible to tell whether the changes in performance and attitude were due to changes in technology or job-design changes. Despite the methodological problems, some authors reported major gains in efficiency. Paul, Robertson, and Herzberg (1969) and Ford (1969) reported improvements in satisfaction, turnover, and production after introduction of job-change programs. However, not all reports

© 1975 Newspaper Enterprise Association, Inc.

were positive. Maher and Overbagh (1971) reported short-term improvements in satisfaction and performance, but after one year, these variables returned to preprogram levels. There was thus some evidence that reported changes in worker response were due more to a Hawthorne effect.

The incomplete research designs and inability to determine causes for change led people to question the value of job enrichment and enlargement. It seemed that both strategies produced changes in worker response but for unclear reasons. Further, changes often lasted for a limited time. As a result, attention was focused on the changes in specific parts of jobs and how these affected behavior and attitudes. More research was directed at explaining why job design succeeded or failed. There were fewer large-scale job-enlargement and job-enrichment programs. Researchers began to identify the structure of jobs and how changing structure would lead to changes in performance.

Task Attributes

As the name suggests, research on *task attributes* was meant to identify characteristics of the task components of jobs that influence worker behavior. In an early study, Turner and Lawrence (1965) identified six task attributes that they thought were related to satisfaction and attendance: variety, autonomy, required interaction, optional interaction, knowledge and skill required, and responsibility. They conducted interviews and made field observations of these six attributes for 47 different jobs. Each attribute was scaled, yielding a score reflecting "how much" of it was present in each job. Jobs that scored high on these variables were positively correlated with high worker satisfaction and attendance. Yet, a curious finding also emerged: this relationship held only for workers from factories in small towns and not for urban workers. Turner and Lawrence concluded that worker reactions to task attributes were influenced by cultural factors. This gave impetus to investigating what "types" of people respond most positively to redesigned jobs. The findings from such studies will be discussed shortly.

Following the Turner and Lawrence study, other researchers investigated how certain task attributes influence performance. Hackman and Lawler (1971) identified four *core* dimensions of jobs: variety, autonomy, identity, and feedback. They concluded that jobs high on these core dimensions, performed by individuals desiring satisfaction of higher-order needs (in the Maslow sense of achievement, recognition, and so on), yielded the greatest satisfaction, motivation, attendance, and performance. A later study by Brief and Aldag (1975) repeated the findings.

It was apparent that motivation was influenced by job structure. Further, it seemed possible to design jobs so as to increase motivation. Research by Steers and Porter (1974), Steers (1975), and Steers and Spencer (1977) produced evidence that jobs providing variety, autonomy, identity, and feedback increased motivation among some employees. This manifested itself in greater organizational commitment and job involvement, as well as in increased attendance and job satisfaction.

It also became apparent that not *all* people responded in the same way. Why people differed in responses to jobs with comparable task attributes had to be explained. Researchers focused on the role of *human needs* in determining the "type" of job a person would want. It was thought that people trying to satisfy *higher-order* needs would want more stimulating jobs. They would thus respond more positively to enriched jobs. Jobs providing high levels of certain task attributes seemingly satisfied such needs.

Several scales were developed to identify people who would want an enriched job and would respond positively to (be more motivated by) it. Hackman and Oldham (1975) developed one such scale: the *Higher Order Need Strength Questionnaire B*. Sample items are presented in Figure 13–2. The relative strength of growth needs is reflected in the choice of jobs characterized by opportunities for decision making, need for a variety of skills and abilities, freedom and independence, and factors such as high pay, fringe benefits, job security, and friendly coworkers (Aldag & Brief, 1979). Results of studies testing the effect of these needs suggest that people with strong higher-order needs do derive more satisfaction from enriched jobs (Hackman & Lawler, 1971). Similarly, both Wanous (1974) and Oldham, Hackman, and Pearce (1976) found that differences in strength of higher-order need moderated the relationship between job characteristics and feelings of satisfaction. However, not all research has been supportive. Stone, Mowday, and Porter (1977) reported little difference in the attitudes and behavior of people with high versus low growth needs. It appears that an individual's desire (need) to be challenged at work does affect reactions to an enriched job, but this alone does not account for all variance.

Job Characteristics Model

Clearly, there has been no one theoretical explanation of why and how task attributes affect workers. The way jobs influence motivation could be partially explained by several existing theories, including Maslow's need hierarchy, Herzberg's two-factor theory, and expectancy theory (Steers & Mowday, 1977). To integrate and synthesize much of the literature on this topic, a model was proposed by Hackman and Oldham (1976) to explain how jobs influence attitudes and behavior. It is called the *job characteristics model* and is probably the most researched explanation of job enrichment.

INSTRUCTIONS

People differ in what they like and dislike in their jobs. Listed below are several pairs of jobs. For each pair, you are to indicate which job you would prefer. Assume that everything else about the jobs is the same—pay attention only to the characteristics actually listed for each pair of jobs.

If you would prefer the job in the left-hand column (Column A), indicate how much you prefer it putting a check mark in a blank to the left of the neutral point. If you prefer the job in the right-hand column (Column B), check one of the blanks to the right of neutral. Check the neutral blank only if you find the two jobs equally attractive or unattractive. Try to use the neutral blank rarely.

Column A   **Column B**

1. A job which offers little or no challenge.

   Strongly prefer A   Neutral   Strongly prefer B

   A job which requires you to be completely isolated from co-workers.

2. A job where the pay is very good.

   Strongly prefer A   Neutral   Strongly prefer B

   A job where there is considerable opportunity to be creative and innovative.

3. A job where you are often required to make important decisions.

   Strongly prefer A   Neutral   Strongly prefer B

   A job with many pleasant people to work with.

4. A job with little security in the somewhat unstable organization.

   Strongly prefer A   Neutral   Strongly prefer B

   A job in which you have little or no opportunity to participate in decisions which affect your work.

5. A job in which greater responsibility is given to those who do the best work.

   Strongly prefer A   Neutral   Strongly prefer B

   A job in which greater responsibility is given to loyal employees who have the most seniority.

Figure 13–2   Sample Items from the Higher Order Need Strength Questionnaire B

SOURCE: J. R. Hackman and G. R. Oldham, "Development of the Job Diagnostic Survey," *Journal of Applied Psychology, 60* (1975), pp. 159–170.

According to Hackman and Oldham, any job can be described by five core dimensions:

1. *Skill variety.* The number of different activities, skills, and talents the job requires.

2. *Task identity.* The degree to which a job requires completion of a whole, identifiable piece of work—that is, doing a job from beginning to end, with visible results.

3. *Task significance.* The job's impact on the lives or work of other people, whether within or outside the organization.

4. *Autonomy*. The degree of freedom, independence, and discretion in scheduling work and determining procedures that the job provides.

5. *Task feedback*. The degree to which carrying out the activities required results in direct and clear information about the effectiveness of performance.

The second part of the model deals with the effect of the core job dimensions on the individual. They are said to influence three critical *psychological states*. The *experienced meaningfulness of work* is high when the job involves skill variety, task identity, and significance. The *experienced responsibility for work outcomes* is influenced mainly by the amount of autonomy. *Knowledge of results of work activities* is a function of feedback. According to the theory, high levels of the critical psychological states will lead to favorable personal and work outcomes. These include high internal motivation, work performance, satisfaction, and low absence and turnover (Dunham, 1979).

The final part of the Hackman and Oldham model is an individual difference variable called *growth-need strength* (GNS); it reflects a desire to fulfill higher-order needs. As had others before them, Hackman and Oldham felt that people with high needs for personal growth and development should respond more positively to jobs high on the core dimensions. Only people with high GNS should strongly experience the critical psychological states associated with such jobs. The entire job characteristics model is portrayed in Figure 13–3.

Hackman and Oldham developed an equation for indexing the potential of a job to motivate its holder. The equation is based on the five core dimensions. Hackman and Oldham refer to their index as the *motivating potential score* (MPS) and define it as

$$\text{MPS} = \frac{\text{Skill variety} + \text{Task identity} + \text{Task significance}}{3} \times \text{Autonomy} \times \text{Feedback}$$

The first three core dimensions are averaged because they all contribute to the experienced meaningfulness of work, the first critical psychological state. The other two dimensions, autonomy and feedback, reflect the remaining critical states and thus are not averaged.

The job's motivating potential will be very high when each component of the formula is high. Because the components are multiplied, low scores on any one will yield a low motivating potential score. In this extreme, a score of zero on any of the major components (for example, a job completely lacking in autonomy) reduces the MPS to zero; the job has no potential for motivating incumbents.

Finally, as shown in Figure 13–3, the entire effect of the job characteristics model is moderated by the strength of growth need. Only employees trying to satisfy higher-order needs will respond favorably to a job high in motivating potential.

Empirical Tests of the Model.   A number of studies have tested the relationships and predictions of the model. Empirical support is mixed. Certain parts of the model are substantiated more than others.

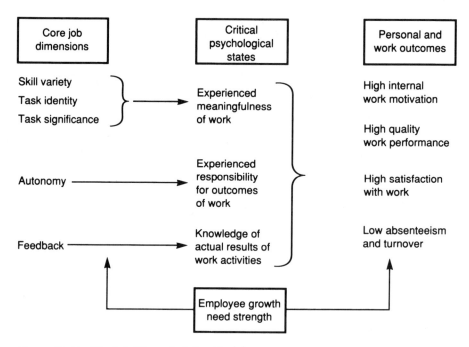

Figure 13–3   The Job Characteristics Model

SOURCE: J. R. Hackman and G. R. Oldham, "Motivation
Through the Design of Work: Test of a Theory," *Organizational
Behavior and Human Performance, 16* (1976), pp. 250–279.

Hackman and Oldham (1976) provided validation evidence for their own theory. In general, the results were moderately supportive:

1. The core job dimensions relate to the critical psychological states. Skill variety, task identity, and task significance combined to predict the level of perceived meaningfulness. The authors were thus able to identify those factors contributing to "meaningful work," a frequent desire of employees.

2. The three critical psychological states related to selected personal and work outcomes. In particular, high levels were associated with satisfaction and internal motivation.

3. Individual differences in GNS have a moderating effect, as Hackman and Oldham suggested. In particular, high-GNS employees were more likely to have favorable personal and work outcomes after experiencing the critical psychological states.

However, not all findings were supportive:

1. The core dimensions of autonomy and feedback were not clearly related to the corresponding critical psychological states of experienced responsibility and knowledge of results. Some of the other dimensions predicted these states as well or better.

2. The critical psychological states were only weakly related to absence and performance.

In general, the results showed that jobs high on the core job dimensions were associated with high levels of personal and work outcomes. Individuals with high GNS responded most favorably to these types of jobs. The importance of the intervening critical psychological states was not strongly supported.

Other studies have tested the validity of the job characteristics model. Evans, Kiggundu, and House (1979) reported mild support for GNS as a moderator of the core job dimensions-psychological states relationship. As with research on expectancy theory, the validity and superiority of multiplying the parts of the MPS formula were not supported. It seemed that a simpler model (perhaps adding the parts) would yield equally good or better predictions. Kiggundu (1983) felt the critical psychological state of "experienced responsibility for work outcomes" could be divided into responsibility for one's own work versus responsibility for others' work. He proposed conceptual refinement based upon *task interdependence*: the extent to which workers facilitate the work of others. Finally, based upon a review of over 200 studies that tested the model, Fried and Ferris (1987) arrived at the following three conclusions. Research suggests the existence of multiple job characteristics, but it is not clear as to how many there are. Second, the linkage between the job characteristics and the critical psychological states is not as strong as originally hypothesized. Third, the personal and work outcomes specified in the model are indeed related to the job characteristics.

While the research on the job characteristics model is not totally supportive of its validity, several points should be kept in mind. First, the model is quite new. As with all explanatory models, modifications will probably be made as empirical tests warrant. Second, the model incorporates a broad range of variables. It proposes relationships among jobs (core dimensions), intervening constructs (psychological states), and work behavior (personal and work outcomes), all moderated by individual differences (GNS). Given such an array, some problems with validity should be expected. A few researchers (for example, Roberts & Glick, 1981) also feel that some research does not directly follow the relationships proposed in the model. If the model has indeed been "misinterpreted," it is not surprising that results have been less than fully supportive. Finally, as always in I/O psychology and science in general, accuracy of measurement is crucial. Many of the concepts are not particularly easy to measure. Thus, the model's accuracy is weakened in proportion to weaknesses in assessing the variables. Problems and issues in measuring job-design variables are discussed in the next section.

Measurement of Job-Design Variables

It is virtually impossible to get pure, objective measures of task characteristics. The variety and autonomy present in a job are usually best ascertained by asking incumbents. In the final analysis, what is important is how workers perceive their jobs, for it is on the basis of these perceptions that they develop feelings about their work.

Therefore, many measurement issues involve the extent to which workers see common dimensions in their jobs.

When Hackman and Oldham (1976) proposed the job characteristics model, they also developed a questionnaire called the *Job Diagnostic Survey* (JDS). This assessed the variables in the model. Hackman and Oldham (1975) felt the JDS would provide a reliable and valid assessment of core dimensions, critical psychological states, and strength of individual growth needs. Perhaps the most critical issue was the number and nature of core job dimensions, for it is these that supposedly are the basis for enriched and meaningful work. Hackman and Oldham proposed five core job dimensions; other researchers tried to confirm their existence.

In testing the validity of the JDS, Dunham (1976) could find little difference in the measures of variety and autonomy. This suggests that the two dimensions are not as distinct as Hackman and Oldham proposed. Dunham also felt that all five dimensions could be subsumed in a single dimension reflecting *job complexity* without losing the meaning of enriched work; that is, it could be said that an enriched job is simply more complex than a routine job. In another study of the JDS, Dunham, Aldag, and Brief (1977) found the concept of enriched work could be defined in terms of two, three, four, and sometimes five factors, depending on its nature. The five core factors proposed by Hackman and Oldham did not appear every time. I/O psychologists seem to agree that certain key factors define enriched work, but they do not seem to concur on what or how many factors there are. There has also been research on other instruments useful in job design (for example, Sims, Szilagyi, & Keller, 1976). But exactly what factors we should measure in designing jobs is also debatable. Sims and associates identified six core job factors, using an instrument they called the Job Characteristics Inventory. As did Hackman and Oldham, they identified variety, autonomy, feedback, and task identity as four core job factors. However, they also identified two factors unique to their study: dealing with others and friendship. Other authors have developed job-design instruments based on a combined theoretical orientation. For example, Campion and Thayer (1985) created the Multimethod Job Design Questionnaire based on motivational, mechanistic, work physiology, and perceptual/motor perspectives. These authors found considerable support for job design based on their tenets.

In summary, attempts to determine the important variables in job design have been only moderately successful. In a general way, we know the types of variables critical to enriched work. Precisely what these variables are for different types of jobs is not consistent. So long as measurement problems persist, it will be difficult to develop a single verifiable model as the foundation for job design. Our limited ability to generalize across different jobs necessitates a more situation-specific approach. This will not preclude "reshaping holes," but it will certainly not make our job any easier (see Field Note 1).

Field Note 1

The process of job enrichment produces an interesting paradox from the monetary-

compensation standpoint. Let us say we have a boring, distasteful job that pays $6 per hour. We decide to enrich the job, making it more inherently pleasurable and satisfying to perform. The changed job now involves greater skill variety and decision-making responsibility. The question now becomes, in which direction should we alter the wage paid to this job after the enrichment? The more common answer would be to *increase* the wage, perhaps to $7 per hour, because the job now requires more talents and responsibility. However, one can also argue the wage should be *decreased*, perhaps to $5 per hour. Here is why.

There are two major forms of compensation or reward: extrinsic (financial) and intrinsic (nonfinancial) rewards. Because the job initially provided very little intrinsic re-

ward, it was necessary for the employer to offer a substantial wage. However, after enrichment the job became more intrinsically rewarding. Thus, to keep the overall level of compensation (extrinsic *and* intrinsic) constant, the extrinsic compensation should be lowered. The extreme case of this logic would be a job that is so intrinsically gratifying that we will perform it for free (that is, no extrinsic compensation at all).

How do you feel about this paradox? Do enriched jobs provide a certain level of their own (intrinsic) reward such that increases in financial compensation are not necessary? Or do we "double dip"—pay higher wages for jobs that are also more satisfying to perform?

How to Redesign Jobs

Given some understanding of what constitutes an enriched job, the next step is actually changing a job to make work more stimulating. The process of job redesign is by no means simple or routine; many factors must be considered. Aldag and Brief (1979) recommend the following procedures for redesigning a job:

1. Assessment of need is the first step. Presumably there is a reason to alter a job, like unsatisfactory turnover, absence, performance, or accident levels. If such a need exists, the redesigned job should meet the following criteria:

   a. It should be simple, demanding a low skill level and short-cycle completion sequences. Such a job is often seen as monotonous.

   b. Altering production methods and procedures should be economically feasible. If redesign entails huge new capital investments (for example, in equipment and facilities), the expected gains in performance might not offset the costs of technology.

   c. Jobholders should accept and be ready for job redesign. This means seeing increased variety, autonomy, and so on, as desirable. The incumbents must also have (or be capable of learning) the aptitudes and skills needed to perform the redesigned work.

2. If a job meets these criteria, a committee or task force should be formed to investigate the prospects further. The task force should include management and labor, as well as outsiders as needed. Those holding the job in question are ideal candidates. The main responsibility of the task force is to study intently the job in question, particularly the tasks to be performed. The best source of

information is a structured job analysis, which may already have been done for another reason, like personnel selection, performance appraisal, or training. The task force should identify exactly the activities that will directly contribute to perceptions of task attributes like autonomy, variety, and feedback. Since the job was chosen because it was seen as monotonous, efforts should be made to understand what it is about it that produces lack of autonomy, task identity, feedback, and so on. The task force should focus on the link between activities performed and holders' reactions to the job along core task dimensions.

3. The task force should then plan some possible redesign aimed at improving the job in terms of task attributes—that is, changes in work performance that can increase feelings of autonomy, variety, feedback, and task identity. Perhaps different changes would contribute to each task attribute. The goal of this phase is to come up with new procedures that will allow workers to get their jobs done and also result in stronger perceptions of the task attributes. The changes may involve expanding the scope of job duties, new sequences of work procedures, or developing a new production system.

4. The task force should choose the criteria used to judge whether redesign has succeeded. Many factors can be included: employee attitudes; objective individual indexes like absence, turnover, and performance; and organization indexes like cost efficiency. These factors will be the "scorecard" for the redesign program. Changes should then be made and employees performance closely monitored. If the efforts were successful, thought might be given to expanding the program to other jobs.

The entire job redesign strategy is presented in Figure 13–4.

Job redesign takes a fairly long time to plan, execute, and monitor—months or years rather than days or weeks. Rigid standards for evaluating the program are also necessary. An organization must be sure that job redesign is truly "worth it" before undertaking major changes. If the changes are attributable only to a Hawthorne effect, the organization would be wise to tread softly; that is, it should be sure that the changes are not due to simply the novelty of new ways of working. Intelligent decisions can be made only by using good information; this in turn necessitates using appropriate evaluation procedures.

Finally, it is not uncommon for changes in one area to have repercussions through the whole organization. Job redesign should not be done in a vacuum. We will shortly examine how job redesign can have "ripple effects."

Example of Job Redesign.   Huse (1980) describes an example of a job redesign and its outcome. A company manufactured laboratory hot plates, which are used in scientific research. The task of assembling the hot plates was highly fractionated; individual employees would repeatedly add one component to each unit as it passed before them in a continuous assembly line. This method of production was highly routinized, according to the concepts of work simplification and standardization.

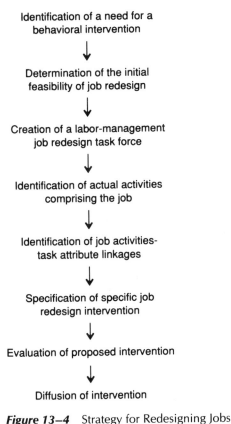

Figure 13–4   Strategy for Redesigning Jobs

SOURCE: R. J. Aldag and A. P. Brief, *Task Design and Employee Motivation* (Glenview, Ill.: Scott, Foresman, 1979). Copyright © 1979, Scott, Foresman and Company. Reprinted by permission.

However, the company was dissatisfied with the level of productivity, the number of defective products, and the degree of absenteeism.

As a means of enhancing efficiency, the company took steps to redesign the job by forming new and larger modules of work. All of the previously separate tasks were combined so that each hotplate could be completely assembled, inspected, and shipped by each operator. The operators could attach their personal name tags to each hotplate. The redesigned job resulted in a 84% improvement in productivity, controllable rejects dropped from 23% to fewer than 1%, and absenteeism dropped from 8% to less than 1%.

A later, sophisticated analysis indicated that the changes were due to the intervention. In accordance with the tenets of the job-characteristics model, the process of combining tasks increased the variety of skills used on the job. Allowing the employees to attach their name tags and personally ship the finished product increased task identity. Self-inspection of the product added greater task significance, autonomy, and feedback from the job itself. While not all job redesign efforts are as successful as this one was, major gains in organizational efficiency can be attained through job redesign.

Effectiveness of Job-Redesign Programs

Does job redesign "work?" Does it produce the intended positive outcomes? We are just beginning high-quality research on the effectiveness of job redesign and taking a hard look at whether it succeeds.

Umstot, Bell, and Mitchell (1976) conducted a field experiment comparing the attitudes (for example, satisfaction) and performance of workers in both enriched and unenriched jobs. The job in question involved identifying and coding land with appropriate zoning codes. The five core dimensions (task attributes) of the job-characteristics model were experimentally manipulated to create both enriched work (high in autonomy, skill variety, and so on) or unenriched work (low on these dimensions). Both male and female employees were represented in both conditions. After two days, employee attitudes and performance were assessed. Those with enriched work were more satisfied, but there were no productivity differences among groups. In the second phase of the study, the routine work was redesigned. Following this, satisfaction increased significantly, but level of performance did not. Umstot and associates concluded that job redesign is effective in producing more satisfying work but not in increasing productivity.

A study with quite different results was done by Locke, Sirota, and Wolfson (1976). The authors conducted a carefully controlled field experiment involving clerical jobs in a federal agency. A redesign program was introduced after careful diagnosis of the work situation; the authors used both experimental and control groups to evaluate effectiveness. In this study, the behavior (productivity and absence) of those with enriched jobs improved significantly, but there were no differences in satisfaction. However, the authors were skeptical about the real cause for the change in worker behavior. They believed that rather than because of enriched work, productivity increased because of more efficient use of personnel, and absenteeism decreased because employees expected to be rewarded for better attendance. When the employees discovered there were no rewards (promotions or raises) for improved performance, they became very angry and bitter. Locke and associates concluded that employees value enriched work not because it is more stimulating or pleasing but only because it is seen as a way of increasing rewards.

The final study we will discuss was done by Hackman, Pearce, and Wolfe (1978). A number of clerical jobs in a bank were redesigned because of technological innovation, which gave the authors a chance to assess the effects of the changes on employees. Some jobs became more complex and challenging, others became less so, and still others remained unchanged. Measures of attitudes and work behavior were collected before and after the changes. Results showed that job satisfaction was directly related to changes in job characteristics; changes in performance and absence depended on employee growth needs. In general, the results supported both the job characteristics model and the concept of job enrichment. The changes in employee attitudes and behavior were as predicted.

As the number of studies conducted on job enrichment has increased in recent years, we are now in a position to examine their cumulative findings. It appears the major outcome of redesigned work is an increase in job satisfaction. Loher, Noe, Moeller, and Fitzgerald (1985) reported average correlations between scores on the five core job dimensions of the job characteristics model and reported job satisfaction around .40. In other words, it seemed that the more jobs are enriched (defined as higher scores on the core job characteristics), the more satisfied are the people who perform them. However, Caldwell and O'Reilly (1982) caution against interpreting causality from correlational findings. They argue that it is perhaps that more satisfied workers simply describe their jobs more favorably in terms of job characteristics rather than that job satisfaction is the product of enriched work. Mowday and Spencer (1981) found that jobs with higher motivating potential scores (MPS) incurred less absenteeism and turnover among incumbents than less motivating jobs. Finally, the research relating job characteristics to changes in job performance has produced mixed findings. Locke, Feren, McCaleb, Shaw, and Denny (1980) estimated that across all jobs there is a 17% improvement in productive output after enrichment. However, other authors (Griffin, Welsh, & Moorhead, 1981) report less supportive findings. Griffin and associates feel that poorly designed measures of job performance contribute to the ineffectiveness of some job-enrichment programs.

What can we conclude about the effectiveness of job redesign? Probably the safest conclusion is that results vary depending on the criterion and we cannot simply assume that such programs will have a common outcome. Most studies report mixed findings (improvements in some areas but not others), but total failures have also been cited (Frank & Hackman, 1975). Job redesign is complex; it is hard to generalize findings across diverse situations. Differences can exist not only in redesign techniques but also in employees (age, experience, education, skill level) and workplace (jobs, organizations, union status). In trying to improve the worker-workplace fit by changing the workplace, we should exercise the same caution and concern used in evaluating workers. Just as we know that a given test is not valid for hiring many different kinds of workers, we should also realize that a given job-redesign technique will not always work for different jobs. Unfortunately, there are no universal procedures for selecting or modifying pegs or for reshaping holes. Research on job redesign is still in its infancy, and we are just beginning to understand what determines its effectiveness.

Organizational Implications of Job Redesign

As discussed in Chapter 8, organizations are complex systems composed of interdependent parts. If you alter one part of an organization, changes (often unanticipated) in other parts will likely ensue. As a simple example, suppose job redesign were successful in increasing the output of a production department. The organization would have to accommodate the growing supply of manufactured goods—a warehousing and space problem. It would likely be pressured to increase the sale of these goods as the stockpile increased. If the sales department were successful, the responsibility of the accounting and bookkeeping departments would be increased. Thus, changes in production would have implications for the rest of the organization; such *ripple effects* are not at all uncommon. Organizations often do not understand the consequences of making changes in selected areas.

Dunham (1977) reported a study illustrating this point. He found that jobs characterized by higher scores on the core job dimensions were also associated with higher aptitude levels and higher pay. When an organization wants to make jobs more challenging, they should realize that they will need people with more talent and ability to perform them. Further, increased employee talent will also demand more pay; more talented people are worth more. Schneider, Reichers, and Mitchell (1982) confirmed that elevating the core characteristics of jobs also increased the aptitudes of individuals needed to perform the jobs successfully. Schneider and associates feel that some job-enrichment programs may fail because they increase the aptitude requirements beyond the levels incumbents possess. These types of relationships have often been overlooked in job-design literature. An organization cannot hope simply to make work more interesting without affecting anything else. To the extent that ripple effects are anticipated and beneficial, change strategies like job redesign can be of great value to an organization. However, if their potential impact on the entire organization is not fully comprehended, they may do little more than exchange a headache for an upset stomach (see Field Note 2).

Field Note 2

The study by Campion and Thayer (1985) reveals a contradiction between two fundamental approaches to work design, both of which have a strong psychological heritage. The first approach is called the *human-factors paradigm* (and is presented in greater detail in Chapter 15). This approach emphasizes the design of work in terms of increasing efficiency. It typically involves designing tasks so as to avoid complicated movements, intensive decisions, and other factors that often lead to errors. In general the human-factors paradigm strives to maintain functional simplicity, forthrightness, and directness in the design of task duties. The more complicated the system, the more things that can go wrong; thus, designers strive to keep things simple and straightforward. This philosophy tends to produce tasks that are easy to perform (with the ultimate goal of being "goof-proof") or at least as uncomplicated as possible.

The second approach is the *job-enrichment paradigm*; it, too, seeks to enhance efficiency. However, its tack is very different from the human-factors approach. The job-enrichment paradigm seeks to provide a sense of challenge and stimulation to work. It is precisely *because* many jobs have been designed with simplicity in mind that they are perceived as boring and monotonous. Thus, using a job-enrichment rationale, tasks are designed so as to provide some diversity of human response and, in the process, literally increase the variability in operator behavior—the very thing that the human-factors paradigm seeks to minimize.

As Campion and Thayer discovered, these two approaches make almost polar opposite recommendations for task design. Is there a middle-ground resolution to these conflicting views? Not directly. In the extreme, both approaches are dysfunctional. If every work task were designed to be so simple that it required no human thought or discretion, we would have created a very sterile and unappealing environment. On the other hand, when I get behind the wheel of my car, I am grateful that human-factors psychologists have designed the steering mechanism such that when I want the car to turn left, I simply turn the wheel to the left. I would not want the steering mechanism "enriched" to the point where it would take simultaneous foot, knee, hand, and arm movements to get the car to turn left. In short, each approach has its place in work design, but there are occasions and situations in which it is not clear which paradigm should prevail.

Organization Development

In the first part of this chapter, we discussed job design: changing jobs to make them more interesting and meaningful for the worker. Job design is one way of improving organization effectiveness but by no means the only way. Sometimes the problems facing organizations require solutions beyond making a *job* the unit of change. The topic of *organization development*, often referred to as simply *OD*, concerns the ways in which organizations can grow, change, and develop to function more effectively. In this part of the chapter, we will examine OD.

What Is OD?

A formal subdiscipline of I/O psychology, OD is a new area. It is diverse and rapidly evolving; thus, it has no single all-encompassing definition. Perhaps one of the best definitions has been supplied by the American Society for Training and Development (1975): OD is "an effort planned, organization-wide, managed from the top, to increase organization effectiveness and health through planned intervention in the organization using behavioral science knowledge." There are five key parts to this definition:

1. OD is a *planned* activity since it involves diagnosing problems, implementing a plan, and mobilizing resources to carry out the plan.

2. OD efforts affect the *entire* organization, though the total organization may not be its focal point.

3. OD effects must be managed and supported from the *top*. Like personnel training, discussed in Chapter 6, without support and commitment from top management, OD will fail.

4. OD programs are meant to improve the *health* and *effectiveness* of the organization. Organization health is like individual health: healthy entities can perform at high levels; lack of health precludes this.

5. Goals flow from deliberate *interventions*; procedures may range from altering physical layout to providing sensitivity training for certain organization members.

As the foregoing suggests, OD is broadly based, intentionally designed to facilitate the organization's well-being. As we will soon see, there are many issues to be considered in an OD program.

The Need for OD

Why must organizations be "developed" periodically? This is due not to organization characteristics per se but rather to the rapidly changing environments (technological, social, political, and so on) in which organizations exist. Changing environments exert pressure on organizations; to perform effectively (sometimes just survive), they must change to cope with environments. There are few creatures in life durable and adaptable enough *not* to change over time and still survive. Organizations have a greater need to change now than ever before for at least three major reasons (Huse, 1980):

1. *The knowledge explosion.* For centuries, the amount of knowledge remained at a fairly constant level. From 1600 to 1800, that amount doubled, and again doubled by 1900. As a culture, we now double our knowledge far more often (now estimated at every 50 years) because of tremendous advances in medicine, communication, technology, and so forth. As a result, knowledge quickly became obsolete and organizations dependent on it equally so.

2. *Rapid product obsolescence.* As new knowledge is acquired, old knowledge and products quickly become obsolete. With growing emphasis on research and development, products are quickly replaced by newer versions or models. The design of automobiles, medical instruments, and computers provides three examples of revolutionary changes. Only flexible organizations are likely to compete successfully in such a dynamic market and to continue providing jobs for their workers.

3. *Changing composition of the labor force.* The types of people filling jobs are rapidly changing. Members of today's work force are better educated, and want more from their jobs than did their relatively uneducated counterparts 60 years ago. There are more women and racial minorities in the work force, and they are assuming jobs that they typically did not hold earlier. Two-career families are common, and many people hold more than one job. Organizations must find ways to cope with the changing work force, because people are organizations' life blood.

Given the pressures from legislation, foreign competition, the domestic economy, and social concerns, there is a growing need for organizations to learn to change. Inability to change can have serious implications. Since OD involves organi-

Automation has simplified many jobs, but the work often becomes monotonous—the case of postal workers verifying ZIP codes. How would you enrich this job?   United States Postal Service

zation change, and the need to change is increasingly necessary, OD will probably increase in importance.

Three Basic Concepts

Three concepts are invariably evident in all OD literature. Each has been the subject of extensive investigation; each is also an integral part of any OD effort. Collectively, they are the ingredients of all OD programs.

The Change Agent.   The *change agent* (sometimes referred to as the *interventionist*) is the person who initiates the change. This is usually someone outside the organization (for example, a hired consultant), but occasionally it may be a person within it. The agent is usually involved in diagnosing and classifying problems, identifying courses of action, recommending change procedures, and in some cases actually implementing the changes.

Glickman (1974) proposed that effective change agents possess the following qualities: diagnostic ability, basic knowledge of behavioral science, empathy, knowledge of the theories and methods of their own disciplines, goal-setting ability, and problem-solving skills. Agents must strive to build trust among organization members; they must be seen as being sincerely concerned with improving the organization's well-being. Without this trust, organization members will resist attempts at change.

Also, as Harrison (1970) observed, the agent must intervene only to the extent required for effecting enduring solutions to the problem at hand. If the agent's role is to help the organization diagnose problems and plan strategies for improvement, he or she should not impose predetermined "solutions" with supposed "guaranteed" results. The change agent should never try to exceed the limits of his or her role; these should be mutually agreed on at the start of the program.

The Client.   The *client* is the recipient of the change effort. This may be an individual, a group, or possibly the entire organization. You might not think it would be a problem, but sometimes it is not exactly clear who the client is. For example, an organization may at first hire a consultant to diagnose why an important manager suffers from excessive role overload. It is also agreed that the consultant may offer strategies for alleviating the problem. In diagnosing the problem, the consultant discovers that the manager had assumed increasingly more responsibility because his or her subordinates were seen as incompetent. Rather than overseeing a poor job, the manager gradually assumes responsibility for doing it. At this point, there are three parties (besides the consultant) involved: the manager, the subordinates, and the organization employing these people.

As French and Bell (1978) stated, an agent, in order to help people, must interact with and influence them. If the agent's authority does not extend to interacting with subordinates, the real problem probably will not be resolved. Perhaps the true issue in the situation described is incompetent subordinates, but it could also be a manager who has distorted views of the quality of subordinates' work. Perhaps the manager is not good at delegating, irrespective of subordinates' merits. In this case, how can the consultant help the client, and who in fact *is* the client? In practice, there may be more than one client. The manager may be the *key* client, but there may be various ancillary clients, all part of the total organization. In some cases, helping one client may conflict with enhancing the well-being of another. The agent must decide how the organization can best be helped, realizing that this is not always an easy decision.

The Intervention.   *Intervention* is what the change agent does on behalf of the client. The change agent can engage in a broad range of activities. French and Bell described the major types, including:

1. *Diagnostic activities:* fact-finding to ascertain the state of the system, the status of a problem, the "way things are."

2. *Intergroup activities:* to improve effectiveness of interdependent groups.

3. *Education and training activities:* to improve skills, abilities, and knowledge.

4. *Coaching and counseling activities:* working with people to help them (1) define learning goals; (2) learn how others see their behavior; and (3) learn new behavior to see whether it improves goal attainment.

5. *Life- and career-planning activities:* to enable individuals to focus on life and career objectives and how they might achieve them.

Each of these includes many activities and exercises. They all use conceptual material and actual experience with the phenomenon being studied. Some are directed toward specific targets, problems, or processes. For example, intergroup activities are directed toward work teams; life-planning activities, toward individuals. In general, interventions are structured activities in which selected units (target groups or individuals) engage in a series of tasks directed toward organization improvement.

Generalized Models of Change

How do organizations change? Are there any guidelines for helping consultants see consistencies in the change process? Researchers have tried to formulate theories explaining change; there seem to be repeatable patterns in the process. Since there are so many types of change, it seems impossible to generate an exact and precise "theory" to which all change efforts rigidly conform. As such, they are more "conceptual guidelines" and are referred to as *generalized models* of change.

One of the simplest and oldest was proposed by the eminent social psychologist Kurt Lewin. He saw change as a three-step process: (1) unfreezing, (2) change, and (3) refreezing. *Unfreezing* means weakening the structural support of the system needing change—getting the system to "open up." *Change* refers to moving the system in a new direction. *Refreezing* means reinforcing the changes made—providing support and stability to prevent the system from slipping back to its previous form. While this three-step process is abstract, it is the basis for virtually all successful OD programs.

At a lower level of abstraction, two models of change are endorsed. Again, these models are nothing more than the rationale behind a change agent's efforts. Both try to facilitate change, but each has distinctive characteristics.

Planned Change. The first model is referred to as *planned change* and closely mirrors Lewin's model. It was first developed by Lippitt, Watson, and Westley (1958), and has since been modified and refined by Huse (1980). The basic concept is the dynamic, seven-step process shown in Figure 13–5. The figure also shows Lewin's original notion of unfreezing, change, and refreezing superimposed on the more refined model of planned change. The seven-step process consists of scouting, entry, diagnosis, planning, action, stabilization and/or evaluation, and termination. In the process, consultant and client may change strategies and modify approaches based on continuing diagnosis of the client's problems. This rediagnosis and reformulation is reflected by the feedback arrow 1 in Figure 13–5. If the consultant terminates one program but indicates that other problems needing further work have been identified, the consultant-client relationship may begin anew, as indicated by feedback arrow 2.

The planned-change model has both strengths and weaknesses. It does not emphasize the diagnosis and problem identification of OD, but it quite strongly emphasizes using specific changes to solve specific problems (Sashkin, Morriss, & Horst, 1973). This approach is often based on using a planned-intervention strategy, such as sensitivity training. Other change models are more flexible; strategy evolves

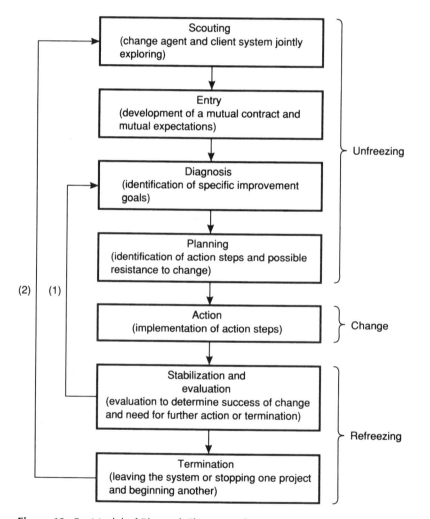

Figure 13–5   Model of Planned Change and Lewin's Concept of Change

from problem diagnosis. Some intervention strategies are widely applicable, but it is not advisable to select a solution before thoroughly analyzing the problem. This is like the personnel training situation in which a training technique is selected before the organization's training needs have been ascertained.

Action Research. *Action research* is the second model of change. Unlike planned change, which *may* have feedback or cyclical properties, action research is based on a cyclical process. The model emphasizes data gathering and preliminary diagnosis before planning and implementing action and developing *new* behavioral science knowledge that can be applied in other organizational settings. The concept was originally proposed by Lewin but has since been expanded by others (for example, Frohman, Sashkin, & Kavanagh, 1976).

Figure 13–6 is a model of action research (French, 1969). While the model seems to have many parts, there are in fact, only seven major components, repeated cyclically.

1. *Identification of problem(s).* This begins when a key person senses one or more problems that might be alleviated by a change agent.

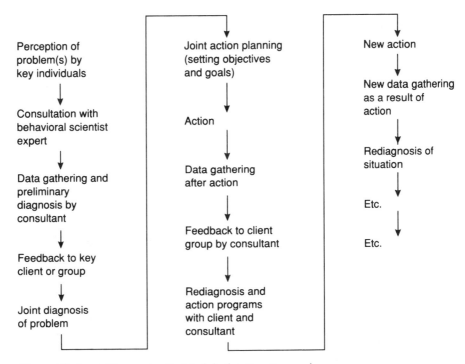

Figure 13–6 A Diagrammatic Model of Action Research

SOURCE: W. French, "Organization Development Objectives, Assumptions and Strategies," *California Management Review, 12* (2) (1969), pp. 23–34.

2. *Consultation with an expert.* The change agent and client establish an atmosphere of trust and openness and establish a collaborative relationship.

3. *Data gathering and preliminary diagnosis.* This is usually done by the consultant to assess the current status of the organization. The most common methods are interviews, observation, questionnaires, and organization performance data.

4. *Feedback to key client.* The results of data gathering are given to the client; this is the change agent's attempt to tell the client about itself. Usually, the change agent is concerned with helping the client determine strengths and weaknesses of the unit in which the change agent is working.

5. *Joint diagnosis of problem(s).* At this point, the change agent and the client discuss the feedback and try to define the real problems that need change. The change agent does *not* "tell" the client what the problem is, as a doctor would do with a patient, but helps the client determine what it is.

6. *Planning and action.* The change agent and client agree on action to be taken. This begins the unfreezing process, as the client starts to move to a different equilibrium.

7. *Data gathering after action.* Since action research is cyclical, data must also be collected to assess the effects of action taken. These new data are again fed back to the client; in turn, this leads to rediagnosis and new action. The entire process is repeated until the consultant-client relationship is ended.

Action research emphasizes evaluation of results, which is why it is called action *research*. Results are evaluated as a basis for further collaborative efforts with the client in the cyclical process of diagnosis, action, and rediagnosis. The method also generates new knowledge that can be used elsewhere. One strength of action research is its emphasis on diagnosis; it analyzes problems from many perspectives. This is especially attractive when problems are not clearly understood or are interdependent. A second advantage is its emphasis on evaluation. Strategies are selected based on the success of preceding strategies. However, one drawback is the model's painstaking approach to problem resolution; this can greatly extend the total change process and create client dependency on the change agent. At some point, the client must be sufficiently "cured" for the change agent to leave the system. It is particularly difficult to end a consultant-client relationship when the client is deeply enmeshed in a cycle.

A few points should be added about planned change and action research. First, not all change agents prefer one or the other. Some agents may favor one approach but use both. Second, certain problems may lend themselves more to one approach than the other. In fact, while each model has distinguishing characteristics, they are not totally different strategies of change. Finally, these are general models, not unyielding operating standards. Depending on the nature of the problem, there may be deviation and certain steps may be more heavily emphasized. In any case, planned change and action research are two rational approaches to OD.

Typology of OD Intervention

Change agents deal with different kinds of clients (individuals, groups, total organizations), fill different roles, and direct their efforts to different problems. Consequently, researchers have tried to integrate the various OD interventions into a typology. A *typology* is a classification of types of things, usually in graphic form, used to promote better understanding of relationships among them. In OD, typologies have classified interventions on such factors as role of the change agent, type of client, types of problems addressed, kinds of interventions, and so on. A typology of OD inteventions based on the research of Blake and Mouton (1976) and White and Mitchell (1976) is shown in Figure 13–7.

A cube is created from the three dimensions of OD interventions. The first dimension is the recipient of the change effort: the client. Basically, agents try to change either selected *individuals, groups of workers,* or *entire organizations*. The second dimension is the level or nature of change. This can be *conceptual* (new information or knowledge), *behavioral* (new skill), *procedural* (new policy or practice), or *structural* (including organization reporting relationships). Finally, four roles of the change agent are presented. In an *acceptant* role, the consultant offers passive support, permitting clients to explore problems and feelings in the presence of an accepting outsider. In a *catalyst* role, the consultant stimulates self-examination by providing feedback on the client's problems; in general, the agent functions as a catalyst for change. The consultant challenges client attitudes or procedures in the

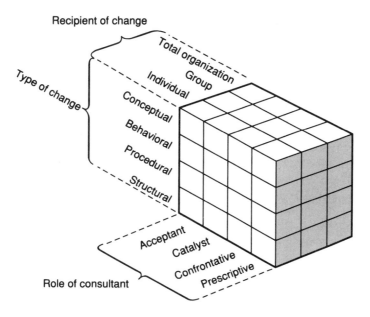

Figure 13–7 Typology of Organization Development Interventions

confrontational role by asking probing questions, presenting discrepant data, and proposing alternatives that will motivate clients. Finally, in the *prescriptive* role, the consultant serves as an expert, controls the situation, and prescribes what should be done.

As reseachers have commented, a change agent's intervention will not fit neatly into one of the boxes in the cube. In an intervention, the key client may be an individual, but that person's relationship to a subgroup may also become an issue. Especially with the action-research model, changes may be sequential and incremental and may affect the way work is performed. Finally, a consultant may, during the intervention, support, stimulate, challenge, or direct the client, depending on the problem and stage of intervention. Nevertheless, a typology is often helpful in ordering the dimensions of a concept. The reader may find that Figure 13–7 serves such a purpose, recognizing that it is only a graphic representation and not a mirror of reality.

Major OD Interventions

As noted, there are many intervention strategies for a consultant to draw on. It is beyond our scope to describe all or even most of them. However, three OD interventions deserve explication.

Process Consultation. *Process consultation* was proposed by Schein (1969) as a means for helping groups to understand the process of interacting with one another. The recipient is the work group. In fact, in the majority of OD interventions, the work group is probably the client. In process consultation, there is an almost exclusive focus on diagnosis and management of interpersonal and group processes. The consultant's role is that of observing groups in action, helping them diagnose the nature and extent of their problems, and helping them better solve the problems.

According to Huse (1980), process consultation focuses on several types of activities. In each case, the consultant's job is to provide feedback to the group about its conduct, with the expectation that tendencies that hamper its effectiveness will be revealed. One area is communication within the group. The consultant observes a group meeting and notes such factors as who does most of the talking, whether people are cut off or are invited to speak, and discrepancies between verbal and nonverbal messages. Another activity concerns the roles of group members. Some members may find themselves presenting factual information, others may provide judgments (for example, "I don't like that idea"), and still others may verify or refute comments. The consultant may videotape a meeting to study members' roles. In many cases, the same people fill the same roles over many meetings. What is fascinating is that the members are rarely (if ever) formally *assigned* these roles; they are *assumed* as a result of the group's dynamics. Yet another activity involves group norms. As discussed in Chapter 8, norms are group standards of behavior. The consultant can assist the group in identifying its own norms and determining whether those norms are helpful.

In many cases, members become so immersed in the group that they fail to "see" communication patterns, role prescriptions, and norm development. For this reason, the consultant serves as an independent outsider. Group members are often surprised at what the consultant observes. Many factors influencing group behavior are subtle. The consultant identifies these influences, describes how they affect interaction, and then allows the group to decide whether changes are warranted. A good process consultant has to be very sensitive and aware of group dynamics. The consultant can feed back only what he or she has observed. Like all skills, observation has to be well developed before it can be effective.

Team Building.   Organizations require the cooperation of many people if work is to be done effectively. Consequently, groups or teams come together permanently or temporarily to accomplish work. The primary purpose of a team is problem solving. However, in many cases problems are ill defined and dependent on other organizational problems and issues. The problem-solving effectiveness of groups can be lowered by many factors, including role conflict and ambiguity, confusion about assignments, and lack of imagination and motivation. An OD consultant may then be called in to strengthen the team's effectiveness. The name given to this intervention strategy is *team building*.

Beer (1976) describes a twofold goal in team building: (1) the immediate barriers to group effectiveness must be removed, and (2) the group must develop self-sufficiency in managing future processes and problems. The consultant's main job is to increase cohesiveness and synchronization, from which benefits follow. Team building relies on diagnosis by the group and setting goals that provide unity of purpose. In most team-building activities, groups spend time examining and finding ways to improve how they structure their approach to work. In many cases, work groups are concerned with effective time use. The group may examine present planning methods, introduce better ones, and identify ways of more effectively using skill and knowledge. As the group develops, it becomes more aware of the need for action about specific problems or tasks as well as for better self-diagnosis of the processes used to accomplish tasks (Huse, 1980).

Team building is one of the more challenging intervention strategies. There are many forces, both temporal and longitudinal, that limit a group's problem-solving ability. Team building is a generic strategy in that different groups have problems for very different reasons. The consultant must be adept at having team members diagnose these problems and develop plans for dealing with them. Team building is not a one-shot process—it usually involves many follow-up interventions (Beer, 1976). The factors contributing to group ineffectiveness are usually not static; thus, team-building strategies may be continuous. The importance of the group and the severity of its problems influence the nature and extent of a consultant's efforts.

Survey Feedback.   A widely used intervention strategy involves systematically collecting data and feeding them back to individuals and groups at all levels. The recipients' task, facilitated by the consultant, is to analyze and interpret the data and develop corrective action based on the results. These activities are called *survey feedback* (French & Bell, 1978). There are two major components: use of attitude surveys and feedback workshops. Survey feedback may be used as part of team building, but it generally serves a much broader purpose.

Many organizations use attitude surveys to assess current feelings; survey feedback involves more than administering attitude surveys. Most attitude surveys have limited value for improving organization effectiveness. The survey feedback approach is potentially a very powerful intervention strategy. French and Bell compared the two uses of attitude surveys—traditional and survey feedback—as presented in Table 13–1. As can be inferred, survey feedback requires more "work," but the benefits are also greater.

Neff (1966) stated that in order for change to take place, three things must happen. First, the work group must accept the data as being *accurate*. People often resist data about their organization, asserting, "Employees really don't feel that way—they were just letting off steam." This defensiveness must be overcome. Second, the work group must *accept responsibility* for its part in the problems identified. There can be a tendency to shirk this responsibility, saying, in effect, that dealing with the problem rests with someone else. Third, the work group must commit itself to *solving problems*. It is not enough to identify problems; steps must be taken to resolve them, when possible. Not all problems can be solved. For example, although most employees may be unhappy because a plant is located 20 miles from their home town, the plant cannot be moved to decrease commuting time. However, other steps

TABLE 13–1   *Two Approaches to the Use of Attitude Surveys*

	Traditional Approach	**Survey Feedback or OD Approach**
Data collected from	Rank and file, and maybe supervisors	Everyone in the system or subsystem
Data reported to	Top management, department heads, and perhaps to employees through newspaper	Everyone who participated
Implications of data are worked on by	Top management (maybe)	Everyone in work teams, with workshops starting at the top (all superiors with their subordinates)
Third-party intervention strategy	Design and administration of questionnaire, development of a report	Obtaining concurrence on total strategy, design and administration of questionnaire, design of workshops, appropriate interventions in workshops
Action planning done by	Top management only	Teams at all levels
Probable extent of change and improvement	Low	High

SOURCE: W. L. French and C. H. Bell, *Organization Development: Behavioral Science Interventions for Organization Improvement*, 2nd ed. (Englewood Cliffs, N.J.: Prentice-Hall, 1978). Copyright © 1978. Reprinted by permission of Prentice-Hall, Inc.

might be taken, such as company-sponsored car pools. If *some* of the problems are not dealt with, employees will regard the attitude survey as a farce and treat it as such. The leaders of each work group guide feedback, discussion, diagnosis of problems, and problem-solving action. The consultant's role is to work with leaders, acting as a resource and a facilitator.

Survey feedback has been shown to be an effective change technique in OD. Bowers (1973) reported that it is more effective than process consultation or sensitivity training. Further, Solomon (1976) found that survey feedback is seen as being most effective when the information is negative. Positive information per se does not inspire or direct movement; negative information suggests that movement is desirable and the direction is implied. Solomon feels that survey feedback is particularly useful if an organization is having many problems and the need for change is particularly acute.

When we say that change occurs as a result of OD, there are actually several kinds involved. The first type is called *alpha* change and refers to movement along a scale that reflects relatively stable dimensions. Increased organizational profit following an OD intervention would be one example of alpha change. *Beta* change involves the recalibration of the scale intervals by which change is measured. Managers, prior to leadership development, may see themselves as outstanding leaders. Following development, the same managers may have lower scores on the same assessment instrument because they will have recalibrated themselves and then have a more realistic view of how things are; thus, such lower scores may actually mean successful change rather than failure. *Gamma* change is the most complex type. It basically involves redefining the relevant conceptual problem as a consequence of an OD intervention. In essence, the framework within which the phenomenon is viewed changes. Measuring gamma change is very difficult since the pre-OD measurement is no longer applicable and the post-OD measurement is "off the scale." An example of gamma change would be something like an initial measurement of a work group's problem-solving effectivenss followed by an OD intervention such as team building. The team-building intervention may cause the abandonment of the initial issue—problem solving—and the emergence of a whole new one, such as lack of trust among group members. Research has shown that it is difficult to measure these three types of change accurately (Randolph, 1982), yet it's these very changes that occur when OD is effective. Armenakis, Bedeian, and Pond (1983) laud OD efforts that attempt to assess these types of change, for change is the basic concept that OD tries to bring about in organizations.

An Illustrative Example

My own experience as an OD consultant may help the reader understand the OD process. About 25 years ago, a man developed a new storm door. He found that some people in his town needed it. Because he was mechanically inclined, he built the doors himself. Each morning, he would build two storm doors by hand; in the afternoon, he would install the doors. Soon word about his doors spread, and he got more orders than he could fill. He then rented out a small building and hired two people to assist him in production, while he retained the responsibility for hanging the doors and keeping the company records. As business grew, he was forced to move to a larger building, take on more help, distribute his products over a wider area, and maintain more records.

He discovered there was also a market for storm windows, and he began producing them. Business continued to grow. He opened a second production facility and put his son in charge. Today there are four production facilities and several warehouse distribution centers, along with a total work force of close to 200. The founder and his son felt they could move into more product lines and newer markets, but because they were each working about 70 hours a week, they did not know where they would get the time or energy. At this point, I was called in as a consultant.

I began with lengthy discussions with key people. I discovered that top management was suffering from role overload; there was simply too much to do and not enough time to do it. I learned that as the business grew, top management personally had taken on more and more responsibility. The company president and his son did such things as (1) maintaining the financial records; (2) hiring all personnel; (3) developing new sales territory; (4) designing new products (with a drafting board and pen); (5) responding to all salespeople who called on the company; and (6) ordering materials. It was hardly surprising that there was no time left for planning and growth, which are typical responsibilities of top management. The two top people literally did just about everything but physically stand on the production line. I asked why they took on such wide responsibilities. They told me this was how the company had started; the system had "worked" all along, so why tamper with success? The president and his son were reluctant to give up what they had been doing for years.

It was only after I collected data revealing that employees were not satisfied with their treatment by top management that there was an impetus for change. Employees complained they had only five minutes of contact with the boss each day; they felt they needed more guidance. The feeling was not surprising, given top management's workload. The major impetus for change occurred when I convinced the two top men that only *they* could decide to expand the company (which they wanted to do). If they did not do it, it would never get done. Obviously, something had to give. I got them to see the need for hiring several key people to assume some of their duties. This included a product design engineer, a personnel manager, a sales manager, and a comptroller. By giving up some self-imposed duties, the two top men had more time for activities that would lead to further growth and development.

Let us review some of the text material in the context of this case. Here the client was the total organization, but the focal point of my intervention was top management. Decisions made later would affect many other people in the organization. My role was to first diagnose the *cause* of the problems and then help top management see the need for change. Once the need was recognized, I proposed various alternatives. They would not give up some duties but would consider relinquishing others. I could not tell them what to do, but I did explain the consequences for themselves and the company of the courses of action selected. Once decisions were made, other issues had to be addressed. New jobs had to be created and the right people hired and trained.

I might add that all the changes did not occur overnight. It was almost two years from the time I was first contacted to the hiring of the last major person that completed the company's reorganization. Change is still taking place as new markets and products are found. Both the company and I learned from this experience that change is (1) necessary, (2) difficult, (3) slow, and (4) continuous. OD facilitates change, and for that reason it is a valuable tool for the I/O psychologist. However, there is nothing mystical about organizational change. It is based on careful deliberation and insight and not magic wands or snake oil.

Research on OD

As White and Mitchell (1976) observed, in recent years the *practice* of OD has far surpassed *research* on the subject. With any method or technique we must ask whether it works, to what degree, and whether it is cost effective. Answers can be provided only through research, and OD research is still embryonic. It may be tempting to castigate I/O psychologists for this lack of development, but it is often very difficult to do high-quality OD research. In the case study I reported, it would have been virtually impossible to find a second company of the same size, technology, history, and so on to use as a control. Yet, it is such things as sample size, use of control groups, random assignment of people to experimental conditions, and so on that define "good" research. Given the difficulties in an OD context, it is not surprising that the quality of OD research is not as high as, for example, personnel selection research. Nevertheless, we still must determine the adequacy of our interventions, recognizing that this is sometimes difficult.

The relatively small amount of OD research indicates—not suprisingly—that our methods sometimes succeed, sometimes fail, and often are mixed. Porras and Berg (1978) reviewed the results of 35 empirical studies of OD activities and found them to be mixed. Among the findings were that worker satisfaction does not always increase following intervention; change more often affects *outcomes* (what gets done) than *processes* (how it is enacted); and *individuals* are more likely to change than are *groups*.

White and Mitchell (1976) asked whether many of the positive changes brought about by OD intervention might be due to a Hawthorne effect. This question is unanswerable without appropriate research. It does seem very possible that changes in organization effectiveness might result from any number of strategies rather than from just the one used in a given case. However, this would not totally discount the value of OD. It suggests that OD is effective as a change method, but we may be fooling ourselves about the respective merits of a given OD strategy. Of course, if changes are short-lived, we face a far more serious situation. In such a case, we have a classic Hawthorne effect, and the effectiveness of both a given strategy and the entire OD process will be suspect. Eden (1986) raised the possibility that OD interventions are successful to the extent that they raise expectations for improved performance within the company. That is, interventionists are perceived to elevate the client's expectations for its own improved performance, thus, OD becomes somewhat of a self-fulfilling prophecy. Eden suggests interventionists should be as obtrusive as possible in their change-making efforts to raise these expectations that result in improved productivity. In such a case the consequences of OD are not seen as Hawthorne effects but, rather, the presence of the interventionist is perceived as a catalyst for inducing change.

Terpstra (1981) reported an interesting study directly addressing the relationship between quality of OD research and reported outcomes of intervention. Terpstra evaluated 52 OD studies on such variables as sample size, use of control groups, and sampling strategy. After "scoring" each study on quality of research design, he examined whether the study produced (1) uniformly positive findings, (2) uniformly negative findings, or (3) mixed results. The results are shown in Table 13–2. The higher the average methodology/design score, the better the research. Uniformly positive findings are associated with the lowest-quality research and uniformly negative findings with the highest-quality research. Terpstra's results indicate that we should be hesitant to conclude that OD interventions are effective when we have not carefully determined whether such a conclusion is warranted.

Nicholas and Katz (1985) feel that one reason some OD programs have been ineffective is that certain kinds of dependent (criterion) variables have been used in places in which OD could not possibly have an effect. An example would be production rate, which is premised on the belief that the amount of production is a function of individual efforts. As we saw in Chapter 10, productivity is limited by situational constraints, and many OD programs are not aimed at altering technology. Furthermore, as Bass (1983) illustrates, short-term versus long-term interests may determine whether OD has been successful.

Nicholas (1982) assessed three classes of OD intervention in terms of their reported use and effectiveness. Technostructural approaches (for example, job enrichment) were found to have the greatest impact on worker behavior at the group level but were not effective at the organizational level. Human process interventions (for example, process consultation) were found to be most effective when aimed at salaried workers. Multifaceted interventions (for example, the use of survey feedback followed by team building) were found to be most successful when all levels of the

TABLE 13–2 *Average Methodology/Design Scores for OD Studies Classified by Outcome*

OD Outcome	Number of Studies	Average Score
Uniformly positive	35	2.66
Mixed	12	3.25
Uniformly negative	5	4.80

SOURCE: D. E. Terpstra, "Relationship between Methodological Rigor and Reported Outcomes in Organization Development Evaluation Research," *Journal of Applied Psychology, 66* (1981), pp. 541–543.

organization were involved. Nicholas concluded that no one change technique or class of techniques works well in all organizational settings. Whatever techniques are used, the goal is to enhance the effectiveness with which organizations operate (see Field Note 3).

Field Note 3

It has been my professional experience that OD problems are among the most ambiguous that I/O psychologists can face. The high degree of ambiguity in a problem can be as vexing for the change agent as it is for the client. Here is a problem presented to me by one of my clients, a large insurance company that has been in business for a long time.

Over the past few years, the insurance business has become deregulated, which means there are no longer restrictions placed on the types of companies that can enter the insurance business. Furthermore, other types of businesses are also being deregulated, such as the financial industry. The upshot of all this change in the legal and political environment is that industries no longer have any clear notion of their own "turf." Everybody suddenly is getting into everybody else's business. For example, insurance companies are now offering financial services, banks are offering stockbroker services, retail merchandise outlets are selling insurance, and so on. The old rules and standards simply are no longer operative as the marketplace has become highly turbulent.

My client had observed these changes and said to me, "We realize we have to change with the times. Everything we have ever done has been premised on the way things used to be, but those days are proba-bly gone forever. Furthermore, we anticipate the future will bring even greater changes than we have witnessed to date. What we want from you is to help us decide what we as an organization should be like in terms of structure, staff, and mission *fifteen years from now*. Tell us what we should be so we can compete, survive, and prosper in a world that no one today can even visualize."

In my consulting career, I have taken on a wide variety of "fuzzy" projects, but this one was by far the most ambiguous. Here was an example of a client who was ready for change but had little idea as to where it would or should wind up. Change is often difficult to bring about, even when you know what the objective is. This was a case where, given my inability to predict accurately a most unpredictable future, even the objective was not clear. In such a situation, OD becomes one of the few strategies that change agents can use to bring clients through traumatic and uncertain times. However, even the most skilled interventionists must accept the high degree of ambiguity inherent in some situations. As tempting as it may be to push the client into seeing a more tangible and immediate problem, it will rarely serve the client's best interests. You must use your best professional judgment to solve your client's problems—there is really no other way.

What are the characteristics of successful organizations? Vaill (1982) has identified eight defining characteristics as shown in Table 13–3. It is these characteristics that all OD programs, directly or indirectly, try to develop in organizations.

TABLE 13–3   *Characteristics of High-Performing Organizations*

They are performing excellently against a known external standard.

They are performing excellently against what is assumed to be their potential level of performance.

They are perfoming excellently in relation to where they were at some earlier time.

They are judged by informed observers to be doing substantially better qualitatively than other comparable systems.

They are doing whatever they do with significantly fewer resources than it is assumed are needed.

They are perceived as exemplars of the way to do whatever they do, and this becomes a source of ideas and inspiration for others.

They are perceived to fulfill at a high level the ideals for the culture within which they exist—that is, they have mobility.

They are the only organization that has been able to do what they do at all, even though it might seem that what they do is not that difficult or mysterious a thing.

SOURCE: P Vaill, "The Purposing of High-Performing Systems," *Organizational Dynamics, 2* (2) (1982), pp. 23–39.

Values and Ethics in OD

It is appropriate to end the discussion of OD with a comment on values and ethics. Whenever change is deliberate, someone's value and beliefs are being acted on. The act of change itself is based on a value (that is, change is good or necessary). OD is saturated with values. Sometimes these are implicit, sometimes they are explicit, and sometimes they clash (Connor, 1977). Among the values operative in OD are that cooperation is preferable to conflict, openness is preferable to suppression, and the level of trust and support in most groups and organizations is lower than necessary or desirable. Psychologists have long known that behavior manifests values. The behavior of the change agent and client in an OD intervention is also guided by values. All parties involved should discuss their values before discussing possible choices. Some conflicts over strategies occur because participants disagree about fundamental values. Many times agreement is assumed when, in fact, it does not exist. A manager I knew preferred creating a feeling of competition among his subordinates to see who would come up with the best idea for a project. It would have been foolish to engage in team building to enhance intragroup cooperation when that value was not endorsed by the manager.

The issue of ethics is also vitally important to the OD consultant. Like any professional working with people's lives, the OD consultant must have integrity. Conflicts can arise that directly involve ethical issues. One of the toughest decisions for a change agent is that of when to end a consultant-client relationship (White & Wooten, 1983). On the one hand, the consultant likes to "be there" to help; on the other, there comes a point when the client must break free of the consultant. If the consultant leaves the system too soon, the client may not have the internal resources with which to solve problems. If the consultant prolongs the relationship (all the while being paid a fee), he or she may create a state of being "needed" by the client to survive. When to end a relationship is a matter of professional judgment. No formula will provide the answer. While ethical matters are rarely a case of black or white, they are the substance of the consultant's professional character.

Summary

Seldom in life are we dealt a "pat hand," a set of circumstances so right that changes are never needed. This also true in the work world. Forces affecting work necessitate changes. These forces may come from the workers, the job, or the organization's environment. It is thus necessary to change the workplace to cope with these forces. In this chapter, we looked at two general methods of changing work. Job design involves altering a person's job, usually to make it more satisfying and rewarding. The second method is organization development, a much broader approach. Job design may be considered one part of organization development; in many cases of OD, the unit of change is much greater than a job.

In trying to improve the fit between worker and job, it is necessary to modify either the "pegs" or the "holes." This chapter reviewed the theories, methods, and results of changing the "holes" to fit the "pegs." Ultimately, the fit between the two is a product of knowing when and how to change both.

MAJOR CHAPTER OBJECTIVES IN REVIEW

After having read this chapter, you should know:

1. Rationale of job design as reflected in job enlargement and job enrichment.

2. Logic and formulation of the job characteristics model.

3. Effectiveness of job-redesign programs to improve worker-workplace fit.

4. Rationale of organization development.

5. Concepts of the change agent, the client, and the intervention.

6. Major OD intervention strategies.

7. Values and ethics of OD.

CASE STUDY—How Do I Create Teamwork?

Alex Rowland gazed pensively out of his office, which overlooked the production area of his company. Seven years ago, he had founded Microtechnics, Inc., a high-tech company that produced microchips for use in computers. Rowland, an engineer by training, prided himself on assembling one of the finest engineering design departments in his industry. He handpicked his people from the finest universities in the country, gave them a free hand in product design, and paid them extremely well. While many companies feared losing their engineers to competitors, Rowland had the luxury of knowing many engineers were just waiting for a chance to join his company. In an industry where product quality and capacity were critical, Microtechnics was regarded as an industry leader in product design.

But all was not well at Microtechnics. What was once the strongest asset of the company was bordering on becoming a liability. Rowland wondered if he had created a monster. The problem was that the company was lagging far behind in production, and in having its products hit the market at opportune times. The apparent cause of the problem was the engineering department, the very department that had put Microtechnics on the map. The engineers were very prideful and territorial. They would not release a new product for production until they thought it was perfect down to the last detail. The engineers did not want the production department grabbing one of their "babies" until they were ready to release it. There was a constant struggle between the engineering and production departments regarding the release of products for manufacturing and distribution. While Rowland knew the value of superior products, he also knew that consumers paid for products, not great ideas, and if Microtechnics didn't put the product in the consumer's hands, soon there would be no Microtechnics. The production department repeatedly approached Rowland about missed production deadlines. Sales were way down because other companies were getting their products out the door first. They often lacked the quality of a Microtechnics product, but they still made great inroads into new markets by being there first. Microtechnics was developing a reputation of being the caboose in product delivery, and in a highly competitive industry its tardiness was killing the company financially.

The engineering department viewed production as a bunch of bureaucrats, people who failed to understand the importance of superior workmanship. The engineers at Microtechnics had earned numerous patents on their products, and in the span of seven short years had garnered three industry awards for product design. They were good, they knew it, everyone knew it. The problem was that Microtechnics wasn't just in the business of thinking up new products. It also had to produce them, and get people to buy them.

Rowland stared out over a cup of coffee. He felt he was running two separate companies: one in engineering, the other in production. They certainly weren't working together. Rowland knew he couldn't kill the goose that laid his golden eggs. Without his engineers, his company would be nothing. But if he couldn't get his engineers to realize they were in the manufacturing business and to facilitate the production process, they wouldn't stay in business.

Rowland felt trapped. He couldn't live without his engineers, and he wasn't living too well with them. If he couldn't find a way to unite his company, he knew it wouldn't be long before he joined a long list of former company presidents who had great ideas but didn't know how to run a business.

Questions

1. What exactly is the problem facing Microtechnics?

2. What factors are operating to reinforce the way the engineering department is operating?

3. What intervention strategies do you feel might benefit Microtechnics, and how would you implement them?

4. Do you believe the situation at Microtechnics requires the involvement of a change agent external to the company, or should Rowland create a permanent job within the company to address this situation? Why do you feel as you do?

5. If the intervention strategy is successful, how would the operation of Microtechnics be conducted differently than it is now?

14

Union/Management Relations

Over the years, I/O psychologists have been involved in a broad range of topics relating to work. Strangely enough, one not often addressed is union/management relations. This area cannot be dismissed as "tangential" to work; for many organizations, union-related issues are among the most crucial. Many authors (for example, Dubno, 1957; Stagner, 1961; Shostak, 1964) have observed that there is a great imbalance in I/O psychologists' interest between union and management problems. The two are not mutually exclusive, but I/O psychology seems more aligned with management. A listing of some of the professional activities of I/O psychologists testifies to this: managerial consulting, management development, using assessment centers to identify those with management ability, and determining the criteria of managerial success. However, I/O psychology has not spurned the advances of unions or been unreceptive to them. The relationship was described by Shostak (1964) as "mutual indifference." Unions appear reluctant to approach I/O psychologists for help in solving their problems. Rosen and Stagner (1980) think this is caused partly by the belief that I/O psychologists are not truly impartial and partly by reluctance to give outsiders access to union data.

The reasons for the unions' attitudes are not totally clear. One explanation is that the development of industrial psychology is closely tied to the work of Frederick Taylor. Criticisms of "Taylorism" have been raised by union workers; they see it as exploiting workers to increase company profits. There can be an adversarial relationship between unions and management, a "we/them" perspective. Unions may still see I/O psychology as a partner of "them." Also, some factors may appear to place I/O psychologists more in the management camp. I/O psychologists are often placed in management-level positions. It is also invariably *management* who sees the need for, explains problems to, and pays the consultant. In short, I/O psychology has been more involved with management than with unions (to the point that some authors refer to I/O psychology as a "management tool"). This is most apparent in the conspicuous absence of psychological research on unions. A summary of the major reasons that I/O psychologists have not worked well with unions was offered by Huszczo, Wiggins, and Currie (1984) and is presented in Table 14–1.

TABLE 14–1 *Reasons Why Unions Distrust I/O Psychologists*

Their association with management.

Their association with F. W. Taylor's scientific management (i.e., emphasis on efficiency, time and motion studies).

Unions are ignored in textbooks and journals of I/O psychology.

Their association with moralistic intellectuals who want social reform.

Methods (e.g., attitude surveys) have been used to avoid or beat union-organizing attempts or lower pay demands.

Their association with job enrichment techniques that interfere with job classification and standards systems.

Methods of psychological testing emphasize differentiation among workers (hence, antisolidarity and antiseniority systems).

Many psychologists have not had work experience similar to union members', which causes suspicion and communication barriers.

SOURCE: G. E. Huszczo, J. G. Wiggins, and J. S. Currie, "The Relationship between Psychology and Organized Labor: Past, Present, and Future." *American Psychologist, 39* (1984), 432–440.

In the past several years interest in unions has increased. Whether the "thaw" will continue and grow remains to be seen. I suspect current interest stems from the realization that worker-workplace problems need not be dealt with from an either/or perspective. Unions and management can benefit from solving problems that affect them jointly. If our discipline is successful in overcoming its "promanagement" image, we can and will make greater inroads in understanding unions. Current research suggests that such changes are beginning (see Field Note 1).

In this chapter, we will examine the nature of unions, factors influencing union/ management relations, recent research on unions, and how unionization affects many topics discussed earlier.

Field Note 1

I am of the opinion that unions have been given inadequate attention by educators. When the topic of labor unions comes up, students are more likely to have heard of Jimmy Hoffa (a union leader with reputed criminal connections) than Walter Reuther (a major contributor to organized labor). Why? There are probably many reasons, but one seems fundamental. Schools, colleges, and higher education in general are founded on scholarly intellectual values. They produce learned people, many of whom rise to become business leaders. Unions, on the other hand, got their start representing relatively uneducated workers—rank-and-file employees—rather than business leaders. Rightly or wrongly, unions have had the image of representing the "common man" in labor over the "privileged intellectuals." Some union leaders become suspicious and skeptical of the motives of formally educated people, feeling they are more likely to share values held by management.

Textbooks that offer more than a passing look at organized labor are rarely found in this country. It seems the "we/they" dichotomy that exists between labor and management has also filtered down into textbook writing; unions simply are infrequently discussed in books. *This* book, in fact, is one of the few I/O psychology textbooks to devote a chapter to union/management issues. However, the anti-intellectual attitude that some unions hold is costing them in ways beyond exposure in education. Unions will rarely hire outside professionals; they generally promote from within their own ranks. If you were an I/O psychologist who wanted to work full-time for a union, I doubt if you would have many employment possibilities. Furthermore, unions are currently experiencing a decline in membership, an un-

precedented number of unions are being decertified, and unions are losing their effectiveness compared to previous years in negotiating for desired employment conditions. In short, I feel unions are in need of some fresh ideas. They could benefit from some OD-type interventions. But unless they are willing to look beyond their own ranks for expertise, I doubt that they (like any organization) will have sufficient internal strength to pull themselves up by the bootstraps. The paradoxical split between I/O psychology (the study of people at work) and labor unions (which represent a large portion of workers) has been detrimental to both parties.

What Is a Union?

According to Tannenbaum (1965), "unions are organizations designed to promote and enhance the social and economic welfare of their members" (p. 710). Basically, unions were created to protect workers from exploitation. Unions originally sprang from the abysmal working conditions in this country 75 to 100 years ago. Workers got little pay, had almost no job security, had no benefits, and, perhaps most important, worked under degrading and unsafe conditions. Unions gave unity and power to employees. This power forced employers to deal with workers as a group, thereby providing a basis for improvement in the workers' welfare. It should also be realized that certain federal laws *forced* employers to stop certain activities (such as employing children) and engage in others (such as making Social Security contributions). Collectively, labor unions and labor laws brought about many changes in the workplace. While the problems facing the North American worker today are not as severe as they were 75 years ago, unions continue to give a sense of security and increased welfare to their members.

Why do workers join unions? What can unions accomplish? According to several authors, unions have consistently contributed to the attainment of certain outcomes. Bok and Dunlop (1970) feel unions have made the following contributions to worker welfare:

1. They have increased wages; in turn, employers have raised the wages of some nonunion workers.

2. They have bargained for and gotten benefits such as pensions, insurance, vacations, and rest periods.

3. They have provided formal rules and procedures for discipline, promotion, wage differentials, and other important job-related factors. This has led to less arbitrary treatment of employees.

Sherman (1969) adds the following reasons for joining unions: they provide better communication with management, better working conditions, increased employee unity, and higher morale. Other authors cite social reasons, like belonging to a group with whom workers can share common experiences and fellowship. Thus, there are both economic and personal reasons for joining unions.

Unions as Organizations

According to Glueck (1974), approximately 20 million U.S. citizens belong to labor unions, representing about 25% of the nonagricultural work force. In Canada, membership is over 2 million. The largest labor union is the American Federation of Labor-Congress of Industrial Organizations (AFL-CIO). Of all union members, 83% belong to an AFL-CIO affiliate. Other large unions include the United Auto Workers and the United Mine Workers. While unions are strongest among blue-collar employees, some white-collar workers (particularly government employees and teachers) are also being unionized, as witnessed by the growth of the American Federation of State, County, and Municipal Employees. In recent years, there has been a decline in unionization as the number of service jobs has increased and the number of manufacturing jobs (a traditional union stronghold) has dissipated.

Each union has a headquarters, but its strength is its many locals. A *local* may represent members in a geographic area (for example, all tollbooth collectors in Philadelphia) or a particular plant (for example, Amalgamated Beef Packers at Armour's Dubuque, Iowa, slaughterhouse). The local elects officials. If it is large enough, it affords some officials full-time jobs. Other officials are full-time company employees who may get time off for union activities. The *shop*, or *union*, steward has a union position equivalent to that of a company supervisor. The steward represents the union on the job site; he or she handles grievances and discipline. Usually the steward is elected by members for a one-year term.

A union represents an organization (for example, a labor organization) within another organization (the company). The local depends on the company for its existence. Large companies often have a multiunion labor force and thus multiple organizations within themselves. In this case, the employer must deal with several collectively organized groups, for example, production workers, clerical workers, and truck drivers. Each union negotiates separately, trying to improve the welfare of its members. A large, multiunion employer is a good example of how organizations are composed of interdependent parts. Each union has a certain degree of power, which can influence the behavior of the total organization.

Union members pay membership dues, which are the union's chief resource. The union can also collect money for a strike fund, a pool members can draw from if they are on strike and do not get paid. (We will discuss strikes in more detail shortly.)

Unions use their funds to offer members such things as special group automobile insurance rates or union-owned vacation facilities. Unions are highly dependent on their members. Increased membership gives a union more bargaining clout, generates more revenue, and provides a greater range of services for members. Without members, a union cannot exist—indeed, declining membership can threaten its very survival.

The Formation of a Union

When employees want to consider joining a union, they follow a standard procedure. The first step involves inviting representatives to solicit union membership. Federal law allows organizers to solicit membership as long as this does not endanger employees' safety or performance. Solicitations usually occur over lunch or at break time. It is illegal for employers to threaten physically, interfere with, or harass organizers. It is also illegal to fire employees for prounion sentiments.

Both the union and the company will typically mount campaigns on behalf of their positions. The union will stress how it can improve the workers' lot. The company will mount a countercampaign stressing how well off the employees already are, the costs of union membership, and loss of freedom. A federal agency, the National Labor Relations Board (NLRB), gets involved. The NLRB sends a hearing officer to oversee the union campaign and monitor further developments.

Employees are asked to sign cards authorizing a union election. If fewer than 30% sign the authorization cards, the process ends. If 30% or more sign, the next step is an election to determine whether a union will represent the employees. The NLRB officer must determine which employees are eligible to be in the union and thus eligible to vote. Management personnel (supervisors, superintendents, and managers) are excluded. The hearing officer schedules the election, provides secret ballots and ballot boxes, counts the votes, and certifies the election. If more than 50% of the voters approve, the union is voted in. If the union loses the election, it can repeat the entire process at a later date. A union that lost a close election would probably do so.

Brief and Rude (1981) proposed that the decision to accept or reject a union is not unlike other choices facing an individual. Employees will support a union to the extent that they see it as a way of getting outcomes important to them without prohibitive costs. Bakke (1945) stated this most eloquently:

> The worker reacts favorably to union membership in proportion to the strength of his belief that this step will reduce his frustrations and anxieties and will further his opportunities relevant to the achievement of his standards of successful living. He reacts unfavorably in proportion to the strength of his belief that this step will increase his frustrations and anxieties and will reduce his opportunities relevant to the achievement of such standards [p. 38].

DeCotiis and LeLouarn (1981) developed the model of the determinants of unionization shown in Figure 14–1. The work context includes employee reaction to work, organization climate, perceived organization structure, and supervision. Personal characteristics include age, sex, and race, as well as feelings of job satisfaction.

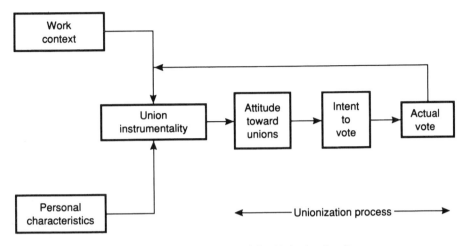

Figure 14–1   A Model of the Determinants of the Unionization Process

SOURCE: T. A. DeCotiis and J. Y. LeLouarn, "A Predictive Study of Voting Behavior in a Representation Election Using Union Instrumentality and Work Perceptions," *Organizational Behavior and Human Performance, 27* (1981), pp. 103–118.

The work context and personal characteristics determine union instrumentality, that is, the extent to which a union is seen as improving the employee's welfare. Instrumentality affects the employee's attitude toward unions; in turn, this affects the employee's intent to vote for a union. The actual vote is determined by the sequence shown in the model. DeCotiis and LeLouarn were able to explain over 54% of the variance in perceptions of union instrumentality on consideration of the concepts in their model.

Summers, Betton, and DeCotiis (1986) found that union instrumentality can be lowered when different unions are competing among themselves for the right to represent employees. They discovered employees are likely to take antiunion information more seriously if its source is another union rather than management. Premack and Hunter (1988) carefully studied the unionization decision by means of elaborate statistical methods. The authors concluded that some employees hold strong attitudes toward unions, both pro and con, and their attitudes are usually not altered one way or the other during the course of the organizing campaign. However, other employees are uncertain about their attitudes toward unions, and it is these people whose attitudes can be altered by the behavior of both parties during the organizing campaign. Premack and Hunter note that the votes of these employees are critical to the outcome of the election because most union representation elections are decided by a small number of votes.

The Labor Contract

Once a union is recognized, its officials are authorized to negotiate a labor contract. This is a formal agreement between union and management, specifying conditions of employment over a set period.

Both sides prepare a preliminary list of what they want included; the union presents its demands and the employer its offers. The union tends to ask for more than it knows it can get; management tends to offer less. While both sides seek a satisfactory agreement, they often resort to bombast, which is a hallmark of such negotiations. Union officials may allege management is making huge profits and taking advantage of workers. Management may allege that malicious union leaders have duped the good workers and that their policies may force the company into bankruptcy. Over time, both sides usually come to an agreement; the union often gets less than it wanted and management gives more. When agreement is not reached (an *impasse*), other steps are taken, as will be discussed.

Contract negotiations take place between two teams of negotiators. The union side typically consists of local union officials, shop stewards, and perhaps a representative of the national union. Management usually fields a team of a few personnel and production managers, who follow preset guidelines. The contract contains many articles; there are also many issues to bargain over. The issues can generally be classified into five categories: (1) compensation and working conditions; (2) employee security; (3) union security; (4) management rights; and (5) contract duration (Glueck, 1974). Table 14–2 gives examples of these and the positions typically taken by each side.

In the process, each bargaining team checks with its members to see whether they will compromise on initial positions. Each side may be willing to yield on some points but not others. Eventually, they reach a tentative agreement. Union members then vote on the contract. If they approve it, the contract is *ratified* and remains in effect for the agreed-upon time (typically two to three years). If members reject the contract, further negotiation will be necessary.

TABLE 14–2   *Typical Bargaining Issues and Associated Positions Taken by Union and Management*

Issue	Union's Position	Management's Position
Compensation and working conditions	Higher pay, more fringe benefits, cost-of-living adjustments	Limit company expenditures by not yielding to all union demands
Employee security	Seniority is the basis for promotions, layoffs, and recall decisions	Merit or job performance is the basis for these decisions
Union security	A union shop in which employees must join the union when hired	An open shop in which employees can choose to join the union
Management rights	Union wants more voice in setting policies and making decisions that affect employees	Management feels certain decisions are its inherent right and does not want to share them with the union
Contract duration	Shorter contracts	Longer contracts

Determining whether a contract will be ratified typically depends on (1) industry practices, (2) community practices, and (3) recent trends. If the union represents truck drivers and a critical issue is wages, the union will collect data needed to judge the proposal. What other companies in the industry pay truck drivers, what other companies in the community pay them, and whether prices and wages are rising or falling will be considered. Stagner and Rosen (1965) refer to the area of compromise as the *bargaining zone*; this is presented in Figure 14–2. Both parties must move toward a compromise without exceeding their tolerance limits; this is the point beyond which the contract will be unacceptable. If both parties reach a compromise within their expectations, there will be agreement. If, however, one side exceeds its tolerance limit, the proposed contract will not be acceptable.

Both sides will use whatever external factors are available to influence the contract in their favor. If there is high unemployment and the company could replace workers who go on strike, management has an advantage. If the company does much of its business around Christmas, the union may choose that time to negotiate a contract, knowing the company can ill afford a strike then. Each side looks for factors that will bolster its position.

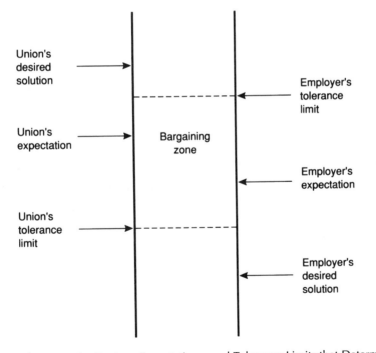

Figure 14–2 Desires, Expectations, and Tolerance Limits that Determine the Bargaining Zone

SOURCE: R. Stagner and H. Rosen, *Psychology of Union-Management Relations* (Belmont Calif.: Wadsworth, 1965), p. 96. Reprinted by permission of the publisher. Brooks/Cole Publishing Company, Pacific Grove, California.

Collective Bargaining and Impasse Resolution

Whether or not the bargaining process runs smoothly is often due to the parties' approaches. Walton and McKersie (1965) distinguish between distributive and integrative bargaining postures. *Distributive* bargaining is predominant in the United States. This assumes a win-lose relationship; whatever the employer gives the union, the employer loses and vice versa. Because both sides are trying to minimize losses, movement toward a compromise is often painful and slow.

The alternative is *integrative bargaining*. Both sides work to improve the relationship while the present contract is in effect. Contract renewal is not seen as the time and place for confrontation. Instead, both parties seek to identify common problems and propose acceptable solutions that can be adopted when the contract expires.

These bargaining postures are not formally chosen; rather, they are implied by behavior in the workplace. While it is not always a strictly either/or decision, it appears that distributive bargaining is far more characteristic of union/management relations than is integrative bargaining.

What happens if the two parties cannot reach an agreement? In some cases, the labor contract may stipulate what will be done if an impasse is reached. In other cases, union and management must jointly determine how to break the impasse. In either case, there are three options, all involving third parties.

Mediation. According to Kochan (1980), mediation is the most used yet the most informal third-party option. A neutral third party (a mediator) assists union and management in reaching voluntary agreement. A mediator has no power to impose a settlement; rather, he or she facilitates bringing both parties together.

Where do mediators come from? The Federal Mediation and Conciliation Service (FMCS) provides a staff of qualified mediators. An organization contacts FMCS for the services of such a person. The mediator need not be affiliated with FMCS, any third party acceptable to labor and management may serve. Generally, however, both parties prefer someone with training and experience in labor disputes, so FMCS is often called on.

How a mediator intervenes is not clear-cut. Mediation is voluntary; thus, no mediator can function without the trust, cooperation, and acceptance of both parties. Acceptance is important since the mediator must obtain any confidential information that the parties have withheld. If the information is used indiscriminately, the parties' bargaining strategy and leverage could be weakened. The mediator tries to reduce the number of disputed issues; ideally, he or she reaches a point where there are no disputes at all. The mediator encourages information sharing to break the deadlock. Without a mediator, it is often difficult for parties to "open up" after assuming adversary roles. The mediator facilitates the flow of information and progression toward compromise. If the mediator is unsuccessful, both parties may engage in the next phase: fact finding.

Fact-Finding. Fact-finding is more formal than mediation. A qualified mediator may also serve as a fact finder, but his or her role will change. In fact-finding, the third party reviews the facts, makes a formal recommendation to resolve the dispute, and makes the recommendation public. It is presumed that if the recommendation is public, pressure will be brought on the parties to accept it or use it for a negotiated settlement. However, according to Kochan (1980), fact-finding has not produced the desired pressure. Public interest is apparently aroused only when a strike threatens or actually imposes direct hardship on the public.

Fact-finding may be most useful when one party faces internal differences and needs recommendations from an expert to overcome opposition to a settlement. There appears to be a difference in the effectiveness of fact-finding between private- and public-sector employers. In the public sector, fact-finding has met with limited success. Parties learn that rejecting a fact-finding recommendation is not politically or economically costly, so they are unlikely to value the opinion of the fact finder. In the private sector, fact-finding can be helpful primarily because the final technique of settlement (arbitration) is strongly opposed by unions and management. However, fact-finding generally is not used very often in the private sector.

Arbitration. Arbitration is the final and most formal settlement technique. Both parties *must* abide by the decision of the neutral third party. "Final and binding" is usually associated with arbitration. The outcome of arbitration is *binding* on both parties. Use of arbitration may be stipulated in the labor contract; it may also be agreed upon informally. This is called *interest* arbitration because it involves the interests of both parties in negotiating a new contract.

Arbitrators must have extensive experience in labor relations. The American Arbitration Association (AAA) maintains the standards and keeps a list of qualified arbitrators. Arbitrators listed by AAA often also serve as mediators listed by FMCS. Effective mediators, fact finders, or arbitrators all need the same skills. What distinguishes the services is the clout of the third party.

There are many forms of interest arbitration. With *voluntary* arbitration, the parties *agree* to the process. It is most common in the private sector in settling disputes arising while a contract is still in effect. *Compulsory* arbitration is *legally required*. It is most common in the public sector.

There are other types of arbitration. With *conventional* arbitration, the arbitrator creates the settlement he or she deems appropriate. In *final-offer* arbitration, the arbitrator must select the proposal of either union or management; no compromise is possible. For example, suppose the union demands $8 per hour, and the company offers $7. In conventional arbitration, the arbitrator could decide on any wage but will probably split the difference and decide on $7.50. In final-offer arbitration, the arbitrator must choose between the $7 and the $8. An additional variation also holds for final-offer arbitration: the arbitrator may make the decision on a *total package*; he or she must choose the complete proposal of either the employer or the union on all issues. The decision may also be made on an *issue-by-issue* basis. In this case, the arbitrator might choose the employer wage offer but select the union demand on vacation days. Decisions on voluntary versus compulsory arbitration, conventional versus final-offer arbitration, and total package versus issue-by-issue resolution are determined by law for public-sector employers and by mutual agreement in the private sector (see Field Note 2).

Interest arbitration is more common in the public sector. The private sector historically has been opposed to outside interference in resolving labor problems that are "private" affairs. Thus, private-sector employers will readily seek the *advice* of a mediator but shun strategies that *require* certain courses of action. The public sector, however, is quite different. Strikes in the public sector (for example, police) can have devastating effects on the general public. Since they are often prohibited by law, other means of settlement (fact-finding, arbitration) are provided. Some public-sector employees have gone on strike (sometimes legally but usually illegally), but strikes are more often the outcome of impasses in the private sector.

We will next consider the options available if no settlement is reached through standard procedures.

Field Note 2

Interest arbitration can be a seductively simple means of resolving impasses—so simple, in fact, that some people fear it is overused. Let us say the union wants a 50-cents-per-hour pay increase and management offers 10 cents per hour. Both sides believe from past experience that an arbitrator would likely split the difference between the two, settling on 30 cents per hour. It has been suggested that the more arbitration is used to resolve impasses and the more splitting that occurs, the more likely it is that parties will not bargain seriously between themselves; that is, they will opt for the effortless remedy, arbitration. Thus, the parties will disregard the mediation and fact-finding stages and go directly to arbitration. Arbitration becomes an addictive response to impasse; this phenomenon has been labeled the "narcotic effect" of arbitration.

How do you weaken the narcotic effect of arbitration? One solution is to have arbitrators *not* split the difference in making decisions. However, arbitrators are free to fashion whatever decisions they think are fair. Splitting the difference is often perceived as the fairest thing to do, and also increases the acceptability of the arbitrator for future cases

since neither party will have received preferential treatment. Thus, with each split decision, the narcotic effect becomes stronger. One way to weaken the narcotic effect is to prohibit split decisions, which is what happens in final-offer arbitration. Here, the arbitrator is bound to accept either the 50-cents or 10-cents position and not any figure over, under, or in between. Given this, it has been hypothesized that negotiators will offer more serious, reasonable proposals, knowing the alternative is to have an arbitrator choose one position over the other. An absurd offer would never get chosen. In total-package, final-offer arbitration the arbitrator must chose the entire package of either the union or management, which tends to drive both parties into compromise. The alternative version of issue-by-issue final-offer arbitration has been found to produce its own type of split decisions; that is, since there can be no *within* issue splits, the arbitrator splits *between* issues. Thus, the union position is accepted on one issue and management's position on another. The creation of total-package final-offer arbitration is presumed to have most greatly decreased reliance on arbitration for impasse resolution.

Responses to Impasse

Consider the situation in which union and management cannot resolve their disputes. They may or may not have used a mediator. Assume the private sector is involved because mediation, fact-finding, and arbitration might be required in the public sector. What happens if the two parties cannot agree?

Collective bargaining entails realizing that both sides can take action if they are not pleased with the outcome. These actions are weapons with which to bring about favorable settlements. What the union can do is to strike. Union members must vote for a strike. If members support a strike and no settlement is reached, they will stop work at a particular time. That point is typically the day after the current contract expires. Taking a strike vote during negotiations brings pressure on management to agree to union demands.

The right to strike is a very powerful tool. The losses from a long strike may be greater than the concessions made in a new contract. Also, unions are skilled in scheduling their strikes (or threatening to do so) when the company is particularly vulnerable (such as around Christmas for the airline industry). If employees do strike, the company is usually closed down completely. There may be limited production if management performs some jobs. It is also possible to hire workers to replace those on strike. These replacements are called "scabs." Given the time it takes to recruit, hire, and train new workers, replacements will not be hired unless a long strike is predicted.

While a strike hurts management, it is unpleasant for the workers as well. Since they are not working, they do not get paid. The employees may have contributed to a strike fund, but such funds are usually only a fraction of regular wages. A strike is the price employees pay to get their demands. It sometimes also limits their demands. By the time a union faces a strike, it is usually confronted with two unpalatable options. One is to accept a contract it does not like; the other is to strike. Employees may seek temporary employment while they are on strike, but such jobs are not always available. On the basis of labor economists' studies of the costs of strikes to both the employees and employers, it is safe to say that strikes rarely benefit either party. Sometimes the company suffers the most; in other cases, the union does. There are rarely any "winners" in a strike. Stagner and Rosen (1965) have illustrated the consequences for both union and management in accepting each other's alternatives, particularly as they relate to a strike (see Figure 14–3)

One study examined some of the dynamics associated with strikes. Stagner and Effal (1982) looked at the attitudes of unionized automobile workers at several times, including when contracts were being negotiated, during an ensuing strike, and seven months after the strike ended. The authors found that union members on strike (1) had a higher opinion of the union and its leadership than before the strike; (2) evaluated the benefit package more highly after the strike; (3) became more militant toward the employer during the strike; and (4) reported more willingness to engage in union activities. The results of this study support predictions based on theories of conflict and attitude formation.

Management is not totally defenseless in case of a strike. If it anticipates a strike,

Company	Union
Alternative 1	
Perceived consequences of giving in to union demands:	Perceived consequences of accepting company counteroffer:
1. Lessening of investor return.	1. Loss of membership support.
2. Loss of competitive standing.	2. Loss of status within union movement.
3. Setting bad precedent.	3. Setting bad precedent.
4. Avoiding costly strike.	4. Avoiding costly strike.
5. Avoiding government and public ill will.	5. Avoiding government and public ill will.
Alternative 2	
Perceived consequences of refusing to accede to union demands:	Perceived consequences of sticking to original demands:
1. Due to potential strike, loss of investor return.	1. Prove strength and determination of union to members.
2. Due to potential strike, loss of competitive standing.	2. Due to potential strike, loss of member income.
3. Loss of government and public good will.	3. Due to potential strike, loss of member support.
4. Maintenance of company prerogatives.	4. Loss of government and public good will.
5. Breaking union power.	5. Teach company a "lesson."

Figure 14–3 Illustration of Union and Company Alternatives and Related Consequences

SOURCE: R. Stagner and H. Rosen, *Psychology of Union-Management Relations* (Belmont, Calif.: Wadsworth, 1965), p. 103. Reprinted by permission of the publishers, Brooks/Cole Publishing Company, Pacific Grove, California.

it might boost production beforehand to stockpile goods. Most public-sector employees, on the other hand, perform services, and services cannot be stockpiled. This is one reason strikes are illegal in some parts of the public sector. Sometimes a strike uncovers information about the quality of the work force. When one company replaced strikers with temporary help, new production records were set. In this case, the strike revealed a weakness in the employees.

A strike is not the only option available to the union. Work *slowdowns* have also been used. Workers operate at lower levels of efficiency. They may simply put out

THE WIZARD OF ID   by Brant parker and Johnny hart

By permission of Johnny Hart and News America Syndicate

less effort and thus produce less, or they may be absent to reduce productivity. Since strikes are illegal in the police force, police officers dissatisfied with their contracts have called in sick en masse with what has become known as the "blue flu." Such tactics can exert great pressure on management to yield to union demands.

Sabotage is another response to impasse in negotiations. Stagner and Rosen (1965) describe a situation in which factory production was increased from 2,000 to 3,000 units per day by modifying a drill press. However, wages were not increased, and workers resented it. They found that bumping the sheet metal against the drill would eventually break the drill. The employee handling the drill would have to wait idly for a replacement. By some curious accident, average production continued around 2,000 units per day. However, management got the "message." While sabotage is not a sanctioned union activity like a strike, it is a way of putting pressure on management to accept demands.

Management also has a major tactic to get the union to acquiesce. It is called a *lockout* and is considered the employer's equivalent of a strike. The company threatens to close if the union does not accept its offer. Employees cannot work and thus "pay" for rejecting the employer's offer. A threatened lockout may put the pressure of a majority of workers on a minority holding out against a contract issue. Like strikes, lockouts are costly to both the company and the union, and they are not undertaken lightly. They are management's ultimate response to an impasse.

Before we leave this topic, note that strikes, slowdowns, sabotage, and lockouts represent failures in the collective bargaining process. These actions have been taken because a settlement was not reached. Like most responses to frustration, in the long run they are rarely beneficial. Some unions may want to "teach the company a lesson"; some companies want to break a union; but both parties have a symbiotic relationship. A company cannot exist without employees, and without a company, employees have no jobs. Collective bargaining reflects the continual tussle for power, but neither side can afford to be totally victorious. If a union exacts so many concessions that the company goes bankrupt, it will have accomplished nothing. As Estey (1981) put it, "Labor does not seek to kill the goose that lays the golden eggs; it wants it to lay more golden eggs, and wants more eggs for itself" (p. 83).

If management drives employees away by not making enough concessions, it will not have a qualified work force. Industrial peace is far more desirable for all parties than warfare. Conflict can provide opportunities for change and development; if conflict gets out of hand, it can be devastating. Union/management relations are not all typified by infighting and power plays. Nothing unites opposing factions faster than a common enemy. Because the United States is losing some economic battles to foreign competition, some union/management relations have become far more *integrative*. For example, in 1982, unions in the auto industry gave up some concessions gained before the current contract expired. The industry, in turn, used the money saved to become more competitive. By remaining solvent, the industry continued to provide jobs. Both management and labor could pursue some common goals. Collective bargaining is a delicate process. Neither side should lose sight of the total economic and social environment, even though short-term, narrow issues are often at the heart of disputes.

Disputes over Contract Interpretation

Collective bargaining is mainly directed toward resolving disputes over new labor contracts; however, disputes also occur over contracts currently in effect. No matter how clearly a labor contract is written, there invariably are disagreements over its meaning or extent. Developing a clear and precise contract involves writing skills in their highest form. Despite the best intentions of those involved, events occur that are not clearly covered in a labor contract. For example, companies often include a contract clause stating that sleeping on the job is grounds for dismissal. A supervisor notices that an employee's head is resting on his arms and his eyes are closed. The supervisor infers the employee is asleep and fires him. The employee says he was not sleeping but felt dizzy and chose to rest for a moment rather than risk falling down. Who is right?

If the supervisor dismissed the employee, the employee would probably file a grievance. A *grievance* is a formal complaint. The firing decision can be appealed through a grievance procedure, which is usually a provision of a labor contract (Ash, 1970). First, the employee and supervisor try to reach an understanding. If they do not, the shop steward represents the employee in negotiating with the supervisor. This is often done whether or not the steward thinks the employee has a "case"—for the steward's job is, above all, to represent union members. If not resolved, the case may then be taken to the company's director of industrial relations. This person will hear testimony from both sides and issue a verdict. This may be a compromise—the employee keeps his or her job but is put on probation. The final step is calling in an arbitrator. This person examines the labor contract, hears testimony, and renders an opinion. This is called *rights* or *grievance* arbitration; it involves the rights of the employee. The labor contract usually specifies that union and management share the cost of arbitration, which may be $1,000 per hearing. This is done to prevent all grievances from being routinely pushed to arbitration. Each side must believe it has a strong case before calling in an arbitrator (see Field Note 3).

The arbitrator must be acceptable to both sides; this means being seen as neither prounion nor promanagement. The arbitrator may decide in favor of one side or issue a compromise decision. The decision is final and binding. If an arbitrator hears many cases in the same company and repeatedly decides in favor of one side, he or she may become unacceptable to the side that always loses. Articles of the labor contract that are repeated subjects of grievance (due mainly to ambiguous language) become prime candidates for revision in the next contract.

Field Note 3

For many years rights arbitration has been used as a means of resolving disputes over grievances filed in unionized companies. The arbitrator is called in, hears both sides of the story, and renders a decision. This decision is final and binding to both parties. Why? Because both have agreed to this means of dispute settlement in the labor contract and therefore must accept the arbitrator's decision.

Over the past few years, the arbitration model of dispute settlement has been used to resolve an ever-widening range of problems. These problems are not limited to unionized companies, to employment issues, or even to any companies. Actually, all that is needed are two (or more) disputants, an acceptable third party who will serve as an arbitrator, and an agreement by the parties to accept the arbitrator's decision.

Here is an example. Let us say you take your car to a repair shop. It charges you $500 for the work, which you pay, but you discover the car still does not run properly. You want either to get your money back or to have the car fixed to your satisfaction, but the repair people say your car must have a new problem because it worked fine when it left the shop. You now have a dispute on your hands.

What can you do about it? One approach would be to try to work it out with the repair shop, but you probably will not get too far since the repair people already feel strongly about their position. Another approach would be for you to bring a legal suit against the repair shop. This could take a long time, and both parties would have to pay associated legal fees. A third alternative would be to use an arbitrator, someone whose opinion both you and the repair people would respect and by whose decision you would agree to abide. You and they would further agree to share the cost of the arbitrator's fee.

What if you did not like the arbitrator's decision and later decided to seek relief in court? Could you? Possibly—but it would be brought to the court's attention that you reneged on the arbitrator's decision, which would certainly detract from your perceived honesty and credibility. Arbitrators generally offer disputants greater speed and less cost in reaching a resolution than many other systems of dispute settlement. Is there any guarantee that you will be satisfied with the resolution? No, but if you did not like the solution, you probably would not consider that arbitrator an acceptable choice for any future disputes. Such is the way arbitrators are found unsatisfactory in industrial disputes: they have alienated one of the disputing parties.

A number of studies examined determinants of grievances. The most common are characteristics of grievants, personalities of the union stewards, and the nature of the environment in which grievances are filed. Several studies (for example, Eckerman, 1948, Sulkin & Pranis, 1957) have tried to ascertain the "type" of person who submits a grievance. The design usually calls for comparing grievants and nongrievants on a variety of factors. Using this method, Sulkin and Pranis (1957), for example, reported that grievants had more education, were more active in the union, had a higher absence rate, and received lower wages with fewer net increases. The characteristics of grievants seem stable within a given company but inconsistent across companies (Kissler, 1977).

Dalton and Todor (1979) examined the relationship between personality characteristics of the union steward and propensity to file a grievance. The union steward is instrumental in the grievance process. Dalton and Todor discovered wide differences in the conduct of stewards toward grievances. Some stewards will advise employees to file a grievance; others try to resolve problems on the plant floor to keep them from

Umpires function as arbitrators in a baseball game. Sometimes the disputants express their displeasure over a decision. UPI/Bettman

becoming formal grievances. Further, the more dominant the steward's personality, the more likely he or she is to file a grievance in an employee's behalf.

Dalton and Todor's (1982) model of the grievance process emphasizes the role of the union steward. This is shown in Figure 14–4. Some incident occurs that is seen as a possible grievance. A management representative may try to reduce grievances by resolving the problem informally with the union steward's consent. If the employee wants to pursue a grievance (has a positive propensity), the steward might discourage this but would probably support the action. If the worker has a negative propensity to file a grievance, the steward may encourage the individual or may file in the name of the union without the worker's consent. Finally, the bottom link in the model shows a steward can bypass any worker propensities (positive or negative) and file a grievance in the name of the union. In such a case, it is the steward's propensity alone that determines the action. Dalton and Todor feel the union steward holds a key role in the union member-grievance relationship, one that until recently has not been well understood.

A few studies have examined the extent to which the work environment contrib-

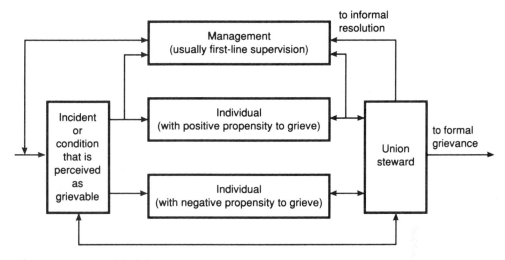

Figure 14–4 Model of the Grievance Process

SOURCE: D. R. Dalton and W. D. Todor, "Antecedents of Grievance Filing Behavior: Attitude/Behavioral Consistency and the Union
Steward," *Academy of Management Journal, 25* (1982), pp. 158–169.

utes to number and types of grievances. Ronan (1963) studied grievance activity over
a five-year period in two plants manufacturing heavy equipment. He found the plants
did have a significant effect on the number of grievances but the kind of work did not.
Employees at both plants submitted grievances for similar reasons and seemed to
follow the same pattern in terms of rate. Muchinsky and Maassarani (1980) found
that depending on the type of work, certain articles of a contract are more likely to be
grieved. Public employees who work as prison guards and attendants in state mental
hospitals were more likely to file grievances about their own safety and disciplinary
actions than were employees in a transportation department. On the other hand,
transportation department employees filed more grievances about hours of work and
wages. Thus, allegations are directly related to type of work. The most "sensitive"
aspects of work are likely to differ from one organization to another.

One may think of grievances as a somewhat contaminated index of the quality of
union/management relations. In general, when the working relationship is good,
grievances will be fewer. However, as Gordon and Miller (1984) have noted, in some
organizations work problems get resolved informally between the conflicting parties
and never develop into formal grievances. While formal grievances are usually indicative of conflict, their absence does not always reflect a problem-free work environment. It is also true that the more ambiguous the labor contract, the more likely
conflicts will ensue. A poorly written or inconsistently interpreted contract invites
grievances (Werther, 1974). There can be much grievance activity in a recently
unionized organization; employees will use grievances to "test" management's
knowledge of the labor contract (Muchinsky & Maassarani, 1981). Particularly in the
public sector, where collective bargaining is relatively new, officials are expected to
act as "management" even though they have little or no training in dealing with labor

(Redenius, 1976). Such an imbalance contributes to errors in contract administration. There is much publicity about strike-related issues, but members feel the union's highest priority should be better ways of handling grievances (Kochan, 1979). Unions serve many purposes; however, it seems the most pressing need they fill is that of ensuring fair treatment in employment. Of course, this is a primary reason that unions appeal to workers.

Influence of Unions on Nonunionized Companies

Even though they do not have unionized employees, companies are still sensitive to union influence. Companies unresponsive to employees' needs invite unionization. A nonunion company that wants to remain so must be receptive to the ideas and complaints of its workers. If a company can satisfy employees' needs, a union is not necessary. Said another way, the company voluntarily does what would be forced on it by a labor union. In a given community or industry, there is often a mix of union and nonunion companies. If unionized employees get concessions from management on wages, benefits, hours, and so on, these become reference points for nonunionized employees. Thus, a nonunion company may feel compelled to raise wages, for example, to remain competitive. If a labor contract calls for formal grievance procedures, a nonunion company may well follow suit. Workers are aware of employment conditions in other companies, which gives them a frame of reference for judging their own. If a company does not offer comparable conditions, employees may see a union as a means of improving their welfare. This is not to say that nonunion companies must offer *identical* conditions. There are costs associated with a union (for example, dues); a nonunion company might set wages slightly below those paid in a unionized company so the net effect (higher wages minus dues) is comparable. What economists call the "union/nonunion wage differential" has been the subject of extensive research.

While a prudent nonunion employer will keep abreast of employment conditions in the community and the industry, a company cannot act to keep a union out "at all costs." There is much labor relations legislation. Many laws (like the National Labor Relations Act) were enacted to prohibit unfair practices on both sides. For example, an employer cannot fire a worker just because he or she supports a union. The history of labor relations is full of cases of worker harassment by unions or management to influence attitudes toward unionization. But both sides can suffer for breaking the law.

Behavioral Research on Union/Management Relations

Thus far, we have examined the structure of unions, collective bargaining, and various issues in union/management relations. For the most part, we have not discussed psychological issues; with the exception of grievances, there is little behavioral research on union/management relations. However, over the past few years, interest in this area has increased. We are beginning to see an interdisciplinary approach to topics that historically were treated with parochialism (Brett, 1980). In the next few pages, we will examine research on union/management relations with a strong behavioral trust.

Employee Support for Collective Bargaining

A number of studies have dealt with why employees support a union, particularly with regard to personal needs and job satisfaction. Feuille and Blandin (1974) sampled the attitudes toward unionization of over 400 college professors at a university experiencing many financial and resource cutbacks. The items measured were satisfaction with areas like fairness of the university's personnel decisions, adequacy of financial support, representation of faculty interests in the state legislature, and salary. The professors were also asked to rate their inclination to accept a union. Professors dissatisfied with employment conditions were much more likely to support a union. Respondents also were consistent in their attitude toward a union and perception of its impact and effectiveness. Those who favored a union saw it as an effective way of protecting employment interests and as having a positive impact. In general, results indicated that unionization is attractive as employment conditions deteriorate.

Using a similar research design and sample, Bigoness (1978) correlated measures of job satisfaction, job involvement, and locus of control with disposition to accept unionization. Bigoness also found that feelings of dissatisfaction related to acceptance of unionization. In particular, dissatisfaction with work, pay and promotions each correlated .35 with attitude toward unionization. Additionally, unionization was more appealing to people who were less involved in their jobs and had an external locus of control. Combining all independent variables in a multiple regression equation, Bigoness accounted for over 27% of the variance in attitudes toward unionization.

Studies by Hamner and Smith (1978) and Schriesheim (1978) have already been discussed, but both merit a brief review. Hamner and Smith (1978) examined union activity in 250 units of a large organization. In half the units, there had been some union activity; in the other half, no activity was reported. Using an immense sample of over 80,000, the authors found that employee attitudes were predictive of level of unionization activity. The strongest predictor was dissatisfaction with supervision. Schriesheim (1978) found that prounion voting in a certification election was positively correlated with dissatisfaction; dissatisfaction with economic facets was also more predictive than dissatisfaction with noneconomic factors. Furthermore, research by Youngblood, De Nisi, Molleston, and Mobley (1984) and Zalesny (1985) showed the importance of two other factors in union support. The first is a person's attitude toward collective bargaining in general. The more acceptable unions are in general to a person, the more likely will he or she vote for unionization. Second, unions must be perceived as being instrumental in enhancing worker welfare. Employees may not be satisfied with their employment conditions but may feel that unions can do little to aid them.

What these studies have in common is that they all show that dissatisfaction with employment conditions is predictive of support for unionization. The more satisfied workers are, the less likely they are to think a union is necessary or that it will improve their welfare. These results are not surprising. They do reveal the facets of dissatisfaction associated with a disposition toward unions. Some authors tout the social benefits of unions (for example, association with similar people). But it is mainly the perceived *economic* advantages that give unions their appeal. However, not all support for unions is based on dissatisfaction with economic conditions. Hammer and Berman (1981) found that the faculty at one college wanted a union mainly because they distrusted administrative decision making and were dissatisfied with work content. Prounion voting was motivated by a faculty desire for more power in dealing with the administration.

One myth about unions is that they appeal mostly to blue-collar workers; white-collar employees supposedly have more needs met on the job and thus are not disposed to unionization. The fallacy of this is evident in the growing number of white-collar employees, mainly in the public sector, becoming unionized (Angel, 1982). Bass and Mitchell (1976) also provide evidence to refute this. They asked a sample of business managers to rate on a nine-point scale the perceived need for unionization among scientists in their organization. The managers' average rating was 2.8; they did not think scientists would be positive about a union. Yet, the scientists' average rating was 5.8, reflecting a moderately strong need. The managers clearly believed the myth that scientists (among other professionals) are not interested in unionization. The data indicate that scientists, like other groups, will accept unions if they are seen as improving employment conditions. Although the *degree* of support for unions may vary for different occupations, no group seems categorically opposed to them.

Union Influence

What influence do unions have on enhancing employee welfare? Various studies have produced somewhat different conclusions. Gomez-Mejia and Balkin (1984) found that samples of unionized and nonunionized college teachers were equally satisfied with all job facets except pay, with which unionized faculty were more satisfied. Carillon and Sutton (1982) found a strong positive relationship between judged union effectiveness in representing teachers and their reported quality of work life. One alleged fear of college administrators is that faculty unionization will affect organization effectiveness. A study by Cameron (1982) dealt with this in 41 colleges. Faculty were unionized in 18 colleges and nonunionized in 23. Cameron proposed nine indexes of effectiveness for a college involving student academic development, faculty and administrator satisfaction, and ability to acquire resources. Nonunion colleges were significantly more effective on three of the nine indexes; unionized colleges were not significantly more effective on any. Cameron also collected attitude data from faculty members on five factors relating to their work. These results are presented in Figure 14–5. Faculty power and red tape were seen as increasing since unionization;

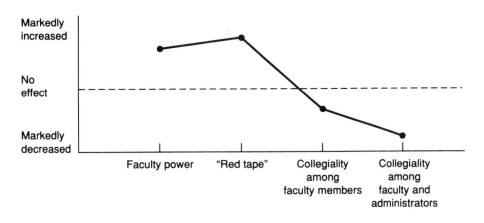

Figure 14–5 Perceptions of the Effects of Faculty Unionization

SOURCE: K. Cameron, "The Relationship between Faculty Unionism and Organizational Effectiveness," *Academy of Management Journal,* 25 (1982), p. 13.

collegiality was seen as decreasing. The study revealed some major differences in effectiveness of union and nonunion colleges; however, the cause was not determined. Unionization may "cause" colleges to be less effective, which would be a strong argument against unions. However, the less effective colleges may turn to unions for improvement, which is obviously an argument supporting unionization. As discussed in Chapter 2, causality is difficult to determine. In this context, the relationship between faculty unionization and college effectiveness awaits more research.

In the preceding chapter, we discussed job enrichment and its cost to the organization. Giles and Holley (1978) examined how often union workers wanted contract negotiations to involve five issues: pay, fringe benefits, working conditions, job security, and job enrichment. Employees at two plants, one manufacturing and the other food processing, were asked to indicate their preferences. The results are shown in Table 14–3. Job enrichment received the lowest mean rating at both plants. This suggests that members do not particularly want unions to bargain actively for job

TABLE 14–3 *Perceptions of the Time Representatives Should Devote to Certain Issues of Union Members at Two Plants*

Negotiation Issue	Plant A	Plant B
Fringe benefits	28%	17%
Pay	24	47
Job security	18	14
Working conditions	16	13
Job enrichment	13	9

SOURCE: W. F. Giles and W. H. Holley, "Job Enrichment versus Traditional Issues at the Bargaining Table: What Union Members Want," *Academy of Management Journal,* 21 (1978), p. 728.

enrichment. It is not that union workers are absolutely *uninterested* in enriched jobs; rather, job enrichment is relatively unimportant compared to other issues. In both plants, traditional economic issues of pay and fringe benefits got higher ratings than the noneconomic issues of working conditions, job security, and job enrichment. An alternative explanation is that union employees did not see job enrichment as a legitimate union function and thus did not give it a high rating. Indeed, Holley, Feild, and Crowley (1981) reported that union members expressing a strong preference for job enrichment also indicated a strong preference for more union and management cooperation in addressing work problems. Some union members seem supportive of job enrichment, but they look to joint union management participation to attain it.

Hammer (1978) proposed that a union's strength as indexed by the members' wages is related to members' views of various work-related outcomes. In studying 17 unions, Hammer found that the stronger the union was measured to be, the more likely were members to feel they would be promoted, hold secure jobs, and receive good pay. In stronger unions, workers collaborated more with one another (for example, sought co-workers' advice on problems, accepted supervisor's advice) than in weaker unions. In general, Hammer felt that a union's strength influences workers' motivation, performance, and satisfaction. Hammer developed a model showing the union's role in shaping attitudes and behavior (see Figure 14–6). Understanding of motivation, performance, and satisfaction is improved by knowledge of union char-

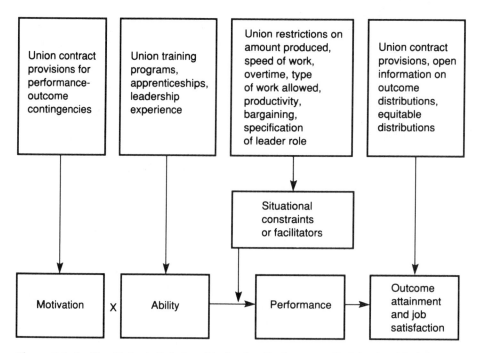

Figure 14–6 The Union's Role in a Motivation-Performance-Satisfaction Model

SOURCE: T. H. Hammer, "Relationships between Local Union Characteristics and Worker Behavior and Attitudes," *Academy of Management Journal, 21* (1978), p. 573.

acteristics. For example, unions can affect the ease with which employees perform their jobs by offering special training, requiring apprenticeships, or giving members leadership experience in union activities. Through labor contracts, the amount of work (such as flight hours per month for airline pilots), speed (controlling the assembly line), overtime per worker, or kinds of tasks an employee can perform (production workers cannot repair broken equipment) can also be restricted. Hammer's model clearly indicates that unions play a significant role in areas traditionally studied by I/O psychologists; to date, this has rarely been acknowledged.

Dispute Settlement

As you might imagine, I/O psychologists have examined the process by which disputes are settled in both laboratory and field settings. As in some other areas of I/O research, the generalizability of laboratory findings in this area are somewhat limited. Gordon, Schmitt, and Schneider (1984) feel the value of laboratory studies is to prepare people for undertaking actual collective bargaining in the future and to help develop questionnaires for later field use in dispute settlement. The authors noted that the limitations of laboratory and field research on dispute settlement are the classic ones discussed in Chapter 2: There is questionable generalizability from laboratory studies, and field studies fail to identify causal relationships.

Recently, there have been several studies on mediation and arbitration as means of dispute settlement. Bazerman and Neale (1982) asked whether strategies of personnel selection and training can improve negotiating effectiveness. They proposed selecting negotiators on the basis of their ability to take a broad perspective on problems and training them not to be overconfident about effecting a resolution. The authors found training increased the number of concessions negotiators were willing to make and concluded that it may be a useful tool in dispute settlement. Neale (1984) determined that when the costs of arbitration are high, negotiators are more likely to reach a resolution on their own before resorting to arbitration. However, when cost is not much of an issue, they are more likely to accept arbitration. Researchers have also discovered the behavioral implications of the different types of arbitration. Starke and Notz (1981) reported that subjects anticipating final-offer arbitration were closer to agreement at the conclusion of their bargaining than subjects anticipating conventional arbitration. In fact, Grigsby and Bigoness (1982) concluded that final-offer, conventional, total-package, and issue-by-issue arbitration all produced different bargaining outcomes even though they are all variations of the same resolution process (arbitration). These behavioral studies on dispute settlement have enhanced our understanding in ways that traditional labor economic research has been unable to do.

Commitment to the Union

The concept of employee commitment to a union addresses the notion of *dual loyalty*: Can a person be loyal to both a labor union and the employing company? Union commitment is a parallel concept to organizational commitment, a topic addressed in Chapter 8. For several years, researchers have examined the antecedents of both union and company commitment. For example, Fukami and Larson (1984) discovered that it was more difficult to explain workers' commitment to their union than their commitment to their employer.

A big stride in our understanding of union commitment was made through a major study by Gordon, Philpot, Burt, Thompson, and Spiller (1980). These authors developed a questionnaire for measuring commitment that was completed by more than 1800 union members. Responses were factor analyzed, and union commitment was found to be composed of four dimensions: (1) loyalty, (2) responsibility to the union, (3) willingness to work for the union, and (4) belief in unionism. The research had at least two major benefits for unions. First, unions could use questionnaires to assess the effect of their actions and estimate solidarity, especially before negotiations. Second, the research revealed the importance of socialization to new union members. The authors felt that union commitment increases when both formal and informal efforts are made to involve a member in union activities soon after joining. Co-worker attitudes and willingness to help are crucial to the socialization process. Improving the socialization of new members improves their commitment, which is one index of union strength. In a follow-up study by Ladd, Gordon, Beauvais, and Morgan (1982), the questionnaire was administered to nonprofessional and professional members of a white-collar union. The results revealed the same factors as those found in the original study despite the sample differences, although other researchers have arrived at somewhat different conclusions (Friedman & Harvey, 1986).

More recently, the research of Angle and Perry (1986) and Gordon and Ladd (1989) suggests the strength of dual commitment within an organization is related to its climate. When there is strong conflict between the two parties (as typically when a union is first voted in), workers tend to align themselves with one party or the other, thus precluding dual commitment. However, where mature collective bargaining relationships exist and there is little hostility between the parties, workers can feel a sense of allegiance to both the union and the company. Thus, the strength of dual commitment can be viewed as a barometer of the degree of cooperation between the parties.

Unions and the Content of I/O Psychology

This book is organized around areas of I/O psychology. At the start of this chapter, we said that unions have a strong influence on the work world. It is thus instructive to examine some of the ways in which unions affect the areas of I/O psychology. While this presentation is not intended to be exhaustive, it will reveal the pervasive union influence on the substantive topics addressed by I/O psychology.

Personnel Selection

In both union and nonunion companies, management determines the knowledge, skills, and abilities needed to fill jobs. The personnel office usually determines fitness for employment in lower-level jobs. For higher-level jobs, responsibility is spread through various units of the company. However, in a union company, the labor contract may stipulate that those hired for jobs represented by the union *must* join the union. This is a *union shop*; the employee has no choice about joining.[1] In other unionized companies, the employee has the *choice* of joining a union; these are *open shops*. However, considerable pressure can be brought on an employee to join. In many cases, it is also to the employee's advantage to join the union for the benefits and protection it affords.

Union influence in personnel selection can affect both applicants and companies. Those who do not endorse unions (or who are uncertain about them) may not apply for jobs in unionized companies. Obviously, the applicant pool for unionized companies will be reduced if such feelings are widespread. The extent of this problem will vary with antiunion sentiment and availability of other jobs.

Union influence can also work in reverse. One company I know of prides itself on remaining nonunionized. It believes unionization is encouraged by employees with prior union experience, and therefore carefully screens job applicants for union membership. Those who have been members are not considered (however, they are not told why). The company wants applicants with the talent needed, but places a higher priority on avoiding unionism. Whether the company can continue this without adversely affecting the quality of the work force will depend on the job openings and the number of applicants for employment with the company. Thus, from the perspectives of both the applicants and the company, unions can and do ultimately influence who gets hired.

Personnel Training

One area in which unions have direct and significant influence is personnel training. One of the oldest forms of training is apprenticeship, and unions have a long history of this kind of training, especially in trades and crafts. Apprenticeship is governed by law; at the national level, it is administered by the U. S. Department of Labor. The Bureau of Apprenticeship and Training works closely with unions, vocational schools, state agencies, and others. According to the U. S. Department of Labor (1977), there are over 425 appreticed occupations employing over 250,000 apprentices. Apprentices go through a formal program of training and experience. They are supervised on the job and are given the facilities needed for instruction. There is a progressive wage schedule over the course of apprenticeship, and the individual is well versed in all aspects of the trade. Some authors (for example, Franklin, 1976) think apprenticeship training is unnecessarily long; but there is little doubt that such programs turn out highly skilled artisans.

Most apprentice programs are in heavily unionized occupations (construction, manufacturing, transportation); thus, unions work closely with the Bureau of Apprenticeship and Training. For example, Figure 14–7 shows the cooperation among various organizations and agencies in the carpentry trade. Though not all unions are

---

[1] However, some states have "right-to-work" laws prohibiting union shops.

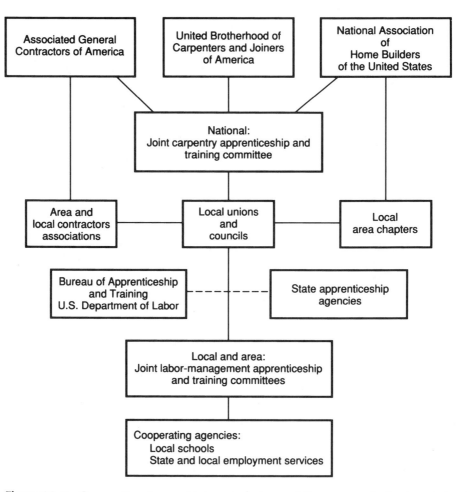

Figure 14–7 Cooperation Among Unions, Industry, and Government in the Apprenticeship System of the Carpentry Trade

SOURCE: U.S. Department of Labor, *Apprenticeship: Past and Present* (Washington, D.C.: U.S. Government Printing Office, 1977), p. 25.

involved in apprentice programs, the link between unions and apprenticeship is one of the oldest in the history of American labor.

Performance Appraisal

A labor contract might specify the dimensions of job performance that will be evaluated. Management may prefer certain aspects, like attendance, while the union may feel that quality of work is salient. Together they decide which aspects will be appraised and the uses of the resulting appraisal information. Pay raises usually are based on merit and seniority; the union may negotiate the contribution of merit in the wage decision. It is obviously beneficial to the union to appraise the "relevant" aspects of work (particularly to supply workers with feedback on performance), but union and management may not agree on the relevant aspects. As with all disputes, disagreements over performance appraisal must be negotiated.

Job Satisfaction

We have already discussed at some length research showing that worker dissatisfaction is associated with a disposition toward unionism. Other research, most notably by Hammer (1978), has shown that satisfaction with pay, working conditions, and security is associated with union status. Unions are seen as *instrumental*; they help employees attain certain outcomes. Thus, these findings are not surprising. In fact, if better pay, fringe benefits, job security, and so on, were *not* related to union status, it is unlikely that unions would survive.

There are no studies that definitely show whether unionized employees are more or less satisfied. Differences in personal characteristics, type of company, union strength, and many other factors would probably moderate this relationship. It should also be recalled that job satisfaction is multifaceted. Union workers may feel more satisfied with certain aspects (like job security) but less satisfied with others (like autonomy). Satisfaction is influenced by unions. Dissatisfaction with employment conditions invites unionization; workers dissatisfied with their unions can vote to expel them. This is called *union decertification*.

Motivation

From various theoretical perspectives, unions should influence motivation. The direction of influence is debatable. According to need theory, unions should fill basic or existence needs; this allows employees to seek fulfillment of higher-order needs. According to expectancy theory, unions are instrumental in attaining desired outcomes like good pay, job security, and fringe benefits. The union enhances instrumentality, which according to the theory, provides for greater motivation.

Some authors think unions suppress motivation. For example, to the extent that a union enhances group solidarity, the strength of a group norm to limit productivity may be greater in a union than a nonunion company. One can think of limiting production as an artificial restriction on outputs, which is a component of the equity theory approach to motivation. However, the norm of production limitation has been observed in both union and nonunion companies; we cannot conclude that unions per se "cause" production limits.

One allegation of college administrators is that unionization of professors would decrease intrinsic motivation. Professionals are supposedly intrinsically motivated by love of their work; it is feared that unions will weaken this and lower output. To date, there is little evidence that professors are any less (or more) productive after unionization. If we infer motivation from productivity, we may conclude, as research suggests, that unionization does not have an appreciable effect on the motivation of college professors. The question of whether unions *cause* increases or decreases in motivation must be solved by complex, longitudinal research; no definitive *empirical* study has answered it. From a *theoretical* perspective, unions should influence motivation.

Leadership

There is little research on how leadership is affected by unions. As part of the validation of the Leader Behavior Description Questionnaire from the Ohio State leadership studies, Fleishman and Harris (1962) showed that the amount of supervisor consideration and initiation of structure influenced the turnover and grievances of unionized employees. However, these findings probably would have been replicated irrespective of union status.

Other areas are ripe for investigation. Union members vote for shop stewards and officials to represent them in collective bargaining. Union members seem to believe that certain characteristics are more effective in bargaining and vote for those who best exemplify them (Stagner, 1956). There are differences in preferences for elected union leaders: some unions favor more outspoken, militant types; others, more experienced and diplomatic types. Management also seeks certain types of leaders with whom it feels it can deal, especially during contract negotiations. In short, there is little doubt that certain leader characteristics are desired by both union and management; the exact nature has yet to be studied empirically.

Organizational Communication

Unions influence communication within organizations. One of the major reasons that employees accept a union is better communication with management. Management must formally direct its comunication to the aggregated work force if the latter is organized.

Grievances are a major channel of organization communication. Workers communicate formal complaints, and management must respond. Some authors contend that grievances are partially meant to "keep management on its toes" and keep it aware of the union. Another major form of union-inspired communication is contract negotiation and administration. Communication is particularly intense during negotiation, but even day-to-day contract interpretation and administration can involve continuous union/management communication. One of the major duties of the shop steward is to communicate employees' cases to management. Other examples of union-based communication include union newsletters, union/management committees, interactions between the local union and the national union, and solicitation of new members. In keeping with the concept of a union as "an organization within an organization," union communication can be classified as *intraorganziational* (communication within the local union), *interorganizational* (communication with management), and *extraorganizational* (communication with the national union). Communication is clearly a dominant thread in the union/management fabric.

Summary

In this chapter, we have examined a topic long neglected by I/O psychologists. Whatever the legitimate or illegitimate reasons, the tide appears to be turning. It is hoped that interest in research on unions over the past ten years will continue. Because I/O psychologists profess interest in human problems in the work world, we simply cannot ignore the impact of unions in this environment. Indeed, as Gordon and Nurick (1981) stated, knowledge of organization behavior is incomplete without an understanding of union influence.

The first part of this chapter reviewed union/management relations. Most of this material is not psychological; it is of great importance in understanding unions, collective bargaining, and union/management relations. Next we examined some recent research on unions. In this area, psychology is beginning to make a contribution. Finally, we reviewed how unions have influenced the basic areas of I/O psychology: employee selection, training, performance appraisal, motivation, satisfaction, and communication.

MAJOR CHAPTER OBJECTIVES IN REVIEW

After having read this chapter, you should know:

1. Nature and formation of a labor union.

2. Labor contracts.

3. Strategies of impasse resolution in the collective bargaining process.

4. Responses to impasse.

5. Grievances and grievance arbitration.

6. Behavioral research results on union/management relations.

CASE STUDY—Should We Let in a Labor Union?

Carl Dwyer and Ann Stovos were faculty members at Springdale College. The college had been in existence for about 30 years, and Dwyer had been on the staff almost since the beginning. Stovos was a relative newcomer, just completing her third year as a faculty member. For the past two years, there had been talk about unionizing the faculty. Much of the interest was sparked by two events.

First, the college had experienced financial cutbacks due to low enrollment. Without tuition revenue, it was facing hardships paying the faculty. As a result, six teaching positions had been eliminated. The faculty understood the college's financial problems, but they felt cutbacks should be made in other areas, like eliminating some administrative positions. The faculty was also critical of how the college determined which teaching positions were eliminated. The other event was that for the third year in a row, the faculty were given only a 5% raise. Other colleges in the state were giving bigger raises, and some of the Springdale faculty felt they were getting the short end of the stick.

Various union representatives had been on campus; there was enough support for a representation election to be held in about a month. The faculty really seemed divided. Some openly supported a union; some were openly opposed; but the majority did not voice their sentiments. Dwyer was opposed to the idea of collective bargaining; Stovos supported it. Since they were office mates, the topic came up quite often. On this particular day, they were discussing whether the goals of unions were compatible with the goals of higher education.

Dwyer began the conversation: "I just don't think there is any place in a college for burly picketers carrying placards and threatening to beat up anyone who crosses the picket line. A college is a place for quiet, scholarly thought, an opportunity to teach interested students, and to contemplate some of the deeper values. I've been here since we had only five buildings and a staff of 20. I don't want to see this place turned into a playground for skull crushers."

"You've been watching too many movies, Carl," Stovos replied. "No one is going to turn Springdale into a battlefield. I want the same things you do. I didn't come here to be physically intimidated. I wouldn't like that any more that you do. But I also want to be treated fairly by the administration. I'd like some security from arbitrary decisions. There's nothing immoral about that, is there?"

"Do you think a union can prevent layoffs and get us 25% yearly raises?" Dwyer asked facetiously.

"No, I don't." Stovos countered, "but a union can force the drafting of fair and equitable policies if layoffs have to occur. And if everyone else is getting 10% raises, maybe they can help us there, too. A union won't work miracles, but it can help to prevent injustice."

"You don't understand, Ann. A college is not a factory. Different ideals run a college. It's not profit but scholarship. We have to foster a climate for inquisitive minds, learning, and personal growth. If I were interested only in making a buck, I wouldn't have become a college professor," Dwyer replied.

"Whether you like it or not, Carl, we are employees like all other working people. What's wrong with trying to ensure fair treatment at work? We have bills to pay and families to support just like everyone else. I don't understand why a college is somehow 'different' from all other employers."

"That's the problem in a nutshell," Dwyer rejoined. "A college is not just an *employer,* and we just don't have *jobs.* We have *careers,* and the success of our career depends on an environment that supports what we are trying to do. Union organizers, picket lines, labor contracts, and mediators have no place in a college."

"I don't see why a college is somehow 'immune' from having to treat its employees fairly like every other employer. What makes a college so special?" Stovos asked.

"Twenty years ago—ten years ago, even—the very thought of a union would have been absurd. The fact that we're now considering one is just proof the quality of education in this country is going downhill. I can just see it now: 'Sorry class, this is our last meeting. I'm going on strike Monday,'" Dwyer fumed. He got up from his desk, grabbed his coat and hat, and headed off for a meeting.

Stovos shot back, "I suppose you'd feel better if you met your class for the last time because *you* were one of the ones whose position got eliminated."

Dwyer didn't answer, but he slammed the door on the way out.

Questions

1. Do you feel that Dwyer is correct in believing a union would interfere with the goals of higher education?

2. What benefits does Stovos see from unionization?

3. Do you believe that some organizations, because of their purpose and goals, should not have unionized employees? If so, which ones, and why?

4. Do you think the respective lengths of time that Dwyer and Stovos had spent at the college have any relation to their attitudes? Why or why not?

5. When you think of unions, what thoughts come to mind? Why do you feel as you do?

15

Work Conditions

People work under a broad array of conditions. For example, most people work indoors, but some work outdoors. Some jobs require exposure to intense heat, cold, and noise; others offer temperate conditions. Many people work from 8:00 A.M. to 5:00 P.M., but other hours are also common. Some jobs involve a high risk of injury or illness; others are low risk. How do these different conditions affect attitudes and behavior? What have I/O psychologists learned about responses to variations in working conditions? This chapter is devoted to how work conditions affect the employee.

Before we begin, it should be acknowledged that research in this area has been conducted in a wide range of professions. Though I/O psychology has made many contributions to the area, so have engineering, physiology, and medicine. Engineers have designed tools, equipment, and work procedures to minimize employee stress and fatigue. Physiologists have studied the effect of heat, cold, noise, and other forms of physical stress on the human body. Physicians studying industrial medicine examine the relationship between certain illnesses and types of work, such as black lung disease among coal miners and cancer among asbestos workers. Thus, research on working conditions and employee behavior is interdisciplinary. Many of the questions addressed extend beyond I/O psychology, but our profession is a primary contributor to the area.

Physical Stressors in the Workplace

As discussed in Chapter 8, stress is highly complex and multifaceted. According to the approach of Beehr and Newman (1978), the causes of stress include work demands, role pressures, and organization characteristics. We discussed how role pressures contribute to stress in Chapter 8. In this chapter we will examine how work demands (noise, heat, and cold) and some organization characteristics (most notably work hours) contribute. There are wide individual differences associated with perceptions of stress. That is, one person may feel stressed by a hectic schedule; another may enjoy the challenge and variety. Any stimulus (for example, work pace, noise, role pressure) that elicits a stress response is a *stressor*. Stressors associated with the physical conditions of work elicit fairly consistent stress responses. However, the *degree* of stress is often moderated by individual differences.

Noise

Noise is defined as "unwanted sound." But before we present the effects of noise on performance, we must understand the characteristics of sound. Two physical characteristics are *frequency* and *intensity*; their psychological counterparts are *pitch* and *loudness*. Sound emanates in waves. If the sound is "pure" (like a tuning fork), a graph of the wave looks like a sine (sinusoidal) wave. Low-frequency sounds have fewer wave repetitions per unit of time than high-frequency sounds. In fact, the number of waves per second is the frequency. Frequency is usually measured in cycles per second (cps), or Hertz (Hz). Impure sounds have more complex wave patterns because they are composed of differing frequencies. The psychological analogue of frequency is pitch; we recognize this by saying that a tenor has a different pitch than a soprano.

Intensity of sound is usually measured in decibels (dB) and reflects differences in sound energy. The decibel scale is constructed such that a change of 10 dB means a tenfold change in sound power. Differences in frequency are represented by differences in waves per second; differences in intensity are represented by differences in the height of the waves. "Loud" sounds have more intensity than "soft" sounds. Figure 15–1 shows various sounds and associated decibel values.

It is difficult to say definitely what effect noise has on performance since "performance" has been examined in many contexts. Some aspects of performance are more affected by noise than others. Early research on noise stress (for example, Broadbent, 1957) suggested that only when levels exceeded 90 dB was there an appreciable decrease in performance. However, later research indicates that lower levels can disrupt certain dimensions of performance. In particular, Cohen (1968) found that tasks requiring concentration are more likely to be adversely affected by noise.

Additional research added to our knowledge of how noise affects people, and revealed the complexity of this relationship. Fiedler and Fiedler (1975) compared the verbal and behavioral reactions of people living near a large airport and those in communities out of the airport's noise range. In general, people who lived near the airport developed ways of coping with, adjusting to, or ignoring the noise. There were few differences between the two groups on such variables as headaches or nervousness, disruption of social lives, and length of residence. This indicates that some people, at least, can adjust to noise. The authors also found wide individual differences in noise tolerance. Some people complained of noise-induced headaches, irritability, and sleeplessness even though they lived in areas free of aircraft-related noise or noise from heavy highway traffic. The proportion of people complaining about noise was equivalent in the two groups. The results suggest that aircraft-related noise did not systematically affect many lives.

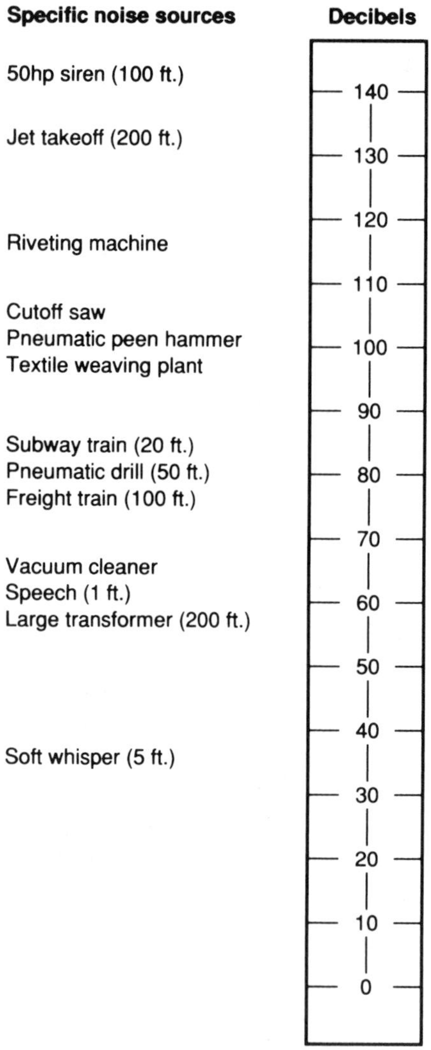

Specific noise sources	Decibels
50hp siren (100 ft.)	140
Jet takeoff (200 ft.)	130
	120
Riveting machine	110
Cutoff saw Pneumatic peen hammer Textile weaving plant	100
	90
Subway train (20 ft.) Pneumatic drill (50 ft.) Freight train (100 ft.)	80
	70
Vacuum cleaner Speech (1 ft.) Large transformer (200 ft.)	60
	50
	40
Soft whisper (5 ft.)	30
	20
	10
	0

Figure 15–1 Decibel Levels for Various Sounds

SOURCE: A. P. Petersen and F. E. Gross, *Handbook of Noise Measurement,* 8th ed. (New Concord, Mass.: GenRad, 1978).

Noweir (1984) examined the effects of noise (80–99 dB) on employees in three textile mills. Employees with high noise exposure (above 90 dB) had more disciplinary actions, accidents, and absenteeism and less productivity than employees with less noise exposure. Noise appeared to affect the quality of work, as reflected by disciplinary actions for material damage, and was particularly evident for spinning operations involving vigilance.

Weinstein (1978) studied sensitivity of college students to noise in a dormitory.

A sample of college freshmen completed a self-report measure of noise sensitivity before they arrived on campus. Two groups were created based on the scores: a noise-sensitive and a noise-insensitive group. Performance of both groups on a number of variables was monitored during freshman year. Sensitive students were much more bothered by dormitory noise and became increasingly disturbed by noise over the year. They also had less academic ability, felt less secure socially, and had a greater desire for privacy. Unlike those in the airport study, college students couldn't adjust to or ignore dormitory noise. The results suggest that colleges might consider providing noise-sensitive students with special housing. A related finding was reported by Topf (1985), who examined personal and environmental predictors of patient disturbance due to hospital noise. Topf found that personal sensitivity to noise was as valid a predictor of noise disturbance as was the objectively measured noise level in the hospital. As Weinstein found, it seems some people can tolerate noise in their lives better than others.

It should be apparent that there are no simple relationships between noise and human performance. Noise adversely affects performance on some tasks but not others. Additionally, some people are more sensitive to noise than others. To the extent that I/O psychologists can (1) identify tasks whose performance will be impaired by noise, and (2) identify people sensitive to noise, steps can be taken to improve the worker-workplace fit. Headphones and sound-proofed construction materials can be used in jobs prone to interference from noise. People can be hired based on their sensitivity to noise. As stated, with differences in both jobs and people, the I/O psychologist's job is to get as good a match as possible between abilities and work requirements.

Hearing Loss from Work. Employees exposed to intense noise over long periods of time usually lose a portion of their hearing. If the noise is of a particular frequency, partial or complete hearing loss to tones of that frequency is quite possible. Employees exposed to intense noise over the full spectrum of frequencies may suffer a general hearing decrease.

A study by La Benz, Cohen, and Pearson (1967) provides empirical evidence of work-related hearing loss. They examined hearing capacity for earth-moving equipment operators repeatedly exposed to noise levels ranging from 90 to 120 dB. They gave hearing tests and compared results with estimates of hearing loss typical for individuals of comparable age. Figure 15–2 shows the respective losses for three groups of operators differing in year of exposure, corrected for age. The hearing loss was particularly acute at higher frequencies (that is, voice range) for more experienced workers.

To protect workers in noisy jobs (like airline ground employees, construction workers, and data processors) from hearing loss, companies provide headphones or earplugs. Many labor contracts specify that not wearing such safety equipment is grounds for dismissal. Some companies also approach the problem of noise stress by means of personnel selection, hiring partially or totally deaf people for noisy jobs.

Noise stress is a major concern for some companies. Noisy equipment may have to be reengineered or housed in certain areas to lessen disruptive influences. Special

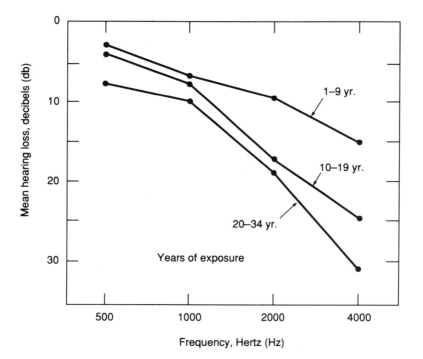

Figure 15–2 Mean Hearing Loss of Three Groups of Earth-Moving Equipment
Operators Varying in Years of Exposure

SOURCE: P. LaBenz, A. Cohen, and B. Pearson, "A Noise and Hearing Survey of Earth-Moving Equipment
Operators," *American Industrial Hygiene Association Journal, 28* (March-April 1967), pp. 117–128.

ear protection has been devised, eliminating the intensity of unwanted noise while
still permitting communication among workers. Employees suffering from work-
related hearing impairment are eligible for special compensation from employers;
some victims of hearing loss have sued employers for not providing safe working
conditions. Fortunately, risk of hearing impairment is slight in most jobs, but in
those where it is a problem, corrective measures are necessary.

Heat

Discomfort from heat is due not only to high temperatures. Adjustment to heat is a
function of three variables: air temperature, humidity, and airflow. High temperatures, high humidity, and a lack of airflow are most uncomfortable. Some research
(for example, Pepler, 1958) indicated that humidity may be the most important
variable in determining discomfort. With high temperature and humidity, rapid air
movement can make the situation tolerable. Because the sensation of heat cannot be
adequately measured by simply recording air temperature, other indexes have been
developed. One used in enclosed environments is the wet-bulb globe temperature

(WBGT). This takes into account the effects of humidity in combination with air temperature. The WBGT is a more sensitive index of discomfort than simple air temperature.

Heat stress is a problem not only for those who work outdoors but also for people working around furnaces, boilers, dryers, and other heat-producing equipment. Heat stress can greatly impair productivity of those doing strenuous work. Workers lose stamina because their bodies are taxed by the combination of heat and physical exertion. However, heat stress can also impair performance in tasks requiring little physical effort, even those limited to mental skills. For example, Fine and Kobrick (1978) compared performance of individuals working on problem-solving tasks under different heat-stress conditions. The treatment group worked under 95° F and 88% humidity; the control group worked under 70° F and 25% humidity. Performance was monitored for seven hours. Results are shown in Figure 15–3. The number of errors made by the treatment group was considerably greater, and the extent of the difference became greater over time.

Organizations are aware of the effects of heat and expend a lot of money to cope

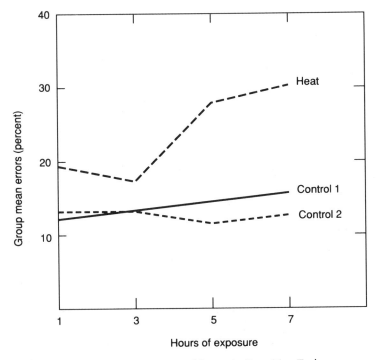

Figure 15–3 Mean Percentage of Errors in Cognitive Tasks over a Seven-Hour Period for a Group Working Under Heat and for Two Control Groups

SOURCE: B. J. Fine and J. L. Kobrick, "Effects of Altitude and Heat on Complex Cognitive Tasks," *Human Factors, 20* (1978), pp. 115–122. Copyright 1978 by The Human Factors Society, Inc., and reproduced by permission.

with the problem. Central air-conditioning is a standard feature of most new office buildings. Dehumidifiers are installed where humidity may affect performance or damage sensitive equipment (like computers). Industrial fans are often installed to draw off the heat (and noxious fumes) associated with some types of manufacturing. However, in many cases, the climate cannot be controlled or modified, as in outdoor work. In such cases, workers may be allowed more rest breaks or may be relieved by other crews. Given rising energy costs, it is increasingly expensive to maintain ideal climates. Recent federal rulings specify thermostat levels (65° in the winter, 78° in the summer) for office buildings as a means of limiting energy consumption. How do people react to these temperature conditions? Vickroy, Shaw, and Fisher (1982) studied the effect of employees' clothing (suit, long-sleeved or short-sleeved shirts) on performance and satisfaction at the two temperature levels. They found that employees who wore appropriate clothing for the temperature showed higher levels of performance and satisfaction with the working conditions than did those wearing inappropriate clothing.

Cold

Both mental and physical tasks are affected by cold; however, there is evidence that people can adapt to cold over time (Teichner & Kobrick, 1955). Prolonged exposure constricts blood vessels, which reduces blood flow to the skin surface and reduces skin temperature. Under such conditions, exposed skin and extremities (fingers and toes) become numb. Under more extreme conditions, total body temperature will be lowered. Manual performance is adversely affected by lowered body temperature, even when hands are kept warm (Lockhart, 1966). Similar results have been reported for tasks requiring concentration (Poulton, Hitchings, & Brooke, 1965). In attempting to explain this, Fox (1967) suggested that cold causes other stimuli to compete for the individual's attention. Cooling of the extremities, with the resulting threat of injury, distracts the worker from the task at hand, thus lowering performance. In particular, tasks requiring fine finger dexterity are more susceptible to impairment from the cold than grosser types of manual activity.

With outdoor activities, wind chill can be a major factor affecting workers. The *wind chill index* provides a means for making a quantitative comparison of combinations of temperature and wind speed. Table 15–1 shows the cooling effects of combinations of certain temperatures and wind speeds derived from the index, these being expressed as equivalent temperatures. An *equivalent temperature* refers to the sensation of cold and wind. For example, an air temperature of 10° F with a 20-mph wind produces the same cooling sensation as a temperature of -25° F under calm wind conditions. Extreme cold produced by a windchill increases numbness and reaction time (Ellis, 1982). However, visual performance (as measured by speed or precision in responding) is generally not impaired by exposure to cold. Continued exposure to extremely cold temperatures produces frostbite, a danger encountered by outdoor workers, especially in the Midwest. In Midwest states the temperature gets down to -20° F, and with the strong wind that blows across the plains of 30 to 40 mph, the windchill temperature can reach -70° F. Prolonged exposure to such temperatures by

TABLE 15–1   *Cooling Effects of Temperature and Wind Speed*

Wind Speed, mph	Air Temperature, °F					
	40	**20**	**10**	**0**	**−10**	**−30**
Calm	40	20	10	0	−10	−30
5	37	16	6	−5	−15	−36
10	28	4	−9	−21	−33	−46
20	18	−10	−25	−39	−53	−67
30	13	−18	−33	−48	−63	−79
40	10	−21	−37	−53	−69	−85

individuals who must work outdoors (as do highway maintenance crews) can ultimately produce death. Special clothing and footwear have been designed for the workers' protection. Additionally, some workers receive extra compensation for working in the cold. Fortunately, few indoor jobs involve exposure to extremely cold temperatures.

Multiple Stressors

Stressors need not exist in isolation. If they exist jointly, a worker must contend with their *additive* or *interactive* effects. For example, if the noise level and the heat level each decrease performance by 10%, the combined effect of a hot, noisy workplace may reduce performance 20%. These two stressors have an *additive* effect. However, in some cases, stressors have an *interactive* effect; their combined effect may exceed the sum of the independent effects.

I recall an episode from a job analysis that illustrates the effect of multiple stressors. A construction worker described his job in the summer as being "hot and noisy." I wanted to observe him at work. He was using a pneumatic air drill to remove street pavement, and the temperature was 90° F. However, the heat radiating off the pavement made the temperature at street level over 110° F. The noise from a pneumatic drill (at a range of about 15 feet) was over 100 dB. After observing this worker for about five minutes and taking notes on his job duties, the effect of the heat and noise made me feel faint and nauseated. While the construction worker could perform under those conditions, I could not. I found the noise worse than the heat, but the combined effect made me abandon my efforts, I also learned that simple descriptive phrases like "hot and noisy" mean different things to different people.

From a practical standpoint, stressors occurring in combination create a far more dangerous work environment than stressors occurring in isolation. Attempts to minimize the effects of one stressor may compound the effects of the other. While protective headgear can reduce noise, the extra covering can increase the effects of heat. Headgear for protecting a worker from cold may also impair hearing and may cause accidents. Action taken to minimize stressor effects must not make the worker vulnerable to other potential hazards.

Fatigue

Fatigue is quite elusive, yet it is a major symptom associated with poor worker-workplace fit. There are several kinds of fatigue, and they all have physiological and psychological characteristics. The I/O psychologist studies fatigue not to understand its physiological basis but to eliminate as many of its effects, particularly on performance and satisfaction, as possible.

The symptoms of fatigue include tiredness, diminished willingness to work, and boredom. Fatigue is a physiological phenomenon meaning a reduction in performance capability that can be restored by rest. In contrast, boredom is a psychological phenomenon meaning a reduction in mental performance capability, which is the result of monotony. However, fatigue is not synonymous with being bored or tired; such feelings may be short-lived and can be "cured" by a diversion or a night's sleep. Fatigue is more generalized and enduring. Also, distinguishing various kinds of fatigue is difficult because of interrelated effects.

Several authors (for example, Grandjean, 1968) attempted to isolate different kinds of fatigue; there seem to be four major varieties. The most distinct type is *muscular* fatigue, caused by prolonged and demanding physical activity. This is associated with biochemical changes and is an acute pain in the muscles. *Mental* fatigue is more closely aligned with feelings of boredom associated with monotonous work. *Emotional* fatigue results from intense stress and is generally characterized by a dulling of emotional responses. Finally, *skills* fatigue is associated with a decline in attention to certain tasks. With skills fatigue, standards of accuracy and performance become progressively lower (McFarland, 1971). The decline is thought to be a major cause of accidents, particularly involving automobiles and airplanes.

All four kinds of fatigue are associated with neurochemical changes in the blood. They serve to create an inhibiting system in the body that operates in contrast to our arousal system. The inhibiting system tends to retard our normal functioning, such that mentally, physically, and emotionally we operate in a more subdued fashion. That is, our physiological mechanisms protect us in response to some previous form of overstimulation that precipitated the fatigue. Our ability to react normally to job contexts becomes retarded when we suffer from fatigue. In particular, both our sense of timing and vigilance are often impaired. *Timing* involves the precise coordination of integrated behaviors into a pattern or sequence. Typing on a typewriter or driving a car would be two examples. *Vigilance* refers to alertness in monitoring and responding to critical stimuli in the environment. Reading the text material to be typed and paying attention to traffic, road conditions, and pedestrians would be examples of vigilance. Fatigue has been found to impede our sense of timing and our capacity to be vigilant. Individuals can more readily endure the effects of fatigue in jobs that require little timing or vigilance, but these components are critical to the conduct of many jobs.

I/O psychologists are concerned with all four types of fatigue, though their response to each is different. Muscular fatigue is best dealt with through new work procedures so people will not overexert themselves. It may involve redesigning a piece of equipment or finding other, less strenuous ways to perform the task. Mental fatigue is addressed through job redesign that attempts to make work more stimulating and challenging. However, as we saw in Chapter 13, individuals differ widely in what they think is boring. Emotional fatigue is usually caused by factors external to the workplace, but an increasing number of organizations are providing counseling services for employees. Companies are doing this because performance can be affected by problems either within or outside the workplace. Skills fatigue is a major concern for those in jobs with a small margin for error. For a pilot or air-traffic controller, the consequences of lower standards can be severe and tragic. Such employees are continually monitored for skills fatigue, and are given time off when necessary.

People differ in susceptibility to fatigue and jobs differ in inducing fatigue. I/O psychologists still have much to learn about fatigue, particularly treatment and prediction. Muscle fatigue is easier to remedy than mental fatigue, at least on a long-term basis. We can better predict the type of person who will be fatigued on a *group* basis. Fatigue is the product of a poor match between our abilities and environmental demands.

Ergonomic Approaches to Work Design

Ergonomics is the study of people's behavior to their work. Ergonomics is also sometimes referenced as "human factors engineering." The purpose of ergonomics is the adaptation of work conditions to the physical and psychological nature of people. Note that the ergonomic perspective on achieving person-environment congruence is to hold the individual as a constant, and mold the work environment to the person. The theory behind ergonomics is that environments are more malleable than people; thus, it is the environment that is adapted to the limitations and qualities of people. The personnel selection and training approaches take the opposite perspective—that is, people are either selected or "shaped" to fit the environment. In reality, of course, successful person-environment fits require a combination of all three approaches.

Grandjean (1986) presents four major objectives of ergonomics:

1. Fitting the demands of work to the efficiency of people to reduce stress;

2. Designing machines, equipment, and installations so that they can be operated with great efficiency, accuracy, and safety;

3. Working out proportions and conditions of the workplace to ensure correct body posture; and

4. Adapting lighting, air-conditioning, noise, and so on, to suit people's physical requirements.

You should note the "environment" can take on a wide variety of physical situations: the physical conduct of work, equipment design, workplace lay out—in short, the arena in which people operate. When I/O psychologists speak of an environment (that is, a machine or work site) as having been "ergonomically designed," we mean it was developed or designed with special regard for its impact on the physical or psychological well-being of the operator (see Field Note 1).

Field Note 1

The field of ergonomics is experiencing a rejuvenation. About 30 years ago our nation's interest in the space program triggered a large outpouring of interest in ergonomics. Designing space capsules that could be operated by an astronaut captivated a great deal of attention. In one space flight the astronauts were instructed to flip a switch "up" to conduct some flight operation. Upon doing so the capsule began to shake violently, so the astronauts flipped the switch "down," contrary to what they were supposed to do. The capsule's operation returned to normal, and no one knew what went wrong. Then someone figured it out. In the weightlessness of space, the astronauts happened to be floating upside-down at the time. Thus, the "up" and "down" positions of the switch became reversed from their vantage point. This was a condition no one on gravity-bound Earth had anticipated when the system was being designed.

The military has been a continual user of ergonomic research, but after our nation's interest in the space program began to wane, there was a concomitant reduction of interest in ergonomics. However, that trend appears to be reversing again. With the boom in high-tech equipment, such as computers, copiers, and electronic recreational products, there is renewed interest in designing these products from a human perspective—that is, to be "user friendly,"—a phrase reflecting an ergonomic orientation. I continue to witness a growing number of jobs for psychologists in the field of ergonomics. What the space program did for ergonomics in the 1960s is being recreated by the high-tech companies of the 1980s and 1990s.

There are three fundamental paradigms that guide the ergonomic analysis and design of work. As was noted at the start of this chapter, researchers from many disciplines other than psychology contribute to ergonomics. These disciplines have contributed heavily to the development and utilization of these paradigms. They are the anthropometric, biomechanical, and physiological bases of work design. Each will be briefly explained, and illustrative examples of work design from each paradigm will be presented.

Anthropometrics

Anthropometry is the study of people in terms of their physical dimensions. It includes the measurement of human body characteristics, such as size, breadth, girth, and distance between anatomical points. Anthropometrists take a very large number of measurements (for example, the distance between shoulder and elbow, the distance between the eyes, and so forth) on individuals to create a sizable data base. The measurements are categorized by demographic variables such as sex, age, and ethnicity, because of their relationship to the variables being measured. That is, males are typically physically bigger than females, our bodies change shape as we get older, and different races have differing physical proportions. Figure 15–4 shows the measurement of two body characteristics, one using a caliper and the other an anthropometer. With descriptive statistics as percentiles, figures are calculated representing major points in the distribution of anthropometric data. Thus, we can describe individuals according to their body characteristics compared to their norm group. For example,

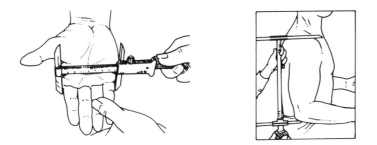

Figure 15–4 Two Instruments Used to Assess Body Measurements: A Caliper and an Anthropometer

SOURCE: K.H. Kroemer, H.J. Kroemer, and K.E. Kroemer-Elbert, *Engineering Physiology*, (New York: Elsevier, 1986).

a person who is at 80th percentile in height but 30th percentile in weight would have a tall slender build.

The compilation of anthropometric measurements becomes the basis for equipment design, used in either work or leisure. Countless examples abound for the application of anthropometric measures. The size of the keys on a typewriter and the spacing between the keys was determined through anthropometry. Men with stubby fingers sometimes have difficulty typing because most keyboards were designed for people with smaller hand features. Figure 15–5 shows ten hand-object couplings. The size of the object would be designed in accordance with anthropometric data about people's hands. The width of airline and theatre seats were similarly determined through examination of the measures on the associated relevant body parts. The leisure industry (that is, sports equipment) also draws heavily on anthropometric data to determine the size of football helmets, golf clubs, tennis racquets, and so forth.

The military also makes great use of anthropometrics. Because people in the military come in a broad range of sizes, weapons and equipment have to be designed to accommodate a broad range of individual differences. I once heard a ergonomist comment on the problems of designing an adjustable monitor screen and chair that could accommodate operators (either male or female) who were in the 10th percentile in height and 90th percentile in weight, or vice versa. Thus, this system had to be workable (that is, a readable screen and a comfortable chair) for people who were short and heavy, tall and thin, or anything in between.

As a final note on anthropometrics, the collection of such information over time is a subtle way to trace the changing physical characteristics of a society. For example, anthropometricians have long known that people get wider in the britches as they get older. However, there are data to suggest that as a society we are changing our shape in that area. Americans of any certain age and gender (for example, 40-year-old males) are about 1 inch wider in the buttocks than their counterparts of just 25 years ago. We do not know why this is happening, and speculation has ranged from changing diets to having more sedentary jobs to changing exercise patterns. For whatever the reason, our prototypical physical shape is slowly being altered. Perhaps in the forthcoming decades airlines will not be able to place six seats across in an aisle (unless they make the planes wider, too).

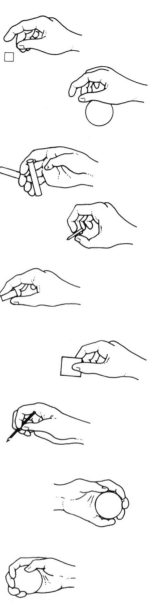

1. Finger Touch:
   One finger touches an object without holding it.

2. Palm Touch:
   Some part of the inner surface of the hand touches the object without holding it.

3. Finger Palmar Grip (Hook Grip):
   One finger or several fingers hook(s) onto a ridge, or handle. This type of finger action is used where thumb counterforce is not needed.

4. Thumb-Fingertip Grip (Tip Grip):
   The thumb tip opposes one fingertip.

5. Thumb-Finger Palmar Grip (Pinch or Plier Grip): Thumb pad opposes the palmar pad of one finger (or the pads of several fingers) near the tips. This grip evolves easily from coupling #4.

6. Thumb-Forefinger Side Grip (Lateral Grip) or Side Pinch: Thumb opposes the (radial) side of the forefinger.

7. Thumb-Two-Finger Grip (Writing Grip): Thumb and two fingers (often forefinger and index finger) oppose each other at or near the tips.

8. Thumb-Fingertips Enclosure (Disk Grip): Thumb pad and the pads of three or four fingers oppose each other near the tips (object grasped does not touch the palm). This grip evolves easily from coupling #7.

9. Finger-Palm Enclosure (Collet Enclosure): Most, or all, of the inner surface of the hand is in contact with object while enclosing it.

10. Power Grasp:
    The total inner hand surface is grasping the (often cylindrical) handle which runs parallel to the knuckles and generally protrudes on one or both sides from the hand.

Figure 15–5   Ten Couplings Between Hand and Object

SOURCE: K.H. Kroemer, H.J. Kroemer, and K.E. Kroemer-Elbert, *Engineering Physiology,* (New York: Elsevier, 1986).

Biomechanics

Biomechanics is defined as the application of mechanical principles (such as levers and forces) to the analysis of body-part structure and movement. Where anthropometrics is utilized in equipment design, biomechanics helps to determine the physical movements required in work. Furthermore, as opposed to body measurements, biomechanics is concerned with the effect of movement and force upon human muscles, tendons, and nerves. Its focus is how the conduct of work affects these bodily parts, and in turn, the best way to design work to minimize stress, pain, or fatigue.

Biomechanics entails the use of complex sensing instruments designed to measure the effects of movements on the body. For example, there are instruments that measure how much force your arms can exert as a function of the angle of your elbow, how much stress is applied to your shoulders as a function of the position of your arms, and so on. Extensive use is also made of motion pictures and video recorders that focus upon close-up views of the body while performing work. Through this information biomechanics provides a way to design work that is most compatible with the physical limits of the human body. An example of the biomechanical approach to work design is presented in Figure 15–6.

Note the right arm of the individual in both photographs. In *a*, the man's wrist is held at a pronounced angle, and his arm extends directly outward from his shoulder. It was concluded that work performed in this way produces strain on both the

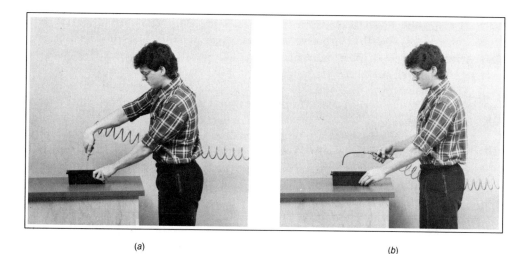

(a)   (b)

Figure 15–6   Air Gun Designs and Muscle Usage

Two versions of air gun design are shown in use cleaning a mold. In *a*, the air gun barrel and handle are straight. This posture is uncomfortable and reduces gripping strength, which results in the force applied to the trigger being a greater percentage of maximum strength. In *b*, the air gun barrel has been bent down at a 90-degree angle; the handle is also bent down at about 70 degrees. The trigger has been replaced with a levered bar that requires less force to operate.

SOURCE: Eastman Kodak Company, *Ergonomic Design for People at Work*, vol. 2 (New York: Van Nostrand Reinhold, 1986).

wrist and the shoulder. Repeated exposure to this pattern of movement can cause a very painful condition in the wrist called carpal tunnel syndrome. In *b*, note the wrist is not held at such an extreme angle, and the right arm hangs by the worker's side. Modifying the shape of the air gun used to perform the job shown in the photographs made it no longer necessary for the worker to "modify" his body position and movements in ways that could cause injury.

The biomechanical approach to work design goes well beyond the domain of psychology into such disciplines as physics and human anatomy. As such, biomechanics is an interdisciplinary approach to designing work; as its very name would suggest, a fusion of mechanical principles and living organisms. In many ways the biomechanical approach to work design is the classic human-factors perspective: the design of the physical requirements of work to be compatible with the capabilities and limitations of the human body.

Physiological

The physiological approach to work design focuses upon the underlying systemic aspects of the body, such as circulation, respiration, and metabolism. From this perspective work is designed with regard to such parameters as oxygen flow, blood flow, heart rate, and blood pressure. As is characteristic of ergonomics in general, there is extensive reliance on measurement, in this case the measurement of physiological responses of the body. Rather than speaking about such issues as muscle fatigue or back strain, physiologists address the specific neurochemical conditions that produce the symptoms of fatigue and strain. Therefore, "work" is thought of in terms of the flow of nerve impulses, sugar metabolism, and acid secretion.

A good illustration of the physiological perspective is shown in Figure 15–7. Pictured are three ways to carry a satchel, and their associated effect on oxygen consumption. Carrying the satchel like a backpack (*a*) results in the lowest amount of oxygen (and thus energy) consumption. Carrying the satchel slung over the shoulder (*b*) consumes 82% more energy. Finally, carrying the satchel as a briefcase (*c*) is the most consumptive of energy. It would also be instructive to use Figure 15–7 to compare the anthropometric, biomechanical, and physiological approaches to work design. Anthropometrics would seek to design the satchel to be approximately equal to the width of a person's back, biomechanics would consider the strain caused by the satchel on the body, and physiologists would address themselves to energy depletion.

Another example of the physiological perspective would be the analysis of the causes of muscle fatigue. Muscle fatigue is caused by the body's producing lactic acid at a faster rate than oxygen can be delivered through the circulation system. Energy is provided by the body as a result of burning nutrients from food with oxygen (aerobic) and without (anaerobic). Most of the oxygen is delivered to the muscle cells from the circulatory system, with blood flow to the muscles matching the muscular demands for oxygen after a few minutes of work. By measuring the amount of oxygen a person uses during work, the amount of aerobic metabolism taking place can be calculated. Thus, work tasks requiring moderate or heavy effort are designed

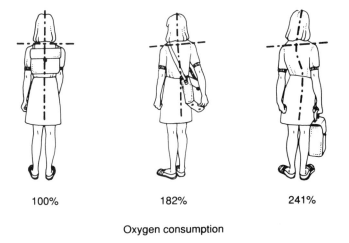

Oxygen consumption

Figure 15–7 Effect of Effort on Energy Consumption (Measured by Oxygen Consumption) for Three Ways of Carrying a School Satchel

SOURCE: M.S. Malhotra and J. Sengupta, "Carrying of School Bags by Children," *Ergonomics 8*, (1965), pp. 55–60.

to keep the demands low enough to permit aerobic metabolism to supply the necessary energy. If the demands exceed what aerobic metabolism can provide, the anaerobic metabolic system helps to produce energy but also produces lactic acid in the process. Hence, it is common for workers in jobs requiring intense bursts of energy (such as firefighters) to experience fatigue quickly. Work designers therefore try to distribute the intensity and duration of peak energy demands to reduce these fatigue-producing conditions. In jobs where intense energy bursts are unavoidable, attention would be given to the use of equipment to help ease the energy demand, or providing backup personnel to permit adequate recovery.

The physiological perspective approaches work design from the most molecular perspective. As with biomechanics, it embraces scientific methods not usually found in the more traditional areas of I/O psychology. Because all work activities have an inherent physiological basis to them, this perspective is particularly well adapted to studying all types of jobs. With the recent advances of computerization, many people now make use of video display terminals (VDTs) in their jobs. There is a growing body of literature that suggests that extensive use of VDTs leads to visual strain and physical discomfort in the neck-shoulder area (Stellman, Klitzman, Gordon, & Snow, 1987). Grandjean (1987) has examined the physiological effects of VDTs on vision as a function of various characteristics of VDTs, such as brightness, contrast, and flicker. He reports definite patterns between photometric characteristics and physiological responses, and recommends that VDTs be designed from an ergonomic perspective as well as from a purely mechanical one. Grandjean also has studied the effects of hand placements and positions, and believes they also contribute to operator efficiency and satisfaction. He believes the VDT workstation has become the launch vehicle for ergonomics in the office world.

Overview

The anthropometric, biomechanical, and physiological perspectives in work design are simply three ways to modify the environment to accommodate the characteristics and limitation of people. While each approach has its own distinctive focus, they are not mutually exclusive. Anthropometric information can be of great help in the design of work from a biomechanical perspective. However, you should think of approaches as three tacks researchers have found useful to modify the environment to fit people in the conduct of work. Anthropometrics relies on a descriptive inventory of bodily measurements, biomechanics examines major body parts and movements in terms of mechanical principles; and the physiological perspective deals with the effect of work on the body's fundamental systems.

Safety and Accidents

Industrial safety and accidents are among the oldest topics in I/O psychology, dating back to the turn of the century. One of the first responsibilities of psychologists was developing safer working conditions. Engineers also contribute greatly, particularly in equipment design and plant layout. While we have made big strides in improving work safety, industrial accidents still are a major concern. The National Safety Council has published some alarming statistics (De Reamer, 1980):

1. Approximately 1 million productive person-*years* are lost annually through work accidents.

2. Accidents cost the nation at least $51.1 billion in lost wages, medical expenses, property damage, and insurance costs.

3. One American worker dies every eight minutes from an industrial accident.

4. Injuries to U.S. workers each year have the same economic impact as if the nation's entire industrial community shut down for one full week.

5. In the United States, loss of life from accidents during this century far exceeds that from wars, earthquakes, floods, tornadoes, and other natural catastrophies *combined.*

Researchers in different disciplines address the problem of industrial accidents from many perspectives, but all are concerned with reducing frequency and severity. I/O psychologists focus on individual characteristics associated with accidents, and investigate various traditional approaches (personnel selection, work design, and training) in accident reduction. Industrial hygienists view occupational diseases as consequences of recurring events or accidents. Safety engineers see accidents as results of a sequence of acts or events with undesirable consequences like personal injury, property damage, or work interruption.

Accidents and injuries are not synonymous. Injury is the consequence of an accident, but many "no-injury" accidents also occur. Though psychologists are concerned with accidents whether or not they result in injury, they generally pay more attention to those accidents involving injuries.

Safety Legislation

There are state and federal laws to protect the welfare of the worker. The major one is the Occupational and Safety Health Act (OSHA). OSHA became effective in 1971; it was meant to integrate federal and state legislation under a federal program establishing uniform codes, standards, and regulations. The purpose of the act is "to assure, as far as possible, every working woman and man in the nation safe and healthful working conditions, and to preserve our human resources." To accomplish this, there are provisions for safety and health standards, research, information, and education and training in occupational safety and health (De Reamer, 1980).

OSHA is comprehensive, covering such things as record keeping, inspection, compliance, and enforcement of safety standards (Nothstein, 1981). It lists over 5,000 safety and health standards. Standards are specified ranging from density of particles in the air to the height at which a fire extinguisher is to be mounted. Some critics suggest that the act is too concerned with "Mickey Mouse" standards that burden employers without really protecting workers. Others consider OSHA one of the most important and influential pieces of legislation ever enacted. The law provides

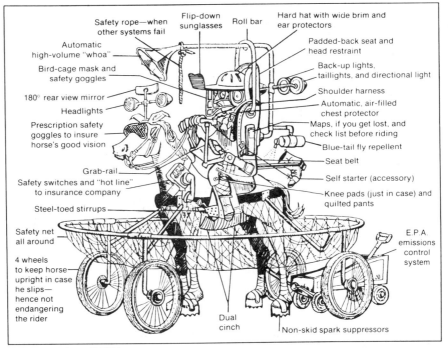

Cowboy after OSHA

for safety inspections and fines for noncompliance. Over 100,000 inspections are conducted annually by trained officers. Companies can be fined for maintaining improper safety records, and for the willful violation of safety standards. In 1987, financial penalties totaling over $3 million, the largest sum ever levied against an employer, were proposed against a beef packing plant for having over 100 serious safety violations.

Other laws involving safety (for example, workers' compensation) exist, but none of them has the far-reaching impact of OSHA. OSHA made the whole realm of occupational safety and health more visible. It has given new status and responsibility to safety and health practitioners. OSHA has increased concern among employers and unions over safety and health problems, as well as compliance with safety regulations. Has OSHA been effective in enhancing industrial safety? While opinions are mixed, much evidence supports its value. Mendeloff (1979) evaluated cumulative safety records and concluded that OSHA has had a significant impact on reducing injuries directly attributable to violations of standards. In an empirical study Cooke and Gautschi (1981) found that OSHA citations had substantially reduced the number of days lost due to on-the-job injuries in companies employing 200 or more production workers. While both of these studies substantiate the effectiveness of OSHA in reducing injuries, other evaluative research reveals less positive outcomes.

Psychological Approaches to Accident Reduction

Throughout this book, we have stressed three approaches to achieving a better fit between worker and workplace. The first is based on individual differences and involves selecting people who have the characteristics thought necessary or desirable for specified work demands. This is the personnel-selection approach, the analogue of finding the right "pegs" to fit the "holes." The second approach is that of training people in the necessary skills, knowledges, or attitudes. This is the personnel-training approach, the analogue of "reshaping the pegs" to fit the "holes." The third approach is modifying the workplace to provide a better match with abilities and characteristics. This is the engineering psychology or work-design approach, the analogue of "reshaping the holes" to fit the "pegs." These approaches are all used to reduce industrial accidents, an area whose criterion of interest is that of creating a safer work environment. Given that 50% to 80% of all accidents are attributable to human error (Spettell & Liebert, 1986), an examination of accidents from a human perspective is most reasonable. We will now examine in some detail I/O research to achieve greater person-environment congruence.

Personnel-Selection Approach

The *personnel-selection approach* is the search for individual differences predictive of accidents. This paradigm has proceeded along two paths: group prediction and individual prediction. Group prediction (also called *actuarial* prediction) has been remarkably successful in forecasting accidents. It is the basis upon which insurance companies operate, and it works as follows. Based upon hundreds of thousands of cases from national samples, insurance companies calculate the probability of incurring automobile-driving accidents as a function of many variables, such as age, sex, marital status, and so on. From a purely statistical standpoint, it is calculated that young (under 25), single, male drivers are more likely to incur accidents than are persons with some other combination of characteristics. Therefore, the cost of the insurance sold to members of various cohorts is adjusted to reflect the differential likelihood of having an accident. In the extreme case, an insurance company might refuse to select for coverage people who have extremely high probabilities for accidents. As you can imagine, these demographically constituted categories cover millions of people nationwide, and are very coarse groupings. Consequently, insurance companies, being highly competitive, seek additional predictors of accidents to refine their assessments of people (and thus lower the cost of insurance). For example, if you are a college student with a "B" or better grade-point average, you are a member of a group that has fewer accidents than less academically accomplished students. Accordingly, the cost of your insurance can be reduced somewhat. Some companies offer cost reductions for nonsmokers, infrequent drivers (that is, 7500 miles per year or less), and graduates of driver education classes. They do so because these variables have been found to be predictive of accidents on an actuarial basis.

But what if you are a young, single male who has never had an accident, and you are lumped in with a group who statisically has many? Is it fair for you personally to have to pay a high insurance premium because of your more reckless peers? If you were to complain about such a situation, you would be accusing the insurance company of making what is called an *ecological fallacy*: attributing to you personally a characteristic (that is, probability of an accident) that in fact describes a *group* of people. Until insurance companies can produce an individually tailored equation that uniquely describes *you* (which will never happen), the best they can do is to continue to look for additional actuarial predictors that will result in more refined predictions of accidents.

The second avenue of the personnel-selection approach to accidents is *individual* prediction. Here predictions are made regarding the likelihood of certain individuals' having accidents. This is the approach that I/O psychologists would most likely contribute to. Unfortunately, the results are not nearly as positive for individual prediction as they are for actuarial prediction. A few variables seem to be predictive of accidents, but many have only a slight relationship, and most are unrelated to accidents. For example, a number of studies examined differences in perceptual skill (ability to perceive a figure or object embedded in a complex background) as related to accidents. Barrett and Thornton (1968) found that perceptual skill was predictive of the number of accidents and near-accidents with pedestrians in a simulated driving situation. Those better at finding the hidden figure had fewer accidents. Mihal and Barrett (1976) reported similar findings. They also found that better drivers select certain specific information cues, and other drivers try to process all available information. Williams (1977) also found that three-dimensional, or stereoscopic, perceptual tests were predictive of accidents.

Research on the value of personality tests to predict accidents has been disappointing. For example, Wilson and Greensmith (1983) found that scores on aggression and anxiety scales were unrelated to driving performance. Similar findings have been reported by many other authors, although some exceptions have been reported (Spangenberg, 1968). While it makes intuitive sense that people with certain types of personalities would have more accidents than others, the literature does not support that conclusion. I suspect a major reason is that many of the personality tests that have been used were designed to detect gross personality disorders, and not to make refined predictions among normal adults. As discussed in Chapter 4, I believe the recent new wave of personality tests designed for the working population may be more successful in predicting accidents.

In keeping with the personnel-selection approach, it should be apparent that variables predictive of accidents could be used to hire people for jobs having high accident risk. People could be hired for transportation jobs (chauffeurs, bus drivers, pilots) and jobs having a high risk factor (handling of hazardous chemicals) on their likelihood of having accidents.

Engineering-Psychology Approach

Engineering psychology approaches accident reduction by modifying the workplace. It involves careful analysis of the workplace including design of equipment, tools, and machinery, as well as physical layout, to diagnose unsafe conditions. As Adams (1972) stated, engineering psychologists are not interested in machines per se. They are interested in human behavior and performance, like all psychologists; they use the person/machine interface as a focal point.

It is beyond our scope to present a complete discourse on engineering psychology. The interested reader should refer to McCormick and Sanders (1982) and Chapanis (1976) for more detail. Designing a safer work environment is one of the oldest and most prominent objectives of engineering psychologists. We will review a few examples of their work.

Yoder, Lucas, and Botzum (1973) faced the problem of workers' developing muscle fatigue and a condition called tenosynovitis (inflammation of tendons) because the pliers they used were not well suited for the task. The work consisted of cutting molded plastic parts used in a pharmaceutical plant. The existing pliers depended on primary use of the third and fourth fingers, which caused muscle fatigue, and holding the pliers at an angle, which produced wrist injury. The authors redesigned the pliers to be more compatible with the limitations of the human hand and wrist. The new pliers utilized a greater proportion of the muscles from all fingers and changed the wrist position needed to perform the task. Figure 15–8 shows the original pliers (a) and the redesigned pliers (b) and (c). The authors feel that other tools can be redesigned so as to minimize muscle fatigue and work-related injuries.

Voevodsky (1974) described a study that tried to reduce the number of times taxicabs are struck from behind. Cab drivers often stop faster than drivers behind them anticipate. Voevodsky installed yellow warning lights on the trunks of 343 cabs. These lights began to blink when the cab slowed down. The rate of blinking was

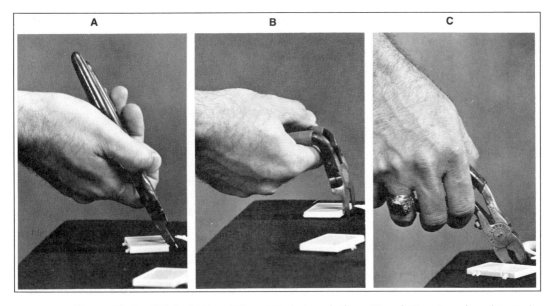

Figure 15–8 Original Pliers (A) and Redesigned Pliers (B and C) as Developed to Reduce Muscle Fatigue and Injury

SOURCE: T. A. Yoder, R. L. Lucas, and G. D. Botzum, "The Marriage of Human Factors and Safety in Industry," *Human Factors, 15* (1973), pp. 197–205.

proportional to the rate of deceleration; faster blinking implied more rapid deceleration. A control group of 160 cabs was not fitted with the lights.

After ten months, accident statistics on the two groups of cabs were compared. On three major performance dimensions (number of rear-end collisions, cost of repairs necessitated, and injuries to cab drivers) the experimental cabs outperformed the control cabs. The size of the difference was also very impressive: Accidents were reduced by over 60%. The statistics on the control cabs were unchanged during the study. To see whether the differences were not due simply to greater caution on the part of the drivers of the experimental cabs, comparisons were made of *front-end* collisions. No significant differences were found between experimental and control cabs. The author thus concluded that the cab drivers did not change their driving, but the motorists behind them had.

Both studies are good examples of the engineering psychology approach to safety. The researchers modified the equipment used, and the changes resulted in fewer accidents and injuries. Engineering psychology showed that performance can be improved by designing the workplace to complement human skills, be it in terms of muscle usage or reaction time.

Personnel-Training Approach

As discussed in Chapter 6, personnel training involves more than selecting a method to improve skills. It also involves creating an atmosphere in which training is supported and trained persons are rewarded for improvement. The *personnel-training approach* to safety involves everything we discussed about other types of training, and represents a major approach toward accident reduction. As is the case in all training, employees must be motivated. With safety training, employees must have a reason for behaving safely. Training is thus directed toward making safety a desirable outcome.

All training programs are conducted within a climate that places some degree of importance on training. In some organizations, training may be highly valued; in others, it may be treated with only mild interest. Three studies have examined the degree that organizational influences relate to safety behavior.

Zohar (1980) developed a questionnaire to assess organizational climates regarding safety. Employees at 20 companies rated their perceptions of the safety climate. A team of four experienced safety inspectors evaluated each organization on safety practices and accident-prevention programs. Scores on the questionnaire were then compared with inspectors' judgments. The results revealed that management's commitment to safety is a major factor in the success of safety programs. Organizations with a strong safety climate have job-training programs, give executive authority to safety officials, have high-level managers on safety committees, and consider safety in job design. Zohar feels that attempts to improve safety, like new regulations or poster campaigns, without management commitment will probably not succeed. As we stated in Chapter 6, the role of management is critical to any training program, and safety training is no exception.

Dunbar (1975) conducted a study that also revealed the importance of management in fostering positive attitudes about safety. The author investigated the extent to which employees' attitudes toward their managers were related to their perception of who was responsible for safety. Dunbar thought that when employees felt their managers were very supportive, they would have stronger feelings of personal responsibility for their own safety. If employees did not have such feelings, they would be dependent on managers to make the work environment safe. Dunbar asked a sample of employees to rate their managers on supportiveness; he also asked them who they felt was ultimately responsible for a safe workplace. The results revealed that managers can exert a strong influence with regard to safety. Employees who felt their managers supported them also believed they were responsible for their own safety behavior; employees who felt little support shifted responsibility to their managers. Dunbar's findings support the idea that management influences employee awareness of responsibilities for safe behavior.

Butler and Jones (1979) also investigated how perceptions of a leader's behavior related to accidents in hazardous work environments. The authors related views of officers among enlisted personnel aboard U.S. Navy ships to accident occurrence. In work environments characterized as recognizably hazardous, the leader's behavior was not highly related to injury-producing accidents. However, when hazards were less evident, the behavior of the leader *was* related. Butler and Jones suggest that in highly hazardous environments, accident prevention might best be realized by directly reducing equipment hazards, mechanically or through training. In less hazardous environments, leadership that involves clarity in defining tasks, structuring work activities, and clarity in job demands would appear to be effective.

These three studies attest the importance of an environment conducive to safety training. Employees quickly pick up cues on the importance of safety. Scrap or waste on the floor, unprotected wires, and failure to wear hard hats contradict bulletin board posters saying "Safety First." Organizational attitudes toward safety are conveyed by what people do. The studies show that management behavior and attitudes relate to employee feelings about safety and to accidents.

In terms of actual safety training, Komaki, Barwick, and Scott (1978) showed the efficacy of goal setting, positive reinforcement, and feedback. They studied employees in two departments of a food manufacturing plant: production (makeup) and wrapping. After analyzing the jobs in both departments, the authors identified safe and unsafe behavior.

They made slides showing safe and unsafe behaviors. Workers saw two slides per task, and discussed each type of behavior. After reviewing their current accident rate, employees in both departments set goals for safe behavior. The goals were plotted on a large graph conspicuously displayed at the work site. The researchers then observed behavior, provided feedback and encouragement, and plotted behavior on the graph.

The results are shown in Figure 15–9. In the wrapping department, the baseline of safe behaviors jumped from 70% to 95% after training; in the makeup department, the percentage increased from 77% to 99%. After termination of the program, safe behavior reverted to its pretraining levels. Komaki and associates (1978) reported that worker motivation was very high throughout the study, and pressure was put on co-workers not to "ruin" the graph. The results clearly indicate that safe behavior can be enhanced through training aimed at increasing motivation and sensitivity. They also indicate that safe behavior requires continuous attention; in this case, unsafe behavior returned to its base rate *immediately* following the end of the program (labeled "Reversal" in the figure).

Other studies document the value of safety training. Reber, Wallin, and Chhokar (1984) developed checklists of safe and unsafe behaviors at work. Employees were asked to set hard but attainable goals for improved safety performance. They were shown slides of the safe and unsafe behaviors, identified by means of the checklists, and were instructed to select the safe behaviors in conducting their jobs. Their safety performance was fed back to them, giving them knowledge of their results on the job. The training produced a 54% reduction in lost-time injuries. In a similar study Haynes, Pine, and Fitch (1982) used feedback, team competition, and incentives to bring about a 75% reduction in accidents for bus drivers.

An interesting common denominator of all these safety-training studies is that they focused on the conduct of positive (safe) behavior rather than railing against violations of safety rules (negative behavior). That is, they all conclude that training should be directed toward the enhancement of safe behavior rather than the simple eradication of unsafe behavior.

Overview

Organizations need not limit themselves to one approach to reducing accidents. In fact, the prudent organization would adopt a comprehensive program using all three approaches together. Each approach has its own merits; when used in combination,

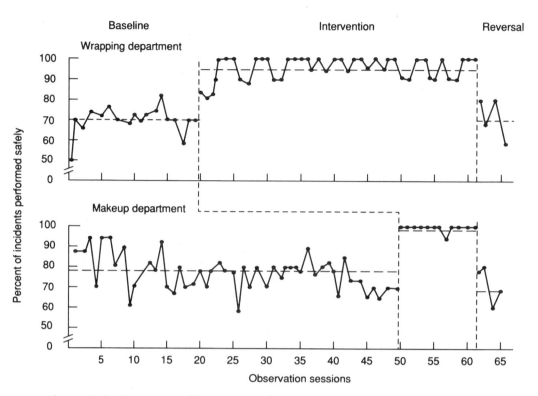

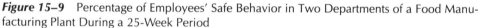

Figure 15–9 Percentage of Employees' Safe Behavior in Two Departments of a Food Manufacturing Plant During a 25-Week Period

SOURCE: J. Komaki, K. D. Barwick, and L. R. Scott, "A Behavioral Approach to Occupational Safety: Pinpointing and Reinforcing Safe Performance in a Food Manufacturing Plant," *Journal of Applied Psychology, 63* (1978), pp. 434–445.

they improve the likelihood of reducing accidents. Research indicates there are some useful variables for predicting which people are most likely to incur accidents. To the extent that these differences can be reliably predicted, we can staff organizations with people who exhibit safe behavior. The engineering-psychology approach entails modifying the tools, equipment, and machinery to eliminate unsafe conditions. Machines must be designed to complement human skills and limitations. The training approach is based on the belief that safety skills, like all skills, can be improved through training. This approach stresses the importance of an environment conducive to safety and of acquiring the knowledge and skills needed to reduce accidents. Each method approaches safety from a different perspective, but all three have proven effective in reducing accidents.

Despite all the advances made in recent years in equipment, tools, machinery, and technology in general, safety is not totally a technical issue per se. Actually, it is primarily a people issue. Smith, Cohen, Cohen, and Cleveland (1978) identified seven factors that were found to differentiate low-accident from high-accident com-

TABLE 15–2 *Characteristics of Successful Safety Programs*

Greater management commitment and involvement in safety programs

A more humanistic approach in dealing with employees stressing frequent positive contact and interaction

Better employee selection procedures

More frequent use of lead workers to train employees versus supervisors

A much greater degree of housekeeping and general plant cleanliness

Better plant environment qualities

Lower turnover and absenteeism among a more stable work force

SOURCE: M. J. Smith, J. H. Cohen, A. Cohen, and R. J. Cleveland, "Characteristics of Successful Safety Programs," *Journal of Safety Research, 10* (1978), pp. 5–15.

panies. These factors are listed in Table 15–2. Note how many relate to people. While the topic of safety certainly transcends individual differences, and the value of technical advances in equipment design should not be underestimated, eventually the ultimate responsibility for maintaining a safe work environment rests with people. Cohen (1977) cogently summarized this point when he said, "Maximally effective safety programs in industry will be dependent on those practices that can successfully deal with 'people' variables" (p. 168). The world's best seat belts will save no lives if people won't wear them or find ways to circumvent their use (see Field Note 2).

Field Note 2

As I mentioned in Chapter 6, I spent some time studying miners of bituminous coal. In the course of my work, I discovered the miners would occasionally feel compelled to take some major risks that could result in accidents and fatal injuries. Here is what would happen.

The machinery used to extract coal from the ground was electrically powered. Down on the mine floor (several hundred feet below the surface), miners would operate tremendously powerful machinery that required very large amounts of electrical current. The electrical current was supplied by a cable that was attached to the rear of the machinery. In much the same way that an upright vacuum cleaner is moved over a carpet, the mining equipment would be moved back and forth on the mine floor to extract the coal from the coal face.

The miners were supposed to mount the electrical cable on hooks elevated above the mine floor. But because there were organizational pressures to extract the coal from the ground as quickly as possible, the miners sometimes would take a "shortcut" and leave the cables on the mine floor. Mounting the cables on hooks would have taken time away from their work, so they would skip this step to save time and be more productive. Why was this important? Returning to the vacuum cleaner analogy, when you are pushing and pulling the vacuum across the carpet, sometimes you may inadvertently back it over the attached electrical cord. However, nothing happens because the weight of the vacuum is not great enough to slice through the cord and thus give you an electrical shock. Mining equipment, on the other hand, is very heavy (several tons) and could easily cut into the power cable. This is precisely what could have happened to the miners. When moving the machinery back and forth, the operator inadvertently could have run over the power cable trailing on the mine floor, which would send several thousand volts of electricity into the machinery, thus electrocuting the operator. The miners told me that as they became more experienced in operating the machinery, they "kind of got the feel" for where the cables were and would not back over them. However, should they have ever "missed" in their judgments, a lethal injury would have awaited them.

Work Schedules

Shift Work

As stated earlier, not all employees work 8:00 A.M. to 5:00 P.M., Monday through Friday. The nature of the services performed may necessitate other schedules. Police officers, fire fighters, and telephone operators provide 24-hour-a-day service. In industrial manufacturing, some technology requires constant monitoring and operation. It isn't practical to shut off furnaces, boilers, and chemical process operations at 5:00 P.M. just because the workers went home. In those cases, it is advantageous to run them continually by having different shifts work around the clock. About 25% of all working hours in the United States are estimated as "nontraditional" (Dunham, 1977). Psychologists have become interested in how different hours—(*shift work*)—affect employee attitudes and behavior.

There are no uniform shift-work hours; various companies use different shifts. Usually, a 24-hour day is broken into three 8-hour work shifts, like 7:00 A.M.– 3:00 P.M. (day shift), 3:00 P.M.–11:00 P.M. (swing or afternoon shift), and 11:00 P.M.–7:00 A.M. (night shift). Some companies have employees work just one shift; but workers generally don't like the swing and night shifts, so many firms rotate the shifts. Employees may work two weeks on the day shift, two weeks on the swing shift, and then two weeks on the night shift. A shift workweek need not be Monday to Friday. Also, there may be an uneven number of days off between shifts, like two days off after the swing shift and three after the night shift.

Psychologists have investigated to what degree workers cope with changes in work time. Research has focused on employee performance, satisfaction with shift work, physiological adjustments to shift work, and social and cultural adjustment. We will briefly examine some of the findings.

Performance.   Malaviya and Ganesh (1976, 1977) examined individual and group productivity of weavers who alternated between day and swing shifts in an Indian textile mill. Half of the weavers worked 13 days on the day shift followed by 12 days on the swing shift; the sequence was reversed for the other half of the sample. The results revealed that for the *group*, productivity was superior during the day shift. However, there were differences in performance of individual weavers over the two shifts. Some produced more during the day shift, others during the swing shift, and for others there was no difference over the two shifts.

Satisfaction.   Many people prefer traditional hours, but some are quite satisfied with aspects of shift work. In a study by de la Mare and Walker (1968), the following was reported about preference in work schedules:

Preference	Percentage
Permanent day work	61%
Rotating shift work	12
Permanent night work	27

In de la Mare and Walker's study, workers favored permanent day work; other researchers report positive preferences for shift work. For example, Wedderburn (1978) reported the following responses from British steelworkers to the question "On the whole, how do you feel about working shifts?"

Responses	Percentage
I like it very much	18%
I like it more than I dislike it	29
I neither like it nor dislike it	22
I dislike it more than I like it	23
I dislike it very much	8

There was large variability in individual worker attitudes. In the same study, Wedderburn obtained responses about perceived advantages and disadvantages of shift work in a number of specific areas. These are reported in Table 15–3. Though advantages and disadvantages are seen with each shift, on par, it seems that more disadvantages are associated with the night shift. The findings reported by Wedderburn are representative of other such studies. Zedeck, Jackson, and Summers (1983) concluded that shift work is not inherently bad for the health of all workers. Some workers adapt and do not allow shift work to lead to medical problems and family disturbances.

Adjustment Problems.   Shift workers experience many problems in physiological and social adjustment. Most physiological problems are associated with interruptions of the *circadian rhythm*; that is, our bodies are "programmed" for a certain time cycle (Aschoff, 1978). Because shift work interrupts the cycle of eating, sleeping, and working, workers often experience physiological problems. They complain of lack of

TABLE 15–3 *Reported Perceptions of Steel Mill Workers Regarding Shift Work*

Descriptive Item	Percentage of "Yes" Responses about*		
	Day Shift	Afternoon Shift	Night Shift
Quickly over	84	38	29
Seems a longer shift	12	40	64
Gives me indigestion	7	4	21
Tiring	58	15	80
Disturbs my sleep	36	2	52
More friendly atmosphere	48	51	21
Makes me irritable	25	18	48
Peaceful	49	62	58
More responsibility at work	28	16	24
More independent	35	26	42
Good for family life	73	19	17
Gives me more spare time	88	15	49
Wastes the day	10	68	55
Starts too early	53	7	20
Restricts my social life	17	79	77
Sexless	13	11	44

* Responses were to the question: "Think of work on _____ shift. How well does each of the above words describe what it is like for you on _____ shift?"
SOURCE: A. A. Wedderburn, "Some Suggestions for Increasing the Usefulness of Psychological and Sociological Studies of Shiftwork," *Ergonomics, 21* (1978), pp. 827–833.

sleep, fatigue, constipation, irritability, and appetite loss. Meers, Maasen, and Verhaagen (1978) reported that the health of a sample of shift workers declined during the first six months of shift work; the decline became more pronounced after four years.

Because most people work during the day and sleep at night, shift workers also have social problems. They often experience difficulties with children, marital relationships, and recreation. Frost and Jamal (1979) reported that shift workers experienced less need fulfillment, were more likely to quit their jobs, and participated in fewer voluntary organizations. Jamal (1981) reported similar findings; workers on fixed work schedules were better off than workers on rotating schedules in terms of mental health, job satisfaction, and social participation.

Shift workers are a relatively small proportion of the population; they are thus forced to fit their schedules around the rest of society. Dunham (1977) makes the interesting point that many social problems would be alleviated by *increasing* shift work. Society would then make more concessions to the needs of shift workers. Changes might be made in such things as hours of television broadcasting, restaurant service, recreational services, and hours of business operation (banks, supermarkets, gas stations, and the like). In fact, convenience food stores and automated bank machines derive much of their business from employees who work nontraditional hours.

Research indicates that shift work has a strong influence on the lives of people who perform it. As long as certain industries require 24-hour-a-day operations, psychologists will continue searching for ways to improve this particularly difficult person-environment fit. Social problems may be lessened by changing some existing patterns in the community. However, physiological problems will be more difficult to overcome.

At least one major source of physiological difficulty is the rotation of workers across shifts. If workers were assigned to a *fixed* shift (day, swing, night), their behavior would be consistent, which would help in adjusting to the circadian rhythm. Some people *prefer* to work afternoons or nights; part of the solution may be personnel selection. Workers could choose a shift; if enough workers of the appropriate skill level were placed in the shift of their choice, both individual and organizational needs would be met. Indeed, Jamal and Jamal (1982) found that employees who worked a fixed shift experienced better mental and physical health than employees on a rotating shift. Rotating shift work seems particularly difficult to adjust to. There is also evidence that backward rotation (from day to night to afternoon shifts) is more difficult to adjust to than forward rotation (from day to afternoon to night). In fact, Freese and Okonek (1984) report that some people who have reached the emotional, mental, and physical breaking point because of rotating shift work are told by their physicians to find jobs with traditional work hours.

Shorter Workweek

Employees traditionally have worked eight hours a day, five days a week, for a 40-hour workweek. However, in the past 20 years, many organizations have adopted a different schedule. Some employees now work 10 hours a day for 4 days. This is popularly known as the "4/40." Poor (1970) estimated that five organizations per day are converting to 4/40.

There are several obvious advantages to a four-day workweek for both the individual and the organization. Individuals have a three-day weekend, which gives them more recreation time, the chance to work a second job, more time for family life, and so on. Organizations have fewer overhead costs because they are open one day less per week. However, there are also possible drawbacks; these include fatigue, fewer productive hours, and more accidents.

There is not much empirical evidence on the subject; several studies have been reported. A few examined worker acceptance of the four-day week. Nord and Costigan (1973) and Goodale and Aagaard (1975) reported favorable reaction. In both studies, over 80% of the workers favored the new systems; acceptance remained high after they had been in effect for a year. The findings also indicated that workers grew more tired toward the end of the day; there were also some adjustment problems in their family lives. Dunham and Hawk (1977) found that support for 4/40 often comes from younger workers with low-level jobs, low income, and relatively low job satisfaction. They felt 4/40 may be supported when it is seen as a partial reprieve from the negative aspects of work.

Fottler (1977) found that continued acceptance of 4/40 is in large part determined by perceptions of changes in jobs. Employees in an urban hospital voted for 4/40. The change was made. Six months later, the employees were asked about their jobs and attitudes toward 4/40. Those who felt the new workweek increased their status and responsibility continued to be supportive. Those who saw the least amount of upgrading following the switch were most negative.

Ivancevich conducted two of the few studies of changes in actual job performance with 4/40. Ivancevich (1974) reported gains in production, employee's effectiveness as team members, and overall job performance 13 months after inception of 4/40. This is positive support for improvements under the shorter workweek. However, Ivancevich and Lyon (1977) presented disconcerting findings in a later study. The results from the 1974 study were replicated over another 13-month period with a different sample; but 25 months later all differences in performance between the five-day and four-day workweeks *disappeared*. The later study indicates that gains with 4/40 may be a Hawthorne effect. However, with so few studies, we do not have a large enough data base from which to draw any firm conclusions. Even if there are no *gains* in productivity, the four-day workweek may provide benefits in other areas, like increasing satisfaction and decreasing turnover and absence. We clearly need more research before we evaluate the four-day workweek.

In a major review of 4/40, Ronen and Primps (1981) reached these conclusions based on many studies. It has a positive effect on home and family life as well as leisure and recreation. There appears to be no change in employee job performance with 4/40. Finally, there are mixed results with regard to absenteeism, but worker fatigue definitely increases. In a few rare instances companies will adopt a 12-hour shift, typically noon to midnight and then midnight to noon. Breaugh (1983) reported workers on 12-hour shifts also incurred substantial fatigue associated with the longer hours. However, the midnight to noon shift felt more out of phase with physiological and social rhythms compared to the noon to midnight shift. Clearly both 12-hour and 10-hour workdays take their toll on worker stamina and attentiveness.

We should add that conversion to 4/40 is not simply a matter of worker preference. Organizations are limited in altering their work schedules by the services they provide and other factors. For example, Goodale and Aagaard (1975) feel 4/40 is not viable if customer service must be provided five days a week. Success of organizations providing services partially depends on accessibility. If an organization cannot do the same business volume in four ten-hour days, conversion to 4/40 is counterproductive. Internal factors may not favor the shorter workweek. Goodale and Aagaard suggest if employees work in groups and supervisors must be available during all working hours, 4/40 may not be applicable. Dunham, Pierce, and Castaneda (1987) cautioned against blanket support for the 4/40; its success depends upon the type of organization and the people in it.

We will undoubtedly see more research on shorter workweeks in the future. Organizations prematurely rushing to 4/40 may encounter more problems than anticipated. Research to date has revealed some advantages, but we clearly need answers to many more questions.

Flexible Working Hours

Another variation in work schedules is flexible working hours, popularly known as *flextime*. According to one report, approximately 23% of private-sector organizations have adopted a form of flextime since it was introduced in the early 1970s (Nollen & Martin, 1978). According to Ronen (1981b), the main objective of flextime is to create an alternative to the traditional, fixed working schedule by giving workers some choice in arrival and departure times. The system is usually arranged so that everyone must be present during certain designated hours ("coretime"), but there is latitude in other hours ("flexband"). For example, coretime may be 9:00 A.M. to 3:00 P.M. However, flexband may range from 6:00 A.M. to 6:00 P.M. Some employee may start working at 9:00 A.M. and work until 6:00 P.M., some may end at 3:00 P.M. by starting at 6:00 A.M., or any combination in between. Problems with family commitments, recreation, second jobs, commutation, and stress may be alleviated by flexible working hours. Lateness is virtually eliminated since the workday begins with arrival. Workers can be late only if they arrive after coretime has begun. The concept of flexible working hours is relatively new, and psychologists are just beginning to understand its effect.

While there is not yet much research on flextime, the results appear quite positive—at least no very adverse effects have yet been reported. The variables examined include satisfaction, productivity, absence, and turnover. Some studies reported more positive results than others. Golembiewski and Proehl (1978) summarized findings of several studies on flextime; they reported that worker support for adoption or continuation of flextime across nine samples of workers ranged from 80 to 100%. It thus appears that many employees are highly receptive to the idea.

Hicks and Klimoski (1981) found that employees did *not* become more satisfied with their work after flextime was adopted. Nevertheless, they reported other benefits like easier travel and parking, less interrole conflict, more feelings of control in the work setting, and more time for leisure activities. The findings on flextime's effect on productivity are mixed, but only a few studies have dealt with this issue. Schein, Maurer, and Novak (1977) examined the degree to which the performance of clerical employees improved under flextime. Out of five production units, performance increased in two and remained unchanged in the others. Schein and associates (1977) were cautious in saying that flextime *increased* productivity; they were confident that it did not lower performance. Kim and Campagna (1981) found that performance over four months of flextime increased in three out of four divisions of a county welfare agency. The authors also reported that flextime had a very positive impact in reducing short-term, unpaid absence (leave without pay for two hours or less a day). Ronen (1981a) reported that in a sample of government workers in Israel, lateness was reduced with flextime. After beginning flextime, late arrivals decreased from an average of 6 to 0.67 times per worker per month.

More recently, some additional studies have further expanded our understanding of flextime. Ralston, Anthony, and Gustafson (1985) reported one of the rare cases that showed flextime improved group productviity. The authors found that flexible hours resulted in a 24% improvement in productivity among computer programmers. They concluded that flextime can increase productivity when the workers must share limited physical resources; otherwise it has no effect on productivity. Orpen's (1981) study would support this conclusion because he found flextime increased employee satisfaction but had a negligible effect on performance. Narayanan and Nath (1982) examined the impact of flextime at two organizational levels: lower-level and professional employees. They concluded flextime primarily benefited lower-level employees by giving them more flexibility in their schedules. For professional employees, the flextime system merely formalized the already existing informal system they had with the company.

A number of points should be made about the effect of flextime. First, we don't really have a wealth of data; definite conclusions about its effectiveness would be somewhat premature. Second, reported gains in productivity may be Hawthorne effects. As with the Ivancevich and Lyon (1977) study on 4/40, it may take up to two years for Hawthorne effects to dissipate. Third, even if productivity gains are Hawthorne effects, this is not necessarily an indictment of flextime. Organizations should state what they hope to gain with flextime; gains in productivity may not be a main objective. As Hicks and Klimoski (1981) reported, employees seem to benefit from flextime. Only in utopia will organization changes have uniformly positive effects—increasing productivity and satisfaction, decreasing absence, lateness, and turnover; and increasing contentment with aspects of nonwork life. Trade-offs must always be made; thus, organizations must set priorities. Finally, flextime may have negative effects on teamwork and superior-subordinate relationships (see Field Note 3). If employees must work as a team, flextime, with continual coming and going, may not be viable (a finding supported by Narayanan & Nath, 1982). As with 4/40, more research must be done in the future. For the present, however, flextime appears to be beneficial and workable in certain organizations.

Field Note 3

Flextime is certainly a popular alternative to traditional hours of work, and is favored by large numbers of employees. Indeed it should be, for it was designed to accommodate their needs. However, flextime can produce a particular problem that is not encountered with traditional work hours.

Let us say coretime is 9:00 A.M. to 3:00 P.M., and the flexband is from 6:00 A.M. to 6:00 P.M. Thus, employees are free to come and go within this 12-hour period. In all likelihood some employees will arrive early and leave early (6:00 A.M. to 3:00 P.M.); others will arrive late and leave late (9:00 A.M. to 6:00 P.M.).

The problem relates to supervision. Because supervisors cannot work 12-hour days, there will be times when the employees are unsupervised. Let us assume the normal hours for a supervisor are 8:00 A.M. to 5:00 P.M., the typical 8-hour day. This means that from 6:00 to 8:00 A.M. and 5:00 to 6:00 P.M., the work force will be unsupervised. As we discussed in Chapter 12, sometimes the job itself provides direction for employees so that they do not need a boss present. However, in many cases there are no substitutes for leadership, and employees simply need some guidance. In this case the unsupervised hours may be very unproductive from the organization's standpoint.

Without a supervisor, employees may also become lax in performing their duties during these hours since they are not being monitored. Finally, it is also possible that flextime may weaken supervisor-subordinate relations in general, since they will not see each other as often (that is, their two 8-hour days do not overlap completely). The organization would either have to have supervisors work longer hours, have more supervisors to "cover" the 12-hour day, or accept having an unsupervised work force for a portion of the day. While flextime solves a lot of problems, it can create a few as well.

Alcoholism and Drug Abuse in the Workplace

Alcoholism and drug abuse are international problems affecting all arenas of life. While we have long been aware of issues pertaining to their treatment, only recently have we begun to examine their impact in the workplace. Due to the sensitivity and confidentiality of substance abuse, we do not have a very strong research foundation upon which to base our knowledge. That is, it is difficult to collect reliable and valid data on substance abuse, given the delicacy of the issue. What follows is a brief overview of some of the major dimensions of this complex social problem.

The term *substance abuse* covers a broad array of substances, but usually includes alcohol, prescription drugs, and illegal drugs. Some people include tobacco (both smoking and chewing) within the domain of substance abuse. Most of our knowledge is limited to alcoholism and illegal drugs. It has been estimated that there are over 10 million American alcoholic workers. Tyson and Vaughn (1987) report that approximately two-thirds of the people entering the work force have used illegal drugs. Four to 5 million people in the United States use cocaine monthly. Frequency of use of marijuana is much higher. Every year $50 billion is spent on cocaine in the United States—the same amount of money that companies spend annually on substance abuse programs for their employees. By any reasonable standard substance abuse is a major problem in industry today.

While I/O psychologists may approach the area of substance abuse from several perspectives, a primary area of concern is performance impairment—that is, the extent to which substance abuse contributes to lower job performance. Experts in the area of employee assistance programs estimate that as much as 50% of absenteeism and on-the-job accidents are related to drugs and alcohol. Drug addiction has also contributed to employees' stealing from the company to support their habits. Thus, we have some knowledge about how substance abuse affects the more global performance criteria of absence, accidents, and theft. Our knowledge of the effects of substance abuse on skill decay is more tentative. Much of our knowledge is based upon industrial accidents in which alcohol or drug usage was confirmed. It is also very difficult to make categorical statements about "drugs" in general because of their variety, duration of effects, and interactive properties with other substances. We do know that cognitively related skills such as vigilance, monitoring, reaction time, and decision making are adversely affected by many kinds of drugs. We do not know if these drugs simply lengthen the amount of time needed to perform these cognitive functions, or whether they cause attention to be focused on irrelevant or competing stimuli. Jobs involving the use of these skills in areas like the transportation industry (for example, pilots and railroad engineers) have regrettably contributed to our knowledge through tragic accidents. Some drugs (such as anabolic steroids) have been found to enhance aspects of physical performance (most notably strength and speed), but their long-term effects can be very harmful to the individual. McDaniel (1988) reported the greater the frequency of use of drugs in general and the earlier the age at which drugs were first used, the greater is the probability of a person's being classified unsuitable as an employee.

It is very difficult for I/O psychologists to conduct high-quality research on substance abuse. Administration of alcohol or drugs in an experimental setting can be conducted only under the most restrictive conditions, given ethical concerns. Reliance on self-report measures are problematic, given issues associated with social desirability and accuracy. There are also civil and legal issues associated with drug testing, be it the constitutional rights of individuals to submit to drug testing or the accuracy of the drug tests themselves (see Chapter 4). As with most complex social problems, researchers and scholars from many professions (such as pharmacology, toxicology, law, and genetics) must take an interdisciplinary approach to addressing these issues. While I/O psychologists will contribute but a small piece of the total picture, I envision our efforts will be concentrated in two traditional areas: issues relating to individual assessment and performance measurement. Perhaps in 20 years an evaluation of working conditions may also include the propensity of certain jobs to induce substance abuse and the likelihood your co-worker is under the influence of drugs or alcohol. Whether we are ready for it or not, I believe society will expect I/O psychologists to help provide information on problems our predecessors could scarcely have imagined.

Concluding Comments

This chapter examined many factors relating to work conditions. Factors like stress caused by physical conditions, accidents, and work schedules all directly affect work lives. I/O psychologists have responded to this by trying to improve the fit between human needs and work demands. Instead of adopting a strict personnel-selection approach (searching for the "right people" to fit a static work environment), advances like the 4/40 workweek and flextime hours show that it is possible to modify the workplace to accommodate the worker. I/O psychologists constantly seek to reduce unnecessary demands in the workplace and to select and train people to cope better with demands that cannot be changed. People and work demands are constantly changing; thus, searching for ways to improve the worker-workplace fit will be an ongoing responsibility for I/O psychology.

It is also noteworthy that the entire area of human-factors psychology is experiencing somewhat of a rejuvenation in recent years. After a period of time in which the "organizational" perspective on work was dominant, the I/O profession seems to be returning to human factors as a means of solving problems of person-environment congruence. Additionally, these problems are not limited to highly technical issues of equipment and machine design. For example, Oldham and Rotchford (1983) examined the best way to design an office to maximize positive employee reactions. The authors examined five characteristics of office design: (1) openness (a function of how many interior walls and partitions bounded the total office); (2) office density (average space per employee); (3) work space density (how closely co-workers were packed together); (4) architectural accessibility (number of walls and partitions that surrounded each employee's work space; and (5) darkness (amount of illumination and color of walls). The employee reactions assessed included work, social, and office satisfaction, discretionary time spent in the office (that is, where workers spend their breaks), and use of spatial markers (for example, plants and posters). The authors found that every one of the five office-design characteristics affected at least one of the employee reactions. In particular, workers were dissatisfied with high office and workspace density, disliked darkness, and used spatial markers to combat lowered accessibility. This study is a classic example of the human factors approach to work problems: designing the work environment to be compatible with human preferences.

As a final example of the human-factors paradigm, Parsons and Kearsley (1982) addressed the issue of division of labor between humans and a growing segment of the work force: robots. They recommend studying the relationship between humans and robots with regard to not only performance and output but also human-robot communication, job satisfaction, and organizational impact. Chao and Kozlowski (1986) found low-skill workers reacted negatively toward implementation of robots, perceiving them largely as threats to their job security. High-skill workers reacted more positively toward robots, and perceived their implementation as providing opportunities to expand their skills. It has been suggested that research on the human-robot interface may become the Hawthorne studies of the future.

MAJOR CHAPTER OBJECTIVES IN REVIEW

After having read this chapter, you should know:

1. Physical stressors in the workplace.

2. Anthropometric, biomechanical, and physiological approaches to work design.

3. Psychological approaches to accident reduction.

4. Effects of shift work on employees.

5. Shorter workweek and flexible working hours.

6. Work related issues associated with substance abuse.

CASE STUDY—Will Life Ever Get Back to Normal?

Janet Ryder sat at her kitchen table reading the entertainment section of the local newspaper. A movie was playing that she had heard a lot about, and she was hoping it would stay in town for at least two weeks. Her husband, Mark, had recently changed jobs and was now working for St. Regis Aluminum, a large manufacturer of lightweight metal products. The company worked shifts, and Mark was starting a two-week stint on the night shift. Neither Janet nor Mark had any previous experience with shift work, and the switch from conventional hours was difficult for both of them.

Janet tried to plan their family life around Mark's changing hours, but she couldn't get the hang of it. Little things kept cropping up that had never been a problem before. For example, the boy next door had been taking trumpet lessons for about two months. He would practice after school. Janet heard the notes straining from the trumpet, but after a while the sounds seemed to blend in with the rest of the neighborhood noise, and she could ignore them. When Mark was sleeping in the afternoon, the noise of the trumpet often woke him up. They had had two arguments about whether they should call the boy's mother and ask that he practice at another time.

Yesterday there had been a sale on roast beef, which was one of their favorite dinners. Janet liked to fix a fancy dinner when there was something special to eat. However, with Mark's schedule, she had to "time" special meals when he worked the day shift. While Mark might be ready to sit down to a full meal at 7:00 A.M. after working the night shift, Janet couldn't quite handle either fixing it or eating it after just getting up. The roast beef would sit in the freezer, waiting for a time when they both could enjoy it.

It was also awkward for their friends. They had been in a biweekly poker club that met on Friday nights. They got together with some other couples at 8 o'clock, and the party would break up around midnight. When Mark worked afternoons, there was no way they could play. When he worked the night shift, they would have to leave at 10 o'clock, just when things were going great. Only when he worked the day shift could they make it. Now they played in the poker club about once every two months, and their friends got another couple to sub for them.

Janet started to feel guilty about feeling sorry for herself. It had been no bargain for Mark either. The weekend the long-awaited Custom Boat and Trailer Show arrived in town, Mark was working the swing shift. He got to visit the show for about a half hour before he had to leave for work. It seemed that on Saturdays and Sundays just when he found something he liked to do, it was time to go to the plant.

Their ten-year-old son Billie wandered into the kitchen. Billie was holding a Little League schedule in his hand. "Mom" he said, "in three weeks there's the regional tournament in Union City. Will you and Dad make it to my game?"

Janet got up and checked Mark's work schedule, which was posted on the cupboard. "I can make it, Billie, but Dad will be working the afternoon shift that week," Janet said.

Billie looked downcast. "I never get to see Dad very much any more," he said, as he slowly walked out of the kitchen.

Questions

1. Think of Chapter 9 on job satisfaction. Do you see any relationship between work and nonwork satisfaction for shift workers?

2. What other disruptions in family life might you predict for the Ryder family as a result of shift work?

3. Are there things the St. Regis Aluminum Company could do to alleviate some of the problems of shift workers? What might they be?

4. Are there things the community might do to make life easier for shift workers? What might they be?

5. How long would you guess it takes for a family to get into the "rhythm" of shift work?

References

Chapter 1

Adair, J. G. (1984). The Hawthorne effect: A reconsideration of the methodological artifact. *Journal of Applied Psychology, 69,* 334–345.

Bingham, W. V. (1917). Mentality testing of college students. *Journal of Applied Psychology, 1,* 38–45.

Blum, M. L., & Naylor, J. C. (1968). *Industrial psychology: Its theoretical and social foundations.* New York: Harper & Row.

Bryan, W. L. (1904). Theory and practice. *Psychological Review, 11,* 71–82.

Bryan, W. L., & Harter, N. (1897). Studies in the physiology and psychology of the telegraphic language. *Psychological Review, 4,* 27–53.

Bryan, W. L., & Harter, N. (1899). Studies of the telegraphic language. *Psychological Review, 6,* 345–375.

Chapanis, A., Garner, W. R., & Morgan, C. T. (1949). *Applied experimental psychology.* New York: Wiley.

Ferguson, L. W. (1962). *The heritage of industrial psychology.* Hartford, CT: Finlay.

Fretz, B. R., & Mills, D. H. (1980). *Licensing and certification of psychologists and counselors.* San Francisco: Jossey-Bass.

Ghiselli, E. E., & Brown, C. W. (1955). *Personnel and industrial psychology.* New York: McGraw-Hill.

Grether, W. F. (1968). Engineering psychology in the United States. *American Psychologist, 23,* 743–751.

Gross, S. J. (1978). The myth of professional licensing. *American Psychologist, 33,* 1009–1016.

Guion, R. M. (1965). Industrial psychology as an academic discipline. *American Psychologist, 20,* 815–821.

Hall, G. S. (1917). Practical relations between psychology and the war. *Journal of Applied Psychology, 1,* 9–16.

Hall, G. S., Baird, J. W., & Geissler, L. R. (1917). Foreword. *Journal of Applied Psychology, 1,* 5–7.

Handbook of human engineering data. (1949). Medford, MA: Tufts College and United States Naval Training Devices Center.

Hess, H. F. (1977). Entry requirements for professional practice of psychology. *American Psychologist, 32,* 365–368.

Hoffman, P. J. (1980). On the establishment of an appropriate length for the EPPP. *Professional Psychology, 11,* 784–791.

Howard, A. (1986). Characteristics of Society members. *The Industrial-Organizational Psychologist, 23*(3), 41–47.

Howard, A., & Lowman, R. L. (1985). Should industrial/organizational psychologists be licensed? *American Psychologist, 40,* 40–47.

Howard, A., Pion, G. M., Gottfredson, G. D., Flattau, P. E., Oskamp, S., Pfafflin, S. M., Bray, D. W., & Bursten, A. G. (1986). The changing face of American psychology: A report from the Committee on Employment and Human Resources. *American Psychologist, 41,* 1311–1327.

Katzell, R. A., & Guzzo, R. A. (1983). Psychological approaches to productivity improvement. *American Psychologist, 38,* 468–472.

Matarazzo, J. D. (1977). Higher education, professional accreditation, and licensure. *American Psychologist, 32,* 856–859.

Matarazzo, J. D. (1987). There is only one psychology, no specialities, but many applications. *American Psychologist, 42,* 893–903.

Mateer, F. (1917). The moron as a war problem. *Journal of Applied Psychology, 1,* 327–320.

Mayfield, E. C. (1975). *Preparation for work in business and industry: The results of a survey of recent graduates.* Unpublished manuscript.

Meyer, H. H. (1972). The future for industrial and organizational psychology: Oblivion or millenium? *American Psychologist, 27,* 608–614.

Muchinsky, P. M. (1973). Graduate training in industrial psychology: One more time. *Professional Psychology, 4,* 286–295.

Muchinsky, P. M. (1976). Graduate internships in industrial psychology: A success story. *Professional Psychology, 7,* 664–670.

Münsterberg, H. (1913). *Psychology and industrial efficiency.* Boston: Houghton Mifflin.

Murray, H. A., & MacKinnon, D. W. (1946). Assessment of OSS personnel. *Journal of Consulting Psychology, 10,* 76–80.

Napoli, D. S. (1981). *The architects of adjustment: The history of the psychological profession in the United States.* Port Washington, NY: Kennikat.

Naylor, J. C. (1970). Training patterns in industrial psychology. *Personnel Psychology, 23,* 192–198.

Naylor, J. C. (1971). Hickory, dickory, dock? Let's turn back the clock! *Professional Psychology, 2,* 217–224.

Norton, S. D., & Gustafson, D. P. (1982). Industrial/organizational psychology as applied to human resources management. *Professional Psychology, 13,* 904–917.

Pickard, C. O. (1945). Absentee control plans. *Personnel Journal, 23,* 271–276.

Rodgers, D. A. (1964). In favor of separation of academic and professional training. *American Psychologist, 19,* 675–680.

Roethlisberger, F. J., & Dickson, W. J. (1943). *Management and the worker.* Cambridge, MA: Harvard University Press.

Scott, W. D. (1903). *The theory of advertising.* Boston: Small, Maynard.

Scott, W. D. (1908). *The psychology of advertising.* New York: Arno Press.

Scott, W. D. (1911a). *Increasing human efficiency in business.* New York: Macmillan.

Scott, W. D. (1911b). *Influencing men in business.* New York: Ronald Press.

Stagner, R. (1981). Training and experiences of some distinguished industrial psychologists. *American Psychologist, 36,* 497–505.

Stagner, R. (1982). Past and future of industrial/organizational psychology. *Professional Psychology, 13,* 892–903.

Stapp, J., Tucker, A. M., & VandenBos, G. R. (1985). Census of psychological personnel: 1983. *American Psychologist, 40,* 1317–1351.

Task Force on the Practice of Psychology in Industry. (1971). Effective practice of psychology in industry. *American Psychologist, 26,* 974–991.

Taylor, F. W. (1911). *The principles of scientific management.* New York: Harper.

Viteles, M. S. (1932). *Industrial psychology.* New York: W. W. Norton.

Chapter 2

American Psychological Association. (1981). Ethical principles of psychologists. *American Psychologist, 36,* 633–638.

Argyris, C. (1968). Some unintended consequences of rigorous research. *Psychological Bulletin, 70,* 185–197.

Bobko, P., & Karren, R. (1979). The perception of Pearson product moment correlations from bivariate scatterplots. *Personnel Psychology, 32,* 313–326.

Boehm, V. R. (1980). Research in the "real world"—A conceptual model. *Personnel Psychology, 33,* 495–504.

Campbell, J. P., Daft, R. L., & Hulin, C. L. (1982). *What to study: Generating and developing research questions.* Newbury Park, CA: Sage.

Daft, R. L. (1983). Learning the craft of organizational research. *Academy of Management Review, 8,* 539–546.

Dipboye, R. L., & Flanagan, M. F. (1979). Research settings in industrial and organizational psychology. *American Psychologist, 34,* 141–150.

Dunnette, M. D. (1966). Fads, fashions, and folderol in psychology. *American Psychologist, 21,* 343–352.

Flanagan, M. F., & Dipboye, R. L. (1981). Research settings in industrial and organizational psychology: Facts, fallacies, and the future. *Personnel Psychology, 34,* 37–47.

Fromkin, H. L., & Streufert, S. (1976). Laboratory experimentation. In M. D. Dunnette (Ed.), *Handbook of industrial and organizational psychology.* Skokie, IL: Rand McNally.

Ghiselli, E. E. (1974). Some perspectives for industrial psychology. *American Psychologist, 29,* 80–87.

Goodale, J. G., & Aagaard, A. K. (1975). Factors relating to varying reactions to the 4-day workweek. *Journal of Applied Psychology, 60,* 33–38.

Gordon, M. E., Kleiman, L. S., & Hanie, C. A. (1978). Industrial-organizational psychology: Open thy ears O House of Israel. *American Psychologist, 33,* 893–905.

Gordon, M. E., Slade, L. A., & Schmitt, N. (1986). The "science of the sophomore" revisited: From conjecture to empiricism. *Academy of Management Review, 11,* 191–207.

Greenberg, J. (1987). The college sophomore as guinea pig: Setting the record straight. *Academy of Management Review, 12,* 157–159.

Guzzo, R. A., Jette, R. D., & Katzell, R. A. (1985). The effects of psychologically based intervention programs on worker productivity: A meta-analysis. *Personnel Psychology, 38,* 275–291.

Hegarty, W. H., & Sims, H. P., Jr. (1978). Some determinants of unethical decision behavior: An experiment. *Journal of Applied Psychology, 63,* 451–457.

Jahoda, M. (1981). Work, employment, and unemployment: Values, theories and approaches in social research. *American Psychologist, 36,* 184–191.

Kaplan, A. (1964). *The conduct of inquiry.* New York: Harper & Row.

Kelman, H. C. (1972). The rights of the subject in social research: An analysis in terms of relative power and legitimacy. *American Psychologist, 27,* 989–1016.

Latham, G. P., & Kinne, S. B. (1974). Improving job performance through training in goal setting. *Journal of Applied Psychology, 59,* 187–191.

Lawler, E. E. (1982). Strategies for improving the quality of work life. *American Psychologist, 37,* 486–493.

Locke, E. A. (Ed.). (1985). *The generalizability of laboratory experiments: An inductive study.* Lexington, MA: D.C. Heath.

London, M., & Bray, D. W. (1980). Ethical issues in testing and evaluation for personnel decisions. *American Psychologist, 35,* 890–901.

Lowman, R. L. (Ed.). (1985). *Casebook on ethics and standards for the practice of psychology in organizations.* College Park, MD: Society for Industrial and Organizational Psychology, Inc., Division 14 of the American Psychological Association.

Miner, J. B. (1984). The validity and usefulness of theories in an emerging organizational science. *Academy of Management Review, 9,* 296–306.

Mirvis, P. H., & Seashore, S. E. (1979). Being ethical in organizational research. *American Psychologist, 34,* 766–780.

Mitchell, T. R. (1985). An evaluation of the validity of correlation research conducted in organizations. *Academy of Management Review, 10,* 192–205.

Mook. D. G. (1983). In defense of external invalidity. *American Psychologist, 38,* 379–387.

Muldrow, T. W., & Bayton, J. A. (1979). Men and women executives and processes related to decision accuracy. *Journal of Applied Psychology, 64,* 99–106.

Stevens, S. (1958). Problems and methods of psychophysics. *Psychological Bulletin, 55,* 177–196.

Stone, E. F. (1986). Research methods in industrial and organizational psychology: Selected issues and trends. In C. L. Cooper and I. T. Robertson (Eds.), *International review of industrial and organizational psychology.* London: Wiley.

Strasser, S., & Bateman, T. S. (1984). What we should study, problems we should solve: Perspectives of two constituencies. *Personnel Psychology, 37,* 77–92.

Thomas, K. W., & Tymon, W. G., Jr. (1982). Necessary properties of relevant research: Lessons from recent outcomes of the organizational sciences. *Academy of Management Review, 7,* 345–352.

Williams, L. K., Seybolt, J. W., & Pinder, C. C. (1975). On administering questionnaires in organizational settings. *Personnel Psychology, 28,* 93–103.

Chapter 3

Arvey, R. D., & Begalla, M. E. (1975). Analyzing the homemaker job using the PAQ. *Journal of Applied Psychology, 60,* 513–517.

Arvey, R. D. (1986). Sex bias in job evaluation procedures. *Personnel Psychology, 39,* 315–335.

Arvey, R. D., Passino, E. M., & Lounsbury, J. W. (1977). Job analysis results as influenced by sex of incumbent and sex of analyst. *Journal of Applied Psychology, 62,* 411–416.

Ash, R. A., & Edgell, S. L. (1975). A note on the readability of the PAQ. *Journal of Applied Psychology, 60,* 765–766.

Barrett, G. V., Caldwell, M. S., & Alexander, R. A. (1985). The concept of dynamic criteria: A critical reanalysis. *Personnel Psychology, 38,* 41–56.

Bass, B. M. (1962). Further evidence on the dynamic character of criteria. *Personnel Psychology, 15,* 93–97.

Belcher, D. W. (1974). *Wage and salary administration.* New York: Prentice-Hall.

Blum, M. L., & Naylor, J. C. (1968). *Industrial psychology: Its theoretical and social foundations.* New York: Harper & Row.

Brogden, H. E., & Taylor, E. K. (1950a). The dollar criterion—applying the cost accounting concept to criterion construction. *Personnel Psychology, 3,* 133–153.

Brogden, H. E., & Taylor, E. K. (1950b). The theory and classification of criterion bias. *Educational and Psychological Measurement, 10,* 159–186.

Cain, P. S., & Green, B. F. (1983). Reliabilities of selected ratings available from the Dictionary of Occupational Titles. *Journal of Applied Psychology, 68*, 155–165.

Cascio, W. F. (1982). *Applied psychology in personnel management* (2nd ed.). Reston, VA: Reston.

Conley, P. R., & Sackett, P. R. (1987). Effects of using high- versus low-performing job incumbents as sources of job analysis information. *Journal of Applied Psychology, 72*, 434–437.

Cornelius, E. T., DeNisi, A. S., & Blencoe, A. G. (1984). Expert and naive raters using the PAQ: Does it matter? *Personnel Psychology, 37*, 453–464.

Doverspike, D., Carlisi, A. M., Barrett, G. V., & Alexander, R. A. (1983). Generalizability analysis of a point-method job evaluation instrument. *Journal of Applied Psychology, 68*, 476–483.

Dunnette, M. D. (1963). A note on *the* criterion. *Journal of Applied Psychology, 47*, 251–254.

Dyer, L., Schwab, D. P., & Theriault, R. D. (1976). Managerial perceptions regarding salary increase criteria. *Personnel Psychology, 29*, 233–242.

Freeberg, N. E. (1976). Criterion measures for youth-work training programs: The development of relevant performance dimensions. *Journal of Applied Psychology, 61*, 535–545.

Garvin, D. A. (1986). Quality problems, policies, and attitudes in the United States and Japan: An exploratory study. *Academy of Management Journal, 29*, 653–673.

Ghiselli, E. E. (1956). Dimensional problems of criteria. *Journal of Applied Psychology, 40*, 1–4.

Ghiselli, E. E., & Haire, M. (1960). The validation of selection tests in the light of the dynamic character of criteria. *Personnel Psychology, 13*, 225–231.

Gomez-Mejia, L. R., & Balkin, D. B. (1983). Classifying work-related and personal problems of troubled employees. In K. Pearlman, F. L. Schmidt, & W. C. Hamner (Eds.), *Contemporary problems in personnel.* New York: Wiley.

Gomez-Mejia, L. R., Page, R. C., & Tornow, W. W. (1982). A comparison of the practical utility of traditional, statistical, and hybrid job evaluation approaches. *Academy of Management Journal, 15*, 790–809.

Guion, R. M. (1961). Criterion measurement and personnel judgment. *Personnel Psychology, 14*, 141–149.

Heneman, R. L. (1986). The relationship between supervisory ratings and results-oriented measures of performance: A meta-analysis. *Personnel Psychology, 39*, 811–826.

Hollinger, R., & Clark, J. (1983). *Theft by employees.* Lexington, MA: Lexington Books.

Hulin, C. L. (1962). The measurement of executive success. *Journal of Applied Psychology, 46*, 303–306.

Jenkins, J. G. (1946). Validity for what? *Journal of Consulting Psychology, 10*, 93–98.

Lawler, E. E., III. (1967). The multitrait-multirater approach to measuring managerial job performance. *Journal of Applied Psychology, 51*, 369–381.

Lent, R. H., Aurbach, H. H., & Levin, L. S. (1971). Predictors, criteria, and significant results. *Personnel Psychology, 24*, 519–533.

Levine, E. L., Ash, R. A., Hall, H., & Sistrunk, F. (1983). Evaluation of job analysis methods by experienced job analysts. *Academy of Management Journal, 26*, 339–347.

Lopez, F. M., Kesselman, G. A., & Lopez, F. E. (1981). An empirical test of a trait-oriented job analysis technique. *Personnel Psychology, 34*, 479–502.

Mahoney, T. A. (1983). Approaches to the definition of comparable worth. *Academy of Management Review, 8*, 14–22.

McCormick, E. J. (1976). Job and task analysis. In M. D. Dunnette (Ed.), *Handbook of industrial and organizational psychology.* Skokie, Ill.: Rand McNally.

McCormick, E. J., Jeanneret, P. R., & Mecham, R. C. (1972). A study of job characteristics and job dimensions as based on the Position Analysis Questionnaire (PAQ). *Journal of Applied Psychology, 56,* 347–368.

Milkovich, G. T., & Newman, J. M. (1984). *Compensation.* Plano, TX: Business Publications.

Mobley, W. H., Griffeth, R. W., Hand, H. H., & Meglino, B. M. (1979). Review and conceptual analysis of the employee turnover process. *Psychological Bulletin, 86,* 493–522.

Morsh, J. E., & Archer, W. B. (1967). *Procedural guide for conducting occupational surveys in the United States Air Force.* Lackland Air Force Base, TX: Personnel Research Laboratory, Aerospace Medical Division, PRL-TR-67-11.

Muchinsky, P. M. (1975a). A comparison of three analytic techniques in predicting consumer installment credit risk: Toward understanding a construct. *Personnel Psychology, 28,* 511–524.

Muchinsky, P. M. (1975b). Consumer installment credit risk: A need for criterion refinement and validation. *Journal of Applied Psychology, 60,* 87–93.

Muchinsky, P. M. (1977). Employee absenteeism: A review of the literature. *Journal of Vocational Behavior, 10,* 316–340.

Muchinsky, P. M. (1979). Human resource management of employee absenteeism. In V. V. Veysey & G. S. Hall, Jr. (Eds.), *The new world of managing human resources.* Burbank, Calif.: North Hollywood Printing.

Muchinsky, P. M., & Morrow, P. C. (1980). A multidisciplinary model of voluntary employee turnover. *Journal of Vocational Behavior, 17,* 263–290.

Muchinsky, P. M., & Tuttle, M. L. (1979). Employee turnover: An empirical and methodological assessment. *Journal of Vocational Behavior, 14,* 43–77.

Nagle, B. F. (1953). Criterion development. *Personnel Psychology, 6,* 271–289.

Nicholson, N. (1977). Absence behavior and attendance motivation: A conceptual synthesis. *Journal of Management Studies, 14,* 213–252.

Pedalino, E., & Gamboa, V. U. (1974). Behavior modification and absenteeism: Intervention in one industrial setting. *Journal of Applied Psychology, 59,* 694–698.

Prien, E.P., & Ronan, W. W. (1971). Job analysis: A review of research findings. *Personnel Psychology, 24,* 371–396.

Pursell, E. D., Dossett, D. L., & Latham, G. P. (1980). Obtaining valid predictors by minimizing rating errors in the criterion. *Personnel Psychology, 33,* 91–96.

Ronan, W. W. (1963). A factor analysis of eleven job performance measures. *Personnel Psychology, 16,* 255–267.

Rothe, H. F. (1946). Output rates among butter wrappers: I. Work curves and their stability. *Journal of Applied Psychology, 30,* 199–211.

Rothe, H. F. (1947). Output rates among machine operators: I. Distributions and their reliability. *Journal of Applied Psychology, 31,* 484–489.

Rothe, H. F. (1951). Output rates among chocolate dippers. *Journal of Applied Psychology, 35,* 94–97.

Rothe, H. F. (1970). Output rates among welders: Productivity and consistency following removal of a financial incentive system. *Journal of Applied Psychology, 54,* 549–551.

Rothe, H. F. (1978). Output rates among industrial employees. *Journal of Applied Psychology, 63,* 40–46.

Rothe, H. F., & Nye, C. T. (1958). Output rates among coil winders. *Journal of Applied Psychology, 42,* 182–186.

Rynes, S. L. & Milkovich, G. T. (1988). Wage surveys: Disspelling some myths about the "market wage." *Personnel Psychology, 39,* 71–90.

Sackett, P. R., & Harris, M. M. (1985). Honesty testing for personnel selection: A review and critique. In H. J. Bernardin & D. A. Bownas (Eds.), *Personality assessment in organizations.* New York: Praeger.

Schmidt, F. L., & Kaplan, L. B. (1971). Composite vs. multiple criteria: A review and resolution of the controversy. *Personnel Psychology, 24,* 419–434.

Schwab, D. P., & Grams, R. (1985). Sex-related errors in job evaluation: A "real-world" test. *Journal of Applied Psychology, 70,* 533–539.

Schwab, D. P., & Wichern, D. W. (1983). Systematic bias in job evaluation and market wages: Implications for the comparable worth debate. *Journal of Applied Psychology, 68,* 60–69.

Seashore, S. E., Indik, B. P., & Georgopoulos, B. S. (1960). Relationship among criteria of job performance. *Journal of Applied Psychology, 44,* 195–202.

Smith, P. C. (1976). Behavior, results, and organizational effectiveness: The problem of criteria. In M. D. Dunnette (Ed.), *Handbook of industrial and organizational psychology.* Skokie, Ill.: Rand McNally.

Spool, M. D. (1978). Training programs for observers of behavior: A review. *Personnel Psychology, 31,* 853–888.

Steers, R. M., & Rhodes, S. R. (1978). Major influences on employee attendance: A process model. *Journal of Applied Psychology, 63,* 391–407.

Taber, T. D., & Hackman, J. D. (1976). Dimensions of undergraduate college performance. *Journal of Applied Psychology, 61,* 546–558.

Taylor, C. W., Price, P. B., Richards, J. M., & Jacobsen, T. L. (1964). An investigation of the criterion problem for a medical school faculty. *Journal of Applied Psychology, 48,* 294–301.

Taylor, C. W., Price, P. B., Richards, J. M., & Jacobsen, T. L. (1965). An investigation of the criterion problem for a group of medical general practitioners. *Journal of Applied Psychology, 49,* 339–406.

Taylor, L. R. (1978). Empirically derived job families as a foundation for the study of validity generalization: The construction of job families based on the component and overall dimensions of the PAQ. *Personnel Psychology, 31,* 325–340.

Thorndike, R. L. (1949). *Personnel selection.* New York: Wiley.

Toops, H. A. (1944). The criterion. *Educational and Psychological Measurement, 4,* 271–297.

Turner, W. W. (1960). Dimensions of foreman performance: A factor analysis of criterion measures. *Journal of Applied Psychology, 4,* 216–223.

U.S. Department of Labor, Employment, and Training Administration. (1977). *Dictionary of occupational titles* (4th ed.). Washington, D.C.: U.S. Government Printing Office.

Wallace, S. R. (1965). Criteria for what? *American Psychologist, 20,* 411–417.

Weitz, J. (1961). Criteria for criteria. *American Psychologist, 16,* 228–231.

Wherry, R. J. (1957). The past and future of criterion evaluation. *Personnel Psychology, 10,* 1–5.

Chapter 4

American Psychological Association. (1981). Ethical principles of psychologists. *American Psychologist, 36,* 633–638.

Anastasi, A. (1976). *Psychological testing* (4th ed.). New York: Macmillan.

Arvey, R. D. (1979). Unfair discrimination in the employment interview: Legal and psychological aspects. *Psychological Bulletin, 86,* 736–765.

Arvey, R. D. & Campion, J. E. (1982). The employment interview: A summary and review of recent literature. *Personnel Psychology, 35,* 281–322.

Bass, B. M. (1954). The leaderless group discussion. *Psychological Bulletin, 51,* 465–492.

Bennett, G. K. (1940). *Test of Mechanical Comprehension.* New York: Psychological Corporation.

Ben-Shakhar, G., Bar-Hillel, M., Bilu, Y., Ben-Abba, E., & Flug, A. (1986). Can graphology predict occupational success? Two empirical studies and some methodological ruminations. *Journal of Applied Psychology, 71,* 645–653.

Bentz, V. J. (1985). Research findings from personality assessment of executives. In H. J. Bernardin & D. A. Bownas (Eds.), *Personality assessment in organizations.* New York: Praeger.

Bersoff, D. N. (1981). Testing and the law. *American Psychologist, 36,* 1047–1056.

Bingham, W. V. D., & Moore, B. V. (1941). *How to interview* (3rd ed.). New York: Harper & Row.

Blum, M. L., & Naylor, J. C. (1968). *Industrial psychology: Its theoretical and social foundations.* New York: Harper & Row.

Brugnoli, G. A., Campion, J. E., & Basen, J. A. (1979). Racial bias in the use of work samples for personnel selection. *Journal of Applied Psychology, 64,* 119–123.

Buros, O. K. (Ed.). (1970). *Personality tests and reviews.* Highland Park, NJ: Gryphon Press.

Buros, O. K. (Ed.). (1974). *Tests in print II.* Highland Park, NJ: Gryphon Press.

Campbell, D. P. (1977). *Manual for the Strong-Campbell Interest Inventory T325 (merged form).* Stanford, CA: Stanford, CA: Stanford University Press.

Campion, J. E. (1972). Work sampling for personnel selection. *Journal of Applied Psychology, 56,* 40–44.

Carlson, R. E. (1968). Employment decisions: Effect of mode of applicant presentation on some outcome measures. *Personnel Psychology, 21,* 193–207.

Carlson, R. E. (1972). The current status of judgmental techniques in industry. Paper presented at the symposium Alternatives to Paper and Pencil Personnel Testing, University of Pittsburgh.

Cascio, W. F. (1975). Accuracy of verifiable biographical information blank responses. *Journal of Applied Psychology, 60,* 767–769.

Cascio, W. F. (1976). Turnover, biographical data, and fair employment practice. *Journal of Applied Psychology, 61,* 576–580.

Cascio, W. F. (1982). *Applied psychology in personnel management* (2nd ed.). Reston, VA: Reston.

Cascio, W. F., & Phillips, N. F. (1979). Performance testing: A rose among thorns? *Personnel Psychology, 32,* 751–766.

Ceci, S. J., & Peters, D. (1984). Letters of reference: A naturalistic study of the effects of confidentiality. *American Psychologist, 39,* 29–31.

Childs, A., & Klimoski, R. J. (1986). Successfully predicting career success: An application of the biographical inventory. *Journal of Applied Psychology, 71,* 3–8.

Crawford, J. E., & Crawford, D. M. (1946). *Small Parts Dexterity Test.* New York: Psychological Corporation.

Cronbach, L. J. (1970). *Essentials of psychological testing.* New York: Harper & Row.

Equal Employment Opportunity Commission. (1978). Adoption by four agencies of uniform guidelines on employee selection procedures. *Federal Register, 43,* 38290–38309.

Frederiksen, N. (1968). *Organization climates and administrative performance.* Princeton, NJ: Educational Testing Service.

Ghiselli, E. E. (1966). *The validity of occupational aptitude tests.* New York: Wiley.

Ghiselli, E. E. (1973). The validity of aptitude tests in personnel selection. *Personnel Psychology, 26,* 461–477.

Ginton, A., Daie, N., Elaad, E., & Ben-Shakhar, G. (1982). A method for evaluating the use of the polygraph in a real-life situation. *Journal of Applied Psychology, 67,* 131–137.

Gough, H. G. (1984). A managerial potential scale for the California Psychological Inventory. *Journal of Applied Psychology, 69,* 233–240.

Green, S. B., Lissitz, R. W., & Mulaik, S. A. (1977). Limitations of coefficient alpha as an index of test unidimensionality. *Educational and Psychological Measurement, 37,* 827–838.

Guion, R. M. (1978). "Content validity" in moderation. *Personnel Psychology, 31,* 205–213.

Guion, R. M., & Gottier, R. F. (1965). Validity of personality measures in personnel selection. *Personnel Psychology, 18,* 135–164.

Haney, W. (1981). Validity, vaudeville, and values: A short history of social concerns over standardized testing. *American Psychologist, 36,* 1021–1034.

Hathaway, S. R., & McKinley, J. C. (1943). *Minnesota Multiphasic Personality Inventory* (rev. ed.). New York: Psychological Corporation.

Hogan, J., Hogan, R., & Busch, C. M. (1984). How to measure service orientation. *Journal of Applied Psychology, 69,* 167–173.

Holland, J. L. (1965). *Manual for the vocational preference inventory.* Palo Alto, CA: Consulting Psychologists Press.

Hollander, E. P. (1965). Validity of peer nominations in predicting a distant performance criterion. *Journal of Applied Psychology, 49,* 434–438.

Hunter, J. E., & Hunter, R. F. (1984). Validity and utility of alternative predictors of job performance. *Psychological Bulletin, 96,* 72–98.

Kalleberg, A. L., & Kluegel, J. R. (1975). Analysis of the multitrait-multimethod matrix: Some limitations and an alternative. *Journal of Applied Psychology, 60,* 1–9.

Kane, J. S., & Lawler, E. E. (1978). Methods of peer assessment. *Psychological Bulletin, 85,* 555–586.

Knouse, S. B. (1983). The letter of recommendation: Specificity and favorability of information. *Personnel Psychology, 36,* 331–341.

Landy, F. J. (1986). Stamp collecting versus science: Validation as hypothesis testing. *American Psychologist, 41,* 1183–1191.

Lawshe, C. H. (1975). A quantitative approach to content validity. *Personnel Psychology, 28,* 563–575.

Lee, R., & Booth, J. M. (1974). A utility analysis of a weighted application blank designed to predict turnover for clerical employees. *Journal of Applied Psychology, 59,* 516–518.

Levy, L. (1979). Handwriting and hiring. *Dun's Review, 113,* 72–79.

Likert, R., & Quasha, W. H. (1941–1948). *Revised Minnesota Paper Form Board Test.* New York: Psychological Corporation.

Lykken, D. T. (1974). Psychology and the lie detection industry. *Psychological Bulletin, 79,* 725–739.

Mayfield, E. C. (1972). Value of peer nominations in predicting life insurance sales performance. *Journal of Applied Psychology, 56,* 319–323.

Mitchell, T. W., & Klimoski, R. J. (1982). Is it rational to be empirical? A test of methods for scoring biographical data. *Journal of Applied Psychology, 67,* 411–418.

Mount, M. K., Muchinsky, P. M., & Hanser, L. M. (1977). The predictive validity of a work sample: A laboratory study. *Personnel Psychology, 30,* 637–645.

Muchinsky, P. M. (1975). The utility of work samples in complying with EEOC guidelines. *Personnel Journal, 54,* 218–220.

Muchinsky, P. M. (1979). The use of reference reports in personnel selection: A review and evaluation. *Journal of Occupational Psychology, 52,* 287–297.

Nagle, B. F. (1953). Criterion development. *Personnel Psychology, 6,* 271–289.

Olian, J. D. (1984). Genetic screening for employment purposes. *Personnel Psychology, 37,* 423–438.

Otis, A. S. (1922–1929). *Self-Administering Tests of Mental Ability.* Tarrytown-on-Hudson, NY: World.

Owens, W. A., & Schoenfeldt, L. F. (1979). Toward a classification of persons. *Journal of Applied Psychology, 65,* 569–607.

Pace, L. A., & Schoenfeldt, L. F. (1977). Legal concerns in the use of weighted applications. *Personnel Psychology, 61,* 159–166.

Paterson, D. G. (1930). *Minnesota Spatial Relations Test.* Chicago: Stoelting.

Rafaeli, A., & Klimoski, R. J. (1983). Predicting sales success through handwriting analysis: An evaluation of the effects of training and handwriting sample content. *Journal of Applied Psychology, 68,* 212–217.

Reilly, R. R., & Chao, G. T. (1982). Validity and fairness of some alternative employee selection procedures. *Personnel Psychology, 35,* 1–62.

Robertson, I. T., & Kandola, R. S. (1982). Work sample tests: Validity, adverse impact and applicant reaction. *Journal of Occupational Psychology, 55,* 171–183.

Schmidt, F. L., Greenthal, A. L., Berner, J. G., Hunter, J. E., & Seaton, F. W. (1977). Job sample vs. paper-and-pencil trades and technical tests: Adverse impact and examinee attitudes. *Personnel Psychology, 30,* 187–198.

Schmitt, N. (1976). Social and situational determinants of interview decisions: Implications for the employment interview. *Personnel Psychology, 30,* 79–101.

Schmitt, N., Gooding, R. Z., Noe, R. D., & Kirsch, M. (1984). Meta-analyses of validity studies published between 1964 and 1982 and the investigation of study characteristics. *Personnel Psychology, 37,* 407–422.

Society for Industrial and Organizational Psychology, Inc. (1987). *Principles for the validation and use of personnel selection procedures* (3rd ed.). College Park, MD: Author.

Standards for educational and psychological testing. (1985). Washington, DC: American Psychological Association.

Tenopyr, M. L. (1977). Content-construct confusion. *Personnel Psychology 30,* 47–54.

Tiffin, J. (1941). *Purdue Pegboard.* Chicago: Science Research Associates.

Verplank, W. S. (1955). The control of the content of conversation: Reinforcement of statements of opinion. *Journal of Abnormal and Social Psychology, 51,* 668–676.

Waid, W. M., & Orne, M. T. (1980). Individual differences in electrodermal liability and the detection of information and deception. *Journal of Applied Psychology, 65,* 1–8.

Wernimont, P. F., & Campbell, J. P. (1968). Signs, samples, and criteria. *Journal of Applied Psychology, 53,* 372–376.

Wonderlic, E. F., & Hovland, C. I. (1939). The personnel test: A re-standardized abridgement of the Otis S. A. test for business and industrial use. *Journal of Applied Psychology, 23,* 685–702.

Zedeck, S., Tziner, A., & Middlestadt, S. E. (1983). Interviewer validity and reliability: An individual analysis approach. *Personnel Psychology, 36,* 355–370.

Chapter 5

Barrett, G. V., Phillips, J. S., & Alexander, R. A. (1981). Concurrent and predictive validity designs: A critical reanalysis. *Journal of Applied Psychology, 66,* 1–6.

Blum, M. L., & Naylor, J. C. (1968). *Industrial psychology: Its theoretical and social foundations*. New York: Harper & Row.

Boudreau, J. W. (1983). Economic considerations in estimating the utility of human resource productivity improvement programs. *Personnel Psychology, 36,* 551–576.

Breaugh, J. A. (1981). Relationships between recruiting sources and employee performance, absenteeism, and work attitudes. *Academy of Management Journal, 24,* 142–147.

Breaugh, J. A. (1983). Realistic job previews: A critical appraisal and future research directions. *Academy of Management Review, 8,* 612–619.

Brogden, H. E. (1951). Increased efficiency of selection resulting from replacement of a single predictor with several differential predictors. *Educational and Psychological Measurement, 11,* 183–196.

Brown, S. H. (1981). Validity generalization and situational moderation in the life insurance industry. *Journal of Applied Psychology, 66,* 664–670.

Burke, M. J. (1984). Validity generalization: A review and critique of the correlational model. *Personnel Psychology, 37,* 93–116.

Cascio, W. F. (1978). *Applied psychology in personnel management.* Reston, VA: Reston.

Cascio, W. F. (1987). *Costing human resources: The financial impact of behavior in organizations* (2nd ed.). Boston: Kent.

Cascio, W. F., Alexander, R. A., & Barrett, G. V. (1988). Setting cutoff scores: Legal, psychometric, and professional issues and guidelines. *Personnel Psychology, 41,* 1–24.

Cattin, P. (1980.). Estimation of the predictive power of a regression model. *Journal of Applied Psychology, 65,* 407–414.

Chacko, T. I.(1982). Women and Equal Employment Opportunity: Some unintended effects. *Journal of Applied Psychology, 67,* 119–123.

Cronbach, L. J., & Gleser, G. C. (1965). *Psychological tests and personnel decisions* (2nd ed.). Urbana, IL: University of Illinois Press.

Dean, R. A., & Wanous, J. P. (1984). Effects of realistic job previews on hiring bank tellers. *Journal of Applied Psychology, 69,* 61–68.

Dudycha, A. L., Dudycha, L. W., & Schmitt, N. W. (1974). Cue redundancy: Some overlooked analytical relationships in MCPL. *Organization Behavior and Human Performance, 11,* 222–234.

Dugoni, B. L., & Ilgen, D. R. (1981). Realistic job previews and the adjustment of new employees. *Academy of Management Journal, 24,* 579–591.

Einhorn, H. J. (1970). The use of nonlinear, noncompensatory models in decision making. *Psychological Bulletin, 73,* 221–230.

Gannon, M. J. (1971). Sources of referral and employee turnover. *Journal of Applied Psychology, 55,* 226–228.

Ghiselli, E. E. (1956). The placement of workers: Concepts and problems. *Personnel Psychology, 9,* 1–16.

Guion, R. M. (1965). *Personnel testing.* New York: McGraw-Hill.

Hawk, R. H. (1967). *The recruitment function.* New York: American Management Association.

Heilman, M. E., & Herlihy, J. M. (1984). Affirmative action, negative reaction? Some moderating considerations. *Organizational Behavior and Human Performance, 33,* 204–213.

Heilman, M. E., Simon, M. C., & Repper, D. P. (1987). Intentionally favored, unintentionally harmed? Impact of sex-based preferential selection in self-perceptions and self-evaluations. *Journal of Applied Psychology, 72,* 62–68.

Landy, F. J., Farr, J. L., & Jacobs, R.R. (1982). Utility concepts in performance measurement. *Organizational Behavior and Human Performance, 30,* 15–40.

Monahan, C. J., & Muchinsky, P. M. (1983). Three decades of personnel selection research: A state-of-the-art analysis and evaluation. *Journal of Occupational Psychology, 56,* 215–225.

Mosier, C. I. (1951). Problems and designs of cross validation. *Educational and Psychological Measurement, 11,* 5–11.

Pearlman, K., Schmidt, F. L., & Hunter, J. E. (1980). Validity generalization results for tests used to predict job proficiency and training success in clerical occupations. *Journal of Applied Psychology, 65,* 373–406.

Reilly, R. R., Brown, B., Blood, M. R., & Malatesta, C. Z. (1981). The effects of realistic previews: A study and discussion of the literature. *Personnel Psychology, 34,* 823–834.

Rothe, H. F. (1947). Distributions of test scores of industrial employees and applicants. *Journal of Applied Psychology, 32,* 484–489.

Schmidt, F. L., Gast-Rosenberg, I., & Hunter, J. E. (1980). Validity generalization results for computer programmers. *Journal of Applied Psychology, 65,* 643–661.

Schmidt, F. L., & Hunter, J. E. (1978). Moderator research and the law of small numbers. *Personnel Psychology, 31,* 215–232.

Schmidt, F. L., & Hunter, J. E. (1980). The future of criterion-related validity. *Personnel Psychology, 33,* 41–60.

Schmidt, F. L., & Hunter, J. E. (1981). Employment testing: Old theories and new research findings. *American Psychologist, 36,* 1128–1137.

Schmidt, F. L., Hunter, J. E., & Caplan, J. R. (1981). Validity generalization results for two job groups in the petroleum industry. *Journal of Applied Psychology, 66,* 262–273.

Schmidt, F. L., Hunter, J. E., McKenzie, R. C., & Muldrow, T. W. (1979). Impact of valid selection procedures on work-force productivity. *Journal of Applied Psychology, 64,* 609–626.

Schmidt, F. L., Hunter, J. E., Outerbridge, A. N., & Trattner, M. H (1986). The economic impact of job selection methods on size, productivity, and payroll costs of the federal work force: An empirically based demonstration. *Personnel Psychology, 39,* 1–29.

Schmidt, F. L., Mack, M. J., & Hunter, J. E. (1984). Selection utility in the occupation of U.S. park ranger for three models of test use. *Journal of Applied Psychology, 69,* 490–497.

Schmidt, F. L., Pearlman, K., Hunter, J. E., & Hirsh, H. R. (1985). Forty questions about validity generalization and meta-analysis. *Personnel Psychology, 38,* 697–798.

Schoenfeldt, L. F. (1974). Utilization of manpower: Development and evaluation of an assessment-classification model for matching individuals with jobs. *Journal of Applied Psychology, 59,* 583–592.

Taylor, M. S., & Schmidt, D. W. (1983). A process-oriented investigation of recruitment source effectiveness. *Personnel Psychology, 36,* 343–354.

Tenopyr, M. L. (1981). The realities of employment testing. *American Psychologist, 36,* 1120–1127.

Zaharia, E. S., & Baumeister, A. A. (1981). Job preview effects during the critical initial employment period. *Journal of Applied Psychology, 66,* 19–22.

Chapter 6

Baldwin, T. T., & Ford, J. K. (1988). Transfer of training: A review and directions for future research. *Personnel Psychology, 41,* 63–105.

Bartlett, C. J. (1978). Equal employment opportunity issues in training. *Human Factors, 20,* 179–188.

Bass, B. M., & Barrett, G. V. (1981). *People, work, and organizations* (2nd ed.). Boston: Allyn & Bacon.

Bass, B. M., & Vaughan, J. A. (1966). *Training in industry: The management of learning.* Pacific Grove, CA: Brooks/Cole.

Brethower, K. S. (1976). Programmed instruction. In R. L. Craig (Ed.), *Training and development handbook* (2nd ed.). New York: McGraw-Hill.

Bunker, K. A., & Cohen, S. L. (1977). The rigors of training evaluation: A discussion and field demonstration. *Personnel Psychology, 30,* 525–541.

Burke, M. J., & Day, R. R. (1986). A cumulative study of the effectiveness of managerial training. *Journal of Applied Psychology, 71,* 232–246.

Campbell, J. P. (1971). Personnel training and development. *Annual Review of Psychology, 22,* 565–602.

Campion, M. A., & Campion, J. E. (1987). Evaluation of an interviewee skills training program in a natural field experiment. *Personnel Psychology, 40,* 675–691.

Catalanello, R. E., & Kirkpatrick, D. L. (1968). Evaluating training programs: The state of the art. *Training and Development Journal, 22,* 2–9.

Cooper, C. L., & Levine, N. (1978). Implicit values in experimental learning groups: Their functional and dysfunctional consequences. In D. L. Cooper & C. Alderfer (Eds.), *Advances in experimental social processes.* New York: Wiley.

Coppard, L. C. (1976). Gaming simulations and the training process. In R. L. Craig (Ed.), *Training and development handbook* (2nd ed.). New York: McGraw-Hill.

Dossett, D. L., & Hulvershorn, P. (1983). Increasing technical training efficiency: Peer training via computer-assisted instruction. *Journal of Applied Psychology, 68,* 552–558.

Dupre, V. A. (1976). Human relations laboratory training. In R. L. Craig (Ed.), *Training and development handbook* (2nd ed.). New York: McGraw-Hill.

Eden, D., & Shani, A. B. (1982). Pygmalion goes to boot camp: Expectancy, leadership, and trainee performance. *Journal of Applied Psychology, 67,* 194–199.

Ford, J. K., & Wroten, S. P. (1984). Introducing new methods for conducting training evaluation and for linking training evaluation to program redesign. *Personnel Psychology, 37,* 651–666.

Franklin, W. S. (1976). Are construction apprenticeships too long? *Labor Law Journal, 27,* 99–106.

Fredericksen, N. (1961). In-basket tests and factors in administrative performance. In H. Guetzkow (Ed.), *Simulation in social science: Reading.* Englewood Cliffs, NJ: Prentice-Hall.

Freeberg, N. E. (1976). Criterion measures for youth-work training programs: The development of relevant performance dimensions. *Journal of Applied Psychology, 61,* 537–545.

Goldstein, I. L. (1974). *Training: Program development and evaluation.* Monterey, CA: Brooks/Cole.

Goldstein, I. L. (1978). The pursuit of validity in the evaluation of training programs. *Human Factors, 20,* 131–144.

Goldstein, I. L. (1980a). Training and organizational psychology. *Professional Psychology, 11,* 421–427.

Goldstein, I. L. (1980b). Training in work organizations. *Annual Review of Psychology, 31,* 229–272.

Hand, H. H. & Slocum, J. W., Jr. (1972). A longitudinal study of the effects of a human relations training program on management effectiveness. *Journal of Applied Psychology, 56,* 412–417.

Hickey, A. E. (1976). Computer-assisted and computer-managed instruction. In R. L. Craig (Ed.), *Training and development handbook* (2nd ed.). New York: McGraw-Hill.

Hinrichs, J. (1976). Personnel training. In M. D. Dunnette (Ed.), *Handbook of industrial and organizational psychology*. Skokie, IL: Rand McNally.

Hughes, J. L., & McNamara, W. J. (1961). A comparative study of programmed and conventional instruction in industry. *Journal of Applied Psychology, 45,* 225–231.

Ilgen, D. R., Fisher, C. D. & Taylor, M. S. (1979). Consequences of individual feedback on behavior in organizations. *Journal of Applied Psychology, 64,* 349–371.

Kidd, J. S. (1961). A comparison of two methods of training in a complex task by means of a task simulation. *Journal of Applied Psychology, 45,* 165–169.

Kirkpatrick, D. L. (1976). Evaluation of training. In R. L. Craig (Ed.), *Training and development handbook* (2nd ed.). New York: McGraw-Hill.

Koerner, J. (1973). Educational technology: Does it have a future in the classroom? *Saturday Review Supplement, 1,* 42–46.

Konz, S. A., & Dickey, G. L. (1969). Manufacturing assembly instructions: A summary. *Ergonomics, 12,* 369–382.

Landy, F. J., & Trumbo, D. A. (1980). *Psychology of work behavior* (rev. ed.). Chicago, IL: Dorsey Press.

Latham, G. P., & Saari, L. M. (1979). The application of social learning theory to training supervisors through behavioral modeling. *Journal of Applied Psychology, 64,* 239–246.

Lefkowitz, J. (1970). Effect of training on the productivity and tenure of sewing machine operators. *Journal of Applied Psychology, 54,* 81–86.

Mathieu, J. E., & Leonard, R. L. (1987). Applying utility concepts to a training program in supervisory skills: A time-based approach. *Academy of Management Journal, 30,* 316–335.

McGehee, W. (1979). Training and development theory, policies, and practices. In D. Yoder & H. G. Heneman, Jr.(Eds.), *ASPA handbook of personnel and industrial relations*. Washington, DC: Bureau of National Affairs.

McGehee, W., & Thayer, P. W. (1961). *Training in business and industry*. New York: Wiley.

Mirvis, P. H., & Lawler, E. E. (1977). Measuring the financial impact of employee attitudes. *Journal of Applied Psychology, 62,* 1–8.

Moore, M. L., & Dutton, P. (1978). Training needs analysis: Review and critique. *Academy of Management Review, 3,* 532–545.

Morrison, J. H. (1976). Determining training needs. In R. L. Craig (Ed.), *Training and development handbook* (2nd ed.). New York: McGraw-Hill.

Nash, A. N., Muczyk, J. P., & Vettori, F. L. (1971). The relative practical effectiveness of programmed instruction. *Personnel Psychology, 24,* 397–418.

Noe, R. A. (1986). Trainees' attributes and attitudes: Neglected influences on training effectiveness. *Academy of Management Review, 11,* 736–749.

Noe, R. A., & Schmitt, N. (1986). The influence of trainee attitudes on training effectiveness: Test of a model. *Personnel Psychology, 39,* 497–523.

A new approach to management's role in back safety. (1966). Hicksville, NY: Advanced Learning Systems.

Parker, T. C. (1976). Statistical methods for measuring training results. In R. L. Craig (Ed.), *Training and development handbook* (2nd ed.). New York: McGraw-Hill.

Raia, A. P. (1966). A study of the educational value of management games. *Journal of Business, 39,* 339–352.

Robertson, I., & Downs, S. (1979). Learning and the prediction of performance: Development of trainability testing in the United Kingdom. *Journal of Applied Psychology, 64,* 42–50.

Russell, J. S. (1984). A review of fair employment cases in the field of training. *Personnel Psychology, 37*, 261–276.

Smith, P. B. (1975). Controlled studies of the outcome of sensitivity training. *Psychological Bulletin, 82*, 597–622.

Solomon, R. L. (1949). An extension of control group design. *Psychological Bulletin, 46*, 137–150.

Suppes, P., & Morningstar, M. (1969). Computer-assisted instruction. *Science, 166*, 343–350.

Sussman, M., & Robertson, D. U. (1986). The validity of validity: An analysis of validation study designs. *Journal of Applied Psychology, 71*, 461–468.

Welsh, P., Antoinetti, J. A., & Thayer, P. W. (1965). An industry-wide study of programmed instruction. *Journal of Applied Psychology, 49*, 61–73.

Wohlking, W. (1976). Role playing. In R. L. Craig (Ed.), *Training and development handbook* (2nd ed.). New York: McGraw-Hill.

Chapter 7

Anderson, C. C., Warner, J. L., & Spencer, C. C. (1984). Inflation bias in self-assessment examinations: Implications for valid employee selection. *Journal of Applied Psychology, 69*, 574–580.

Banks, C. G., & Murphy, K. R. (1985). Toward narrowing the research-practice gap in performance appraisal. *Personnel Psychology, 38*, 335–345.

Barnes-Farrell, J. L., & Weiss, H. M. (1984). Effects of standard extremity on mixed standard scale performance ratings. *Personnel Psychology, 37*, 301–316.

Barrett, G. V., & Kernan, M. C. (1987). Performance appraisal and terminations: A review of court decisions since Brito v. Zia with implications for personnel practices. *Personnel Psychology, 40*, 489–503.

Barrett, R. S. (1966). *Performance ratings.* Chicago: Science Research Associates.

Bartlett, C. J. (1983). What's the difference between valid and invalid halo? Forced-choice measurement without forcing a choice. *Journal of Applied Psychology, 68*, 218–226.

Bass, A. R., & Turner, J. N. (1973). Ethnic group differences in relationship among criteria of job performance. *Journal of Applied Psychology, 57*, 101–109.

Bernardin, H. J., & Kane, J. S. (1980). A second look at behavioral observation scales. *Personnel Psychology, 33*, 809–814.

Bernardin, H. J., & Pence, E. C. (1980). Effects of rater training: Creating new response sets and decreasing accuracy. *Journal of Applied Psychology, 65*, 60–66.

Blanz, F., & Ghiselli, E. E. (1972). The mixed standard rating scale: A new rating system. *Personnel Psychology, 25*, 185–199.

Blum, M. L., & Naylor, J. C. (1968). *Industrial psychology.* New York: Harper & Row.

Boehm, V. R. (1977). Differential prediction: A methodological artifact? *Journal of Applied Psychology, 62*, 146–154.

Borman, W. C. (1974). The rating of individuals in organizations: An alternative approach. *Organizational Behavior and Human Performance, 12*, 105–124.

Borman, W. C. (1978). Exploring upper limits of reliability and validity in performance ratings. *Journal of Applied Psychology, 63*, 135–144.

Borman, W. C. (1982). Validity of behavioral assessment for predicting military recruiter performance. *Journal of Applied Psychology, 67*, 3–9.

Borman, W. C., & Vallon, W. R. (1974). A view of what can happen when behavioral expectation scales are developed in one setting and used in another. *Journal of Applied Psychology, 59*, 197–201.

Bray, D. W. (1982). The assessment center and the study of lives. *American Psychologist, 37,* 180–189.

Bray, D. W., Campbell, R. J., & Grant, D. L. (1974). *Formative years in business.* New York: Wiley.

Burke, R. J., Weitzel W., & Weir, T. (1978). Characteristics of effective employee performance review and development interviews: Replication and extension. *Personnel Psychology, 31,* 903–920.

Burke, R. J., & Wilcox, D. S. (1969). Characteristics of effective employee performance review and development interviews. *Personnel Psychology, 22,* 291–305.

Byham, W. C. (1970). Assessment centers for spotting future managers. *Harvard Business Review, 48,* 150–167.

Campbell, D. J., & Lee C. (1988). Self-appraisal in performance evaluation: Development versus evaluation. *Academy of Management Review, 13,* 302–314.

Campbell, J., Dunnette, M., Arvey, R., & Hellervik, L. (1973). The development and evaluation of behaviorally based rating scales. *Journal of Applied Psychology, 57,* 15–22.

Campion, J. E. (1972). Work sampling for personnel selection. *Journal of Applied Psychology, 56,* 40–44.

Cascio, W. F., & Silbey, V. (1979). Utility of the assessment center as a selection device. *Journal of Applied Psychology, 64,* 107–118.

Cederblom, D. (1982). The performance appraisal interview: A review, implications and suggestions. *Academy of Management Review, 7,* 219–227.

Cederblom, D., & Lounsbury, J. W. (1980). An investigation of user acceptance of peer evaluations. *Personnel Psychology, 33,* 567–580.

Cooper, W. H. (1981). Ubiquitous halo. *Psychological Bulletin, 90,* 218–244.

Davis, B. L., & Mount, M. K. (1984). Effectiveness of performance appraisal training using computer assisted instruction and behavior modeling. *Personnel Psychology, 37,* 439–452.

Dickinson, T. L., & Zellinger, P. M. (1980). A comparison of the behaviorally anchored rating and mixed standard scale formats. *Journal of Applied Psychology, 65,* 147–154.

Fay, C. H., & Latham, G. P. (1982). Effects of training and rating errors. *Personnel Psychology, 35,* 105–116.

Feild, H. S., & Holley, W. H. (1982). The relationship of performance appraisal system characteristics to verdicts in selected employment discrimination cases. *Academy of Management Journal, 25,* 392–406.

Feldman, J. M. (1981). Beyond attribution theory: Cognitive processes in performance appraisal. *Journal of Applied Psychology, 66,* 127–148.

Finkle, R. B. (1976). Managerial assessment centers. In M. D. Dunnette (Ed.), *Handbook of industrial and organizational psychology.* Skokie, IL: Rand McNally.

Flanagan, J. C. (1954). The critical incident technique. *Psychological Bulletin, 51,* 327–358.

Gaugler, B. B., Rosenthal, D. B. Thornton, G. C. & Bentson, C. (1987). Meta-analysis of assessment center validity. *Journal of Applied Psychology, 72,* 493–511.

Green, S. G., Fairhurst, G. T., & Snavely, B. K. (1986). Chains of poor performance and supervisory control. *Organizational Behavior and Human Decision Processes, 38,* 7–27.

Greenberg, J. (1986). Determinants of perceived fairness of performance evaluations. *Journal of Applied Psychology, 71,* 340–342.

Guion, R. (1965). *Personnel testing.* New York: McGraw-Hill.

Hedge, J. W., & Kavanagh, M. J. (1988). Improving the accuracy of performance evaluations: Comparison of three methods of performance appraisal training. *Journal of Applied Psychology, 73,* 68–73.

Heilman, M. E., & Stopeck, M. H. (1985). Being attractive, advantage or disadvantage? Performance-based evaluations and recommended personnel actions as a function of appearance, sex, and job type. *Organizational Behavior and Human Decision Processes, 35,* 202–215.

Heneman, H. G., III. (1980). Self-assessments: A critical analysis. *Personnel Psychology, 33,* 297–300.

Hinrichs, J. R. (1978). An eight-year follow-up of a management assessment center. *Journal of Applied Psychology, 63,* 596–601.

Hinrichs, J. R., & Haanpera, S. (1976). Reliability of measurement in situational exercises: An assessment of the assessment center method. *Personnel Psychology, 29,* 31–40.

Holley, W. H., & Feild, H. S. (1975). Performance appraisal and the law. *Labor Law Journal, 26,* 423–430.

Holzbach, R. L. (1978). Rater bias in performance ratings: Superior, self-, and peer assessments. *Journal of Applied Psychology, 63,* 579–588.

Howard, A. (1974). An assessment of assessment centers. *Academy of Management Journal, 17,* 115–134.

Huck, J. R. (1973). Assessment centers: A review of their external and internal validities. *Personnel Psychology, 26,* 191–212.

Huck, J. R., & Bray, D. W. (1976). Management assessment center evaluations and subsequent job performance of white and black females. *Personnel Psychology, 29,* 13–31.

Ilgen, D. R., & Favero, J. L. (1985). Limits in generalization from psychological research to performance appraisal processes. *Academy of Management Review, 10,* 311–322.

Ilgen, D. R., Fisher, C. D., & Taylor, M. S. (1979). Motivational consequences of individual feedback on behavior in organizations. *Journal of Applied Psychology, 64,* 349–371.

Ilgen, D. R., Mitchell, T. R., & Fredrickson, J. W. (1981). Poor performers: Supervisors' and subordinates' responses. *Organizational Behavior and Human Performance, 27,* 386–410.

Ilgen, D. R., Peterson, R. B., Martin, B. A., & Boeschen, D. A. (1981). Supervisor and subordinate reactions to performance appraisal sessions. *Organizational Behavior and Human Performance, 28,* 311–330.

Ivancevich, J. M. (1982). Subordinates' reactions to performance appraisal interviews: A test of feedback and goal-setting techniques. *Journal of Applied Psychology, 67,* 581–587.

Kane, J. S., & Bernardin, H. J. (1982). Behavioral observation scales and the evaluation of performance appraisal effectiveness. *Personnel Psychology, 35,* 635–641.

Kane, J. S., & Lawler, E. E., III. (1978). Methods of peer assessment. *Psychological Bulletin, 85,* 555–586.

Kay, E., Meyer, H. H., & French, J. R. P., Jr. (1965). Effects of threat in a performance appraisal interview. *Journal of Applied Psychology, 49,* 311–317.

Kingstrom, P. O., & Bass, A. R. (1981). A critical analysis of studies comparing behaviorally anchored rating scales (BARS) and other rating formats. *Personnel Psychology, 34,* 263–289.

Kleiman, L. S., & Durham, R. L. (1981). Performance appraisal, promotion and the courts: A critical review. *Personnel Psychology, 34,* 103–121.

Klimoski, R. J., & Brickner, M. (1987). Why do assessment centers work? The puzzle of assessment center validity. *Personnel Psychology, 40,* 243–260.

Klimoski, R. J., & Strickland, W. J. (1977). Assessment Centers—Valid or merely prescient? *Personnel Psychology, 30,* 353–361.

Kujawski, C. J., & Young, D. M. (1979). Appraisals of "people" resources. In D. Yoder & H. G. Heneman, Jr. (Eds.), *ASPA handbook of personnel and industrial relations.* Washington, DC: Bureau of National Affairs.

Landy, F. J., & Trumbo, D. A. (1980). *Psychology of work behavior* (rev. ed.). Pacific Grove, CA: Brooks/Cole.

Latham, G. P. (1986). Job performance and appraisal. In C. L. Cooper & I. T. Robertson

(Eds.), *International review of industrial and organizational psychology—1986*. London: Wiley.

Latham, G. P., Fay, C. H., & Saari, L. M. (1979). The development of behavioral observation scales for appraising the performance of foremen. *Personnel Psychology, 32*, 299–311.

Latham, G. P., & Pursell, E. D. (1975). Measuring absenteeism from the opposite side of the coin. *Journal of Applied Psychology, 60*, 369–371.

Latham, G. P., Saari, L. M., & Fay, C. (1980). BOS, BES, and baloney: Raising Kane with Bernardin. *Personnel Psychology, 33*, 815–821.

Latham, G. P., & Wexley, K. N. (1977). Behavioral observation scales for performance appraisal purposes. *Personnel Psychology, 30*, 255–268.

Latham, G. P., & Wexley, K. N. (1981). *Increasing productivity through performance appraisal*. Reading, MA: Addison-Wesley.

Latham, G. P., Wexley, K. N., & Pursell, E. D. (1975). Training managers to minimize rating errors in the observation of behavior. *Journal of Applied Psychology, 60*, 550–555.

Latham, G. P., & Yukl, G. A. (1975). A review of research on the application of goal setting in organizations. *Academy of Management Journal, 18*, 824–845.

Lawshe, C. H., Kephart, N. C., & McCormick, E. J. (1949). The paired comparison technique for rating performance of industrial employees. *Journal of Applied Psychology, 33*, 69–77.

Lent, R. H., Aurbach, H. H., & Levin, L. S. (1971). Predictors, criteria, and significant results. *Personnel Psychology, 24*, 519–533.

Levine, E. L., Flory, A., & Ash, R. A. (1977). Self-assessment in personnel selection. *Journal of Applied Psychology, 62*, 428–435.

Lopez, F. M., Jr. (1966). The blood, sweat, and tears of employee performance evaluation. Paper presented at the annual conference of the Public Personnel Association.

Love, K. G. (1981). Comparison of peer assessment methods: Reliability, validity, friendship bias, and user reaction. *Journal of Applied Psychology, 66*, 451–457.

Mabe, P. A., & West, S. G. (1982). Validity of self-evaluation of ability: A review and meta-analysis. *Journal of Applied Psychology, 67*, 280–296.

Maier, N. R. F. (1976). *The appraisal interview*. La Jolla, CA: University Associates.

McCormick, E. J., & Bachus, J. A. (1952). Paired comparison ratings: I. The effect on ratings of reductions in the number of pairs. *Journal of Applied Psychology, 36*, 123–124.

McEvoy, G. M., & Buller, P. F. (1987). User acceptance of peer appraisals in an industrial setting. *Personnel Psychology, 40*, 785–797.

McGregor, D. (1957). An uneasy look at performance appraisal. *Harvard Business Review, 35*, 89–94.

Meyer, H. H. (1980). Self-appraisal of job performance. *Personnel Psychology, 33*, 291–296.

Meyer, H. H., Kay, E., & French, J. R. P., Jr. (1965). Split roles in performance appraisal, *Harvard Business Review, 43*, 123–129.

Mitchel, J. O. (1975). Assessment center validity: A longitudinal study. *Journal of Applied Psychology, 60*, 573–579.

Mitchell, T. R., & Kalb, L. S. (1982). Effects of job experience on supervisor attributions for a subordinate's poor performance. *Journal of Applied Psychology, 67*, 181–188.

Mitchell, T. R., & Linden, R. C. (1982). The effects of the social context on performance evaluations. *Organizational Behavior and Human Performance, 29*, 241–256.

Mobley, W. H. (1982). Supervisor and employee race and sex effects on performance appraisals: A field study of adverse impact and generalizability. *Academy of Management Journal, 25*, 598–606.

Moses, J. L., & Boehm, V. R. (1975). Relationship of assessment center performance to management progress of women. *Journal of Applied Psychology, 60*, 527–529.

Mount, M. K. (1984). Psychometric properties of subordinate ratings of managerial performance. *Personnel Psychology, 37,* 687–702.

Muchinsky, P. M. (1974). Performance ratings of engineers: Do graduates fit the bill? *Engineering Education, 65,* 187–188.

Muchinsky, P. M. (1977). Employee absenteeism: A review of the literature. *Journal of Vocational Behavior, 10,* 316–340.

Murphy, K. R., Martin, C., & Garcia, M. (1982). Do behavioral observation scales measure observation? *Journal of Applied Psychology, 67,* 562–567.

Podsakoff, P. M. (1982). Determinants of a supervisor's use of rewards and punishments: A literature review and suggestions for further research. *Organizational Behavior and Human Performance, 29,* 58–83.

Prince, J. B., & Lawler, E. E. (1986). Does salary discussion hurt the developmental performance appraisal. *Organizational Behavior and Human Decision Processes, 37,* 357–375.

Pulakos, E. D. (1984). A comparison of rater training programs: Error training and accuracy training. *Journal of Applied Psychology, 69,* 581–588.

Pulakos, E. D. (1986). The development of training programs to increase accuracy with different rating tasks. *Organizational Behavior and Human Decision Processes, 38,* 76–91.

Ritchie, R. J., & Moses, J. L. (1983). Assessment center correlates of women's advancement into middle management: A 7-year longitudinal analysis. *Journal of Applied Psychology, 68,* 227–231.

Saal, F. E. (1979). Mixed standard rating scale: A consistent system for numerically coding inconsistent response combinations. *Journal of Applied Psychology, 64,* 422–428.

Saal, F. E., Downey, R. G., & Lahey, M. A. (1980). Rating the ratings: Assessing the psychometric quality of rating data. *Psychological Bulletin, 88,* 413–428.

Saal, F. E., & Landy, F. J. (1977). The mixed standard rating scale: An evaluation. *Organizational Behavior and Human Performance, 18,* 18–35.

Sackett, P. R., & Dreher, G. F. (1982). Constructs and assessment center dimensions: Some troubling empirical findings. *Journal of Applied Psychology, 67,* 401–410.

Schmitt, N. (1977). Interrater agreement in dimensionality and combination of assessment center judgments. *Journal of Applied Psychology, 62,* 171–176.

Schmitt, N., & Lappin, M. (1980). Race and sex as determinants of the mean and variance of performance ratings. *Journal of Applied Psychology, 65,* 428–435.

Schwab, D., Heneman, H. G., III., & DeCotiis, T. (1975). Behaviorally anchored rating scales: A review of the literature. *Personnel Psychology, 28,* 549–562.

Smith, P. C., & Kendall, L. M. (1963). Retranslation of expectations: An approach to the construction of unambiguous anchors for rating scales. *Journal of Applied Psychology, 47,* 149–155.

Steel, R. P., & Ovalle, N. K. (1984). Self-appraisal based upon supervisory feedback. *Personnel Psychology, 37,* 667–686.

Thornton, G. C., III. (1980). Psychometric properties of self-appraisals of job performance. *Personnel Psychology, 33,* 263–272.

Turnage, J. J., & Muchinsky, P. M. (1982). Transsituational variability in human performance within assessment centers. *Organizational Behavior and Human Performance, 30,* 174–200.

Turnage, J. J., & Muchinsky, P. M. (1984). A comparison of the predictive validity of assessment center evaluations versus traditional measures in forecasting supervisory job performance: Interpretive implications of criterion distortion for the assessment paradigm. *Journal of Applied Psychology, 69,* 595–602.

Tziner, A., & Dolan, S. (1982). Validity of an assessment center for identifying future female officers in the military. *Journal of Applied Psychology, 67,* 728–736.

Vetter, H. J. (1969). *Language behavior and communication.* Itasca, IL: F. E. Peacock.

Wesley, K. N., Singh, J. P., & Yukl, G. A. (1973). Subordinate personality as a moderator of the effects of participation in three types of appraisal interviews. *Journal of Applied Psychology, 58,* 54–59.

Wiersma, U., & Latham, G. P. (1986). The practicality of behavioral observation scales, behavioral expectation scales, and trait scales. *Personnel Psychology, 39,* 619–628.

Wollowick, H. B., & McNamara, W. J. (1969). Relationship of the components of an assessment center to management success. *Journal of Applied Psychology, 53,* 348–352.

Zedeck, S., & Cascio, W. F. (1982). Performance appraisal decisions as a function of rater training and purpose of the appraisal. *Journal of Applied Psychology, 67,* 752–758.

Chapter 8

Angle, H. L., & Perry, J. L. (1981). An empirical assessment of organizational commitment and organizational effectiveness. *Administrative Science Quarterly, 16,* 1–14.

Barnett, G. A. (1988). Communication and organizational culture. In G. M. Goldhaber & G. A. Barnett (Eds.), *Handbook of Organizational Communication,* Norwood, NJ: Ablex.

Bateman, T. S., & Strasser, S. (1984). A longitudinal analysis of the antecedents of organizational commitment. *Academy of Management Journal, 17,* 95–112.

Beehr, T. A., & Newman, J. E. (1978). Job stress, employee health, and organizational effectiveness: A facet analysis, model, and literature review. *Personnel Psychology, 31,* 665–699.

Berger-Gross, V., & Kraut, A. I. (1984). "Great expectations": A no-conflict explanation of role conflict. *Journal of Applied Psychology, 69,* 261–271.

Beutell, N. J., & Greenhaus, J. H. (1983). Integration of home and nonhome roles: Women's conflict and coping behavior. *Journal of Applied Psychology, 68,* 43–48.

Burke, R. J., & Deszca, E. (1982). Preferred organizational climates of Type A individuals. *Journal of Vocational Behavior, 21,* 50–59.

Caplan, R. D. (1987). Person-environment fit theory and organizations: Commensurate dimensions, time perspectives, and mechanisms. *Journal of Vocational Behavior, 31,* 248–267.

Chusmir, L. H. (1982). Job commitment and the organizational woman. *Academy of Management Review, 7,* 595–602.

Dipboye, R. L. (1977). A critical review of Korman's self-consistency theory of work motivation and occupational choice. *Organizational Behavior and Human Performance, 18,* 108–126.

Eden, D. (1982). Critical job events, acute stress, and strain: A multiple interrupted time series. *Organizational Behavior and Human Performance, 30,* 312–329.

French, J. R. P., & Raven, B. (1960). The basis of social power. In D. Cartwright & A. F. Zander (Eds.), *Group dynamics* (2nd ed.). Evanston, IL: Row & Peterson.

Greenhaus, J., & Badin, I. (1974). Self-esteem, performance, and satisfaction: Some tests of a theory. *Journal of Applied Psychology, 59,* 722–726.

Gupta, N., & Jenkins, G. D., Jr. (1984). Substance use as an employee response to the work environment. *Journal of Vocational Behavior, 24,* 84–93.

Hamner, W. C., & Tosi, H. L. (1974). Relationship of role conflict and role ambiguity to job involvement measures. *Journal of Applied Psychology, 59,* 497–499.

Higgins, N. C. (1986). Occupational stress and working women: The effectiveness of two stress reduction programs. *Journal of Vocational Behavior, 29,* 66–78.

House, R. J., & Rizzo, J. R. (1972). Role conflict and ambiguity as critical variables in a model of organizational behavior. *Organizational Behavior and Human Performance, 7,* 467–505.

Ivancevich, J. M., & Matteson, M. T. (1980). *Stress and work: A managerial perspective.* Glenview, IL: Scott, Foresman.

Jackson, S. E., & Maslach, C. (1982). After-effects of job-related stress: Families as victims. *Journal of Occupational Behavior, 3,* 63–78.

Jackson, S. E., & Schuler, R. S. (1985). A meta-analysis and conceptual critique of research on role ambiguity and role conflict in work settings. *Organizational Behavior and Human Decision Processes, 36,* 16–78.

Jackson, S. E., Schwab, R. L., & Schuler, R. S. (1986). Toward an understanding of the burnout phenomenon. *Journal of Applied Psychology, 71,* 630–640.

Kahn, R. L., Wolfe, D. M., Quinn, R. P., Snoek, J. D., & Rosenthal, R. A. (1964). *Organizational stress: Studies in role conflict and ambiguity.* New York: Wiley.

Kast, F. E. & Rosenzweig, J. E. (1972). General systems theory: Applications for organization and management. *Academy of Management Journal, 15,* 444–465

Katz, D., & Kahn, R. L. (1978). *The social psychology of organizations* (2nd ed.). New York: Wiley.

Keller, R. T. (1975). Role conflict and ambiguity: Correlates with job satisfaction and values. *Personnel Psychology, 28,* 57–64.

Korman, A. (1970). Toward a hypothesis of work behavior. *Journal of Applied Psychology, 54,* 31–41.

Korman, A. (1977). An examination of Dipboye's "A critical review of Korman's self-consistency theory of work motivation and occupational choice." *Organizational Behavior and Human Performance, 18,* 127–128.

Lodahl, T. M., & Kejner, M. (1965). The definition and measurement of job involvement. *Journal of Applied Psychology, 49,* 24–33.

Luthans, F., McCaul, H. S., & Dodd, N. (1985). Organizational commitment: A comparison of American, Japanese, and Korean employees. *Academy of Management Journal, 28,* 213–218.

Maslach, C., & Jackson, S. E. (1981). The measurement of experienced burnout. *Journal of Occupational Behavior, 2,* 99–113.

Matteson, M. T., Ivancevich, J. M., & Gamble, G. O. (1987). A test of the cognitive social learning model of Type A behavior. *Journal of Human Stress, 13,* 23–31.

Matteson, M. T., Ivancevich, J. M., & Smith, S. V. (1984). Relation of Type A behavior to performance and satisfaction among sales personnel. *Journal of Vocational Behavior, 25,* 203–214.

Meier, S. T. (1983). Towards a theory of burnout. *Human Relations, 36,* 899–910.

Mowday, R. T., Steers, R. M., & Porter, L. W. (1979). The measurement of organizational commitment. *Journal of Vocational Behavior, 14,* 224–247.

Muchinsky, P. M., & Monahan, C. J. (1987). What is person-environment congruence? Supplementary versus complementary models of fit. *Journal of Vocational Behavior, 31,* 268–277.

Naylor, J. C., Pritchard, R. D., & Ilgen, D. R. (1980). *A theory of behavior in organizations.* New York: Academic Press.

Nelson, D. L., & Quick, J. C. (1985). Professional women: Are distress and disease inevitable? *Academy of Management Review, 10,* 206–218.

O'Reilly, C. A. (1977). Personality-job fit: Implications for individual attitudes and performance. *Organizational Behavior and Human Performance, 18,* 36–46.

Parker, D. F., & DeCotiis, T. A. (1983). Organizational determinants of job stress. *Organizational Behavior and Human Performance, 32*, 160–177.

Pervin, L. A. (1968). Performance and satisfaction as a function of individual-environment fit. *Psychological Bulletin, 69*, 56–68.

Porter, L. W., Steers, R. M., Mowday, R. T., & Boulian, P. V. (1974). Organizational commitment job satisfaction, and turnover among psychiatric technicians. *Journal of Applied Psychology, 59*, 603–609.

Rabinowitz, S., & Hall, D. T. (1977). Organizational research on job involvement. *Psychological Bulletin, 84*, 265–288.

Rizzo, J. R., House, R. J., & Lirtzman, S. I. (1970). Role conflict and ambiguity in complex organizations. *Administrative Science Quarterly, 15*, 150–163.

Russell, D. W., Altmaier, E., & Velzen, D. V. (1987). Job-related stress, social support, and burnout among classroom teachers. *Journal of Applied Psychology, 72*, 269–274.

Saal, F. E. (1978). Job involvement: A multivariate approach. *Journal of Applied Psychology, 63*, 53–61.

Schein, E. (1985). *Organizational culture and leadership.* San Francisco: Jossey-Bass.

Schneider, B. (1987). The people make the place. *Personnel Psychology, 40*, 437–454.

Schneider, B., & Reichers, A. E. (1983). On the etiology of climates. *Personnel Psychology, 36*, 19–39.

Schuler, R. S. (1975). Role perceptions, satisfaction, and performance: A partial reconciliation. *Journal of Applied Psychology, 60,.* 683–687.

Schuler, R. S. (1977a). The effects of role perceptions on employee satisfaction and performance moderated by employee ability. *Organizational Behavior and Human Performance, 18*, 98–107.

Schuler, R. S. (1977b). Role conflict and ambiguity as a function of the task-structure-technology interaction. *Organizational Behavior and Human Performance, 20*, 66–74.

Scott, W. G., Mitchell, T. R., & Birnbaum, P. H. (1981). *Organization theory: A structural and behavioral analysis.* Homewood, IL: Richard D. Irwin.

Steers, R. M. (1977) Antecedents and outcomes of organizational commitment. *Administrative Science Quarterly, 22*, 46–56.

Szilagyi, A. D., Sims, H. P., & Keller, R. T. (1976). Role dynamics, locus of control, and employee attitudes and behavior. *Academy of Management Journal, 19*, 259–276.

Tharenou, P. (1979). Employee self-esteem: A review of the literature. *Journal of Vocational Behavior, 15*, 316–346.

Wiener, Y. (1982). Commitment in organizations: A normative view. *Academy of Management Review, 7*, 418–428.

Chapter 9

Andrisani, P. J., & Shapiro, M. B. (1978). Women's attitudes toward their jobs: Some longitudinal data on a national sample. *Personnel Psychology, 31*, 15–34.

Baird, L. S. (1976). Relationship of performance to satisfaction in stimulating and nonstimulating jobs. *Journal of Applied Psychology, 61*, 721–727.

Beehr, T. A. (1986). The process of retirement. A review and recommendations for future investigation. *Personnel Psychology, 39*, 31–55.

Ben-Porat, A. (1981). Event and agent: Toward a structural theory of job satisfaction. *Personnel Psychology, 34*, 523–534.

Berger, C. J., Olson, C. A., & Boudreau, J. W. (1983). Effects of unions on job satisfaction: The role of work-related values and perceived rewards. *Organizational Behavior and Human Performance, 32,* 289–324.

Brayfield, A. H., & Crockett, W. H. (1955). Employee attitudes and employee performance. *Psychological Bulletin, 52,* 396–424.

Carsten, J. M., & Spector, P. E. (1987). Unemployment, job satisfaction, and employee turnover: A meta-analysis test of the Muchinsky model. *Journal of Applied Psychology, 72,* 374–381.

Cherrington, D. J., Reitz, H. J., & Scott, W. E. (1971). Effects of contingent and non-contingent reward on the relationship between satisfaction and task performance. *Journal of Applied Psychology, 55,* 531–536.

Dachler, H. P., & Hulin, C. L. (1969). A reconsideration of the relationship between satisfaction and judged importance of environmental and job characteristics. *Organizational Behavior and Human Performance, 4,* 252–266.

De Wolff, C. J., & Shimmin, S. (1976). The psychology of work in Europe: A review of a profession. *Personnel Psychology, 29,* 175–195.

Dubin, R. (1956). Industrial workers' worlds: A study of "Central Life Interests" of industrial workers. *Social Problems, 3,* 131–142.

Dubin, R., & Champoux, J. E. (1977). Central life interests and job satisfaction. *Organizational Behavior and Human Performance, 18,* 366–377.

Dunham, R. B., & Herman, J. B. (1975). Development of a female faces scale for measuring job satisfaction. *Journal of Applied Psychology, 60,* 629–632.

Dyer, L., & Theriault, R. (1976). The determinants of pay satisfaction. *Journal of Applied Psychology, 61,* 596–604.

Ewen, R. B. (1964). Some determinants of job satisfaction: A study of the generality of Herzberg's theory. *Journal of Applied Psychology, 48,* 161–163.

Ewen, R. B. (1967). Weighting components of job satisfaction. *Journal of Applied Psychology, 51,* 68–73.

Fisher, C. D. (1980). On the dubious wisdom of expecting job satisfaction to correlate with performance. *Academy of Management Review, 5,* 607–612.

Gibson, J. L., & Klein, S. M. (1970). Employee attitudes as a function of age and length of service: A reconceptualization. *Academy of Management Journal, 13,* 411–425.

Gillet, B., & Schwab, D. P. (1975). Convergent and discriminant validities of corresponding Job Descriptive Index and Minnesota Satisfaction Questionnaire scales. *Journal of Applied Psychology, 60,* 313–317.

Hammer, T. H., Landau, J. C., & Stern, R. N. (1981). Absenteeism when workers have a voice: The case of employee ownership. *Journal of Applied Psychology, 66,* 561–573.

Hammer, T. H., & Stern, R. N. (1980). Employee ownership: Implications for the organizational distribution of power. *Academy of Management Journal, 13,* 78–100.

Hamner, W. C., & Smith, F. J. (1978). Work attitudes as predictors of unionization activity. *Journal of Applied Psychology, 63,* 415–421.

Herzberg, F., Mausner, B., & Snyderman, B. B. (1959). *The motivation of work.* New York: Wiley.

Hinrichs, J. R., & Mischkind, L. A. (1967). Empirical and theoretical limitations of the two-factor hypothesis of job satisfaction. *Journal of Applied Psychology, 51,* 191–200.

Hoppock, R. (1935). *Job satisfaction.* New York: Harper & Row.

Hulin, C. L. (1966). Job satisfaction and turnover in a female clerical population. *Journal of Applied Psychology, 50,* 280–285.

Hulin, C. L. (1968). Effects of changes in job satisfaction levels on employee turnover. *Journal of Applied Psychology, 52,* 122–126.

Hulin, C. L., & Smith, P. C. (1964). Sex differences in job satisfaction. *Journal of Applied Psychology, 48,* 88–92.

Hulin, C. L., & Smith, P. C. (1965). A linear model of job satisfaction. *Journal of Applied Psychology, 49,* 209–216.

Hunt, J. W., & Saul, P. N. (1975). The relationship of age, tenure, and job satisfaction in males and females. *Academy of Management Journal, 18,* 690–702.

Iaffaldano, M. T., & Muchinsky, P. M. (1985). Job satisfaction and job performance: A meta-analysis. *Psychological Bulletin, 97,* 251–273.

Ilgen, D. R., & Hollenback, J. H. (1977). The role of job satisfaction in absence behavior. *Organizational Behavior and Human Performance, 19,* 148–161.

Ivancevich, J. M. (1978). The performance to satisfaction relationship: A causal analysis of stimulating and nonstimulating jobs. *Organizational Behavior and Human Performance, 22,* 350–365.

Ivancevich, J. M. (1979). High and low task stimulation jobs: A causal analysis of the perform- ance-satisfaction relationship. *Academy of Management Journal, 22,* 206–222.

Jacobs, R., & Solomon, T. (1977). Strategies for enhancing the prediction of job performance from job satisfaction. *Journal of Applied Psychology, 62,* 417–421.

Jamal, M., & Mitchell, V. F. (1980). Work, nonwork, and mental health: A model and a test. *Industrial Relations, 19,* 88–93.

Janson, R., & Martin, J. K. (1982). Job satisfaction and age: A test of two views. *Social Forces, 60,* 1089–1102.

Jones, A. P., James, L. R., Bruni, J. R., & Sells, S. B. (1977). Black-white differences in work environment perceptions and job satisfaction and its correlates. *Personnel Psychology, 30,* 5–16.

Kabanoff, B. (1980). Work and nonwork: A review of models, methods, and findings. *Psychological Bulletin, 88,* 60–77.

King, N. (1970). Clarification and evaluation of the two-factor theory of job satisfaction. *Psychological Bulletin, 74,* 18–31.

Klein, K. J. (1987). Employee stock ownership and employee attitudes: A test of three models. *Journal of Applied Psychology, 72,* 319–332.

Kraut, A. I., & Ronen, S. (1975). Validity of job facet importance: A multinational, multicrit- eria study. *Journal of Applied Psychology, 60,* 671–677.

Kunin, T. (1955). The construction of a new type of attitude measure. *Personnel Psychology, 8,* 65–77.

Landy, F. J. (1978). An opponent process theory of job satisfaction. *Journal of Applied Psychology, 63,* 533–547.

Landy, F. J., & Trumbo, D. A. (1980). *Psychology of work behavior* (rev. ed.). Pacific Grove, CA: Brooks/Cole.

Lawler, E. E. (1971). *Pay and organizational effectiveness: A psychological view.* New York: McGraw-Hill.

Locke, E. A. (1969). What is job satisfaction? *Organizational Behavior and Human Perform- ance, 4,* 309–336.

Locke, E. A. (1976). The nature and causes of job satisfaction. In M. D. Dunnette (Ed.), *Handbook of industrial and organizational psychology.* Skokie, IL: Rand McNally.

Long, R. J. (1982). Worker ownership and job attitudes: A field study. *Industrial Relations, 21,* 196–215.

Lounsbury, J. W., & Hoopes, L. L. (1986). A vacation from work: Changes in work and nonwork outcomes. *Journal of Applied Psychology, 71,* 392–401.

Lorenzi, P. A. (1978). A comment on Organ's reappraisal of the satisfaction-causes-performance hypothesis. *Academy of Management Review, 3,* 380–384.

McCabe, D. J., Dalessio, A., Briga, J., & Sasaki, J. (1980). The convergent and discriminant validities between the IOR and the JDI: English and Spanish forms. *Academy of Management Journal, 23,* 778–786.

McCormick, E. J., & Ilgen, D. R. (1980). *Industrial psychology* (7th ed.). Englewood Cliffs, NJ: Prentice-Hall.

Mikes, P. S., & Hulin, C. L. (1968). Use of importance as a weighting component of job satisfaction. *Journal of Applied Psychology, 52,* 394–398.

Miller, H. E., & Terborg, J. R. (1979). Job attitudes of part-time and full-time employees. *Journal of Applied Psychology, 64,* 380–386.

Mirvis, P. H., & Lawler, E. E. (1977). Measuring the financial impact of employee attitudes. *Journal of Applied Psychology, 62,* 1–8.

Mobley, W. H. (1977). Intermediate linkages in the relationship between job satisfaction and employee turnover. *Journal of Applied Psychology, 62,* 237–240.

Mobley, W. H., Horner, S. O., & Hollingsworth, A. T. (1978). An evaluation of precursors of hospital employee turnover. *Journal of Applied Psychology, 63,* 408–414.

Mobley, W. H., & Locke, E. A. (1970). The relationship of value importance to satisfaction. *Organizational Behavior and Human Performance, 5,* 463–483.

Moch, M. K. (1980). Racial differences in job satisfaction: Testing four common explanations. *Journal of Applied Psychology, 65,* 299–306.

Muchinsky, P. M. (1977). Employee absenteeism: A review of the literature. *Journal of Vocational Behavior, 10,* 326–340.

Muchinsky, P. M., & Morrow, P. C. (1980). A multidisciplinary model of voluntary employee turnover. *Journal of Vocational Behavior, 17,* 263–290.

Muchinsky, P. M., & Tuttle, M. L. (1979). Employee turnover: An empirical and methodological assessment. *Journal of Vocational Behavior, 14,* 43–77.

Nicholson, N., Brown, C. A., & Chadwick-Jones, J. K. (1976). Absence from work and job satisfaction. *Journal of Applied Psychology, 61,* 728–737.

Nord, W. R. (1977). Job satisfaction reconsidered. *American Psychologist, 32,* 1026–1035.

Odewahn, C. A., & Petty, M. M. (1980). A comparison of levels of job satisfaction, role stress, and personal competence between union members and nonmembers. *Academy of Management Journal, 23,* 150–155.

Opinion Research Corporation. (1981). *Strategic planning for human resources: 1980 and beyond.* Princeton, NJ: Arthur D. Little.

Organ, D. W. (1977). A reappraisal and reinterpretation of the satisfaction-causes-performance hypothesis. *Academy of Management Review, 2,* 46–53.

Orpen, C. (1978). Work and nonwork satisfaction: A causal-correlational analysis. *Journal of Applied Psychology, 63,* 530–532.

Phillips, J. C., & Benson, J. E. (1983). Some aspects of job satisfaction in the Soviet Union. *Personnel Psychology, 36,* 633–645.

Porter, L. W. (1962). Job attitudes in management: I. Perceived deficiencies in need fulfillment as a function of job level. *Journal of Applied Psychology, 46,* 375–384.

Porter, L. W., & Steers, R. M. (1973). Organizational, work, and personal factors in employee turnover and absenteeism. *Psychological Bulletin, 80,* 151–176.

Rhodes, S. R. (1983). Age-related differences in work attitudes and behavior: A review and conceptual analysis. *Psychological Bulletin, 93,* 328–367.

Ronen, S. A. (1977). A comparison of job facet satisfaction between paid and unpaid industrial workers. *Journal of Applied Psychology, 62,* 582–588.

Salancik, G. R., & Pfeffer, J. (1977). An examination of need satisfaction models of job satisfaction. *Administrative Science Quarterly, 22,* 427–456.

Sauser, W. J., & York, C. M. (1978). Sex differences in job satisfaction: A reexamination. *Personnel Psychology, 31,* 537–547.

Scarpello, V., & Campbell, J. P. (1983). Job satisfaction: Are all the parts there? *Personnel Psychology, 36,* 577–600.

Schaffer, R. H. (1953). Job satisfaction as related to need satisfaction in work. *Psychological Monographs, 67,* (304).

Schmitt, N., & Bedeian, A. G. (1982). A comparison of LISREL and two-stage least squares analysis of a hypothesized life-job satisfaction reciprocal relationship. *Journal of Applied Psychology, 67,* 806–817.

Schneider, B., & Dachler, H. P. (1978). A note on the stability of the Job Descriptive Index. *Journal of Applied Psychology, 63,* 650–653.

Schriesheim, C. A. (1978). Job satisfaction, attitudes toward unions, and voting in a union representation election. *Journal of Applied Psychology, 63,* 548–552.

Seybolt, J. W. (1976). Work satisfaction as a function of the person-environment interaction. *Organizational Behavior and Human Performance, 17,* 66–75.

Sheridan, J., & Slocum, J. W. (1975). The direction of the causal relationship between job satisfaction and work performance. *Organizational Behavior and Human Performance, 14,* 159–172.

Slocum, J. W., & Strawser, R. H. (1972). Racial differences in job attitudes. *Journal of Applied Psychology, 56,* 28–32.

Smith, F. J. (1977). Work attitudes as predictors of attendance on a specific day. *Journal of Applied Psychology, 62,* 16–19.

Smith, P. C., Kendall, L. M., & Hulin, C. L. (1969). *The measurement of satisfaction in work and retirement.* Skokie, IL: Rand McNally.

Smith, P. C., Smith, O. W., & Rollo, J. (1974). Factor structure for blacks and whites of the Job Descriptive Index and its discrimination of job satisfaction. *Journal of Applied Psychology, 59,* 99–100.

Steers, R. M., & Rhodes, S. R. (1978). Major influences on employee attendance: A process model. *Journal of Applied Psychology, 63,* 391–407.

Terborg, J. R., Lee, T. W., Smith, F. J., Davis, G. A., & Turbin, M. S. (1982). Extension of the Schmidt and Hunter validity generalization procedure to the prediction of absenteeism behavior from knowledge of job satisfaction and organizational commitment. *Journal of Applied Psychology, 67,* 440–449.

Vroom, V. H. (1964). *Work and motivation.* New York: Wiley.

Wanous, J. P. (1974). A causal-correlational analysis of the job satisfaction and performance relationship. *Journal of Applied Psychology, 59,* 139–244.

Wanous, J. P., & Lawler, E. E. (1972). Measurement and meaning of job satisfaction. *Journal of Applied Psychology, 56,* 95–105.

Weaver, C. N. (1977). Relationships among pay, race, sex, occupational prestige, supervision, work autonomy, and job satisfaction in a national sample. *Personnel Psychology, 30,* 437–445.

Weaver, C. N. (1978a). Black-white correlates of job satisfaction. *Journal of Applied Psychology, 63,* 255–258.

Weaver, C. N. (1978b). Job satisfaction as a component of happiness among males and females. *Personnel Psychology, 31,* 831–840.

Weaver, C. N. (1978c). Sex differences in the determinants of job satisfaction. *Academy of Management Journal, 21,* 265–274.

Weaver, C. N. (1980). Job satisfaction in the United States in the 1970s. *Journal of Applied Psychology, 65,* 364–367.

Weaver, C. N., & Holmes, S. L. (1975). A comparative study of the work satisfaction of females with full-time employment and full-time housekeeping. *Journal of Applied Psychology, 60,* 117–118.

Weiner, N. (1980) Determinants and behavioral consequences of pay satisfaction: A comparison of two models. *Personnel Psychology, 33,* 741–757.

Weiss, D. J., Dawis, R. V., England, G. W., & Lofquist, L. H. (1967). *Manual for the Minnesota Satisfaction Questionnaire* (Minnesota Studies on Vocational Rehabilitation, vol. 22). Minneapolis: University of Minnesota, Industrial Relations Center, Work Adjustment Project.

Weiss, H. M., & Shaw, J. B. (1979). Social influences on judgments about tasks. *Organizational Behavior and Human Performance, 24,* 126–140.

Wiggins, R. L., & Steade, R. D. (1976). Job satisfaction as a social concern. *Academy of Management Review, 1,* 48–55.

Yeager, S. J. (1981). Dimensionality of the Job Descriptive Index. *Academy of Management Journal, 14,* 205–212.

Zedeck. S. (1987). Work, family, and organization: An untapped research triangle. Paper presented at the American Psychological Association, New York.

Chapter 10

Adams, J. S. (1965). In L. Berkowitz (Ed.), *Advances in experimental social psychology* (Vol. 2). New York: Academic Press, 267–299.

Adams, J. S., & Rosenbaum, W. B. (1962). The relationship of worker productivity to cognitive dissonance about wage inequities. *Journal of Applied Psychology, 46,* 161–164.

Alderfer, C. P. (1969). An empirical test of a new theory of human needs. *Organizational Behavior and Human Performance, 4,* 142–175.

Alderfer, C. P. (1972). *Existence, relatedness, and growth: Human needs in organizational settings.* New York: Free Press.

Arnold, H. J., & Evans, M. G. (1979). Testing multiplicative models does not require ratio scales. *Organizational Behavior and Human Performance, 24,* 41–59.

Betz, E. L. (1984). Two tests of Maslow's theory of need fulfillment. *Journal of Vocational Behavior, 24,* 204–220.

Broedling, L. A. (1975). Relationship of internal-external control to work motivation and performance in an expectancy model. *Journal of Applied Psychology, 60,* 65–70.

Campbell, J. P., & Pritchard, R. D. (1976). Motivation theory in industrial and organizational psychology. In M. D. Dunnette (Ed.), *Handbook of industrial and organizational psychology,* Skokie, IL: Rand McNally.

Carrell, M. R., & Dittrich, J. E. (1978). Equity theory: The recent literature, methodological considerations, and new directions. *Academy of Management Review, 3,* 202–210.

Dachler, H. P., & Mobley, W. H. (1973). Construct validation of an instrumentality-expectancy task-goal model of work motivation: Some theoretical boundary conditions. *Journal of Applied Psychology, 58,* 397–418.

Deci, E. L. (1972). The effects of contingent and noncontingent rewards and controls on intrinsic motivation. *Organizational Behavior and Human Performance, 8,* 217–229.

Deci, E. L. (1975). *Intrinsic motivation.* New York: Plenum Press.

De Leo, P. J., & Pritchard, R. D. (1974). An examination of some methodological problems in testing expectancy valence models with survey techniques. *Organizational Behavior and Human Performance, 12,* 143–148.

Dyer, L., & Parker, D. F. (1975). Classifying outcomes in work motivation research: An examination of the intrinsic-extrinsic dichotomy. *Journal of Applied Psychology, 60,* 455–458.

Erez, M. (1977). Feedback: A necessary condition for the goal setting-performance relationship. *Journal of Applied Psychology, 62,* 624–627.

Garland, H. (1984). Relation of effort-performance expectancy to performance in goal-setting experiments. *Journal of Applied Psychology, 69,* 79–84.

Georgopoulos, B. S., Mahoney, G. M., & Jones, N. W. (1957). A path-goal approach to productivity. *Journal of Applied Psychology, 41,* 345–353.

Goodman, P. S., & Friedman, A. (1971). An examination of Adams' theory of inequity. *Administrative Science Quarterly, 16,* 271–288.

Graen, G. (1969). Instrumentality theory of work motivation: Some experimental results and suggested modifications. *Journal of Applied Psychology Monograph, 53*(2).

Hall, D. T., & Nougaim, K. E. (1968). An examination of Maslow's need hierarchy in an organizational setting. *Organizational Behavior and Human Performance, 3,* 12–35.

Hamner, W. C., & Foster, L. W. (1975). Are intrinsic and extrinsic rewards additive: A test of Deci's cognitive evaluation theory of task motivation. *Organizational Behavior and Human Performance, 14,* 398–415.

Hamner, W. C., & Hamner, E. P. (1976). Behavior modification on the bottom line. *Organizational Dynamics, 4,* 8–21.

Hollenbeck, J. R. & Klein, H. J. (1987). Goal commitment and the goal-setting process: Problems, prospects, and proposals for future research. *Journal of Applied Psychology, 72,* 212–220.

Huseman, R. C., Hatfield, J. D., & Miles, E. W. (1987). A new perspective on equity theory: The equity sensitivity construct. *Academy of Management Review, 12,* 222–234.

Ilgen, D. R., Nebeker, D. M., & Pritchard, R. D. (1981). Expectancy theory measures: An empirical comparison in an experimental simulation. *Organizational Behavior and Human Performance, 28,* 189–223.

Ivancevich, J. M., & McMahon, J. T. (1977). Black-white differences in a goal-setting program. *Organizational Behavior and Human Performance, 20,* 287–300.

Jablonsky, S. F., & De Vries, D. L. (1972). Operant conditioning principles extrapolated to the theory of management. *Organizational Behavior and Human Performance, 7,* 340–358.

Janz, T. (1982). Manipulating subjective expectancy through feedback: A laboratory study of the expectancy-performance relationship. *Journal of Applied Psychology, 67,* 480–485.

Kennedy, C. W., Fossum, J. A., & White, B. J. (1983). An empirical comparison of within-subjects and between-subjects expectancy theory models. *Organizational Behavior and Human Performance, 32,* 124–143.

Kerr, S. (1975). On the folly of rewarding A, while hoping for B. *Academy of Management Journal, 18,* 769–783.

Kim, J. S., & Hamner, W. C. (1976). Effect of performance feedback and goal setting on productivity and satisfaction in an organizational setting. *Journal of Applied Psychology, 61,* 48–57.

Landy, F. J., & Trumbo, D. A. (1980). *Psychology of work behavior* (rev. ed.). Pacific Grove, CA: Brooks/Cole.

Latham, G. P., & Baldes, J. J. (1975). The practical significance of Locke's theory of goal setting. *Journal of Applied Psychology, 60*, 122–124.

Latham, G. P., & Marshall, H. A. (1982). The effects of self-set, participatively set and assigned goals on the performance of government employees. *Personnel Psychology, 35*, 399–404.

Latham, G. P., & Yukl, G. A. (1975a). A review of research on the application of goal setting in organizations. *Academy of Management Journal, 18*, 824–845.

Latham, G. P., & Yukl, G. A. (1975b). Assigned versus participative goal-setting with educated and uneducated wood workers. *Journal of Applied Psychology, 60*, 299–302.

Lawler, E. E., & Porter, L. W. (1967). Antecedent attitudes of effective managerial performance. *Organizational Behavior and Human Performance, 2*, 122–142.

Lawler, E. E., & Suttle, J. L. (1972). A causal correlational test of the need hierarchy concept. *Organizational Behavior and Human Behavior, 7*, 265–287.

Lied, T. L., & Pritchard, R. D. (1976). Relationship between personality variables and components of the expectancy-valence model. *Journal of Applied Psychology, 61*, 463–467.

Locke, E. A. (1968). Toward a theory of task motivation and incentives. *Organizational Behavior and Human Performance, 3*, 157–189.

Locke, E. A. (1977). The myths of behavior mod in organizations. *Academy of Management Review, 1*, 543–553.

Locke, E. A., Shaw, K. N., Saari, L. M., & Latham, G. P. (1981). Goal setting and task performance: 1969–1980. *Psychological Bulletin, 90*, 125–152.

Lord, R. G., & Hohenfeld, J. A. (1979). Longitudinal field assessment of equity effects in the performance of major league baseball players. *Journal of Applied Psychology, 64*, 19–26.

Maslow, A. H. (1954). *Motivation and personality.* New York: Harper & Row.

Maslow, A. H. (1970). *Motivation and personality* (2nd ed.). New York: Harper & Row.

Matsui, T., Kagawa, M., Nagamatsu, J., & Ohtsuka, Y. (1977). Validity of expectancy theory as a within-person behavioral choice model for sales activity. *Journal of Applied Psychology, 62*, 764–767.

Mawhinney, T. C. (1975). Operant terms and concepts in the description of individual work behavior: Some problems of interpretation, application, and evaluation. *Journal of Applied Psychology, 60*, 704–712.

Mawhinney, T. C. (1979). Intrinsic × extrinsic work motivation: Perspectives from behaviorism. *Organizational Behavior and Human Performance, 24*, 411–440.

McConkie, M. L. (1979). A clarification of the goal setting and appraisal processes in MBO. *Academy of Management Review, 4*, 29–40.

McCormick, E. J., & Ilgen, D. R. (1980). *Industrial psychology* (7th ed.). Englewood Cliffs, NJ: Prentice-Hall.

Mento, A. J., Steel, R. P., & Karren, R. J. (1987). A meta-analytic study of the effects of goal setting on task performance: 1966–1984. *Organizational Behavior and Human Decision Processes, 39*, 52–83.

Middlemist, R. D., & Peterson, R. B. (1976). Test of equity theory by controlling for comparison co-workers' efforts. *Organizational Behavior and Human Performance, 15*, 335–354.

Miner, J. B. (1980). *Theories of organizational behavior.* Hinsdale, IL: Dryden Press.

Mitchell, T. R. (1974). Expectancy models of job satisfaction, occupational preference and effort: A theoretical, methodological, and empirical appraisal. *Psychological Bulletin, 81*, 1053–1077.

Mitchell, T. R. (1982). Motivation: New directions for theory, research, and practice. *Academy of Management Review, 7*, 80–88.

Mitchell, T. R., & Knudsen, B. W. (1973). Instrumentality theory predictions of students' attitudes towards business and their choice of business as an occupation. *Academy of Management Journal, 16,* 41–51.

Mitchell, V. F., & Mougdill, P. (1976). Measurement of Maslow's need hierarchy. *Organizational Behavior and Human Performance, 16,* 334–349.

Muchinsky, P. M. (1977). A comparison of within- and across-subjects analyses of the expectancy-valence model for predicting effort. *Academy of Management Journal, 20,* 154–158.

Muchinsky, P. M., & Taylor, M. S. (1976). Intrasubject predictions of occupational preference: The effect of manipulating components of the valence model. *Journal of Vocational Behavior, 8,* 185–195.

Nord, W. (1969). Beyond the teaching machine: The neglected area of operant conditioning in the theory and practice of management. *Organizational Behavior and Human Performance, 4,* 375–401.

Pedalino, E., & Gamboa, V. U. (1974). Behavior modification and absenteeism. *Journal of Applied Psychology, 59,* 694–698.

Perry, J. L., & Porter, L. W. (1982). Factors affecting the context for motivation in public organizations. *Academy of Management Review, 7,* 89–98.

Phillips, J. S., & Lord, R. G. (1980). Determinants of intrinsic motivation: Locus of control and competence information as components of Deci's cognitive evaluation theory. *Journal of Applied Psychology, 65,* 211–218.

Pinder, C. C. (1977). Concerning the application of human motivation theories in organizational settings. *Academy of Management Review, 2,* 384–397.

Porter, L. W. (1961). A study of perceived need satisfaction in bottom and middle management jobs. *Journal of Applied Psychology, 45,* 1–10.

Porter, L. W., & Lawler, E. E. (1968). *Managerial attitudes and performance.* Homewood, IL: Richard D. Irwin.

Pritchard, R. D. (1969). Equity theory: A review and critique. *Organizational Behavior and Human Performance, 4,* 176–211.

Pritchard, R. D., Campbell, K. M., & Campbell, D. J. (1977). The effects of extrinsic financial rewards on intrinsic motivation. *Journal of Applied Psychology, 62,* 9–15.

Pritchard, R. D., De Leo, P. J., & Von Bergen, C. W. (1976). A field experimental test of expectancy-valence incentive motivation techniques. *Organizational Behavior and Human Performance, 15,* 355–406.

Pritchard, R. D., Dunnette, M. D., & Jorgenson, D. O. (1972). Effects of perceptions of equity and inequity on worker performance and satisfaction. *Journal of Applied Psychology, 56,* 75–94.

Pritchard, R. D., Hollenback, J., & De Leo, P. J. (1980). The effects of continuous and partial schedules of reinforcement on effort, performance, and satisfaction. *Organizational Behavior and Human Performance, 25,* 336–353.

Pritchard, R. D., Leonard, D. W., Von Bergen, C. W., & Kirk, R. J. (1976). The effect of varying schedules of reinforcement on human task performance. *Organizational Behavior and Human Performance, 16,* 205–230.

Pritchard, R. D., & Sanders, M. S. (1973). The influence of valence, instrumentality, and expectancy on effort and performance. *Journal of Applied Psychology, 57,* 55–60.

Saari, L. M., & Latham, G. P. (1982). Employee reactions to continuous and variable ratio reinforcement schedules involving a monetary reward. *Journal of Applied Psychology, 67,* 506–508.

Schmidt, F. L. (1973). Implications of a measurement problem for expectancy theory research. *Organizational Behavior and Human Performance, 10,* 243–251.

Schwab, D. P., Olian-Gottlieb, J. D., & Heneman, H. G. (1979). Between-subjects expectancy theory research: A statistical review of studies predicting effort and performance. *Psychological Bulletin, 86,* 139–147.

Scott, W. E. (1976). The effects of extrinsic rewards on "intrinsic motivation." *Organizational Behavior and Human Performance, 15,* 117–129.

Stahl, M. J., & Harrell, A. M. (1981). Modeling effort decisions with behavioral decision theory: Toward an individual differences model of expectancy theory. *Organizational Behavior and Human Performance, 27,* 303–325.

Steers, R. M., & Porter, L. W. (1974). The role of task-goal attributes in employee performance. *Psychological Bulletin, 81,* 434–452.

Steers, R. M., & Porter, L. W. (Eds.). (1975). *Motivation and work behavior.* New York: McGraw-Hill.

Terborg, J. R. (1977). Validation and extension of an individual differences model of work performance. *Organizational Behavior and Human Performance, 18,* 188–216.

Tubbs, M. E. (1986). Goal setting: A meta-analytic examination of the empirical evidence. *Journal of Applied Psychology, 71,* 474–483.

Vroom, V. H. (1964). *Work and motivation.* New York: Wiley.

Wahba, M. A., & Bridwell, L. T. (1976). Maslow reconsidered. A review of research on the need hierarchy theory. *Organizational Behavior and Human Performance, 15,* 212–240.

Wanous, J. P., & Zwany, A. (1977). A cross-sectional test of need hierarchy theory. *Organizational Behavior and Human Performance, 18,* 78–97.

Wherry, R. J., & South, J. C. (1977). A worker motivation scale. *Personnel Psychology, 30,* 613–636.

Yukl, G. A., & Latham, G. P. (1975). Consequences of reinforcement schedules and incentive magnitudes for employee performance: Problems encountered in an industrial setting. *Journal of Applied Psychology, 60,* 294–298.

Yukl, G. A., Latham, G. P., & Pursell, E. D. (1976). The effectiveness of performance incentives under continuous and variable ratio schedules of reinforcement. *Personnel Psychology, 29,* 221–232.

Chapter 11

Ashour, A. S. (1973). The contingency model of leader effectiveness: An evaluation. *Organizational Behavior and Human Performance, 9,* 339–355.

Barrow, J. C. (1977). The variables of leadership: A review and conceptual framework. *Academy of Management Review, 2,* 231–251.

Bartol, K. M., Evans, C. L., & Stith, M. T. (1978). Black versus white leaders: A comparative review of the literature. *Academy of Management Review, 3,* 293–304.

Bartol, K. M., & Wortman, M. S. (1975). Male versus female leaders: Effects of perceived leader behavior and satisfaction in a hospital. *Personnel Psychology, 28,* 533–547.

Brown, J. A. (1954). *The social psychology of industry.* New York: Penguin Books.

Cartwright, D. (1965). Influence, leadership, control. In J. G. March (Ed.), *Handbook of organizations.* Skokie, IL: Rand McNally.

Csoka, L. S., & Bons, P. M. (1978). Manipulating the situation to fit the leader's style: Two validation studies of Leader Match. *Journal of Applied Psychology, 63,* 295–300.

Dansereau, F., Graen, G., & Haga, W. (1975). A vertical dyad linkage approach to leadership in formal organizations. *Organizational Behavior and Human Performance, 13,* 46–78.

Dienesch, R. M., & Liden, R. C. (1986). Leader-member exchange model of leadership: A critique and further development. *Academy of Management Review, 11,* 618–634.

Evans, M. G., & Dermer, J. (1974). What does the Least Preferred Co-worker scale really measure? A cognitive interpretation. *Journal of Applied Psychology, 59,* 202–206.

Faley, R. H. (1982). Sexual harassment: Critical review of legal cases with general principles and preventive measures. *Personnel Psychology, 35,* 583–600.

Fiedler, F. E. (1951). A method of objective quantification of certain counter-transference attitudes. *Journal of Clinical Psychology, 7,* 101–107.

Fiedler, F. E. (1964). A contingency model of leadership effectiveness. In L. Berkowitz (Ed.), *Advances in experimental social psychology* (Vol. 1). New York: Academic Press.

Fiedler, F. E. (1965). Engineer the job to fit the manager. *Harvard Business Review, 43*(5), 115–122.

Fiedler, F. E. (1967). *A theory of leadership effectiveness.* New York: McGraw-Hill.

Fiedler, F. E. (1971). Validation and extension of the contingency model of leadership effectiveness: A review of empirical findings. *Psychological Bulletin, 76,* 128–148.

Fiedler, F. E., & Garcia, J. E. (1987). *New approaches to leadership: Cognitive resources and organizational performance.* New York: Wiley.

Fiedler, F. E., & Mahar, L. A. (1979a). The effectiveness of contingency model training: A review of the validation of Leader Match. *Personnel Psychology, 32,* 45–62.

Fiedler, F. E., & Mahar, L. A. (1979b). A field experiment validating contingency model training. *Journal of Applied Psychology, 64,* 247–254.

Field, R. H. (1979). A critique of the Vroom-Yetton contingency model of leadership behavior. *Academy of Management Review, 4,* 249–258.

Field, R. H. (1982). A test of the Vroom-Yetton normative model of leadership. *Journal of Applied Psychology, 67,* 523–532.

Fleishman, E. A., & Harris, E. F. (1962). Patterns of leadership behavior related to employee grievances and turnover. *Personnel Psychology, 15,* 43–56.

Foti, R. J., & Lord, R. G. (1987). Prototypes and scripts: The effects of alternative methods of processing information on rating accuracy. *Organizational Behavior and Human Decision Processes, 39,* 318–340.

Fulk, J., & Wendler, E. R. (1982). Dimensionality of leader-subordinate interactions: A path-goal investigation. *Organizational Behavior and Human Performance, 30,* 241–264.

Graen, G., Alvares, K., Orris, J. B., & Martella, J. A. (1970). Contingency model of leadership effectiveness: Antecedents and evidential results. *Psychological Bulletin, 74,* 285–296.

Graen, G., Liden, R. C., & Hoel, W. (1982). Role of leadership in the employee withdrawal process. *Journal of Applied Psychology, 67,* 868–872.

Green, S. G., & Nebeker, D. M. (1977). The effects of situational factors and leadership style on leader behavior. *Organizational Behavior and Human Performance, 19,* 368–377.

Greene, C. N. (1975). The reciprocal nature of influence between leader and subordinate. *Journal of Applied Psychology, 60,* 187–193.

Greene, C. N. (1979). Questions of causation in the path-goal theory of leadership. *Academy of Management Journal, 22,* 22–41.

Greene, C. N., & Schriesheim, C. A. (1980). Leader-group interactions: A longitudinal field investigation. *Journal of Applied Psychology, 65,* 50–59.

Heilman, M. E., Hornstein, H. A., Cage, J. H., & Herschlag, J. K. (1984). Reactions to prescribed leader behavior as a function of role perspective: The case of the Vroom-Yetton model. *Journal of Applied Psychology, 69,* 50–60.

Hemphill, J. K. (1950). *Leader behavior description.* Columbus: Ohio State University Personnel Research Board.

Herold, D. M. (1977). Two-way influence processes in leader-follower dyads. *Academy of Management Journal, 20,* 224–237.

Hill, T. E., & Schmitt, N. (1977). Individual differences in decision making. *Organizational Behavior and Human Performance, 19,* 353–367.

Hollander, E. P., & Julian. J. W. (1969). Contemporary trends in the analysis of the leadership process. *Psychological Bulletin, 71,* 387–397.

House, R. J. (1971). A path-goal theory of leader effectiveness. *Administrative Science Quarterly, 16,* 321–338.

House, R. J. (1985). Research contrasting the behavior and effect of reputed charismatic versus reputed non-charismatic U.S. Presidents. Paper presented at the Annual Meeting of Administrative Science Association. Montreal, Canada.

House, R. J., & Mitchell, T. (1974). Path-goal theory of leadership. *Journal of Contemporary Business, 3,* 81–98.

House, R. J., & Singh, J. V. (1987). Organizational behavior: Some new directions for I/O psychology. *Annual Review of Psychology, 38,* 669–718.

Howell, J. P., & Dorfman, P. W. (1981). Substitutes for leadership: Test of a construct. *Academy of Management Journal, 24,* 714–728.

Hunt, D. M., & Michael, C. (1983). Mentorship: A career training and development tool. *Academy of Management Review, 8,* 475–485.

Jago, A. G., & Ragan, J. W. (1986). The trouble with Leader Match is that it doesn't match Fiedler's contingency model. *Journal of Applied Psychology, 71,* 555–559.

Jago, A. G., & Vroom, V. H. (1977). Hierarchical level and leadership style. *Organizational Behavior and Human Performance, 18,* 131–145.

Jago, A. G., & Vroom, V. H. (1982). Sex differences in the incidence and evaluation of participative leader behavior. *Journal of Applied Psychology, 67,* 776–783.

Kabanoff, B. (1981). A critique of Leader Match and its implications for leadership research. *Personnel Psychology, 34,* 749–764.

Keller, R. T. (1989). A test of the path-goal theory of leadership with need for clarity as a moderator in research and development organizations. *Journal of Applied Psychology, 74,* 208–212.

Kennedy, J. K. (1982). Middle LPC leaders and the contingency model of leadership effectiveness. *Organizational Behavior and Human Performance, 30,* 1–14.

Kerr, S., & Jermier, J. M. (1978). Substitutes for leadership: Their meaning and measurement. *Organizational Behavior and Human Performance, 22,* 375–403.

Kipnis, D., & Cosentino, J. (1969). Use of leadership powers in industry. *Journal of Applied Psychology, 53,* 460–466.

Klimoski, R. J., & Hayes, N. J. (1980). Leader behavior and subordinate motivation. *Personnel Psychology, 33,* 543–555.

Konrad, A. M., & Gutek, B. A. (1986). Impact of work experiences on attitudes toward sexual harassment. *Administrative Science Quarterly, 31,* 422–438.

Kram, K. E., & Isabella, L. A. (1985). Alternatives to mentoring: The role of peer relationships in career development. *Academy of Management Journal, 28,* 110–132.

Larson, L. L., Hunt, J. G., & Osborn, R. N. (1976). The great hi-hi leader behavior myth: A lesson from Occam's razor. *Academy of Management Journal, 19,* 628–641.

Leister, A., Borden, D., & Fiedler, F. E. (1977). Validation of contingency model leadership training: Leader Match. *Academy of Management Journal, 20,* 464–470.

Likert, R. (1961). *New patterns of management.* New York: McGraw-Hill.

Lord, R. G. (1985). An information processing approach to social perceptions, leadership, and behavioral measurement in organizations. *Research in organizational behavior, 7,* 87–128.

Lord, R. G., Foti, R. J., & Phillips, J. S. (1982). A theory of leadership organization. In J. G. Hunt, U. Sekaran, & C. Schriesheim (Eds.), *Leadership: Beyond establishment views.* Carbondale: Southern Illinois University.

Lowin, A., & Craig, J. R. (1968). The influence of level of performance on managerial style: An experimental object-lesson in the ambiguity of correlational data. *Organizational Behavior and Human Performance, 3*, 441–458.

Manz, C. C. (1986). Self-leadership: Toward an expanded theory of self-influence. *Academy of Management Review, 11*, 585–600.

Mawhinney, T. C., & Ford, J. D. (1977). The path-goal theory of leader effectiveness: An operant interpretation. *Academy of Management Review, 2*, 398–411.

Meindl, J. R., & Ehrlich, S. B. (1987). The romance of leadership and the evaluation of organizational performance. *Academy of Management Journal, 30*, 91–109.

Noe, R. A. (1988). Women and mentoring: A review and research agenda. *Academy of Management Review, 13*, 65–78.

O'Leary, V. E. (1974). Some attitudinal barriers to occupational aspirations in women. *Psychological Bulletin, 81*, 809–826.

Peters, L. H., Harthe, D. D., & Pohlmann, J. T. (1985). Fiedler's contingency theory of leadership: An application of the meta-analysis procedures of Schmidt and Hunter. *Psychological Bulletin, 97*, 274–285.

Pfeffer, J. (1977). The ambiguity of leadership. *Academy of Management Review, 2*, 104–112.

Phillips, J. S., & Lord, R. G. (1981). Causal attribution and prescriptions of leadership. *Organizational Behavior and Human Performance, 28*, 143–163.

Pierce, J. L., Dunham, R. B., & Cummings, L. L. (1984). Sources of environmental structuring and participant responses. *Organizational Behavior and Human Performance, 33*, 214–242.

Random House College Dictionary (1984). New York: Random House.

Rice, R. W. (1978). Construct validity of the Least Preferred Co-worker (LPC) score. *Psychological Bulletin, 85*, 1199–1237.

Rice, R. W. (1981). Leader LPC and follower satisfaction: A review. *Organizational Behavior and Human Performance, 28*, 1–25.

Schriesheim, C. A., House, R. J., & Kerr, S. (1976). Leader initiating structure: A conciliation of discrepant research results and some empirical tests. *Organizational Behavior and Human Performance, 15*, 297–321.

Schriesheim, C. A., & Kerr, S. (1974). Psychometric properties of the Ohio State leadership scales. *Psychological Bulletin, 81*, 756–765.

Schriesheim, C. A., & Stogdill, R. M. (1975). Differences in factor structure across three versions of the Ohio State leadership scales. *Personnel Psychology, 28*, 189–206.

Shiftlett, S. (1981). Is there a problem with the LPC score in Leader Match? *Personnel Psychology, 34*, 765–769.

Stinson, J. E., & Tracy, L. (1974). Some disturbing characteristics of the LPC score. *Personnel Psychology, 27*, 477–485.

Stogdill, R. M. (1948). Personal factors associated with leadership. *Journal of Psychology, 25*, 35–71.

Stogdill, R. M., & Coons, A. E. (Eds.). (1957). *Leader behavior: Its description and measurement.* Columbus: Ohio State University Bureau of Business Research.

Strube, M. J., & Garcia, J. E. (1981). A meta-analytic investigation of Fiedler's contingency model of leadership effectiveness. *Psychological Bulletin, 90*, 307–321.

Tscheulin, D. (1973). Leader behavior measurement in German industry. *Journal of Applied Psychology, 57*, 28–31.

Vecchio, R. P. (1977). An empirical examination of the validity of Fiedler's model of leadership effectiveness. *Organizational Behavior and Human Performance, 19*, 180–206.

Vecchio, R. P. (1982). A further test of leadership effects due to between-group variation and within-group variation. *Journal of Applied Psychology, 67*, 200–208.

Vecchio, R. P., & Gobdel, B. C. (1984). The vertical dyad linkage model of leadership: Problems and prospects. *Organizational Behavior and Human Performance, 34,* 5–20.

Vroom, V. H., & Jago, A. G. (1978). On the validity of the Vroom-Yetton model. *Journal of Applied Psychology, 63,* 151–162.

Vroom, V. H., & Yetton, P. W. (1973). *Leadership and decision-making.* Pittsburgh: University of Pittsburgh Press.

Weissenberg, P., & Kavanagh, M. (1972). The independence of initiating structure and consideration: A review of the literature. *Personnel Psychology, 25,* 119–130.

Wilkinson, I., & Kipnis, D. (1978). Interfirm use of power. *Journal of Applied Psychology, 63,* 315–320.

Chapter 12

Arps, G. F. (1920). Work with knowledge of results versus work without knowledge of results. *Psychology Monograph, 28* (3, Whole No. 125).

Ashford, S. J., & Cummings, L. L. (1983). Feedback as an individual resource: Personal strategies of creating information. *Organizational Behavior and Human Performance, 32,* 370–398.

Athanassiades, J. (1973). The distortion of upward communication in hierarchical organizations. *Academy of Management Journal, 16,* 207–226.

Bacharach, S. B., & Aiken, M. (1977). Communication in administrative bureaucracies. *Academy of Management Journal, 10,* 365–377.

Barnard, C. I. (1938). *The functions of the executive.* Cambridge, MA: Harvard University Press.

Berlo, D. K. (1960). *The process of communication.* New York: Holt, Rinehart and Winston.

Burgess, R. L. (1968). Communication networks: An experimental re-evaluation. *Journal of Experimental Social Psychology, 4,* 324–337.

Burke, R. J., Weitzel, W., & Weir, T. (1978). Characteristics of effective performance review and development interviews: Replication and extension. *Personnel Psychology, 31,* 903–919.

Dance, F. E. (1970). The "concept" of communication. *Journal of Communication, 20,* 201–210.

D'Aprix, R. (1982). The oldest (and best) way to communicate with employees. *Harvard Business Review, 60*(5), 30, 32.

Davis, K. (1953). A method of studying communication patterns in organizations. *Personnel Psychology, 6,* 301–312.

De Meuse, K. P. (1987). Employee nonverbal cues: Their effects on the performance appraisal process. *Journal of Occupational Psychology, 60,* 207–226.

Farace, R. V., & MacDonald, D. (1974). New directions in the study of organizational communication. *Personnel Psychology, 27,* 1–19.

Fielden, J. (1964). "What do you mean I can't write?" *Harvard Business Review, 42*(3), 144–148.

Fielden, J. S. (1982). "What do you mean you don't like my style?" *Harvard Business Review, 60*(3), 128–138.

Flesch, R. (1948). A new readability yardstick. *Journal of Applied Psychology, 32,* 221–233.

Flesch, R. (1974). *The art of readable writing.* New York: Harper & Row.

Gaines, J. (1980). Upward communication in industry: An experiment. *Human Relations, 33,* 929–942.

Galbraith, J. (1973). *Designing complex organizations.* Reading, MA: Addison-Wesley.

Gifford, R., Ng, C. F., & Wilkinson, M. (1985). Nonverbal cues in the employment inter-view: Links between applicant qualities and interviewer judgments. *Journal of Applied Psychology, 70,* 729–736.

Greenbaum, J. H. (1974). The audit or organizational communication. *Academy of Management Journal, 17,* 739–754.

Greller, M. M., & Herold, D. M. (1975). Sources of feedback: A preliminary investigation. *Organizational Behavior and Human Performance, 13,* 244–256.

Guetzkow, H. (1965). Communication in organizations. In J. G. March (Ed.), *Handbook of organizations.* Skokie, IL: Rand McNally.

Gupta, N., & Beehr, T. A. (1979). Job stress and employee behaviors. *Organizational Behavior and Human Performance, 23,* 373–387.

Hanser, L. M., & Muchinsky, P. M. (1978). Work as an information environment. *Organizational Behavior and Human Performance, 21,* 47–60.

Hanser, L. M., & Muchinsky, P. M. (1980). Performance feedback information and organizational communication: Evidence of conceptual convergence. *Human Communication Research, 7,* 68–73.

Hatfield, J. D., & Huseman, R. C. (1982). Perceptual congruence about communication as related to satisfaction: Moderating effects of individual characteristics. *Academy of Management Journal, 25,* 349–358.

Hicks, H. G. (1967). *The management of organizations.* New York: McGraw-Hill.

Ilgen, D. R., Fisher, C. D., & Taylor, M. S. (1979). Consequences of individual feedback on behavior in organizations. *Journal of Applied Psychology, 64,* 349–371.

Imada, A. S., & Hakel, M. D. (1977). Influence of nonverbal communication and rater proximity on impressions and decisions in simulated employment interviews. *Journal of Applied Psychology, 62,* 295–300.

Jablin, F. M. (1979). Superior-subordinate communication: The state of the art. *Psychological Bulletin, 86,* 1201–1222.

Knapp, M. L. (1972). *Nonverbal communication in human interaction.* New York: Holt, Rinehart & Winston.

Lawrence, P. R., & Lorsch, J. W. (1967). *Organizational and environment: Managing differentiation and integration.* Boston: Harvard University Graduate School of Business.

Leavitt, H. J. (1951). Some effects of certain communication patterns on group performance. *Journal of Abnormal and Social Psychology, 46,* 38–50.

Levine, E. L., & Flory, A. (1975). Evaluation of job applications—a conceptual framework. *Public Personnel Management,* November/December 1975, 378–385.

Marion, B. W., & Trieb, S. E. (1969). Job orientation: A factor in employee performance and turnover. *Personnel Journal, 48,* 799–804, 831.

Meier, R. (1963). Communication overload: Proposals from the study of a university library. *Administrative Science Quarterly, 7,* 521–544.

Miller, J. G. (1960). Information input, overload and psychopathology. *American Journal of Psychiatry, 116,* 367–386.

Morrow, W. R., Lowenberg, G., Larson, S., Redfearn, M., & Schoone, J. (1983). Evaluation of business memos: Effect of writer sex and organizational position, memo quality, and rater sex. *Personnel Psychology, 36,* 73–86.

Muchinsky, P. M. (1977a). An intraorganizational analysis of the Roberts and O'Reilly organizational communication questionnaire. *Journal of Applied Psychology, 62,* 184–188.

Muchinsky, P. M. (1977b). Organizational communication: Relationships to organizational climate and job satisfaction. *Academy of Management Journal, 20,* 592–607.

Mudd, S. A., & McCormick, E. J. (1960). The use of auditory cues in a visual search task. *Journal of Applied Psychology, 44,* 184–188.

Nemeroff, W. F., & Wexley, K. N. (1977). Relationships between performance appraisal interview characteristics and interview outcomes as perceived by supervisors and subordinates. Paper presented at the meeting of the National Academy of Management, Orlando, FL.

O'Reilly, C. A. (1978). The intentional distortion of information in organizational communication: A laboratory and field approach. *Human Relations, 31,* 173–193.

O'Reilly, C. A. (1980). Individuals and information overload in organizations: Is more necessarily better? *Academy of Management Journal, 23,* 684–696.

O'Reilly, C. A., & Pondy, L. R. (1979). Organizational communication. In S. Kerr (Ed.), *Organizational behavior.* Columbus, OH: Grid.

O'Reilly, C. A., & Roberts, K. H. (1974). Information filtration in organizations: Three experiments. *Organizational Behavior and Human Performance, 11,* 253–265.

O'Reilly, C. A., & Roberts, K. H. (1976). Relationships among components of credibility and communication behaviors in work units. *Journal of Applied Psychology, 61,* 99–102.

O'Reilly, C. A., & Roberts, K. H. (1977a). Communication and performance in organizations. *Proceedings of the Academy of Management,* 375–379.

O'Reilly, C. A., & Roberts, K. H. (1977b). Task group structure, communication, and effectiveness in three organizations. *Journal of Applied Psychology, 62,* 674–681.

Pace, R. (1962). Oral communication and sales effectiveness. *Journal of Applied Psychology, 46,* 321–324.

Pettigrew, A. (1972). Information control as a power resource. *Sociology, 6,* 187–204.

Porter, L. W., & Roberts, K. H. (1976). Communication in organization. In M. D. Dunnette (Ed.), *Handbook of industrial and organizational psychology.* Skokie, IL: Rand McNally.

Powell, J. D., Heimlich, K. T., & Goodin, E. H. (1980). Training executives for today's communication challenges. Paper presented at the meeting of the National Academy of Management, Detroit.

Randle, C. W. (1956). How to identify promotable executives. *Harvard Business Review, 34*(3), 122–134.

Redfield, C. E. (1953). *Communication in management.* Chicago: University of Chicago Press.

Roberts, K. H., & O'Reilly, C. A. (1974). Failures in upward communication: Three possible culprits. *Academy of Management Journal, 17,* 205–215.

Roberts, K. H., & O'Reilly, C. A. (1978). Organizations as communication structures: An empirical approach. *Human Communication Research, 4,* 283–293.

Roberts, K. H., O'Reilly, C. A., Bretton, G., & Porter, L. W. (1974). Organizational theory and organizational communication: A communication failure? *Human Relations, 27,* 501–524.

Rogers, C. R., & Farson, R. E. (1969). Active listening. In R. C. Huseman, C. M. Logue, & D. L. Freshley (Eds.), *Readings in interpersonal and organizational communication.* Boston: Holbrook Press.

Rogers, E. M., & Agarwala-Rogers, R. (1976). *Communication in organizations.* New York: Free Press.

Schmitt, N. (1976). Social and situational determinants of interview decisions: Implications for the employment interview. *Personnel Psychology, 29,* 79–101.

Schmitt, N., Coyle, B. W., & Saari, B. B. (1977). Types of task information feedback in multiple cue probability learning. *Organizational Behavior and Human Performance, 18,* 316–328.

Schwartz, D., & Jacobson, E. (1977). Organizational communication network analysis: The liaison communication role. *Organizational Behavior and Human Performance, 18,* 158–174.

Scott, W. G., & Mitchell, T. R. (1976). *Organizational theory: A structural and behavioral approach.* Homewood, IL: Richard D. Irwin.

Shaw, M. E. (1964). Communication networks. In L. Berkowitz (Ed.), *Advances in experimental social psychology.* New York: Academic Press.

Simpson, R. L. (1959). Vertical and horizontal communication in formal organizations. *Administrative Science Quarterly, 4,* 188–196.

Sims, H. P., & La Follette, W. R. (1975). An assessment of the Litwin and Stringer organization climate questionnaire. *Personnel Psychology, 28,* 19–38.

Snyder, R. A., & Morris, J. H. (1984). Organizational communication and performance. *Journal of Applied Psychology, 69,* 461–465.

Steckler, N. A., & Rosenthal, R. (1985). Sex differences in nonverbal and verbal communication with bosses, peers, and subordinates. *Journal of Applied Psychology, 70,* 157–163.

Tushman, M. (1978). Technical communication in research and development laboratories: The impact of project work characteristics. *Academy of Management Journal, 21,* 624–645.

Watson, K. M. (1982). An analysis of communication patterns: A method for discriminating leader and subordinate roles. *Academy of Management Journal, 25,* 107–120.

Whitely, W. (1984). An exploratory study of managers' reactions to properties of verbal communication. *Personnel Psychology, 37,* 41–60.

Wilcox, R. P. (1959). Characteristics and organization of the oral technical report. *General Motors Engineering Journal, 6,* 8–12.

Woocher, F. D. (1977). Did your eyes deceive you? Expert psychological testimony on the unreliability of eyewitness identification. *Stanford Law Review, 29,* 969–1030.

Zand, D. D. (1972). Trust and managerial problem solving. *Administrative Science Quarterly, 17,* 229–240.

Chapter 13

Aldag, R. J., & Brief, A. P. (1979). *Task design and employee motivation.* Glenview IL: Scott, Foresman.

American Society for Training and Development. (1975). *Characteristics and professional concerns of OD practitioners.* Madison, WI: American Society for Training and Development.

Armenakis, A. A., Bedeian, A. G., & Pond, S. B. (1983). Research issues in OD evaluation: Past, present, and future. *Academy of Management Review, 8,* 320–328.

Bass, B. M. (1983). Issues involved in relations between methodological rigor and reported outcomes in evaluations of organizational development. *Journal of Applied Psychology, 68,* 197–199.

Beer, M. (1976). The technology of organization development. In M. D. Dunnette (Ed.), *Handbook of industrial and organizational psychology.* Skokie, IL: Rand McNally.

Blake, R., & Mouton, J. (1976). *Consultation.* Reading, MA: Addison-Wesley.

Bowers, D. G. (1973). OD techniques and their results in 23 organizations: The Michigan ICL study. *Journal of Applied Behavioral Science, 9,* 21–43.

Brief, A. P., & Aldag, R. J. (1975). Employee reactions to job characteristics: A constructive replication. *Journal of Applied Psychology, 60,* 182–186.

Caldwell, D. F., & O'Reilly, C. A. (1982). Task perceptions and job satisfaction. A question of causality. *Journal of Applied Psychology, 67,* 361–369.

Campion, M. A., & Thayer, P. W. (1985). Development and field evaluation of an interdisciplinary measure of job design. *Journal of Applied Psychology, 70,* 29–43.

Connor, P. E. (1977). A critical inquiry into some assumptions and values characterizing OD. *Academy of Management Review, 2*, 635–644.

Dunham, R. B. (1976). The measurement and dimensionality of job characteristics. *Journal of Applied Psychology, 61*, 404–409.

Dunham, R. B. (1977). Relationships of perceived job design characteristics to job ability requirements and job value. *Journal of Applied Psychology, 62*, 760–763.

Dunham, R. B. (1979). Job design and redesign. In S. Kerr (Ed.), *Organizational behavior.* Columbus, OH: Grid.

Dunham, R. B., Aldag, R. J., & Brief, A. P. (1977). Dimensionality of task design as measured by the Job Diagnostic Survey. *Academy of Management Journal, 20*, 209–221.

Eden, D. (1986). OD and self-fulfilling prophecy: Boosting productivity by raising expectations. *Journal of Applied Behavioral Science, 22*, 1–13.

Evans, M. G., Kiggundu, M. N., & House, R. J. (1979). A partial test and extension of the job characteristics model of motivation. *Organizational Behavior and Human Performance, 24*, 354–381.

Ford, R. N. (1969). *Motivation through the work itself.* New York: American Management Association.

Frank, L. L., & Hackman, J. R. (1975). A failure of job enrichment: The case of change that wasn't. *Journal of Applied Behavioral Science, 11*, 413–436.

French, W. L. (1969). Organization development: Objectives, assumptions and strategies. *California Management Review, 12*(2), 23–34.

French, W. L., & Bell, C. H. (1978). *Organization development: Behavioral science interventions for organization improvement* (2nd ed.). Englewood Cliffs, NJ: Prentice-Hall.

Fried, Y., & Ferris, G. R. (1987). The validity of the job characteristics model: A review and meta-analysis. *Personnel Psychology, 40*, 287–322.

Frohman, M., Sashkin, M., & Kavanagh, M. (1976). Action research as applied to organization development. *Organization and Administrative Sciences, 7*, 129–142.

Glickman, B. (1974). Qualities of change agents. Paper presented at Boston College, Chestnut, MA.

Griffin, R. W., Welsh, A., & Moorhead, G. (1981). Perceived task characteristics and employee performance: A literature review. *Academy of Management Review, 6*, 655–664.

Hackman, J. R., & Lawler, E. E. (1971). Employee reactions to job characteristics. *Journal of Applied Psychology, 55*, 259–286.

Hackman, J. R., & Oldham, G. R. (1975). Development of the Job Diagnostic Survey. *Journal of Applied Psychology, 60*, 159–170.

Hackman, J. R., & Oldham, G. R. (1976). Motivation through the design of work: Test of a theory. *Organizational Behavior and Human Performance, 16*, 250–279.

Hackman, J. R., Pearce, J. L., & Wolfe, J. C. (1978). Effects of changes in job characteristics on work attitudes and behaviors: A naturally occurring quasi-experiment. *Organizational Behavior and Human Performance, 21*, 289–304.

Harrison, R. (1970). Choosing the depth of organizational intervention. *Journal of Applied Behavioral Science, 6*, 181–202.

Huse, E. F. (1980). *Organization development and change* (2nd ed.). New York: West.

Kiggundu, M. N. (1983). Task interdependence and job design: Test of a theory. *Organizational Behavior and Human Performance, 31*, 145–172.

Lawler, E. E. (1969). Job design and employee motivation. *Personnel Psychology, 22*, 426–435.

Lippitt, R., Watson, J., & Westley, B. (1958). *The dynamics of planned change.* New York: Harcourt Brace Jovanovich.

Locke, E. A., Feren, D. B., McCaleb, V. M., Shaw, K. N., & Denny, A. T. (1980). The relative effectiveness of four methods of motivating employee performance. In K. Duncan, M. Gruneberg, & D. Wallis (Eds.), *Changes in working life.* New York: Wiley.

Locke, E. A., Sirota, D., & Wolfson, A. D. (1976). An experimental case study of the successes and failures of job enrichment in a government agency. *Journal of Applied Psychology, 61,* 701–711.

Loher, B. T., Noe, R. A., Moeller, N. L., & Fitzgerald, M. P. (1985). A meta-analysis of the relation of job characteristics to job satisfaction. *Journal of Applied Psychology, 70,* 280–289.

Maher, J. R., & Overbagh, W. B. (1971). Better inspection performance through job enrichment. In J. R. Maher (Ed.), *New perspectives in job enrichment.* New York: Van Nostrand Reinhold.

Mowday, R. T., & Spencer, D. G. (1981). The influence of task and personality characteristics on employee turnover and absenteeism incidents. *Academy of Management Journal, 24,* 634–642.

Neff, F. W. (1966). Survey research: A tool for problem diagnosis and improvement in organizations. In A. W. Gouldner & S. M. Miller (Eds.), *Applied sociology.* New York: Free Press.

Nicholas, J. M. (1982). The comparative impact of organization development interventions on hard criteria measures. *Academy of Management Review, 7,* 531–542.

Nicholas, J. M., & Katz, M. (1985). Research methods and reporting practices in organization development: A review and some guidelines. *Academy of Management Review, 10,* 737–749.

Oldham, G. R., Hackman, J. R., & Pearce, J. L. (1976). Conditions under which employees respond to enriched work. *Journal of Applied Psychology, 61,* 395–403.

Paul, W. J., Robertson, K. B., & Herzberg, F. (1969). Job enrichment pays off. *Harvard Business Review, 41*(2), 61–78.

Porras, J. I., & Berg, P. O. (1978). The impact of organization development. *Academy of Management Review, 3,* 249–266.

Randolph, W. A. (1982). Planned organizational change and its measurement. *Personnel Psychology, 35,* 117–139.

Roberts, K. H., & Glick, W. (1981). The job characteristics approach to task design: A critical review. *Journal of Applied Psychology, 66,* 193–217.

Sashkin, M., Morriss, W., & Horst, L. (1973). A comparison of social and organizational change models: Information flow and data use processes. *Psychological Review, 80,* 510–526.

Schein, E. (1969). *Process consultation: Its role in organization development.* Reading, MA: Addison-Wesley.

Schneider, B., Reichers, A. E., & Mitchell, T. M. (1982). A note on some relationships between the aptitude requirements and reward attributes of tasks. *Academy of Management Journal, 25,* 567–574.

Sims, H. P., Szilagyi, A. D., & Keller, R. T. (1976). The measurement of job characteristics. *Academy of Management Journal, 19,* 195–212.

Solomon, R. J. (1976). An examination of the relationship between a survey feedback OD technique and the work environment. *Personnel Psychology, 29,* 583–594.

Steers, R. M. (1975). Effects of need for achievement on the job performance—job attitude relationship. *Journal of Applied Psychology, 60,* 678–682.

Steers, R. M., & Mowday, R. T. (1977). The motivational properties of tasks. *Academy of Management Review, 2,* 645–658.

Steers, R. M., & Porter, L. W. (1974). The role of task-goal attributes in employee perform-ance. *Psychological Bulletin, 81,* 434–452.

Steers, R. M., & Spencer, D. G. (1977). The role of achievement motivation in job design. *Journal of Applied Psychology, 62,* 472–479.

Stone, E. F., Mowday, R. T., & Porter, L. W. (1977). Higher-order need strength as a moderator of the job scope-job satisfaction relationship. *Journal of Applied Psychology, 62,* 466–471.

Terpstra, D. E. (1981). Relationship between methodological rigor and reported outcomes in organization development evaluation research. *Journal of Applied Psychology, 66,* 541–543.

Turner, A. N., & Lawrence, P. R. (1965). *Industrial jobs and the worker: An investigation of response to task attributes.* Cambridge, MA: Harvard University Press.

Umstot, D. D., Bell, C. H., & Mitchell, T. R. (1976). Effects of job enrichment and task goals on satisfaction and productivity: Implications for job design. *Journal of Applied Psychol-ogy, 61,* 379–394.

Vaill, P. (1982). The purposing of high-performing systems. *Organizational Dynamics, 2(2),* 23–39.

Wanous, J. P. (1974). Individual differences and reactions to job characteristics. *Journal of Applied Psychology, 59,* 616–622.

White, L. P., & Wooten, K. C. (1983). Ethical dilemmas in various stages of organizational development. *Academy of Management Review, 8,* 690–697.

White, S. E., & Mitchell, T. R. (1976). Organization development: A review of research content and research design. *Academy of Management Review, 1(2),* 57–73.

Chapter 14

Angel, M. (1982). White-collar and professional unionization. *Labor Law Journal, 33,* 82–101.

Angle, H. L., & Perry, J. L. (1986). Dual commitment and labor-management relationship climates. *Academy of Management Journal, 29,* 31–50.

Ash, P. (1970). The parties to the grievance. *Personnel Psychology, 23,* 13–37.

Bakke, E. W. (1945). Why workers join unions. *Personnel, 22,* 37–46.

Bass, B. M., & Mitchell, C. W. (1976). Influences on the felt need for collective bargaining by business and science professionals. *Journal of Applied Psychology, 61,* 770–773.

Bazerman, M. H., & Neale, M. A. (1982). Improving negotiation effectiveness under final offer arbitration: The role of selection and training. *Journal of Applied Psychology, 67,* 543–548.

Bigoness, W. J. (1978). Correlates of faculty attitudes toward collective bargaining. *Journal of Applied Psychology, 63,* 228–233.

Bok, D., & Dunlop, J. (1970). *Labor and the American community.* New York: Simon & Schuster.

Brett, J. M. (1980). Behavioral research on unions and union management systems. In B. M. Staw & L. L. Cummings (Eds.), *Research in organizational behavior.* Greenwich, CT: JAI Press.

Brief, A. P., & Rude, D. E. (1981). Voting in a union certification election: A conceptual analysis. *Academy of Management Review, 6,* 261–267.

Cameron, K. (1982). The relationship between faculty unionism and organizational effective-ness. *Academy of Management Journal, 25,* 6–24.

Carillon, J. W., & Sutton, R. I. (1982). The relationship between union effectiveness and the quality of members' worklife. *Journal of Occupational Behavior, 3,* 171–179.

Dalton, D. R., & Todor, W. D. (1979). Manifest needs of stewards: Propensity to file a grievance. *Journal of Applied Psychology, 64,* 654–659.

Dalton, D. R., & Todor, W. D. (1982). Antecedents of grievance filing behavior. Attitude/behavioral consistency and the union steward. *Academy of Management Journal, 25,* 158–169.

De Cotiis, T. A., & Le Louarn, J. Y. (1981). A predictive study of voting behavior in a representation election using union instrumentality and work perceptions. *Organizational Behavior and Human Performance, 27,* 103–118.

Dubno, P. (1957). The role of the psychologist in labor unions. *American Psychologist, 12,* 212–215.

Eckerman, A. C. (1948). An analysis of grievances and aggrieved employees in a machine shop and foundry. *Journal of Applied Psychology, 32,* 255–269.

Estey, M. (1981). *The unions: Structure, development, and management* (3rd ed.). New York: Harcourt Brace Jovanovich.

Feuille, P., & Blandin, J. (1974). Faculty job satisfaction and bargaining sentiment: A case study. *Academy of Management Journal, 17,* 678–692.

Fleishman, E. A., & Harris, E. F. (1962). Patterns of leadership behavior related to employee grievances and turnover. *Personnel Psychology, 15,* 43–56.

Franklin, W. S. (1976). Are construction apprenticeships too long? *Labor Law Journal, 27,* 99–106.

Friedman, L., & Harvey, R. J. (1986). Factors of union commitment: The case for a lower dimensionality. *Journal of Applied Psychology, 71,* 371–376.

Fukami, C. V., & Larson, E. W. (1984). Commitment to company and union: Parallel models. *Journal of Applied Psychology, 69,* 367–371.

Giles, W. F., & Holley, W. H. (1978). Job enrichment versus traditional issues at the bargaining table: What union members want. *Academy of Management Journal, 21,* 725–730.

Glueck, W. F. (1974). *Personnel: A diagnostic approach.* Plano, TX: Business Publications.

Gomez-Mejia, L. R., & Balkin, D. B. (1984). Faculty satisfaction with pay and other job dimensions under union and nonunion conditions. *Academy of Management Journal, 27,* 591–602.

Gordon, M. E., & Ladd, R. T. (1989). Dual allegiance: Renewal, reconsideration, and recantation. Unpublished manuscript.

Gordon, M. E., & Miller, S. J. (1984). Grievances: A review of research and practice. *Personnel Psychology, 37,* 117–146.

Gordon, M. E., & Nurick, A. J. (1981). Psychological approaches to the study of unions and union-management relations. *Psychological Bulletin, 90,* 293–306.

Gordon, M. E., Philpot, J. W., Burt, R. E., Thompson, C. A., & Spiller, W. E. (1980). Commitment to the union: Development of a measure and an examination of its correlates. *Journal of Applied Psychology, 65,* 479–499.

Gordon, M. E., Schmitt, N., & Schneider, W. G. (1984). Laboratory research on bargaining and negotiations: An evaluation. *Industrial Relations, 23,* 281–233.

Grigsby, D. M., & Bigoness, W. J. (1982). Effects of mediation and alternative forms of arbitration on bargaining behavior: A laboratory study. *Journal of Applied Psychology, 67,* 549–554.

Hammer, T. H. (1978). Relationships between local union characteristics and worker behavior and attitudes. *Academy of Management Journal, 21,* 560–577.

Hammer, T. H., & Berman, M. (1981). The role of noneconomic factors in faculty union voting. *Journal of Applied Psychology, 66,* 415–421.

Hamner, W. C., & Smith, F. J. (1978). Work attitudes as predictors of unionization activity. *Journal of Applied Psychology, 63,* 415–421.

Holley, W. H., Feild, H. S., & Crowley, J. C. (1981). Negotiating quality of worklife, productivity, and traditional issues: Union members' preferred roles of their union. *Personnel Psychology, 34,* 309–328.

Huszczo, G. E., Wiggins, J. G., & Currie, J. S. (1984). The relationship between psychology and organized labor: Past, present and future. *American Psychologist, 39,* 432–440.

Kissler, G. D. (1977). Grievance activity and union membership: A study of government employees. *Journal of Applied Psychology, 62,* 459–462.

Kochan, T. A. (1979). How American workers view labor unions. *Monthly Labor Review, 102*(4), 23–31.

Kochan, T. A. (1980). *Collective bargaining and industrial relations.* Homewood, IL: Richard D. Irwin.

Ladd, R. T., Gordon, M. E., Beauvais, L. L., & Morgan, R. L. (1982). Union commitment: Replication and extension. *Journal of Applied Psychology, 67,* 640–644.

Muchinsky, P. M., & Maassarani, M. A. (1980). Work environment effects on public sector grievances. *Personnel Psychology, 33,* 403–414.

Muchinsky, P. M., & Maassarani, M. A. (1981). Public sector grievances in Iowa. *Journal of Collective Negotiations, 10,* 55–62.

Neale, M. A. (1984). The effects of negotiation and arbitration cost salience on bargainer behavior: The role of the arbitrator and constituency in negotiator judgment. *Organizational Behavior and Human Performance, 34,* 97–111.

Premack, S. L., & Hunter, J. E. (1988). Individual unionization decisions. *Psychological Bulletin, 103,* 223–234.

Redenius, C. (1976). Public employees: A survey of some critical problems on the frontier of collective bargaining. *Labor Law Journal, 27,* 588–599.

Ronan, W. W. (1963). Work group attributes and grievance activity. *Journal of Applied Psychology, 47,* 38–41.

Rosen, H., & Stagner, R. (1980). Industrial/organizational psychology and unions: A viable relationship? *Professional Psychology, 11,* 477–483.

Schriesheim, C. A. (1978). Job satisfaction, attitudes toward unions, and voting in a union representation election. *Journal of Applied Psychology, 63,* 548–552.

Sherman, V. C. (1969). Unionism and the non-union company. *Personnel Journal, 48,* 413–422.

Shostak, A. B. (1964). Industrial psychology and the trade unions: A matter of mutual indifference. In G. Fisk (Ed.), *The frontiers of management psychology.* New York: Harper & Row.

Stagner, R. (1956). *Psychology of industrial conflict.* New York: Wiley.

Stagner, R. (1961). Implications of psychology in labor-management relations: Comments on the symposium. *Personnel Psychology, 14,* 279–284.

Stagner, R., & Effal, B. (1982). Internal union dynamics during a strike: A quasi-experimental study. *Journal of Applied Psychology, 67,* 37–44.

Stagner, R., & Rosen, H. (1965). *Psychology of union-management relations.* Belmont, CA: Wadsworth.

Starke, F. A., & Notz, W. W. (1981). Pre- and post-intervention effects of conventional versus final offer arbitration. *Academy of Management Journal, 24,* 832–850.

Sulkin, H. A., & Pranis, R. W. (1957). Comparison of grievants with nongrievants in a heavy machinery company. *Personnel Psychology, 10,* 27–42.

Summers, T. P., Betton, J. H., & De Cotiis, T. A. (1986). Voting for and against unions: A decision model. *Academy of Management Review, 11,* 643–655.

Tannenbaum, A. S. (1965). Unions. In J. G. March (Ed.), *Handbook of organizations*. Skokie, IL: Rand McNally.

U.S. Department of Labor. (1977). *Apprenticeship: Past and present*. Washington, DC: U.S. Government Printing Office.

Walton, R. E., & McKersie, R. B. (1965). *A behavioral theory of labor negotiations*. New York: McGraw-Hill.

Werther, W. B. (1974). Reducing grievances through effective contract administration. *Labor Law Journal, 25*, 211–216.

Youngblood, S. A., De Nisi, A. S., Molleston, J. L., & Mobley, W. H. (1984). The impact of work environment, instrumentality beliefs, perceived labor union image, and subjective norms on union voting intentions. *Academy of Management Journal, 17*, 576–590.

Zalesny, M. D. (1985). Comparison of economic and noneconomic factors in predicting faculty vote preference in a union representation election. *Journal of Applied Psychology, 70*, 243–256.

Chapter 15

Adams, J. A. (1972). Research and the future of engineering psychology. *American Psychologist, 27*, 615–622.

Aschoff, J. (1978). Features of circadian rhythms relevant to the design of shift schedules. *Ergonomics, 21*, 739–754.

Barrett, G. V., & Thornton, C. L. (1968). The relationship between perceptual style and driver reaction to an emergency situation. *Journal of Applied Psychology, 52*, 169–176.

Beehr, T. A., & Newman, J. E. (1978). Job stress, employee health, and organizational effectiveness: A facet analysis, model, and literature review. *Personnel Psychology, 31*, 665–699.

Breaugh, J. A. (1983). The 12-hour work day: Differing employee reactions. *Personnel Psychology, 36*, 277–288.

Broadbent, D. S. (1957). Effect of noise on behavior. In C. M. Harris (Ed.), *Handbook of noise control*. New York: McGraw-Hill.

Butler, M. C., & Jones, A. P. (1979). Perceived leader behavior, individual characteristics, and injury occurrence in hazardous work environments. *Journal of Applied Psychology, 64*, 299–304.

Chao, G. T., & Kozlowski, S. W. (1986). Employee perceptions on the implementation of robotic manufacturing technology. *Journal of Applied Psychology, 71*, 70–76.

Chapanis, A. (1976). Engineering psychology. In M. D. Dunnette (Ed.), *Handbook of industrial and organizational psychology*. Skokie, IL: Rand McNally.

Cohen, A. (1968). Noise effects on health, production, and well-being. *Transactions of the New York Academy of Sciences, Series II, 30*, 910–918.

Cohen, A. (1977). Factors in successful occupational safety programs. *Journal of Safety Research, 9*, 168–178.

Cooke, W. N., & Gautschi, F. H. (1981). OSHA, plant safety programs, and injury reduction. *Industrial Relations, 20*, 245–257.

De la Mare, G., & Walker, J. (1968). Factors influencing the choice of shift rotation. *Occupational Psychology, 42*, 1–21.

De Reamer, R. (1980). *Modern safety and health technology*. New York: Wiley.

Dunbar, R. L. (1975). Managers' influence on subordinate thinking about safety. *Academy of Management Journal, 18*, 364–369.

Dunham, R. B. (1977). Shift work: A review and theoretical analysis. *Academy of Management Review, 2,* 626–634.

Dunham, R. B., & Hawk, D. L. (1977). The four-day/forty-hour week: Who wants it? *Academy of Management Journal, 20,* 644–655.

Dunham, R. B., Pierce, J. L., & Castaneda, M. B. (1987). Alternative work schedules: Two field quasi-experiments. *Personnel Psychology, 40,* 215–242.

Eastman Kodak Company (1986). *Ergonomic design for people at work* (Vol. 2). New York: Van Nostrand Reinhold.

Ellis, H. D. (1982). The effect of cold on the performance of serial choice reaction time and various discrete tasks. *Human Factors, 24,* 589–598.

Fiedler, F. E., & Fiedler, J. (1975). Port noise complaints: Verbal and behavioral reactions to airport-related noise. *Journal of Applied Psychology, 60,* 498–506.

Fine, B. J., & Kobrick, J. L. (1978). Effects of altitude and heat on complex cognitive tasks. *Human Factors, 20,* 115–122.

Fottler, M. D. (1977). Employee acceptance of a four-day workweek. *Academy of Management Journal, 20,* 656–668.

Fox, W. F. (1967). Human performance in the cold. *Human factors, 9,* 203–220.

Freese, M., & Okonek, K. (1984). Reasons to leave shiftwork and psychological and psychosomatic complaints of former shiftworkers. *Journal of Applied Psychology, 69,* 509–514.

Frost, P. J., & Jamal, M. (1979). Shift work, attitudes and reported behaviors: Some association between individual characteristics and hours of work and leisure. *Journal of Applied Psychology, 64,* 77–81.

Golembiewski, R. T., & Proehl, C. W. (1978). A survey of the empirical literature on flexible workhours: Character and consequences of a major innovation. *Academy of Management Review, 3,* 837–853.

Goodale, J. G., & Aagaard, A. K. (1975). Factors relating to varying reactions to the 4-day workweek. *Journal of Applied Psychology, 60,* 33–38.

Grandjean, E. (1968). Fatigue: Its physiological and psychological significance. *Ergonomics, 11,* 427–436.

Grandjean, E. (1986). *Fitting the task to the man: An ergonomic approach.* London: Taylor & Frances.

Grandjean, E. (1987). *Ergonomics in computerized offices.* London: Taylor & Frances.

Haynes, R. S., Pine, R. C., & Fitch, H. G. (1982). Reducing accident rates with organizational behavior modification. *Academy of Management Journal, 25,* 407–416.

Hicks, W. D., & Klimoski, R. J. (1981). The impact of flexi-time on employee attitudes. *Academy of Management Journal, 24,* 333–341.

Ivancevich, J. M. (1974). Effects of the shorter workweek on selected satisfaction and performance measures. *Journal of Applied Psychology, 59,* 717–721.

Ivancevich, J. M., & Lyon, H. L.(1977). The shortened workweek: A field experiment. *Journal of Applied Psychology, 62,* 34–37.

Jamal, M. (1981). Shift work related to job attitudes, social participation and withdrawal behavior. A study of nurses and industrial workers. *Personnel Psychology, 34,* 535–548.

Jamal, M., & Jamal, S. M. (1982). Work and nonwork experiences of employees on fixed and rotating shifts: An empirical assessment. *Journal of Vocational Behavior, 20,* 282–293.

Kim, J. S., & Campagna, A. F. (1981). Effects of flexitime on employee attendance and performance: A field experiment. *Academy of Management Journal, 24,* 729–741.

Komaki, J., Barwick, K. D., & Scott, L. R. (1978). A behavioral approach to occupational safety: Pinpointing and reinforcing safe performance in a food manufacturing plant. *Journal of Applied Psychology, 63,* 434–445.

Kroemer, K. H., Kroemer, H. J., & Kroemer-Elbert, K. E. (1986). *Engineering physiology: Physiologic bases of human factors/ergonomics.* New York: Elsevier.

La Benz, P., Cohen, A., & Pearson, B. (1967). A noise and hearing survey of earth-moving equipment operators. *American Industrial Hygiene Association Journal, 28,* 117–128.

Lockhart, J. M. (1966). Effects of body and hand cooling on complex manual performance. *Journal of Applied Psychology, 50,* 57–59.

Malaviya, P., & Ganesh, K. (1976). Shift work and individual differences in the productivity of weavers in an Indian textile mill. *Journal of Applied Psychology, 61,* 774–776.

Malaviya, P., & Ganesh, K. (1977). Individual differences in productivity across type of work shift. *Journal of Applied Psychology, 62,* 527–528.

Malhotra, M. S., & Sengupta, J. (1965). Carrying of school bags by children. *Ergonomics, 8,* 55–60.

McCormick, E. J., & Sanders, M. S. (1982). *Human factors in engineering and design.* New York: McGraw-Hill.

McDaniel, M. A. (1988). Does pre-employment drug use predict on-the-job suitability. *Personnel Psychology, 41,* 717–729.

McFarland, R. A. (1971). Understanding fatigue in modern life. *Ergonomics, 14,* 1–10.

Meers, A., Maasen, A., & Verhaagen, P. (1978). Subjective health after six months and after four years of shift work. *Ergonomics, 21,* 857–859.

Mendeloff, J. (1979). *Regulating safety: An economic and political analysis of occupational safety and health policy.* Cambridge, MA: MIT Press.

Mihal, W. L., & Barrett, G. V. (1976). Individual differences in perceptual information processing and their relation to automobile accident involvement. *Journal of Applied Psychology, 61,* 229–233.

Narayanan, V. K., & Nath, R. (1982). Hierarchical level and the impact of flextime. *Industrial Relations, 21,* 216–230.

Nollen, S. D., & Martin, V. H. (1978). *Alternative work schedules, part I: Flextime.* New York: AMA-COM.

Nord, W. R., & Costigan, R. (1973). Worker adjustment to the four-day week: A longitudinal study. *Journal of Applied Psychology, 58,* 60–66.

Nothstein, G. Z. (1981). *The law of occupational safety and health.* New York: Free Press.

Noweir, M. H. (1984). Noise exposure as related to productivity, disciplinary actions, absenteeism, and accidents among textile workers. *Journal of Safety Research, 15,* 163–174.

Oldham, G. R., & Rotchford, N. L. (1983). Relationships between office characteristics and employee reactions: A study of the physical environment. *Administrative Science Quarterly, 28,* 542–556.

Orpen, C. (1981). Effect of flexible working hours on employee satisfaction and performance. *Journal of Applied Psychology, 66,* 113–115.

Parsons, H. M., & Kearsley, G. P. (1982). Robotics and human factors: Current status and future prospects. *Human Factors, 24,* 535–552.

Pepler, R. D. (1958). Warmth and performance: An investigation in the tropics. *Ergonomics, 2,* 63–88.

Petersen, A. P., & Gross, F. E. (1978). *Handbook of noise measurement* (8th ed.). New Concord, MA: GenRad.

Poor, R. (1970). *Four days, forty hours: Reporting a revaluation in work and leisure.* Cambridge, MA: Bursk & Poor.

Poulton, E. C., Hitchings, N. B., & Brooke, R. B. (1965). Effect of cold and rain upon the vigilance of lookouts. *Ergonomics, 8,* 163–168.

Ralston, D. A., Anthony, W. P., & Gustafson, D. J. (1985). Employees may love flextime, but what does it do to the organization's productivity? *Journal of Applied Psychology, 70,* 171–179.

Reber, R. A., Wallin, J. A., & Chhokar, J. S. (1984). Reducing industrial accidents: A behavioral experiment. *Industrial Relations, 23,* 119–125.

Ronen, S. (1981a). Arrival and departure patterns of public sector employees before and after the implementation of flextime. *Personnel Psychology, 34,* 817–822.

Ronen, S. (1981b). *Flexible working hours: An innovation in the quality of working life.* New York: McGraw-Hill.

Ronen, S., & Primps, S. B. (1981). The compressed work week as organizational change: Behavioral and attitudinal outcomes. *Academy of Management Review, 6,* 61–74.

Schein, V. E., Maurer, E. H., & Novak, J. F. (1977). Impact of flexible working hours on productivity. *Journal of Applied Psychology, 62,* 463–465.

Smith, M. J., Cohen, H. H., Cohen, A., & Cleveland, R. J. (1978). Characteristics of successful safety programs. *Journal of Safety Research, 10,* 5–15.

Spangenberg, H. H. (1968). The use of projective tests in the selection of bus drivers. *Traffic Safety Research Review, 12,* 118–121.

Spettell, C. M., & Liebert, R. M. (1986). Training for safety in automated person-machine systems. *American Psychologist, 41,* 545–550.

Stellman, J. M., Klitzman, S., Gordon, G. C., & Snow, B. R. (1987). Work environment and the well-being of clerical and VDT workers. *Journal of Occupational Behavior, 8,* 95–114.

Teichner, W. H., & Kobrick, J. L. (1955). Effects of prolonged exposure to low temperature on visual-motor performance. *Journal of Experimental Psychology, 49,* 122–126.

Topf, M. (1985). Personal and environmental predictors of patient disturbance due to hospital noise. *Journal of Applied Psychology, 70,* 22–28.

Tyson, P. R., & Vaughn, R. A. (1987). Drug testing in the work place: Legal responsibilities. *Occupational Health and Safety,* April, 24–36.

Vickroy, S. C., Shaw, J. B., & Fisher, C. D. (1982). Effects of temperature, clothing, and task complexity on task performance and satisfaction. *Journal of Applied Psychology, 67,* 97–102.

Voevodsky, J. (1974). Evaluation of a deceleration warning light for reducing rear end automobile collisions. *Journal of Applied Psychology, 59,* 270–273.

Wedderburn, A. A. (1978). Some suggestions for increasing the usefulness of psychological and sociological studies of shiftwork. *Ergonomics, 21,* 827–833.

Weinstein, N. D. (1978). Individual differences in reactions to noise: A longitudinal study in a college dormitory. *Journal of Applied Psychology, 63,* 458–466.

Williams, J. R. (1977). Follow-up study of relationships between perceptual style measures and telephone company vehicle accidents. *Journal of Applied Psychology, 62,* 751–754.

Wilson, T., & Greensmith, J. (1983). Multivariate analysis of the relationship between drivometer variables and drivers' accident, sex, and exposure status. *Human Factors, 25,* 303–312.

Yoder, T. A., Lucas, R. L., & Botzum, G. D. (1973). The marriage of human factors and safety in industry. *Human Factors, 15,* 197–205.

Zedeck, S., Jackson, S. E., & Summers, E. (1983). Shift work schedules and their relationship to health, adaptation, satisfaction, and turnover intention. *Academy of Management Journal, 26,* 297–310.

Zohar, D. (1980). Safety climate in industrial organizations. Theoretical and applied implications. *Journal of Applied Psychology, 65,* 96–102.

Author Index

Subject Index